AMERICAN MERCHANT SEAMAN'S MANUAL

S.S. *Mallory Lykes*. One of three sister ships, the Constellation Class *Mallory Lykes* is operated by Lykes Bros. Steamship Co., from New Orleans. Her principal characteristics: length overall 665 feet, beam 75 feet, service speed 21 knots, steam turbine, capacity 700 twenty-foot containers. Courtesy Lykes Bros. Steamship Co.

AMERICAN MERCHANT SEAMAN'S MANUAL

For Seamen By Seamen

Based on the original edition edited by
Felix M. Cornell and Allan C. Hoffman

Sixth Edition

EDITOR IN CHIEF

William B. Hayler, Master Mariner

ASSOCIATE EDITORS

John M. Keever, Master Mariner
Paul M. Seiler, Boatswain

CORNELL MARITIME PRESS

Centreville, Maryland

Library of Congress Cataloging-in-Publication Data

Main entry under title:

American merchant seaman's manual.

"Based on the original edition edited by Felix M. Cornell and Allan C. Hoffman."
    Includes index.
    1. Seamanship—Handbooks, manuals, etc. 2. Merchant marine—Handbooks, manuals, etc. I. Hayler, William B., 1921-   II. Keever, John M. III. Seiler, Paul M. IV. Cornell, Felix M.
American merchant seaman's manual.
VK541.C67 1981   623.8'8'0202   80-25488
ISBN 0-87033-267-8

Manufactured in the United States of America

First edition, 1938. Sixth edition, 1981; third printing, 1990

To Captain William H. Aguilar, Master Mariner
onetime Commanding Officer, T.S. *Golden Bear*

With best wishes

CONTENTS

PREFACE TO THE FIRST EDITION

DURING THE PAST TEN YEARS, spent in selling nautical books and learning the requirements and desires of seamen, the editors have been impressed with the need and demand for a manual that would contain under one cover all of the information necessary and of vital interest to seamen to sell for a price well within their reach.

With the view of publishing such a manual we have kept notes for many years of their criticisms, both favorable and unfavorable, on all of the recognized standard works on seamanship.

When these notes were sufficiently complete to afford an accurate guide to the actual requirements and needs of merchant seamen, a direct approach to American Merchant Seamen was made in the form of a contest appearing in their trade paper. The question, "What do you think the ideal Merchant Seaman's Manual should contain?" was asked and the response was gratifying and unexpectedly large. Hundreds of letters were received and many seamen and officers came personally to express their views and offer their assistance in preparing such a manual.

Guided by our notes and the suggestions made by these seamen and officers, and assisted by them, we have prepared this manual, and believe that it will fill the need for a manual written expressly for seamen and by seamen.

The Editors

New York City
October, 1938

PREFACE TO THE SIXTH EDITION

THE *American Merchant Seaman's Manual* has been the primary seamanship text and reference book of our American Merchant Marine for more than forty years. During this time it has served generations of merchant seamen and cadets in three periods of crisis and national emergency. In the last ten years it has become increasingly apparent that a complete updating is necessary, however, if the Manual is to retain its usefulness in the face of the revolution of modern technology which is rejuvenating our Merchant Marine.

The changes which have taken place since 1938 when the Manual first appeared, and since 1957 when the fifth edition was published, are almost too numerous to mention. For example, the introduction of containerization and RO/RO (Roll-on Roll-off) ships has given the American Merchant Marine an opportunity to regain the position of preeminence it enjoyed at the end of World War II. Ships have been made safer and more efficient by the use of Radar, Loran, Satellite Navigation, the Stuelcken boom, and voice radio. The development of Cardiopulmonary Resuscitation (CPR) has become an important factor in the administration of First Aid.

In 1978 the current editors met with the publisher to see how the Manual could best be revised to assure its continuing usefulness. Much of the material was by this time outmoded, and many of the illustrations were outdated. The editors have utilized their own seagoing background as well as their classroom experience to help blend the old and the new into a seamanship textbook which we trust will be as useful to the present generation of seamen as the original was to their fathers and grandfathers.

Anyone familiar with older editions will have no difficulty finding his way around in the new. The numbering of the chapters is identical, but some of the titles have been broadened to portray more accurately their scope. Chapter VI, for example, is now "Canvas and Leather Work" instead of "Canvas Work"; Chapter XVII is now "Maritime Environment" instead of simply "Weather."

Differences between navy and merchant practice in anchoring, line handling, and basic terminology are noted. The treatment of the Rules of the Road has been abbreviated and contains only items of prime interest to the able seaman. The editors recommend that the serious student be always familiar with the most recent Coast Guard publication on Rules of the Road, since a general seamanship text such as the *American Merchant Seaman's Manual* cannot always be current in this regard.

Although the Sixth Edition is intended primarily for the merchant seaman and cadet, it should also prove of interest to anyone who goes to sea for a living or for recreation. Navy personnel, fishermen, and yachtsmen will find information here that may escape their notice in other texts.

W.B. Hayler

J.M. Keever

P.M. Seiler

T.S. Golden Bear
At Sea
February, 1980

ACKNOWLEDGMENTS

SEAMANSHIP IS A BROAD SUBJECT, and anyone who undertakes to write or edit a text needs assistance from many quarters. The editors have been extremely fortunate in having an abundance of cooperation from their colleagues at the California Maritime Academy and from the maritime industry in the San Francisco Bay area and elsewhere. We wish to acknowledge the assistance of Commander Fred Newton and Commander William Knodle for proofreading the Navigation and Maritime Environment chapters, Mr. Albert McLemore and Mr. Albert Reignierd for their suggestions on steering gear, Mrs. Lindy M. Keever for her assistance on the tanker chapter, Midshipman R.L. Schopp and Midshipman J.P. Jackson for their excellent photographs, Midshipman Eric Pett and Mr. Scott Duncan for their many sketches, Midshipman Michael A. Yinger for assistance on the index, Mrs. Harriet Millett who helped proofread and type the manuscript, and Rear Admiral J.P. Rizza for his encouragement.

Many individuals and firms in the maritime world have contributed photographs, sketches, and suggestions. In particular we thank Mr. Charles Regal, Matson Navigation Company; Mr. Seth E. Hargrave, Exxon Co.; Mr. William F. Schill, Chevron Shipping Company; Captain George D. Dunham, Delta Steamship Lines Inc.; Commander Robert A. Moore, American President Lines; Mr. Ronald A. Williams, American Hawaii Cruises; Ms. Renee R. Kristoff, Totem Ocean Trailer Express, Inc.; Mr. Larry C. Manning, Military Sealift Command; Commander R.T.E. Bowler, U.S. Naval Institute; and Captain Thomas J. Patterson, Maritime Administration. Acknowledgment appears by each photograph or sketch which is new to this edition.

In addition we owe our special thanks to:

Mr. Dick Saxton of Tubbs Cordage Company for suggestions and proofreading of the material on synthetic and natural fiber rope. Mr. Warren Myers of Bethlehem Steel Corporation for material on wire rope. Mr. M.L. Fisher of the Naval Education and Training Development Center for his assistance in supplying sketches from the *Navy Training Manual for Boatswain's Mate 3 & 2* as well as for obtaining permission to utilize the Canvas and Leather chapter in that manual as a basis for this text.

Mr. Donald Cook and Mr. Donald Todd of Devoe and Raynolds Co., Inc., for their suggestions and proofreading of the chapter on painting. Mr. J.P. Snyder of Sperry Marine Systems for the circuit information on steering gear as well as for photographs of modern installations.

Captain D.E. Hand, United States Coast Guard, and Mr. Mike Walsh of the Merchant Vessel Personnel Divison, United States Coast Guard, for their timely suggestions and information about the forthcoming edition of the *Manual for Lifeboatmen, Able Seamen, and Qualified Members of*

Engine Department, CG-175. Mr. L.J. Adams of C.J. Hendry Co. for material on the Sea-Jay Elliot inflatable life raft.

Rear Admiral J.E. Snyder, Jr, Oceanographer of the Navy, for his assistance in the Communications chapter and for the plates from the *International Code of Signals* (H.O. 102). Mr. Ernest B. Brown, Chief, Scientific Navigation Branch, Defense Mapping Agency, Hydrographic/ Topographic Center, for making photographs and drawings available from the *American Practical Navigator*.

Dr. Frank A.M. Bryant and Mr. Louis C. Jacobi for updating and rewriting the chapter of Ship Sanitation and Medical Procedures. Mr. Richard Belt, United States Department of State, for making available information on Consular Services from the *Foreign Service Manual*. Captain R.W. Hayler for proofreading much of the text and Captain Joe Taussig for his technical assistance and encouragement at the end of the project.

Attribution for the material in the General Information chapter is listed separately at the beginning of that chapter, but we must extend special thanks to Mr. George E. Delury of the *World Almanac* and Rear Admiral Harley Nygren of the National Oceanic and Atmospheric Administration for their contributions. Finally, to the staff at the Harry Lundeberg School for their article as well as for the photographs taken at Piney Point.

W. B. H.

J. M. K.

P. M. S.

October 1980

INTRODUCTION

THE NEW MERCHANT SEAMAN going aboard ship for the first time should know as much as he possibly can about his job, his ship, the sea, and the Merchant Marine. This manual, encompassed in one volume, is intended to provide knowledge the seaman will need to embark on his career.

Generally speaking, the Merchant Marine is comprised of all the commercial ships of a country together with the personnel who man them. From the seaman's viewpoint there are important differences between the Merchant Marine and the Navy. A sailor enlists in the Navy for a period of years either ashore or afloat and is paid by the United States government. The merchant seaman, on the other hand, is a civilian and usually signs on for a single voyage or at the most for a period of a few months. He is paid by a private shipping company for his service and his job will always be at sea. The United States government does own some merchant ships which are assigned to the Military Sealift Command or other agencies, but these ships are also manned by civilians.

A steamship company is a private enterprise organized and managed to make money for its stockholders. If the company fails in this objective, its ships are laid up, and jobs are lost. The company, therefore, wishes to have its ships at sea as continuously as possible, carrying cargo and sometimes passengers on those trade routes which are the most profitable.

It is useful for the merchant seaman to know a little about the organization of a steamship company. Most companies have an Operating Department which supervises the actual operation of the vessels. In the Operating Department are divisions which roughly correspond to the organization of each vessel in a company's fleet of ships. For example, a company's shore department may include a Port Captain (sometimes called a Marine Superintendent), a Port Engineer, and a Port Steward. The men who head up these shore divisions are veteran ship's officers thoroughly familiar with the problems of ships and their crews.

At the top of the administrative organization aboard ship is the Master, usually called the Captain, or sometimes, "the old Man." He is not a member of any department but has held all the jobs in the Deck Department from Third Mate through Chief Mate. He may have received his first license by coming up "through the hawsepipe" from able seaman, or he may be a graduate of one of the maritime academies. He stands no watches but is always available and on call. He is responsible for the ship, crew, and cargo. The personal responsibility he has for his ship has no parallel in the shoreside world. It can only be compared with that of the President of the United States for the country.

At the head of the Deck Department is the Chief Officer or Chief Mate. If there are only three mates, the Chief Mate will stand a watch on the bridge. Whether he stands a watch or not, the Chief Mate is responsible to the Master for the efficient running of the ship and for the cargo. The Second Mate is usually assigned as navigator and stands the 4 to 8 watches. The Third Mate stands the 8 to 12 watches and performs other duties assigned him by the Captain and Chief Mate. It is obvious that the day's duties of the licensed officers do not end with the completion of their watches and that both licensed and unlicensed personnel must be available for overtime work which will greatly increase their take-home pay.

While the deck crew, headed by the Boatswain, is under and responsible to the Master, its work is usually supervised by the Chief Officer, and in most of the routine the Boatswain works directly under him. Under the Boatswain are the seamen and the ship's carpenter and deck storekeeper, if the ship carries them.

Also under the Master are the Chief Engineer, the Radio Officer, and Chief Steward each of whom is a highly trained and experienced specialist responsible to the Master for the proper operations and functioning of his respective department. Passenger ships have, in addition, a Purser's department, headed by a Chief Purser, and a Medical Department under the ship's doctor, a graduate and registered physician.

The work and responsibility of the departments are separate and distinct although it is plain that a ship functions as a complete organization, not as a group of unrelated departments. A ship at sea, therefore, is a complete and complex organization of men and machinery in which the various departments function as units of the whole structure. If a part of any unit breaks down, the smooth operation of the whole machine is interrupted, if not seriously endangered.

One of the most important contrasts between the merchant seaman's job afloat and a job shoreside is that on a voyage the merchant seaman can neither quit nor be discharged. At sea there are no readily available replacements. The modern merchant ship is sparsely manned, and if the seaman whose name is opposite the article number of a particular job is sick or incapacitated, that function or assignment can only be done at the extreme inconvenience of someone else. Some other member of the crew will have to do *his* work as well as his own. This has given rise to one of the oldest traditions of the sea. The good seaman and shipmate will always be "ready, willing, and able" to do his own job and lend a hand where necessary. Whatever the seaman's job may be, he should realize that if his job were not important, he would not have been hired to do it. The most important attribute of the seaman is a feeling of responsibility for his job.

In the past the only qualifications needed by a merchant seaman were a knowledge of marlinespike seamanship and an iron constitution to stand up to the rigors of life under the most primitive conditions. One hundred day voyages were commonplace. Death and crippling of seamen through scurvy and other disease, maltreatment, freezing weather, typhoons, and accidents were the rule rather than the exception. There were no labor unions and no government agencies to safeguard the welfare and rights of seamen. The practice of "shanghaiing" crews was commonplace and the expression "being shanghaied" still has its place in the dictionary as a synonym for being taken on a voyage by trickery or force. All hands stood twelve hours of watch a day (four hours on and four hours off) in addition to doing the ship's work while not on watch. The word "overtime" had not been invented.

The reform of these conditions has been a slow, uphill, and painful process, but the results have been tremendous. The seaman of one hundred or even fifty years ago would not believe the living conditions his successors now enjoy aboard ship.

Today sailing in the Merchant Marine takes its place with other respected professions. The contribution which the Merchant Mariner makes to his country and to civilization are vital and well recognized. He is entitled, among other things, to medical and dental care at United States Public Health Hospitals. His rights to join a union and to bargain collectively for higher wages and better conditions are guaranteed.

A merchant seaman is one of the few individuals in the world whose opportunities to rise in his profession are limited only by his own ability and ambition. If he is willing to study and to take advantage of training offered by the Maritime Administration, the unions, and private institutions, there is no reason why he cannot one day be Master of his own ship or hold a responsible job in a steamship company ashore.

Best wishes for fair winds and following seas.

W. B. H.

J. M. K.

P. M. S.

California Maritime Academy
August 1980

CHAPTER I

MARLINESPIKE SEAMANSHIP

MARLINESPIKE SEAMANSHIP is a general term that covers all phases of rope work. It includes the care, handling, knotting and splicing of both fiber and wire rope of all sizes. A thorough knowledge of marlinespike seamanship is of great importance to every seaman, as rope in its many forms is used constantly aboard ship. Every seaman should be capable of making an eye splice in both fiber and wire rope, a short splice, a chain splice, a long splice in fiber rope, and a round seizing with both wire and hemp seizing stuff. He should also be able to tie the half dozen important knots in the dark.

To become an expert in this art of handling rope, a seaman must have a clear understanding of all the fundamentals of rope work together with the experience that comes with practice.

We have tried in this chapter to supply all the fundamental information necessary but must leave the practice to the individual.

NATURAL FIBER ROPE

Under this heading come Manila, sisal, hemp, coir, cotton, and flax. It takes its name from the species of plant from whose fiber it is made. Fiber rope is impregnated with oil when manufactured which adds about 10 percent to its actual weight. The oil lengthens the life of the rope by keeping out heat and moisture. As the oil leaves it, the rope tends to deteriorate more rapidly. The strength of fiber rope becomes less with use and a used rope is deceptive. Unlike a wire rope the strands do not wear flat, thereby giving a visible sign of weakness. The fibers stretch and untwist but this does not plainly indicate weakness. Do not place a maximum strain on a rope which has been under a load for a long period, or has been close to the breaking point. Rope safety decreases rapidly with constant use, depending upon the working conditions and amount of strain.

Manila is a hard fiber which comes from the bark of the abaca plant. It is the most important natural rope in the world. It grows almost exclusively in the Philippines and takes its name from the port from which it is exported. It possesses a lightness, strength, and durability with which no other natural fiber can compare. It is glossy, has a brilliant sheen, and is smooth and pliable. Saltwater has little effect on it, and therefore it is used almost exclusively for marine cordage. Until the advent of synthetic fibers it was used primarily for mooring lines, and it still finds considerable use aboard ship.

The abaca plant and the banana plant are very closely related and resemble each other in appearance and habits of growth. The plant is a large tree-like herb 15 to 20 feet high. The stalk is from 6 to 22 feet in length and from 6 to 18 inches in diameter. The bark is formed in ribbonlike strips of fiber over a fleshy core. The fiber is removed, cleaned and dried, and then baled for shipment to the mill. Manila fiber absorbs oils and preservatives directly into the fiber. Consequently it resists deterioration from bacterial rot for a long time.

Sisal is made from a hard fiber obtained from the leaves of *Agave sisalana*. It is sometimes known as sisal hemp, but is entirely different from true hemp. True sisal comes mainly from East Africa, the Dutch West Indies, and Haiti. Henequen is sometimes called Yucatan or Cuban sisal but this is not correct. Sisal fibers are white to yellowish-white in color. Unlike Manila, sisal lacks gloss, is stiff and harsh to the touch, and is easily injured by exposure to the weather. The length of the fiber is 2 to 4 feet as opposed to 6 to 10 for Manila. It is only about 80 percent as strong as Manila. During World War II when Manila was not available, sisal was substituted. Because of its stiffness and tendency to kink, seamen breathed a sigh of relief when Manila came back on the market. Aboard ship today it is little used except as small stuff although some finds its way aboard yachts. Sisal fiber takes only a surface coating of oil or preservatives. These leach out rapidly.

Hemp comes from the *Cannabis sativa* plant. There is only one true species of hemp but considerable confusion arises about its correct name because there are many other somewhat similar fiber-producing plants. The commercial fibers obtained from them are frequently—and incorrectly—called hemp. Several of these are Manila hemp, sisal hemp, New Zealand hemp, and Mauritius hemp. Hemp is grown in the United States, USSR, Italy, France, and Korea. It was probably the first fiber used for manufacturing rope in this country in Boston about 1640. Hemp fiber is coarse and about 80 percent as strong as Manila, but is used for entirely different purposes. It was formerly used for standing rigging, and still may be used on the ratlines of the few remaining square-riggers where its stiffness is an asset. When tarred it stands up well in wet weather. In the present day, however, most all hemp is made up as marline and is used extensively in the bos'n's locker where small stuff is appropriate.

Coir rope is made from coconut husk fiber and is a buoyant rope that does not become waterlogged. It has about half the strength of Manila. It was formerly used on tugs for lashing lighters and barges together, but has fallen into disuse and today is almost unknown in the maritime industry.

Cotton and **flax** ropes are made of common cotton and flax, respectively. Only smaller sizes are used aboard ship. Cotton signal halyards and leadlines are common. Flax cordage was commonly used for boltrope on sails because of its soft and flexible qualities. It has now largely been replaced by synthetics, but some flax sail twine may still be found.

Flax is extremely strong when wet. It gains approximately 100 percent tensile strength over dry strength. Its wet strength is comparable to that of nylon. Flax and hemp ropes are very stable and have low elongation and elasticity comparable to Manila.

CONSTRUCTION

Rope is made by first twisting fibers into yarns or threads, then twisting the yarns into strands, and finally twisting the strands together to form the finished rope. As the rope is built up, each part successively is twisted in an opposite direction; thus, when the yarns are twisted in a right-hand direction, the strands are twisted left-handed and the rope is twisted right-handed. This forms a right-handed plain-laid rope. If three or more of these right-handed plain-laid ropes are used as strands to form another rope, it will be a left-handed hawser, or cable-laid rope.

When a rope has four or more strands, it is customary to put a core or line in the center to retain the rounded form of its exterior. This core or line is called the heart.

Rope is designated as right-laid or left-laid according to the direction in which the strands are twisted. To determine which way the rope is laid, look along the rope and if the strands advance to the right or in a clockwise direction, the rope is right-laid; if the strands advance to the left or in a counterclockwise direction, the rope is left-laid.

Lay means the amount and direction of the twist put into a rope— expressed as hard-laid, common- or regular-laid, soft-laid, boltrope, sail- maker's lay. Generally speaking, the softer the lay, the stronger the rope; the harder the lay, the more resistant to chafing.

The average line is made of three strands which can be separated into yarns or threads, so it is called 6-thread, 9-thread, 12-thread, etc. Line is measured by thread up to 21-thread in the Merchant Marine. All line after this is measured by its circumference. Line larger than 5 inches in circum- ference is commonly called hawser.

SMALL CORDAGE

Small stuff is the common term for a line 1 3/4 inches in circumference or less. It is generally designated by the number of threads of which it is made, 24-thread stuff being the largest. Aside from being known by the number of threads, various kinds of small stuff have their own names, such as:

Spun yarn is the cheapest and most commonly used for seizing, serving, etc., where neatness is not important. It is laid up loosely and left-handed and is 2-, 3-, or 4-stranded. It is tarred.

Marline has the same uses as spun yarn but makes a neater job. It is 2-stranded and laid up left-handed. Untarred marline is used for sennit, a braided cord or fabric made of plaited yarns. Tarred yacht marline is used in rigging lofts.

SYNTHETIC FIBER ROPE

Natural fibers were mentioned first in this chapter because until com- paratively recently they were the only fibers available. They still have many uses aboard ship.

After World War II, rope made out of petroleum products appeared and began to replace Manila for use in mooring lines. The introduction of these

THREE-STRAND LAID AND EIGHT-STRAND PLAITED

NOMINAL SIZE		MANILA				POLYPROPYLENE			
Dia-meter	Circum-ference	Linear Density[1] (lbs./100 ft.)	New Rope Tensile Strength[2] (lbs.)	Safety Factor	Working Load[3] (lbs.)	Linear Density[1] (lbs./100 ft.)	New Rope Tensile Strength[2] (lbs.)	Safety Factor	Working Load[3] (lbs.)
3/16	5/8	1.50	406	10	41	.70	720	10	72
1/4	3/4	2.00	540	10	54	1.20	1,130	10	113
5/16	1	2.90	900	10	90	1.80	1,710	10	171
3/8	1-1/8	4.10	1,220	10	122	2.80	2,440	10	244
7/16	1-1/4	5.25	1,580	9	176	3.80	3,160	9	352
1/2	1-1/2	7.50	2,380	9	264	4.70	3,780	9	420
9/16	1-3/4	10.4	3,100	8	388	6.10	4,600	8	575
5/8	2	13.3	3,960	8	496	7.50	5,600	8	700
3/4	2-1/4	16.7	4,860	7	695	10.7	7,650	7	1,090
13/16	2-1/2	19.5	5,850	7	835	12.7	8,900	7	1,270
7/8	2-3/4	22.4	6,950	7	995	15.0	10,400	7	1,490
1	3	27.0	8,100	7	1,160	18.0	12,600	7	1,800
1-1/16	3-1/4	31.2	9,450	7	1,350	20.4	14,400	7	2,060
1-1/8	3-1/2	36.0	10,800	7	1,540	23.8	16,500	7	2,360
1-1/4	3-3/4	41.6	12,200	7	1,740	27.0	18,900	7	2,700
1-5/16	4	47.8	13,500	7	1,930	30.4	21,200	7	3,020
1-1/2	4-1/2	60.0	16,700	7	2,380	38.4	26,800	7	3,820
1-5/8	5	74.5	20,200	7	2,880	47.6	32,400	7	4,620
1-3/4	5-1/2	89.5	23,800	7	3,400	59.0	38,800	7	5,550
2	6	108.	28,000	7	4,000	69.0	46,800	7	6,700
2-1/8	6-1/2	125.	32,400	7	4,620	80.0	55,000	7	7,850
2-1/4	7	146.	37,000	7	5,300	92.0	62,000	7	8,850
2-1/2	7-1/2	167.	41,800	7	5,950	107.	72,000	7	10,300
2-5/8	8	191.	46,800	7	6,700	120.	81,000	7	11,600
2-7/8	8-1/2	215.	52,000	7	7,450	137.	91,000	7	13,000
3	9	242.	57,500	7	8,200	153.	103,000	7	14,700
3-1/4	10	298.	69,500	7	9,950	190.	123,000	‹7	17,600
3-1/2	11	366.	82,000	7	11,700	232.	146,000	7	20,800
4	12	434.	94,500	7	13,500	276.	171,000	7	24,400

CAUTION! WORKING LOADS ARE GUIDELINES ONLY.

See Footnotes at bottom.

Figure 1-1. Specifications of Manila and various synthetic fiber rope.

[1] **LINEAR DENSITY**

Linear Density (pounds per 100 feet) shown is "average." Maximum is 5% higher.

[2] **NEW ROPE TENSILE STRENGTHS**

New Rope Tensile Strengths are based on tests of new and unused rope of standard construction in accordance with Cordage Institute Standard Test Methods.

[3] **WORKING LOADS** are for rope in good condition with appropriate splices, in non-critical applications, and under normal service conditions. Working loads should be exceeded only with expert knowledge of conditions and professional estimates of risk. Working loads should be reduced where life, limb, or valuable property are involved, or for exceptional service conditions such as shock, loads, sustained loads, etc.

Manila rope tensile and weight specifications are based upon federal specification T-R-605B Amendment 3 four-strand standard lay is approximately 7% heavier and has approximately 95% of the strength of three-strand manila size for size.

Specifications for other ropes are available upon request.

[1] **CAUTION: USE OF WORKING LOADS**

Because of the wide range of rope use, rope condition, exposure to the several factors affecting rope behavior, and the degree of risk to life and property involved, it is impossible to make blanket recommendations as to working loads. However, to provide guidelines, working loads are tabulated for rope in good condition with appropriate splices, in non-critical applications and under normal service conditions.

A higher working load may be selected only with expert knowledge of conditions and professional estimate of risk and if the rope has not been subject to dynamic loading or other excessive use, has been inspected and found to be in good condition and is to be used in the recommended manner, and the application does not involve elevated temperatures, extended periods under load, or obvious dynamic loading (see explanation below) such as sudden drops, snubs, or pickups. For all such applications and for applications involving more severe

(Standard Construction)

DACRON SILVERLON				NOMINAL	ESTERLENE				NYLON			
Linear Density[1] (lbs./100 ft.)	New Rope Tensile Strength[2] (lbs.)	Safety Factor	Working Load[3] (lbs.)	DIA-METER (inches)	Linear Density[1] (lbs./100 ft.)	New Rope Tensile Strength[2] (lbs.)	Safety Factor	Working Load[3] (lbs.)	Linear Density[1] (lbs./100 ft.)	New Rope Tensile Strength[2] (lbs.)	Safety Factor	Working Load[3] (lbs.)
1.20	900	10	90	3/16	.94	720	10	72	1.00	900	12	75
2.00	1,490	10	149	1/4	1.61	1,130	10	113	1.50	1,490	12	124
3.10	2,300	10	230	5/16	2.48	1,710	10	171	2.50	2,300	12	192
4.50	3,340	10	334	3/8	3.60	2,440	10	244	3.50	3,340	12	278
6.20	4,500	9	500	7/16	5.00	3,160	9	352	5.00	4,500	11	410
8.00	5,750	9	640	1/2	6.50	3,780	9	440	6.50	5,750	11	525
10.2	7,200	8	900	9/16	8.00	4,600	8	610	8.15	7,200	10	720
13.0	9,000	8	1,130	5/8	9.50	5,600	8	720	10.5	9,350	10	935
17.5	11,300	7	1,610	3/4	12.5	7,650	7	1,080	14.5	12,800	9	1,420
21.0	14,000	7	2,000	13/16	15.2	8,900	7	1,310	17.0	15,300	9	1,700
25.0	16,200	7	2,320	7/8	18.0	10,400	7	1,540	20.0	18,000	9	2,000
30.4	19,800	7	2,820	1	21.8	12,600	7	1,870	26.4	22,600	9	2,520
34.4	23,000	7	3,280	1-1/16	25.6	14,400	7	2,180	29.0	26,000	9	2,880
40.0	26,600	7	3,800	1-18	29.0	16,500	7	2,480	34.0	29,800	9	3,320
46.2	29,800	7	4,260	1-1/4	33.4	18,900	7	2,820	40.0	33,800	9	3,760
52.5	33,800	7	4,820	1-5/16	35.6	21,200	7	3,020	45.0	38,800	9	4,320
67.0	42,200	7	6,050	1-1/2	45.0	26,800	7	3,820	55.0	47,800	9	5,320
82.0	51,500	7	7,350	1-5/8	55.5	32,400	7	4,620	66.5	58,500	9	6,500
98.0	61,000	7	8,700	1-3/4	66.5	38,800	7	5,550	83.0	70,000	9	7,800
118.	72,000	7	10,300	2	78.0	46,800	7	6,700	95.0	83,000	9	9,200
135.	83,000	7	11,900	2-1/8	92.0	55,000	7	7,850	109.	95,500	9	10,600
157.	96,500	7	13,800	2-1/4	105.	62,000	7	8,850	129.	113,000	9	12,600
181.	110,000	7	15,700	2-1/2	122.	72,000	7	10,300	149.	126,000	9	14,000
204.	123,000	7	17,600	2-5/8	138.	81,000	7	11,600	168.	146,000	9	16,200
230.	139,000	7	19,900	2-7/8	155.	91,000	7	13,000	189.	162,000	9	18,000
258.	157,000	7	22,400	3	174.	103,000	7	14,700	210.	180,000	9	20,000
318.	189,000	7	27,000	3-1/4	210.	123,000	7	17,600	264.	226,000	9	25,200
384.	228,000	7	32,600	3-1/2	256.	146,000	7	20,800	312.	270,000	9	30,000
454.	270,000	7	38,600	4	300.	171,000	7	24,400	380.	324,000	9	36,000

Courtesy: Tubbs Cordage Company.

exposure conditions, or for recommendations on special applications, consult the manufacturer.

Many uses of rope involve serious risk of injury to personnel or damage to valuable property. This danger is often obvious, as when a heavy load is supported above one or more workmen. An equally dangerous situation occurs if personnel are in line with a rope under excessive tension. Should the rope fail, it may recoil with considerable force—especially if the rope is nylon. Persons should be warned against standing in line with the rope. IN ALL CASES WHERE ANY SUCH RISKS ARE PRESENT, OR THERE IS ANY QUESTION ABOUT THE LOADS INVOLVED OR THE CONDITIONS OF USE, THE WORKING LOAD SHOULD BE SUBSTANTIALLY REDUCED AND THE ROPE BE PROPERLY INSPECTED.

DYNAMIC LOADING VOIDS WORKING LOAD AS TABULATED ABOVE.

Working loads are not applicable when rope is subject to significant dynamic loading. Whenever a load is picked up, stopped, moved or swung there is an increased force due to dynamic loading. The more rapidly or suddenly such actions occur, the greater this increase will be. In extreme cases, the force put on the rope may be two, three, or even more times the normal load involved. Examples could be picking up a tow on a slack line or using a rope to stop a falling object. Therefore, in all such applications as towing lines, lifelines, safety lines, climbing ropes, etc., working loads as given **do not apply**.

Users should be aware that dynamic effects are greater on a low elongation rope such as manila than on a high elongation rope such as nylon, and greater on a shorter rope than on a longer one. The working load listed contains provision for very modest dynamic loads. This means, however, that when this working load has been used to select a rope, the load must be handled slowly and smoothly to minimize dynamic effects and avoid exceeding the provision for them.

NATURAL AND SYNTHETIC FIBERS — COMPARISON OF CHARACTERISTICS

Fiber Type	Nylon	Polyester	Polypropylene	Polyethylene	Manila
* Bulk Strength[1]	1.0	.9 — 1.1	.55	.55	.33
* Weight	1.0	1.21	.80	.83	1.21
Elastic Elongation	1.0	.6	.8	.6	
Coefficient[3] of Friction	.10 — .12	.13 — .15	.15 — .22	.08	.15
Melt Point	480 °F	480 °F	330 °F	280 °F	Chars-350 °F
Critical Temperature[4]	350 °F	350 °F	300 °F	250 °F	180 °F
Specific Gravity	1.14	1.38	.91	.95	1.38
Cold-Flow (Creep)	Neg.	Neg.	High	High	Neg.
Water Absorption into Fiber	up to 9%	less than 1%	Zero	Zero	

* (Using Nylon as a Basis of 1.0)
[1] Bulk strength is defined as strength per circumference squared.
[3] Coefficient of friction is based on reluctance to slip or slide.
[4] Critical temperature is defined as the point at which degradation is caused by temperature alone.
Table courtesy of **Samson Ocean Systems, Inc.**

Figure 1-2. Comparison of natural and synthetic fibers. Note that the format and information shown vary somewhat from the preceding plate. Both are representative of the information cordage manufacturers make available. Strengths tabulated by the manufacturer should always be used in preference to the strength calculated by formula.

synthetic fibers was gradual, but their use became prevalent during the early 1960s. Since then the use of synthetics has become widespread.

Synthetics have far more elongation than Manila. It is necessary to adapt to its elasticity and different handling, particularly with nylon, which was first on the market.

The development of synthetic fibers has brought about a continual flow of new and competitive products on the market.

Available synthetic blends of two or more different filaments have characteristics which lie somewhere between their parent ingredients. Because nylon was the first of the synthetics to appear aboard ship, some mariners refer to any synthetic as "nylon." This is a misnomer and can be dangerous because characteristics vary widely. Using a wrong name may implant an inaccurate impression as to how a line will react.

Basically there are four synthetic fibers in use at the present time, nylon, polyester, polypropylene, and polyethelene. An example of a brand blend is "Esterlene," a combination of polypropylene and polyester. In Europe, much of the polyethelene is waxy in finish and is a "chemical cousin" to polypropylene. This has approximately the same properties except that polypropylene has excellent splice-holding and knot-holding properties, but these properties for polyethelene are rated only "fair."

Nylon will stretch about 40 percent of its length and still return to its original length after tension is removed. It is also about two and a half times as strong as Manila, tends to deteriorate in the sun, and is destroyed by acid. Since some oils have an acid content, it is seldom used on tankers.

Polyester has an elongation close to Manila, resists deterioration from the sun, and unlike nylon it attracts moisture. It is the most expensive of synthetics and approximates nylon in strength. One of the new polyesters, for example, is approximately 20 percent stronger than nylon. A view is that your dollar goes farther with polyester.

Polyester brand names include such as Dacron and Silverlon.

Polypropylene is about one and a half times stronger than Manila and is very light and wiry. It actually costs less than Manila per fathom because of its very low linear density even though its price per pound can be higher. All synthetics have a far longer useful life than Manila. Despite the initial high expense on some products, the annual cost is far less. A table of the characteristics of various synthetics as well as Manila is contained in Figure 1-1. It will be noted that some trade names also are included.

CONSTRUCTION

Synthetics are "laid up" or constructed in one of three ways as illustrated in Figure 1-3. The first is 3-strand which probably will be laid up right-handed or clockwise. There is no difference in the manner in which this is done and the way conventional Manila is laid up. It is entirely suitable for mooring lines, but if a weight is suspended from a pendant made up of a single part of 3-strand line, the line will tend to unlay and elongate.

The second manner in which synthetic rope may be constructed is by plaiting. When this is done, four strands are left-hand laid and four are right-hand laid. These are paired off, laid parallel, and are braided together. This is known as "plaited" or "plaited-braid" rope. Rope made in this manner has no tendency to unwind or hockle and is very flexible whether it is wet or dry. It is used for large mooring lines and for towing and can be spliced without too much difficulty. Seamen the world over are now familiar with the splicing method.

Double-braided rope is the third type of construction. This is very expensive but still in use. It may be made from nylon, polyester, or their combination. As is true with other articles, different manufacturers have their own names for essentially the same product. Two common ones are Samson's Two-In-One Braid and Tubbs's Dubl-Braid. Double-braided rope is non-rotational and torque-free as is true for plaited rope. It is very flexible, fakes down, and pays out without snagging. It has a rather complicated splice requiring special tools. Detailed splicing instruction pamphlets are usually provided by the various manufacturers.

DO'S AND DON'TS

A good seaman will learn all that he can about the characteristics of mooring lines, falls, guys and tackles in use aboard ship as soon as possible after going aboard. As noted previously, the characteristics of the various synthetics differ enormously.

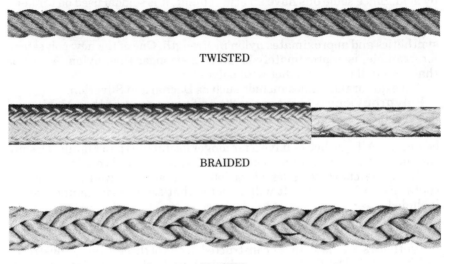

TWISTED

BRAIDED

PLAITED

Figure 1-3. Types of rope construction. Courtesy: Tubbs Cordage Company.

There need be no fear of any rope or wire. But a healthy respect is mandatory. This is true for any fiber or wire rope under tension, and especially true for synthetic rope. Nylon can stretch up to 40 percent of its original length when wet without parting and has a very low coefficient of friction. Stated more simply, nylon stretches more than anything else on the market and is extremely slippery to hold on to. Furthermore, if a line is under tension, and you try to slack or ease it out, the line will probably not run as freely as Manila and will bind on the bitts. If it cannot be "started," it may tend to fuse and turn into something which looks much like glass. If at this point the tension keeps increasing and the line cannot be started, it may carry away. A nylon which parts will immediately return to its original length with a vicious snap back or backlash which can seriously injure or kill anyone in a direct line with it. So . . . have respect for a synthetic line under tension. Since synthetics are more difficult to hold than Manila, take an extra round turn on the bitts before beginning figures-of-eight, and when splicing, take an extra tuck.

Heat build up from friction of moving lines through cleats, bitts, or H bars (and even working in hawseholes) can reach a point where a synthetic line will melt or a Manila line will burn. Polypropylene turns to liquid at approximately 300 degrees Fahrenheit. Nylon and polyester reach this point at approximately 500 degrees Fahrenheit. When synthetic fiber becomes liquid it actually becomes a lubricant. This causes a line to hop, skip, and jump or even carry away in its movement through cleats or bitts.

This is one reason why products like Esterlene have been developed. The high-melting point of the polyester cover protects the low-melting point of the polypropylene core-yarns.

It is a legend to never stand in the bight of a line, and this bears repeating. The reason is obvious, but accidents happen when seamen are hurried, tired, careless, or angry. The woods are full of one-legged seamen who know better. For this reason the Navy recommends the use of a separate safety observer for mooring operations. In the merchant service the licensed officer in charge of a mooring station must be vigilant to insure that through carelessness his men do not subject themselves to a hazard. Further information on line handling is covered in Chapter IV.

CARE AND HANDLING

To open a new coil of natural fiber rope, loosen the burlap cover, saving the lashings, and lay the coil on the flat side with the inside end near the deck. Then reach down through the eye (the opening in the center of the coil) and draw the tagged end up and out of the coil. As it comes out, it should uncoil counterclockwise. Do not uncoil from the outside or take the end from the top of the coil because kinks will result. Rope manufacturers recommend that lashings around the coil be cut from inside the eye and the burlap covering left on the coil. Deck storekeepers will find that this will keep their coils of rope in shape and keep the storeroom more orderly.

Synthetics will probably come aboard on a reel in the same manner as wire, differing from Manila which comes in a coil covered with burlap. To guard against kinking, synthetic rope should be unreeled in the same manner as wire. The reel should be mounted on a reel-holder. Synthetics, given a chance, will kink at the first opportunity, and the result is loss of strength and damage as serious as when it happens with wire.

Natural fiber rope shrinks in length when wet as the fibers swell. A rope taut when dry should be slacked off in wet weather to prevent it from parting under the added strain. Even a heavy dew at night will penetrate an oil line that the oil has left and may create a dangerous situation.

Natural fibers are subject to deterioration from heat, sunlight, and mildew rot. They also are damaged by chemicals, acids, alkalies, paints, soaps, and vegetable oils. Do not store when wet. Store in a well ventilated, cool, and dark area. If stowed topside they should be under an overhang and covered with canvas or other waterproof material. Most synthetic fibers are affected by sunlight, fluorescent light, and chemicals. Do not stow nylon in strong sunlight for extended periods. It should be covered. Keep away from temperatures above 250 degrees Fahrenheit and strong chemicals. Synthetics can be stowed wet if necessary. Polyester and polypropylene are not damaged by sunlight.

Should dark red, brown, or black spots be noted between the strands of natural fiber rope, and a sour, musty, or acidic odor be detected, the rope is no longer useful. Rotting rope should not be stored near new rope.

Both natural and synthetic fiber rope should be kept clear of rusty iron surfaces. Although this is more injurious to natural fiber, rusting iron can result in the loss of 40 percent of nylon's breaking strain in one month. Rust stains which can be removed with soap have no adverse affect on rope strength. Rope containing rust stains which cannot be removed should be taken out of heavy service.

The age of natural fiber rope is important. If over five years old, it is not safe for heavy use. If Manila or sisal feel harsh, dry, or dead, the quality of the rope is doubtful. An accumulation of grease also affects rope strength.

Wet synthetic fiber hawsers under heavy strain will wring out steam-like water vapor. This is normal under safe-working loads and helps cool fibers.

A hockle in a synthetic rope should be cut out as it reduces breaking strength by approximately 30 percent. The portion of a rope containing cuts also should be removed.

Rope should be parceled with canvas to protect it from chafing at any point where it rubs against a heavy object.

An old rule a prudent seaman still observes states that not more than 1/6 the breaking strain should be placed on an old line and not more than 1/4 the breaking strain on a new line.

COILING

For a **straight coil** lay a circular bight of secured end on deck and lay additional bights on top of it, using up the entire amount of line. Keep out kinks and turns. Capsize entire coil and it will be clear for running.

To **flemish down** a line, make a small circle of free end and continue to lay down circles around it until all the line is down and resembles a coiled clock spring. This is the neatest method.

To **fake down** a rope lay out the free end in a straight line, then turn back a loop to form a close flat coil and continue to lay flat coils with the ends on top of ends of preceding coil. Always coil a line with the lay.

Right-handed rope should always be coiled "with the sun," that is in a clockwise direction.

Left-handed rope should always be coiled "against the sun," that is in a counterclockwise direction.

To remove turns in a line, coil down against the lay, bring lower end up through the center of the coil and then coil down clockwise. If there are many turns in the rope, coil small, if few, coil large.

STRENGTH OF ROPE

Whenever the question arises as to how strong rope is or what weight it can withstand, the best means of finding out is to go to the manufacturer's specifications. Figure 1-1 is an example showing results of tests made on new and unused rope.

Manufacturers may vary in systems of size measure, methods of listing tensile strengths (minimum, approximate average, plus-or-minus 10 percent), and linear density weights. It is important to understand that total fiber content in any so-called "size" of a rope in hawser sizes is the total function of its strength. The weight or linear density of amount of fiber that can be circumscribed within a circumference of a rope determines the strength of that size.

If the manufacturer's specifications are not available for the specific rope about to be used, refer to a general table (see Figure 1-1) or to any other good seamanship text. If no appropriate table can be found, the following empirical formula is surprisingly accurate. It is for Manila only, but nylon is about two and a half times as strong as Manila. Thus the formula can be used by multiplying the result by 2 1/2 or 2.5. The Coast Guard requires that candidates for licenses be able to utilize this formula. In any case, whichever method is used, it is important to note that rope which is not new, not stored properly, or otherwise abused, is less strong than when it left the factory. It will be less strong, therefore, than shown by the tables or formulas.

DEFINITIONS AND ABBREVIATIONS

B = **Breaking Strain** (same as tensile strength), in terms of long tons or pounds, as specified.

SWL or **P** = **Safe Working Load** = (note Figure 1-1) safety requires that less stress be placed on the rope or wire than is required to break it, otherwise gear would frequently be carried away with resulting loss of life and property. If the **SWL** of Manila is used as 20 percent of **B**, and **B** of a 5 inch Manila is 20,250 pounds, then the **SWL** will be 4,050 pounds.

SF = **Safety Factor** = the relationship between the Breaking Strain and the Safe Working Load. If the **SWL** of Manila is taken as 20 percent of B, the **SF** is 5.

EMPIRICAL FORMULAS

$$B = \frac{C^2}{2.5} \qquad \text{or} \qquad B = 900C^2$$

where B = Breaking Strain in long tons (2,240 pounds = 1 long ton)

and C = Circumference of rope in inches

where B = Breaking Strain in pounds

and C = Circumference in inches

SWL $= \dfrac{B}{SF}$ In this formula both SWL and B must be in the same units. If SWL is in tons, B must be in tons. If SWL is in pounds, B must be in pounds.

Example: Using the preceding formulas, what is the Breaking Strain for 5 inch Manila in pounds?

$$B = 900C^2 = 900 \times 5^2 = 900 \times 25 = 22,500 \text{ pounds}$$

Note that this is about 10 percent more than the 20,200 pounds given in Figure 1-1.

Suppose we wished to know the Safe Working Load of this line using a Safety Factor of 5:

$$\text{SWL} = \frac{\text{B}}{\text{SF}} = \frac{22,500}{5} = 4,500 \text{ pounds}$$

Example: Using the preceding formulas, what is the Breaking Strain for 3 inch Manila in tons?

What would be the Safe Working Load if a Safety Factor of 6 were used? (The greater the SF, the safer you are.)

$$\text{B} = \frac{\text{C}^2}{2.5} = \frac{3^2}{2.5} = \frac{9}{2.5} = 3.6 \text{ long tons}$$

$$\text{SWL} = \frac{\text{B}}{\text{SF}} = \frac{3.6}{6} = .6 \text{ long tons}$$

Note: Referring to Figure 1-1 again, this time the formula and the table both yield the same results,

$$\text{B} = 8,100 \text{ pounds}$$

or

$$\frac{8,100}{2,240} = 3.61 \text{ long tons}$$

TERMS

Against the sun—A nautical term meaning rotation in a counterclockwise, or left-handed direction.

Backhanded rope—Rope in which the yarns and strands are both twisted in the same direction (clockwise), and the strands are then laid up left-handed (counterclockwise). It is very pliable because the strands and yarns have the same twist.

Becket—A rope eye for the hook of a block. A rope grommet used as a rowlock; any small rope or strap serving as a handle.

Becket bend—An efficient bend used for uniting the two ends of a rope or the end of a rope to an eye. It jams tight with the strain, will not slip, and is easily cast off.

Beeswax—Honeycomb wax taken from beehives, used extensively in canvas work. It is applied to sail twine to prevent the small threads from fraying as the twine is pulled through the canvas. Usually it is in the form of a wad.

Belay—To make a rope or line fast by winding it in figure-eight fashion around a cleat, a belaying pin, or a pair of bitts. Also, to stop or cease.

Belaying pin—A pin of either wood or metal, set in pinrails, upon which to belay a rope or secure the running rigging.

Bend—The twisting or turning of a rope so as to fasten it to another rope or to some object, as a spar or ring.

Bight—A loop in a rope, as that part of the rope between the end and the standing part, formed by bringing the end of the rope around, near to, or across its own part.

Bitt—One or more heavy cylindrical fittings, usually set vertically in the deck of a vessel, to secure mooring lines and tow lines.

Bitt a cable—To make a line fast by a turn under the thwartship piece and again around the bitthead; to weather-bitt a cable, an extra turn is taken; to double-bitt is to secure by passing a line around a pair of bitts.

Bitthead—The upper part of a bitt, or its head or top.

Bitter end—The inboard end of a cable or rope; in an anchor chain, the last link, which is made fast to the bottom or side of the chain locker.

Bollard—A heavy piece of wood or metal, set on the dock, to which the mooring lines are made fast.

Boltrope—Hemp or cotton cordage sewed into the edge of a piece of canvas or a sail to give added strength and to prevent canvas from ripping. The name is also applied to a good quality of long-fiber Manila or hemp rope.

Braid—To plait or interweave strands, yarns, ropes, or cords.

Bridle—Any span of rope with its ends secured.

Cable—A heavy rope used in attaching anchors or in towing.

Cable-laid—Cable-laid rope is made up of three ropes laid up left-handed; the ropes comprising the strands being laid up right-handed. It is also called hawser-laid rope.

Catch a turn—To take a turn, as around a capstan or bitt, usually for holding temporarily.

Cavil—A strong timber, bollard, or cleat used for making fast the heavier lines of a vessel. Also called kevel.

Chafe—To wear the surface of a rope by rubbing against a solid object.

Chafing gear—A winding of small stuff, rope, canvas, or other materials around spars, rigging, ropes, etc., to prevent chafing.

Chafing mat—A mat made from woven ropes or cordage to prevent chafing.

Cleat—A heavy piece of wood or metal having two horns around which ropes may be made fast or belayed. Usually secured by bolts or lashings to some fixed object, as the deck of a vessel or the dock.

Clothes stop—Small cotton line used for stopping clothes to a line or for securing clothes rolled up in bags or lockers.

Coil—To lay down rope in circular turns.

Cord—A small rope made by twisting several strands together.

Cordage—Ropes or cords; anything made of ropes or cords; used collectively as in speaking of that part of the rigging of a ship composed of ropes, etc.

Core—A small rope run through the center of heavier rope or wire. It is usually found in 4-strand rope, giving it a smooth, round appearance.

Cow's-tail—Frayed end of rope. Same as Irish pennant.

Cross turns—Turns taken around a rope at right angles to the turns of the lashings or seizing.

Dead man—A timber or other heavy object buried in the ice to which a ship can be moored for Arctic operations; an anchor or any heavy object buried ashore to which a mooring line can be run and made fast.

Dead rope—A rope in a tackle not led through a block or sheave.

Eye—A loop in the end of a rope, usually made permanent by splicing or seizing.

Eye seizing—A seizing used for shortening an eye, the turns of the seizing stuff being taken over and under each part and the ends crossed over the turns.

Fag end—An unraveled or untwisted end of rope, or as applied to flags and pennants, the ragged end.

Fake—To lay down a length of line so that it will run out rapidly without kinking. The coils are laid with ends over the ends of each preceding one.

Fiber—The smallest threadlike tissue of a rope, cord, or thread, as the fibers of flax, cotton, hemp, Manila, etc., which are twisted to make the yarn out of which the rope is made.

Fid—A tapered wooden pin used to separate the strands when splicing heavy rope.

Flemish—To coil a rope on deck in tight concentric coils with the free end in the center.

Frap—To bind or draw together and secure with ropes, as two slack lines.

Frapping—Lines passed around boat falls to steady the boat when hoisting or lowering.

Frapping turns—Cross turns; turns taken around and perpendicular to the turns of a lashing or seizing.

Hawser—Any large rope used principally for towing, mooring, warping, or kedging. It would customarily be 5 inches in circumference or greater.

Hawser-laid—Left-handed rope of nine strands laid up in the form of three 3-stranded, right-handed ropes.

Heart—The inside center strand of a rope. Same as core.

Heave—To haul or pull on a line; to throw a heaving line.

Heave taut—To haul in a line until it has a strain upon it.

Irish pennant—The loose end of a line; a flying rope yarn. Cow's tail.

Jam—To wedge tight.

Kink—A short bight caused by too much twisting of the rope.

Knittles—Rope yarns twisted and rubbed smooth for pointing and similar purposes. Two or more yarns may be twisted together or one yarn may be split and its halves twisted. Also called nettles.

Knot—A twisting, turning, tying, knitting, or entangling of ropes or parts of a rope so as to join two ropes together or make a finished end on a rope for a certain purpose.

Lanyard—A line used for making anything fast. Also an ornamental braid or plait used by sailors in securing their knives and the like.

Lashing—A binding or wrapping of small stuff used to secure one object or line to another, as an eye to a spar.

Lashing eye—Loops in the ends of two ropes through which are passed the lashings which bind them together.

Lay—The direction in which the strands of a rope are twisted. This may be right-handed (clockwise), or left-handed (counterclockwise). It also refers to the degree of tightness with which the strands are twisted, as soft, medium, common, plain, and hard lay.

Left-handed—Opposite to right-handed; applied to rope in which the strands wind spirally from right to left.

Line—Term for rope when it is used aboard ship. In general, seamen refer to either natural or synthetic fiber rope as line. More exactly, line refers to a piece of rope that is used for a specific purpose such as a mooring line, lifeline, heaving line, or lead line. Traditional exceptions are a boat rope, footrope, manrope, boltrope, and bell rope. Wire, however, is referred to simply as wire, or wire rope.

Loop—*See* Bight.

Marlinespike—An iron or steel tool that tapers to a sharp point, used to splice strands of rope or wire.

Marry—Temporarily binding two lines together side by side or end to end.

Nip—To pinch or close in upon.

Part—(verb) To break; (noun) A length or line or wire. A part of line is commonly considered to be a single part of line, a line that is not doubled up.

Pass a lashing—Make the necessary turns to secure a line or an object.

Pass a line—Carry a line to or around an object; reeve through and make fast.

Pass a stopper—To reeve and secure a stopper.

Pay out—To slack off on a line or let it run out.

Plain-laid rope—Built up by twisting each part in the opposite direction, as: yarn twisted right-handed, strands twisted left-handed, and then laid up right-handed.

Plait—*See* Braid.

Pointing—Any of numerous ways of working the end of a rope into a stiff cone shaped point.

Pricker—A light piece of metal like a marlinespike, but with a handle. Used for the same purposes as a marlinespike.

Rack—To seize two ropes together with cross turns of spun yarn or small stuff.

Rack seizing—Small stuff rove around two lines in an over and under figure-eight fashion.

Reeve—To pass the end of a rope through an eye or an opening, as through a block, thimble, or bight.

Render—To pass through freely. Said of a rope when it runs easily through a fairlead or a sheave.

Riders—A second layer of turns placed over the first layer of turns of a seizing. Also called riding turns.

Rigging—A term applied to ship's ropes generally.

Right-handed—Turning from left to right, clockwise and with the sun; opposite to left-handed, counterclockwise or against the sun.

Right-handed rope—*See* Plain-laid rope.

Rope—A general term used to describe any cord more than 1 3/4 inches in circumference.

Rope yarn—Untwisted strands of a rope used for rough seizings.

Round turn—To pass a line completely around a spar, bitt, or another rope.

Secure—To attach, fasten, or make fast.

Secured end—The part of a line that is attached or secured to an object.

Seize—To put on or clap on a seizing. That is, bind with small stuff, as one rope to another, a rope to a spar, etc. Seizings are named according to their construction and application, as throat seizing, flat, and round seizing.

Seizing stuff—Small stuff.

Selvagee strop—A selvagee strop is made of many turns of rope yarns, marline, or other small stuff seized together with marline and used to hook a tackle to a hawser or shroud, etc.

Sennit—Braided spun or rope yarns commonly named according to their shape or design.

Shroud-laid—4-stranded rope laid up right-handed over a core.

Slack—The part of a rope hanging loose; the opposite of taut.

Snake lines—Common name for short pieces of rope with a cringle or thimble spliced in one end of them. They are usually made of small stuff and are used to provide a lead for a larger rope, such as a gantline, in the rigging. When working aloft they are handy in preventing the bos'n's chair gantline from swinging about in the wind or holding it against the roll of the ship.

Splice—To join the ends of ropes together, or the end of a rope to its standing part to form an eye, by interweaving the strands. If properly spliced, the diameter of the rope is only slightly increased.

Standing part—That part of a line which is secured. In knotting, that part of the main rope distinguished from the bight and the end.

Stop— To seize or lash, usually temporarily.

Stopper—A short line, one end of which is secured to a fixed object, used to check or stop a running line, as a boat-fall stopper.

Strap—A rope or wire sling used to handle heavy objects. Small straps are used to attach a handybilly to the hauling part of a line.

Take a turn—To pass a line around a cleat or belaying pin to hold on.

Taut—Tight, snug, tightly-drawn; opposite of slack.

Thimble—An iron ring with a groove on the outside for a rope grommet or splice.

Throat seizing—A seizing used to lash an eye in a rope; to hold it around a thimble, or to seize two parts of rope together at the point where they cross each other.

Thrums—Short pieces of small stuff secured by their bights to pieces of canvas for use as chafing gear. The verb thrum means to attach the small stuff.

Toggle—A small piece of wood or bar of iron inserted in a knot to make it more secure, or more readily unfastened or slipped.

Trice—To haul up and secure.

Turn—A single winding of rope, as around a bollard or cleat.

Unlay—To separate the strands of a rope.

Unreeve—The opposite of reeve.

Veer—To allow rope or chain to run out; to slack off.

Veer and haul—To slack off and pull alternately.

Whip—To lash the end of a rope to prevent it from unlaying. Also used to designate different kinds and arrangements of blocks and tackles.

Whipping—The lashings on the end of a rope or the small stuff used for shipping.

With the sun—Rotation in the same direction as the sun, clockwise or right-handed; opposite to against the sun, counterclockwise or left-handed.

KNOTS AND SPLICES

The safety of a vessel and its crew frequently depends on the knots and splices used in joining lines together. For this reason no man can consider himself a seaman until he has mastered the methods of quickly and properly tying those knots and making those splices commonly used.

The *Manual for Lifeboatmen, Able Seamen, and Qualified Members of the Engine Department*, Coast Guard Pamphlet, CG-175, sets forth the requirements for able seamen and lists the "principal knots, bends, splices, and hitches" which the candidate for A.B. must know. In the list which follows, those knots contained in CG-175 are indicated by an asterisk (*).

The seaman should also be able to make the following splices in Manila rope: eye, short, and long. In addition, he should be able to tie other knots, including some of the various wall and crown, and should also be able to splice wire cables, as well as make other splices in Manila. He should be able to make proper mousings and seizings, and be familiar with methods of parceling and serving. He should be thoroughly familiar with the use of the sailmaker's palm, fid, and marlinespike.

The illustrations and descriptions here are of the most widely known and useful knots. The illustrations have been planned so that a minimum of description is required and it should be possible to make most of the knots by carefully following the presentations.

For clearness the knots are shown in their open state, that is, before they have been pulled taut, and hence some knots will, when pulled tight, present a somewhat different appearance than the drawings show.

There are many instances of a knot being known by more than one name, especially when used for different purposes. Where possible, this has been noted. Many knots are made in slightly different ways by different classes of people using them. The illustrations in this book generally show the most universally accepted forms so far as it has been possible to determine them.

In learning to make these knots a 6-foot length of 9-thread Manila rope may be used, with the ends whipped as shown in Figure 1-5. The Manila rope may be a little hard to handle at first, but since Manila rope will be the type most often encountered in actual practice, it is just as well to become accustomed to its use. It is also advisable to practice tying knots in awkward positions and in the dark, as this may be necessary aboard ship.

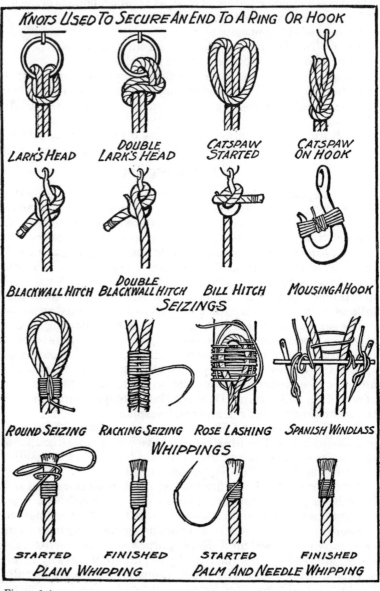

Figure 1-4.

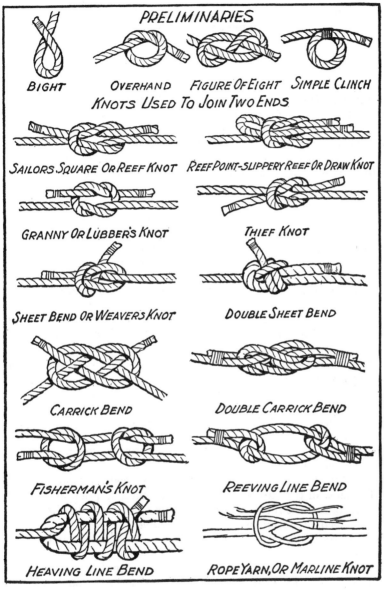

Figure 1-5.

When tying knots, it is customary to speak of different parts of the rope as follows: The *end* is, as the name implies, the very end of the rope. The *bight* is a loop or half loop formed by turning the rope back on itself. The *standing part* is the long unused portion of the rope.

KNOTS

The **Overhand Knot***, with the **Figure of Eight** or **Flemish Knot**, is the simplest of all knots. Both are occasionally used to keep the end of a rope from fraying or as a "stopper knot" to keep a rope from pulling through a hole. They form a part of many other knots.

Simple Clinch is used to form various types of running knots.

The **Sailor's Reef***, or **Square Knot**, is probably the most useful of all knots. It is strong, easily tied, will not slip, and is easily untied by pushing the standing parts and ends toward the middle of the knot.

When an end of the sailor's knot is passed back through the adjacent bight it becomes a reef point.

The **Reef Point** is used extensively for reefing sails. Its virtue lies in the fact that it can be untied very quickly by jerking the end.

The **Granny** or **Lubber's Knot** is usually made by mistake when trying to make the sailor's knot. It is a poor knot, slips easily and should never be used.

The **Thief Knot** is identical with the sailor's except that the standing parts of the two ropes are on opposite sides of the knot. Because of this it is likely to shift its position under strain.

The thief or bread knot supposedly derived its name in an interesting fashion. In galleys of the old sailing vessels, the cook, it is said, used to fashion the bread container by means of a sailor's knot. In the cook's absence the cabin boy on one ship used to slip into the galley to steal food and on leaving, instead of tying a true sailor's knot, invariably tied the modification now known as "thief." The cook on seeing his bread box fastened with an improper knot always knew whom to blame, much to the cabin boy's surprise.

The **Sheet Bend*** (also call **Becket Bend**) is used for fastening the "sheet" to the clew of the sail. It is also good to make a quick and secure joining of two ropes that must withstand a heavy strain. This knot is of exactly the same construction as the *Weaver's knot*.

The **Double Sheet Bend*** is a more secure method of accomplishing the same purpose.

The **Carrick Bend*** is a useful as well as an ornamental knot. Its main use is for joining large hawsers. It is good for piecing large ropes, because when pulled taut the knot contains no sharp bends that would injure the rope.

The **Double Carrick Bend** is a variation of the carrick bend used for bending heavy hawsers together.

The **Fisherman's Knot** is commonly used for joining gut leaders.

The **Reeving-line Bend** is used to connect two hawsers so that they will offer little resistance when rove through an opening. Take a half hitch with each end around the other hawser and seize to finish off.

The **Heaving-line Bend** is used to tie a small rope to a large rope, generally as the name implies, to make a heaving line fast to a hawser.

The **Rope-yarn** or **Marline Knot** makes a small tight knot in joining two pieces of rope yarn or marline together.

The **Bowline*** is probably the best known and most useful of the eye knots. It is easily made by forming a bight in the rope and passing the end up through the bight, under the standing part and down through the bight again.

The **Running Bowline*** is merely a bowline, the large loop of which is made around the standing part of the rope, forming a slipping noose similar to that used on a lariat.

The **Bowline on a Bight*** is a method of making a loop in a rope, both ends of which are fastened. Double up the center of the rope and form a double bight. Pass the very end of the loop up through this bight. Draw this loop back down over the large loop until it finally reaches the position shown in Figure 1-6.

The **French Bowline*** makes a safe sling if it is necessary to send a man over the side on dangerous work, into a smoke-filled hold, or hold suspected of containing gas, or any job at which he will need the use of both hands. First make a regular bowline but instead of turning the end about the standing part at once, give it a round turn about the *bight* of the eye, then finish the knot as you would a regular bowline. You now have two loops connected loosely through the gooseneck so that a man may sit in one loop while the other loop fits under his arm pits with the knot at his breast.

The **Spanish Bowline*** is a method of forming two loops in a rope, neither of which will slip.

The **Fisherman's Eye** is a variation of the fisherman's knot used to form a loop.

The **Crabber's Eye** is another type of loop knot, not so very well known. Its virtue lies in the fact that once made correctly, it seldom slips.

The **Openhand Knot** is a method of forming a loop that is seldom used because it will jam under strain.

The **Midshipman's Hitch** is a form of running noose that becomes tight when the knot passes against an object within the noose.

The **Jug Sling** or **Hackamore**, another form of noose knot, may be used to carry a jug by placing the neck in the center of the knot and using the loop and ends for handles. As a hackamore knot, it is used as a temporary bridle.

The **Tomfool's Knot** is a knot in which two loops are formed. A practical application of this knot is to use the two loops as rope handcuffs.

The **Jury Masthead Knot** is a multiple noose knot in which four loops are formed. In use it is placed over the top of a jury mast and the four loops are used to hold the stays.

Sheepshanks*—The first type illustrated is the most universally used for shortening ropes. The shortening will remain secure as long as there is a strain on the rope.

The **Knotted Sheepshank** has a number of forms, one of which is illustrated. Its advantage lies in the fact that it will not loosen if the rope is slackened.

The **Toggled Sheepshank** has the same virtues as the knotted sheepshank and in addition can be made when both ends of the rope are secure. It is made by simply forming a marlinespike hitch on each end of the plain sheepshank.

The **Sheepshank with Reef** is more secure than the ordinary variety, can be made more quickly, and in addition is quite ornamental.

The **Clove Hitch*** is used to make a line fast to a spar or post. When used on a post it is tied by throwing two half hitches over the post. When it is used on a spar, stanchion, etc., it is made by passing the end around twice to form the hitch as illustrated.

The **Slip Hitch** is a variation of the clove hitch that can be instantly released by pulling the free end.

The **Timber Hitch*** is used where a quick fastening is desired, as in hauling or lifting timber, pipe or rails, or for temporarily securing a rope to a spar.

The **Killick Hitch** is the timber hitch with a half hitch added to steady long timber, pipe, rails or other long objects while handling with a single sling. The half hitch may be placed as far away from the timber hitch part as needed, in order to steady the end of the load.

The **Rolling Hitch*** is used to bend a rope to a spar or standing part of another rope, especially when it is necessary to shift the rope along the spar without removing it. This knot is made by passing the end twice round the spar or rope, each time crossing the standing part on the top. A hitch round the spar or rope on the opposite side of the turns finishes it off.

The **Stopper Hitch** is similar to the rolling hitch except that the second turn is crossed over the first turn. Tied in this manner it is more secure than the rolling hitch. Take several turns around spar or other object with the free end and retain your grasp as a safety measure.

The **Lifting Hitch** is used when the strain is to come parallel to the spar. A lifting hitch may be made with a strap as shown in Figure 1-7.

Two Half Hitches* is a widely used knot for making a line fast temporarily to a spar or ring.

Round Turn and Two Half Hitches is another method of making a line fast to a spar or ring. It is more secure than two half hitches alone.

The **Fisherman's Bend*** is a reliable, secure method of making a line fast to a spar or ring.

The **Stuns'l Tack Bend** or **Buntline Hitch** is a bend that will jam and remain secure as long as a strain or tension is kept on the line. This was the regulation hitch for the studding-sail tack and the buntline in making fast these ropes to the sail in square-rigger days. Also called a "back hitch" by the boys in the schooners.

The **Stuns'l Halyard Bend** is made by taking a round turn with the end

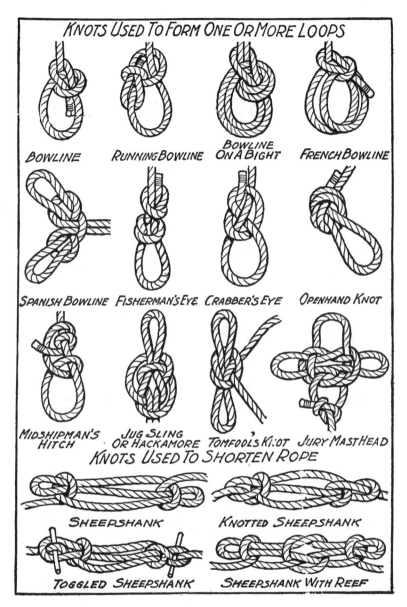

Figure 1-6.

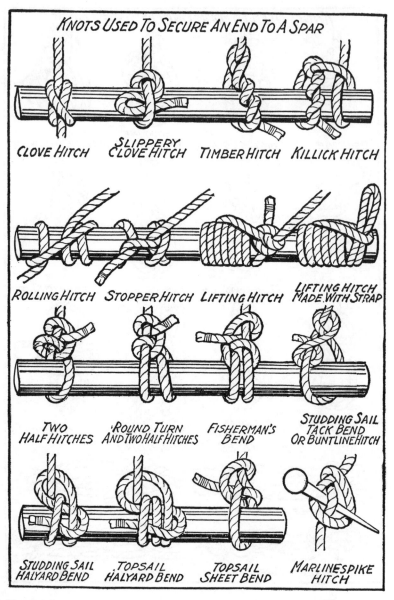

Figure 1-7.

coming around the standing part, then under both turns and tucked over and under the turns.

The **Topsail Halyard Bend** is used on yachts for fastening a rope to a spar.

The **Topsail Sheet Bend** is the yachtsman's version of the buntline hitch, studding-sail tack bend, or back hitch. It is exactly the same thing. It is ordinarily used to bend the sheet to the clew of a sail.

The **Marlinespike Hitch** is used to get a grip on a line with a marlinespike so that the line may be pulled taut.

The **Lark's Head** is used to fasten a line to a ring when there is to be an even strain on both parts. Also known as Cow Hitch.

The **Double Lark's Head** is a more secure knot serving the same purpose as a lark's head.

The **Cat's Paw**, which is also called by various other names, is made by forming two bights in a rope, one with either hand. The bights are then twisted on themselves and may be slipped over a hook or other object. It is quite secure.

The **Blackwall Hitch** is a quick and secure method of attaching a rope to a hook, provided the rope will be constantly taut when in use. The **Single Blackwall** is best when the rope and the hook are the same size. Use the **Double Blackwall Hitch** when the rope is smaller than the hook.

The **Bill Hitch** is another method for securing a line to a hook. It will hold only while a continuous strain is on the line, and should not be used when the rope is of smaller diameter than the hook.

Mousing a Hook is a method used to prevent a sling or hitch from accidentally coming off the hook.

The **Round Seizing** is used to hold two lines together. It is made by passing eight or ten turns of seizing stuff tightly around the two lines and securing them with two or more frapping turns.

The **Racking Seizing** is another method used to hold two lines together. It is made by first passing turns around the two lines, in figure-eight manner, and then going back over and between these turns with round turns. A good racking on two parts of a tackle, to hold the stress while slacking up the hauling parts, can be made with a few round turns of stout tarred spun yarn.

The **Rose Lashing** is a method used to secure an eye to a spar. The manner in which it is made is clearly shown in Figure 1-5.

The **Spanish Windlass** is a device used to pull two taut ropes together. Rarely seen today, its use is much the same as that of the rigging screw. The two parts of the rope are hove together by this means preparatory to putting on a round seizing.

The **Plain Whipping** is used to prevent the ends of a rope from fraying or becoming unlaid. There are several methods of making plain whippings, the most common is shown in Figure 1-5.

The **Palm and Needle**, or **Sail Maker's Whipping** serves the same purpose and is used when a neat permanent job is required.

The **Crown*** is used to start a back splice and as a base for more complicated end knots. It is shown in an open state to illustrate the method of forming the knot.

The **Back Splice**, used to prevent an end from fraying, is made by first forming a crown and then tucking each strand over and under the strands of the standing part. This method increases the diameter of the line and should not be used when the line must be rove through a block.

The **Wall Knot*** is used at the end of a line and as a part of other end knots. It is shown both in an open and a finished state in Figure 1-8.

The **Double Wall Knot** is made from the wall knot by following each strand around again until the end comes out at the top.

The **Wall and Crown** is used mainly as a base for a manrope knot.

The **Manrope Knot** is one of the wall and crown combinations. A single crown is first made on the rope. A wall knot is then made underneath this, around the rope's standing part.

The **Diamond Knot** is made the same as the wall knot except that each strand is brought up through the bight of the second strand.

The **Matthew Walker Knot** is of the same general type as the foregoing but of somewhat more complicated construction.

The **Three-Strand Turk's Head*** is an ornamental knot. It can be made by weaving the line as illustrated in its flat form in Figure 1-8. Figure 1-8 also shows the same type of knot made around a post or mast. In this latter form it is useful for holding together a partly broken or splintered mast or post as the knot covers considerable area and can be drawn very tight.

The **Four-Strand Turk's Head** is almost impossible to illustrate with a drawing or photograph and is very difficult to learn from a book; you can learn it by studying the following instructions and with a little aid from someone who already knows how to make it: Start with an overhand knot; open it and pass end of the rope farthest from you down under the bight, crossing it, up through the knot, lying close against you; now dip the end over and back through the middle opening and against the standing part, then lay the left bight over to the right and dip the end over and under; now switch the next bight from right to left and dip over and under till the ends meet lying against each other.

Worming is filling up the lays of a rope with spiral windings of small stuff preparatory to parceling in order to make a round, smooth surface.

Parceling consists of protecting a rope from the weather by winding strips of canvas or other material around it with the lay, before serving.

Serving is covering a rope with small stuff wound closely and snugly over the worming and parceling. The turns of the serving are made against the lay of the rope and each one must be taut. To keep the serving taut and the turns close, a serving board and serving mallet are used.

"Worm and Parcel with the Lay
Turn and Serve the Other Way."

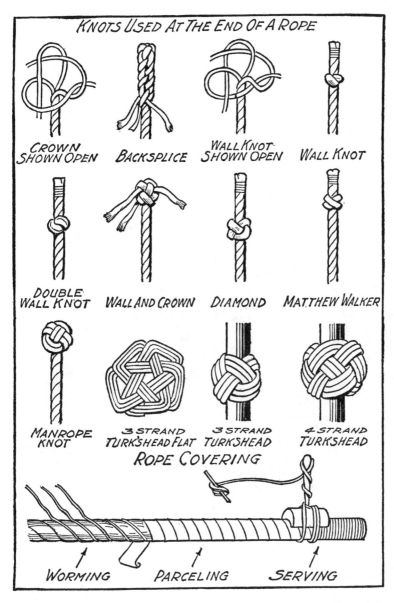

Figure 1-8.

SPLICING

It is very often desirable to join two rope ends together in a neater manner than can be accomplished by the use of knots. For this purpose various methods of "splicing" are employed. Another reason for this type of joining is the fact that a well made splice very nearly approaches the strength of the rope itself, whereas even the best knots do not.

Small ropes can be spliced by opening the strands with the fingers. For the larger ropes use a marlinespike or fid.

Figure 1-9. Trainees at the Harry Lundeberg Seamanship School making up a towboat fender. Courtesy: Harry Lundeberg Seamanship School, Inc.

Short Splice*—Unlay for a sufficient distance, the strands of the two rope ends to be spliced. Then intertwine the strands as shown at the left in Figure 1-10. Fasten the ends temporarily in this position by passing a rope yarn or string securely around the outside of the joining. The actual splicing is now ready to begin. This is accomplished by passing or "tucking" each strand over and under its companions in the opposing rope end. After this has been done with all six strands, one round of "tucks" has been made. To hold well a short splice must usually be composed of three or more rounds of "tucks."

The **Long Splice*** is useful when it is necessary to have a joining less bulky than the short splice. To make this splice, unlay the two rope ends for quite a distance and put the ends together in the same manner as in the short splice, but do not tie them. Now unlay one of the strands still further and follow the space left between the remaining two with a strand from the other rope end. This strand should be twisted into the space so that after twisting has been accomplished the rope appears as it did originally, but instead of consisting of three strands from the same rope, it now is made up of two strands from one rope and one from the other rope. Do this same thing again with the other four strands, unlaying one and following the space made with the opposing strand from the other rope end. The rope should now appear as in the illustration. Make overhand knots with each set of strand ends. Next part the ends of each strand, tucking one half under and over the adjacent strands on one side of the knot and the remainder under and over the adjacent strands on the other side of the knot.

Three-Strand Eye Splice*—Unlay the rope 12 to 24 inches, depending on size of rope. Form the eye of desired size by bending the crotch of the strands back onto standing part with eye toward you. Now with center strands up and the other two strands on either side, tuck center strand under the strand directly below it; left-hand strand passes over the strand under which the first strand was tucked and then under the next strand. Turn the splice over and twist the last strand with the lay to tighten the yarn and tuck it under the remaining strand. Remember that all strands are tucked from right to left. After you have taken full tucks with the three strands, tuck each of them over and under twice more. If splice is to be served, it is well to cut out one third of the yarns before making the last tucks.

Four-Strand Eye Splice—First or left strand tucks under two (first tuck only); other strands each under one. Direction of tucks from right to left.

Flemish Eye Splice—To make a Flemish eye splice first unlay all strands a short distance, and then unlay one strand further. Form an eye by bending the two strands back to the point where the single strand has been unlaid. Lay up the single strand in its own groove but in the opposite direction. Finish the splice by tucking the three strands in the same manner as in an ordinary eye splice.

The **Cut Splice** is made by placing the two ropes side by side and splicing the ends into each other's standing parts as in an eye splice. If a special size eye is desired, take the measurement from throat to throat. (This splice is used for a quick joining of two ends of a parted wire hawser.) Always see that the two sides of the eye are equal in length.

Sailmaker's Eye Splice—In making the sailmaker's eye splice the first tuck is made in the same manner as an ordinary eye splice and then each strand is tucked around and around the strands of the standing part, with the lay of the rope. The splice should be tapered by cutting out a portion of each strand at each tuck after the first.

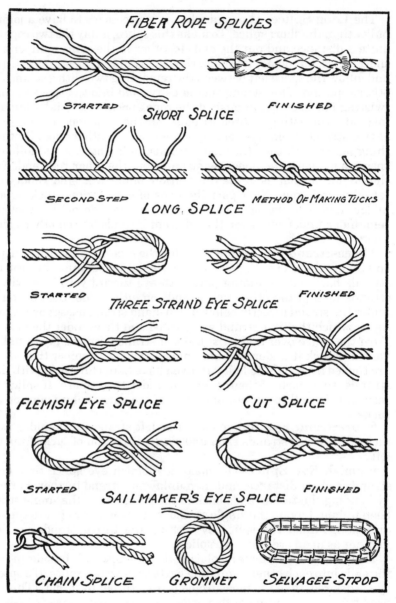

Figure 1-10.

Chain Splice—Unlay the end and reeve two of the strands through the end link; unlay the third strand and follow it up as in a long splice with one of the other strands; marry these two and tuck the ends as in the long splice. The remaining strand, which was rove through the link, is tucked in the rope in the same way as the eye splice. If the rope is a four-strand one, proceed as before, except that two strands will be handled as in the long splice. This splice is put in so that the rope's bulk will not obstruct the reeving of the rope and chain through a block or other lead; the ordinary eye splice would be too bulky in such a case.

Grommet—A grommet is a ring or strap made of rope and has many uses. It is made of one continuous strand of rope by crossing the strand to form a ring and then following the lay of the rope with each end until three complete turns are formed. The ends are then tucked as in a long splice. "Stropping a block" was the old term for fitting a grommet around the shell of the block. Today almost every block is fitted with a strop (or strap) of steel or iron and is *inside* the shell.

Selvagee Strop—A selvagee strop is made of many turns of rope yarns, marline, or other small stuff seized together with marline. When making a selvagee strop, care should be taken to give each turn an equal tension. The illustration in Figure 1-8 shows the marline hitches used to secure the turns. This strop is a better holder than the ordinary rope strop when used as a means of hooking a tackle to a hawser, shroud, etc. It is always free of twists or kinks.

*Contained in *Manual for Lifeboatmen, Able Seaman, and Qualified Members of the Engine Department,* Coast Guard Pamphlet, *CG-175.*

CHAPTER II

WIRE AND WIRE SPLICING

WIRE ROPE

WIRE ROPE was introduced into use aboard ship about one hundred years ago. Wire rope, made from steel, comes in a variety of sizes depending upon its intended function. It is made up of a number of individual wires twisted together uniformly around a core of wire or fiber.

Tensile strength and quality of wire depends largely upon the carbon content of the wire. The kind of wire rope used is of two general classes— Improved Plow Steel and Extra Improved Plow Steel. Improved Plow Steel has a carbon content of about 0.70 percent to 0.80 percent; and Extra Improved Plow Steel has a carbon content of about 0.70 percent to 0.85 percent. However, since the carbon content varies with the manufacturer, these figures are representative.

Flexibility, as well as tensile strength, depends upon the number and size of wires in each strand and the number of strands in the rope. A 6x19 rope has 6 strands with 19 wires in each strand. A 6x37 wire rope has the same diameter, but the individual wires are far smaller. Consequently the wire rope itself is more flexible. Most wire rope used aboard ship is six-strand.

CORES

All wire rope has a core around which the strands are laid up. The core may be natural or synthetic fiber, wire strand, or independent wire rope. Whatever type core is used, its purpose is to support the strands which are laid up around it.

Fiber core, which may be synthetic, Manila, sisal, or hemp, provides a necessary foundation, adding to the flexibility and elasticity of the rope. In addition, when manufactured, the core is permeated with a lubricant which helps to keep the entire rope lubricated. If flexibility is not an important factor, or if the rope is to be used where high operating temperatures are expected, or additional strength is desired, a wire core may be used.

LAY

The term "lay" is used two ways. The first describes the appearance or construction of wire rope according to direction of the spiral. The second describes the length or distance it takes for an individual strand to make a complete spiral of the rope. Thus, if a strand takes 18 inches to make a complete revolution, the length of the lay is 18 inches.

Showing how "one rope lay" is the lengthwise distance in which a strand makes one complete turn around the rope.

Figure 2-1. Wire rope lays. Courtesy: Bethelehem Steel Corporation.

Although there are several ways in which wire may be laid up, the most common is right-regular lay. In right-regular lay the individual wires are laid up in the strands to the left (or in a direction opposite to the direction in which the strands rotate around the axis of the rope), and the strands are laid up to the right. This has the effect of causing the individual wires to point along the axis of the rope. A left-regular lay wire rope shows the individual wires lined up with the axis of the rope, but laid up to the right in individual strands, while the strands are laid up to the left.

Lang lay is the reverse of regular lay. In lang lay both the individual wires and the strands rotate in the same direction. This makes it appear that the individual wires make an angle of about 45 degrees or more with the axis of the rope. Lang lay can be either right or left as indicated in Figure 2-1. However, lang lay is rarely found aboard ship. Finally, there is a reverse lay in which the wire rope is composed of alternate regular and lang lay strands. This type also is seldom seen.

WIRE ROPE SIZE

Unlike fiber rope which is measured by its circumference, wire is measured by its diameter. Although there appears to be a "short" and a "long" diameter, the greatest diameter should be measured, as shown in Figure 2-2.

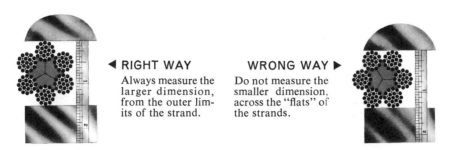

◀ RIGHT WAY

Always measure the larger dimension, from the outer limits of the strand.

WRONG WAY ▶

Do not measure the smaller dimension, across the "flats" of the strands.

Figure 2-2. Measuring wire rope. Courtesy: Bethelehem Steel Corporation.

PREFORMED WIRE ROPE

Wire rope is either "preformed" or "non-preformed." If the rope is preformed, the wires and strands have been preshaped to conform to the curvature which they will take in the finished rope. This helps eliminate locked-up stress and strain which exists in non-preformed rope, and reduces the tendency to kink. Pre-forming also reduces the tendency of the rope to rotate about its own axis. Preformed rope is easier to splice. A most important advantage of preformed rope is that its tendency to unlay or fly apart violently when cut is greatly reduced. Although non-preformed wire is still used, 95 percent of all wire rope sold for shipboard use is now preformed. Originally more expensive than non-preformed, its cost is now almost comparable. There is no difference in the appearance of preformed and non-preformed wire. The difference cannot be determined until the wire is cut. Preformed or not, a seizing should be placed on the wire before cutting.

GALVANIZING

To protect it against salt water and weather, wire rope may be galvanized (zinc coated). This process, however, tends to make the rope stiffer and to reduce its strength by about 10 percent. Galvanized wire is generally used for standing rigging or towing hawsers because it will lose its zinc coating if constantly run through blocks.

CHARACTERISTICS AND USE OF WIRE ROPE

Several examples of the more common wire ropes are shown in Figure 2-3, and a sampling of a few sizes and uses of wire are as follows:

6x7   Galvanized. Permanent standing rigging.

6x12   Galvanized. Guys, boat ladders, Jacob's ladders, boom pendants, wire mooring line. Phosphor bronze. Life lines, wheel ropes.

6x19   For its size, this is the strongest of all the wire ropes. Galvanized. Standing rigging, guys, boat slings, topping lifts for booms. Ungalvanized. Heavy hoisting. Useful on derricks and dredges.

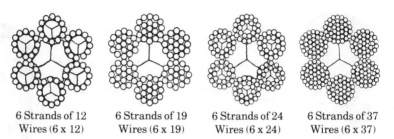

| 6 Strands of 12 Wires (6 x 12) | 6 Strands of 19 Wires (6 x 19) | 6 Strands of 24 Wires (6 x 24) | 6 Strands of 37 Wires (6 x 37) |

Figure 2-3. Examples of the more common wire ropes. Courtesy: U.S. Navy.

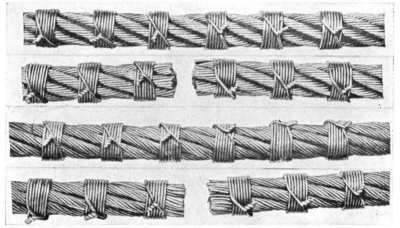

Figure 2-4. Seizings on wire rope. (Top) regular lay rope. (Bottom) lang lay rope.

	Phosphor bronze. Life lines, wheel ropes, rigging, radio antennas.
6x24	Stronger than 6x12 construction and about as flexible. Used mainly in the larger sizes.
6x37	Galvanized. Steering gear, transmission rope, boatcrane falls, hawsers, towing hawsers, bridles.
	Ungalvanized. Very flexible when not galvanized. Cranes, heavy hoisting.
Spring lay or Swedish	A combination of wire and fiber rope. Six main strands laid around a fiber core. Each main strand consists of three preformed wire strands and three fiber strands. Measured by its diameter. Used for mooring lines.

CARE AND PRESERVATION

Before storing, wire should be cleaned and lubricated. It should not be stored in places with acid, or where acid has been kept.

Wire rope should *not* be unreeled from a reel on its side. The reel must be on a pipe or rod so that it will turn easily. If wire is placed back on a reel, remember that a right lay wire will roll to the left. Avoid reverse bends. If

wire is spooled from reel to drum, it should be spooled only from the top of
the reel to the top of the drum.

Kinks are the greatest enemy of wire rope. If a line becomes kinked, and
its strands take a permanent set, the strength is reduced by 50 percent.
Kinks should be cut out and the wire spliced. A kink should not be pulled
out by placing a strain on it. As soon as noticed, grasp the part of each side
of the wire outside of the kink and try to enlarge the kink by pushing and
working the wire into a loop. Then turn the bent portion over, place on a
firm object, and push until the kink straightens out as much as possible.
Then, the area should be placed on a flat surface and pounded smooth with
a wooden mallet.

Finally the wire should be wound on a sheave of the proper size. Because
manufacturers suggest different size sheaves, the rule of thumb used by
the U.S. Coast Guard that the diameter of the sheave should not be less
than twenty times the diameter of the wire is advisable. In addition, the
stiffer the wire rope, the larger the sheave diameter must be. Finally, some
manuals point out that just as a sheave too small will increase friction and
pinch the rope, so will a sheave too large fail to support and guide the rope.
Bethlehem Steel Corporation makes the following recommendations for
sheave and drum size:

Diameter of rope in inches	Diameter of sheave or drum in inches		
	6x19	6x37	8x19
1/4	6	4 1/2	5
5/16	7 1/2	5 5/8	6 1/4
3/8	9	6 3/4	7 1/2
7/16	10 1/2	8	8 3/4
1/2	12	9	10
9/16	13 1/2	10	11 1/4
5/8	15	11 1/4	12 1/2
3/4	18	13 1/2	15
7/8	21	16	17 1/2
1	24	18	20
1 1/8	27	20	22 1/2
1 1/4	30	22 1/2	25

Even new wire may have some fishhooks, and for this reason gloves
should always be worn when handling wire. A few fishhooks will not
destroy the strength of the wire, but more fishhooks are obviously an
indication of wear. The Navy recommends that if 4 percent of the individual wires in the length of one lay of the rope are broken or have
fishhooks, the rope is unsafe.

As is true with any important piece of equipment, wire should be inspected periodically. Fishhooks, kinks, and worn and corroded spots
should be looked for. The diameter of the wire rope should be measured in

several places as well as the diameter of one of the individual wires. If the measurement of the original diameter is less by half the diameter of an individual wire, the strength of the rope has been reduced significantly. If the measurement of the original diameter is less by the diameter of the individual wire, it is time to replace the rope.

The importance of lubricating wire is obvious. Every time the rope bends or straightens, the position of the strands and the individual wires change. Lubrication keeps these "moving parts" from wearing each other out. Lubrication also helps prevent corrosion.

Wire should be cleaned before lubrication. This can be done with a wire brush, compressed air, or steam. Even fresh water helps. There is no point in applying new lubricant on top of old dirt or grit. A good lubricant for running rigging is medium graphite grease. Fish oil, raw linseed oil, or motor oil may be used, but graphite grease is preferable because it resists salt water corrosion. There are also commercial lubricants on the market.

Sometimes wire rope fails. There is always a reason. In most cases causes for this failure can be prevented. To keep wire rope useable, it is a good idea to know the common reasons for failure:

- Using the wrong size wire.
- Failing to maintain wire properly.
- Failing to lubricate.
- Using the wrong size sheaves.
- Overriding or crosswinding on drums.
- Jumping off sheaves.
- Subjecting to moisture or acid.
- Subjecting to severe or continuing overloads.
- Operating winch too fast.
- Kinking.
- Allowing excessive internal wear because of grit penetrating the strands.
- Permitting to untwist.
- Being careless.

SAFE WORKING LOAD, SAFETY FACTOR AND BREAKING STRAIN

As is true for fiber rope, the best means of finding the breaking strain of wire rope is to consult Occupational Safety and Health Administration (OSHA) standards or the manufacturer's specifications. It should be noted that these specifications are calculated on the basis of tests performed on new wire. If the wire used is not new, or has been subjected to abuse, it is not as strong as when it left the factory. Rated capacities for 6x19 and 6x37 wire rope are shown in the following table:

EXTRACTS FROM TABLES G-2 AND G-4, OCCUPATIONAL SAFETY AND HEALTH ADMINISTRATION (OSHA) STANDARDS PUBLISHED BY AMERICAN IRON AND STEEL INSTITUTE, 1974. THESE TABLES SHOW OSHA-RATED CAPACITIES FOR IMPROVED PLOW STEEL WIRE ROPE.

Diameter (inches)	6x19		Diameter (inches)	6x37	
	Ind. wire rope core	Fiber core		Ind. wire rope core	Fiber core
1/4	0.53	0.49	1 1/4	10.0	9.8
3/8	1.1	1.1	1 3/8	13.0	12.0
1/2	2.0	1.8	1 1/2	15.0	14.0
5/8	3.0	2.8	1 3/4	20.0	19.0
3/4	4.2	3.9	2	26.0	25.0
7/8	5.5	5.1	2 1/4	33.0	-
1	7.2	6.7			
1 1/8	9.0	8.4			

Notes
1. Rated capacities are in tons of 2,000 pounds. Rated capacity has the same meaning as Safe Working Load (SWL).
2. Capacity assumes single leg vertical pull using a hand tucked splice attachment. Capacity would be greater for a socket or swaged terminal attachment or a mechanical sleeve attachment.
3. OSHA standards require that the SWL of running ropes not exceed one-fifth to one-fourth of the Breaking Strain depending upon the weight involved.
4. OSHA standards do not permit wire rope to be used for a vessel's cargo gear if in any length of 8 diameters the total number of visible broken wires exceeds 10 percent of the total number of wires. Except for eye splices in the ends of wires, each wire rope used in hoisting or lowering shall consist of one continuous piece without knot or splice.
5. In the event that OSHA-approved tables for the SWL of wire rope have not been developed, the SWL recommended by the manufacturer shall be used provided that a safety factor (SF) of not less than 5 is maintained.

If the manufacturer's specifications or OSHA standards are not available, the following empirical formulas similar to those discussed in Chapter I for Manila may be used:

$$B = 2.5\,C^2 \qquad \text{or} \qquad P \text{ or } SWL = \frac{C^2}{2.5}$$

There are some things to watch out for, however, in applying these formulas. Remember that wire is measured by the *diameter*. These formulas require the use of the *circumference*. Thus, it is necessary to convert diameter to circumference by using the formula $C = pi \times D$ where pi = 3.14. The formula for P or SWL assumes a safety factor of 6.25 which is adequate. However, on a Coast Guard licensing examination a slightly different formula may be furnished. It may be that the 2.5 will be replaced by 3.0 or another similar figure, or a different safety factor will be required. The above formulas hold good only for 6x12 plow steel or 6x24 cast steel wire. Therefore, a change in the formula is necessary.

Problem: What is the breaking strain of a 1.25 inch 6x12 plow steel wire? If the Safety Factor is 6.25, what is its Safe Working Load (SWL)?

$$B = 2.5\,C^2 \qquad B = 2.5 \times (3.14 \times 1.25)^2 = 38.51 \text{ tons}$$

$$P = SWL = \frac{C^2}{2.5} = \frac{(3.14 \times 1.25)^2}{2.5} = 6.16 \text{ tons}$$

There is a variation to this problem. You might be given the Safe Working Load or Breaking Strain and asked for the smallest size wire you could use.

Problem: Given the formula $SWL = C^2 \div 2.5$, what size wire should be used to insure a SWL of 15 tons?

$$SWL = \frac{C^2}{2.5} \quad \text{or} \quad C^2 = SWL \times 2.5$$

$$C^2 = 15 \times 2.5 = 37.5$$
$$C = \sqrt{37.5} = 6.12$$
$$\text{But } C = \text{pi} \times D$$
$$\text{So } 6.12 = 3.14 \times D$$
$$D = \frac{6.12}{3.14} = 1.95$$

So, you know you must use a wire of at least 1.95 inch in diameter. Since there is no 1.95 inch diameter wire, you must round off to the next *larger* size, or 2 inches.

SEIZINGS

In the manufacture of wire rope, great care is exercised to lay each wire in the strand and each strand in the rope under uniform tension. If the ends of wire rope are not properly secured, the original balance of tension will be disturbed and maximum service will not be obtained because some strands will be carrying a greater portion of the load than others.

Before cutting steel wire rope, it is essential to place at least three sets of seizings each side of the intended cut to avoid disturbing the uniformity of the rope. On large diameter ropes more seizings are necessary.

It is important to use the proper size and grade of wire for seizing. We advocate using annealed iron wire in these sizes:

WIRE SIZES AND NUMBER OF SEIZINGS

	Number of Seizings for Wire Rope		
Rope Diameter	*Annealed Iron Seizing Wire Diameter*	*Regular Lay with Hemp Center*	*Lang Lay and Rope with Strand or I.W.R.C.*
1/2'' and smaller	.035''	3	4
9/16'' to 7/8'' inclusive	.063''	3	4
1'' to 1 1/2'' inclusive	.092''	4	5
1 5/8'' to 2 1/8'' inclusive	.120''	5	6
2 1/4'' and larger	.135''	5	6

INSTRUCTIONS FOR PUTTING ON SEIZING

1. Wind uniformly and use good tension on wire. Unless a serving mallet is used there is no advantage in making more than ten wraps of wire per seizing.

2. Cross the ends over the seizing and twist the wires counterclockwise.

3. Grasp ends with wire cutters and twist up slack. Do not try to tighten up on seizing by twisting.

4. Draw up on seizing and twist up slack again.

5. Cut ends and pound back as in Figure 2-4.

WIRE ROPE CLIPS

Although wire rope clips are not recommended to take the place of an eye splice, they can be used on a temporary basis. If the clip connection is made properly, breaking strength of the rope will be approximately 80 percent of its original value. If an insufficient number of clips is used, or if the nuts are not properly set up, it will be less. The minimum number of clips recommended is shown in the following table. Figure 2-5 shows the right and wrong way to use wire clips.

MINIMUM NUMBER OF CLIPS REQUIRED

Rope Diameter	*All 6x7 Ropes; All Ropes with Independent Wire Rope Centers*	*All 6x19 6x37 Rope*	*Proper Torque To Be Applied To Nuts of Clips (ft/lb)*
3/8	4	3	25
1/2	4	3	40
5/8	4	3	65
3/4	5	4	100
7/8	5	4	165
1	6	5	165
1-1/8	6	5	165
1-1/4	7	6	250
1-3/8	7	6	375
1-1/2	8	7	375
1-3/4	8	7	560

Courtesy of U.S. Navy

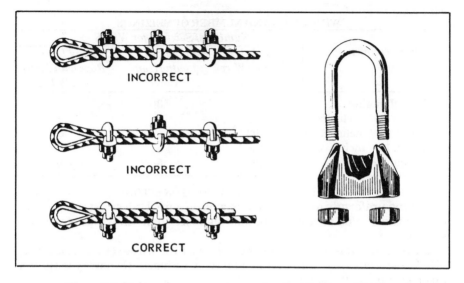

Figure 2-5. Right and wrong way to use wire clips. Courtesy: U.S. Navy.

Note that the correct way of using clips is to place the U-bolts on the short or dead end of the rope. This is because the live or stress-bearing end of the rope should be protected against crushing and abuse. The bearing seats and extended prongs of the body offer such protection. As a safety measure it is wise to check all clips after an hour's running time and at regular intervals because rope tends to compress and the clips to loosen under operating conditions. If clips have been installed on the same rope for a long time, they should be removed and the rope underneath examined for the presence of broken wires. If any broken wires are found, the damaged part should be cut out and a new connection made.

TOOLS FOR WIRE ROPE SPLICING

1. Two "T" shaped splicing pins.
2. Two round splicing pins.
3. One tapered spike for opening the strands and taking out the hemp center.
4. A knife for cutting the hemp core.
5. A pair of wire cutters for cutting off ends of strands.
6. Two wooden mallets to hammer down any uneven surfaces.
7. A piece of hemp rope spliced endless.
8. A hickory stick about the size of an ordinary hammer handle, which will be used to untwist the strands, as shown in some of the following illustrations.

It will be noted that a tapered spike is shown on following pages. Many rope splicers prefer to use the "T" shaped splicing pin for this work.

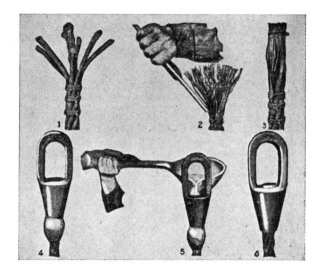

HOW TO ATTACH A WIRE ROPE SOCKET

1. Measure from end of rope a length equal to basket of socket. Serve at this point with not less than three seizings. Cut out the hemp center but do not cut out wire rope or strand when used as a center. Open strands.
2. Separate wires in strands. Straighten by means of iron pipe. Cleanse all wires carefully with kerosene oil from ends to as near first serving as possible. Wipe dry.
3. Dip wires, for three quarters of the distance to the first seizing, into one half muriatic acid, one half water (use no stronger solution and take extreme care that acid does not touch any other part of the rope). Keep wire in long enough to be thoroughly cleaned. Wipe dry. Serve end so that socket covers all wires.
4. Then slip socket over wires. Cut top seizing wire and distribute all wires evenly in basket and flush with top. Be sure socket is in line with axis of rope. Place fire clay around bottom of socket.
5. Pour in molten zinc. Use only high grade zinc, preferably heated not above 830°F. Do not use babbitt or other antifriction metal. Remove all seizings except one nearest socket. Cool slowly.

Figure 2-6. Attaching a wire rope socket.

EYE SPLICES

An eye splice formed around a thimble is called a thimble or hard eye splice. If no thimble is used, it is sometimes called an open or soft eye splice. Three common open splices are the Liverpool splice (which originated on

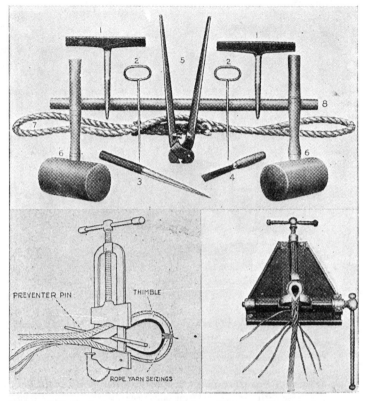

Figure 2-7. Tools for wire rope splicing. (Bottom left) Rigger's screw. (Bottom right) Rigger's vise.

the Liverpool docks), the West Coast or Logger's splice (used by loggers in snaking out heavy logs), and the Gun Factory splice (used in handling heavy guns at a gun factory). The thimble, Liverpool, and West Coast splices will be discussed.

THIMBLE SPLICE

1. Measure off 2 to 4 feet from the end of the rope, depending upon the size of the rope, and bend it at that point. Lay the proper size thimble into the bend and clamp in a splicing vise, as illustrated in Figure 2-8, with the loose end of the rope at the right when looking toward the vise.

2. The tools, also shown in Figure 2-8, consist of two wooden mallets, a spike, a serving iron, knife, nippers, a piece of pipe and some hemp rope.

3. Unlay the rope back to the thimble, serve ends of strands with fine annealed wire, bend four strands to the right and two to the left and cut out the hemp center as shown in Figure 2-9. A strand or independent wire rope center should be cut in the same manner as a hemp center, but not quite so close to the thimble.

4. Untwist the lay of the rope somewhat by means of the hemp rope and pipe as shown in Figure 2-10. Then drive the spike under the 2 top strands of the main part of the rope and insert the strand lying on top (i.e., under the point of the thimble) through the opening. The spike should be driven from right to left and the strand put through in the same direction. To make this clearer, a section of the rope and of the loose ends are shown in Figure 2-11A.

The strands in the main rope are numbered 1 to 6 and in the loose end **a** to **f** (Figure 2-11A). The first step then, as stated, is to drive the spike in between 1 and 2 and out between 6 and 5 (Figure 2-11B) and insert end **a** through this opening.

Next pull the strand up tight and force it back by twisting the spike up along the lay toward the thimble.

5. Then tuck in the other ends thus: Follow strand 1 around to where it lies on the bottom of the rope (see Figure 2-12) and drive the spike under it (i.e., between 1 and 6 and 1 and 2) from the right (Figure 2-11C) and force end **b** through from the left, bringing it over the rope. Twist the spike back along the lay toward the thimble, after having pulled end up tight, until the strand can be worked up no farther. Next drive the spike from the right under 2 where it is at the bottom of the rope, force end **c** through from the left and work back as before; and so on, **d** under 3, **e** under 4, **f** under 5.

6. All the ends having thus been tucked whole once, they are tucked whole a second time. This second tucking consists merely in wrapping each end once around the strand from under which it comes out, and then forcing the tuck back as close to the thimble as possible. Thus **a** lies under 1 and 6 as a result of the first tuck just described (Figure 2-11B).

Lift 6 by means of spike (Figure 2-11D), bring **a** around and back under 6 and pull up tight. Strand **b** lies under 1 and is wrapped once around in the same way, and so on for **c, d, e,** and **f**. Figure 2-10 shows the splice while **b** is being tucked the second time. The strands **a** and **b** are given one more tuck each in exactly the same way as for the second tuck. When **this** operation is finished strands **a** and **b** will have had three whole tucks each and strands **c, d, e,** and **f** two whole tucks each.

7. All the ends having been tucked whole as described, they are split. That is, by means of a knife the wires are separated into two parallel bundles for each strand, as shown in Figure 2-13. *One* bundle from each end is then wrapped *three* times around the strand from under which it comes out, in a manner exactly the same as the second tucking of the whole end was done. (See under paragraph 6.) After this operation is finished, the splice appears as shown in Figure 2-14.

8. Cut off the loose ends as close as possible except the two half strands **a** and **d** as shown in Figure 2-14. These 2 strands should be cut off long enough to reach to the thimble after being opened up and hammered back. (See Figure 2-15.)

9. Take a coil of seizing strand, fasten one end loosely to the thimble, and have an assistant hold the coil itself in the location shown in Figure 2-15.

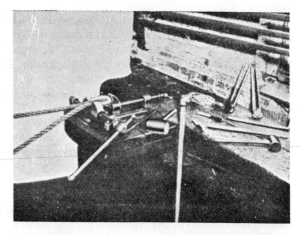

Figure 2-8. Preparing for a thimble splice.

Figure 2-9. Thimble splice.

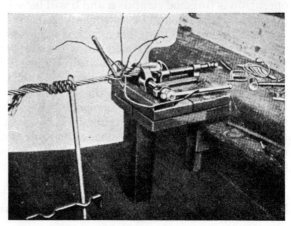

Figure 2-10. Thimble splice.

A   B

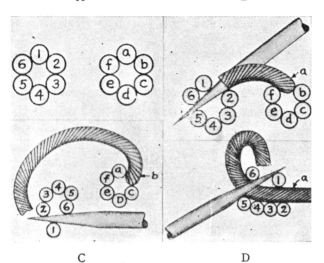

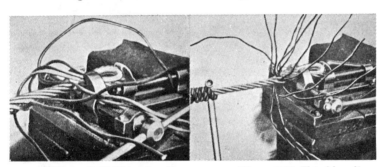

Figure 2-11.
Thimble splice.

C   D

Figure 2-12. Thimble splice.   Figure 2-13. Thimble splice.

Then, using the serving iron as illustrated in the same figure, apply the serving. When up to the thimble, twist the ends together and cut off.

10. Then completed, the thimble splice will appear as in Figure 2-16. If properly made and correctly used there is no danger of it ever pulling out, and under excessive load such a splice would develop about 60 to 90 percent of the ultimate strength of the rope, depending upon the size. The only reason it will not carry up to the full breaking strength is that the wires nick each other under heavy stress where the strands cross inside the tuck and are slightly weakened thereby. The weakest part of the splice is in the vicinity of the last set of tucks, and for this reason it is very important not to hammer or otherwise distort this section more than is absolutely necessary.

Note: If no seizing strand is to be used, all strands are given four instead of the three tucks mentioned under 7. All of the ends are then cut short and the finished splice hammered lightly.

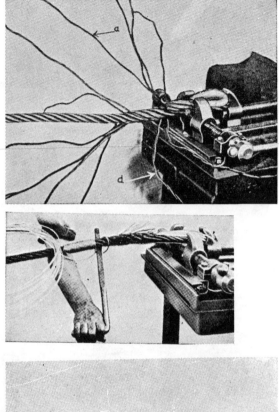

Figure 2-14. Thimble splice.

Figure 2-15. Thimble splice.

Figure 2-16. Thimble splice.

DIRECTIONS FOR MAKING LIVERPOOL EYE SPLICE

1. Measure off 2 to 4 feet from the end of the rope and seize wire with marline to prevent unraveling while splicing. Unlay the strands back to the seizing, cut out the heart close to the seized end and whip the end of each of the six strands.

2. Bend the wire to form an eye of desired size and seize the 2 parts together with marline.

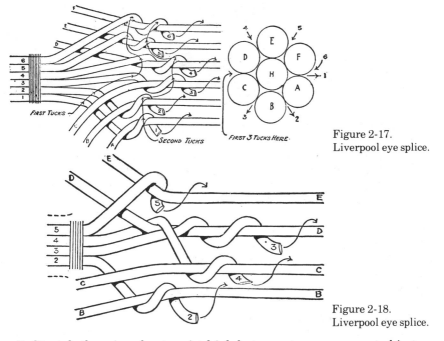

Figure 2-17.
Liverpool eye splice.

Figure 2-18.
Liverpool eye splice.

3. Stretch the wire about waist high between two permanent objects; a selvage strap and a handybilly should be used to make the stretch taut.

4. With the strands lying about parallel to the part of the wire through which they are to be tucked and the eye in a vertical position, stand with the eye on your left side and face in the direction in which the tucks are to be made.

5. Divide the tucking strands so that three are on each side of the standing part.

6. Open the standing part through the center with a marlinespike and tuck the top strand over the right side through the opening. This step is shown in Figure 2-17 where tucking strand 1 passes under the strands C, B, and A of the standing part.

7. The next strand on the right is tucked through the same opening but comes out under two strands on the right. This step is shown in Figure 2-17 where tucking strand 2 passes under the strands C and B of the standing part and comes out between strands B and A.

8. The last strand on the right also is tucked through the same opening but comes out under one strand. This step is shown in Figure 2-17 where tucking strand 3 passes under strand C of the standing part and comes out between strands C and B.

9. The top tucking strand on the left side is now passed over and around the top strand on the left side of the standing part. This step is shown in Figure 2-17 where tucking strand 4 passes over and around strand D of the standing part.

Figure 2-19.
West Coast eye splice.

10. The next tucking strand on the left is now passed over and around the next strand in the standing part. This is shown in Figure 2-17 where tucking strand 5 is passed over and around strand E of the standing part.

11. The last tucking strand is passed over and around the last strand of the standing part. This is shown in Figure 2-17 where tucking strand 6 passes over and around strand F of the standing part.

This completes the first tuck of all 6 strands. The second tuck for each strand is made by passing the tucking part around and under the strands of the standing part, following the lay of the wire. This second tuck is shown in Figure 2-17 by the small arrow marked second tuck.

To finish the splice, take one more tuck with each strand in the same manner, pound splice into shape, and cut off ends of tucking strands close to the splice.

Figure 2-17 shows diagrammatically the method of making this splice. The tucking strands are numbered 1 to 6 in the order that they are tucked. The strands in the standing part are lettered A to F, as illustrated in the cross section at the right of the figure.

A variation of the foregoing eye splice is shown in Figure 2-18. This is sometimes called a "locked" splice because the position of strands 3 and 4 have been reversed, forming a lock.

WEST COAST SPLICE

The West Coast or Logger's splice is a locked splice made by passing each tucking strand successively under two strands, back over and around one strand and out again under two strands. This is clearly shown in Figure 2-22 where the lettered strands A to F are the tucking strands and the numbered strands 1 to 6 are the strands in the standing part.

A second tuck is made with the last four tucking strands in the same manner as the first tuck, completing the splice. Figures 2-19, 2-20, and 2-21 further illustrate the West Coast splice.

LONG AND SHORT SPLICES

Two types of splices are commonly used for joining six-strand ropes. The standard "short" splice is used for ordinary conditions, and the "long" splice for ropes for haulages or inclines or whenever the duty is particularly severe. Splices should never be used in vertical shafts and are not recommended on inclines where the steepest grade is greater than 45

Figure 2-20. West Coast eye splice.   Figure 2-21. West
                                               Coast eye splice.

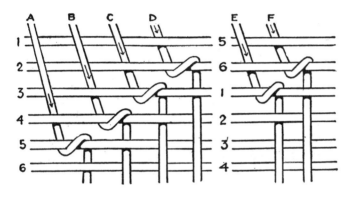

Figure 2-22. West Coast eye splice.

degrees. Additionally, as is true with fiber rope, a long splice is used if an increase in diameter cannot be tolerated.

Splices should be used in running rigging with extreme caution and only in emergency situations. A long splice will tend to unlay if required to run through a block frequently. Its use is severely limited by OSHA regulations.

In the explanations which follow only six-strand rope will be considered since it is the most common. Because lang lay is so little used today, special instructions for lang lay only will not be given.

In making a splice, a length of rope equal to half the length of the finished splice is consumed on each of the 2 ends. This length is indicated as "Distance to Unlay" in Tables A and B in the table below, and it is necessary to allow twice this amount of extra rope for making the splice.

Tables A and B give the distance to unlay and length of tuck recommended for both "short" and "long" splices in regular lay ropes. For lang lay ropes both of these values should be increased 20 percent over those specified for "long" splices.

SPLICES IN REGULAR LAY SIX-STRAND WIRE ROPES

Rope Diameter	Short Splice Table A		Long Splice Table B	
	Distance to Unlay	Length of Tuck	Distance to Unlay	Length of Tuck
1/4 inch	7 feet	10 inch	15 feet	15 inch
3/8 "	8 "	12 "	18 "	18 "
1/2 "	9 "	14 "	21 "	21 "
5/8 "	10 "	16 "	24 "	24 "
3/4 "	11 "	18 "	27 "	27 "
7/8 "	12 "	20 "	30 "	30 "
1 "	13 "	22 "	33 "	33 "
1 1/8 "	14 "	24 "	36 "	36 "
1 1/4 "	15 "	26 "	39 "	39 "
1 3/8 "	16 "	28 "	42 "	42 "
1 1/2 "	17 "	30 "	45 "	45 "

SHORT SPLICE

Place temporary seizings 2 to 3 feet from end of each rope, depending on size of rope. Unlay strands back to the seizings and marry them. Place a temporary seizing around the joining point and remove seizing from one rope. Clamp the married portion in a vise and select any strand and tuck over one and under two *against the lay*. Make four rounds of tucks and then divide the strands into two parts and bend one half of each strand back in the clear and take two tucks with the other halves. This makes six tucks, all *against the lay* over one and under two. Now turn the wire in the vise, remove the temporary seizing on the other rope, and repeat the same tucking procedure as before. Pull each strand tight after tucking.

Remove temporary seizing and beat out the splice well, working from the center each way. The cut off strands to finish splice.

LONG SPLICE

It is extremely important, in the making of a long splice in wire rope, to use great care in laying the various rope strands firmly into position. If, during any of the various operations, some of the strands are not pulled tightly into their respective places in the finished splice, it is doubtful if satisfactory results will be obtained.

When such a poorly made splice is put into service the strands which are relatively slack will not receive their full share of the load, thus causing the remaining strands to be excessively stressed. This unbalanced condition will result in a distorted relative position of the rope strands, so that some of these will project above the nominal diameter of the rope and be subjected to excessive abrasion and abuse. In addition, of course, the unequal stress distribution will decrease the ultimate strength of the finished splice.

It is strongly recommended, therefore, that during each of the steps described in the following method, particular attention be paid to maintaining, as nearly as possible, the same degree of tightness in all of the strands in the splice.

When ropes are to be used in places where failure would endanger human life, the splicing should be done only by men who are experienced in such work. It is good practice to test such splices to at least twice their maximum working load, before placing them in service.

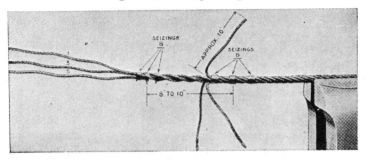

Figure 2-23. Splicing 6-strand rope.

DIRECTIONS FOR SPLICING SIX-STRAND WIRE ROPE
(hemp center)

1. Measure back, from each of the two ends to be spliced, a distance 8 to 10 inches more than that indicated in Tables A and B on the preceding table. At these points, marked D in Figure 2-23, place three seizings of wire firmly around the rope to prevent the strands from unlaying further back. Now unlay three alternate strands at each end back to these binding wires. It is important that the strands should be alternate, that is, if we assume them to be numbered for one end of rope and lettered for the other end, as shown in Figure 2-24, either strands 1, 3 and 5 or 2, 4, and 6 and also A, C, and E or B, D and F should be unlaid.

2. Figure 2-25 shows one end of rope after three strands have been unlaid. The other end of rope should be similarly prepared.

3. Cut off at each end of the rope the three strands, which have just been unlaid, leaving the ends projecting about 10 inches.

4. Apply three more seizings of wire at B in Figure 2-23 in order to hold firmly in place the three strands which have not been unlaid. Then separate these three strands as far as seizings B, and cut off the hemp center close to the first of seizings B (see Figure 2-26). This will make each of the two ends of rope have three strands separated from each other for a distance of 11 feet for regular lay ropes, one-inch diameter, and 22 feet for lang lay ropes, or as indicated in Tables A and B, in the preceding table.

5. Place one end of the rope securely in a vise as shown in Figure 2-27 and assemble the other end so that corresponding strands from each end

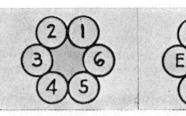

Figure 2-24.
Splicing 6-strand rope.

Figure 2-25.
Splicing 6-strand rope.

interlock regularly with each other in a manner similar to that in which the fingers will interlock when those of one hand are pushed between those of the other. It is *extremely important* that the two ends of rope be forced firmly against one another and be held in this manner until the next two operations are completed. It is advisable, therefore, for one man to hold the ropes tightly together while another man does the splicing. Next, apply seizing F, Figure 2-27, so as to bind the two ropes firmly together.

6. Remove those seizings B and D which are to the left of seizing F (Figure 2-27). Unlay any one strand A (Figure 2-28) and follow up with strand No. 1 from the other end, laying it tightly in the open groove left by the unwinding of A, making the twist of the strand agree exactly with the lay of the open groove. In order to get the best results, strand No. 1 should be rotated several times so as to tighten the wires. This will permit it to be fitted into place more easily.

7. When all but a short end of No. 1 has been laid in, the strand A should be cut off, leaving an end equal in length to No. 1. (See Figure 2-29.) This length should be, for a 1-inch diameter rope, about 18 inches for regular lay ropes, and 24 inches for lang lay ropes. For a smaller rope this may be slightly decreased, and for a larger diameter an increased length is desirable.

After this stage has been reached it is no longer necessary for one man to hold the two ends of rope together since the splice will be sufficiently formed to prevent slippage.

Figure 2-26. Splicing 6-strand rope.
Figure 2-27. Splicing 6-strand rope.
Figure 2-28. Bottom left. Splicing 6-strand rope.
Figure 2-29. Bottom right. Splicing 6-strand rope.

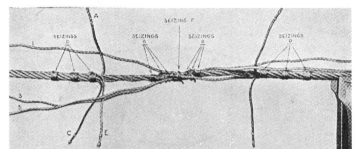

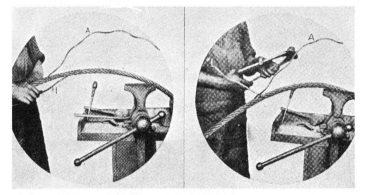

8. Unlay another strand C in the same manner that A was unlaid and follow up with strand No. 3, stopping, however, back of the ends of A and No. 1. The unlaid strand C should be cut off as A was cut, leaving two short ends C and No. 3, equal in length to those of A and No. 1.

9. Proceed in a similar manner with the third set of strands, E and No. 5. Figure 2-30 now shows the relative position of strands C and No. 3 with respect to strands E and No. 5 and Figure 2-31 shows the relative position of strands A and No. 1 also.

The distance between the points where the ends project should be about 3 1/2 feet for regular lay ropes and 4 1/2 feet for lang lay ropes. There now

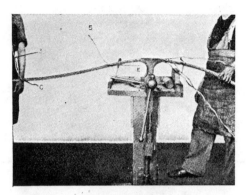

Figure 2-30. Splicing 6-strand rope.

Figure 2-31. Splicing 6-strand rope.

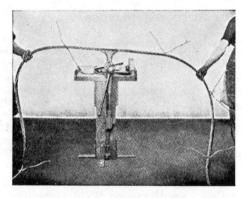

Figure 2-32. Splicing 6-strand rope.

remain the three strands on the other side, which must be laid in the same way.

10. When all six strands have been laid in, as directed, the splice will appear as indicated in Figure 2-32. There will now be six places at which the ends of the strands extend 18 inches or 24 inches for regular or lang lay respectively. These ends must be secured without increasing the rope's diameter, as follows:

11. Place the rope in a vise at the point where the ends A and No. 1 extend.

12. Wrap the endless piece of Manila rope around the wire rope as shown in Figure 2-33 and insert stick in the loop. Pull the end of the stick so that the wire rope will be unlaid between vise and stick.

13. By means of the stick, the rope may be unlaid sufficiently to insert the point of the spike under two strands. Use the pin to force the hemp core into such a position that it may be reached by the knife and cut. It will be noticed that the end of strand No. 1, which is to be laid in, has been bent back toward the vise. As this end must follow the twist of the rope and occupy the space left vacant by the removal of the hemp core, the end itself

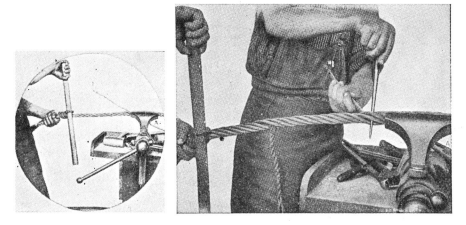

Figure 2-33.
Splicing 6-strand rope.

Figure 2-34.
Splicing 6-strand rope.

should have some tendency to twist in the proper direction. Bending the end back, and giving it one twist so as to loosen the wires, will impart this tendency. In addition the strand should be straightened so as to remove any curvature left in it.

14. Figure 2-34 shows the rope after the end of strand No. 1 has been laid in place. Strand A must be laid in the same manner but in the opposite direction. This is done by tucking strand A in *back* of strand No. 1 by placing spike *over* strand A and *under* strands No. 2 and No. 3. Proceed in the same manner as with strand No. 1. Bend and twist strand A the same as strand No. 1.

SPLICING WIRE WITH AN INDEPENDENT WIRE ROPE CENTER

On rare occasions it may be necessary to splice a rope with a wire heart strand. If such an occasion does occur, placing a rope with a wire heart strand can be done in the same general manner as that employed when splicing hemp-center rope.

CHAPTER III

BLOCKS AND TACKLES

BLOCKS

BLOCKS are one of the most important fittings aboard ship. They are made of either wood or metal and their construction and use should be thoroughly understood. When being lowered away in a lifeboat, life and safety depend upon the blocks in the lifeboat falls. Therefore, the nomenclature of a typical block should be understood (Figure 3-1).

The frame is also known as the shell. The opening between the shell and the top of the sheave is known as the swallow.

Blocks take their names from the number of sheaves; a single block has one sheave, a double block has two, and so on. They are identified by their shape or construction and also by the use or place they occupy aboard ship.

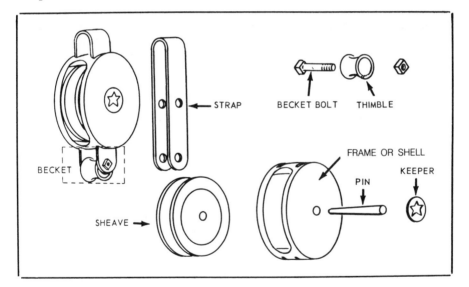

Figure 3-1. Parts of a typical wood-framed block.

Cheek blocks are usually placed in fixed positions to perform a specific duty (Figure 3-2). The hauling part of the lifeboat falls runs through cheek blocks which act as fairleads to the winch. The cheek blocks at the base of a sailboat mast act as fairleads for the cleats to which the halyards are secured. Figures 3-3 and 3-4 show examples of various kinds of blocks.

Figure 3-2. Self-adjuster heel block fitting with star cup tension spring and pin for cargo hoisting.

The size of the block is governed by the size of the rope to be used with it. The length of a wooden block in inches should be about three times the circumference of the fiber rope to be used with it (*See* table following). Sizes of small wood shelled blocks such as tail blocks, snatch blocks, and blocks used by men working aloft are often determined by the length of the wood shell. This also applies to small, all-steel shelled blocks as used on handy-billies.

TABLE OF BLOCK SIZES

Length Shell Inches	Size Sheave Inches	For Dia. Rope Inches
3	1 3/4 × 1/2 × 3/8	3/8
4	2 1/4 × 5/8 × 3/8	1/2
5	3 × 3/4 × 3/8	5/8
6	3 1/2 × 1 × 1/2	5/8-3/4
7	4 1/4 × 1 × 1/2	7/8
8	4 3/4 × 1 1/8 × 5/8	1
9	5 1/2 × 1 1/8 × 5/8	1
10	6 1/4 × 1 1/4 × 5/8	1 1/8
12	8 × 1 3/8 × 3/4	1 1/4
14	9 1/2 × 1 5/8 × 7/8	1 3/8

Blocks for use with wire rope are not so well standardized; see page 5, Chapter II, which indicates a manufacturer's recommendations for proper size of sheaves and drums for wire rope. However, if a manufacturer's table is not available, the general Coast Guard rule is used—the diameter of the sheave should be 20 times the diameter of the wire.

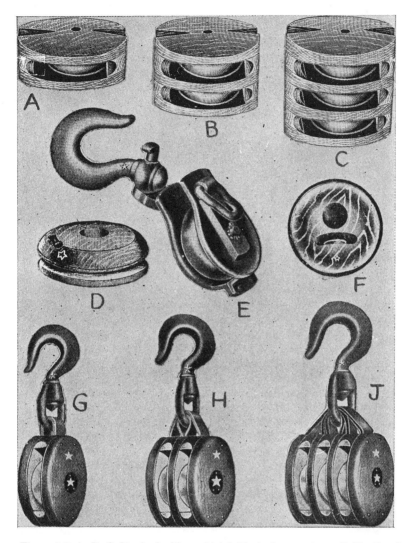

Figure 3-3. A., B., C. Single, double, and triple blocks for rope straps; D. Masthead truck; E. Snatch block; F. Masthead ball; G., H., J. Common iron strapped wood blocks.

TACKLES

A tackle or purchase is an assembly of ropes (falls) and blocks used to multiply power or to gain a better lead as in the use of a single whip, making it easier to handle light loads but gaining no power or mechanical advantage. If the whip is reversed and the block is attached to the weight to be moved, the whip is then called a runner (Figure 3-5, drawing A), and the power or mechanical advantage is doubled.

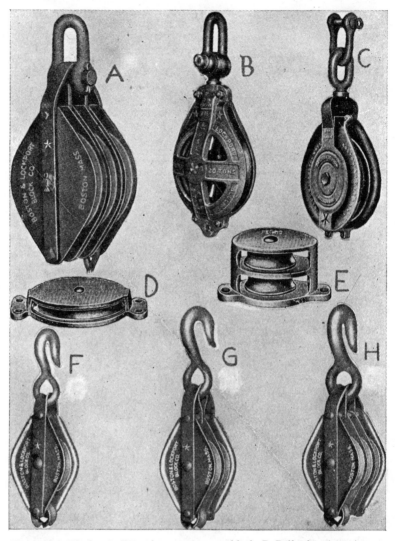

Figure 3-4. Blocks: A. Extra-heavy wire rope block; B. Roller bearing wire rope hoister; C. Farrall wire rope cargo shackle; D., E. Single and double cheek blocks; F., G., H. Steel blocks for Manila rope.

Stationary blocks give no increase in power, serving only as a convenient lead for rope. All increase in mechanical advantage is derived from movable blocks. An easy way to determine the mechanical advantage is to count the number of parts of line supporting the movable block. A tackle is said to be rigged "to advantage" when hauling on the part of a line that leads through a *movable* block, and "to disadvantage" when the hauling end leads first through a *fixed* block.

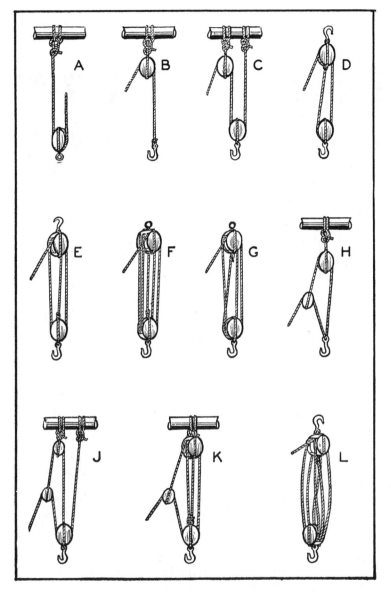

Figure 3-5. A. Runner; B. Single whip; C. Double whip; D. Gun tackle; E. Watch or single luff tackle; F. Double luff tackle; G. Twofold purchase; H. Single Spanish Burton; J. Double Spanish Burton; K. Double Spanish Burton (second method); L. Threefold purchase.

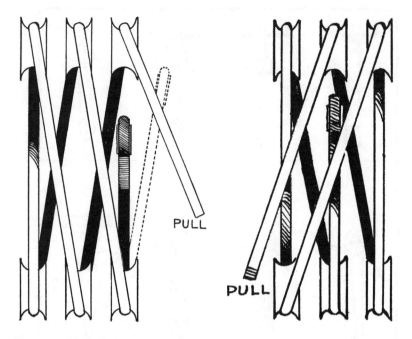

Figure 3-6. Method of reeving two triple blocks.

Figure 3-5 shows various tackles which may be found aboard ship. Although never seen aboard a *modern* ship, the single and double Spanish burtons are a matter of historic interest. They were used to "sweat up" the shrouds on square-rigged sailing ships and are now a relic of the past.

Tackles, like blocks, get their names from the number of sheaves in the blocks. Thus tackles are designated as two-fold, three-fold, etc. They are also named from the use to which they are put, such as gangway tackle, guy tackle, and stay tackle.

There are many combinations for reeving tackle, generally based on type of blocks, number of sheaves, and the particular kind of work for the tackle.

Figure 3-6 illustrates two practical methods of reeving two three-fold blocks, commonly used for boat falls. Reeving two four-fold blocks is shown in Figure 3-7. Note the position of becket and lead of pull rope or hauling part. This arrangement gives even distribution of load.

The block on the left is resting on the edges of its plates and sheaves. The block on the right is resting on its side, with plates parallel to floor. Start to reeve at point marked "pull rope," proceeding as follows:

Under & Over Sheave No. 2; Over & Under Sheave No. 7; Over & Under Sheave No. 3; Under & Over Sheave No. 6; Under & Over Sheave No. 1; Over & Under Sheave No. 8; Over & Under Sheave No. 4; Under & Over Sheave No. 5; To becket.

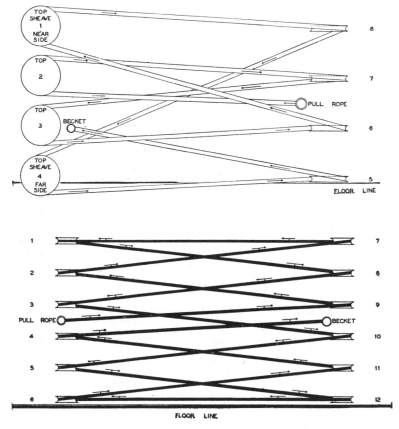

Figure 3-8. Method of reeving two sixfold blocks parallel to each other.

In Figure 3-8 is shown one method of reeving two six-fold blocks for a jumbo lift of 60 tons with 3/4 inch first-grade wire hoisting rope.

Both blocks are resting on their sides with plates parallel to floor. Start to reeve at point marked "pull rope," proceeding as follows:

Over & Under No. 9; Under & Over No. 2; Over & Under No. 7; Over & Under No. 1; Under & Over No. 8; Over & Under No. 3; Under & Over No. 10; Over & Under No. 5; Under & Over No. 12; Under & Over No. 6; Over & Under No. 11; Under & Over No. 4; To becket.

TERMS

Falls—That part of tackle made up of rope.

Reeve—To pass the rope around the sheaves of the block.

Rove—Past tense of reeve.

Standing part—That part of the falls made fast to one of the blocks.

Hauling part—The end of the falls to which power is applied.

Overhaul—To separate the two blocks.
Round in—To bring the two blocks together.
Two-blocked—When the two blocks are close together.
Chockablock—Same as above.
Handy-billy—Small light tackle made up of wood or steel blocks and used for miscellaneous light work.

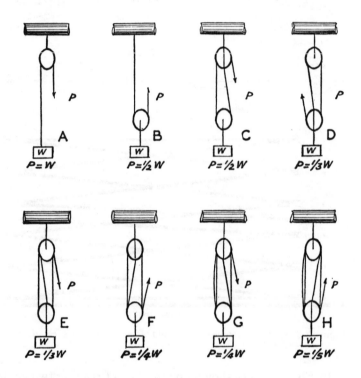

Figure 3-9. Purchases.

PROBLEM SOLVING

The **mechanical advantage** (MA) of a block and tackle is the ratio of the weight lifted to the amount of power or force exerted to lift it. When friction is *disregarded*, mechanical advantage will be the *theoretical mechanical advantage* (TMA in formula). *With* friction it will be the *actual mechanical advantage* (AMA). For example, in Figure 3-9, the TMA of the gun tackle purchase of C is 20 ÷ 10 or 2. The AMA is 20 ÷ 12 or 1.66. Friction is generally considered to be 10 percent for each sheave. In other words, when pulling through a single whip with 100 pounds of effort, the capacity to lift would be only 90 pounds. While friction may be less, this is a convenient estimate used on Coast Guard licensing examinations.

Note that mechanical advantage of the same basic rig depends upon whether it is "inverted," and note the gun tackle purchases in sketches C and D.

The TMA can be easily obtained by counting the number of parts of line which support the weight or movable block. In C, two parts of line support the movable block, in D there are three; therefore, the TMA in C is 2 and in D it is 3. It is commonly said that C is a gun tackle purchase rigged to *disadvantage*, and that D is a gun tackle purchase rigged to *advantage*.

The ratios of Power or Force to Weight (reciprocal of mechanical advantage) is as follows:

	Friction Not Considered	*Friction Considered*
A—Single whip	$P = W$	$\dfrac{P}{W} = \dfrac{11}{10}$
B—Single whip with block at weight	$\dfrac{P}{W} = \dfrac{10}{20}$	$\dfrac{P}{W} = \dfrac{11}{20}$
C—Gun tackle purchase	$\dfrac{P}{W} = \dfrac{10}{20}$	$\dfrac{P}{W} = \dfrac{12}{20}$
D—The same inverted	$\dfrac{P}{W} = \dfrac{10}{30}$	$\dfrac{P}{W} = \dfrac{12}{30}$
E—Luff tackle	$\dfrac{P}{W} = \dfrac{10}{30}$	$\dfrac{P}{W} = \dfrac{13}{30}$
F—The same inverted	$\dfrac{P}{W} = \dfrac{10}{40}$	$\dfrac{P}{W} = \dfrac{13}{40}$
G—Double purchase	$\dfrac{P}{W} = \dfrac{10}{40}$	$\dfrac{P}{W} = \dfrac{14}{40}$
H—The same inverted	$\dfrac{P}{W} = \dfrac{10}{50}$	$\dfrac{P}{W} = \dfrac{14}{50}$

When working block and tackle problems, rather than relying on memory, it is simple to follow this basic formula:

$$\frac{P}{W} = 1 + \frac{\dfrac{\text{number of sheaves}}{10}}{\text{TMA}}$$

P and W can be in any unit of weight, but they must both be in the *same* units. If P is in tons, W must be in tons.

Example: Find how much power (force) is needed to lift a 500-pound weight using a double or two-fold purchase rigged to *advantage*. Consider friction loss to be 10 percent for each sheave. First, write the basic formula. Second, sketch the H purchase. Next, consider the facts:

   Weight to be lifted is 500 pounds. (W = 500).
   There are 4 sheaves.
   Five parts of line are supporting the movable block (TMA = 5).
Then arrange the formula like this:

$$\frac{P}{500} = 1 + \frac{\frac{4}{10}}{5} \quad \text{This we can simplify} \ .. = \frac{\frac{14}{10}}{5}$$

$$\text{and simplify further} \ .. = \frac{14}{50}$$

Rewritten:

$$\frac{P}{500} = \frac{14}{50} \quad \text{and} \ldots P = \frac{14 \times 500}{50} = 140 \text{ lbs}$$

If friction is *not* considered, the problem is easier. Essentially, the same formula is used, but with *no* sheaves, so the expression on the top, right-hand side of the equation becomes 1.

$$\frac{P}{W} = \frac{1}{5} \quad \text{and substituting} \ldots \frac{P}{500} = \frac{1}{5}$$
$$\text{Therefore, P = 100 lbs}$$

With any block and tackle problem, it helps to remember three things:

   1. The number of parts of a line supporting the load determines the mechanical advantage.

   2. The ratio between the distance the hauling end is moved and the distance weight is actually moved can also determine the mechanical advantage.

   3. If one tackle is bent onto another (Figure 3-10), multiply the individual mechanical advantage of each to get the total mechanical advantage of the combined system.

NOTES

A tackle is "two-blocked" or "chockablock" when blocks are jammed together and the fall cannot be hauled any closer.

Fleeting is to draw both blocks of a tackle as far apart as possible without having the hauling part of the falls run through the block.

To make up a **deck tackle**, haul through the fall until the blocks are about 3 feet apart. Place blocks down, points of hooks up (hooks should always point the same way) and coil the fall around the blocks. Then clove

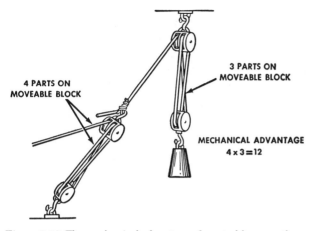

Figure 3-10. The mechanical advantage of one tackle on another is the product of one times the other. Courtesy: U.S. Navy.

Figure 3-11. Chain hoists. Courtesy: Dresser Industries, Inc.

hitch the end of the fall around the whole tackle between the blocks. The tackle is then safe to be carried about or hung up in the bos'n's locker.

Should **falls** become **twisted**, first try to remove the twist by swinging the blocks about until the lines are clear; if this does not work, it is sometimes necessary to capsize the lower block through the falls to clear it.

When **lifting** a heavy weight with a tackle, have a stopper loosely applied around the falls between blocks ready for tightening in case of trouble.

Remember one very important thing: "Use the right tackle for the right job." Using a very light tackle for a heavy lift is foolish, as the falls will soon be "long jawed" (so pulled out of shape that the strands appear separate, rather than part of the whole). If turns develop in a fall, coil the excess of the hauling part counterclockwise near the block and lead the end down through; this will thoroughfoot the fall and help to clear it.

Parbuckling is a form of purchase which, like Spanish burton, belongs to the past. It consists of rolling a cylindrical object up an inclined plane by passing lines around it and back to the vessel. The object revolves within the lines and is thus hauled aboard. This is how Captain Bligh loaded extra spars, casks of water, and perhaps rum aboard HMS *Bounty* before sailing for Tahiti.

CHAIN HOISTS

Chain hoists are occasionally required to hoist heavy equipment within a confined space. A typical example would be the lifting of turbine casing or removal of a pump from its foundation in the engine room. Anyone may well be called upon to assist in rigging such a hoist. Being prepared to assist means knowing all the tools of the trade and using chain hoists is one.

The safe working load is marked on the hoist. It should not be exceeded. The mechanical advantage of the hoist is so great that one man can lift the required weight, and there is sufficient friction so that the weight will not lower itself when he removes his hands from the chains. There are a number of types of chain hoists on the market. Figure 3-11 illustrates some of the most common.

CHAPTER IV

DECK SEAMANSHIP

A true seaman:
Every bone in his body a spar,
every tooth in his head a marlinespike,
every hair on his head a ropeyarn.
When he spits, he spits tar.
—*Anon.*

Figure 4-1. View from the bridge of S.S. *Santa Maria* looking forward. Ship is alongside in her San Francisco berth. Gantry crane in foreground. Starboard boom loading cargo by yard and stay rig. Photo: Midn. J.P. Jackson, California Maritime Academy.

ELEMENTARY DECK SEAMANSHIP is covered in the Examination Guide for Lifeboatmen and Able Seamen (Chapter X). This chapter contains information on the masts, booms and rigging of a ship, together with the accepted methods of performing the various jobs required of the men on deck. As the equipment on each ship varies, it is impossible to describe exactly the equipment or procedure in every case. However, the principles and methods in general apply to all ships and need only to be adapted to the equipment at hand. The ability to adapt the equipment at hand to his needs is one of the prime requisites of a good deck seaman.

It is suggested that Chapter V—Cargo Stowage and Handling—be read before beginning this section. In Chapter V newer methods of handling cargo are discussed, and a sketch of the yard and stay rig (Figure 5-17) which has been the mainstay of the conventional dry cargo ship is shown. This chapter covers rigging and nomenclature in more detail.

MASTS

Steel masts and king posts have long since replaced wooden masts and sails. The most important function of masts and king posts is to support cargo booms. If a vessel has masts rather than king posts, they are known as the *fore, main,* and *mizzen.* King posts take their name from the hold which they serve.

Masts are usually curved steel plates welded together and strengthened inside with stiffeners of angle iron. Masts are stepped as low as possible. On small ships they run through to the keelson, and on larger ships they are stepped through one or two decks. At the points where the mast runs through the deck, the deck plates and the plates on the mast are doubled for strength.

Some masts have structures around their base. If open, the structure may be called a mast platform. If enclosed, it is called a masthouse and may be used for storage or may contain resistor panels for electric deck machinery. Masts are steadied by standing rigging. Attached to the mast are the fittings necessary for the working of cargo. Topping lift blocks are secured to hound bands (metal bands with links) on the mast. Most masts are fitted with ladders. Through the truck (top of the mast) may be rove a light halyard or dummy gantline for use when a bos'n's chair is needed. Cargo lights are attached to the mast to illuminate the deck when cargo is being worked or the ship is anchored. On some modern ships masts may be large enough that the lookout can enter from the main deck level and climb to his lookout platform (called a "crow's nest" in the past).

King posts are short, sturdy masts without yards or crosstrees. They are stepped athwartships from each other and may be joined together by a steel beam or spanner stay. These used to be called "pair masts," but the term has fallen into disuse. Booms are fitted to both king posts (or to each side of the king post or samson post). The tackle spanning the ends has been called a *lazy guy, span guy, schooner guy,* or *midship guy.* These booms may be worked singly or in unison. On many ships king posts serve as ventilators as well as support for booms.

STANDING RIGGING

Stays, shrouds, and **backstays**, which are heavy galvanized wire ropes, support the masts. Stays support masts from forward. The forestay or head stay runs from mast to forecastle deck and is usually shackled to the top of the stem. Shrouds lead from mast to sides and are secured to gunwhale or bulwarks. Several shrouds are used on either side of the mast and are spaced from fore to aft in a manner to interfere as little as possible with the swinging of the cargo booms. Backstays support the mast from aft.

They are led directly aft if possible, but if led to the sides will also be placed where they will least interfere with the cargo booms. **Preventer stays** are wire ropes rigged temporarily to supplement the regular stays when an extremely heavy lift is to be handled. They should be led as nearly as possible opposite the direction of the greatest load on the mast.

BOOMS

Since the days of sail, the original purpose of booms has undergone change, and their sole use today is to handle cargo and stores. Booms normally have circular steel plate construction similar to masts.

The fittings of a boom consist of a gooseneck at the heel that provides a universal joint support for the lower end of the boom, and a spider band at the head of the boom that provides eyes by which topping lifts, guys and cargo falls are attached to the boom.

If goosenecks are not kept well lubricated, especially when the booms are not used for some time, they will "freeze," which means that rust and corrosion have "taken charge," in which case kerosene oil will generally cut the rust so that free movement is obtained. Goosenecks have been known to freeze so tightly that a heavy jack was required to break them loose. Some goosenecks are self-lubricating, others are fitted with alemite connections for grease gun, and still others must be lubricated with an oil can.

A good practice is to remove the gooseneck and have the machinist cut spiral grooves in the shank of the pin so that the lubricant can find its way to all wearing parts.

The head of the boom is supported by a topping lift which may be either a tackle or a single wire span provided with means of using a tackle at or near the deck.

To control the swing of the boom and to hold it in place when handling cargo, guys consisting of a tackle, or a pendant and a tackle, are provided on either side of the boom. When booms are used individually each guy is led from the head of the boom to the deck or bulwarks in a direction as nearly as possible at right angles to the direction of the boom. When two booms are used as a pair the usual practice is to use guy tackles on the outboard side of each boom and a smaller tackle, called a schooner or midship guy, between the heads of the two booms.

JUMBO BOOM

Although still considered a heavy-lift boom designed and rigged with a capacity to handle loads up to 50 tons, the term jumbo boom has lost much of its significance in recent years. Generally it was a single swinging boom like the rig in Figure 4-2. Today, however, when modern ships have Stuelcken booms with capacities of several hundred tons as in Figure 5-19 (Chapter V), one realizes the jumbo boom belongs to an earlier era. Then, the height of sophistication in cargo handling was to stow barrels in a hold "bung up and bilge free."

Figure 4-2. Jumbo boom of T.S. *Golden Bear*. A jumbo or single swinging boom is too slow for modern commercial use. Photo: Midn. J.P. Jackson, California Maritime Academy.

TOPPING LIFTS

On very small vessels topping lifts may be of fiber, but on a ship of any size topping lifts are always wire rope. The seaman should acquaint himself with various rigs and become familiar with their operation.

Single-span—The single-span topping lift is still seen occasionally. Its function is to raise or lower the booms. It is characterized by a single wire which runs from the spider band on the boom to a block secured to the crosstrees of the stub-mast, and from thence down along the mast where it is secured to a triangular piece of boiler plate (bail). This fitting has a hole drilled through each corner. In the upper corner, the wire previously mentioned is attached. To the lower corners are attached the bull rope and the bull chain. The bull chain is a length of 6-inch links of 1-inch chain. In operation, the bull rope is taken to the gypsyhead of the winch, after passing through a snatch-block fairlead. Then the boom can be raised or lowered. The bull chain serves as a stopper.

Stopping off—The single-span topping lift is stopped off when the boom is at the required height. It is done in this fashion: The bull chain is shackled to a pad eye on the deck. The strain is then taken off the bull rope and the bull chain bears the full weight of the boom and lift.

Multiple-purchase topping lift—This consists of two double or triple sheaved blocks. The blocks are secured to the spider band of the boom and to the hound band on the mast. Wire is used to make this tackle because of its strength.

The multiple-purchase topping lift is passed through a snatch block below the gooseneck and the line is taken to the winch. When the boom is hauled as high as desired, it must be "stopped off." This is done by using a chain stopper on the wire. The stopper is taken to the wire and half hitches are thrown about the lift. The hitches are 12 to 18 inches apart so that they will not jam. The fiber tail of the stopper is passed about the wire opposite to the lay, and is held in place by hand. The winch is backed off until the chain stopper takes the full strain. Then the snatch block is capsized and the wire freed. The wire is then passed around a cleat secured to the mast or house. At least two-and-a-half round turns and three figure eights are made to hold the wire. Where the wires cross on the cleat they are tied together with rope yarn or a special line.

Inverted multiple-purchase—This consists of a wire pennant (or pendant) from the spider band on the boom to a block on the mast, then down to a purchase (usually three-fold). The purchase is commonly of fiber and is stopped off with a fiber stopper.

WORKING DETAILS OF BOOMS

Booms may be worked singly or in pairs. If they are worked in pairs, the one that is spotted over the hatch is called the hatch boom. The one over the side is called the yard boom. When booms are worked together the runners are shackled together at a central cargo hook. By hauling on one and slacking on the other, movement in the direction of the hauling part is observed. When experienced men handle booms under these conditions, a sling load of cargo (draft) is moved swiftly from the dock to the hold of the ship. In some places, a single fall is used to handle the cargo, but the most common system is to use the split fall system. When a ship enters port, the booms are roughly spotted by the crew, then the longshoremen spot them just as they are needed.

Figure 4-3. Side port of S.S. *Santa Maria*. She works cargo by three methods, all of which can be seen in this photograph. Fork lifts are used to discharge cargo from the side ports, the ship's own gantry cranes handle containers, and the boom in the background is used for loading and unloading palletized cargo by the yard and stay rig. The *Santa Maria* and her three sister ships are the last passenger ships under the American flag. They are operated by Delta Lines and provide liner service for passengers and cargo between Vancouver, Tacoma, San Francisco, Los Angeles, and around South America. Photo: Midn. J.P. Jackson, California Maritime Academy.

Topping the boom—Raising the boom above the deck the desired height.

Cradling the boom—Lowering the boom to the boom support on deck and lashing or clamping the boom in place. Usually the gear is secured alongside the boom by lashings. On long ocean crossings the gear is removed, inspected and overhauled, and replaced when necessary.

Housing the boom—The process of securing a boom for sea, where the boom is hauled aloft close to the mast and secured. The gear may be lashed to the boom or removed as in cradling.

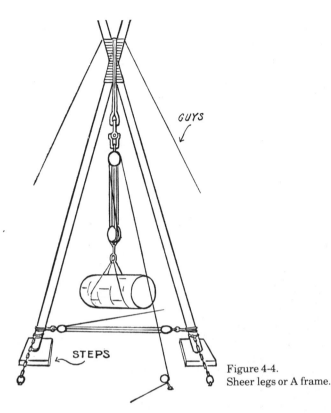

Figure 4-4.
Sheer legs or A frame.

Spotting the boom—The process of swinging the boom horizontally over the desired spot and securing.

FALLS

Cargo falls are used for the raising and lowering of drafts of cargo. They may be a single wire or a tackle. The single wire is called a cargo whip or runner.

Cargo falls are usually five-eights-inch steel wire. They have an eye splice in one end and the other end is secured to the drum of the winch by a clamp or shackle. All cargo falls should be of sufficient length to allow a few turns to remain on the winch drum, even with the draft lowered to the bottom of the hold. Falls should be kept well greased at all times. A little grease in the proper place will prolong the working life of the steel wire.

Falls may be used in several ways. First, the single fall may be attached to the cargo hook with the boom spotted over the side. The cargo may be hauled aboard the ship by the single fall. The other boom is spotted over the hatch. As the draft comes aboard, the first hook is let go, and the second hook picks up the cargo and lowers it into the hold.

Another system is to have both falls meet at a single hook (Western or Seattle). The booms are spotted over the hatch and over the side.

SHEER LEGS AND GIN POLES

Sheer legs (Figure 4-4) may be used for a specific lift when no boom or dockside crane is available. Although traditionally consisting of an A

Figure 4-5. Tug coming alongside to assist ship to her berth. Courtesy Sanders Towboat Service.

frame supported by guys, a tripod can be rigged in an emergency or as a result of an accident or casualty. Depending upon the object to be lifted, the decks should be shored up to distribute the weight over as large an area as possible. Lash the spars securely so that the legs cannot slip. A block and tackle or chain falls might be used to do this. The safety-wise seaman takes on a strain with care, raises the load a few inches, and then lowers it to inspect the entire rigging. The only time one of the editors has seen this used was in the removal of a live bomb which had penetrated several decks but failed to detonate. Sheer legs were rigged and the bomb was gingerly lifted to the main deck. Fortunately, it did not explode.

In contrast to sheer legs, a gin pole consists of a single spar supported vertically by guys in the same manner as sheer legs. It is rarely if ever used.

MOORING A SHIP

One of the seaman's most important and frequent duties is to assist in mooring the ship when coming into port and to help in getting her underway when leaving.

The number of mooring lines a ship will use depends upon its size and other factors such as the weather, the duration of the stay, the configura-

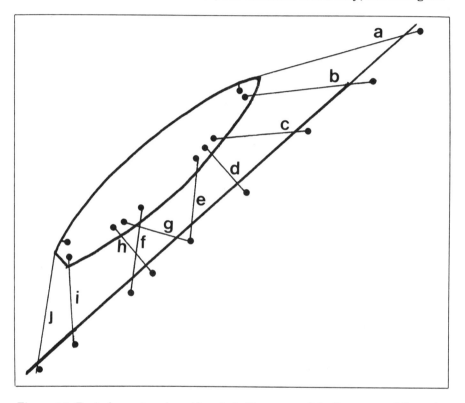

Figure 4-6. Typical mooring alongside a dock. The names of the lines are as follows: A. Offshore bow line; B. Inshore or onshore bow line; C. Bow cross spring; D. Bow breast line; E. Bow spring; F. Quarter cross spring; G. Quarter spring; H. Quarter breast line; I. Inshore stern line; J. Offshore stern line. Drawing: Scott Duncan.

tion of the dock, the rise and fall of the tide, the strength of the current, whether the ship will surge, etc. Consequently, Figure 4-6 only indicates typical mooring alongside a dock. However, the process of mooring a ship becomes clear once the names and uses of the lines are understood.

Mooring lines may be grouped into *bow lines, breast lines, spring lines, cross spring lines,* and *stern lines.* They can be natural fiber, synthetic, Swedish or spring-lay, or wire rope. In the past Manila was widely used but now most mooring lines are synthetic or wire.

Bow lines—Also known as "head lines." There may be both offshore and inshore bow lines. If a vessel has very bluff bows, an offshore line will lead from the outboard chocks to a bollard far enough down the dock so that there will be no danger of it chaffing on the stem. The angle the bow (and stern) lines make with the centerline of the ship is sometimes called *drift*. It should be at least 30 degrees if the placement of bollards or bitts on the dock permit.

Breast lines—May be used from the bow, midships, or stern. Their function is to keep the ship snug against the dock. When used, breast lines should lead as far away from the ship as possible so that they will not have to be tended with the rise and fall of the tide.

Spring lines—In the merchant service a spring line makes an angle with the dock and leads toward midships. If it is a bow spring, it will lead aft; if it is a quarter spring (or located on the stern), it will lead forward. In the Navy the term is used to denote any line at an angle with the centerline of the ship regardless which way it leads. Spring lines are among the most useful for handling vessels alongside docks, whether for mooring, warping, undocking, or "springing" a ship away from the dock. The spring line is one of the first lines sent out when mooring and often the first. As its name implies, it "springs in" and "springs out" a vessel and, for the purpose of warping, may lead from any chock. The bow spring gets the brunt of the work in docking a ship.

Cross spring lines—Lead across the spring lines, sometimes called "back spring lines." The bow cross spring leads toward the bow, and the quarter cross spring leads toward the stern. Cross spring lines will generally be parallel to the bow or stern line depending on where located. They are extremely useful when mooring a ship and keep her in position once alongside. If the ship is moving forward alongside the dock and needs to be slowed or stopped, checking the bow spring and quarter cross spring will help do the trick.

Stern lines—There may be both offshore and onshore stern lines as well as bow lines. The stern line serves exactly the same function on the stern that the bow line does on the bow.

A close watch should be kept on the mooring lines until a ship is well secured in her berth. It may be necessary to adjust some of the lines, either taking in slack or paying them out to prevent parting.

Navy nomenclature—There are differences in Merchant Marine and Navy nomenclature. The Navy does not use the term "cross spring". Instead, adjectives are added to describe which spring line is meant, where it is, and in which direction it is tending. For example, the "forward-bow spring" would be the bow spring which is leading forward—in the same direction as the bow line. In the merchant service this is called the bow-cross spring. The "after-bow spring" leads aft, and in the merchant service is called the bow spring. On the stern what is called the quarter spring becomes the forward-quarter spring. Or if the term "aft" were used, instead of "quarter," it might be the "after-forward" spring. In any event there seems to be room for misunderstanding, and good seamanship and safety require that misunderstandings not happen. In order to remove any shade of doubt as to which line is meant, use the terms "bow," "stern," or "quarter."

If the navy's system of applying names to lines seems cumbersome, their system of numbering lines is very simple. A given ship will probably tie up about the same way each time, and the lines are numbered from forward to aft beginning with No. 1, the bow line, No. 2, the bow spring, and so on.

Fairleads—Fairleads are used when the lead of the line is not in direct line with the hauling apparatus. Fairleads may be chocks, bollards, cleats, snatch blocks or any other device used to lead a hauling line fair and true to the winch, capstan, or gypsyhead. Fairleads may cause some friction loss, but far less than hauling a line around a sharp object which is unseamanlike, unsafe, and hard on the line.

Swinging a ship from a dock by use of a fire warp—If a ship is moored with no power on her engines, it is good practice to run a hawser from her forward winch to the stream or seaward end of the dock so that if a fire breaks out on the dock, it is possible to warp the ship to safety by heaving around on her winch. She could then drop anchor, or a tug could move her farther away from danger.

Some harbor regulations require that if a ship is tied up alongside a dock, a wire with an eye splice be led through a chock on the off-dock side of the ship so that in the event of an emergency a tug can come alongside, take the wire without requiring assistance from the vessel, and pull her away from danger. This is sometimes called an "insurance wire," but the terms are not exact and some seamen may also think of this as a fire warp.

BENDING TWO HAWSERS TOGETHER

When paying out a mooring line always see that the line is long enough. If the wind is setting the ship off the dock, or if there is a strong current which the engines cannot overcome, the distance may open up, and the makings of an emergency develop. Another line must be bent on the mooring line so that it will not be lost or parted. This calls for fast action. The best method is to join the lines by two bowlines although a double sheet bend or a single or double carrick bend may also be used. If the carrick bend is used the ends should be secured, another detail to be taken care of when time is running out. Binding together the eyes of two hawsers as shown in Figure 4-7 is sometimes used by tankers making up to offshore moorings. In this case, however,the smaller line binding the two hawsers together may be dacron and have an eye splice on both instead of just one end. These eye splices are then shackled together. This has the advantage of keeping the line in reasonable shape to pay out or bring in on a gypsyhead without snarling.

COMMANDS TO LINES

Commands given when handling lines are standard both to the Merchant Marine and to the Navy. These must be learned and should become second nature:

Slack the bow spring—Pay out the bow spring and allow it to form an easy bight.

Take a strain on the bow lines—Heave in on the bow line and place it under tension. If the line is not on the winch already, take several turns on the gypsyhead and heave around. This command means about the same thing as "heave 'round."

Take in the slack on the bow line—Heave around on the bow line just enough to take out most of the slack, but do not take a strain.

Ease the bow cross spring—Pay out or start to slack the bow cross spring, but do not take off all the tension.

Avast heaving (around)—Stop heaving.

Hold the stern line—Take enough turns on the gypsyhead to hold the stern line where it is. Do not pay any line out. If the line begins to take an excessive strain and is in danger of parting, report this to the bridge.

Check the stern line—Hold the stern line, but if it begins to take on an excessive strain, pay out enough line so that it is in no danger of parting.

Double up and secure—Run additional lines or bights (parts) or line as needed to make the mooring secure.

Single up—Take in all lines but a single standing part at each station. On some ships when this command is given, the additional meaning to take in all except one or two designated lines forward and aft is understood.

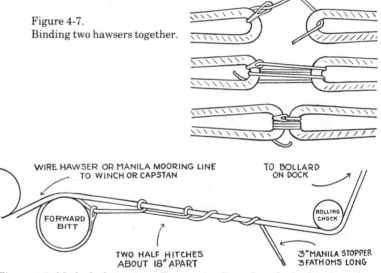

Figure 4-7.
Binding two hawsers together.

Figure 4-8. Method of stopping off a mooring line when the lead is through or around bitts to the winch or capstan.

Stand by your lines—This command alerts the mooring stations to the fact that the ship is ready to get underway, and is about to leave her berth.

Let go, Take in, Cast off—Essentially these commands mean the same thing. The proper command to the dock is "cast off." Technically, the bridge should tell the mooring station, "Take in the bow line." "Let go" formerly meant the line should be slacked smartly so that the dock hands could cast it off.

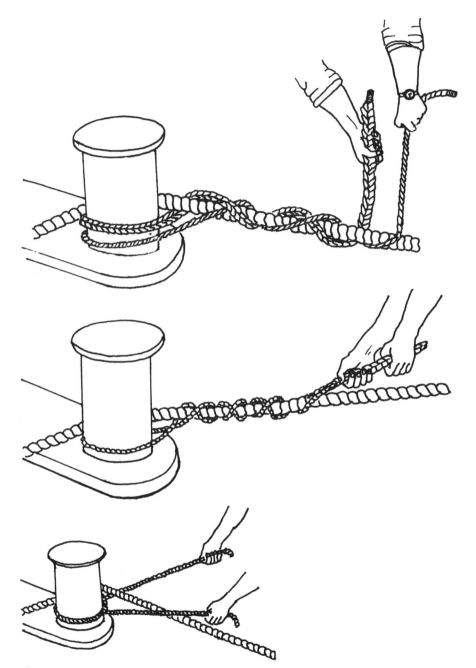

Figure 4-9. "Chinese" stoppers for mooring lines. A. A regular stopper; B. A regular Chinese stopper with no back up; C. The wrong way to start a stopper. The overhand knot around the bitt reduces the strength of the stopper by about half. Drawings: Scott Duncan.

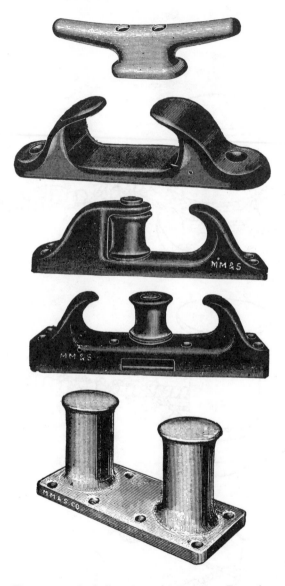

Figure 4-10. Deck fittings used in mooring. Top to bottom: cleat, open chock, single roller chock, double roller chock, bitts.

STOPPERS

When a ship is secured the lines are removed from the gypsyheads or winches and made up around the bitts. Stoppers are used to hold the line temporarily while it is being moved from the winch to the bitts without permitting any slack to get into the line. After the mooring line is made up on the bitts, the stopper is removed. Fiber stoppers were formerly made of 3-inch Manila and secured, sometimes with minor variations, as shown in Figure 4-8. When used on a mooring line a standard stopper hitch tends to jam and frequently must be cut to be removed. A standard stopper hitch is limited to hoisting small boats or on smaller lines.

Over the last several years the so-called "Chinese" stoppers have come into wide use for mooring lines and are strongly recommended (Figure 4-9 A, B, and C). They do not jam, and are quick and safe. Sinnet stoppers have better holding power than regular stoppers, but should be oversized if used. In any case, a stopper should be of the same material as the mooring line on which it is used. If Swedish wire is employed, a Manila or synthetic stopper is desirable because chain would chew or cut the wire. However, for conventional wire rope a chain stopper should be used. If used on wire rope, a regular stopper hitch rather than a "Chinese" stopper is recommended.

CHOCKS AND BITTS

Figure 4-10 shows the deck fittings which are used in mooring a ship. Not shown is a "closed" or "Panama Canal" chock.

Securing a mooring line to a bitt deserves some attention. The first turn(s) should be made around both bitts, and then the Figure eights should be started. As discussed in Chapter I, synthetic line is far more difficult to hold than Manila, and it is necessary to take more round turns with it than with Manila. When securing a synthetic hawser to the bitts, take three round turns and then three figure eights. With Manila, one round turn and four figure eights are generally adequate.

If wire is made up on bitts it should be given three complete round turns around both bitts and the figure eights made in the same manner as with synthetic. In addition, lashing should be placed around the wire between the bitts to keep it in place. If wire is used on a gypsyhead, five turns should be taken to insure against its slipping.

FLEMISHING, COILING, FAKING

Although the definitions for flemishing, coiling, and faking down a line are given in Chapter I, these terms deserve mention here. The object of making up line by any method is to stow it on deck in an orderly fashion and have it available for running if needed. A line dumped on deck, besides being unsightly, becomes snarled or fouled so that it will not be able to be run through a chock or bitts. This is dangerous. Flemishing a line is rarely seen except as a means of making up the halyards of sailboats. Mooring lines are sometimes coiled, but are more often faked down as shown in Figure 4-12.

Heaving line—A light, flexible line with a heavy knot (a monkey fist) in one end which helps get distance and accuracy in the heave. Its most common use is in passing a hawser to the dock when tying up, but it is also useful when passing a heavy line for any purpose. The working end of the heaving line should be bent on the hawser or messenger with a bow line before heaving.

Figure 4-11. Synthetic mooring line made up on bitts. Three round turns around both bitts are recommended before taking the figure eights. Photo: Midn. J.P. Jackson, California Maritime Academy.

Line handling line —Sometimes a short length of smaller line will be bent to the inboard end of the eye splice of a hawser to make it easier to handle.

A **Monkey fist** is best made of 9- to 12-thread line. First wind four turns around your open hand; remove them from your hand and wind four more turns around these at right angles, keeping the turns flat in a four over four position. Now pass the end of the line under the first four turns, then over the second four and under the first four again; now in going under the second four turns again you complete one turn of a third series of four; continue until the third series of four is complete and you have a loosely made ball. A core of old nuts, bolts or metal to make weight is inserted, and the turns are overhauled one by one till you have a tight, compact ball. Cut the two tails about 10 or 12 inches long and splice them together with a short splice, leaving a bight of about 6 inches in which to bend the heaving line. Dipping the monkey fist in paint will help preserve it and serve as a means of identification.

Messengers are lines sent out to lead heavier lines, such as leading a mooring line through the shackle of a mooring buoy; or to lead a towing hawser to a disabled vessel. Another good example is in rigging a breeches buoy.

SEAMANSHIP LORE

The seaman is frequently occupied with jobs other than coming alongside or handling cargo or stores. Some of the equipment and rigging he will

Figure 4-12. Fo'c'sle of S.S. *Santa Maria.* Placement of anchor windlass and bitts are clearly shown. Fairleads abaft anchor brakes are not in use. Ends of offshore and onshore bow lines are faked down inside bulwarks, and spring line is faked down just forward of the two automatic tension winches which are in foreground. Photo: Midn. J.P. Jackson, California Maritime Academy..

use at these times is discussed on the following pages. For want of a better expression this section is called "Seamanship Lore."

Tail straps are small stoppers which are frequently used when painting masts, the sides of the ship, or stacks. They hold the stage or bos'n's chair snug to the side of the ship or help prevent it from swinging. If they have a cringle or thimble in the eye they are commonly called *snake lines* or *lizards.*

A **Bull rope** is any heavy Manila, synthetic, or wire rope used to heave, haul, or lift a load without benefit of the multiplying power of tackle blocks. A bull rope might be used if an anchor had jammed its shank in the hawsepipe and it was desirable to apply a pull to force it out.

A **Gantline** may be defined as a light all-round bull rope usually of about 2 3/4 inch Manila or synthetic. It will get its name from the work it is required to do, as in the case of a *staging gantline.*

Bos'n's Chair—This ever handy "tool" is a standard piece of gear on all ships. The storekeeper generally makes them up and keeps several on hand at all times. They are used when painting aloft or over the side, or for lowering a man into a hold. Figure 4-13 shows a drawing of the chair with permanent bridle and gantline bent on, with the hauling part bent around the bridle loosely.

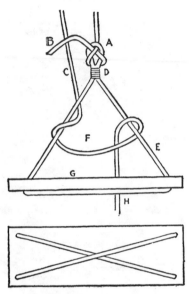

Figure 4-13. Bos'n's chair: A. Sheet bend in bridle eye; B. Tail of sheet bend, handy for frapping line; C. Hauling part of gantline, leads up through block and back to bend in chair; D. Throat seizing of marline on bridle, forming eye; E. Rope bridle, spliced to chair seat; F. Hitch to hold chair and control lowering; G. Wood seat; H. Slack of gantline.

With a man in the chair the bend would close up and lay just below the throat with the hauling part in a vertical line with the standing part.

The standing part is bent to the eye with a single or double sheet or becket bend. Leave a 3- or 4-foot tail; it will be handy as a short frapping line and can be used to advantage in many ways.

Now, to make yourself fast aloft: You have been hauled up to the truck on the topmast, and are sitting in the chair facing the mast; reach up above the bend in the bridle eye and seize *both* the hauling part and the standing part of the gantline together with your left hand; make sure you have a good grip and can hold your weight. Now ask the man on deck to slack the hauling part; reach well down with your right hand and get a working gantline by butting them end to end and passing a few turns of yarn or marline back and forth through the strands from one to the other and seizing the throat with half hitches. Lines bent together in this manner will easily overhaul through the swallow of a topmast block.

Rigging a stage—A safe working stage is an excellent insurance policy, but if being worked by a novice or a careless person it becomes a number one death trap. Learn to rig and work on a stage properly. Another thing that is very important: never play jokes on anyone *working on or connected with* a staging.

A safe stage can be made with a 12-inch plank, 2 inches thick and about 12 feet long; it should be straight-grained yellow pine or spruce and free of knots. Horns of 1 1/2 x 3 inch hardwood are bolted to the under side about 18 inches from each end and extending 12 to 15 inches on either side. Secure stage lines around plank at horns with a marlinespike hitch; bend a bowline in the standing part forming a bridle.

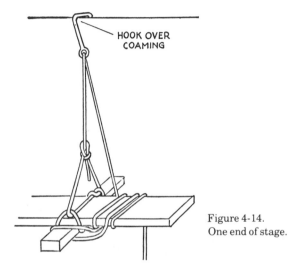

HOOK OVER
COAMING

Figure 4-14.
One end of stage.

Some bos'ns will fit their stages with permanent bridles; in which case bend the stage lines to the bridles. If rigging a fixed stage, secure the lines to cleats or some other strong support with a round turn and two half hitches. If the stage is to be raised or lowered by the men working upon it, secure tail blocks, stage hooks or lizards in a safe manner and reeve the stage lines through them; secure the hauling part to the stage with two or three round turns and belay around the horns. Drop a manrope about midway between the stage lines and rig a Jacob's ladder at one end of the stage.

If, in working a stage low over the bow or stern, it hangs too far outboard, pass heaving lines from the deck to both ends of the stage and heave into desired position. You could also breast the stage in with frapping lines and hooks placed in porthole rims. Tail straps work equally well.

Boat rope or **line** is commonly 2 1/2- to 3-inch Manila put over the side forward of accommodation ladders, pilot ladders or sideports. It hangs in a long bight close to the water and is made fast well aft of such ladders. This line is used by pilot boats and small launches to take holding turns on while taking on or discharging persons, and is particularly handy when there is a seaway such as is found off pilot stations.

Pendants are short lines or wires having an eye spliced in both ends. Pendants are used in many ways about a ship and are usually named according to their use, such as guy pendants, clear hawse pendants, etc.

Guy pendants are pendants that connect the head of a boom with a guy tackle and serve to shorten the length of the guy tackle. Some guy pendants are fitted with swivels at each end to keep the guy tackle free of turns.

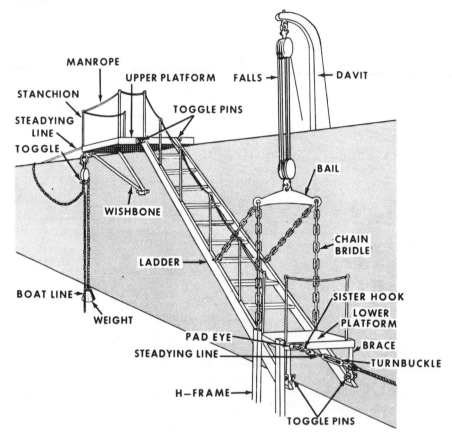

Figure 4-15. Parts of the accommodation ladder. Courtesy: U.S. Navy.

Clear hawse pendants are usually made of heavy wire and are used in the process of clearing hawse, i.e., taking turns out of anchor chains.

Bridles may be described as wire, steel or Manila hangers that resemble an inverted "V." They are used to sling an object by two or more points to keep it trim when handling. Examples: Accommodation ladders and automobile slings have bridles, and the rope part of a bos'n's chair is also a bridle.

Preventer guys and **stays**, as the names imply, are used as precautionary measures when handling heavy cargo.

Preventer guys supplement the regular guys and consist usually of a single part of wire or rope. The wire or rope should be of sufficient strength to hold the boom alone if the regular guy carries away.

Bails may also be called *yokes* and are commonly of steel, though sometimes referred to as spreaders when made of wood. Example: a bail is

Figure 4-16. Motor launch lowered into the skids by jumbo gear aboard *Golden Bear*. Research ships, training ships, and navy ships frequently use cargo gear to pick up their utility boats.
Photo: Editors.

used to span or bracket two bridles on the accommodation ladder. Another use is when a topping lift is attached to a triangular bail and to it is bent the bull rope for topping booms and the open link chain which shackles to a pad eye on the deck to hold the boom at the desired height. An example of a bail is shown on the drawing of the accommodation ladder, Figure 4-15.

Accommodation ladder is used when a ship is anchored in a harbor. It may be used instead of a brow when the ship is alongside a dock (drawing, Figure 4-15). If alongside a dock the topping lift, bail, and bridle can be removed and the weight of the entire ladder supported by the dock itself.

Rigging an accommodation ladder like the one shown is somewhat tedious and time-consuming. However, safety should not be sacrificed to save time. No one should be permitted to use the ladder until it is fully rigged and handrails are in place. Newer ships may have automated or power equipment which makes rigging simple.

Although pilots are happy to use a pilot ladder, frequently customs and quarantine officials require the accommodation ladder to be rigged before they consent to come aboard.

A **Boat boom** is a boom swung out from a ship's side when at anchor and to which boats can secure. Boat booms are not needed on merchant ships. They are only necessary when a ship is equipped with many boats, has a large crew, and is frequently anchored in a bay or harbor. Navy ships and training ships have use for them. A description of their operation can be found in a navy training or seamanship manual.

PRECAUTIONARY HINTS

Keep clear of any line under a strain. A line under extreme tension may creak, make snapping sounds, and may smoke. If it parts, it will snap back fast and can take off a leg or a head. Have great respect for the power of all lines—fiber, synthetics and wire.

Have the utmost respect for an automatic tension winch if your ship is so equipped. Insure that you are instructed in its operation before you use it. If you are by yourself, and get caught in the turns of the line as they lead into the gypsyhead, it may kill you.

Place chafing gear at all wearing points of mooring lines. This may be old strips of canvas wrapped around the lines and seized with marline. An old piece of fire hose works even better.

Place rat guards on all lines of ships moored to docks. These are two-piece metal disks which are lashed to the lines to prevent rats from coming aboard. Rat guards are required in most ports.

Never step on a line that is running out rapidly and never stand or step in the bight of a line. Keep clear of any working line.

Always carry a knife and make sure it is sharp! You may never need it, but it might save your life.

CHAPTER V

CARGO STOWAGE AND HANDLING

THE ASPIRING SEAMAN needs to be familiar with all types of cargo stowage and cargo handling. In recent times there has been a revolution in this aspect of marine service. The specialized carriers of today, with their diverse cargoes, methods of loading and stowage and necessary safety precautions, make this a complex task. Both seamen and officers aboard

Figure 5-1. Modern cargo loading operation. Barges being loaded aboard the stern of the S.S. *Almeria Lykes*. Courtesy: Lykes Bros. Steamship Co., Inc.

any particular ship need to understand thoroughly the cargo operations for that ship as well as any problems which may result from the differing types of cargo carried.

As in the past, the main objective of a merchant ship is to load, carry, and discharge cargo from one place to another safely and profitably. Although considerable responsibility falls on the operations department of a shipping company and on longshoremen, it is ultimately the ship's officers and crew who must insure that no damage occurs to the ship or the ship's cargo during these operations.

Today the modern merchant ship is usually a highly sophisticated, specialized carrier. To transport cargo containers of various types, several kinds of specialized ships have developed. First on the seas was the break-bulk ship with container capability. Then came the full container ship. For various types of trade in different areas of the world, further improvements on the container ship were introduced, including LASH, Seabee, and RO/RO, or Roll-on-Roll-off. Each of these cargo systems has its own problems which will be discussed.

Figure 5-2. Modern break-bulk ship with capability of handling containers on deck. This Lykes Lines ship has high capacity booms. Courtesy: Lykes Bros. Steamship Co., Inc.

THE CONTAINER SHIP

The container and container ship as they exist today have been the greatest single advance in the Merchant Marine since the shift from sail to steam. The military were the first to use containers. They utilized odd-sized conex (container-express) boxes as well as ammunition boxes similar in construction although smaller than the present containers. Larger boxes of standardized size evolved but most of them were carried on the decks of standard break-bulk ships. Securing these boxes was a problem, and loading them was difficult and time consuming. Finally, cargo gear was often not adequate to pick up a containerized load.

A few United States companies began to standardize the size of their containers and build or convert ships for carrying them. Container cells were installed in the holds with special gantry cranes designed for rapid and efficient handling of containers.

As the state of the art improved and facilities were developed in most large ports of the world, cranes were no longer put aboard ship. All loading

Figure 5-3. Floating crane picking up heavy unitized cargo. The use of floating cranes is sometimes necessary. Courtesy: Lykes Bros. Steamship Co., Inc.

and discharging was done by dockside crane. Again, the use of multiple cranes made the loading and discharge even faster.

From the beginning the rapid turn-around time proved to be an economic windfall to the shipping company. Greatly reduced port costs enabled ships to make additional voyages. Although labor disputes caused concern, these problems were worked out through negotiation to the mutual advantage of the operator and the worker.

As containerization became more popular, other advantages were realized. International Size Standards were set so that containers could be easily interchanged from one ship to another. (The current International Size Standards are 8 feet x 8 feet x 20 feet, or 8 feet x 8 feet x 40 feet.) Most companies use these sizes or are converting to them. Shippers realized that the container system offered cargo far more protection than break-bulk.

Figure 5-4. Shoreside gantry crane with capability of rapidly loading containers. Container ships require the use of highly specialized dockside facilities. Courtesy: Matson Navigation Company.

Loaded and sealed at the factory, the commodity stayed in its container with no further handling until it reached its consignee. Less breakage through handling resulted and pilferage was reduced.

Reefer containers were also developed so that a container had its own refrigeration unit. A reefer cargo no longer poses a threat of loss during the loading operation. All that is necessary is to ensure that the box is kept at its desired temperature during loading and until plugged in aboard ship.

The ease of loading and discharging containers and the increased security of the container has brought into being an entirely new cargo concept

Figure 5-5. Modern built-for-the purpose container ship. S.S. *Maui* on her maiden voyage. Courtesy: Matson Navigation Company.

Figure 5-6. Containership discharging with multiple cranes. S.S. *Sea-Land Commerce* alongside at the Port of Oakland, California. Courtesy: Sea-Land Service, Inc.

known as the Intermodal Transportation, or Land Bridge system. Cargo bound from the Far East to New York no longer has to transit the Panama Canal. Instead, the container is loaded at the factory, trucked to the ship, loaded, transported across the ocean, unloaded onto a rail car, transported across the country, and delivered to its consignee. Much time is saved. Anyone who intends to follow a career in the Merchant Marine will profit from a special study of intermodal transportation.

The job of the ship's officers and seamen is somewhat different when working on a container ship. Individual items of cargo are no longer a problem since special cargo is already secure in a locked container. What is of prime importance to the container ship deck officer is that reefer containers are loaded within the proper temperature range and connected aboard ship. This operation must be checked routinely throughout the voyage. The ship's officers also insure that the proper boxes are loaded and discharged, noting the time operations start and stop. They are concerned about damage to the ship, ship's gear, cargo, and containers and inspect and accept for sea the lashing and securing of all containers.

With appropriate planning, a well-organized shore staff can greatly simplify and speed up the loading and discharging of a container ship. However, the master and crew are still responsible for the cargo while aboard ship and must take all necessary precautions to insure its safety. Damaged or lost cargo not only results in expensive insurance claims, but in the loss of a good customer.

LASH, SEABEE AND RO/RO

The container revolution in the dry cargo industry spurred the development of several new classes of ships.

The first used the container idea, enlarged upon it, and provided containers that could be transported by water rather than land after being discharged from the ship. The two most successful types of barge-carrying vessels are LASH (lighter aboard ship) and Seabee (named for "Can Do," Navy CB's). Both require large vessels designed to carry self-contained barges loaded astern. The prime difference in the two types is in the method of loading and stowage. LASH uses a large straddle crane which picks up the barge at the stern and rolls it on tracks to the cell where the barge is stowed. Seabee uses a large hydraulic elevator lift. The barge is floated over the elevator which raises it, and then moves it to its designated stowage position. Of prime importance to this type of ship is the reliability of the barge loading gear. Since only one way exists to load and unload barges, a break-down gear can make the ship helpless. The hydraulic elevator has proved more reliable than the crane.

With use of the LASH and Seabee concept advantage can be taken of an extensive system of water ways minimizing port calls and port time for the mother ship. But markets should be studied carefully before a LASH ship is put into operation because in some trades barge transportation has the reputation of handling low-value cargo. In some areas, this leads to putting conventional containers in barges or converting barge space to container space. Both of these operations are very costly.

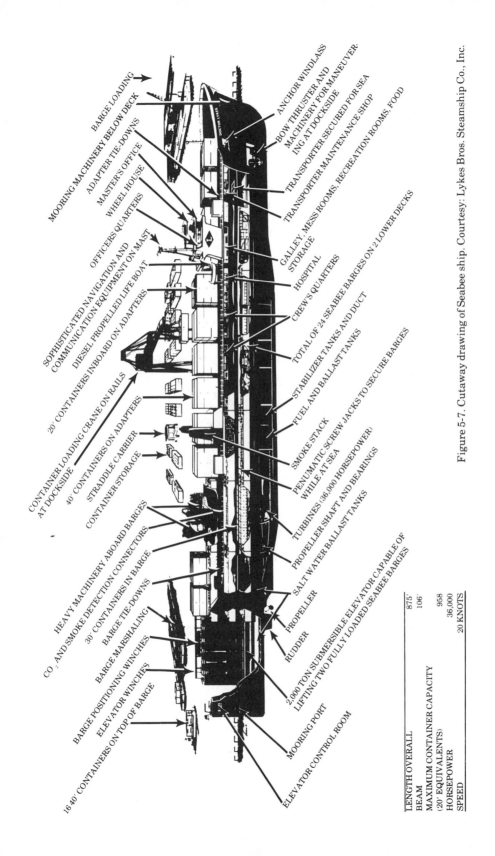

BARGE LOADING

MOORING MACHINERY BELOW DECK

ADAPTER TIE-DOWNS

MASTER'S OFFICE

WHEEL HOUSE

OFFICERS' QUARTERS

SOPHISTICATED NAVIGATION AND
COMMUNICATION EQUIPMENT ON MAST

DIESEL PROPELLED LIFE BOAT

20' CONTAINERS INBOARD ON ADAPTERS

CONTAINER LOADING CRANE ON RAILS
AT DOCKSIDE

40' CONTAINERS ON ADAPTERS

STRADDLE CARRIER

CONTAINER STORAGE

HEAVY MACHINERY ABOARD BARGES

CO₂ AND SMOKE DETECTION CONNECTORS

30' CONTAINERS IN BARGE

BARGE TIE-DOWNS

BARGE MARSHALING

BARGE POSITIONING WINCHES

ELEVATOR WINCHES

16-40' CONTAINERS ON TOP OF BARGE

ANCHOR WINDLASS

BOW THRUSTER AND
MACHINERY FOR MANEUVER-
ING AT DOCKSIDE

TRANSPORTER SECURED FOR SEA

TRANSPORTER MAINTENANCE SHOP

GALLEY, MESS ROOMS, RECREATION ROOMS, FOOD
STORAGE

HOSPITAL

CREW'S QUARTERS

TOTAL OF 24 SEABEE BARGES ON 2 LOWER DECKS

STABILIZER TANKS AND DUCT

FUEL AND BALLAST TANKS

SMOKE STACK

PENUMATIC SCREW JACKS TO SECURE BARGES
WHILE AT SEA

TURBINES (36,000 HORSEPOWER)

PROPELLER SHAFT AND BEARINGS

SALT WATER BALLAST TANKS

PROPELLER

RUDDER

2,000 TON SUBMERSIBLE ELEVATOR CAPABLE OF
LIFTING TWO FULLY LOADED SEABEE BARGES

MOORING PORT

ELEVATOR CONTROL ROOM

LENGTH OVERALL	875'
BEAM	106'
MAXIMUM CONTAINER CAPACITY (20' EQUIVALENTS)	958
HORSEPOWER	36,000
SPEED	20 KNOTS

Figure 5-7. Cutaway drawing of Seabee ship. Courtesy: Lykes Bros. Steamship Co., Inc.

The limitations of the container ship led to the development of the Roll-on-Roll-off ship (RO/RO). RO/RO vessels now come in many shapes and sizes, with different means of loading. However more standardization is coming in newer ships of this class. In some cases ramps are designed as part of the vessel, and in others as part of shore gear. If a part of the ship, ramps may be attached on the bows, the stern, the quarters, or on the sides. Although the first major use of this type of ship was as an automobile carrier, the idea of RO/RO developed for several reasons. One fault of the container ship was that if cargo did not fit into a 8 foot x 8 foot x 40 foot box, it did not fit on a container ship. RO/RO made it possible to load anything that could be driven, towed, or carried up the ramp by a lift truck, including containers either brought aboard by lift truck or on their own chassis.

Figure 5-8. View from spar deck of RO/RO ship unloading trailers. Courtesy: Totem Ocean Trailer Express, Inc.

The RO/RO concept is new and, as is true with any new method, it has some adjustment problems. But RO/RO is growing in popularity and will soon be an even more important part of our merchant fleet.

CONVENTIONAL CARGO VESSELS

Although conventional break-bulk cargo ships are less common in the United States flag trade, many still operate in world trade. Even on the new sophisticated carriers described, the ship's stores are often loaded by conventional means. In addition, should any malfunction occur in special loading systems, the basics of cargo handling are always useful in designing a jury-rig to get the problem solved. Therefore, it is important for the good seaman to understand the principles involved in the conventional cargo vessel. He should also be thoroughly familiar with types of cargo gear installed, and slings used, and he should be able to operate this equipment.

HATCHES

Older break-bulk ships had very simple hatch closures that required large amounts of man hours to open and close. These were not efficient and could be dangerous. In heavy seas these hatch closures frequently admitted some water to the holds and occasionally were swept overboard. Hatches of the construction in Figure 5-9 are typical of ships built in the 1940s and early 1950s, some of which are still seen in service. Hatch terms applying to them follow:

Hatch—Deck openings through which cargo is lowered and raised; numbered fore and aft, No. 1 Hatch, No. 2 Hatch, etc.

Coaming—Raised steel structure around the hatch opening.

Stiffener—Shelf-like top of the coaming, to which cleats are secured.

Coaming stays—Angle iron supports under stiffener.

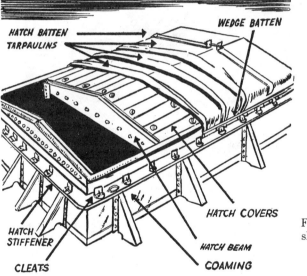

Figure 5-9. Cargo hatch, showing various parts.

Cleats—Metal pieces riveted or welded to stiffener. Wedges are driven against these and wedge batten.

Wedge batten—Long metal strips inserted between cleats and coaming to hold edge of tarpaulin in place.

Tarpaulin—Large waterproofed canvas used to cover hatch. Normally three are used, placed so that their seams run athwartships and overlap faces aft. Corners are tucked in hospital bed fashion.

Wedge—Wooden wedges are driven between cleat and wedge batten to hold tarpaulins in place. When wedges are properly driven the beveled grain is against the wedge batten and the smooth edge against the cleat.

Wedges are driven from forward with small end aft, and from the sides with small end inboard.

Hatch beams—Heavy girders used to cover hatches. Types: King beam, blind beam, strongbacks.

Hatch boards—Lengths of board about 4 1/2 feet long, 2 1/2 feet wide and about 2 inches thick. These are placed over the beams and the tarpaulins cover the hatch boards. Hatch battens (sea battens) are heavy metal bars placed over the tarpaulins over the top of the hatch, secured beneath stiffener and held together at center of hatch by bolts and nuts, or small turnbuckles.

Figure 5-10. Modern hydraulically operated hatch. Wooden hatch boards are a thing of the past. Courtesy: Lykes Bros. Steamship Co., Inc.

Deck cleats—Double-horned metal fittings on deck used to secure lines.

Pad eye—Inverted U-shaped fitting used to shackle gear to deck through the eye.

Ring bolts—Same as pad eyes but with rings.

Never throw a tarpaulin over an open hatch and leave it. Many a man has fallen and been killed because the hatch cover had not been put in place under the tarpaulin.

Hatches on newer vessels are hydraulically controlled and may be opened and closed in a matter of minutes by one man. The hatch seals itself, usually with pneumatic gaskets. This type of hatch is safer, more efficient, and more seaworthy (Figure 5-10). No hold tarp is required.

PREPARATION OF SHIP FOR LOADING

Depth of water—As the ship takes on cargo, she will go down in the water. The water depth must be sufficient to float the ship when loaded, and the loading berth must be clear, i.e., not fouled by rocks or other obstructions.

Ballast tanks and bunkers—Where a ship is to bunker *after* loading, the extra weight of fuel must be taken into consideration in bringing her down to her load line.

Preparing the holds—Cleaning of various compartments may begin as they are cleared of cargo during the process of unloading. Decks, bulkheads, stringers and deck beams should be swept clean, and in some cases, where the odor of previous cargo would damage the new cargo, they must be washed. If so, wash from the top down, using fresh water. Leakage of oil, sirups, etc., may be taken up with sawdust. Remove all crushed and dirty dunnage and stow good dunnage in small piles near where it will be used. Beds or quoins and wedges may be put into sacks to protect them from theft and render them easy to move when desired.

Where cargo such as flour or seeds, or anything subject to damage by moisture, is to be carried, it is necessary to cover the metal beam and hold stanchions with paper, burlap, or matting to prevent the drops of moisture that may condense on them from contacting the cargo.

Separation cloths—These are often used to separate similar cargo destined for different ports, and should always be used under bag cargo to insure that the sweepings will be clean when collected after discharging.

Shifting boards—If bulk grain is to be loaded, shifting boards or temporary wooden bulkheads are built to divide the hold into small compartments, to keep the grain from shifting as the ship rolls. Feeders or wooden hoppers are built in the hatchway to feed grain into the holds as the cargo settles during the voyage.

DUNNAGE

Many cargo claims arise from faulty dunnaging or lack of sufficient or suitable dunnage. Moreover, proper dunnaging is usually necessary to keep cargo from toppling, and so is an integral part of stowage and of great importance to the safety of the crew, the ship and her cargo.

The purposes of dunnage are:

1. To raise the cargo from the deck, providing ventilation and drainage.

2. To separate different consignments; especially needed when different consignments of the same goods are shipped.

3. To bind one tier of cargo so that another may be stowed on top of it.

4. To brace cargo to prevent toppling.

5. To provide a covering over cargo which might be damaged otherwise.

6. To fill in broken stowage.

7. To prevent chafing.

8. To protect cargo from contact with moisture or "sweat" which forms on the ship's sides, frames, bulkheads, side stringers, etc.

Dunnage usually consists of rough strips of wood of equal thickness. Fir, pine, and spruce are used, but fir is preferred because it has less odor. Strong-scented dunnage will taint certain cargoes. Thus dunnage which has soaked up creosote or oil from a previous cargo should not be used again. Bamboo, rattan, staves and even bones, hoofs and horns are sometimes used for dunnage.

General rules for use of dunnage—No hard-and-fast rule covering the amount, kinds and use of dunnage can be given, each cargo being a rule unto itself in this respect. However, bearing in mind the importance of proper dunnaging and the purposes for which it is used, certain general principles are worth bearing in mind and may be summarized as follows:

1. Dunnage must be dry and clean and must not have been in contact with creosote, oil, or other odorous goods.

2. The first layer of dunnage must be laid in the direction of the drains—athwartships if drainage is to the scuppers, fore-and-aft if drainage is to an athwartship cofferdam.

3. Drain water condensing on the sides of the ship into the bilges by placing dunnage across the limber boards up to a point just above the filling boards in the rounding part of the hold.

4. Cover all iron work such as stanchions, coamings, etc. The shaft tunnel is covered only at the square of the hatch, the remainder protected by upright battens and tarpaulins.

5. Lay extra dunnage in the wings of the 'tween decks so that water condensing from the ship's sides will have a clear run to the scuppers.

6. Stringer or wing plates in the 'tween decks should be dunnaged evenly though the decks may not require it.

7. Ships with double bottoms and no bilges require special attention to floor dunnaging to make certain that water condensing on the ship's sides has a free run to the well.

STOWAGE

Cargo plans—A plan showing the amount and type of cargo to be carried, its destination and how it will be stowed, is prepared by the shipping company or stevedore well in advance of loading. Different colors are used to designate cargo for different ports. Cargo is stowed so that the last to be discharged goes in first. In peacetime, cargo is marked with the first letter of its destination; in war, code symbols are used. Cargo plans are usually sent ahead to reach the discharging port ahead of the vessel, and vacant spaces, with measurements, are plainly marked.

Trim—Since the loading and stowage of cargo effects the trim and list of a vessel, these must be checked, so that when ready to sail, she will be in proper trim (slightly down by the stern) and without a list.

Bracing, shoring and chocking—Shifting will damage cargo as well as endanger the safety of the ship and her crew. Many a good ship has rolled over in heavy weather and gone to the bottom because of shifting cargo. To prevent this, partitions or temporary bulkheads are built in the holds. Regulations for each country, and sometimes for each port, specify the scantlings of the lumber to be used. Demountable shifting boards, consisting of bolted uprights and planks for the bulkheads, are most satisfactory.

Broken stowage—That space which is unavoidably "lost" or unoccupied by cargo. It includes: (1) Space between or around packages or containers; (2) space occupied by dunnage; (3) space at the sides, ends and tops of cargo; (4) space occupied by pillars, frames, and other temporary or permanent fixtures. It amounts to 10 to 15 percent of the cargo space and must be taken into account in planning stowage.

Figure 5-11. Log ship at the loading terminal. (Used by permission from *Modern Marine Terminal Operations and Management,* 1983, Port of Oakland, California).

Stowage factor—The number of cubic feet of space required to stow one long ton (2240 pounds) of any commodity is the stowage factor of that commodity.

SPECIAL CARGOES

Cargoes requiring special care in handling, loading and discharge are often put aboard. These require special attention as the shipper pays extra for this care.

Gold, silver, currency and **registered mails** are stowed in the ship's strong box or specially constructed compartments in one of the holds.

Explosives such as ammunition, bombs, mines, torpedoes, gunpowder, picric acid, fireworks, detonating caps, fuses, primers or "warheads" are not stowed as regular cargo. In peacetime ships carrying this type of cargo

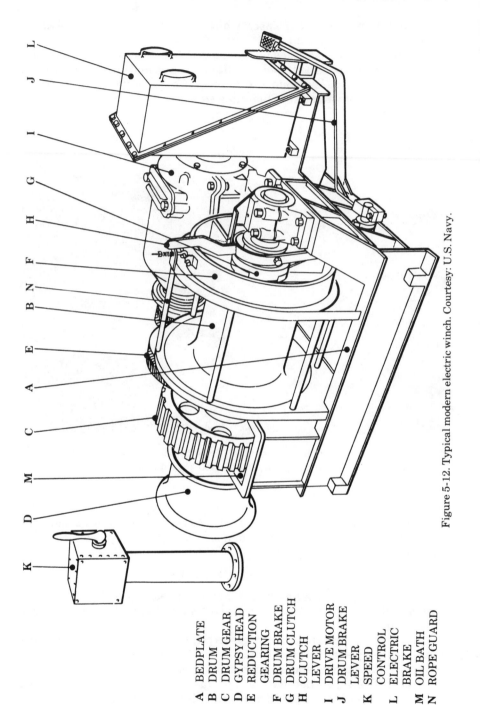

Figure 5-12. Typical modern electric winch. Courtesy: U.S. Navy.

A   BEDPLATE
B   DRUM
C   DRUM GEAR
D   GYPSY HEAD
E   REDUCTION
    GEARING
F   DRUM BRAKE
G   DRUM CLUTCH
H   CLUTCH
    LEVER
I   DRIVE MOTOR
J   DRUM BRAKE
    LEVER
K   SPEED
    CONTROL
L   ELECTRIC
    BRAKE
M   OIL BATH
N   ROPE GUARD

FLUSH HEAD　　OVAL PIN　　EYE SCREW　　HEART

WESTERN　　　　　　SEATTLE

NEW YORK　　LIVERPOOL

PLAIN　　　　　　　　　　HATCH

REVERSE　　　　　　　　SAFETY TONGUE

CHAIN SLING

Figure 5-13. Cargo hooks and shackles.

must have specially built compartments or magazines. However, during wartime, this cargo is often stowed with, and in the same way as, regular cargo.

Petroleum products such as gasoline, kerosene, naphtha, or benzene are carried in drums when loaded aboard a general cargo vessel. These drums should be stowed on end.

Gasoline, naphtha or benzene are not stowed near the engine or boiler room unless a temporary bulkhead of wood is built which will keep these cargoes at least 3 feet away from the bulkhead. The space between the temporary partition and the bulkhead should be filled with an insulating substance, such as asbestos, rock-wool or spun glass. (This will serve to keep the heat from the flammable liquids.)

When this cargo is stowed on deck, it is so placed that it is clear of heat (away from engine room, boiler room, fiddley gratings or smoke-stack).

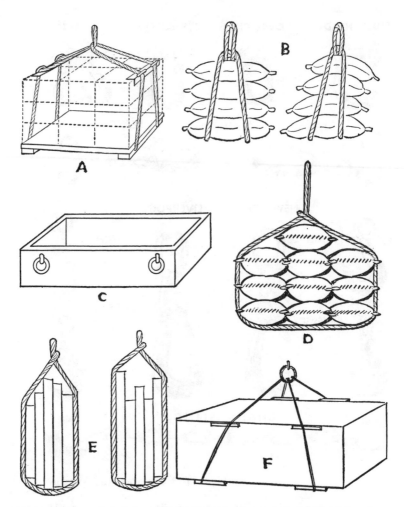

Figure 5-14. Different types of slings. A. Platform; B. Right and wrong way of making up a draft of bags; C. Box; D. Draft of bags; E. Right and wrong way of making up a draft of different boxes; F. Method of slinging cases.

When explosives are being loaded, the red "Bravo" flag is flown and "no smoking, no visitors and no open light" signs are posted at the gangway and other conspicuous spots throughout the vessel.

Acid, although not classed as an explosive, is classed as dangerous cargo. It is usually carried on deck in carboys. The space between carboy and crate is usually filled with chalk or some other absorbent material which is not affected by the acid. It is stowed where it may easily be thrown overboard should a leak develop. If the shipper requests to have it stowed below deck, it is never stowed with other cargo. Before it is placed on the deck, a 2-inch floor of chalk or charcoal should be laid. This will absorb any acid which might leak, and prevent it from damaging other cargoes or eating through the deck.

Odorous goods—Tea, coffee, sugar, flour, spices and many other food-stuffs may be damaged by odors. The principal products whose odors can injure other goods are tobacco, rum, rope, sponges, rags, vinegar, coal, brown sugar, naphthalene, manufactured rubber, fertilizers, especially guano, and vegetables whose fermentation may cause offensive odors.

Dusty goods—Soiling dusts, such as certain dye products, and pulverized cargoes, such as flour, may cause damage to other cargo and perhaps to personnel unless the holds are particularly well cleaned after this type of cargo is hauled. Cement dust may harden from dampness and stop up strainers, efface markings, etc. Men working in holds where grain in bulk is being stowed must wear masks.

Live cargo—Where livestock is carried, the shipper ordinarily has handlers along who feed and water the stock. The seaman's duty to livestock lies in seeing to it that sufficient ventilation is provided for the animals, which are carried in the 'tween decks or on deck, in special stalls built for the purpose. These stalls are better placed athwartships instead of fore and aft so that the vessel's rolling will not throw the animal's flanks against the side of the stall.

Grain—Three primary precautions must be taken when grain is to be loaded. (1) The grain must be protected from moisture. This is accomplished by seeing to it that the bilges are dry and that all metal beams, etc., are covered with burlap. (2) Rose boxes must be protected in such a way that accumulated water may escape while the rose boxes remain clear of grain. This is done by covering the rose boxes with three layers of burlap held in place by a ring of cement. (3) The grain must be prevented from shifting as the ship rolls. This is done by building shifting boards, or temporary wooden bulkheads supported by uprights and shores. Further protection against the shifting of the grain is taken by building feeder boxes which are filled with grain after the cargo has been loaded; then as the grain settles during the voyage, the grain in the feeder boxes seeps out and fills the space.

DECK CARGO

Deck cargo has taken on a new look since the addition of containers. Only large items that will not go into the holds are now stowed on deck without first being put into a container. Examples are locomotives, large tractors, and yachts. Entire cargoes of lumber or logs are also common. Particular attention must be given to the securing of deck cargo because it is exposed to the sea and a shifting of weight this high above the keel in a vessel can be disastrous.

CARGO GEAR

Even on conventional break-bulk ships cargo gear has been changing rapidly. Conventional yard and stay rigs are being replaced by Ebel and Farrell rigs. Swinging cranes are the trend of the future. Old fashioned

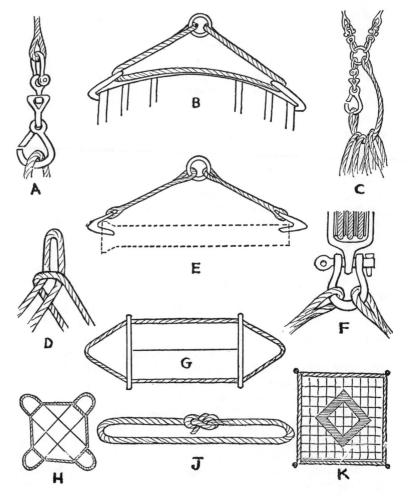

Figure 5-15. Hooks and slings. A. Cargo hook; B. Barrel hooks; C. Cargo hook with snotter; D. Method of fastening sling; E. Hooks for pipes and bales; F. Block and shackle; G. Bag sling; H. Nitrate sling; J. Rope sling; K. Loading net.

winches, whether steam or electric, are no longer being placed on new construction.

Power-driven winches—The principal purpose of winches, in general, is cargo handling. However, they are also used for many purposes involving the handling of lines, including warping operations. Winches usually consist of a large cable-winding drum mounted on a horizontal shaft and upon one or both ends of which a winch head is carried. See Figure 5-12.

Cargo hooks and shackles—Typical cargo hooks and shackles are shown in Figure 5-13. It is important that the hook or shackle be strong enough to support the load it is required to lift. If the Safe Working Load is not available, the following formulas may be used:

Hook   *Shackle*

SWL (tons) = 2/3 d^2 (d in inches)   SWL = 3d^2

The diameter of the hook is taken to be the smallest diameter, and the diameter of the shackle is the smallest part, or just below the pin.

Slings and drafts—Slings are made in all shapes and sizes of Manila, wire, nylon, nets, bars, and hooks. They are worked in combination depending upon the cargo handled. Palletized and unitized cargoes have simplified the types of slings in some loading operations, but in any break-bulk operation many different types of slings will be seen.

Figures 5-14 and 5-15 illustrate some of the cargoes and methods of handling with different types of slings. Cargo nets and platforms, while

Figure 5-16. Small modern forklift designed for in-hold operation. Courtesy: Military Sealift Command.

not in the true sense of the word "slings," are used for handling many small units of cargo in a single draft.

Fork lift or lift truck—The fork lift has become indispensable in handling cargo for break-bulk ships. Fork lifts are very powerful and come in a variety of sizes. They can be powered by gasoline, diesel, propane, or electric battery. Fork lifts are used in the warehouse, on deck, and in the cargo hold (Figure 5-16).

The type of cargo gear used aboard ship is constantly being updated and improved. The standard yard and stay cargo gear pictured in Figure 5-17 is

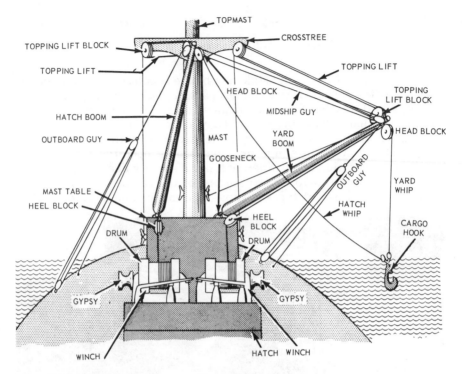

Figure 5-17. Typical cargo gear. Courtesy: U.S. Navy.

Figure 5-18. *State of Andhra Pradesh* unloading in San Francisco. Although common aboard foreign flag ships, shipboard swinging cranes are little used by U.S. flag vessels at the present time. Courtesy: Norton, Lilly & Co., Inc.

Figure 5-19. Stuelcken boom. This Stuelcken mast installation has a lifting capacity of 525 tons. It was installed on the MV *Wakagiku Maru* in 1978 and is the largest in existence. Courtesy: Blohm & Voss A. G.

Figure 5-20. Wishbone type Stuelcken booms. These booms have a capacity of 80 tons. Heavier booms are capable of lifting 320 tons. Courtesy: Lykes Bros. Steamship Co., Inc.

on its way out. After many years of dedicated service it can no longer compete.

Various attempts have been made to improve and mechanize this basic gear. Ebel and Farrell rigs changed from manila to wire guys, eliminated the midships guy, and put all operations on winches. Although this was an improvement, it caused large maintenance problems. Modern shipboard swinging cranes are being used increasingly in new ships to replace the old conventional yard and stay cargo gear. They require less maintenance, their gear is simpler to stow for sea, and they are more reliable to operate. The ship in Figure 5-18 is equipped with rotary or slewing cranes which is an example of an improved shipboard crane.

No chapter on general cargo would be complete without a discussion of heavy lift booms. Although not very common, the heavy lift boom is still in existence and fulfills a definite need. For example, one Stuelcken mast installation has a lifting capacity of 525 tons. A heavy lift boom has yet to be designed to improve upon the features of the Stuelcken model. Although several variations exist in the means of positioning the boom from one hatch to the other, this boom is the ultimate in shipboard heavy lifts.

CHAPTER VI

CANVAS AND LEATHER WORK

CANVAS

CANVAS, OFTEN CALLED DUCK, is a general name for a class of strong, heavy, plain cloth woven of cotton or linen. *Numbered duck* is the canvas encountered most often, but occasionally you see the terms *ounce duck* or *army duck*. Numbered duck runs from No. 1, the heaviest, to No. 12, the lightest. Numbers 7, 9, 11 no longer are issued. Each number means a certain weight in ounces per square yard of cloth. For example, No. 1 is 28.71 ounces per square yard. No. 6 is 20.74 ounces per square yard, and No. 12 is 11.16 ounces per square yard. Canvas in weights besides those designated specifically under the numbered system is called ounce duck. Army ducks are ounce ducks similar to numbered duck, but have finer yarns, higher cloth counts, and usually lighter weights.

Canvas normally is made up in bolts of from 85 to 100 yards, but is issued by the linear yard in widths from 22 to 72 inches.

The lengthwise threads are called the *warps* and the crosswise threads are known as the *welts*. The threads on a good piece of canvas will give and stretch when the canvas is bored through with a fid, but on an old or inferior piece of canvas the threads will break.

TREATED CANVAS

Much canvas is treated to make it resistant to fire, water, weather, and mildew. Some is waterproof and oil- and gasoline-resistant. Current specifications for building ships require that all top-side canvas be treated according to the use to which it is to be put. Canvas to be used below decks is usually white and untreated. Preservatives are available for shipboard use on untreated canvas or for re-treating canvas.

CARE AND STOWAGE

Canvas is very expensive; so learn how to care for it, and make sure you never abuse it. New and unused canvas, spare covers, etc., should be stowed in a clean, dry storeroom. Never store canvas where acid is (or has been) stowed; acid fumes are detrimental to canvas. Every effort should be made to provide a space free from rats, mice, and insects. Wet, painted, or oil-soaked canvas should not be stowed below deck. Occasionally it is necessary to scrub canvas that has become particularly dirty or stained by grease or oil. Use a mild soap solution, rinse thoroughly, and hang it up to dry.

This chapter has been reproduced with little change from the *Navy Training Manual for Boatswain's Mate 3 & 2* by permission of the Navy Education and Training Development Center, Pensacola, Florida.

All covers, awnings, and paulins should be inspected frequently and carefully, and all rips and torn or loose seams should be repaired. If a grommet tears out, sew a patch over the spot and put in another grommet. A larger size grommet may be substituted for one that has torn out, if it is in a spot where appearance is unimportant.

MEASURING CANVAS

Great care should be taken when measuring and cutting canvas. *Measure twice and cut once.* When measuring canvas for items that will be stretched taut (awnings for example), *deduct* one-half inch for each linear foot in both width and length. If the canvas is to be loose (as for hatch hoods and gun covers), *add* one-half inch for each linear foot in both width and length. Use the old article for a pattern whenever possible. When that is not available, make a sketch of the item, showing all the necessary dimensions, and work from that.

RIPPING CANVAS

Spread the canvas on deck and pick up one thread at the measured mark, and with the knife blade (it must be sharp) held at an angle of 30 degrees, press lightly as it is moved forward and at the same time keep a strain on the thread; in this way the thread is removed leaving a straight thin line for the blade to follow as the actual cutting is done.

PERTINENT DATA

The weight of canvas used for the various covers varies, but the information in the accompanying table is more or less standard.

No. of Canvas	Article
1	Sand bags
1	Hammocks
2	Hatch paulins
4	Berth bottoms
4	Sea bags
6	Large boat covers
8	Hose rack covers
8	Soiled clothes bags
8	General-purpose paulins
10	Shower curtains

SEWING CANVAS BY HAND:
TOOLS

Sail needles—Needles are numbered according to size; the higher the number, the smaller the needle. The heavier the canvas, the larger your needle should be. After use, needles should be dried carefully and oiled or stowed in a container of powdered chalk to prevent them from rusting.

Palms—Two types of palms are used: the sailmaker's palm and the roping palm. At first glance you probably see no difference, but if you check the metal slug you can see that the roping palm is designed for larger sized needles. This is the palm to use when jobs require the largest needles—sewing on bolt ropes, for example.

Sailmaker's or bench hook—This hook (Figure 6-1) has a swivel eye. It is used to hold the ends of two pieces of canvas being sewn together, as shown in the illustration.

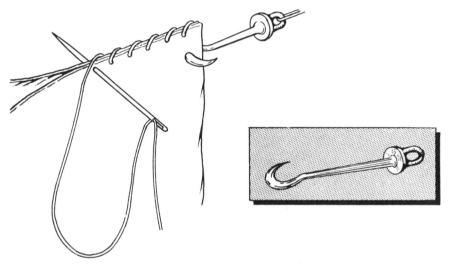

Figure 6-1. Round stitching canvas held by a bench hook. Courtesy: U.S. Navy.

Beeswax—This substance can hardly be called a tool, but it is a necessary item. It reduces the wear on the sail twine while sewing and retards deterioration.

Creasing sticks—This is a wood or metal tool slotted at one end and used to crease the seams.

Rubber—A flat steel tool used for rubbing or smoothing down the seams, this is fitted with a wooden handle.

Pricker—This is a steel tool with a rounded handle and tapered down to a sharp point. It is used for piercing heavy canvas when sewing.

Sail twine—Sail twine is usually made of cotton. It is put up in half-pound balls and its size is designated by the ply, or number of threads. Four- to eight-ply twine is used for sewing canvas, depending on the weight of the canvas.

STITCHES AND THEIR USES

Round stitch—The round stitch is the one used most commonly for joining two pieces of canvas. Turn back the edges, hold the pieces together, and send the needle through both pieces at right angles to the seam, as shown in Figure 6-1.

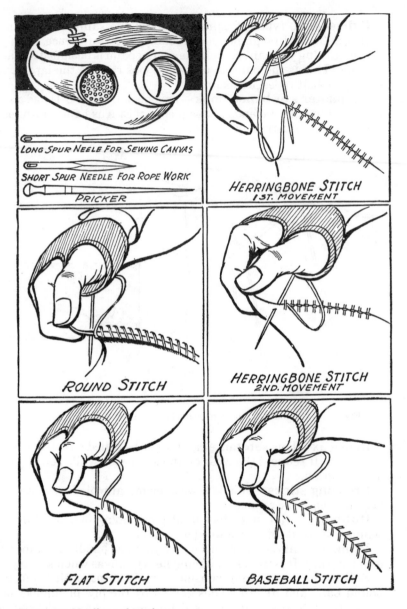

Figure 6-2. Needles and stitches.

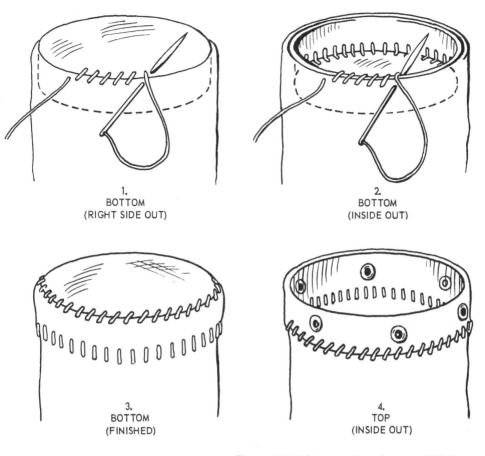

1.
BOTTOM
(RIGHT SIDE OUT)

2.
BOTTOM
(INSIDE OUT)

3.
BOTTOM
(FINISHED)

4.
TOP
(INSIDE OUT)

Figure 6-3. Making a sea bag. Courtesy: U.S. Navy.

Flat stitch—A flat stitch is used when a strong seam is required, as on a paulin or a sail. Pencil a guideline 1 1/2 or 2 inches from the edge of each strip of canvas, depending on how wide you want the seam. Crease each piece on a line slightly less than halfway to the guideline. Make the folds away from the guidelines and interlock the folds (Figure 6-2). Interlocking the edges forms a watertight seam and keeps a ragged edge from showing. Insert needle at the guideline, and stitch diagonally so that stitches appear at right angles to the seam on top but run at an angle on the reverse side. After completing one edge, turn canvas over and sew the other edge of the seam. Flat stitching is used for patching.

Baseball stitch—The baseball stitch is used to mend tears in light and medium canvas. Figure 6-2 shows how it is done.

Herringbone stitch—The herringbone stitch is used to mend tears in heavy or painted canvas. It is also used to sew canvas on lifelines. Figure 6-2 shows the steps in making this stitch.

MAKING A SEA BAG

A sea bag may be any size desired, but 1 foot in diameter and 36 inches in length is about average. Use No. 4 weight canvas that is wide enough for the length of the bag, plus allowance for seams, to avoid sewing an extra seam. A 40-inch width is adequate. Cut a length equal to 3 1/7 times the diameter of the bag plus 3 inches for the seam. Fold back one-half inch at each end and draw a line 1 inch from each fold. Lap the ends and flat stitch each fold to the opposite part along the penciled line as in Figure 6-3.

Now for the bottom: With a piece of sail twine tied to a pencil, draw a circle 1 foot in diameter on a piece of canvas. Cut this out, leaving at least 1 inch outside the circle. Fold 1 inch of the sides down inside the tube. Insert the bottom in the tube and round stitch it in place, sewing along the penciled circle as in step 1 of Figure 6-3. To make the bottom stronger, you can turn the bag inside out as in step 2 and round stitch another seam. If you intend to do this, leave 1 1/2 or 2 inches outside the circle when cutting out the bottom.

With the bag turned inside out, turn down 1 1/2 inches at the top, then fold it again so that you have three thicknesses where the grommets go. Flat stitch this as in step 4. Insert four or six grommets equally spaced around this hem, and your bag is finished. (See the section in this chapter on inserting grommets.)

To make the finished bag soft and pliable, boil it in soapy water for about 30 minutes and rinse well.

SEWING BOLT ROPES TO CANVAS
BY HAND

Bolt ropes are the ropes around the edges of awnings and sails. Their purpose is to take the strain of the stops, clews, reef points, and the like. To sew on a bolt rope, hem the canvas and lay the rope along the edge. Use a round stitch, the size of which is determined by the size of the rope. The rope is sewn strand by strand to the canvas as shown in Figure 6-4. Carefully observe these points when sewing on bolt ropes:

1. Keep the rope taut and canvas slack.

2. Don't bunch the canvas, but hold your needle at such an angle that it goes through the canvas a fraction of an inch ahead of where it comes out from under the strand.

3. Sew each strand to the canvas, making sure the needle goes under, not through, the strands.

4. Don't let your stitches start to creep up around the rope, but keep them coming out of the rope in a straight line along the underside. If you let them creep, the canvas begins to curl around the rope.

5. *Sew the bolt rope tight.*

WATERPROOFING

Canvas may be waterproofed in several ways. A solution that can be made on board ship is as follows: yellow soap and beeswax, two ounces each; lampblack in oil, 10 pounds; distilled or rain water, 3 pints; boiled oil,

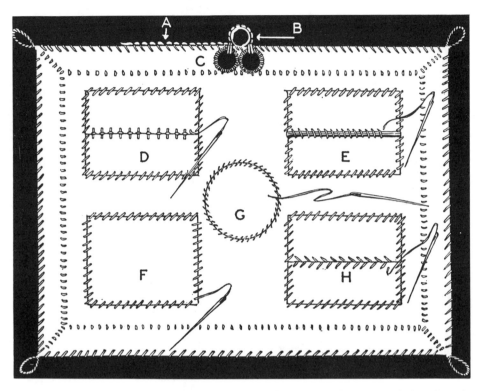

Figure 6-4. Examples of sewing canvas: A. Sewing boltrope to a sail or awning; B. Cringle made around a thimble; C. Hand-worked eyelets; D. Herringbone stitch, used on painted or very stiff canvas; E. Round stitch, used to join two edges together or for quick repair of very heavy canvas; F. Flat stitch on square patch; G. Flat stitch on round patch; H. Baseball stitch, used to sew rips where a snug fit is required.

1 1/2 gallons, and 1/2 pint of drier. The soap and wax are cut up in small pieces and heated in the water until melted; then the oil is added. The lampblack is added next, dissolving thoroughly. When mixing is complete, remove from fire and add drier. This preparation should be well covered when not in use.

It should be remembered that canvas, when wet, will shrink. All canvas should be slacked off in wet weather to prevent carrying away.

GROMMETS

Hand-sewn type—Metal grommets have almost replaced the hand-sewn type, but if you ever should be caught without the proper size of metal grommets, it is well to know how to make them by hand. Properly made and sewn to the canvas, they are almost as strong as the metal type.

The first step is to fashion a two- or three-strand grommet of marline. Stretch this over a fid to make it round and firm. Double your sail twine, twist the two parts together, and wax adequately. Then punch a hole in the canvas slightly smaller than the grommet. Sew the grommet to the canvas, using a round stitch. Pass the needle through the canvas, well back from the edge. After completing the stitches, shape the grommet again with a fid.

Metal grommets—Several different types of metal grommets are in use, but the two that are most familiar are pictured in Figure 6-5. The one

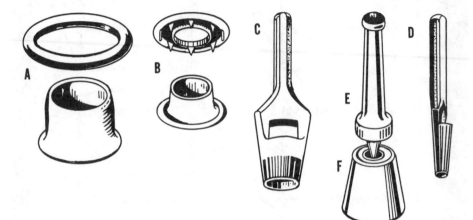

Figure 6-5. Grommets, cutting punches, and inserting punch and die. Courtesy: U.S. Navy.

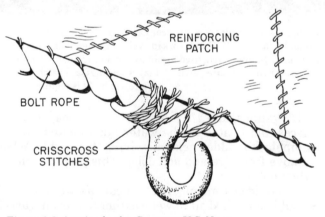

Figure 6-6. Awning hooks. Courtesy: U.S. Navy.

in sketch A is called the eyelet and ring type, and comes in sizes 6 to 15, inclusive, with inner diameters from three-fourths of an inch to 2 inches. Sketch B shows the spur type. It is in sizes 0 to 6, inclusive, with inner diameters from one-fourth to three-fourths of an inch.

The cutting punches show range in diameter from 1 inch down to seven-sixteenths of an inch in the double bow type (sketch C), and from three-eights to one-eighth inch in the single bow type (sketch D). When using these to punch holes in canvas, lay the canvas on a piece of heavy sheet lead, and they will cut a neat, clean hole.

The grommet-inserting punches and dies are available in sets in the same sizes as the grommets; that is, from 0 to 15. Use the same size set as the size of grommet. In Figure 6-5 sketch E shows the punch and F the die.

The proper way to insert the spur-type grommet is to push the eyelet part of the grommet through the hole in the canvas. Place the eyelet on the die and the spur over the eyelet. The punch fits inside the eyelet and when struck with a hammer, curls the edge of the eyelet down over the spur. Don't pound too hard on the punch, because that causes the grommet to cut through the canvas and later it may pull out.

The eyelet and ring type of grommet is especially for awnings and sails. Properly used, this is the best of all types. The ring part is sewn to the canvas the same as the handmade grommet. Then the eyelet is placed in the ring and set with the punch and die.

SEWING METAL FITTINGS TO CANVAS

Most metal fittings that must be sewn to canvas are rings of some sort. When sewing them on, as in making grommets, use your sail twine doubled and twisted together. Use as many round stitches as you can, stitching through the canvas over as great an area as possible, to spread the strain. Usually D-rings are secured to canvas by placing a webbed strap, folded canvas strip, or even a leather strap through the ring and sewing the strap to the canvas, using a flat stitch.

Awning hooks are positioned and held from sliding along the bolt rope by taking several crisscross stitches around the hook. (See Figure 6-6.) Several stitches around the concave pad on each side of the hook will take the strain of the awning lashings.

It is a good idea to sew a reinforcing patch over the edge of canvas every place a metal fitting is to be attached.

AWNINGS

Awnings are canvas coverings spread over the decks of a vessel to protect the crew from sun and weather. The center of the awning is held up by a strong fore-and-aft wire rope jackstay supported by intermediate stanchions. There may be a wooden strongback in place of the jackstay and others leading from it to the rail. The edges of the awning are hauled out and secured to ridge ropes along the rail. The ridge ropes in turn are supported by specially braced stanchions that usually can be taken down when the awnings are not in use. Edges of some awnings are secured to the ridge rope by lacings rove around the ridge rope and through grommets in the awning or awning hooks sewn to the bolt ropes. Other awnings are equipped with stops and earings spliced into the grommets. Earings are larger and longer than the stops and are spliced at the corners and in the grommets that line up with the stanchions.

When spreading an awning, haul it over the jackstay and spread it out fore and aft. If the awning is large and heavy, it may be necessary to rig a block and tackle to haul it taut. Next, man and reeve off the earings. Pull them taut and secure them temporarily to the ridge rope. Reeve off, set taut, and secure the stops temporarily to the ridge rope. It will be necessary to go back and tighten all stops and earings to take the sag from the awning. Earings and stops are secured by wrapping the bitter ends around the parts rove through the grommets and around the ridge rope, tucking the ends between the parts.

During rains, awnings must be housed to allow them to shed water better. This is done by casting off two or more stops between earings and securing them tautly to the lifeline. When awnings are secured by lacings rove through grommets, it is almost impossible to house them. It may be to your advantage to replace the lacings with earings and stops.

LEATHER

Hides and skins, being of animal origin, vary in area, thickness, and weight. Subsequent tanning and finishing processes further alter these features. The following information concerning the areas, thicknesses, and weights is therefore only approximate.

The types of leather include rigging, harness, shoe, chamois, kid, lacing, belting, and various artificial leathers. Of these, the three you are most likely to have need for are rigging, belting, and artificial leathers.

Rigging leather is designated by weight as light, medium, and heavy, and ranges from 6 ounces per square foot to over 10 ounces per square foot. It is issued by the pound. There are approximately 20 square feet per hide, and each one sixty-fourth inch of thickness equals approximately 1 ounce per square foot.

Belting is either round or flat and is issued in any desired length by the linear foot. Round belting comes in two widths, one-fourth inch and three-eights inch. Width is used instead of diameter because, despite the name, it is oval rather than perfectly round. Flat belting may be either single or double ply. Single ply belting is in 1- to 6-inch widths; double ply, from 2 to 12 inches.

The most common types of artificial leathers are used for upholstery and are issued by the square foot.

CARE OF LEATHER

Leather exposed to the elements should be kept well oiled or waxed. Any oil that does not contain harsh chemicals is suitable, but the best is neat's-foot oil. Leather in such places as on lifelines may be kept well preserved by the application of paste wax. Saddle soap, an excellent preservative and cleaner, can be used on holsters, and on shoes, jackets, and other leather wearing apparel. If leather becomes badly soiled and stained, wash it with a mild soap and water solution, rinse well, and dry in a spot away from intense heat. After it is dry, apply saddle soap or neat's-foot oil to replace the natural oils of the leather.

Leather is especially subject to mildew and rotting. It is also highly susceptible to accidental cutting, gouging, and abrading. Excessive heat causes it to shrink considerably, with consequent rending and cracking. Acids, corrosives, or their fumes have a disastrous effect upon leather.

The foregoing conditions should be borne in mind when stowing leather. Rolls must have top stowage to prevent crushing. Stowage must be well clear of any liquids or greases that might stain. To prevent sticking, paper should be placed between hides stowed one on top of the other. Original moistureproof wrappers should be left on as long as possible to prevent mildew. Stowage should always be in a dry, well-ventilated compartment.

SEWING LEATHER

When joining two leather edges by handsewing, the line along which the stitches are to run on each edge is grooved so as to countersink the stitches below the surface. Draw a line parallel and close to the edge first, then

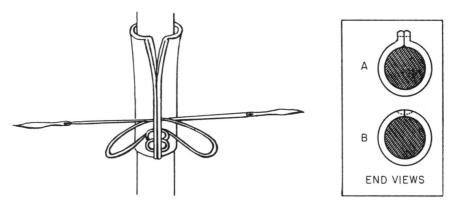

Figure 6-7. Shoemaker's stitch. Courtesy: U.S. Navy.

make your groove with a grooving tool (a dull knife will do). Use a block of wood for a straightedge. Next, punch holes along the grooves for the stitches.

The shoemaker's or cobbler's stitch is shown in Figure 6-7. A variation of this stitch is to cut the leather carefully so that the edges abut. Angle the grooves toward the edges of the leather and sew through the edges. This variation is particularly useful in sewing leathers on the looms of oars, but great care must be taken to trim the leather so that the edges butt and yet the leather is tight around the loom. Inset A of Figure 6-7 shows the end view of the regular shoemaker's stitch. Inset B shows the variation.

Leather, of course, handles and sews much easier if it is soaked in water for a few minutes.

THE SEWING MACHINE

OPERATION

The sewing machine is an ingenious affair, but quite simple to operate. It requires two threads, one of which may be seen on a spool on top; the

Figure 6-8. Threading the needle. Courtesy: Singer Manufacturing Company.

Figure 6-9. Threading the needle (continued). Courtesy: Singer Manufacturing Company.

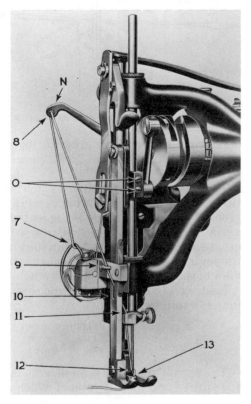

other is wound on a bobbin and inserted in the shuttle on the underside of the machine. The shuttle slides in the shuttle race that is directly under the needle. The top or needle thread is rove through a system of eyelets and a tensioning device fairleading it to the needle. As the needle moves down, it unwinds thread from the spool and draws it down through the material being sewn. When the needle starts to retract, it leaves a small loop of thread on the underside of the material. The shuttle, carrying the bobbin, passes through this loop. As the needle returns to its highest position and the tension spring on back to the end of its arc, the tension spring on the shuttle and the tensioning device in the needle thread system hold their respective threads and the stitch is pulled tight.

As the needle rises, the *lifting presser foot* raises slightly and the *feed dogs* pull the material into position for the next stitch. The material has reached its new position, and the lifting presser foot has come down to hold it there, before the needle again enters the material.

Because the sewing machine illustrated is frequently found in shipboard sail lockers today, this section of the chapter describes its use and care. If your sail locker has a different type of machine, consult the manufacturer's pamphlet to learn about it.

This Singer operates with one needle and one shuttle. It sews up to 550 stitches per minute; never sew at speeds in excess of this. Stitches can be adjusted in length from about 12 per inch to 2 per inch. Length of stitches is varied with the weight of canvas used.

Needles that may be used in this model vary in size from No. 19 to 31 inclusive. But remember: Needle size depends on the size of thread to be used. Needle packets often have stamped on them the size of thread to use with that particular size of needle.

The thread must pass freely through the eye of the needle. Do not use rough or uneven thread or thread that passes with difficulty through the needle eye, because such thread interferes with successful operation of the machine. Thread used in the needle should be left-twist, but either right- or left-twist may be used in the bobbin.

THREADING THE MACHINE

Threading the needle—To thread the needle, turn the balance wheel over toward you until the thread takeup lever (No. 8 in Figure 6-8) moves up to its highest position. Pass the thread from the unwinder through eyelet (1). Raise the lid of the cup (C) and pass the thread through the hole at the end of the thread post (2) under the lid. Close the lid and pass the thread through eyelet (3), and over the thread retainer disk (4). Pull the thread down between the disks. Then the thread goes down and around the tension wheel (5) and through the loop of the thread takeup spring (6). The thread then goes under the staple (7) shown in both Figures 6-8 and 6-9.

Next, pass the thread from back to front through the hole in the thread takeup lever (No. 8 in Figure 6-8 and 6-9), down through the thread guide (9), and into the slot in the vibrating presser bar (10). From there it goes through the thread guide on the needle clamp (11), and from left to right

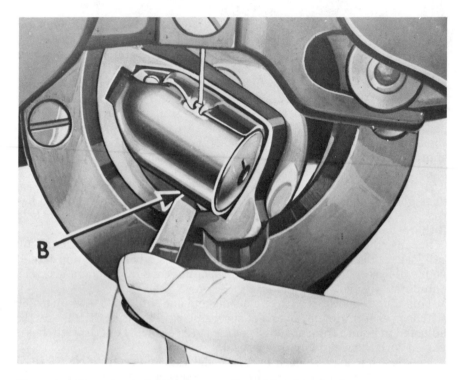

Figure 6-10. Removing the bobbin. Courtesy: Singer Manufacturing Company.

through the eye of the needle (12). Pull about 4 inches of the thread through the hole in the lifting presser foot (13).

Threading the bobbin—To remove the bobbin, turn the balance wheel to bring the needle bar to its lowest position. Insert the small end of the shuttle cylinder opener in the slot (B) in the spring latch beneath the shuttle cylinder, as in Figure 6-10. Press the latch away from the cylinder outward or toward the left as far as it will go and the bobbin will drop out.

To wind the bobbin, place the bobbin on the winder spindle and push it up tight against the shoulder. The small pin in the shoulder must go into the slot in the bobbin. Pass the thread from the unwinder through the hole in the left side of the bobbin. Push the bobbin winder drive wheel against the balance wheel and latch it in position as shown in Figure 6-11. Hold the end of the thread until a few coils are wound on the bobbin, then cut it off. When the bobbin is full, the bobbin winder trips automatically and stops.

To replace the bobbin and thread the shuttle, take the bobbin between the thumb and forefinger of the left hand, with the thread leading off from the underside toward the right as in Figure 6-12. Place the bobbin in the cylinder as far as it will go. Draw the thread into the slot (1) in the cylinder and under the tension spring into the delivery eye (2). Then push the cylinder back until it is locked by the spring latch. Allow about 3 inches of thread to hang free.

Figure 6-11. Winding the bobbin. Courtesy: Singer Manufacturing Company.

With your left hand, grasp the needle thread. Leave it slack. Then, with your right hand, turn the balance wheel toward you, moving the needle through a full cycle. This catches the bobbin thread and, by pulling on the needle thread, you can draw the bobbin thread up through the hole in the throat plate. Lay both threads back under the presser feet, and you are ready to sew.

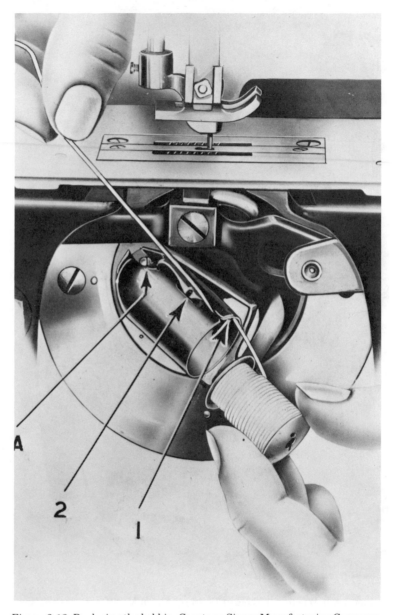

Figure 6-12. Replacing the bobbin. Courtesy: Singer Manufacturing Company.

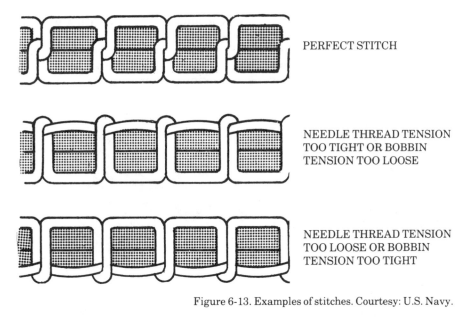

PERFECT STITCH

NEEDLE THREAD TENSION
TOO TIGHT OR BOBBIN
TENSION TOO LOOSE

NEEDLE THREAD TENSION
TOO LOOSE OR BOBBIN
TENSION TOO TIGHT

Figure 6-13. Examples of stitches. Courtesy: U.S. Navy.

ADJUSTMENTS

The perfect stitch has the two threads locking in the middle of the material. If the thread lies along the top of the material, either the needle thread is too tight or the bobbin thread is too loose. The bobbin thread is too tight, or the needle is too loose, if the thread lies along the bottom of the material. To get a perfect stitch, as shown in Figure 6-13, it may be necessary to adjust the tension.

Tension—Tension on the needle thread is adjusted by the knurled nuts on the thread retainer disks and the tension wheel (H and J in Figure 6-14). Tension on the thread retainer disks should be only enough to cause the tension wheel to turn when the thread is taken from the spool.

Tension on the bobbin thread is regulated by the screw holding the tension spring to the bobbin cylinder (A, Figure 6-12). Turning the screw to the right increases the tension; turning it to the left decreases the tension. Before changing tension on the bobbin, try to obtain the desired result by adjusting the needle thread tension.

Length of stitch—The length of the stitch is adjusted by loosening the thumbscrew (G in Figure 6-15) and moving the screw up or down. Move the screw down to lengthen the stitch; up, to shorten the stitch. After adjusting to the desired length, tighten the screw again.

Pressure on material—Pressure on the material should be only enough to allow the feed to move the work along evenly, and to prevent the work from rising with the needle.

To adjust pressure on the material, loosen the hexagon locking nut (E in Figure 6-15) and turn the hexagon screw. Turning the screw to the right increases the pressure; turning it to the left decreases the pressure.

When the pressure is correct, hold the adjusting screw with a wrench and tighten the locking nut against the bracket (F).

Needle bar and shuttle—To adjust the needle bar, loosen the two setscrews (indicated by arrows at 0 in Figure 6-9). Move the bar up or down until the top of the needle eye is approximately one thirty-second inch

Figure 6-14. Oiling points on the back of the machine. Courtesy: Singer Manufacturing Company.

below the shuttle point. This setting can be varied slightly, depending on the size of the needle and thread to be used.

If a change is made from a very small needle to a much larger one, the shuttle point will perhaps pass too close to the needle. Or, the shuttle point will pass too far away from the needle if a change is made from a large to a much smaller needle. Adjustment of the shuttle for proper clearance between shuttle point and the needle is made by loosening the screw (P in Figure 6-16) and turning the shuttle race either right or left. Only a slight movement of the shuttle should be required. Make sure you tighten the clamping screw after the adjustment is made.

Timing the feed—For general sewing conditions, the feed dog should be so timed that it completes its feeding action at approximately the same time the takeup lever (N, Figure 6-9) completes its upward stroke.

Machines are properly timed when they leave the factory, and no adjustment is necessary unless the position of the feed cam is disturbed.

If adjustment should be necessary, remove the arm side cover at the rear of the machine arm. With the arm side cover removed, the feed cam is

Figure 6-15. Oiling points on the front of the machine. Courtesy: Singer Manufacturing Company.

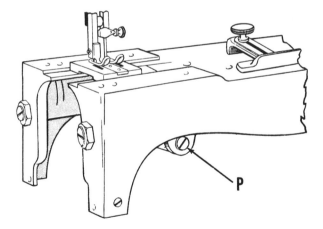

Figure 6-16. Adjusting the shuttle. Courtesy: Singer Manufacturing Company.

easily accessible. This cam is provided with two screws. Loosen the two screws and set the cam for earlier or later movement of the feed dog, as required, by turning the cam about the arm shaft to the required position. Then securely tighten the two screws in the cam.

OILING THE MACHINE

To ensure easy running and to prevent unnecessary wear of the sewing machine, all parts in movable contact need to be oiled. When a machine is in continuous use, oil should be applied frequently. Use only the oil recommended by the manufacturer of the machine. On this Singer, most points to be oiled are indicated by the unlettered arrows in Figures 6-14 and 6-15. Other places requiring oil, but not shown in the illustrations, are the shuttle race and the hole in the hub of the friction driving pulley.

OPERATING HINTS

Following are some hints you will find helpful when operating a sewing machine.

Probably the first indication of trouble to an inexperienced operator is the breaking of the thread. If the needle thread breaks, check the needle first. Make sure that it is inserted and set correctly, that it is not bent, and is not blunt. Then check the thread to be sure it is not too coarse for the needle, improperly threaded, or the tension is not too tight. If the bobbin thread breaks, it may be because the tension is too tight or the bobbin case is threaded improperly. If the trouble is none of these, it probably is in the relationship between the needle and shuttle. Check and adjust whichever is out of adjustment.

Occasionally, light canvas starts to bunch up when being sewn. This is an indication that the stitches are too long.

When sewing together long pieces of light canvas, you will find that the one on top will end up several inches shorter than the other. This is caused by the way the machine feeds. Do not attempt to adjust the machine to correct this, but allow an extra inch per yard when cutting the top piece. Never try to force the material through the machine. Let it feed itself.

Do not use linseed oil in the oil cup, because it causes the machine to gum up. Use any good light grade of oil that is free from acids. No. 10 motor oil will do.

CHAPTER VII

PAINTS AND PAINTING

If it moves, salute it. If it doesn't, paint it.
—*Old saying*

PAINTING ABOARD SHIP is primarily used to preserve surfaces. Because it provides a smooth, washable surface, paint also serves as an aid to cleanliness and sanitation. Although painting improves appearance, a complete coat of paint is only necessary when scrubbing will not remove offensive stains, or when the surface has deteriorated to the point where "spotting in" or a partial application of paint will not serve. This chapter provides basic information about paint, its uses aboard ship, and good painting practices.

Paints have been used since the beginning of civilization. But in the 1900s the manufacturing of paint began to change rapidly. The use of natural colored earths, animal fats, and vegetable oils gave way, particularly since World War II, to complex chemical compounds. In what amounts to an ongoing revolution, new kinds of paints keep coming on the market. New or old, most paints consist of four important elements, *pigment, vehicle, drier,* and *thinner.*

PIGMENT

White lead is the oldest of the opaque white pigments. It is still used in a few foreign commercial paints. Its consumer use in the United States, however, is prohibited by the Environmental Protection Agency. Because of its lead content it is considered poisonous and therefore unsafe. Unfortunately the lead content which makes it unsafe is the reason it is an excellent primer. White lead pigment is made by treating lead with acetic acid and carbon dioxide. The resulting fine white powder is then added to a suitable vehicle (linseed oil, for example) and the paint is ready for use.

Zinc oxide is another white pigment with a very fine texture. Since it does not weather well, zinc oxide is usually mixed with *titanium dioxide* and other pigments to make it strong enough to withstand the extreme changes of outdoor temperatures without cracking and scaling.

Titanium dioxide is a white pigment which has excellent "hiding power" qualities. In combination, zinc oxide and titanium dioxide are now the principal white pigments used aboard ship.

Inert pigments are *paint extenders* which are chemically stable and do not add color to the paint. Some of the more important extenders are barium sulphate, whiting or calcium carbonate, magnesium silicate or asbestine, and silica or silex. They are used to provide a less expensive

Figure 7-1. Tank vessel in drydock for overhaul. Upper photo shows vessel after spot sandblasting and touch up with a buff primer. Note that the existing coatings of black and marine red are still in good condition. Chain has been roused out of chain locker for inspection and sand blasting. Lower photo shows ship after painting has been completed. Courtesy: Devoe & Raynolds Co., Inc.

vehicle for some colors, to reduce the amount of hiding pigments required, and to strengthen and increase the thickness of the paint coat. They also help make a good primer coat. Some of them reduce settling or caking in the container as well.

VEHICLE

The vehicle, also known as the binder, is the liquid portion of the paint which becomes solid and unites the pigment particles. It wets the surface to be painted and penetrates the pores of the surface. The vehicle insures that the film formed by the hardening paint sticks.

Until the 1940s the base of most paints was an oil such as linseed. Today few shipboard paints contain raw oil of any kind. Some have vehicles of processed oils in combination with synthetic resins, and others have vinyl bases. Still others have chlorinated alkyd bases. These vehicles dry by evaporation, and/or oxidation. Two-package coatings dry by polymerization, a process whereby two or more similar molecules combine chemically to form a large molecule of a new substance. As a consequence, these new paints are different from those which contain raw oils. So, if a paint is thick and needs to be thinned, read the label on the can. Do not add anything not recommended.

Water-base paints for shipboard or industrial use are a comparatively recent development although various types have been used for centuries. Water-base paints are now being made from synthetic resins. Therefore, it is unnecessary to use thickeners, stabilizers and other substances formerly needed in water base emulsions.

DRIERS

When some metallic compounds are mixed with oil, they add to the drying properties of paint. These compounds consist mainly of lead, manganese, and cobalt napthenates. A paint drier takes oxygen from the air and adds it to the oil. This speeds up the curing process.

THINNERS

Thinners reduce the consistency of the paint so that it may be applied easily by spraying or brushing. Thinners also increase the penetration of the vehicle into the surface and cut down the gloss. If too much thinner is used, however, the thickness of the film is reduced. Thin films do not protect the surface and also wear out quickly. In flat paints the proportion of the oil is purposely reduced to such an extent that the paint dries without gloss. Thinners must then be added by the manufacturer for application. Mineral spirits are a common type of thinner, but the proper type depends upon the base of the paint. Once again: Read the directions on the can before adding anything.

LACQUERS AND VARNISHES

Lacquers and varnishes deserve mention although their use is limited aboard ship. Any coating that dries by solvent evaporation only is a lacquer. Lacquer can be made of a cellulose resin (such as nitrocellulose or cellulose acetate), resins, or a combination of resins such as methyl methacrylate combined with some of the acrylics. A dye or pigment can be added to the lacquer to give it color.

Varnishes can be divided into resinous varnishes, alkyd-resin varnishes, urethane-resin varnishes and epoxy-resin varnishes depending upon the type of resin used. Resinous varnishes are simply oils cooked with natural or synthetic resins. Linseed, tung, and soybean oils are used as thinners and require solvent evaporation and oxidation to dry.

Enamel is any pigmented finish coat, flat to high gloss, solvent or water base. A few are even high performance. Aboard ship the main use of enamel is on machinery or instruments.

Figure 7-2. Painting the side of the *Golden Bear*. Personnel working over the side must wear life jackets. Photo: Midn. Steven Dirschel, California Maritime Academy.

Shellac, also called a spirit varnish, is really not a true varnish. It is a lacquer made of a specific natural resin, called lac, which is dissolved in alcohol. It is little used aboard ship today.

TYPES OF PAINT

There are many kinds of paint used in different ways for many purposes. Some of the more important types of paints used aboard ship include primers, pretreatment coatings, topside, bottom and boot topping paint.

Primers are paints prepared especially to stick to the surface of the metal or wood which has been properly prepared for painting. The object is to provide a good base for finish coats of paint. Primers for metal include chemicals which help prevent rust.

Two frequently used primers are *oxide of lead* (red lead) and *zinc chromate*. Red lead is used on all metals except aluminum where zinc chromate is used. If the surface has been taken down to the bare metal, two primer coats should be used. It is helpful to use one color for the first coat and another color for the second coat to insure that there are no "holidays." Allow ample drying time between coats.

Pretreatment coatings—One of the early developments in marine paints is pretreatment coating. *Phosphoric acid* is very effective as a pretreatment coating, and several manufacturers have developed products which come in two-package units made up of a film-forming component and an acid solution. The directions on the can should be followed meticulously, and only as much as needed should be mixed.

Pretreatment coatings are an excellent means of protecting the surface to be painted and insuring that maximum life will be obtained from the primer and finish coats applied later. Since pretreatment coatings are not paint, they must be applied in thin films.

All paints, including pretreatment coatings, are highly flammable. Therefore, safety precautions should be enforced. If painting is done in an enclosed area, adequate ventilation should be insured. In any case, read the instructions and note if the painter is advised to wear a respirator.

Topside paints—Both conventional paints and the newer high performance paints are used topside. With the newer paints proper preparation of the surface is particularly important.

The new high performance paints used topside go a long way toward reducing, if not stopping, rust and corrosion aboard ship. Most of these paints consist of *inorganic zinc* although some are *zinc-pigmented coatings.* Similar to synthetic rope, they are frequently known by their trade names. Examples are Devoe and Reynolds' "Catha-Coat" and Americoat Corporation's "Dimetcote."

Corrosion of steel is an electrochemical reaction caused when a cathode (the negative area) and an anode (the positive area) form. Corrosion occurs at the anode. The potential difference between these two points determines how fast the corrosion takes place. The bonding of steel with a conductive zinc metal product makes the steel become the cathode and prevents corrosion. (Zinc becomes the anode and sacrifices itself to protect steel.) The process of galvanizing and the use of zinc anodes to prevent corrosion has been in use for a long time. The use of zinc in a coating to prevent corrosion is similar. Inorganic silicate zinc metal coatings apply very effective cathodic protection to any steel structure and are an important part of the entire protective coating system.

There are two basic types of inorganic zinc coatings—the alkali metal silicates which are water-based and the alkyl silicates which are organic solvent-based. In addition, there are polymer modified inorganic zinc coatings which act like unmodified inorganic zinc coatings but have improved primer and application properties. Epoxy modified inorganic zinc is currently the most effective.

The key factor in preparing steel for the application of inorganic zincs is the removal of all mill scale, rust, oil paint, grease, and other foreign matter. The second factor is the development of a roughness of the metal surface. Inorganic zincs are normally applied in the shipyard where oil and grease are first removed by commercial grease removers and then rinsed by water. Mill scale and rust are removed by grit blasting.

Bottom paints—Although bottom paint is applied at the shipyard, it is important to know something about the paints used. The bottom needs two types of protection against corrosion by salt water and against fouling by marine growth.

There are a number of different types of anti-corrosive paints used on ship bottoms. They have different bases, and rely on different principles. Among these are asphalts (which may be either bitumen or coaltar), tung oil with a phenolic base, chlorinated rubber, and vinyl types.

The high performance paints will probably be epoxy or a modified epoxy of some sort which bond to the metal. High performance paints are tough, have good adhesion qualities and have excellent water resistance.

Figure 7-3. Preparing the surface of the boat deck on the *Golden Bear*. Tedious work, but if not done properly, the paint applied later will be wasted. Photo: Editors.

Marine growth such as algae (seaweed or grass) and slime organisms require sunlight to grow. Consequently, the waterline presents the most serious fouling problem. Extra protection is required on the waterline as well as the bottom sides, rudder area and the bottom flats. To insure extra protection, make certain that better quality or more paint is used and that ample anti-fouling paint is applied where needed. If a high performance system is used, it should be able to last between dry-docking two years apart. If a conventional system is used, more frequent dry-dockings are required.

Boot topping paints—That part of the hull just above and below the waterline is called boot topping. It is punished by sea as well as by air. As a result, the boot topping needs more protection than any other part of the ship, and a seaman can expect to do his share in touching up this area during the course of his time aboard ship. Vinyl anti-fouling or vinyl alkyd enamel have been commonly used for boot topping. Best protection is provided by a high performance anti-corrosive such as modified epoxy and a high performance hard film anti-fouling paint.

SURFACE PREPARATION

No matter how good a paint is, it cannot be expected to stay on a surface that is dirty or rusty. Paint applied over rust does not stop the action of rust. Rusting goes on and loosens paint. Dirt, oil, grease, and rust or mill scale must be removed completely and the surface thoroughly dried. Items used to prepare surfaces include hand tools, power tools, sandblasters and shotblasters, detergents and water. Various paint and varnish removers are used as well.

HAND TOOLS

The most commonly used hand tools are *sandpaper* or *emery paper*, a *steel-wire brush*, a *hand scraper*, and a *chipping hammer*. The size of the abrasive paper is indicated by code numbers ranging from 4 to 5/0 (or 00000). In garnet or artificial abrasives, 4 or 3 would be very coarse and 2/0 to 5/0 would be fine. Sandpaper is a must in cleaning corners. A coarse sandpaper is used first and one of the finer grades is used to finish the job. There is also a waterproof type of sandpaper which can be used with water or oil for "wet" sanding. This is not possible with ordinary sandpaper.

A wire brush is a handy tool for light work on rust or on light coats of paint where power sanding is not possible. It can be used for brushing around welded spots and other places which are too rough for sanding. If a steel surface is pitted, use a steel wire brush to clean out the pits. Do not use common steel wire brushes on stainless steel or aluminum! This causes corrosion.

Scrapers are useful for removing paint and rust from small areas and from plating less than one-fourth inch thick where it is impossible to use power tools. Sometimes a chipping hammer is necessary, but make sure only enough force is used to remove the paint. Too much force may scar the surface. If a great deal of force is necessary to remove the paint, the paint is probably still good. If so, feather the edges and paint after preparing the bare metal.

POWER TOOLS

Although hand tools are frequently necessary, power tools should be used whenever possible. They are quicker, easier, and more efficient. A word of caution about a power wire brush, however, is in order. It can be detrimental in burying rust. If the surface is rough, and there is a rust pocket in a pit, the wire brush can curl over the lip of the pit and hide the rust.

One of the more versatile power tools is the portable grinder, shown in Figure 7-4. It can be equipped with a wheel wire brush, a rotary cup brush, or an emery wheel.

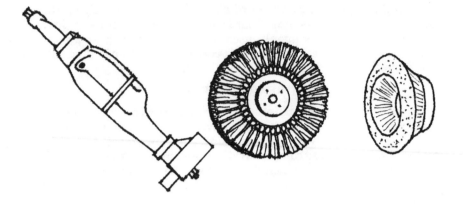

Figure 7-4. Electric portable grinder and wire brushes. Emery wheel is shown mounted in grinder. Wheel brush is shown at left, cap brush at right. Drawings: Scott Duncan.

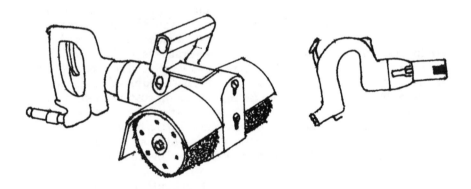

Figure 7-5. Power scaling tools. "Jitterbug" or "rattler" is shown above. Pneumatic hammer (without chisel) is shown below. Drawings: Scott Duncan.

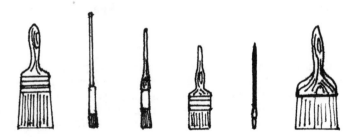

Figure 7-6. Types of brushes. From left to right: flat, fitch, sash tool, flat varnish, lettering, and painter's duster. Drawings: Scott Duncan.

Scaling may be done by any of the tools shown in Figure 7-5. A chisel about 8 inches long and 1 1/4 inches wide is used with the pneumatic hammer. It is held so that the chisel strikes the surface at an angle of about 45 degrees. It is even more important to avoid denting the surface with the pneumatic hammer than it is with the hand chipping hammer.

The rotary scaling and chipping tool, sometimes called a "jitterbug" or "rattler," comes in a variety of sizes. It has a bundle of cutters or chippers mounted in each side and is pushed along the surface. The rotating chippers do the hard work.

An electric disc sander is almost mandatory as a final step in preparation of a surface. Extreme care has to be taken so that the disc does not stay too long in one place and scar the surface.

POWER TOOL SAFETY PRECAUTIONS

Do not be afraid of power tools aboard ship or anywhere else. But, you will live longer if you treat them with the greatest respect. Most power tools are 115 volts, alternating current. It is especially easy to short circuit such a tool and electrocute yourself in a marine environment if the tool is not properly grounded. The following are suggested as safety precautions:

1. Do not operate any tool or equipment unless you have been shown how.

2. All electric power tools used aboard ship are or should be of the three-wire grounded type. If an electric tool is not provided with a ground, *do not use it.*

3. If the insulation or any of the wires looks old, or you can see any bare wire, the tool is *not* safe.

4. You must use the ground. If the ground circuit is not complete and you become grounded, you can receive a fatal shock.

5. Always use goggles when chipping whether you are using hand or power tools. The human eye is very fragile and you might lose it.

7. Keep your mind on the job. Do not let yourself get jolted out of a daydream by a wire brush that has turned on its operator.

GALVANIZED SURFACES

Galvanizing is done by dipping the object to be galvanized in a molten zinc bath. This gives the base metal a protective coating. If you paint galvanized steel you should sand or roughen the surface slightly and remove as little zinc as possible in the process. The surface should receive a coat of pretreatment or epoxy-modified inorganic-zinc coating, but not both, before painting. Old timers used to clean with ammonia or vinegar, but this is detrimental to modern paints and coatings. Welds and damaged galvanized areas should be painted in the same manner as the surrounding galvanized area.

PAINTING

With very few possible exceptions the paint you will use aboard ship—or elsewhere for that matter—will already be in its own can. It will have the necessary ingredients in it, and nothing else need be added. If you think it is too stiff, read the instructions on the can and see what the manufacturer says should be used as a thinner. As you know, when paint stands for long periods of time, the pigment settles to the bottom and the vehicle rises to the top. You must remix before use. If you have a mechanical stirrer, use it. If not, patiently stir the paint with a flat paddle, not a round pole or rod, until it is of a uniform consistency. To make sure the paint is thoroughly mixed, it helps to pour the paint back and forth between two cans. This is sometimes called "boxing" and insures a smooth and even mixture. When you open a can of paint, you may find that "skin" has formed on the surface. It must be removed. In addition, if there are any particles of dirt, pigment, or skin, they should be removed by straining the contents of the can through fine wire mesh or cheese cloth.

PAINTING BY BRUSH

Paint is applied by brush, roller, or spray. The most commonly used types of brushes are shown in Figure 7-6. A good painter using a *flat brush* can paint almost anything aboard ship. A flat brush is wide and thick and carries a large amount of paint. *Sash brushes* are handy for painting small items and hard-to-get-at places and for cutting in corners. The *duster brush* is used in cleaning.

Use of the brush—Basic principles which will make painting by brush easier are listed below:

1. Hold the brush by the handle and not by the stock.

2. Hold the brush at right angles to the surface, with the ends of the bristles alone touching, and lift it clear of the surface when finishing a stroke! Otherwise the surface will be uneven and have laps and spots which give a very poor appearance.

3. Do not cover the brush with the paint; dip the ends of the bristles only. Do not repeat this until the preceding charge has been exhausted.

4. Apply the paint with long strokes parallel to the grain of the wood. If painting along smooth surfaces, draw the brush along the entire surface if not too long, so as to show as few breaks as possible.

5. The successive applications should be applied systematically. Be sure on the second application to cross the preceding work at right angles. In each complete application keep all strokes parallel to each other. During the crossing use a medium pressure; in the final application use a light pressure. The final application should be in the length direction of the work.

6. An overhead surface should be systematized thus: Lay off the ceiling panels fore and aft, and the beams athwartships. However, if the panels contain many pipes running parallel with the beams, lay off the ceiling in general, parallel with the beams.

7. Vertical surfaces, bulkheads, etc., should be painted with the lines vertical. Each succeeding coat of paint should be laid off in the same direction; this is an exception to rule 5.

8. Keep the paint well mixed in the pot during the work.

9. Wait until the preceding coat is entirely dry before applying the second coat. Paint dries after coming in contact with the air; hence a second coat would retard this process. It may also cause the first coat to come up.

Care of brushes—A paint locker should have a container with divided compartments for stowing different types of brushes for short periods of time. The container needs a tight cover and means of hanging brushes so that the entire length of the bristles and lower part of the ferrule are covered by the thinner kept in the container. Brushes should not touch the bottom.

If a brush is to be used the following day, it should be cleaned with the proper thinner and placed in the right compartment of the container. Brushes not to be used temporarily should be cleaned in thinner, washed in detergent and water, rinsed thoroughly in fresh water, and hung up to dry. After drying, brushes should be wrapped in brown paper and stowed flat. A brush used with water-base paint should be washed immediately in detergent and water. Thinner is not to be used.

PAINTING BY ROLLER

After World War II the use of rollers was introduced aboard ship. Rollers are an excellent means of applying paint to a large flat area in a short amount of time. Rollers may be fitted into frames and with extenders (sometimes called "manhelpers") which enable the painter to reach a long way up the side or topside of a ship. However, it is better to cut in the edges first by brush.

Rollers should be cleaned in the same manner as brushes. They too will be ruined if not cared for properly.

SPRAY GUN PAINTING

Although more often used by shipyard workers spray guns are sometimes employed by seamen aboard ship to paint. If used, nearby areas need to be properly masked. The time saved in using a spray gun can be more than used up if it becomes necessary to clean those areas that should have been masked before starting.

A conventional spray gun is a precision tool in which air and paint are separately directed into the same area where the paint is atomized and sprayed out in front the gun. The mixing area may be outside or inside the gun's spray cap. Spray guns are classified according to where the air and paint are mixed. Two of the most frequently used types of spray guns are the external-mix and the internal-mix which are shown in Figure 7-7.

When the trigger of a conventional spray gun is squeezed the air valve opens and admits compressed air through the air inlet. The air passes through the gun to the spray head. In the external-mix type the air does not come into contact with the paint inside the gun but is blown out through small holes drilled in the air cap. Paint is shot out of the nozzle in a thin jet and the force of the air striking it causes the jet to form into a fine spray which can be adjusted.

The handling of a spray gun can be learned only by practice, but some tips are in order.

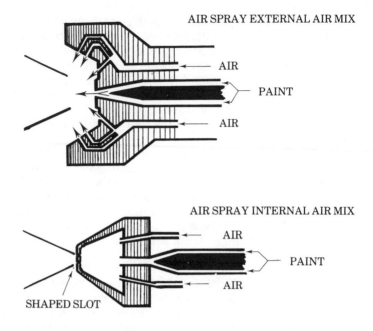

Figure 7-7. Spray guns compared. Courtesy: Devoe & Raynolds Co., Inc.

1. Before starting to spray, check the adjustments and operation of the gun by trying the spray on a surface similar to the one to be painted.

2. Use the minimum pressure necessary to do the work at a distance of about 6 to 10 inches.

3. Keep the gun perpendicular to and at the same distance from the surface being painted. (If the stroke is not perpendicular to the surface, paint will not be deposited in a uniform coat.)

4. Start the stroke before squeezing the trigger and release the trigger before completing the stroke. (If the gun is held too far away from the surface, much of the paint will be dry before it hits the surface, and if the gun is not moving when the trigger is squeezed or released, the paint will build up on the surface.)

5. When spraying corners, stop one or two inches short of the corner on both sides, turn the gun on its side and, starting from the top, spray downwards, coating both sides at once.

6. If spraying a large area into which small parts and pieces protrude, first coat those items lightly before going over the entire surface. This will help eliminate touching up later.

If it is important to clean brushes and rollers after use, it is obvious that it is even more important to clean a precision instrument like the spray gun. The various parts should be disassembled and cleaned carefully following the manufacturer's instructions. A good discussion of the spray gun can be found in the Navy's *Boatswain's Mate 3 & 2 (NAVTRA 10121-E)*.

Figure 7-8. Touching up the anchor of the *Golden Bear.* Only in a shipyard will the anchor and chain be prepared properly for painting. The best you can do is touch up for appearance only and trust it will stay on until the next time. Photo: Editors.

NOTES ON PAINTING

Too much time is wasted on board ship in scraping paint off screw threads, gaskets, and other places which should never have been painted over in the beginning. A little attention to the following common-sense rules will prevent this waste of time and improve the appearance of the ship:

Never, under any circumstances, paint rubber gaskets on watertight doors, manholes, hatches, etc.

Never paint screw threads, compartment name plates, louvres, gauze air screens, zinc protectors on the bottom.

Never, without orders, paint anything that has not been kept painted.

Never paint out lettering without special orders to do so. All the various numbers and letters have definite meanings, and they must not be painted out.

As there is a regulation way in which ships must be painted, never paint anything a different color without orders.

In painting use only a little paint on the brush, and never paint crosswise; that is, never make the strokes cross; they should always be parallel to each other.

Never put the paint on in a thick coat. It will not dry and become hard, but it is easily rubbed off for days afterward, and catches dirt continually. Put it on in thin coats, and it will dry quickly and form a hard surface.

Never paint over a dirty surface, or a rough unprepared surface. Paint is too frequently used to save scrubbing. The surface to be painted must be cleaned and scrubbed down to a smooth surface before any paint is applied. Rags or hands full of clean rope yarns will make excellent soogee rags to help remove any remaining stubborn dirt before painting and to remove paint drippings after painting. Be sure to remove the lint left by rags and yarn. A few turns of rags around a brush handle just above the bristles will stop the paint from working onto the handle. Try this the next time the overhead is to be painted.

Binding a brush is binding the bristles with twine much the same as the straws of a broom are bound, to keep them from spreading.

Generally the brush is held by the handle, but at times the wrist and palm of the hand may get tired and sore, in which case experienced painters have found comfort and ease by changing for a spell and holding the brush by the brindle, or metal band, which allows plenty of play on the brush. Keep the brindle clean.

When painting or washing the forward or after ends of deck houses always start at the windward side; in this way no paint or dirty water will be blown onto the finished surface.

When mixing paint in more than one container, remember to box the contents together to get a uniform paint film. This boxing of paint is very necessary when using colors.

When painting the mast or tarring down the rigging a simple way to control the paint or tar when charging the brush is to fit the paint can inside a water bucket and pack old rags around the paint can to keep it centered. In this way the excess paint that drips from the brush as you wipe it over the edge of the can is taken up by the rags and not splattered on the deck below.

It is necessary to have a hard undercoat for permanence in painting and to attain this do not put too much oil in a priming coat.

While the addition of driers to paint is desirable, too much drier will cause too rapid top-drying, resulting in a wrinkled effect.

One gallon of correctly mixed paint will cover approximately 700 square feet.

Running, streaking and sagging may be caused by improper mixing and stirring as well as by applying the paint too thick.

To prepare ready mixed paint pour off most of the liquid (vehicle) into another can and stir well the pasty pigment which has settled to the bottom. During the stirring process add small amounts of the liquid and continue stirring until all the liquid is used. Box well the mixed paint before using.

Boxing paint means pouring paint back and forth from one can to another until the mixture is smooth and free from lumps.

CHAPTER VIII

GROUND TACKLE

GROUND TACKLE consists of all the equipment used in anchoring. This includes anchors, cables, connecting devices and the windlass.

Figure 8-1. Old-fashioned anchor.

ANCHORS

Ship models found in ancient Egyptian tombs were equipped with crude anchors. Some of these ancient anchors were grooved or perforated stones and some were T-shaped stones. Wooden frames weighted with stones (killicks), another old type of anchor, were used for many years and until recently still in use in the Maritime Provinces of Canada.

In the early part of the 19th century the first modern anchor, featuring curved arms, was introduced. This anchor (Figure 8-1), sometimes called the admiralty or Navy anchor but now simply referred to as the old-fashioned anchor, became standard and was supplied to the British Navy in the 1850s. The American Navy and Merchant Marine used it for many years. Ton-for-ton its holding power is still unmatched by more modern designs.

An anchor will weigh roughly one to one and one-half pounds for each ton of a vessel's displacement. An anchor works like a pick axe. When the pick is driven into the ground, it will require a tremendous amount of force to pull it loose with a straight pull on the handle. By lifting the handle, however, a leverage is obtained which breaks it free. In the same way, an anchor holds because a long cable causes the pull on the anchor to be in line with the shank. When it is desired to break the anchor free, the cable is taken in and this lifts the shank of the anchor, producing a leverage which loosens its hold.

TYPES OF ANCHORS

The old-fashioned anchor was in general use from the mid-19th century until shortly before World War I. It was stowed horizontally on the billboard or on the fo'c'sle. Obviously when hoisted it could not be pulled into the hawsepipe and it was necessary to "fish" and "cat" the anchor in order to secure it for sea. This was a tedious and time-consuming process. Another disadvantage was that one fluke would be buried in the sand or mud and the other would be protruding from the bottom—waiting to foul the anchor chain when the ship swung with the tide. For these reasons the old-fashioned anchor has dropped into disuse. It is now chiefly used as an ornament in front of maritime museums, at the main gate of naval bases, and in chapels whose congregations are largely made up of the seafaring community. Among the last old-fashioned anchors in general use on a ship of any size were those installed on the Coast Guard Training Ship *Eagle*, and these were replaced by patent anchors in the late 1950s. Old-fashioned anchors are still used for boat anchors and by yachtsmen for small craft. Occasionally, they are used in permanent moorings. Replicas are used as the insignia for merchant marine deck officers, midshipmen, and boatswains.

There are several types of patent anchors, sometimes called "stockless anchors" (one exception, the Danforth does have a "stock"). The patent anchor has many advantages over the old-fashioned anchor. It is easier to stow and less apt to foul.

The anchor shown in Figure 8-2 is typical of what is used in the Merchant Marine or U.S. Navy. It is called the **Baldt** anchor and has excellent holding power, stows easily in the hawsepipe, and rarely fouls.

Other types of anchors are shown in Figure 8-3. The **Gruson-Hein** is an old German anchor which carries its flukes close to the shank. This is an advantage when swinging because one objection to the double fluke anchor is the tendency to cant as greater pressure comes on one fluke and then the other. The wider apart the flukes, the greater the canting effect.

The **Danforth** anchor combines the stock of the old-fashioned anchor and the flukes of the patent stockless anchor. It has excellent holding properties and is used as the stern anchor for navy landing ships and landing craft as well as on smaller vessels. It is excellent in a sticky or mud bottom.

The **Northill** anchor is light-weight. It was used in seaplanes and is popular among yachtsmen.

The **Eells** anchor is widely used in salvage operations. With an open back design, it utilizes suction to increase its holding power in soft bottoms.

A comparatively new development of unusual design is the **Bruce** anchor which is of British manufacture. It is coming into use in offshore oil rigs and their supply vessels. It buries itself deeply, and has extremely high holding power. It requires low breakout force.

The **mushroom** anchor is excellent for permanent moorings, channel buoys and other navigational aids. It is also used for submarines. It takes firm hold and remains fixed under adverse conditions. As the anchor oscillates under strains, it buries itself deeper still.

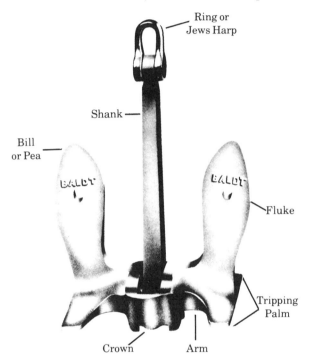

Figure 8-2. Baldt stockless anchor. Courtesy: Baldt, Inc.

A **grapnel** is a small anchor used for dragging purposes, recovering items lost overboard, and picking up chains or cables lost on the bottom. It is frequently used as a boat anchor.

The **mooring** anchor is rarely seen in normal use, but is sometimes used as an ice anchor in arctic operations.

Mooring clumps are not anchors, but are used as anchors and should be mentioned. They are blocks of stone or concrete, and are fitted with iron eyes. They are frequently used to anchor mooring buoys or channel markers.

A **deadman**, any heavy object buried in the ground ashore to which a mooring line or wire can be run, can be an anchor. In ice operations it is a timber or other heavy object frozen in the ice from which a ship can be moored. Its use is preferred to a mooring or ice anchor.

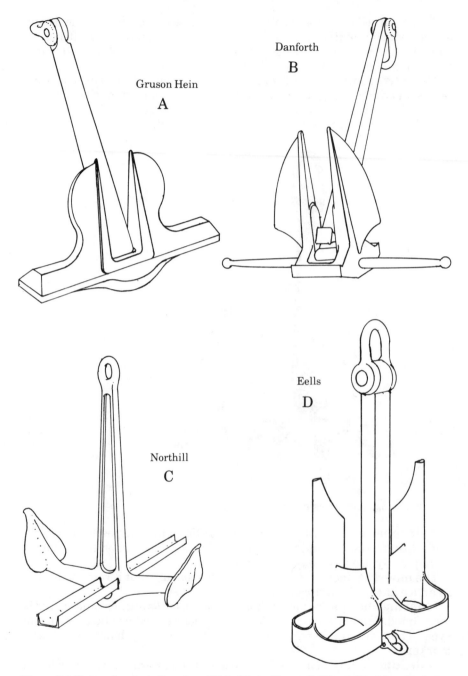

Figure 8-3. Types of anchors. Drawings: Midn. Marty Gipson, California Maritime Academy.

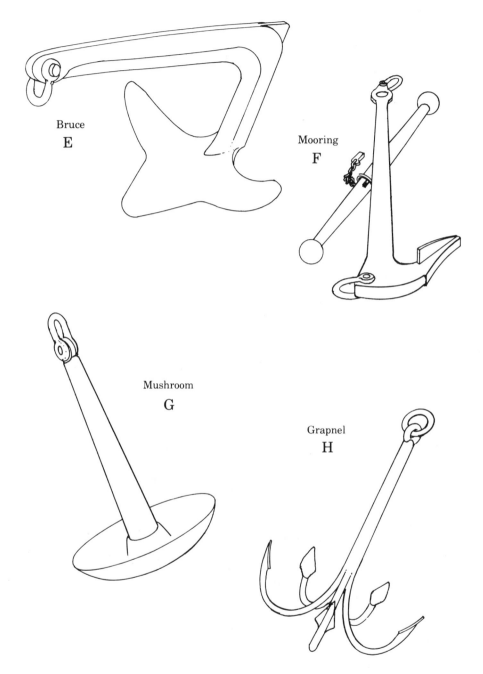

Bruce
E

Mooring
F

Mushroom
G

Grapnel
H

Figure 8-3. Types of anchors (continued).

ANCHOR PARTS

The nomenclature for the parts of the old fashioned anchor are not always adaptable to the patent anchor. Differences in names of the parts of the two anchors are indicated where they exist:

Ring (jews harp or shackle)—The ring to which the cable is bent. It is secured to the top of the shank with a riveted pin.

Stock—The cross-arm below the ring. Although the Danforth anchor has a stock, patent anchors are also called "stockless" anchors.

Shank—The long center part of the anchor running between ring and crown.

Crown—Rounded lower section to which shank is fixed. On patent anchors the crown is fitted with various shaped projecting shoulders (or tripping palms) which turn on the bottom, forcing the anchor to grab. The shank is fitted to the crown with a pivot or ball-and-socket joint which allows a movement of from 30 to 45 degrees either way.

Arms—Pieces which extend from either side of the crown.

Throat—Inner curved part of any arm where it joins shank.

Palm or fluke—On the old-fashioned anchor these terms meant the same thing. On a patent anchor this is not so. As is true on the old-fashioned anchor, the fluke is the broad shield-shaped part of the anchor which digs into the bottom. The palm, or tripping palm, is the shoulder at the end of the crown which, when it drags along the bottom, forces the fluke to dig in.

Blade—This is the back of the palm of an old-fashioned anchor or that part of the arm below the fluke.

Bill or pea—Tip of the fluke.

ANCHORS CARRIED ON SHIPS

Most ships nowadays carry only a port and starboard anchor forward. A few carry a stern anchor. In the sailing era a ship's safety was completely dependent upon the holding power of her anchors once she had furled her sails. She had no engines to help her off a lee shore when her anchor started to drag. The extra anchors she carried had special names, some of which have dropped into disuse but still may find favor among older seamen and on Coast Guard licensing examinations.

Bower anchors—Carried in hawsepipes in the bow. Generally the only anchors installed for ready use. The term "bower" is little used today.

Sheet anchor—Similar to the bower anchor, but carried in a hawsepipe aft of the bower anchor or on deck and kept for an emergency.

Stern anchor—Any anchor carried at the stern.

Stream anchor—Little seen in the modern day. Probably of less weight than the bower anchor and sometimes carried near the stern and dropped to keep the ship from swinging with the tide. If it is carried astern, by definition it becomes a stern anchor.

Kedge anchor—Formerly a smaller anchor carried by boats for the purpose of "kedging" (or moving) the ship ahead a little at a time.

TESTING AND STAMPING OF ANCHORS

The safety of a ship often depends on the ability of its anchor to hold. With this important point in mind the American Bureau of Shipping has laid down a rigid set of regulations governing the manufacturing and testing of anchors.

Every anchor must pass a severe test both as to materials and construction, and must meet the requirements of the A.B.S., after which it is stamped on the fluke and shank by the manufacturer in the following manner:

Old-fashioned anchor—(a) The number of certificate (furnished by the Surveyor). (b) The initials of the Surveyor who witnesses the Proof Test. (c) Month and year of test. (d) Proof Test applied (lbs.). (e) Initials signifying that the testing machine is recognized by the Committee of the American Bureau of Shipping. (f) The weight of anchor, excluding stock (lbs.). (g) The weight of stock (lbs.).

Stockless anchor—(a) The number of certificate (furnished by the Surveyor). (b) The initials of the Surveyor who witnesses the Proof Test. (c) Month and year of test. (d) Proof Test applied (lbs.). (e) Initials signifying that the testing machine is recognized by the Committee of the American Bureau of Shipping. (f) The weight of anchor (lbs.). (g) Initials signifying that the anchor head has been tested by a Surveyor to the American Bureau. (h) The weight of anchor head (lbs.). (i) The initials of the Surveyor who witnesses the Drop Test. (j) The number of Drop Test Certificates (furnished by the Surveyor). (k) Month and year of Drop Test.

Anchors are to be made of forged wrought iron, forged open hearth ingot steel, or cast steel; the shackles may be of wrought iron or of forged steel unwelded.

Anchor stocks are to be in weight equal to one fourth that of the anchor. Stockless anchors may be adopted, subject to the Committee's approval and the addition of one fourth to the weights for ordinary anchors; the weight of the head is not to be less than three fifths of the total weight of the anchor.

No vessel can be classed with letter (e) unless the anchors have been tested and the weights are in accordance with requirements, as to tonnage of vessel.

All anchors are to be tested under the inspection of a surveyor to the American Bureau of Shipping in a machine recognized for such purposes by the committee of the American Bureau of Shipping.

Prior to testing, the actual weight of the anchor is to be ascertained.

ANCHOR CABLES

Anchor cables—The large, heavy chains which support the anchors are called anchor cables. They may also be known as *chain cables* or *ship's cables*.

One end of the anchor cable is bent to the ring of the anchor and the other or *bitter end* passes through the riding chock and over the wildcat of the windlass and down the spillpipe into the chain locker. It is secured in the chain locker by a number of methods, most commonly by shackling it to a ring in the deck. Another method is to cut an opening in the bulkhead between the two chain lockers and shackle the bitter ends of the two cables together.

Some merchant ships and all Navy ships secure the bitter end of the anchor cable by a third method which allows for quick slipping of the cable should the need arise. The end is passed through a ring secured to the deck and brought up to another ring made fast to the overhead where it is secured with rope lashings or a slip hook. A manhole on deck permits quick and easy access to the lashings in an emergency.

The *length* of a *ship's cable* is governed by the American Bureau of Shipping Standards, which are based on length, breadth, tonnage and

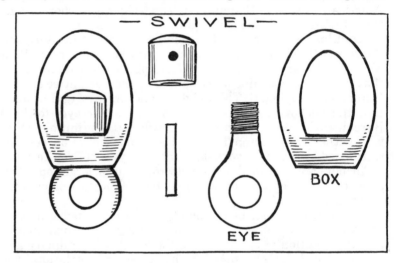

Figure 8-4. Swivel.

freeboard of the vessel. Lengths assigned to ships of 12,000 to 26,500 tons are 165 fathoms to each bower anchor. This length scales downward, according to the size of the ship.

A **cable length** is 120 fathoms, a traditional unit of nautical measure derived from the length of a ship's cable, but bearing no relation to the length of a present-day ship's cable.

Recognized authorities differ in their definitions of a cable length but the majority of them call it 120 fathoms.

MAKING UP ANCHOR CABLES

An anchor cable is an assembly of a number of individual units secured together in a proper manner. They are connected to the anchor by means of a swivel piece composed of shackles, swivels and special links.

Swivel pieces (Figure 8-4) are made up in various combinations. The following sequence is considered good practice, but other combinations may be used.

First, the bending shackle goes next to the anchor and must always be bent on with the bow toward the anchor.

Second, heavy open link or long end stud link.

Third, stud or open link.

Fourth, swivel, connected with bow toward anchor.

Fifth, open or stud link.

Sixth, detachable link, to join the swivel piece to the first shot of cable. This completes the outboard swivel shot or bending shot to which the succeeding 15 fathom shots are connected by other detachable links (Figure 8-5). Formerly connecting shackles or Kenter shackles were used, but the use of the detachable link which has no tendency to foul the wildcat is now universal.

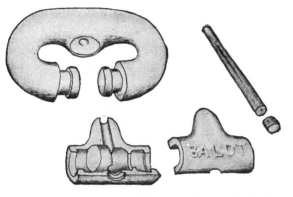

Figure 8-5. Detachable links.

CABLE MARKINGS

It is important to the safety of every ship that her officers know at all times the scope or amount of cable she has out. To make this knowledge quickly available, a system of cable markings is used. These markings consist of a series of turns of wire and stripes of paint.

In the merchant service the wire markings are standard, but mates and carpenters, who actually handle the anchoring equipment, may have their own system of paint markings.

The Navy system of marking is somewhat different from the merchant service. The two are shown for comparison.

Merchant service markings:

15 fathoms, one turn of wire on first stud from each side of detachable link.

30 fathoms, two turns of wire on second stud from each side of detachable link.

45 fathoms, three turns of wire on third stud from each side of detachable link.

60 fathoms, four turns of wire on fourth stud from each side of detachable link.

75 fathoms, five turns of wire on fifth stud from each side of detachable link.

90 fathoms, six turns of wire on sixth stud from each side of detachable link.

In addition to using wire on the stud links near the detachable link to mark the amount of chain in the merchant service, the links near the detachable one are painted white, while the detachable link may be painted red. The system, borrowed from the Navy and now in general practice, works as follows:

15 fathoms, white paint on the stud link on either side of the detachable link.

30 fathoms, white paint on the two links on either side of the detachable link.

45 fathoms, white paint on the three links on either side of the detachable link.

60 fathoms, white paint on the four links on either side of the detachable link.

75 fathoms, white paint on the five links on either side of the detachable link.

90 fathoms, white paint on the six links on either side of the detachable link.

In addition to using white paint on the stud links as described, it is suggested that the detachable links be painted red.

Some companies may paint a number of links white in the first shot because it is used the most and the paint wears off faster. Also, this practice insures that the bos'n or mate will see *some* white go by as the first shot passes through the hawsepipe.

To the landlubber the amount of time spent marking the chain may appear unnecessary, but after being on the fo'c'sle when the anchor has been dropped, trying to see through the clouds of rust, and to hear over the clatter of the anchor chain, it will make more sense.

Navy markings for anchor chains follow. The detachable links are painted red, white, or blue:

Red for 15 fathoms.

White for 30 fathoms.

Blue for 45 fathoms.

Red for 60 fathoms.

White for 75 fathoms, and so on.

The system of painting links white on either side of the detachable link and wrapping wire on the studs is similar to that used in the merchant service. In addition, each link in the next-to-last shot is painted yellow and the last shot is entirely red. These last two shots warn of the approach of the *bitter end* of the cable, an excellent idea and also frequently used in the merchant service.

TESTING CABLE CHAIN

The importance of anchors to the safety of a ship has been mentioned in connection with testing of anchors and can be emphasized here again in conjunction with the importance of anchor cables.

It will readily be seen that no matter how fine the materials and construction of an anchor may be, it will not hold the ship if the cable should carry away.

The American Bureau of Shipping Rules specify that chain, shackles and other connecting devices be given a series of tests to determine their strength and perfection. After passing the tests each separate connecting unit and each 15-fathom shot of continuous chain must be stamped by the

Figure 8-6. Stud link chain.

Figure 8-7. Close link chain.

manufacturer as follows:

A. The number of Certificate (furnished by Surveyor).

B. The Initials of the Surveyor who witnesses the Test.

C. Month and Year of Test.

D. The Breaking Test (lbs.).

E. The Proof Test applied (lbs.).

F. Initials signifying that the Testing Machine is recognized by the Committee of the American Bureau of Shipping.

NOTES ON THE MAKING OF ANCHOR CABLES

The stud link commonly used on large anchors is a comparatively new link having a stud cast or welded across the center on the inside (Figure 8-6). This stud prevents the link from closing under heavy strain. It is estimated that the stud adds 15 percent to the strength of the link. One method of manufacture is known as drop-forging. This means that each link is formed from a straight piece of tested steel bar and welded under a steam-hammer. This requires several operations, for each of which the link must be reheated. The second link is welded into the first and so on until the desired length of chain has been made.

Another method is known as casting. Molds are made of the desired size and the metal is heated to about 3000 degrees Centigrade. This may vary; the metallurgist determines the heat from his specification. The molten metal is swung over the molds in a pouring ladle, handled by a traveling crane. The pouring is done by an experienced man who must control the flow of the metal in such a way as to prevent air bubbles from forming in the casting. After proper cooling time the molds are knocked apart and the chain is ready for cleaning and testing.

A third method is a patented drop-forging process called the Di-Lok (Figure 8-8). The Di-Lok chain is made of links consisting of a male section and a female section. The cold male section is inserted into the heated female section and the joint is struck in a forming die, locking the extra metal of the female around the cold lugs of the male section. This leaves the link drop-forged to shape and size, and the stud is formed as part of the link and not a separate piece. The stud thus formed has a gap in the center. Figure 8-9 shows the parts of chain links before and after they are united by this mechanically forged lock.

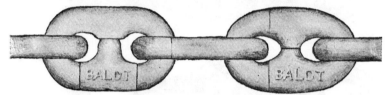

Figure 8-8. Di-Lok chain joined with detachable link.

Figure 8-9. Di-Lok link before and after joining.

CARE OF ANCHOR CABLES

Ground tackle is very important to the safety of a ship and very expensive; therefore, it must be given the best of care. Links should be tested when anchor is weighed and at regular intervals the cable should be ranged (laid out) for inspection and overhauling. The shackle bolts, forelock pins, locking pins, lead rings and swivels must be examined for defects. The shots should be interchanged; the little ones at the bitter end should be transferred to the outboard and vice versa. This change of position of shots when carried out in a systematic manner will insure uniform wear of the entire cable.

The Navy method of examining chain links is to wash the chain with a hose while heaving in slowly. Each link is sounded with a hammer and if one is found with a false ring it is given a close inspection.

Any change in length of the chain should be noted. *The Naval Ships' Technical Manual* states that "the overall length of six links, measuring from every third link, shall be checked and a minus tolerance of one-eighth inch or a plus tolerance of three-quarter inch for each one inch of wire diameter shall be permitted."

One source of possible damage to the chain occurs when anchoring. As the anchor strikes the ground, the end links may drop forcefully on the jews harp. Over a long period of time this action may cause fractures in the links or in the jews harp. This kind of damage can be eliminated by securing a block of wood in the jews harp.

When it has not been practicable to range out the chain for an extended period, pour 5 to 10 gallons of fuel oil over it as it lies in the locker.

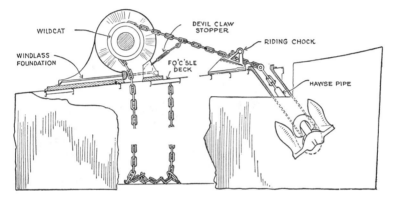

Figure 8-10. A vessel's ground tackle connected as a single unit.

THE WINDLASS

The windlass is a machine used to raise the anchor. It consists primarily of an engine, which may be either steam or electric; the wildcat which is the gear used to grip the chain; suitable controls for connecting the wildcat to the engine, and brakes for controlling the wildcat when it is not engaged with the engine (Figure 8-10).

The accompanying illustrations clearly show the various parts of the electric windlass (Figure 8-11). Gypsyheads are used in handling lines. When fitted to a windlass these are driven by the same engine and usually fitted with controls so that they may be operated independently.

Parts of the equipment used in anchoring, starting at the anchor and working back follow:

Hawsepipe—Openings in eyes or forward part of ship where shank of patent anchor is stowed.

Buckler plate—A heavy metal plate "dogged down" (fastened) by butterfly nuts when the vessel is at sea. Covers hawsepipe opening on deck and prevents water rushing up the hawsepipe.

Riding chock—The metal fairlead for anchor chain. It serves to prevent the chain from fouling on deck, also to hold riding pawl.

Riding pawl—A safety stopper that works like a ratchet on the links of the chain. It is lifted as chain runs out. A bar prevents it from bouncing on the outgoing links. When heaving in, the pawl is dropped in the after side of the riding chock. The pawl bounces over the incoming links, but if an emergency occurs, such as the wildcat jumping out of gear, the pawl will catch on a link and hold the chain.

Devil claws—In the Merchant Marine devil claws (Figure 8-12) are used as a stopper and consist of a metal claw attached to a turnbuckle which in turn is secured at the base of the windlass. In operation, the devil claws are used when the vessel is leaving port and securing for sea. The claws are put on a link of chain and the turnbuckle is set up, acting as a permanent stopper. The devil claws cannot be released under tension.

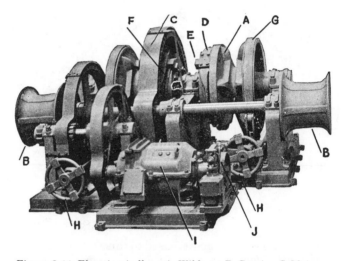

Figure 8-11. Electric windlass: A. Wildcats; B. Gypsies; C. Main gear wheel housing; D. Locking ring; E. Locking ring key; F. Locking ring eccentric rib; G. Brake friction bands; H. Brake compressor wheels; I. Electric motor; J. Automatic motor brake.

Pelican hook—In the Navy a pelican hook (Figure 8-12) is used instead of a devil claw and can be released under tension. A pelican hook is not suited to merchant service use because it is heavy and awkward and requires more men on the fo'c'sle. Both devil claws and pelican hooks are used as stoppers after the ship has anchored.

Wildcat—A sprocketed wheel in the windlass with indentations for the links of the anchor chain. The wildcat, when engaged, either hauls in or pays out the anchor chain. When disengaged the wildcat revolves freely and the only control of the anchor chain is the friction brake and the riding pawl.

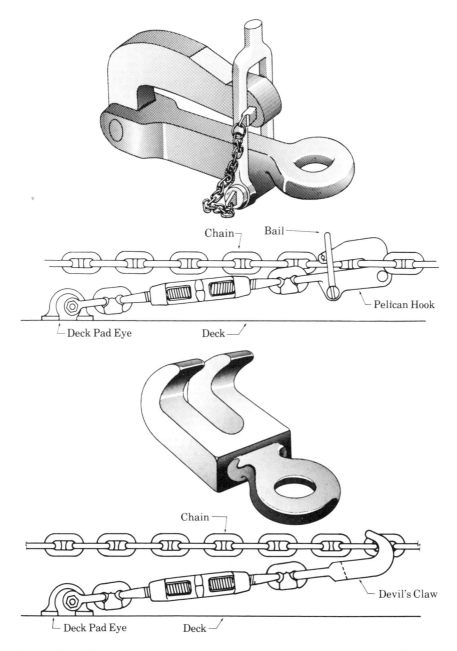

Figure 8-12. Pelican hook and devil claw stopper assemblies compared. Upper two sketches are pelican hook and pelican hook assembly. Lower sketches are devil claw and its assembly. Pelican hook can be released under tension, devil claw cannot. Navy uses pelican hook, Merchant Marine normally uses devil claw. Courtesy: Baldt, Inc.

Friction brake—Consists of a band which bears on a flywheel. By tightening on the band the wildcat can be controlled.

Locking ring—A device with pigeonholes into which a bar is placed to lock the wildcat to the hoisting gear of the engine. The wheel is usually turned forward to disengage the wildcat and turned aft to engage it.

Gypsyheads—Large drums used for the handling of the forward mooring lines.

Spillpipe (Navy pipe)—The opening in deck through which the chain leads to the chain locker.

LETTING GO THE ANCHOR

Assuming the anchors are secure for sea with the spillpipes cemented in, as is the practice where there are many days between ports, the first job is to break out the cement plugs in the spillpipes and free the chain. Now take

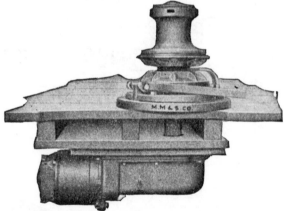

Figure 8-13. Combination capstan and wildcat used on small vessels.

off the devil claws or hooks. If the vessel is equipped with patent riding chocks and pawls the next step is to release these. (Always get both anchors ready, it may save embarrassment later.)

The next step is to make certain that the anchor is not jammed or frozen in the hawsepipe and will let go freely when the brake is released. The best method is to "walk out" the anchor a short distance with the windlass. To do this, first, lock up the windlass by engaging wildcat with the locking keys; second, heave in slightly so that the strain is on the locking keys instead of the brake; third, release the brake; and fourth, veer the chain with the windlass. It is good policy to veer the chain until the anchor is clear of the hawsepipe.

Having freed the anchor, the brake is set tight and the windlass unlocked. The anchor is now ready to let go.

At the proper signal from the bridge the anchor is let go by releasing the brake.

The Navy practice of dropping the anchor differs from that just described because in the Navy the anchor is usually dropped from the pelican hook rather than from the brake. When this is done the brake is released and the weight of the anchor is now carried on the pelican hook which unlike the devil claw can be released under tension. The pin is removed from the pelican hook and a seaman (usually the biggest on the ship) stands ready with a sledge hammer to strike the bail at the command "let go."

The editors favor releasing the anchor from the brake. It is safer because no one is standing near the chain, and because the chain is kept under positive control of the brake from the moment it is released. If the anchor is released from the pelican hook, the man on the brake does not know how much he has to tighten up on the brake before the chain slows or stops. The argument against releasing the anchor from the brake is that you may not know precisely when the anchor will "let go" after the command is given. Further, there may be some fear that the brake band will suffer excessive wear before the chain can pay out freely. In practice neither of these considerations presents a problem.

In any case, once the anchor is released the further steps are governed by the depth of water at anchorage and amount of chain the master wants his vessel to ride to. Usually one can sense when the anchor hits bottom, as there is a noticeable slackening in the speed of the chain paying out. Now tighten the brake a little so that the mate may determine exactly how much chain is out by the markings. If none of these are visible, slack off chain until the first mark that comes out of the locker can be identified. If 60 fathoms, or four shackles, is desired in the water and at first letting go you have put 15 fathoms well in the water, then slack out in shots of 15 fathoms or half shots, until the desired scope is out. Now check the chain with the brake and stand by for further orders. When the chain is "brought up," that is, when the vessel has come to rest in the water, the brake is set as tight as possible and the pawl is dropped on the chain.

SCOPE OF CHAIN

Good practice requires allowing 5 to 7 fathoms of chain for each fathom of depth. In deep water, however, the scope may be less because the ship probably will not have more than 150 fathoms of chain. In bad weather veer up more chain to a scope of 10 or 12 fathoms to one fathom. In extreme cases it may be necessary to drop a second anchor underfoot.

In the Merchant Marine, the master or pilot usually specified the amount of chain in shots. In the Navy, the practice is to give the command in fathoms.

HEAVING IN THE ANCHOR

To heave in the anchor lock up the windlass, release the brake and start heaving. After the anchor is in sight great care should be taken in heaving it home in the hawsepipe. The windlass should be run at its minimum speed and stopped the instant the anchor is snugly nested with its flukes against the side.

Occasionally when heaving in an anchor it may come up with the flukes turned in toward the hull. The flukes must be turned out in order to get the

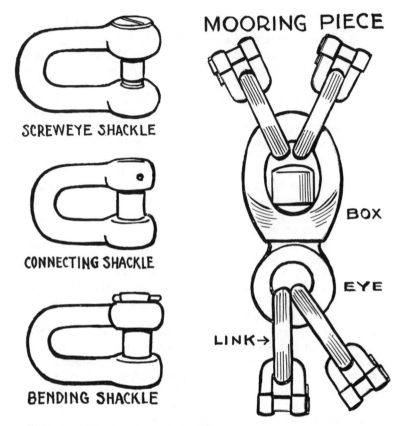

Figure 8-14. Mooring piece and shackles.

anchor home. If the vessel is under way and the chain is veered until the anchor is in the water, the pressure of the water will usually turn out the flukes.

A second method, if the foregoing should fail, is to heave the anchor up until the shank starts to enter the hawsepipe. The anchor crown will now be bearing away from the hull with flukes pointing inward almost at right angles to the ship's side. Lift the pawl and veer the chain with full power until the anchor is clear of the hawsepipe. This sudden reversal will give a quick pendulous movement to the anchor and will in almost every case be successful in turning out the flukes.

FREEING AN ANCHOR JAMMED IN A HAWSEPIPE

There are many reasons why anchors jam. The anchor may be rusted in place or it may have been drawn up too far to fit into the pipe. Sometimes as the shank finds a new seat in the pipe, the friction of iron to iron may cause the anchor to "freeze" so that it will not pay out when the brake is released.

In most cases of jammed anchors a simple jolt, such as starting the windlass at full power, will usually cause enough vibration to free it. Another method used successfully by carpenters is to shake the chain between wildcat and riding chock. Actually the chain will not shake, but a swinging motion can be set up which may vibrate the chain links enough to release the anchor.

MOORING WITH TWO ANCHORS

Mooring with two anchors is rarely done. It is only necessary in a congested harbor so that a vessel will cover less space as she swings with the tide or wind.

Figure 8-15.

The vessel steams slowly to her anchorage and first drops the weather anchor. She backs down, or moves to the point where the lee anchor is to be placed, veering on the weather anchor as she backs. After the lee anchor is dropped, chain is veered on the lee anchor and heaved in on the weather anchor until the ship is riding with an equal span between the two anchors.

If the ship is expected to swing with the tide or wind it may be advisable to place a mooring swivel just outside the hawsepipe so that there will be less danger of the chain snarling or crossing.

Clearing hawse is the tedious process of taking turns out of anchor cables. It will probably be necessary to disconnect one of the chains at the detachable link to get this difficult job done. Patience and good seamanship are required.

CARRYING OUT ANCHORS

Carrying out an anchor is rarely, if ever, necessary in the merchant service, and seldom in the Navy. About the only reason would be to prevent a grounded ship from being washed further ashore. This then becomes an emergency or salvage operation and outside assistance would be needed. Whether a merchant ship's lifeboats could be rigged to support and carry out an anchor is a moot point. A Navy ship equipped with amphibious landing craft would have better luck. Unless specializing in salvage work this is not done.

ANCHOR WATCH

Navigation Safety Regulations require that when a vessel is at anchor in United States waters an anchor watch be maintained. The anchor watch must be alert to detect a dragging anchor and also, should this happen, be ready to veer chain, let go a second anchor, or get underway using a vessel's own engines or tug assistance. The anchor watch should insure that there is sufficient room for the vessel to swing with the tide without striking another vessel (see Figure 8-15), and keep bumboats and unauthorized personnel away from and off the ship. The anchor watch is also responsible for the internal security of the ship and watching for the outbreak of fire.

CHAPTER IX

THE STEERING GEAR AND HELMSMAN

STEERING GEAR

THE TERM "STEERING GEAR" includes everything between the wheel in the pilot house where the helmsman is standing his watch to the rudder which moves in response to his commands. The steering system has to meet very severe demands. There must be provision for the rudder to be held in position even if the steering engine breaks down. In addition, the system must have high mechanical advantage so that the helmsman will be able to move a multi-ton rudder separated from him by more than half the length of the ship away.

When sail disappeared from the oceans and steam was introduced, ships became so large that it was no longer possible to steer them by hand. Even sailing vessels frequently had to use two men on the wheel in order to control the ship's head. However, power steering now makes it possible for one man to steer the largest ship without perspiring.

A number of different steering gears have been in service since power steering was introduced. One of the first was a differential-screw steering gear which was used with a steam and later an electric-steering engine. Steam was used for many years, and there may be a few ships so equipped today. During World War II some tankers and most, if not all, Liberty ships had steam steering. But steam has disadvantages. Among these are the vulnerability of the steam pipes, the relatively poor economy, and the discomfort and loss caused by stray heat.

When the electric-steering gear was introduced, it was a distinct improvement over steam. However, it also has disadvantages. An excessive amount of power is required to start, accelerate, and then stop the motor and screw gear. A distinct improvement is the electrohydraulic system. It is used in all ships of any size today, uses little power, is far more sensitive than the straight electric type, and has little lag. The amount of space required for the hydraulic gear is reasonable, and there is a considerable saving in weight as compared with earlier types.

Since introduced, there have been a number of modifications in electrohydraulic steering resulting in a variety of different arrangements now in service, although all work on the same principle.

There may be one, two, or four hydraulic cylinders and plungers connected to a crosshead, tiller, or quadrant. The cylinders receive hydraulic fluid from one or more power units which consist of a constant-speed electric motor driving a variable-stroke hydraulic pump such as a Hele-Shaw or a Waterbury speed gear.

Figure 9-2 is a schematic of an electrohydraulic steering gear which has one ram. A large tanker may have four rams, but the principle of operation

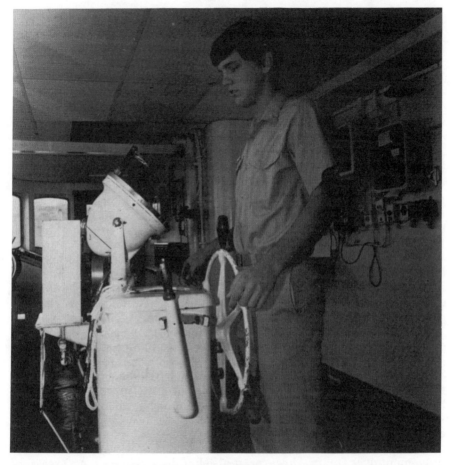

Figure 9-1. Helmsman aboard T.S. *Golden Bear.* Photo: Midn. R.L. Schopp, California Maritime Academy.

is the same. The sketch shows the rudder amidships. When the wheel on the bridge is put over to the right, the motion is carried to the transmitting unit, to the receiving unit, to the differential, and then to the pump which pumps the hydraulic fluid causing the crosshead and rudder stock to move and force the rudder to swing to the right. The pumping operation continues until the rudder lines up with the wheel on the bridge. If either the trick wheel in the steering engine room or the auxiliary steering station (shown on the after deck-house in the diagram) is engaged, the same action will result. The gear train maintains the movement of the rudder in step with the steering wheel by adjusting the pump stroke. It consists of a differential gear and cam arrangement which controls the discharge of fluid from the pump to the steering gear cylinders. Not all installations have both a port and starboard cable (only one of which would be in use at a time). It is standard, however, to have both port and starboard motors and pump. These are operated alternately so that each receives the same amount of service use.

Another type of electrohydraulic steering gear is the rotary vane type. Rotary vane steering gears, a comparatively recent development, have no rams. With these units the rudder torque is developed by the differential pressure that acts across the vanes. These units require less space than the ram type.

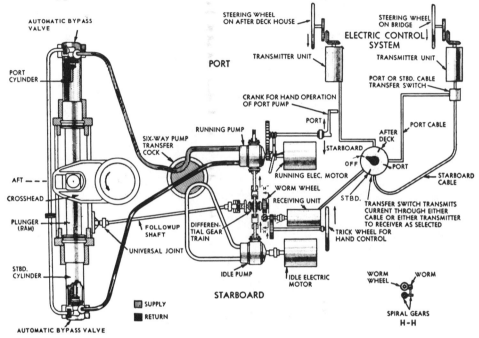

Figure 9-2. Single-ram electro-hydraulic steering gear. Courtesy: U.S. Naval Institute.

The Coast Guard requires that provision be made for an alternate means of steering. Auxiliary steering requires power, and can be accomplished either by the wheel in the steering engine room or one topside aft. Emergency steering may be provided for by simply rigging a block and tackle to the rudder stock and moving the tiller either by manpower or deck machinery. With a very large ship this is obviously cumbersome if not impractical, and emergency steering would be limited to bringing the rudder amidships or to the desired rudder angle after a casualty.

TELEMOTOR

Older ships may have a telemotor for hand steering which is activated when the control lever on the Gyropilot is moved to the "Off" position and the by-pass valve at the front of the large wooden hand wheel is closed. Although an electrical interlock switch exists on the by-pass valve to prohibit the telemotor and electrical steering from being on at the same

Figure 9-3. Typical steering engine room aboard 180,000 DWT tanker. Each cylinder has a 12-inch bore and a 65-inch stroke. Tiller radius is 48 inches. Rudder torque developed is 24,000,000 inch-pounds. Time to place rudder from hardover port to hardover starboard is 28 seconds. Courtesy: Sperry Marine Systems.

time, it is essential that the control lever not be "On" at the same time that the by-pass valve is closed or else the steering gear will get conflicting signals from both the telemotor as well as the receiving unit, and a casualty may result.

GYROPILOT

Practically all merchant ships and some naval vessels use the Gyropilot or "iron mike" which automatically steers the ship on a set course unless the vessel is in restricted waters or in heavy traffic. The Gyropilot is extremely sensitive and conserves fuel. When the Gyropilot is used, the helmsman stands by the wheel to insure that the ship remains on course, and in daytime may act also as lookout.

When the ship is operating on automatic electric, the lever will be on the "Gyro" setting, when in manual or hand electric, it will be on "Hand," and if the ship is equipped with, and using, a telemotor, the lever will be on "Off." In order to shift from one mode to another it is only necessary to throw the lever. This though should not be done unless the rudder is amidships and the rudder angle indicator is "0°." However, on some types of Gyropilots a touch of the wheel no longer controls the rudder angle. Instead, it introduces a change of course important to understand. If the ship is on course 090 degrees when the lever is thrown to "Gyro," the "iron mike" will make whatever changes in the rudder angle are necessary to maintain course 090 degrees. If the helmsman spins the wheel, he will alter the instructions given the "iron mike" to steer 090 degrees, but he will not directly change the rudder angle. If he rotates the wheel one complete revolution to the right, he will change the course 3 degrees, and the new course will be 093 degrees. One spoke will change the course one-half degree. The rudder angle used will be the minimum to make the course change depending upon the "Weather" and "rudder" adjustments. The importance of understanding this is emphasized by the *Torrey Canyon* disaster. That ship was on automatic electric when her position was in doubt. One report indicated that in the excitement of giving the command to change course away from danger, no one immediately realized that the ship was on automatic electric, and the wheel was spun as for a rudder command. Whether the time lost spelled the difference between disaster and safety cannot be known, but the incident does underline the absolute necessity for being alert and completely familiar with the equipment in use.

The fundamentals of the operation of the Gyropilot should be understood. Departures of the ship from the set course are immediately detected by the master compass and transmitted to the repeater motor. The repeater motor, acting through a differential gear and an adjustable lost motion device, turns the contactor roller shown in the center of the diagram. Movement of the contactor roller completes an electrical circuit through one or the other of the contactor rings surrounding the roller. This circuit, acting through electro-magnetic relays, starts an electric motor which moves the rudder in the proper direction to correct the deviation from the course. Movement of the rudder is transmitted back to the gyropilot where,

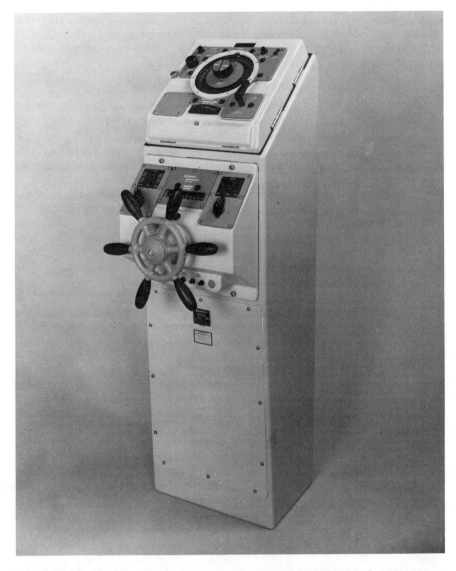

Figure 9-4. The first Gyropilot was installed in the tanker *J.A. Moffat* more than 50 years ago. Since then Gyropilots have become very sophisticated. Merchant ships are normally on automatic electric except when in restricted waters or in maneuvering situations. This console permits steering by hand electric and automatic electric as well as providing for computer generated command heading with the Sperry Integrated Navigation System. Courtesy: Sperry Marine Systems.

acting through another lost motion device, it turns the contactor rings so as to bring the insulated segment over the contactor roller, thus opening the electrical circuits and stopping the motor, leaving a certain amount of rudder applied to return the vessel to the course. As the ship responds, the repeater motor causes the contactor roller to engage with the opposite segment of the contactor ring, thus returning the rudder to the midship position. The elementary action of the gyropilot mechanism will be more clearly understood by referring to Figure 9-5 in which:

(A) shows the ship on a straight course with rudder amidships.

(B) shows that the ship has departed from a straight course, thus causing the roller to make contact with one segment of the contact ring, thereby energizing the steering engine.

(C) shows that the steering engine has moved, corrective rudder has been applied to the ship, and the contact ring has followed the roller, thus stopping the steering engine.

(D) shows that the ship has returned to the set course, thus moving the roller and energizing the steering engine in the reverse direction.

(E) shows that the rudder has moved to the midship position, thus bringing the roller to the neutral position again and stopping the steering engine.

When the lever is set at "Hand" position, it locks the repeater motor and automatically sets both lost motion adjustments to zero.

WEATHER AND RUDDER ADJUSTMENTS

The weather adjustment assists in introducing a dead zone in the response of the control amplifier to helm/rudder orders in gyro-automatic steering mode. The typical range of adjustment is between 0 degrees and 5 degrees. The control (a potentiometer) is usually mounted on the control unit and permits the operator to minimize rudder activity in heavy seas. When positioned to zero, minimum helm/rudder order will activiate the system; when positioned to "10" (relative scale calibration on the more modern installations), as much as 5 degrees of heading drift will be permitted before the system applies corrective rudder. The purpose of the weather adjustment is to allow the ship to yaw and pitch in heavy seas without continually operating the rudder.

The rudder adjustment establishes the ratio between rudder angle and heading error by varying the amount of helm/rudder angle created by the repeatback supplied to the error amplifier. The typical ratio is between 1:1 and 3:1. The potentiometer, located on the gyro-automatic unit only, forms a voltage divider with the load resistor for the helm/rudder angle signal. The purpose of the control is to vary the amount of rudder applied as a function of the order allowing adjustment for maneuvering characteristics caused by ship size, loading or configuration.

RUDDERS

On most ships the rudder is fitted aft on the center line of the ship and secured to the rudder post. The heading of the ship is changed by putting the rudder over to one side or the other. The action of the water on the rudder forces the stern of the vessel to the side, and the vessel changes course. This differs from the action of the steering wheel of the automobile which turns the front wheels. This in turn forces the front of the car to move first, and then the rear wheels follow. As the rudder is moved off the center line, the even flow of the water past the hull is blocked, causing the ship's stern to head in the opposite direction. For example: With *right* rudder, the stern of the ship will be forced to the *left*, resulting in the bow moving to the *right*.

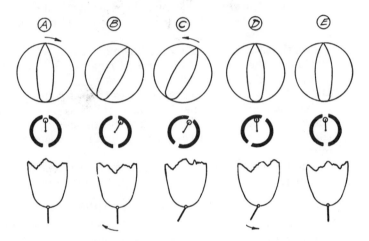

Figure 9-5. Showing contact and follow-up as ship leaves course and is returned by proper rudder action.

Since the action of the rudder depends upon the flow of the water past the hull, the faster the ship is traveling, the more responsive it is to the action of the rudder. Consequently, if the vessel is stopped or nearly stopped, the rudder is of little or no use, and the ship is said to have "lost steerage way." When this happens, the helmsman should report it.

There are three types of rudders shown in Figure 9-6, the unbalanced or ordinary, the semi-balanced, and the balanced. A rudder is said to be unbalanced if the leading edge of the rudder is at the rudder post. This means that the center of pressure of the rudder is considerably aft of the rudder post, and more effort is necessary to move the rudder. The semi-balanced rudder has some area forward of the rudder post, and consequently the center of pressure of the rudder shifts forward. The balanced rudder has the center of pressure at the rudder post, and requires the minimum amount of effort to move the rudder. However, since the center of pressure moves aft as the rudder angle is increased, the design of the rudder and the location of the rudder post is a compromise. Rudders are usually fitted so that they can swing through a total angle of 70 degrees, or 35 degrees either side of the center line.

The bottom of the rudder receives more wash from the propeller than the top because the greater depth of the lower part of the propeller makes that part of it more effective. In short, the wash coming from the bottom of the propeller is stronger than the wash from the top. This causes some tendency for the ship to want to come to port. In an effort to equalize the effect of the propeller on the rudder, the contra-guide rudder was developed and used for a number of years. Liberty ships, Victories, and C-3's were so equipped. Although many ships with contra-guide rudders are still in service, none are known to be under construction.

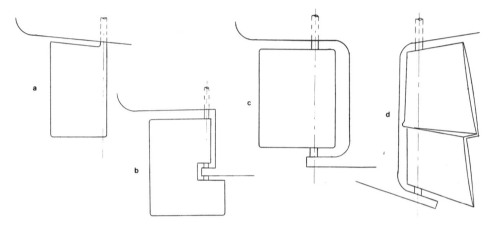

Figure 9-6. Types of rudders: A. Unbalanced; B. Semi-balanced; C. Balanced; D. Contra-guide. Contra-guide rudder can be unbalanced, semi-balanced, or balanced. Drawings: Midn. Eric Pett, California Maritime Academy.

BOW THRUSTER

Since a ship has little if any maneuverability at slow speed, bow thrusters are fitted on many modern ships to assist in docking and undocking. Essentially the bow thruster is a large propeller contained in a tunnel near the forefoot. When the ship is stopped or moving very slowly, the bow thruster can move the bow to the right or left and decrease or do away completely with the requirement to use tugs. The action of the bow thruster can be compared to the action of the sweep oar of a pulling boat.

STANDARD COMMANDS TO THE HELMSMAN

Right (left) rudder—A command to apply right (left) rudder instantly by an indeterminate amount. Must be followed immediately by the amount of rudder desired.

Right (left) full rudder—Put the rudder over to the right (left) very close to the maximum amount. On most ships this is 30 degrees.

Right (left) hard rudder—Put the rudder over to the right (left) all the way. On most ships this will be 35 degrees. The helmsman must be careful not to jam the rudder against the stops. Although the word "hard" has no exact definition, it is understood to be farther over than "full."

Right (left) standard rudder—This command is used only in the Navy to bring the rudder over enough so that the ship will turn in its standard tactical diameter. It would probably be 15-20 degrees. The command is not used in the merchant service.

Right (left) 5, 10, 15, etc. degrees of rudder—Turn the wheel to right (left) until rudder is placed at the number of degrees ordered. This command is frequently used in making changes of course. The helmsman would then be ordered to steer the new course by such a command as: "Steady on course - - -," in time to permit the helmsman to "meet her" on the new course. The complete command would be: "Right 10 degrees rudder, steady on course 275 degrees."

Right (left) handsomely—Turn the rudder a small amount. The term "handsomely" has largely dropped into disuse, but means "carefully, not necessarily slowly."

Give her more rudder—Increase the rudder angle. The command is given with the rudder already over when it is desired to make the ship turn more rapidly. The command should be followed by the exact number of degrees desired for the turn.

Meet her—Use rudder as necessary to check the swing. This command is given when the ship is nearing the desired course.

Ease the rudder to 15, 10, 5, etc. degrees—Decrease the rudder angle. The command is given when the ship is nearing its new heading, and it is desired to slow the swing. The command can be given: "Ease to 5 degrees rudder."

Steady, Steady so, Steady as you go—Steer the course which the ship is heading when you receive the command. This command is given when, in changing course, the new course is reached or the ship is heading as desired.

Rudder amidships—Place the rudder amidships. The command may be given when the ship is turning, and it is desired to make her swing less rapidly.

Shift your rudder—Change from right to left rudder (or vice-versa) an equal amount.

Mind your rudder—A warning that the ship is swinging to the left (right) because of bad steering. Pay attention!

Nothing to the right (left)—Do not let the ship's head move to the right (left) of the ordered course. Command is frequently used in a narrow channel.

How does she head?—A question to the helmsman. He should give the ship's head at the time: "200 degrees, sir."

Keep her so—A command to the helmsman when he reports the ship's heading and it is desired that he steady the ship down on that heading.

Very well—An acknowledgement from the conning officer after the helmsman has reported that an order has been carried out. It is *never* used by the helmsman. "Very well" is used rather than "all right" which might be confused with a command to use right rudder.

Come right (left) to course—Put the rudder over right (left) and steady on course.

HINTS ON STEERING

A good helmsman learns the steering commands so well that they become second nature to him. In addition, he remembers it is the ship that moves, not the compass. The lubber's line, the vertical black line marked on the rim of the compass, lines up with the bow representing the ship's head. Unlike the tiller or steering oar, the steering gear works so that the bow turns in the same direction that the wheel moves. For example, if steering course 250 degrees and ordered to steer 270 degrees, apply right rudder. It may help to remember: "Come right to add. Come left to subtract."

When given a new course to steer and when the ship starts to swing towards that course, the helmsman must take off the rudder before the new course is reached. Otherwise the momentum will cause the ship to swing by the desired course. Steering a ship does not have many parallels to driving a car unless the car is driving across a frozen pond and there is little traction between the wheels and the surface. The ship is many times heavier than a car; and since it "slides" through the water, a ship takes far longer to react.

Some weather conditions will cause a vessel to yaw or swing off her course suddenly. The helmsman can offset this to a degree by "meeting her" as quickly as possible when the swing begins. Vessels have a very noticeable tendency to yaw when the wind and sea are on the quarter. This is the most difficult point of steering.

Vessels sometimes appear to "carry" a small amount of right or left rudder even though the rudder angle indicator is amidships. This may be due to a variety of reasons. For example, if the wind is on the starboard quarter, a few degrees of left rudder will have to be carried to counteract this. On the other hand, the problem may be that the rudder angle indicator is not properly lined up. Steering under these conditions poses no problem as long as the situation is understood. Conditions during the watch may change. It may be that you are carrying a different amount of rudder when you turn the wheel over to your relief than you were when you relieved the wheel. Always tell your relief how much rudder you are carrying before he takes over.

The two most important requirements of the helmsman are to keep the ship on course and to do so by using as little rudder as possible under all ordinary conditions. Steering is a full-time job because the responsibility for the safety of the ship is largely in the hands of the helmsman.

If the helmsman wanders off course more than a few degrees he should inform the watch officer. This is particularly true in pilot waters. Occasionally a new helmsman may glance down at the compass and be horrified to find that he is 10 degrees or 15 degrees off course. In panic he may apply a large amount of rudder in the wrong direction only to find he is now 40 degrees off course! With greater experience the watch officer can bring the ship back on course quickly.

Always know "who has the conn" or is giving commands. If the mate on watch (or watch officer) is the only licensed officer on the bridge, there is no doubt. If the captain is on the bridge, he may be directing the ship's course and speed himself, or he may simply be observing the mate. Only one person can direct the ship. The helmsman must know who is conning. If there is any doubt in his mind it is his responsibility to find out.

Except in the Panama Canal, the pilot, if one is aboard, is in an advisory capacity. He directs the movements of the ship only with the concurrence of the master. Occasionally the master will tell the pilot to step aside. Should the pilot and master give conflicting orders to the helmsman, the helmsman obeys the captain.

The helmsman should always report that he has been relieved. A proper report would be: "I have been relieved by Smith, sir. Steering course 092 degrees, checking 093 degrees."

When the helmsman receives an order, he repeats it exactly. After he has carried out the order he tells the watch officer or master. In this way the helmsman insures his officer that he understands the order, and, in turn, his officer *knows* that his command has been carried out.

CHAPTER X

TEST GUIDE FOR
LIFEBOATMAN AND ABLE SEAMAN

THIS CHAPTER PROVIDES A STUDY GUIDE for the ordinary seaman who wishes to prepare for lifeboatman or able seaman examinations. The prospective able seaman may refer also to the U.S. Coast Guard's up-dated *Manual for Lifeboatmen, Able Seamen, and Qualified Members of Engine Department, CG-175* to supplement this material (see Chapter 23 for Requirements for Members of the Engine Department).

REQUIREMENTS AND EXAMINATION FOR
CERTIFICATE OF EFFICIENCY AS LIFEBOATMAN

Certificate required. Every person employed in a rating as lifeboatman on any United States vessel requiring certificated lifeboatmen shall produce a certificate as lifeboatman or merchant mariner's document endorsed as lifeboatman or able seaman to the shipping commissioner, United States collector or deputy collector of customs, or master before signing articles of agreement. No certificate of efficiency as lifeboatman is required of any person employed on any unrigged vessel, except on a seagoing barge and on a tank barge navigating waters other than rivers and/or canals.

Service or training requirements:

(a) An applicant, to be eligible for certification as lifeboatman, must meet one of the following requirements:

(1) At least 1 year's sea service in the deck department, or at least 2 year's sea service in the other departments of ocean, coastwise, Great Lakes, and other lakes, bays, or sounds vessels;

(2) Graduation from a schoolship approved by and conducted under rules prescribed by the Commandant;

(3) Satisfactory completion of basic training as a Cadet of the United States Merchant Marine Cadet Corps;

(4) Satisfactory completion of 3 years' training at the U.S. Naval Academy or the U.S. Coast Guard Academy including two training cruises;

(5) Satisfactory completion of a course of training approved by the Commandant, and served aboard a training vessel; and

(6) Successful completion of a training course approved by the Commandant, such course to include a minimum of 30 hours' actual lifeboat training: Provided, that the applicant produces evidence of having served a minimum of 3 months at sea aboard ocean or coastwise vessels.

(b) An applicant, to be eligible for certification as lifeboatman, shall be able to speak and understand the English language as would be required in the rating of lifeboatman and in an emergency aboard ship.

Examination and demonstration of ability:

(a) Before a lifeboatman's certificate may be granted, the applicant must prove to the satisfaction of the Coast Guard by oral or written examination and by actual demonstration that:

(1) He has been trained in all the operations connected with the launching of lifeboats and life rafts and the use of oars and sails;

(2) He is acquainted with the practical handling of boats themselves; and,

(3) He is capable of taking command of a boat's crew.

(b) The oral or written examination shall be conducted only in the English language and shall consist of questions regarding:

(1) Lifeboats and life rafts, the names of their essential parts, and a description of the required equipment;

(2) The clearing away, swinging out, and lowering of lifeboats and life rafts, the handling of lifeboats under oars, sails, and power, including questions relative to the proper handling of a boat in a heavy sea; and,

(3) The operation and functions of commonly used types of davits.

(c) The practical examination shall consist of a demonstration of the applicant's ability to carry out the orders incident to launching lifeboats, and the use of the boat's sail, and to row.

General provisions respecting Merchant Mariner's documents endorsed as lifeboatman. A merchant mariner's document endorsed as able seaman shall be considered as the equivalent of a certificate as lifeboatman or an endorsement as lifeboatman and it shall be accepted as a certificate as lifeboatman wherever required by law or regulation.

International provisions respecting Merchant Mariner's documents endorsed as lifeboatman. In addition to the above, recommendations for the 1978 International Conference on Training and Certification of Seafarers will require, when adopted, that every seaman receive additional training in personal survival techniques. The merchant mariner's document shall be endorsed by the Coast Guard to reflect satisfactory completion of this training.

REQUIREMENTS AND EXAMINATION FOR
CERTIFICATE OF SERVICE AS ABLE SEAMEN

Certificate required:

(a) Every person employed in a rating as able seamen on any United States vessel requiring certificated able seamen, before signing articles of agreement, shall present to the United States collector or deputy collector of customs, or master, his certificate as able seaman or his merchant mariner's document endorsed as able seaman.

(b) No certificate as able seaman is required of any person employed on any unrigged vessel except seagoing barges, nor on any tug or towboat on the bays and sounds connected directly with the seas.

(c) No certificate as able seaman is required of any person employed on any sail vessel of less than 500 net tons while not carrying passengers for hire and while not operating outside the line dividing inland waters from the high seas.

General requirements:

   (a) To qualify for certification as able seaman an applicant shall be;

      (1) At least 19 years of age;

      (2) Pass the prescribed physical examination;

      (3) Meet the sea service or training requirements set forth in this part;

      (4) Satisfactorily pass an examination demonstrating his ability as an able seaman and lifeboatmen; and

      (5) Be able to speak and understand the English language as would be required in the rating of able seamen and in an emergency aboard ship.

Physical requirements:

   (a) All applicants for a certificate of service as able seaman shall be required to pass a physical examination given by a medical officer of the United States Public Health Service and present to the Officer in Charge, Marine Inspection, a certificate executed by the Public Health Service Officer. Such certificate shall attest to the applicant's acuity of vision, color sense, hearing and general physical condition. In exceptional cases where an applicant would be put to great inconvenience or expense to appear before a medical officer of the United States Public Health Service, the physical examination and certificate may be made by any other reputable physician.

   (b) The medical examination for an able seaman is the same as for an original license as a deck officer. If the applicant is in possession of an unexpired deck license, the Officer in Charge, Marine Inspection, may waive the requirement for a physical examination.

      (1) Epilepsy, insanity, senility, acute venereal disease or neuro-syphilis, badly impaired hearing, or other defects that would render the applicant incompetent to perform the ordinary duties of an officer at sea are causes for certification as incompetent.

      (2) For an original license as master, mate, or pilot, the applicant must have uncorrected vision of at least 20/100 in both eyes correctable to at least 20/20 in one eye and 20/40 in the other. The color sense will be tested by means of a pseudoisochromatic plate test but any applicant who fails this test will be eligible if he can pass the "Williams" lantern test or equivalent.

Service or training requirements:

   (a) The minimum service or training required to qualify an applicant for certification and the various endorsements as able seamen is listed in this paragraph:

      (1) High seas and inland waters—

         (i) "Any waters—unlimited" Three years service on deck in vessels of 100 gross tons or over operating on ocean or coast-wise routes or on the Great Lakes.

         (ii) "Any waters—unlimited" The period of time spent by an applicant successfully completing a course of able seamen's training in a

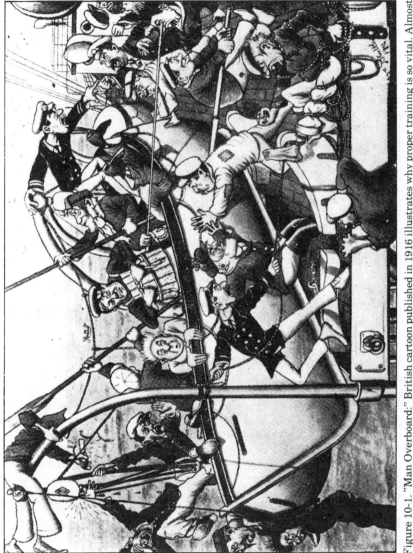

Figure 10-1. "Man Overboard." British cartoon published in 1916 illustrates why proper training is so vital. Almost every example of poor seamanship and safety violation is shown. You need a sense of humor if you are going to sea, but never forget the sea is unforgiving in its treatment of the incompetent, the unwary, and the untrained. *From "Humours of the Mercantile Navy" by E.G.O. Beuttler.* Courtesy: Chief Bos'n Paul M. Seiler, U.S.C.G. (Ret).

training school approved by the Commandant may be accepted as the equivalent of sea service up to a maximum of 1 year of the 3 years required in subdivision (I) of this subparagraph.

(iii) "Any waters—unlimited" Satisfactory completion of 18 months training in a seagoing training ship approved by the Commandant.

(iv) "Any waters—12 months" 12 months service on deck in vessels of 100 gross tons or over operating on ocean or coast-wise routes or on the Great Lakes. (Holders of certification under this provision are limited to one fourth of the number of able seamen required by law to be employed on a vessel.)

(v) "Any waters—12 months" Satisfactory completion of a course of training at a U. S. Maritime Service Training Station of at least 9 months, 6 months of which shall have been served aboard a seagoing training vessel. (Holders of certification under this provision are limited to one-fourth of the number of able seamen required by law to be employed on a vessel.)

(2) Great Lakes and inland waters—

(i) "Great Lakes—18 months' service" 18 months service on deck in vessels of 100 gross tons or over operating on ocean or coastwise routes, or on the Great Lakes, smaller lakes, bays or sound. (Holders of certification under this provision may comprise the required number of able seamen on vessels on the Great Lakes and on the smaller lakes, bays, and sounds.) If the seamen possesses the requisite service for certification under subparagraph (1) (v) of this paragraph, there shall be added "any waters—12 months."

(3) Tugs and towboats—

(i) "Tugs and towboats—any waters." 18 months service on deck in vessels operating on ocean or coastwise routes, or on the Great Lakes, or on the bays and sounds connected directly with the seas.

(4) Bays and sounds—

(i) "Bays and sounds—12 months, vessels 500 gross tons or under not carrying passengers." 12 months service on deck in vessels operating on ocean or coastwise routes, or on the Great Lakes, or on the bays and sounds connected directly with the seas.

(5) Barges—

(i) "Seagoing barges—12 months." 12 months service on deck in vessels operating on ocean or coastwise routes, or on the Great Lakes, or on the bays and sounds connected directly with the seas.

Examination and demonstration of ability:

(a) Before an applicant is certified as able seaman, he shall prove to the satisfaction of the Coast Guard by actual demonstration, his knowledge of seamanship and his ability to carry out effectively all the duties that may be required of an able seaman, including those of a lifeboatman. He shall demonstrate that:

(1) He has been trained in all the operations connected with the launching of lifeboats and life rafts and the use of oars and sail;

(2) He is acquainted with the practical handling of the boats themselves; and

(3) He is capable of taking command of a boat's crew.

(b) The oral or written examination shall be conducted only in the English language and shall consist of questions regarding:

(1) Lifeboats and life rafts, the names of their essential parts and a description of the required equipment;

(2) The clearing away, swinging out, and lowering of lifeboats and life rafts, and handling of lifeboats under oars and sails, including questions relative to the proper handling of a boat in a heavy sea;

(3) The operation and functions of commonly used types of davits;

(4) The applicant's knowledge of nautical terms; boxing the compass, either by degrees or points according to his experience; running lights, passing signals, and fog signals for vessels on the high seas, in inland waters, or on the Great Lakes depending upon the waters on which the applicant has had service; and distress signals; and

(5) The applicant's knowledge of commands in handling the wheel by obeying orders passed to him as "wheelman" and knowledge of the use of engine room telegraph or bell pull signals.

(c) In the actual demonstration, the applicant shall show his ability by taking command of a boat and directing the operation of clearing away, swinging out, lowering the boat into the water, and acting as coxswain in charge of the boat under oars. He shall demonstrate his ability to row by actually pulling an oar in the boat. He shall also demonstrate knowledge of the principle knots, bends, splices, and hitches in common use by actually making them.

(d) Any person who is in valid possession of a certificate as able seaman endorsed, "any waters—12 months" and who can produce documentary evidence of sufficient service to qualify for a certificate as able seaman endorsed, "any waters—unlimited," may be issued a new document bearing this endorsement without additional professional examination. The applicant shall surrender for cancellation the document bearing the limited endorsement. No physical examination will be required at the time of this exchange unless it is found that the applicant obviously suffers from some physical or mental infirmity to a degree that in the opinion of the Officer in Charge, Marine Inspection would render him incompetent to perform the usual duties of an able seaman at sea. If such condition is believed to exist, the applicant shall be required to undergo an examination by a medical officer of the Public Health Service to determine his competency.

General provisions respecting merchant mariner's documents endorsed as able seaman:

(a) The holder of a merchant mariner's document endorsed for the rating of able seaman may serve in any unlicensed rating in the deck department without obtaining an additional endorsement.

(b) A merchant mariner's document endorsed as able seaman will also be considered a certificate of efficiency as lifeboatman without further endorsement.

(c) This type of document will describe clearly the type of able seaman certificate which it represents, e.g.; able seaman—any waters; able seaman any waters-12 months; able seaman Great Lakes—18 months; able seaman—on freight vessels, 500 gross tons or less on bays or sounds, and on tugs, towboats, and barges on any waters.

ORDINARY SEAMEN

The deck department of any vessel is composed of the ordinary seamen, able seamen (including quartermasters, boatswains, and carpenters, who are specialized able seamen), radio operators, cadets, mates and master. Sixty-five percent of the deck crew of an oceangoing vessel must be able seamen. One-fourth of these able seamen may hold 12-month certificates. In addition to this overall requirement of law, wheelmen in restricted waters must be able seamen. Although only necessary for AB and Quartermaster, an able seaman's certificate is good for obtaining a job as carpenter, Bos'n, Deck Maintenance Man, Watchman, and any other ratings that make up the deck force.

Ordinary seaman, the entrance rating in the deck department, requires no professional or physical examination according to the Coast Guard. However, in practice steamship companies and unions require all individuals to take a physical examination before signing shipping articles. Furthermore, it is important for the ordinary seaman to have adequate vision and hearing and to be physically fit to qualify for service in the higher ratings of able seaman and licensed officer. The Public Health Service will give voluntary examinations to ordinary seamen who request it. After a period of training which varies according to the waters served upon, the ordinary seaman is eligible for a rating as able seaman and lifeboatman, and may apply to the Officer in Charge, Marine Inspection, U.S. Coast Guard. When the individual passes the required physical and the written, verbal and practical examinations, he or she is permitted to do any required work on deck no matter what it may be, and to be able to do it not only under favorable conditions, but also in any emergency which may arise. In other words, any duty in the deck department may be performed except actual navigation of the vessel.

After three years at sea an able seaman may take the third mate's examination. If successful, another year's service as third mate qualifies one for a second mate's license. Similarly, a year's service at sea as second and chief mate qualifies that person to sit for chief mate and master respectively.

LIFEBOATS

The modern lifeboat, a so-called "double-ender" or whaleboat, is pointed at both bow and stern. Lifeboats may be open or totally enclosed. They may be propelled by oars, hand propelling equipment, or motor. They may be constructed of galvanized steel, aluminum, or fiberglass reinforced plastic (FRP) (wooden lifeboats are no longer in service on American flag vessels). Much care has gone into the design and construction of lifeboats. Therefore, except for emergency repairs, no changes can be made without Coast

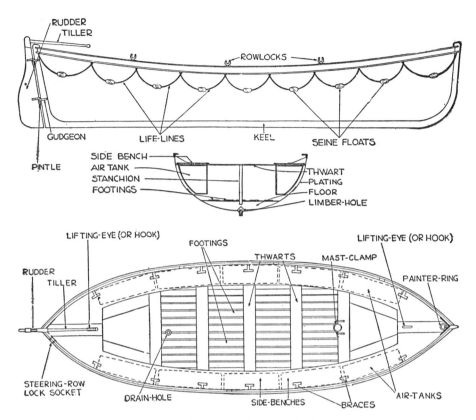

Figure 10-3. Metallic open lifeboat.

Guard approval. Even emergency changes must be reported to the Officer in charge, Marine Inspection, at the first opportunity.

If a lifeboat is intended to be propelled by oars, sails must be provided. A lifeboat of a capacity of less than 60 persons may be propelled by oars, and one of 60 persons or more must be equipped with hand-propelling gear or with a motor. A lifeboat with a capacity of 100 or more must be motor-propelled.

The manufacturer of the lifeboat places a plate marked in letters and numbers at least 1 1/2 inches (3.75 cm) high on the bow indicating the

◄ Figure 10-2. A. Lifeboat secured for sea on gravity davits after boat drill on T.S. *Golden Bear*. Note that gripes have been passed and tricing pendant has been attached. Photo: Editors. B. In most cases enclosed lifeboats are now required for all newly constructed ships. Hull is fire retardant fiberglass. Boat has fuel capacity of 24 hours at 6 knots. Sufficient buoyancy is provided to make boat unsinkable in all conditions up to a full load. Launching procedures differ from open lifeboats. Thorough training is particularly important. Courtesy W. B. Arnold Co., Inc.

cubic capacity as well as the number of persons the lifeboat may carry. The number of persons is also marked or painted on top of at least two thwarts on an open lifeboat and on the tops of enclosed lifeboats and survival capsules. Each lifeboat must have the ship's name and number of the boat painted on the bow in letters not less than 3 inches (7.5 cm) high. Oars are marked with the vessel's name.

The tops of thwarts, side benches and footings of lifeboats are painted international orange with the area near the mechanical disengaging gear control lever painted in a color contrasting with the lever. Numbered in accordance with where they are carried aboard ship, odd numbered lifeboats are on the starboard side, even on the port, with lower numbered boats carried forward, and higher numbered aft. For example, Boats 1 and 3 would be on the starboard side, 2 and 4 on the port. In peacetime each

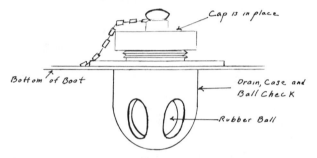

Figure 10-4. Automatic lifeboat drain. Drawing: Midn. Eric Pett, California Military Academy.

lifeboat must have its own set of davits. However, in wartime nesting of lifeboats was authorized with Boat 1-A nested below Boat 1, etc.

Figure 10-3 shows the nomenclature of a metallic, open lifeboat. A fiberglass lifeboat is similar. The keel of a metal boat is made of a heavy metal bar joined to the stem and stern posts to form the backbone of the boat. The stern post is fitted with gudgeons for holding the rudder. The gunwale runs the length of the boat atop the plating and gives strength to the boat. In the gunwales are sockets for the rowlocks. In case it capsizes, the lifeboat has grab rails on the outside for persons to cling to. Where there are no grab rails, some other means of hanging on is provided.

In places where the hull contacts the chocks or cradles, doubler plating (an extra plate) is used to give strength. Frequent inspection and painting are required to protect the plating. Aluminum lifeboats may be damaged by electrolytic action if steel or other metals touch the hull. Electrolysis may occur in salt air even if two dissimilar metals do not actually touch. For this reason no steel or iron tools should be left in aluminum boats.

A lifeboat is fitted with one or more drains (Figure 10-4) to allow water to run out when the boat is in the davits. The drain cap should be screwed on before the boat is placed in the water, but if the cage is kept free from debris, the rubber ball *should* act as a check valve and prevent water from entering the boat.

Thwarts extend from side to side in an open boat. They provide seating for the oarsmen as well as give strength to the hull in the same manner as beams of a ship. Foot rests or stretchers provide a place for the oarsmen to brace their feet when rowing. Additional seating is provided by the side benches. An enclosed boat or survival capsule has seats located in the center with one or more concentric rows of seats around the sides facing inward.

Provision tanks, water tanks and buoyancy compartments (or air tanks) are located below the side benches or thwarts. The air tanks on newer boats are usually filled with cellular foam. Older boats may have air tanks which can be removed for maintenance. Each tank is fitted with a small nipple so that air tightness can be checked with a small air pump. Even without an air pump air can be blown into the tanks to cause the sides of most tanks to bulge if there are no leaks. On a hot day the sides of an airtight tank will probably bulge because of expansion inside. If a tank is holding air pressure, soapy water on top of the nipple will bubble.

On each lifeboat which is provided with a sail, a mast step or clamp is installed. The clamp is attached to a thwart.

Some lifeboats have hand-propelling equipment or Fleming gear, popularly known as "idiot" sticks. This means of propulsion consists of propeller, stern tube, stern gland, gears, and pulling lever handles which the "oarsmen" push back and forth. The bottom of the levers fit into sockets which are connected to a box on each side of the boat. The two bars move cranks on each side of the gear box. Obviously, bars, cranks, and levers for hand-propelled boats must be kept clear to facilitate the stowing of gear.

A motor lifeboat is equipped with a diesel engine although a few older boats may have gasoline engines. The engine should not be run for more than five minutes if the boat is out of water or overheating may result. A reversing gear and clutch enable the propeller to operate ahead, astern, or disengaged. Although engines and fuel systems are designed to minimize danger from fire or explosion, open flames should be kept away from the boat and smoking should not be permitted in or near a lifeboat. If a boat is equipped with a motor, the motor should be operated each time an abandon ship drill is held.

The rudder is attached to the tiller, and, on an open boat, is removable. A toggle pin attached by a small chain keeps the tiller in place. The rudder has pintles which fit into the gudgeons on the stern post. Most rudders are wood, but if metal, there also will be a watertight air casing which provides buoyancy. A test nipple permits testing for watertightness in the same manner as for an air tank. Lifeboats are easy to maneuver because their rudders are proportionately larger than those on a ship. In addition to a rudder, lifeboats are provided with a large steering or sweep oar. Since a rudder has no effect if the boat has no way on, the sweep oar is handy for maneuvering the boat in a confined space or when it is stopped.

The decks near lifeboats must be kept clear of cargo or other material which would interfere with launching. Vessels must have one approved ladder ready for use for each set of davits to enable passengers and crew to descend to lifeboats and rafts. All boats and rafts are stowed so that they can be launched in the shortest possible time and under unfavorable conditions of list and trim. Boat falls and lifelines must be long enough to reach water at the vessel's lightest seagoing draft and with the vessel listed 15 degrees either way.

A licensed deck officer or certified lifeboatman is in charge of each lifeboat or life raft on vessels engaged on ocean or intercoastal voyages.

The signal for boat drill or boat stations consists of seven short blasts and one long blast of the vessel's whistle, and the same signal on the general

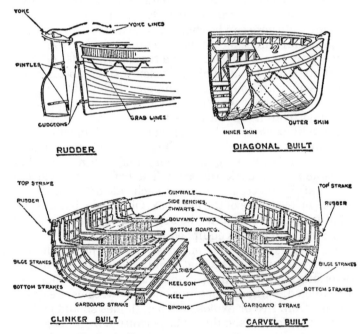

Figure 10-5. Wooden hull construction.

alarm bell. Where whistle signals are used for handling boats, they are as follows: One short blast of the whistle is an order to lower the boats; two short blasts is an order to stop lowering the boats; three short blasts dismisses the crew from boat stations.

A fire and boat drill must be held at least once a week, and on vessels where more than twenty-five percent of the crew has signed on, within twenty-four hours of leaving port. At boat drill, weather conditions permitting, boat covers and strongbacks must be removed, plugs put in, painters let out and tended, boat ladders secured in place, and all the boats must actually be swung out ready for lowering to the embarkation deck and frapped in. The person in charge of each boat must see that all members of its crew are acquainted with their duties. Whenever possible the boats should be lowered to the water and the crew instructed in handling the boats under oars, sail, or other power. At least once every three months every member of the crew of a vessel must participate in a drill in which he actually pulls an oar in a lifeboat.

REQUIRED EQUIPMENT FOR LIFEBOATS

The table on page 10-16 lists the equipment required by the U.S. Government in the Code of Federal Regulation, Title 46, subpart 94.20. A similar listing along with a description of each item is contained in CG-175. All articles must be of good quality, efficient for the purpose they are intended to serve, and kept in good condition.

WOODEN BOAT CONSTRUCTION

Although wood is no longer used for lifeboat construction, occasionally a wooden emergency boat or work boat is used aboard ship. You should know the various types of wooden boat construction. (See Figure 10-5 for the various types.)

DAVITS

Launching equipment consists of davits, winches, blocks, and falls. Davits are usually the high-track (or roller) gravity type. Common types of davits are described and are shown in Figure 10-6 A, B, C, and D. The roller gravity davit is shown in Figure 10-6E and the Miranda gravity davit is shown in Figure 10-6F.

RADIAL DAVITS

Although easily designed and manufactured, radial or round bar davits are found only on small vessels today because they are awkward to use and require excessive manpower. The heads of the davit arms swing in horizontal arcs and do not raise or lower as do the heads of other davit types. The boat is swung aft until the bow clears the forward davit arm and then is swung outboard and forward to the lowering position.

MECHANICAL DAVITS

The common types of mechanical davits largely used on the Great Lakes are the *sheath screw boom,* the *sheath screw crescent,* and the *quadrantal.* Although shaped differently, sheath screw types are similar in operation.

With the sheath screw type, the lifeboat is carried either on chocks under the davits or is cradled between the davits, depending on whether the davit is the straight boom or crescent sheath crew type. In operation, the davit, which is pivoted near the foot so that it will turn in an arc at right angles to the vessel's side, is rotated outboard by a crank operating a sheath screw so that the boat is suspended over the side and frapped in to the embarkation deck. Figure 10-7 shows the T.S. *Golden Bear's* emergency boat swung out on its sheath screw crescent davit.

The quadrantal davit is another mechanical davit which also represented a distinct advance over the radial davit. With this type, the lifeboat

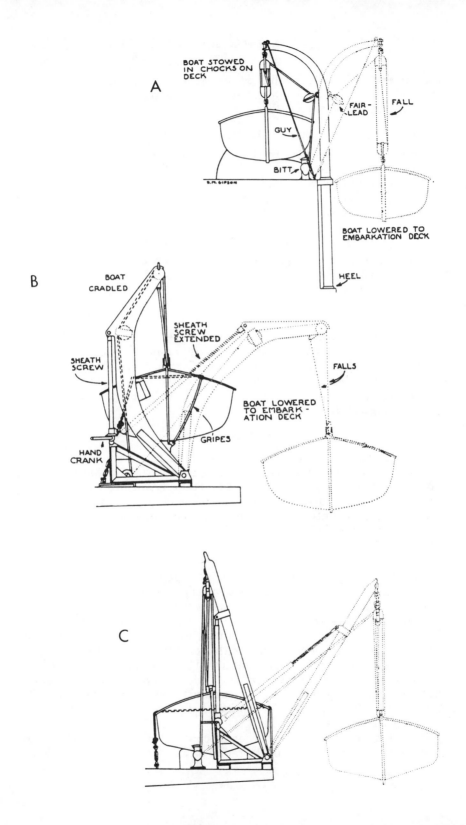

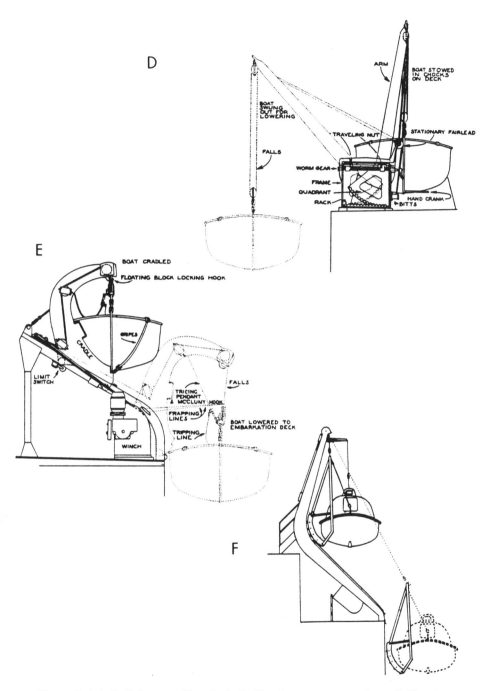

Figure 10-6. A. Radial or round bar davit; B. Sheath screw crescent davit; C. Sheath screw boom davit; D. Quadrantal davit; E. Roller gravity davit; F. Miranda gravity davit. Although little seen on American flag ships currently, it has distinct advantages especially with enclosed lifeboats since it can be launched by personnel in the boat without leaving anyone aboard the parent ship. The Miranda system allows a boat to be launched with the ship listed 30° either way and with a 15° trim.

Letter ID	Item	Ocean and coastwise		Great Lakes		
		Other than sea-barges	Sea-going barges	Vessels carry-ing cargo	Other	Lakes, bays, and sounds; and rivers
a	Bailer	1	None	1	None	None
b	Bilge pump	[1]1	None	None	None	None
c	Boathooks	2	2	1	1	1
d	Bucket	2	1	1	1	1
e	Compass and mounting	1	None	None	None	None
f	Ditty bag	1	None	None	None	None
g	Drinking cups	1	1	None	None	None
h	Fire extinguishers (motor-propelled lifeboats only)	2	2	2	2	2
i	First-aid kit	1	None	None	None	None
j	Flashlight	1	None	1	None	None
k	Hatchets	2	None	2	1	1
l	Heaving line	2	None	None	None	None
m	Jackknife	1	1	None	None	None
n	Ladder, lifeboat, gunwale	1	None	None	None	None
o	Lantern	1	1	1	1	1
p	Lifeline	1	1	1	1	1
q	Life preservers	2	2	2	2	2
r	Locker	1	None	1	None	None
s	Mast and sail (oar-propelled lifeboats only)	1	None	None	None	None
t	Matches (boxes)	2	2	1	1	1
u	Milk, condensed (pounds per person)	1	None	None	None	None
v	Mirrors, signaling	2	None	None	None	None
w	Oars	[2]1 unit	[2]1 unit	[2]1 unit	[2]1 unit	[2]1 unit
x	Oil, illuminating (quarts)	1	None	1	None	None
y	Oil, storm (gallons)	1	None	1	None	None
z	Painter	2	1	2	1	1
aa	Plugs	1	1	1	1	1
bb	Provisions (pounds per person)	2	None	None	None	None
cc	Rowlocks	[2]	[2]	[2]	[2]	[2]
dd	Rudder and tiller	1	1	1	1	None
ee	Sea anchor	1	None	1	None	None
ff	Signals, distress, floating orange smoke	2	None	None	None	None
gg	Signals, distress, red hand flare	[2]1 unit	None	[2]1 unit	None	None
hh	Signals, distress, red parachute flare	[2,3]1 unit	None	[2]1/2 unit	None	None
ii	Tool kit (motor-propelled lifeboat only)	[2]1 unit	[2]1 unit	[2]1 unit	[2]1 unit	[2]1 unit
jj	Water (quarts per person)	3	1	None	None	None
kk	Whistle, signaling	1	None	None	None	None
ll	Fishing kit	1	None	None	None	None
mm	Cover, protecting	1	None	None	None	None
nn	Signals, lifesaving	1	None	None	None	None
oo	Desalting kit	[4]1	None	None	None	None

Figure 10-7. Emergency boat swung out and secured for sea on
sheath screw crescent davits on T.S. *Golden Bear*. This is a Coast
Guard race point type surfboat, but it is not an approved lifeboat.
Photo: Editors.

is carried on chocks under the davits. The davits themselves stand upright
with the tops curved in towards each other so that the ends come directly
above the hoisting hooks of the lifeboat. In operation the davit, which is
pivoted near the foot so that it will turn in an arc at right angles to the
ship's side, is rotated outboard by a crank operating a worm gear so that
the boat is suspended over the side and frapped in to the embarkation deck.
Mechanical davits are frequently used on the Great Lakes, but are rarely
seen in ocean service.

◄   [1]Motor-propelled lifeboats, certified for 100 or more persons, shall be fitted with
an additional hand bilge pump of an approved type or a power bilge pump.
    [2]For description of units, see subpart 94.20-15.
    [3]Vessels in coastwise service need only carry 1 unit for each 5 lifeboats or fraction
thereof.
    [4]Optional equipment. See subpart 94.20-15(jj) water.

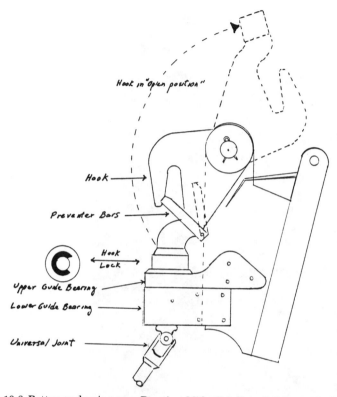

Figure 10-8. Rottmer releasing gear. Drawing: Midn. Eric Pett, California Maritime Academy.

GRAVITY DAVITS

Gravity davits are required for all boats which weigh over 5000 lbs. with their equipment but without passengers or crew. They permit a boat to be launched by one person without motor power. The boats are carried between two heavily constructed davit arms each of which are on rollers and mounted on tracks set at right angles to the ship's side. When released, the rollers permit the davits to roll down the trackways carrying the boat outboard to the lowering position. Tricing pendants pull the boat in to the embarkation deck as it is lowered. At this point the frapping lines are passed to hold the boat in position for the embarkation of passengers. The tricing pendants are cast off by operating the tricing pendant trip (or MacCluney) hooks. The frapping lines restrict the boat from swinging while it is being lowered the rest of the way into the water. *

*On some U.S. flag ships which were built in foreign countries, bowsing tackles may be used instead of frapping lines. These accomplish the same purpose as frapping lines, but are tended from the lifeboat rather than from the embarkation deck of the parent ship. Frequently two-fold purchases are used. The advantage is that only the brakeman need remain aboard ship when the lifeboat is launched. The disadvantage is that bowsing tackles are cumbersome, and more gear must be stowed in the lifeboat.

Before the boat is lowered, the boat commander insures that the cap is screwed on the boat drain (see Figure 10-4), and that the gripes and stopper bar are removed. The power should be turned off the winch, and the trackways cleared. The brakeman gently lifts the winch brake lever and the boat and davit-arm assembly will roll down the trackways to the outboard lowering position.

After the passengers and crew embark, the boat is lowered into the water, the Rottmer releasing gear (see Figure 10-8) is tripped, and the boat rides to the sea painter. Good seamanship dictates that the sea painter is rigged at all times. At periodical drills, rigging should be checked, and lead outboard free of all obstructions so it will not become fouled.

RECOVERING THE LIFEBOAT

Recovering a lifeboat is just as important as launching it, and a lifeboatman should be thoroughly familiar with the process. When the lifeboat comes alongside, the sea painter is passed and tended from the ship so that the lifting pads of the boat match up with the boat falls. If the falls need to be lengthened to reach the boat, they may need to be extended by engaging the hand wheel or crank since merchant ship gravity davits require the weight of the boat to allow the falls to extend. (The decision to disembark anyone while the boat is still in the water depends upon weather and other circumstances, but the time a boat is alongside its parent ship is critical and should be reduced to the minimum.) When the Rottmer release lever is rotated, the releasing gear will close. The frapping lines are tended and kept taut while the boat is being raised to the embarkation station where all remaining personnel are disembarked. The tricing pendants are secured, the frapping lines cast off, and the boat is again raised by power towards its stowed position. Within a foot of the stowed position, or when the white witness marks on the davit arms and trackways line up, the power is removed from the winch, the hand wheel or crank inserted, and the boat brought up to the full stowed position *by hand*.

The importance of raising the lifeboat by hand the last foot of the way to the stowed position cannot be overemphasized even though there is a limit switch (Figure 10-9) designed to cut off power automatically when the boat nears the fully stowed position. If the limit switch fails to function, the boat will continue to rise until the davits go into the stops, the falls will probably part, or be pulled loose, and the boat will go over the side along with anyone in it.

Each time a boat is hoisted on board, a seaman pulls down the limit switch arm with a boathook to test and to insure that it cuts off power to the winch. No one should be aboard the boat when this is being done.

After the boat has reached the embarkation position and the tricing pendants (Figure 10-10) are secured, all hands should leave the boat until after it has reached the secured position. In the secured position, the gripes are passed and the slack removed up on the turnbuckles. The stopper-bar

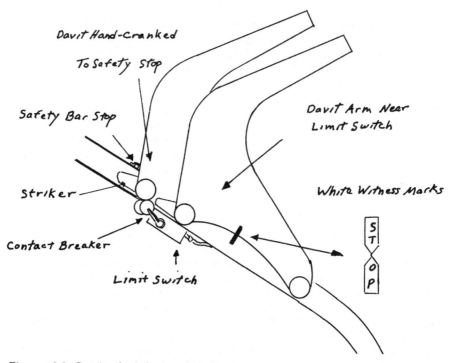

Figure 10-9. Gravity davit limit switch. Drawing: Midn. Eric Pett, California Maritime Academy.

clearing levers are lifted on both the forward and after davits locking the gripes and stopper bars in place. Covers are removed from the drains and the boat is now secure for sea.

It is important to know the proper name and function of each piece of equipment involved in the recovery operation. The *tricing pendants* force the boat to swing inwards towards the embarkation deck. If the brake is kept in the released position too long after the boat is at the embarkation deck, the tricing pendants take too much weight from the falls and cause them to become slack and to part.

After the tricing pendant release lever has been tripped, *frapping lines* hold the boat against the side of the ship. They must be tended as the boat is lowered and again after it has been hooked on when being hoisted. After the boat is stowed in position, *gripes* or wire straps secure it in place for sea. In wartime when two boats are nested for launching by one davit, a *suspension pendant* is used to suspend the top boat while the bottom boat is lowered.

RELEASING GEAR

All lifeboats are required to have a releasing or disengaging gear which will release both forward and after falls at the same time. The gear most

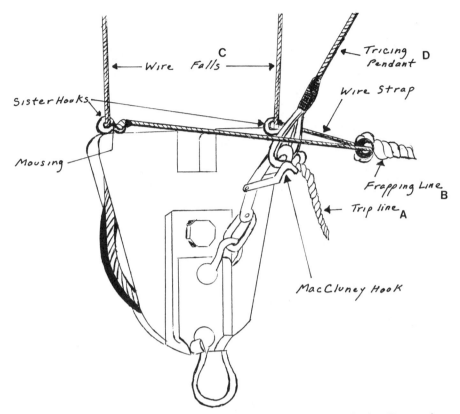

Figure 10-10. Tricing pendant and wire strap frapping line (with sister hooks). Frequently a synthetic tricing pendant or wire rope pendant is used without sister hooks. Large letters A, B, C, D, are for use with Question 33 of Sample Lifeboatman's Examination at the end of this chapter.

frequently used is the Rottmer which is shown in Figure 10-8. The boat is released only on orders from the licensed officer or lifeboatman in charge of the boat. Under his direction one man is assigned this function. The lifeboat release lever is held in place by a toggle pin which prevents it from accidentally turning. On order, the pin is removed. When the boat commander gives the order to release the falls, the release lever is turned. This rotates the shafting which is connected through universal joints to hook locks at both bow and stern. When the hook locks are opened, falls are released even though there is no tension on them. If the lever is rotated by mistake or in panic before the boat reaches the water, the boat will fall the rest of the way causing damage to the boat and injury to its occupants.

INFLATABLE LIFE RAFTS

In addition to lifeboats, modern ships are provided with inflatable life rafts. These have replaced the older rigid balsa or Carley life rafts and

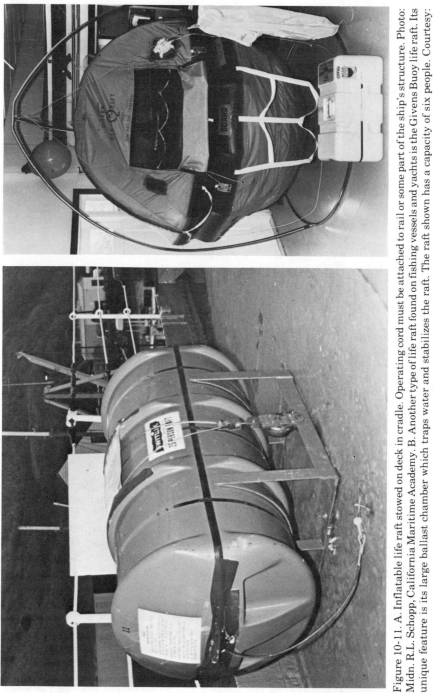

Figure 10-11. A. Inflatable life raft stowed on deck in cradle. Operating cord must be attached to rail or some part of the ship's structure. Photo: Midn. R.L. Schopp, California Maritime Academy. B. Another type of life raft found on fishing vessels and yachts is the Givens Buoy life raft. Its unique feature is its large ballast chamber which traps water and stabilizes the raft. The raft shown has a capacity of six people. Courtesy: Givens Associates.

floats which were in service during World War II and the Korean War. Vessels and tankships that have widely separated accommodations or work areas must have at least one life raft in each such location. Inflatable life rafts have a number of advantages. They are easy to launch; they take up about one-tenth the deck space of a lifeboat of comparable capacity; and, with their proven ability to remain afloat for long periods of time, they provide better survival potential. Disadvantages include limited maneuverability, slow propulsion by paddles, and a propensity to drift because of the boat's lightness.

There are several types of inflatable life rafts on the market, all of which must pass rigid Coast Guard inspection. Depending upon the manufacturer, life rafts have varying characteristics. Some manufacturers provide ladders for boarding. The canopy of one type is rugged enough to permit survivors to jump onto it from the side of the ship. Launching operations also may vary depending upon the particular raft. One example, launching of the Sea-Jay Elliott life raft, is shown in Figure 10-12. Because life rafts have different characteristics, it is especially important that seamen read carefully the instructions for the life rafts on board their ship before sailing.

Life rafts are provided with an impressive amount of survival equipment: ladder, heaving line, jackknife, lifelines, paddles, sea anchor, towing connections, repair kits, sponges, and bailers. They also contain a survival manual with vital information which should be read by everyone aboard.

Carbon dioxide gas is used to inflate life rafts. Heavy concentrations of this gas can result in unconsciousness leading to death. Therefore, the canopy opening must be adjusted to allow for fresh air. After the raft is inflated, the carbon dioxide exhaled by the survivors will cause some discomfort unless the canopy is kept partially open.

Inflatable life rafts must be inspected by personnel at a certified facility annually. Although rugged, life rafts are designed for one purpose only: To save life. If abused or damaged, they may fail when needed. The fiberglass container is designed to protect the life raft and keep it from the weather. Never tamper with a life raft or any other piece of lifesaving equipment. If a life raft is inflated accidentally, it must be repacked at an approved facility.

SURVIVAL CAPSULES

Some artificial islands and mobile offshore drilling rigs are equipped with survival capsules (Figure 10-14). The launching mechanism consists of a hold and launch platform, an electric winch, and a single wire rope fall connected to a Rottmer type hook on top of the capsule. The platform is permanently located so that it extends over the side. Quick launch and recovery operations are possible. Most capsules are equipped with a seawater sprinkling system to provide external fire protection. The capsule is propelled by a diesel engine.

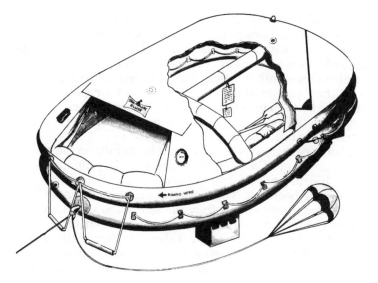

LAUNCHING INSTRUCTIONS

FOR THE

SEA-JAY

INFLATABLE LIFE RAFT

CAUTION

SET FOR OPERATION. DO NOT TAMPER. DO NOT DISTURB METAL BANDS.

1. When stowing raft, always connect the steel link to vessel by shackling painter to cradle using ELLIOT WEAK LINK.

2. Before launching the raft by hand, pull out the painter from the container and make it fast to the cleat provided (on the cradle).

3. If necessary to release painter from cradle, break painter Weak Link manually.

4. Release container by pressing knob on the Hydrostatic Release.

5. Launch life raft complete in container.

6. Gather in painter until taut; give strong pull to inflate raft.

Figure 10-12. Drawing of Sea-Jay Elliot inflatable life raft and launching instructions. Courtesy: C.J. Hendry Co.

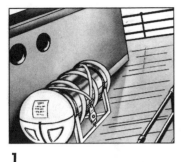

1

The Sea-Jay Elliot life raft is secured to its cradle with a hydrostatic release which, if time permits, can be tripped for manual release and inflation of the raft. If time does not permit manual release and inflation, this is accomplished automatically.

2

As the vessel sinks, pressure of the water at a depth of 10 feet actuates the release mechanism, freeing the raft from its stowage. The life raft is inherently buoyant and will float to the surface.

3

The sinking vessel pulls the operating cord and the life raft inflates. The CO_2 gas expands into the buoyancy chambers in a few seconds so the raft cannot be pulled down by the ship. The sea anchor is streamed automatically when the raft inflates, to reduce drift. All rafts are equipped with a spare sea anchor in the emergency equipment.

4

The Elliot Weak Link* attaches the painter to the ship; this parts and permits the raft to float free of the sinking vessel. The water-activated light comes on to guide survivors to the raft. Once aboard, help others to board, and then read the raft manual to learn details of raft operation and other data to insure survival.
*Patent pending

Figure 10-13. Automatic release and inflation of life raft. Courtesy: C.J. Hendry Co.

PERSONAL FLOTATION DEVICES

In addition to carrying adequate lifeboats and life rafts, all U.S. flag vessels must carry at least one Coast Guard approved personal flotation device (PFD) for each person aboard. These must be inspected annually by the Coast Guard, and those which can no longer pass inspection must be replaced. The Type I PFD is the well known life jacket which comes in adult and child sizes.

The Type IV PFD or ring buoy is not intended to be worn, but is thrown to a person in the water. It is held by the person overboard until rescued. When throwing a life buoy, throw it near, not at, the person.

The Type V PFD (or workvest) is approved for merchant personnel working near or over the water, but it is not a substitute for the Type I, and cannot be counted as a Type I at the annual Coast Guard inspection.

A Cold Water Exposure Suit is a comparatively recent development and is currently available for use. Commercial vessels on the Great Lakes will soon be required to carry one for each person aboard plus extra suits near normal work stations. The suit is watertight and has built-in buoyancy. It provides protection against hypothermia (loss of body heat) for up to 6 hours.

In addition to lifeboats and life rafts, ocean passenger vessels must have life floats or buoyant apparatus for emergency use by the passengers. There must be stowed for quick launchings with lashings capable of being easily cast off. Unless skids are provided, buoyant apparatus and life floats must weigh less than 400 pounds to insure easy launching and are provided with a boat hook, paddles, waterlights, painter, and lifeline.

RADIO

All large oceangoing vessels are provided with lifeboat radios which are carried to a lifeboat for drills or when actually abandoning ship. Lifeboat radio equipment is rugged and easy to operate. The antenna should be strung on the mast in accordance with the instructions. The radio is set to send out distress signals—twelve four-second dashes followed by three SOS groups—on the 500 and 8364 kilohertz (kHz) bands. This signal should activate the automatic alarm of any nearby ship. If the radio operator or person who knows the code is in the boat, the set can also be operated on manual for direct messages between the boat and the rescue vessels of 500 kHz. The silent periods on 500 kHz from 15 to 18 and 45 to 48 minutes past the hour are the best times for distress signals.

All oceangoing vessels are now required to have an emergency position indicating radio beacon (EPIRB). This is a small device which will float free of a sinking vessel and automatically begin operation. It operates on aircraft distress frequencies which are monitored by aircraft on ocean flights, and can usually be received at distances up to 100 miles.

RIG OF SEA PAINTER FOR LIFEBOATS AND EMERGENCY BOATS

The sea painter should be checked at each lifeboat drill to insure that it is still rigged outboard of everything between the boat and where it is secured on deck. The sea painter should be of sufficient length so that when the boat is in the water at her current draft, the boat will lay alongside the ship with its hoisting pad eyes directly below the davits.

Figure 10-15 shows how a sea painter should be secured to the forward thwart by the use of a toggle pin and Figure 10-16 shows a Kings Point Monomoy-type whaleboat towing alongside on a sea painter. The sea

Figure 10-14. Survival capsule. Survival capsules are installed on non-self propelled drilling rigs, self-propelled drilling rigs, fixed structures, and artificial islands. They vary in capacity from 14 to 50 persons. They are launched at the rate of 2 feet/second by a single fall. Capsule can make speeds of up to 6 knots. Courtesy: Whittaker Survival Systems Division.

painter should be secured to the inboard side of the thwart so that the boat will have a tendency to sheer out away from the side of the ship as soon as the releasing gear is tripped. It can be held alongside if necessary by the rudder or steering oar (which should be shipped just before the boat touches the water).

Releasing the sea painter on command and at the right time is essential. The toggle pin should be tapered so that a good tug will be all that is necessary to cast off the boat. (See Figures 10-15 and 10-16.) The shipboard end of the painter should be made fast in a seamanlike manner so that there will be no difficulty in tending it. If the boat is an emergency boat that does *not* have Rottmer releasing gear, the forward and after falls must be hooked on separately. The forward fall should always be hooked on *first*. Otherwise, if the ship has forward way on, and the after falls are hooked on first, the boat will slew around and probably broach, spilling the crew in the water when it overturns or swamps. A final and obvious precaution is to insure that the boat is not permitted to drift back under the quarter and perhaps get chewed up by the propeller.

Figure 10-15. Correct method of securing a sea painter. The end of the lanyard is secured to the thwart, not the sea painter, so that the toggle cannot injure anyone when the sea painter is released.

SEA ANCHOR

Both lifeboats and life rafts are equipped with sea anchors. A lifeboat sea anchor is shown in Figure 10-17. It is equipped with a trip line which permits the sea anchor to be brought back aboard the lifeboat without difficulty. The function of the sea anchor is to check the boat's or life raft's way, keeping her end on to the sea to prevent broaching to and capsizing while encountering heavy seas or breaking surf.

Broaching—The term broaching means that the boat is being thrown broadside onto the sea which can result in it capsizing and swamping. If a boat (or a sailing yacht) is running before the sea, the first effect of an overtaking wave is to lift the stern and depress the bow. If the boat does not have enough way on, the stern will be raised so high that the overtaking wave will push it around broadside to the sea. The bow meanwhile will be buried in the trough and offer far more resistance to being pushed by the wave. A boat is also very apt to broach when it attempts to make a landing through heavy surf. Landing through surf is no job for amateurs as can be appreciated if you glance through Dana's *Two Years Before The Mast*. A sea anchor might assist in keeping the stern into the sea, but it would be better not to make the attempt to land at all. Finally, as discussed in the paragraph on the sea painter, a boat can broach if it is alongside, and the after falls are hooked on before the forward falls.

Emergency sea anchor—If none is available, a sea anchor can be made from anything at hand, a boat bucket, an air tank filled with water, or a combination of oars, spar, and canvas weighted and properly bridled.

Storm oil container—The dotted lines in the apex of the sea anchor of Figure 10-17 represent the storm oil container which is part of lifeboat equipment. This is inserted through the mouth of the sea anchor. There are two lanyards provided at the apex of the sea anchor which are to be secured to the two rings of the container. The cocks at both the large and pointed ends of the oil container are opened slightly to allow the oil to seep out slowly.

The effect of oil in calming the sea has long been known. The oil not only prevents the breaking of the waves, but to a surprising degree prevents them from forming. It will also help in calming the waves to leeward in heavy weather and assist in bringing lifeboats or survivors aboard. Lifeboats must carry one gallon of vegetable, fish, or animal oil in the storm oil container.

TO USE A REAR SIGHT TYPE SIGNALING MIRROR

1. Observer should face a point about halfway between the sun and the observed object.

2. Hold the mirror in one hand about 4 inches from the face and sight the object to be signaled through the hole in the mirror.

3. Hold the other hand about 12 inches behind the mirror in line with the sun and the hole through the mirror, so that a small spot of light appears on the hand. The small spot of light on the hand is reflected on the back face of the mirror (side toward the observer).

4. Now tilt the mirror so that the spot of light on the back face of the mirror disappears through the hole in the mirror, at the same time keeping the observed object sighted through the hole in the mirror. With the mirror in this position the light rays from the sun will be reflected to the observed object.

Note: There are also foresight type and retroreflector type signaling mirrors. Instructions are supplied with all types of signaling mirrors.

WATER LIGHTS

The self-igniting water lights attached to ring buoys, life rafts, and buoyant apparatus may be either chemical or electrical except that tankers are required to use the electric water light because of the fire hazard involved in using chemicals. Formerly used, calcuim carbide is no longer approved for service for this reason.

The chemical water light consists of a metal cylinder, weighted in the bottom to maintain an upright position in the water, and provided with a plug or cap which, when removed, permits sufficient water to ignite the light when it strikes the water. The water light is attached to the ring buoy and arranged so that the plug or device will be removed by the weight of the buoy when the buoy is thrown overboard.

The electric water light consists of a tube containing dry cell batteries. It is mounted in an inverted position so that when it is thrown overboard along with a buoy it will be automatically righted on contact with the water. A mercury or gravity switch closes the circuit and lights the lamp.

Figure 10-16. This Kings Point Monomy-type whaleboat is towing alongside its parent ship. Picture was taken in calm weather in Long Island Sound. It does not take much imagination to realize how different it would be if the weather were less than ideal. The time a boat is alongside is critical and should be as short as possible. The boat should sheer off after launching and should be hooked on and hoisted without delay after its return. Courtesy: U.S. Merchant Marine Academy.

DISTRESS SIGNALS

The distress signals with which lifeboats and life rafts are equipped consist of red flares for night signaling and orange smoke signals for daytime use. The red flare signals are ignited either by removing the cap on the end of the flare, reversing the cap, and using the scratcher on the end of the cap to ignite the button on the head of the flare or by means of a pull wire attached to the cap. Hand smoke signals are ignited in the same way. Floating smoke signs have a pull-wire igniter. Combination flare and smoke signals are hand held and have a flare signal in one end and a smoke signal in the other end, with a pull-wire igniter for each end. Hand held signals should be ignited and burned with back to wind (care being taken not to obscure the signal from the vessel or aircraft being signaled) and held away from the body to avoid burning the operator or persons close by. Floating signals should be thrown overboard to leeward after being ignited. Specific directions for the use of each type of distress signal will be found on the label.

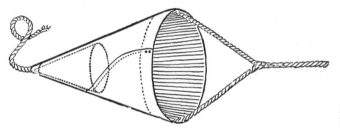

Figure 10-17. Lifeboat sea anchor.

You can expect questions on *lifesaving signals* on the lifeboatman's examination. See the Table of Lifesaving Signals, Figure 13-4 in Chapter 13. Anyone going to sea should also know the *International Distress Signals*. These are contained in Annex IV of the International Rules of the Road, and are reprinted in full in Chapter XIX.

LOOKOUTS

Lookouts are normally stationed on the fo'c'sle head although in heavy weather they may be called back to the bridge to stand their watch. Formerly a lookout might be stationed on the "crow's nest," a platform near the top of the foremast. Both this practice as well as the name "crow's nest" have all but disappeared unless the enclosed lookout station on the stub mast of some tankers would qualify to keep the term "crow's nest" alive.

Lookouts report vessels, land, rocks, shoals, discolored water, buoys, beacons, lighthouses, floating objects, or anything else which might be of interest to the bridge. In the modern day the report is usually made by telephone to the bridge. An older method was to make the report by striking a bell, by hail, or by speaking tube. If a bell is used, one bell indicates that an object has been sighted on the starboard side, two bells for the port side, and three bells for dead ahead. The watch officer will acknowledge the report by whatever method it is made, and the lookout must insure that his report is in fact acknowledged.

In the merchant service sightings are reported in relative bearings by points as indicated in Figure 10-18. In the Navy they will be made in relative bearings by degrees to port or starboard of dead ahead.

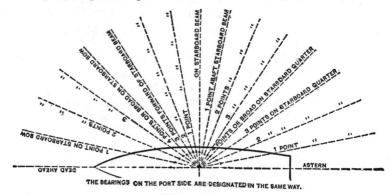

Figure 10-18. Relative bearings from a ship.

General instructions for lookouts:

(1) Be alert and attentive.

(2) Do not give your attention to anything but your own special duty.

(3) Remain at your station until you are regularly relieved.

(4) Keep to your feet and do not lounge.

(5) Do not talk with others except as required by your duty.

(6) When making a report, speak loudly and distinctly.

(7) Repeat a hail or a report until it is acknowledged by the watch officer.

(8) When you are stationed, be sure that you understand what you are supposed to do. If you don't understand your duty ask the officer on watch about it.

(9) Remember that no matter what your station, your duties are important and most necessary. According to the manner in which you perform your duty, you may make yourself of great assistance or absolutely worthless to the watch officer.

Lookouts report to the bridge every half hour by striking the time on the bell and at the same time should observe the running lights and report their conditions to the bridge.

A dim light will be seen quicker at night by looking at the sky a little above the horizon than by looking directly at the horizon. The lookout should sweep the horizon, then sweep the sky just above the horizon. A lookout at night must stand in the dark and must not have any light shine directly in his eyes, nor should there be any bright light forward of him.

Since watching for things is his primary duty, the lookout should see anything that happens, outside the ship, before anyone else. Until he can report things before others see them, he cannot feel that he is "right on the job." Every occurrence should be reported, even if it is believed that it has already been seen by the officer of the watch. It is better to report too many things than to make the mistake of not reporting something because it is believed that it has already been seen or that the officer of the deck would not be interested.

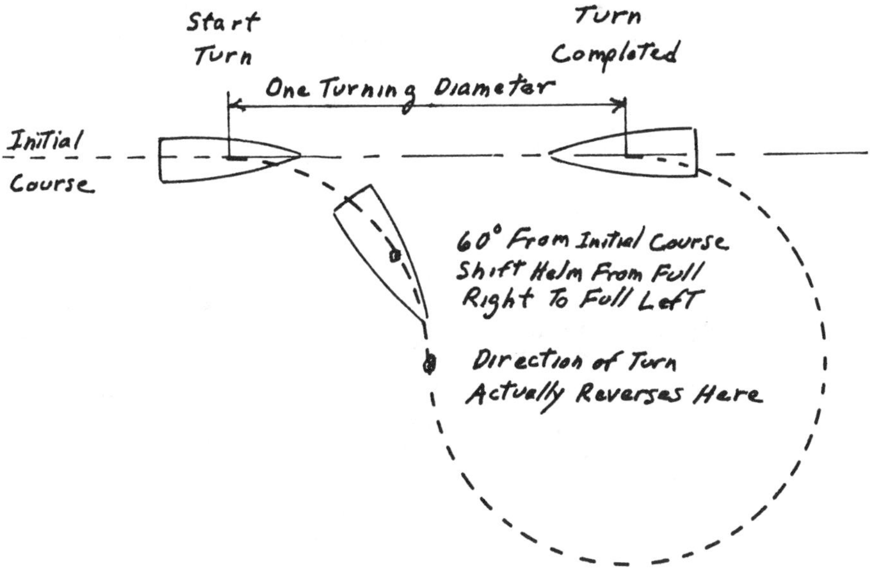

Figure 10-19. Williamson turn.

Often in a heavy fog the lookout on the forecastle can see much farther than anyone on the bridge, and his station in the bow is away from the whistle and the noises on the bridge. No unnecessary noise should be permitted near him. He must listen for all he is worth and report the first sound he hears, for if he waits to hear a faint whistle grow louder, the ship will often be in serious danger before the second sound is heard.

RESCUE OF PERSONS OVERBOARD

At the first cry of "man overboard," a ring buoy should be thrown to mark the spot and to give the person something with which to keep afloat if possible. The rudder should be turned in the direction of the person to prevent the propeller striking him. In the daytime a smoke distress signal will help mark the position of the victim overboard whereas at night a flare or water light attached to the life buoy will serve the same purpose.

At all cost, the person overboard should be kept in sight. Someone on board should be directed to do this and perform no other duty. If the person can be kept in sight, a circle recovery maneuver is the quickest way to bring the victim back aboard in day time. Recovery of a man by ship or by an emergency or lifeboat will depend upon the weather and other factors.

At night the "Williamson turn" (see Figure 10-19), a maneuver borrowed from the Navy, is the best means of bringing the overboard victim aboard even though it takes somewhat longer than a circle recovery. To execute the Williamson Turn, the rudder is put over hard towards the side from which the man has fallen overboard. The rudder is continued full until the ship is 60 degrees from the original heading, and then shifted full to the opposite direction. The ship continues to turn in the new direction until steadied up on the opposite (or reciprocal) of the original course. When the ship is on the reciprocal course, the man should be close aboard the bow on the side from which he fell.

HELICOPTER EVACUATION

The U.S. Coast Guard and rescue services of most foreign countries are able to evacuate personnel who need urgent medical assistance from ships at sea. This is obviously a hazardous undertaking, and requires the utmost skill on the part of the helicopter pilot and his crew as well as the cooperation and fine seamanship of the crew of the merchant ship. The Coast Guard requires that all U.S. flag merchant ships post a helicopter evacuation checkoff list conspicuously in the pilot house. It is reproduced below:

HELICOPTER EVACUATION CHECKOFF LIST:

WHEN REQUESTING HELICOPTER ASSISTANCE

1. Give accurate position, time, speed, course, weather conditions, wind direction and velocity, voice and CW frequencies.

2. If not already provided, give complete medical information, including whether or not the patient is ambulatory.

3. If you are beyond helicopter range, advise your diversion intentions so that a rendezvous point may be arranged.

4. If there are any changes, advise immediately. Should the patient expire prior to arrival of the helicopter, be sure to advise. Remember, the flight crew are risking their lives attempting to help you.

PREPARATIONS PRIOR TO ARRIVAL OF THE HELICOPTER

1. Provide continuous radio guard on 2182 kHz, or specified VOICE frequency if possible. The helicopter cannot operate CW.

2. Select and clear the hoist area, preferably aft, with a minimum 50-foot radius. This must include the securing of loose gear, awnings and antenna wires. Trice up running rigging and booms. If the hoist is aft, lower flagstaff.

3. If hoist is at night, light pickup area as well as possible. BE SURE YOU DO NOT SHINE ANY LIGHTS ON THE HELICOPTER so the pilot is not blinded. If there are obstructions in the vicinity, put a light on them so the pilot will be aware of their positions.

4. Point searchlights vertically to aid in locating the ship, and secure them when helicopter is on scene.

5. Advise location of pickup area BEFORE the helicopter arrives so that he may make his approach aft, amidships or forward, as required.

6. There will be a high noise level under the helicopter, making voice communication almost impossible. Arrange a set of hand signals among the crew who will assist.

HOIST OPERATIONS

1. If possible, move the patient to a position as close to the hoist areas as his condition permits—TIME IS IMPORTANT.

2. Normally, if a litter is required, it will be necessary to move the patient to the special litter which will be lowered by the helicopter. Be prepared to do this as quickly as possible. Be sure patient is strapped in, face, up, WITH LIFEJACKET, IF HIS CONDITION PERMITS.

3. Be sure patient is tagged to indicate what medication, if any, were administered, and when.

4. Have patient's medical record and necessary papers in envelope or package for transfer WITH him.

5. Change course so the ship rides as easily as possible with the wind on the bow, preferably on the port bow. Try to choose a course to keep stack gases clear of the hoist area. Once established, maintain course and speed.

6. Reduce speed if necessary to ease ship's motion, but maintain steerageway.

7. If you do not have radio contact with the helicopter when you are in all respects ready for the hoist, signal the helicopter in with a "come in" by hand, or at night by flashlight.

8. ALLOW BASKET OR STRETCHER TO TOUCH DECK PRIOR TO HANDLING TO AVOID STATIC SHOCK.

9. If a trail line is dropped by the helicopter, guide the basket or stretcher to deck with line—keep line clear at all times.

10. Place patient in basket, sitting with hands clear of sides, or in the litter as described above. Signal hoist operator when ready for hoist. Patient signals by nodding head if he is able. Deck personnel give thumbs up.

11. If necessary to take litter away from hoist point, unhook hoist cable and keep free for helicopter to haul in. DO NOT SECURE CABLE TO VESSEL OR ATTEMPT TO MOVE STRETCHER WITHOUT UNHOOKING.

12. When patient is strapped in stretcher, signal helicopter to lower cable, hook up and signal hoist operator when ready to hoist. Steady stretcher from turning or swinging.

13. If trail line is attached to basket or stretcher, use to steady. Keep feet clear of line. SAVE THIS CHECK LIST—THE INFORMATION CONTAINED HERE IS ESSENTIAL.

STATION BILLS AND EMERGENCY DRILLS

Disaster has a habit of striking suddenly and unexpectedly. In order to avoid loss of life and damage to the ship, all American merchant vessels must have station bills giving alarm signals and emergency duties of each member of the crew. The alarm signals must become second nature. Although some of these signals have been mentioned earlier, all the signals used aboard ship are grouped together below for convenience:

Fire and Emergency—Rapid ringing of the ship's bell and continuous ringing of the general alarm bells for a period of at least ten seconds.

Abandon Ship—More than 6 short blasts and 1 long blast on the whistle and the same signal on the general alarm bells.

Man Overboard—Hail, and pass the word, "Man Overboard" to the bridge. Many masters supplement this by sounding three long blasts on the whistle which will be repeated several times. This is the International one letter signal for "Oscar" which means "Man Overboard."

Dismissal—From *Fire and Emergency stations*: 3 short blasts on the whistle and three short rings on the general alarm bells.

Where whistle signals are used for handling boats: Lower boats—1 short blast on whistle. Stop lowering boats—2 short blasts on whistle. Dismissal from boat stations—3 short blasts on whistle.

Before sailing, station bills and muster lists must be posted in the crew's quarters and in conspicuous places on every passenger vessel and also on every other vessel of more than 500 gross tons which is subject to inspection. The station bill must contain full particulars of the signals which will be used for calling all members of the crew to their stations for emergency duties.

The duties provided for by the station bill include the following:

1. Closing the airports, watertight doors, fire doors and fire screens, covers and all valves of all scuppers, sanitary, and other discharges through the hull below the margin line, and stopping the fans and ventilating system.

2. The extinction of fire.

3. The equipment of boats, rafts, and buoyant apparatus, and their preparation for launching.

4. The muster of passengers, which includes warning the passengers, seeing that they are dressed and have on properly adjusted life preservers, assembling them and directing them to appointed stations, keeping order, and generally controlling their movements.

Special duties shall be allotted to each member of the crew, and the muster lists shall show all these special duties and indicate the station to which each man must go, and the duties he has to perform. The special duties should, as far as possible, be comparable to the regular work of the individual.

The station bill should be prepared in conformity with specimen Standard Form Station Bills, a copy of which may be obtained from the Officer in Charge, Marine Inspection. The emergency signals and instructions have been incorporated in this form.

The continuous ringing of the general alarm bells has but one meaning —fire and emergency. The crew, trained to recognize this signal, shall proceed to their emergency stations immediately and carry out their allotted duties quickly and effectively. In the event of an actual collision, or stranding, those men assigned to fire hose, hydrants, axes, extinguishers, etc., must assist in closing all airports, side scuttles, side ports, watertight doors, and ventilator ducts in the vicinity of their stations.

The General Rules and Regulations provide that the master of any vessel may establish such additional emergency signals as will provide that all the officers, crew, and passengers of the vessel will have positive and certain notice of the existing emergency.

The ten standard instructions provide for emergencies which may occur on board the various types of vessels. Where one or more of these instructions does not apply to a particular type of vessel, they need not be considered. The crew, however, will be familiar with all standard instructions in the event they are transferred to a vessel to which they are applicable.

The advantages of this form are numerous. For instance, when a member of the crew wishes to find his emergency stations, he may look under the respective department in the left-hand column and follow down until he arrives at his rating and number and then read to the right in each column for his station and duties at each emergency drill. With this form in use throughout the merchant service, the personnel become thoroughly familiar with it and need not study and interpret a different form each time they change ships. In this manner, the emergency drills become highly efficient and well organized, as crews become familiar with all standard emergency drill signals and procedures prior to reporting aboard and need only to ascertain the specific post and duties of their assignments.

The object of the standard station bill is to provide a uniform system for training the members of crews of all vessels in the duties that they would be required to undertake in the event of any accident to the vessel which may, if not skillfully handled, involve the abandonment of the vessel. Such uniform training builds up an efficient organization so that in an actual emergency such as fire, stranding, or collision, the appropriate members of the crew will immediately proceed to their allotted stations and carry out the duties assigned to them with a view to dealing with the emergency. Should the abandonment of the vessel become necessary, they will promptly prepare the boats and other lifesaving equipment for use, warn the passengers, and control their movements in the interest of safety.

The preparation of station bills is facilitated by indicating the berth of article number (instead of names) of the individual members of the crew, with the emergency duties assigned to them. A number and card should be fixed to each berth or issued to each member of the crew at the time of signing articles. This supplementary station bill card shows the emergency duties in detail, the location of the station. All signals connected with these duties should be included. In order to provide for a permanent assignment to lifeboats, the station bills should be made up on the basis of maximum passenger and crew capacity.

Station bills must be framed and posted under glass to command the attention of the entire personnel and serve as a guide and constant reminder of what is required and expected of them. On board vessels employing large crews, it is recommended that the station bill be made up in sections and posted in the mess room, quarters, or passageway adjacent to quarters of each department.

The use to which the lifeboats, life rafts, or buoyant appliances which are provided against the contingency of the vessel having to be abandoned, will be put during an emergency depends on the efficiency of the crew. It is not enough that individual members of the crew should be experts in the managment of a boat. Well-organized teamwork is necessary and the organization must cover not only the lowering and handling of the boats or rafts, but also the effective manning of all emergency stations. No amount of material improvement in equipment and arrangement can take the place of a well-instructed, disciplined, and properly organized crew. The establishment of uniformity is essential.

The duties connected with the assisting and controlling of the passengers should normally be assigned to certain members of the steward's department. In emergencies they shall warn all passengers, assist them to obtain and put on life preservers and direct them to the assembly or embarkation stations. They are to keep order in the stairways, passages and doorways, and impress upon passengers the serious danger of injury from leaping overboard. In this connection, the importance of using the side ladders for the purposes of entering the boats should it prove necessary to embark after the boats have been lowered into the water, should be pointed out. At drills they should explain to the passengers the process of abandoning ship and emphasize that the general alarm signal is not itself a signal to abandon ship, but is intended to secure the orderly assembly of passengers at the appointed stations. The steward's department crew should encourage the attendance of all passengers during emergency drills and should be prepared to instruct and assist the passengers. Passengers and crew must be cautioned against attempting to pass through doorways while watertight doors are in motion or the closing signal is sounding.

On all vessels, the allocation of members of the crew to the duties of closing airports and distributing life preservers to the passengers in various parts of the vessel, and preparing and launching the life rafts and buoyant apparatus, should receive special attention.

Cards posted in staterooms for the instruction of passengers must clearly state the various emergency signals and the location of the allotted assembly station of the occupants, or the number of the lifeboats to which they are assigned.

In assigning the crew to stations and duties comparable to their regular work, consideration should be given to the quarters and working station of personnel.

The importance of organizing and training an emergency squad cannot be overemphasized. This squad must be carefully selected from the crew for their experience, intelligence, and endurance. On the signal, the squad assembles near the bridge with fire axes, crowbar, fire extinguishers, extra lengths of hose, gas masks, life lines, first-aid kit, safety-lamp, flashlight, etc., and then proceeds to the scene of action under proper direction and takes over the real work of clearing away wreckage, fighting fires, etc. In the event of a man overboard, the emergency squad shall assist the emergency boat crew clear away and swing out the lee boat and tend the boat falls or winch; assist the boat crew into life preservers and, if necessary, fill in the vacant thwarts to man the boat in the shortest possible time. This squad and all officers should be instructed in the operation of the emergency steering gear, auxiliary lighting system, oxygen-breathing apparatus, steam-smothering and CO_2 control valves and cut-off valves to fuel-oil system. On vessels where the size of the crew permits, the carpenter, plumber, machinist, and electrician should be included in this squad.

Men must be assigned to closing all ports and overboard discharge valves (except those in the engine room) below the bulkhead or main deck under proper direction. Watertight doors shall in all cases be closed immediately upon sounding of the emergency signal. After a collision, the machinery for closing these doors may be damaged.

Men from each lifeboat should be assigned to the embarkation deck to assist passengers entering the boat and capable men must be assigned to lead out and tend painters. Painters should be made fast at the ship's rail in such manner that they may be readily released from that position even if under severe strain. The sea painter should be made fast at a point in its length with due regard to the vessel's draft on each particular voyage so that when the boat is in the water and the sea painter is taking the strain, the boat fetches up abreast a lifesaving net.

The practice of assigning a small group of men in the charge of a deck officer to prepare all lifeboats and swing them out ready for lowering on the emergency signal is to be encouraged. In the event the emergency gets beyond control, the boats will then be ready for abandoning ship and the crew assigned to abandon ship stations accordingly.

Only competent men should be entrusted with the command or as second in command of lifeboats. A comprehensive knowledge of the boat problem is necessary so that under various circumstances a lifeboat may be launched successfully. Hesitation and insufficient leadership are direct incentives to accident. This consideration demonstrates that the boat commander and the man attending the releasing gear have responsible tasks and that skilled cooperation is absolutely necessary. The lifeboat commander has charge of the entire operation and should be in the boat during the operation of lowering because he must decide the opportune moment for releasing the boat falls.

The practice of conducting a combined fire and boat drill has apparently been adopted by ship masters because of its convenience. Emergency drills conducted on specific days at the same hour do not demonstrate crew efficiency. This practice finds the crew waiting for the fire signal with their life belts already on and the engineers warned well in advance of the imminent use of the fire pumps. Boat drills should be separated from fire drills occasionally to insure prompt response to the boat station signals. That portion of the crew who are on watch during these prearranged drills seldom are mustered at their emergency stations during the entire voyage.

The fire pumps shall be started immediately upon sounding of the fire and emergency signal and must be properly attended. The relief valves will dispose of excess pressure.

Although the size of the crew is limited on freight and tank vessels, each member of the crew must be assigned to definite duties in emergencies, such as closing shaft alley doors, attending the steam-smothering system, putting the plug in No. 2 boat or forward fall of No. 1 boat, attending painter, etc.

Many cargo vessels and tank ships are certificated to carry persons in addition to crew. The steward's department should assist these passengers with life preservers and direct them to the allotted lifeboats.

Cargo vessels equipped with watertight doors should have men assigned to close the doors. The crew, divided as equally as possible and assigned to all lifeboats, must be mustered and instructed during these drills. While it is true that these vessels carry sufficient lifeboats on each side for all persons on board, conditions may exist on the vessel whereby the crew cannot reach their respective boats. Therefore, all boats should be manned and as many as possible launched in case of emergency.

EMERGENCY SQUAD

The masters of ocean, coastwise, Great Lakes, bay, sound and river passenger, cargo, and tank ships should organize and train a squad of men for the special duty of handling any emergency that might occur on board ship. This so-called emergency squad, consisting of from 6 to 24 men depending on the size of the crew, should be selected for their skill in their special calling, such as able seamen, quartermasters, boatswains, carpenters, electricians, and deck engineers or oilers. They should be placed under the charge of the chief officer and trained to respond promptly to such emergencies as fire aboard ship, man overboard, steering gear casualties, collision, and to handle emergencies effectively.

SUGGESTIONS FOR SEAMEN

Men at windlass brakes should always wear goggles when dropping anchor, to avoid eye injury due to flying particles. Goggles should be worn at all other times when any work is being done which might be injurious to the eyes.

Riding pawls or devil claws should always be kept in place on anchor chains while a vessel is at pier to prevent injury to persons in the vicinity.

Chains should never be used with links knotted or kinked. They should never be shortened by wiring, tying, or bolting two links together.

Beckets should be used on the eyes of all mooring lines as hand grips when placing eyes over bitts, bollards, etc. This will prevent fingers from being jammed or crushed.

A sufficient number of turns of mooring lines around the gypsy heads should always be taken to hold the strain without slipping. The lines should always lead fair to the gypsy head.

When lowering or topping booms, always take the topping lift fall to the gypsy head with at least four turns.

Runners (cargo falls) should be properly secured to winch drums (preferably by wire clips, and never by rope yarns) before working cargo.

Runners should always be led from the top of the winch drum to the heel block in order to prevent fouling.

Topping lift wires should always be properly secured on cleats to prevent them from jumping off.

Davit crank handles should always be fastened with cotter pins or lock nuts to prevent them from slipping off during operation.

On blocks on boom topping lifts, cargo falls, guys, etc., use only shackles having screw pins with lock nuts and cotter pins. The jaws of other types may open, shearing the pin, and permitting the booms, cargo drafts, etc., to fall.

All wire splices should be parceled and served to prevent hand injury.

When splicing wire, the marlinespike point should always be away from the body.

Chain stoppers should always be used for wire topping lifts.

Snatch blocks should be used only when other blocks cannot be used.

All hooks should be carefully moused. When possible, shackles should be substituted.

When rigging a bos'n's chair on a stay with a shackle, never allow the shackle pin to ride on the stay—it might unscrew.

Strongback bridles should always have a lanyard of suitable length attached to each end above the hook. This will prevent many injuries to hands.

Strongbacks should be stowed as near the bulwarks rail as possible, and on their sides.

Tarpaulins should never be placed over an open hatch, or over one where some of the covers or strongbacks are not in place.

Hatch covers should not be used as skids or discharging platforms. They may be damaged, with consequent injury to men.

When working a hatch section, all covers and strongbacks should be removed. If this is impossible, those remaining should be carefuly secured to prevent unshipping.

Boiler compounds should never be used for washing paint work. They are too powerful for that purpose. They may lead to infection, if improperly handled.

Compartments which have been closed for a long time, especially tanks or double bottoms, should not be entered until tested and found to be gas free and to contain oxygen. When entering such a compartment, another person should always be present.

When painting, or handling paint in a compartment, it should be well ventilated.

During a period of fumigation, no one should remain on board. When fumigation is completed, no one should go on board until all compartments have been thoroughly ventilated.

Bunks should not be turned upside down or reversed so that the protection of the guard rail is lost.

Pilot's and Jacob's ladders should always be kept properly secured—never to the rail—and their rungs intact and free from oil, grease, etc. Pilot's ladders should be used only by pilots.

Men working over the side, or in unprotected and hazardous positions aloft, should always use safety belts or bowlines without slack in the safety lines. These lines should be made fast, independent of the staging, etc.

A safety belt should be put on before going over the side or aloft, and should not be removed until the return on deck.

Extraordinary care should be used when working on smokestacks.

Stagings should be bolted together, not nailed, and should have supports at least every 8 feet.

All staging lines should be securely attached to strong supports, never to rails or stanchions.

When working aloft, all tools should be secured to lanyards.

Loose tools should never be left on gratings or other places from which they might fall.

DONT'S FOR SEAMEN

Never smoke on deck, on barges, or on the pier when fuel oil is being loaded or discharged.

Never smoke in the vicinity of open hatches or in cargo holds.

While cargo lighters are alongside, do not throw lighted matches, cigarettes, etc., over the side or out of portholes.

Never go up and down ladders with both hands full.

Never work in the hot sun without protecting the head.

Never walk on the side where cargo is being worked.

Never walk under heel blocks of winches.

Never walk on carelessly piled hatch boards.

Never walk through unlighted 'tween deck spaces.

Never walk on weather side of decks in heavy sea.

Never walk on wet or oily decks with rubber soles or heels.

Never stand in the bight of an anchor cable or line.

Never work aloft without a safety belt and line.

Never use goggles to protect forehead instead of eyes.

Never enter a gas-filled hold without a life line. Some gas masks have a ring at the back of the harness for a life line; use a French bowline if the type you have does not.

SAMPLE LIFEBOATMAN'S EXAMINATION

The following sample is representative of what to expect on a lifeboatman's examination. However, it is not official. The lifeboatman's examination is made up by the U.S. Coast Guard Institute in Oklahoma City, Oklahoma. It is a multiple-choice type examination and consists of 50 questions. Proper preparation requires a complete understanding of the material covered, a careful study of CG-175, and a study of this and other chapters of this text. Anyone who by some unfortunate chance succeeds in passing his lifeboatman's or able seaman qualification and is not properly prepared will only be a hazard to himself and his shipmates.

1. The way to operate the hand-held distress flare is to:
    a. remove cap and pull ignitor wire
    b. remove cap and scratch handle on hard object
    c. remove cap and scratch button on flare against the surface on the cap
    d. turn cap clockwise
2. Who should test and inspect an inflatable life raft?
    a. Chief Mate
    b. qualified sales and service representative
    c. shipyard personnel
    d. certified lifeboatman
3. Inflatable life rafts are provided with:
    a. a Very pistol
    b. a towing connection
    c. a portable radio
    d. canned milk
4. Life rafts must be overhauled and inspected at least every:
    a. 6 months
    b. 12 months
    c. 18 months
    d. 24 months
5. The purpose of underwater pockets on a life raft is to:
    a. store rain water
    b. stabilize the raft
    c. stow life raft equipment
    d. aid in righting the raft if it inflates upside down
6. Where is the sheath knife in a life raft located?
    a. in the first aid kit
    b. on a line hanging down from the canopy
    c. in the equipment bag
    d. in a pocket on the edge of the raft
7. The primary purpose of the hydrostatic release on a life raft is:
    a. inflate the life raft
    b. test the pressure in the raft
    c. hold raft on its cradle
    d. release the raft if the vessel sinks
8. How do you hand launch a life raft?
    a. pull a cord
    b. cut metal restraining bands
    c. remove elastic packing strap
    d. throw the container overboard

9. The best way to release a life raft from its cradle is by:
   a. cutting the metal straps
   b. the screw turnbuckle on the back of the cradle
   c. lift one end of the raft
   d. push the plunger on the center of the hydrostatic release
10. A life raft should be manually released from its cradle by:
    a. cutting the straps
    b. Rottmer Release
    c. Static release
    d. Hydrostatic release—pushing plunger
11. What position should a person assume if in the sea wearing a life jacket for an extended period of time?
    a. assume spar position; legs extended down, arms spread
    b. legs and arms spread apart lying on back
    c. knees tucked up to chin
    d. lying on stomach face underwater except for breathing
12. A ship's abandon ship signal is:
    a. 6 short blasts and 1 long blast
    b. 1 long for 10 seconds
    c. more than 6 short blasts and 1 long blast
    d. 6 short blasts, more than 1 long blast
13. The lights on the outside of the canopy of an inflatable life raft operate:
    a. by turning on a switch located inside the canopy
    b. only at night
    c. light sensor
    d. automatically
14. When lowering the life raft by hand, what operation should take place?
    a. operating cord detaches automatically
    b. operating cord should be attached to some substantial part of the ship
    c. you should open casing by cutting metal straps
    d. you should inflate the raft on deck first
15. Which operation should be done when launching a portable life raft?
    a. open red valve on CO_2 apparatus
    b. secure operating cord to the vessel
    c. after inflation, detach operation cord from life raft
    d. open life raft casing
16. When a life raft is launched, the operating cord is used for:
    a. a sea painter
    b. cut out and thrown away
    c. to secure the boarding ladder
    d. an emergency fishing line
17. When in a life raft in very cold weather, the greatest danger is:
    a. sharks
    b. freezing
    c. danger of CO_2 from keeping canopy closed
    d. starvation

18. The inflatable bottom on the life raft is to protect you from cold and:
    a. CO_2 asphyxiation
    b. warm water
    c. rough water
    d. to keep the sides of the raft full of air
19. The purpose of oil in the sea anchor is:
    a. to weigh down the anchor
    b. to lubricate the anchor
    c. to repel dangerous fish
    d. to help smooth the sea
20. The operating cord of an inflatable life raft is also used as:
    a. tow line
    b. painter
    c. orange smoke flares
    d. lifeline
21. When reaching ashore in a life raft, the *first* thing to do is:
    a. secure the life raft for possible use as a shelter
    b. go get some firewood
    c. remove the provisions from the life raft
    d. abandon the life raft and send it out to sea in hopes that someone will spot it
22. Signaling device provided in the inflatable life raft is:
    a. Very pistol
    b. orange smoke flares
    c. air horn
    d. lantern
23. The floor of the life raft can be inflated by:
    a. launching raft overboard pull cord
    b. hand pump in tool bag
    c. extra CO_2 canisters for floor
    d. bleeding air out of the sides
24. To haul a life raft back on board, you should:
    a. hook line to eye on raft
    b. pass lines under the raft
    c. hook line to towing bridles
    d. deflate the raft
25. When using the hand held type signaling mirror, one hand is used to hold the mirror and the other:
    a. is held behind the mirror
    b. is held in front of the mirror
    c. used to shield the eyes
    d. used to shield the mirror
26. When lowering boat during rough weather it is advisable to:
    a. avoid the use of frapping lines as it may endanger the boat
    b. lower the boat near the water and have crew board using embarkation ladder
    c. release tricing pendant before removing boat from cradle
    d. have heaving line ready and standing by

27. You are in a raft, drifting at sea, which of the following is an indication of land nearby?
    a. fog
    b. cumulus clouds
    c. birds
    d. flying fish
28. The tricing pendant should be released:
    a. before the boat is lowered
    b. before the passengers get in
    c. after the passengers get in
    d. after the boat is afloat
29. If you are headed 270° True in a life raft, you are going:
    a. north
    b. south
    c. east
    d. west
30. Life rafts are less maneuverable than lifeboats due to their weight, shallow draft and:
    a. large number of appurtenances
    b. large sail area
    c. greater amount of equipment
    d. inability to withstand heavy seas
31. If the inflatable life raft is to be taken in tow, the towline is to be connected to the:
    a. towing connection (bridle)
    b. life line
    c. boarding ladder
    d. all of the above
32. Which of the following would help to survive an extended period in a life raft?
    a. wet clothing to prevent the body from dehydration
    b. keep the raft pumped up as hard as possible
    c. keep busy
    d. all of the above
33. Item "A" refers to:
    a. tripping line
    b. frapping line
    c. boat falls
    d. tricing pendant
    (See Figure 10-10.)
34. The lever for the mechanical disengaging apparatus on a lifeboat shall be marked by:
    a. painting the lever white
    b. painting the area around the lever red
    c. the words "Danger Lever Lowers Boat"
    d. painting the lever red
35. Water should not be issued to occupants (healthy people) of a life raft for:

   a. 8 hours
   b. 10 hours
   c. 24 hours
   d. 48 hours

36. A lifeboat's portable radio telegraph must be able to:
   a. transmit only
   b. take RDF bearings
   c. operate without an antenna
   d. work any ship's auto alarm system

37. The command, in a boat under oars, to complete the stroke and place oars in the boat:
   a. oars
   b. way enough
   c. hold water
   d. in bows

38. After rigging the emergency radio in a lifeboat, the ground wire should be:
   a. secured to the mast
   b. secured to a thwart
   c. secured to a rowlock
   d. put in the water

39. The floating orange smoke signal is ignited:
   a. automatically by water
   b. by a small pull wire
   c. by striking the cap on the striker bottom
   d. by lighting a match

40. When should Manila lifeboat falls be renewed?
   a. every 6 months
   b. every 1 year
   c. every 2 years
   d. every 3 years

41. The purpose of air tanks in a lifeboat is to:
   a. help the lifeboat float
   b. add strength to the lifeboat
   c. keep lifeboat afloat if boat becomes flooded
   d. put in provisions

42. When first using the compass in a lifeboat you must be careful to:
   a. be sure to mount it on the centerline of the boat
   b. add western variation to error
   c. disregard deviation because the lifeboat is so small compared to the ship
   d. check compass for error at noon

43. In Figure 10-20, "C" is the:
   a. footing
   b. floor
   c. provision tank
   d. stuffing box

44. The type of davit most easily lowered by one man is:
    a. radial davit
    b. sheath davit
    c. quadrantal
    d. gravity
45. Which primarily functions as a support?
    a. limber hole
    b. thwart
    c. stanchion
    d. footing

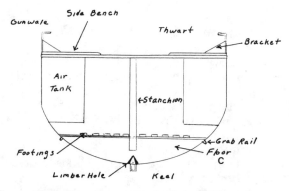

Figure 10-20. Transverse cross section of lifeboat. Drawing: Midn. Eric Pett, California Maritime Academy.

46. What is the length of the heaving line on an inflatable life raft?
    a. 10 fathoms
    b. 15 fathoms
    c. 20 fathoms
    d. 25 fathoms
47. The greatest hazard to survival of a person in the sea is:
    a. weakening of the muscles due to wave action
    b. muscle cramps
    c. exposure to sun and wind
    d. loss of body heat
48. The most commonly used davit on merchant vessels today is:
    a. radial
    b. sheath screw
    c. gravity
    d. quadrantal
49. Limit switches must be tested at least once every:
    a. week
    b. month
    c. 2 months
    d. 3 months

50. Which type of davit stays at the same height when lowering the boat?
    a. gravity
    b. sheath screw
    c. radial
    d. quadrantal
51. What is the most important thing to check before lowering a boat?
    a. oars
    b. life jackets
    c. sea painter
    d. boat plug
52. One short blast of the whistle means:
    a. secure lifeboats
    b. raise boats
    c. lower boats
    d. drill is over
53. When lowering a lifeboat to the embarkation deck, which of the following are used to bring the boat to the side of the ship?
    a. pull lines
    b. boat hooks
    c. tricing pendants
    d. frapping line

ANSWERS TO SAMPLE LIFEBOATMAN'S EXAMINATION QUESTIONS

1. c	20. b	39. b
2. b	21. a	40. c
3. b	22. b	41. c
4. b	23. b	42. a
5. b	24. c	43. b
6. d	25. a	44. d
7. d	26. d	45. c
8. d	27. b	46. a
9. d	28. c	47. d
10. d	29. d	48. c
11. c	30. b	49. a
12. c	31. a	50. c
13. d	32. c	51. d
14. b	33. a	52. c
15. b	34. d	53. c
16. a	35. c	
17. c	36. d	
18. c	37. b	
19. d	38. d	

CHAPTER XI

HANDLING SMALL BOATS UNDER OARS AND POWER

HANDLING SMALL BOATS UNDER OARS

THE ABILITY TO HANDLE A SMALL BOAT under oars is still a necessary skill for the seaman. Mastery of the techniques must be demonstrated before the Coast Guard will certify anyone as lifeboatman. Even though many lifeboats are maneuvered by a motor or a propeller turned by hand propulsion machinery, the necessity of putting an oar propelled boat into the water happens at unexpected times. It is important to be prepared in the event of an emergency.

Figure 11-1. Harry Lundeberg Seamanship School lifeboat crew crossing the finish line to win the 26th International Lifeboat Race in New York Harbor. Race was held 4th of July weekend, 1979. Courtesy: Harry Lundeberg Seamanship School, Inc.

Training with oars is frequently done with emergency boats, surf boats or old Navy whaleboats. The reason is that lifeboats are not very handy or maneuverable although well-suited to their main purpose of keeping a capacity load of survivors safe until rescue.

Manning the boat—Trouble getting the boat into the water usually occurs at the launching stage—the time when the boat is lowered on the falls and before it is completely waterborne. Proper training shortens this period and adds considerably to the successful launching of the boat.

The boat crew acts as a team at all times: when the boat is being launched, when it is in the water, and when it is being recovered. Each

Figure 11-2. Stand by the oars. Lundeberg Seamanship School lifeboat crew getting ready for the 1979 International Lifeboat Race. Courtesy: Harry Lundeberg Seamanship School, Inc.

person knows his own duties as well as those of his shipmates in the boat crew. At lifeboat drill, it is advisable that stations be rotated so that every crew member can perform the duty of any other in an emergency.

OAR, SWEEP OAR, AND SEA PAINTER

A boat is controlled by its oars, sweep oar, and the sea painter when being towed alongside the ship.

The oar—The oar, shown in Figure 11-3, is made of hardwood, probably ash or oak. The part of the loom which rests on the rowlock is called the leather whether the strapping is leather, canvas, or simply bare wood.

To *ship the oar*, first ship the rowlock. Grasp the handle of the oar with the inboard hand. Pick up the oar at the loom with the other hand, using an underhand grip. Lift the oar so that the blade rests on the gunwale forward, inboard of all rowlocks. This is the first step and is done at the command, "Stand by the oars."

The next step, which is taken at the command, "Out oars," is to lift the oar and place it in the rowlock. This brings the boat to the position known as *oars*.

Oars are boated in one step, which is a reversal of the second step used in shipping oars. At the command, *Boat the oars*, reach outside the rowlock, grasp the leather with an underhand grip and, at the exact moment of lifting, force down the handle. This springs the oar upward and makes it easy to toss it to a 45 degree angle, after which it is swung forward and laid on the thwarts. Unship the rowlock. This same operation is done from rowing when the command *Way enough* is given. In this case, the stroke is completed and then the oars are boated.

Stroke oars boat their oars last.

Rowing—Hold the oar horizontal, blades perpendicular, with wrists up and arms extended full length. Lean forward until the knuckles almost touch the back of the man in front. In this position, the oar should be at about a 45 degree angle to the boat's keel. Dip the blade into the water deep enough to immerse the blade but not the loom. Bracing the feet against the

Figure 11-3. Parts of an oar. Drawing: Midn. Marty Gipson, California Maritime Academy.

stretchers, swing the body back, keeping the arms straight until the body is well past perpendicular. Then pull the handle in to the chest, bending the elbows and keeping them close to the body. Bring the oar back until the thumbs touch the chest. Lean well back on oars at the end of each stroke. Feet on the stretchers and the weight of the oar will assist in maintaining balance.

At the end of the stroke, break the oar out of the water steadily. Moving forward for the next stroke, feather the oar by rolling it forward a quarter of a turn by dropping the wrists.

The aft starboard oar is the stroke oar and all of the other oars get their pace from it. The best way to keep in stroke is to watch the back of the man ahead. Do not fall into the habit of watching your own oar. This is a bad habit, easy to form and hard to break. Proper rowing means to pull with the back. Proper cadence means to watch the back of the man ahead.

If the oar is fouled in the water on the recovery stroke, which is called "catching a crab," trail the oar. The coxswain should call *Oars*, to give the trailed oar time to get back in stroke.

The Steering sweep or Sweep oar—This is like the other oars except that it is usually about 2 feet longer. The sweep is always stowed on the thwarts with the blade aft. Sweeps may be shipped on an athwartship piece of wood called a bumpkin with a specially designed metal crutch or closed rowlock, or even a rope becket. Lifeboats usually use a regular rowlock. Sweeps can be marked with a white tip or white strips on the blades and handles to distinguish them from the other oars.

Sweeps can be used for propulsion in an emergency by sculling. Sweeps give more positive control than rudders, and in addition they are effective when the boat has no way on her and the rudder is useless.

The first thing to learn is to balance the sweep. The balancing point will not be midway between the tip of the blade and the end of the handle because the buoyancy of the blade in the water helps to support the sweep. This makes it possible to have a good leverage by keeping the longest part of the sweep outboard from the bumpkin. Balance of the blade can only be learned by "feel."

All boats and all vessels have a "turning axis," that is, a point on the keel on which the boat will pivot and turn when a side force is applied to the bow

Figure 11-4. Towing on the sea painter. Kings Point midshipmen getting ready to bring their Monomoy alongside for recovery. Courtesy: U.S. Merchant Marine Academy.

or stern. This turning point is near the center of the keel or somewhat forward of it, depending on the design of the boat or ship. The side force may be applied by the rudder, by the sweep, or, in the case of large vessels, by a tug. In using the sweep to apply this force, remember that the stern always goes in the direction that the handle moves on the power stroke.

In working a boat around with the sweep while it is under oars, take the power strokes while the oars are on the recovery, or "between strokes," as it is sometimes called.

A novice on the sweep oar will have trouble in maintaining his balance in a choppy sea. A good trick is to learn to feather the sweep oar under water at the end of each stroke. In this way the coxswain can "break water"

Figure 11-5. Using the sweep oar. Sweeps give more positive control than rudders. They are effective when boat has no way on, and a rudder would be useless. A student at Harry Lundeberg Seamanship School demonstrates the correct use of a sweep oar in a Coast Guard approved lifeboat. Courtesy: Harry Lundeberg Seamanship School, Inc.

intentionally, rather than haphazardly, and this will greatly assist him in keeping his balance as well as in keeping the sweep under control. The coxswain should support the handle while making the handle support him.

The Sea Painter—A sea painter should not be confused with the regular boat painter. A boat painter is spliced into a ring or shackle on the stem post and can only be released from the deck of the vessel or cut loose with a hatchet, when the boat is to be freed.

The sea painter is longer than the boat painter. At the boat end, it has an eye about 2 feet in diameter. Just above the splice a wood toggle or fid is attached by a lanyard. Sea painters are made fast at the boat by passing the eye under the thwart from forward to aft, then back over the thwart where the eye is spread over the standing part of the painter and toggled. It should be made fast to the second inboard thwart. (*Note*: In many lifeboats the first thwart is built solid with the foresheets to accommodate the large buoyancy tank which is fitted there. Nevertheless, the after part of this triangular space is considered as the first thwart.)

The sea painter is released at the boat by pulling out the toggle. The pull on the painter, exerting its force aft of the stem of the boat, causes the boat to sheer out away from the side of the vessel, thus removing the danger of having the boat slapped against the side of the ship by the action of the wind or waves.

When making the sea painter fast to the boat, have it outboard of everything and with as little slack as possible, so that the pull will not exert undue strain either on the painter or on the boat. If the sea painter is inboard of anything, the painter will become fouled when it becomes taut.

BOAT COMMANDS

Commands for boats under oars have not undergone change for many years. A seaman of 100 years ago would be at home in a boat today.

While most commands are addressed to both banks of oars, it may often happen that the coxswain desires to give the command only to one bank, or he may want to give one command to one bank and another command to the other. For example, if it is desired to bring the boat about quickly he may do so by giving the command *Give way* to the port bank, and *Starboard back* to the starboard bank. In any case, it is good policy to call the *bank* first, followed by the command, rather than calling the command, followed by the bank which is to execute it. Otherwise one bank may begin to execute a command which is not addressed to it.

When one bank of oars is executing one command and the other bank another, and it is desired to give them a command which will apply to both, call *Oars* first. This cancels the preceding command and gives both banks an opportunity to start the new order in unison.

Give new commands at the beginning of the stroke, *not* at the end. This gives the oars an opportunity to complete the stroke and execute the new command in unison.

The commands and how to execute them:

1. *Stand by the oars*—Stroke oar ships his rowlock, clears his oar and lays in on the gunwale, handle shoved forward to proper position. Immediately each man back of the stroke oar does the same thing, keeping his oar *inboard* of the oar in front of him.

2. *Up oars*—The oars are tossed quickly to a vertical position, blades trimmed in a fore-and-aft plane and in line with that of the stroke oar, handles of oars resting on bottom boards, outboard hand grasping loom of oar at height of chin, wrist of inboard arm resting on inboard thigh and steadying oar.

3. *Toss oars*—Complete the stroke and come to "up oars" position. The difference in meaning between this command and "up oars" has disappeared with the passing of time.

4. *Shove off*—Inboard bowman shoves off smartly from the ship's side with boat hook using the blunt end, shoving the boat ahead, if possible. Outboard bowman takes in the painter. Coxswain sheers off and hauls ahead on the stanchions of the gangway or on the grab rope, assisted as necessary by the inboard stroke oar. Fenders are rigged in by men abreast of them. Bowmen place boat hooks fore and aft, seat themselves and get their oars ready.

5. *Let fall (Out oars or Part oars)*—Given when the boat is clear of the ship's side. As the boat sheers off and away from the ship, it may be necessary to let fall the forward oars before there is room for the after oars

Figure 11-6. Lifeboat instruction at California Maritime Academy. All hands must be certified as lifeboatmen before graduation. Photo: Midn. T. H. Miller, California Maritime Academy.

to clear the ship's side. This would be done by the command *1, 2 and 3 let fall*, or *2 and 3 let fall*. Other oars remain vertical until the command *Let fall*. At this command all oars are dropped, blades outboard, into the rowlock. Slip the inboard hand to the handle and come to the position *Oars* with both hands on the handle. Under no circumstances should the blades dip water in letting fall.

    6. *Give way together*—All oarsmen take a full stroke, keeping cadence with the stroke oar, *by watching the back of the man in front of them*. Feathering of the oar should become habitual and automatic. If stroke oars have not been able to get their oars out in position by the time the command *Give way together* has been given, they will do so quickly and take up the stroke. Continue to pull a strong, steady stroke, using the back, and maintain silence.

    7. *Hold water*—This command is given when way is on the boat and a quick stop is desired. Drop the blades in the water vertically, and hold them perpendicular to the keel line. If considerable way is on, especially in a boat that is heavily loaded, considerable care must be used in holding water, or the force of it may carry away the rowlock, gunwale or the oar itself. Under these conditions, drop the oar in the water at a slight angle, top forward, allowing the water to "slip," and gradually bring the blade vertical as way is lost.

    8. *Port hold water (Starboard hold water)*—If the boat is under way and the oars rowing, a quick turn may be made by giving this command to one side only, the other side continuing with the command *Give way*.

9. *Stern all*—When rowing in ahead motion, complete the stroke, then commence to back water, gradually increasing the depth of immersion of the blades.

10. *Back water*—Row in astern motion. The difference in meaning of the command "stern all" and "back water," if any, is becoming lost with the passage of time. In any event, a good coxswain or boat commander should

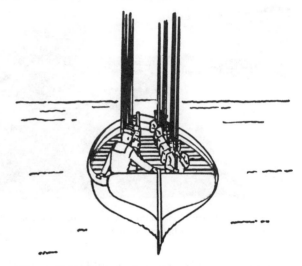

Figure 11-7. "Toss oars."

always give as much warning as possible before giving a new command. He can do this by giving the command, "oars," and then giving the command, "back water." If the boat has any way at all it is good seamanship to give the command "hold water" first to help take way off the boat. Going from ahead to astern without warning may result in broken rowlocks, rowlocks popped out of their sockets, or an oarsman catching a crab. Sometimes the command "port back water" or "starboard back water" is used when it is desired to come about quickly or turn in close quarters. When this is done the other side can either hold water or give way together.

11. *Trail oars*—Used in passing obstructions in which the span of the oars would make passing difficult. It is given when the oars are in the water. Finish the stroke, release the handle of the oar, allowing it to draw fore-and-aft and trail alongside. This command is somewhat awkward to execute, and the oarsman must be careful not to lose his oar. If the boat is in danger of being set down on a dock or other obstruction, oars on that side should be boated to protect them from damage.

12. *Bank oars*—Used to enable oarsmen to rest their arms when laying to and the position of "oars" would be tiresome to hold. Draw the oar through the rowlock until the handle rests on the opposite gunwale. It is given from the command "oars." The command, "Oars across the boat" is sometimes used instead of "Bank oars."

Figure 11-8. "Oars." Kings Point boat crew has completed a stroke and is ready for the next command. Photo: U.S. Merchant Marine Academy.

13. *In bows*—Given as landing is approached, and while the blades are in the water. Bowmen complete the stroke, toss oars and boat them, seize boat hooks, stand erect in bow, facing forward, holding boat hooks vertical in front of them until they are needed.

14. *Way enough*—Given as the boat approaches for a landing, and takes the place of the two commands *Oars* and *Boat oars*. The command is given at the beginning of a stroke. The stroke is completed, oars tossed to about 45 degree angle and boated, forward oar first, stroke oar last. Unship the rowlock. This command may be unnecessary, but can be used to advantage by a good boat commander and a well-trained boat crew.

15. *Oars*—To stop pulling. Given when the coxswain estimates that the boat's headway will carry her to the landing, and while the blades are in the water. Complete the stroke and bring the oars horizontal, at right angles to the keel, blades feathered.

16. *Boat the oars*—Toss the blades to a 45 degree angle, and lay them inside the boat, blades forward, forward oar first, stroke oar last. Unship the rowlock.

LAYING INTO THE BOAT

Fill the outboard thwarts first, starting with the bowmen and working aft, then the inboard thwarts. Coxswain embarks last.

Duties of Each Boatman in Laying in—Outboard bowman stands by forward fall block to release when ordered, which will be when the boat is waterborne. If the boat is equipped with an automatic releasing gear, he sees to it that the block clears the boat and does not foul anyone. If the boat is equipped with split hooks, he removes the turns of the lashing or mousing, except one, and holds this with a "slippery" bight—in other words, pass the end back along the remaining turn, so that on pulling the end the turn is removed and the split hook is tripped.

Inboard bowman stands by the sea painter and lets it go when ordered to do so by the coxswain. He should ignore such commands as *Let go forward* or *Cast off*, since they would cause confusion between the bowmen as to whether the fall or the painter was meant. *There must be no double meanings in boat orders, and it is the coxswain's responsibility to see to it that there are none.*

Figure 11-9. "Out oars."

If a sea painter is not used, the inboard bowman stands by with a boat hook to fend off and the outboard bowman may assist in taking in the regular boat painter. The use of a sea painter usually makes fending off unnecessary.

Up to this point, bowmen have not touched their oars. They man their oars only after the boat is clear of the vessel. When a sea anchor is being used, it is manned by the bowmen.

Oars are numbered fore-to-aft, bowmen being "No. 1 Port oar" and "No. 1 Starboard oar." The first man in the boat puts in the plug or screws home the cap, depending on which is used.

Stroke oars assist the coxswain in clearing and shipping the steering sweep. If a stern fast is used, inboard stroke oar stands by to release it or take it in, and may also assist in fending off.

The outboard stroke oar holds the steering sweep by the handle while the boat is being lowered.

The coxswain attends to the after fall block.

When the coxswain hears *Ready forward* from the bowmen, *Plug in* and *Oars ready* from amidships, and he himself is ready, he reports to the deck, *Boat ready for lowering.*

Laying out of a boat is the reverse of laying in. Inboard thwarts lay out first, except inboard bowman and inboard stroke oar, who remain to assist in hooking on fall blocks if the boat is to be raised. Step from the thwart to the highest accessible rung in the Jacob's ladder. Stepping on the oar looms may result in a sprained ankle, and stepping on the gunwale may cause a crushed foot.

CLEARING THE SHIP OR DEPARTING FROM THE DOCK

All persons should be cautioned against resting arms, hands or fingers on the inboard gunwale while the boat is being lowered or while it is alongside.

Rowlocks should not be shipped at this stage. Aside from the danger of mashed fingers, the rowlocks themselves may be bent or broken and rendered useless.

The boat is lowered on an even keel, slightly down by the stern if the vessel has any headway at all. The moment the boat is waterborne, the coxswain releases the after fall and takes the sweep. He orders *Let go the forward fall*, and as soon as the pull is off the boat it will sheer out on the sea painter. As it does so, he orders *Stand by the oars*.

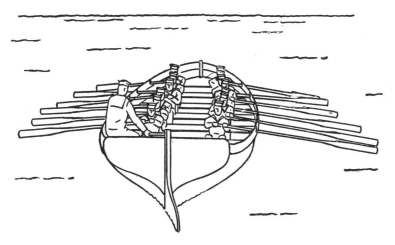

Figure 11-10. Stand by to give way together.

The boat will be allowed to ride the sea painter until it is well clear of the ship's wash, two boat lengths usually being sufficient. The coxswain orders *Let go the sea painter*, and follows this immediately with *Out oars*.

If no sea painter is used, or if the boat is to pull away from a dock, the next problem is shoving it off. Since the boat can be pushed fore-and-aft but cannot be shoved bodily athwartships, it will have to be shoved off either bow first or stern first. Either can be done effectively if the boatmen know their orders.

In moving out bow first there is danger that the coxswain will have to unship his sweep, thus leaving the boat without its most valuable asset for control at the moment when it is most needed, or run the risk of having it snapped off.

Since the port and starboard banks of oars function almost the same as the twin screws of a vessel, they can be used independently. If the port side of the boat is inboard, the starboard oars can be shipped and used to give the boat headway while the inboard bowman pushes the bow out and the coxswain keeps it out with the sweep. At this angle, it will be only a few moments until the boat is sufficiently clear so that both banks of oars can be shipped.

LANDING

Landing is more simple than departure for it involves relinquishing control of the boat rather than gaining control of it.

A good estimation of the way of the boat, the current and the wind is a prime requisite, and when landing to a boat which is underway a good estimation of her headway is necessary for safety.

Come in at an angle, with bow pointing at the point selected for landing. Coxswain should order *In bows* when about five lengths off, in order to give the bowmen ample time to boat their oars and get their boat hooks ready.

The exact moment when *Way enough* should be ordered is important, and it can be learned only by practice. It is essential to order *Way enough* before the inboard oars come too close to the ship's side.

Just before the bow touches the ship (or dock) the coxswain will sheer it off with the sweep. A good landing involves a gradual sheering off so that the boat touches at the waist and with a minimum of bumps.

Inboard bowman takes the painter, which may be a boat rope trailed over the side with a long fore-and-aft bight, or a coiled painter tossed from the deck. He takes a round turn on the same thwart used for the sea painter, making sure that the part in his hand is inboard from the standing part, otherwise it will jam when slacked off. This turn is taken over, then under and back over, the bowman standing aft of the thwart.

The sweep and the fact that the way of the towing vessel will be diminishing will keep the boat from sheering off. The painter may now be slacked until the boat is by a ladder or the fall blocks.

All of the crew lay out except the bowman, one stroke oar and the coxswain.

Landing alongside of docks, quays and jetties is easier than landing alongside a ship, because these places are usually more sheltered and have less wind and current. This does not mean, however, that either the wind or the current can be ignored. Quarters will be closer and other boats may be moving in or out.

Landing at a dock must be as precise as landing to a vessel, for there are definite places having steps or a ladder, and bitts, cleats, etc., for belaying the painter. Landing pontoons are usually low enough to the water so that bowmen can jump out and make the painter fast.

On all landings get the bow well in so that the bowmen will have a good chance to give or receive lines. Once the painter is passed, a few strokes of the sweep will bring the stern in.

When landing between two other boats that are already moored, or in any restricted space, come in at an angle of 45 degrees. In this case, it is better not to use the command *Way enough*, but to come in with the command *Oars*, so that the command *Hold water* can be executed quickly if

Figure 11-11. A 40-foot utility boat coming alongside *Golden Bear* for recovery. Handling a boat under power is not difficult, but it does take practice. Photo: Editors.

the boat has too much way on it. The inboard oars can be boated and when the painter is made fast, back water with the outboard oars and bring the stern in with the sweep.

The use of independent banks of oars is very handy in close quarters and should be encouraged.

Leeway is the drift of a boat to leeward as the result of wind or current or a combination of both. To estimate leeway and to correct for it, observe the point you wish to reach and some prominent object behind it. Keep the point and the object in line and the course is made good even though the bow of the boat is not directly on the point where landing is to be made. The stronger the leeway force, the greater will be the angle of the keel of the boat to the actual dirction it is traveling.

"MAN OVERBOARD"

The approach to a person who is to be picked up in the water is much like the approach to a landing with the added factor that the victim will drift to leeward with the wind and sea while a dock or pier will not.

The parent ship should be to windward of and as close as possible to the victim when the boat is put in the water in order to reduce the time the victim will have to spend in the boat, as well as to shorten the trip the boat will make to pick up the individual in the open ocean.

The most important factor is the safety of the boat because a swamped boat will be of no use to the individual in the water. Whether the approach is made from leeward or windward of the individual will depend upon the circumstances. If the victim overboard is to leeward, then approach from the lee; if to windward, approach from windward. The bowmen should boat their oars a few lengths off and point in the direction of the victim to assist the boat commander in the final approach. Pick up the victim as carefully and gently as possible. The victim may be injured, in a state of shock, or irrational. Therefore, a member of the boat crew should be detailed to tend the victim on the way back to the ship. Voice radio contact between the boat and the ship is very helpful.

HANDLING PROPELLER DRIVEN BOATS

Most newer ships are equipped with either motor-propelled lifeboats or boats fitted with hand propelling equipment which turns a propeller. A few merchant ships and all navy ships have diesel utility boats. The fundamentals of boat handling are much the same whether a boat is propelled by oars or motor, and the same boat etiquette must be observed. However, there are some differences in the maneuverability of the power driven boat.

The following basic rules can normally be used as a foundation for boat handling under power with a right hand propeller:

1. Boat stopped—rudder right—engine ahead——Bow will come right.
2. Boat stopped—rudder left—engine ahead——Bow will come left.
3. Boat stopped—rudder any direction—engine astern——Bow will come right. Stern will come left. (No wind situation)
4. Boat moving astern—rudder left—engine stopped——Stern will come left.
5. Boat moving astern—rudder right—engine stopped——Stern will come right.
6. Boat moving astern—rudder left—engine ahead——Bow will come to left.
7. Boat moving astern—rudder right—engine ahead——Bow will come to right.
8. Boat moving ahead—rudder amidships—engine astern——Stern will come to left or erratic course.

When using a rudder and propeller, the rudder will have no effect when the boat is not moving unless the propeller is in the ahead position causing a wash over the rudder. Boats with a rudder handle very poorly when going astern. The walking effect of the propeller causes a boat with a right-hand propeller to back to port unless this force is overcome by the tendency to back into the wind. If the boat is moving ahead and the engine is shifted astern, a somewhat erratic course may follow. Experience with a specific boat is required before the actual response can be predicted. Even then, the wind and current must be taken into account because they affect the track of the boat.

CHAPTER XII

HANDLING SMALL BOATS UNDER SAIL

Few seamen are boatmen and few boatmen are seamen.
—*Fifth Officer Harold G. Lowe, R.M.S.* Titanic, *1912*

SAILING IS ALMOST A LOST ART in the United States Merchant Marine since steam has replaced sail. With the exception of the few "tall ships" used for training purposes, the sailing vessel has disappeared from the high seas. In the past, a lifeboat launched at sea became a sailboat. When

Figure 12-1. A sight from the past. Danish training ship *Danmark* and U.S. Coast Guard's *Eagle* racing in Kattegat. *Eagle* has stolen *Danmark*'s wind and has pulled ahead. *Danmark* is ship rigged. *Eagle* is a bark. Courtesy: Paul M. Seiler.

the *Titanic* fell victim to an iceberg in the North Atlantic in 1912 all her lifeboats, fitted with sails, enabled those who knew how to use them to fare better than those who did not. Fifth Officer Lowe, both a sailor and a seaman was able to sail his lifeboat to survivors who would otherwise have been lost and to keep a pathetically small group of lifeboats together.

Today, only oar propelled lifeboats must be provided with sails. Large lifeboats are motor driven, and others have hand propelling equipment. So

Figure 12-2. California Maritime Academy sloop *Rubber Duck* crossing the finish line after 1977 trans-Pacific race from Long Beach to Honolulu on California Maritime's first venture in ocean racing. Sailing provides experiences a seaman will acquire in no other way. Also, sailing is fun. Courtesy: John M. Keever.

the compelling reason for knowing how to sail (or to be a boatman as Officer Lowe called it) is gone.

But, there remain excellent reasons for learning how to sail. If you are going to be a seaman or a Merchant Marine officer you will not be happy unless you like the sea. And, if you like the sea, you will want to learn as much about it as possible. There is no better way to learn about tides and currents, weather, or the harbors and bays you will enter and leave on a merchant ship, than by small boat sailing. In the unfortunate event that your ship is lost in either a peacetime or wartime tragedy, small boat experience might save your life—even if your lifeboat has no sails.

Sailing provides a wealth of ship handling experience, useful if you go into tugs or other smaller vessels. As a licensed deck officer or pilot, sailboat experience is priceless.

Although there is not the close association between the Merchant Marine and the yachting world that exists in England, you may be surprised at the respect you, as a professional who earns his living going to sea, will be accorded among yachtsmen. The great number of sailboats in San Francisco Bay, Puget Sound, or Chesapeake Bay indicates that yachting is big business in this country. Opportunities exist for a professional seaman who knows small boats.

Finally, in the 1980's, it has become apparent that there is an energy shortage. The price of fuel oil has gone from $2.50 to more than $30.00 plus a barrel in 1970 to 1980. Newspaper and magazine articles predict that sailing vessels—in some form—will return to the oceans to carry cargo for which speed is not crucial. It is possible your sailing skills will be needed by a large steamship company someday.

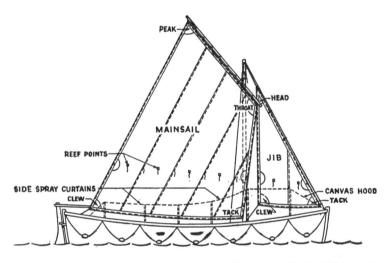

Figure 12-3. Typical lifeboat rig.

The handling of small boats under sail is an ancient art. The first ocean-going boats were small sailing craft, and for approximately 2000 years man depended, for his sailing power, on his ability to harness the wind to his will. This knowledge of the sea and of sailing ships has been handed down through a long succession of seafaring people, from the Phoenicians through the Vikings and the seamen of the Great Age of Exploration to the men of the clipper ships and the modern sailor. Sailing a boat is an art and as such it requires skill which can be achieved only by actual experience; but this skill is founded on considerable knowledge, most of which can be learned before stepping into a boat.

The knowledge, experience and skill of expert seamanship reaches its climax in ocean sailing when land is a thousand miles away. The ocean looks a lot different from the helm of a thirty foot ketch than it does from the bridge of a large container ship or tanker.

There is much for the beginner to learn. One of the most important things is that the average double-end lifeboat is exceptionally seaworthy when handled properly. One should know that, in any kind of a gale, the seaman does not attempt to sail it, but only sees to it that the bow or stern is kept into the seas and that the boat is kept in proper trim.

This chapter will tell the seaman what to do and what not to do. Only by actual sailing will one know how to do it.

To form a sail, strips of canvas in bolt widths are sewed together. In some cases the sails are sewed with the long seam parallel to the leech; in other cases the long seam is perpendiculr to the leech. On the edges they are sewed to ropes called boltropes. Sails are usually strengthened by a tri-angular patch in each corner, and in the wake of the reef points by a canvas strip, or reef band.

Figure 12-4. Rigs of sailing vessels. Courtesy: D. Van Nostrand Company, Inc.

DEFINITIONS OF PARTS OF A SAIL AND ITS ATTACHMENTS

Clew—Lower after corner.
Foot—Lower edge.
Head—Upper edge. In the case of a jib, it is the upper corner.
Leech—After edge.
Luff—Forward edge.
Peak—Upper after corner.
Reef cringle—A thimble attached to the boltrope on the forward and after edges and near the reef points. A line is run through the cringle to assist the reef points in holding a reef.

Reef earing—A piece of line attached to the cringle.

Reef points—Short pieces of line attached in a row across the sail.

Tack—Lower forward corner.

Throat—Upper forward corner. This is also called the nock. A jib has no throat.

RIGS AND RIGGING

Rigs of Sailing Ships—Figure 12-4 shows the rigs of sailing vessels seen on the high seas one hundred years ago. Of historic interest chiefly, the trend from square rigs to fore and aft rigs is indicated. In the later years of sail, many full rigged ships were converted to barks and barkentines in

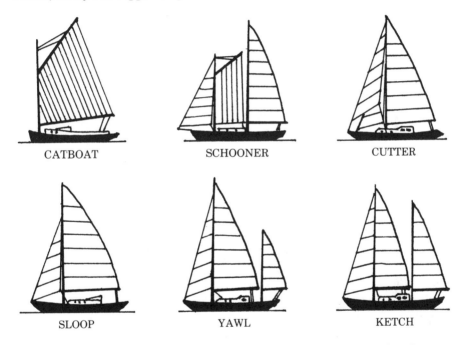

CATBOAT	SCHOONER	CUTTER

SLOOP	YAWL	KETCH

Figure 12-5. Common fore and aft rigs for sailboats and sailing yachts. Drawings: Scott Duncan.

order to permit reduction in the crews. The yachting schooner has given way to the yawl, ketch, and sloop to permit ease of handling and because the "hired hand" has all but disappeared.

Rigs of Sailboats—Figure 12-5 shows the rigs of sailboats. The catboat carries a single sail and has her mast far forward. The schooner is fore and aft rigged, and may have two or more masts although schooners with more than two masts are now rare. The foremast of a schooner is shorter than the mainmast. Both sloops and cutters are "single stickers," and although they differ slightly in appearance, it will not be many years until the difference in definitions of the two will be forgotten. At present the mast of the sloop is mounted farther forward than the cutter whose mast is amidships or just forward of amidships. The cutter frequently carries a forestaysail in addition to her jib. (The term cutter used to apply to a square-sterned ship's boat, but this usage is obsolete.) The two masted rigs which are easily confused are the yawl and ketch. Here again, the difference may disappear in time. The two masts of these boats are known as the mainmast and the mizzen (the latter is sometimes called the jigger). On a yawl the mizzen is smaller and farther aft than on a ketch. As a consequence, on a yawl the helmsman sits forward of the mizzen at the wheel and on a ketch, aft. The novice may think that the mizzen sail is so small it contributes nothing to the boat's speed, but this is not true. Furthermore, it helps in balancing the boat.

Figure 12-6. Areas of much, moderate, and little drive on sails.

(a)   (b)

TYPES OF RIGS

There are a number of types of sailing rigs in use, but only a few will be discussed.

Gaff rig—Originally all fore and aft rigged vessels were gaff rigged. The luff of the sail secured to hardwood or metal rings is free to move up the mast when the sail is raised. Since the mast needs stays and shrouds, the height of the sail is limited by where the mast is stayed. In order to increase the sail area a gaff is used. The gaff increases the sail area, but it is heavy and increases the strain on the mast. In addition, as shown in Figure 12-6, the sail area closer to the mast is the most efficient. Therefore, much of the sail on a gaff rig is of dubious value except when going down-wind.

Marconi rig—About the time of World War I, advancements in metallurgy and design made it possible to attach the luff of the sail to metal slides which were fitted to a track or in a slot on the mast. This permitted staying the mast anywhere it was convenient, and so the height of the sail was no longer limited as illustrated in Figure 12-7. The marconi rig is used on all modern yachts.

Lug rig—The lug rig is a "take-down" rig (Figure 12-3) suitable for lifeboats or small craft not permanently rigged as a sailboat. Instead of being called a "gaff," the spar at the top of the sail is called a "yard." There is a difference between a dipping lug rig and a standing lug rig. One of the two masted luggers in Figure 12-8 has both: A dipping lug is shown on the foremast, and a standing lug on the mizzen. On a dipping lug the tack is forward of the mast and must be "dipped" or passed around the mast when the boat tacks. The other drawing of a lugger shows a standing lug rig on both masts. On the standing lug the tack is secured to the mast so that passing the tack around the mast is not necessary. By modern standards the lug rig is clumsy. However, it is in use in approved rowing lifeboats.

Sprit rig—A sprit rig, also a "take-down" rig, shown in Figure 12-6, is like a lug rig, but one end of the sprit is secured to the peak of the sail and the other end to the mast, a foot or so above the deck. The head is secured to the top of the mast, probably by rovings, and it has no boom. The sprit rig is seldom seen although it is more handy than the lug rig. At one time the dinghy carried by a yacht as a tender might have a sprit rig.

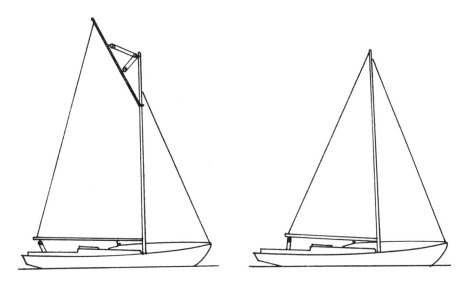

Figure 12-7. Comparison of gaff and marconi rigs. Older gaff rigged sloop is shown at left. If re-rigged as marconi, she appears at right. Drawings: Scott Duncan.

RIGGING

Except for the sprit rig which is said to be loose-footed, the foot of the mainsail is secured to the boom by rovings or by slides attached to a track. The boom in turn is attached to the mast by a gooseneck.

In the gaff and lug rigs the head of each quadrilateral sail is secured to the gaff or yard. The sprit of a sprit rig takes the place of the gaff and is secured to the mast by a rope eye which old salts called a snotter. Marconi-rigged sails are held to the mast by slides which run in a track in the mast as described. Jibs slide up and down on the jib stay secured by snap hooks.

Sails are hoisted by block and tackle arrangements, called halyards. On a larger boat there may be more than one block to make raising the sail

Figure 12-8. Lug rig and sprit rig. Sprit rig is shown at left. Both center and right-hand sketches are luggers, but boat in center has a standing lug rig on both masts. Boat at right has a dipping lug rig on foremast. Its mainsail is a standing lug rig. Drawings: Scott Duncan.

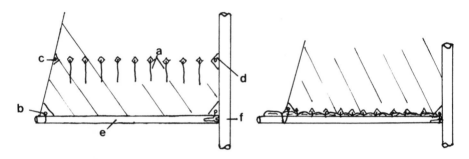

Figure 12-9. Reefing. Letters indicate the following: a. Reef points. b. Clew. c. Clew or leech reef cringle. d. Luff or tack reef cringle. e. Boom. f. Mast. Mast and sail are shown at left before reefing and the reefed mainsail is shown at right. In order to reef it will probably be necessary to luff up into the wind. Sail is dropped until the reef points will reach around the foot of sail. Leech reef cringle is secured to the boom and also pulled as far towards the end of the boom as possible. Tack reef cringle is made snug close to the other end of the boom. It is more seamanlike to secure the reef points around the foot of the sail than to pass them all the way around the boom because they are less apt to become fouled.

easier. Sails may have a line or a tackle which allows a downward pull to be exerted. This is called a *downhaul.*

On a gaff-rigged boat the gaff can be elevated by means of a topping lift which is a purchase attached to it by a bridle.

The outward swing of the boom is controlled by a line called a sheet. This will probably be rigged with a block and tackle.

The heel of the mast rests on the mast-step or some supporting framework. The mast passes through the deck and rests on the keel, or on some boats the mast is stepped on the main deck. Further support is furnished by the standing rigging which is composed of the stays which furnish fore and aft support along with the shrouds which furnish athwartship support. The shrouds are secured to fixtures in the hull called chainplates.

All older sailing vessels, and most of the older sailing yachts, had bowsprits which permitted sails to be rigged farther forward. Handling sails in the cramped space on the bowsprit was difficult and hazardous.

Bowsprits were known as "widow-makers" because many good men were lost when the ship dipped into a big swell.

When the wind is so strong that the lee rail begins to go under, it is time to shorten sail. This is done by reefing. The conventional method of reefing by use of reef points is shown in Figure 12-9.

DEFINITIONS OF SAILING TERMS

Aback—The sails are said to be *aback* when the wind presses their surface aft with a tendency to force the boat astern. This condition may be brought about when the boat has been headed into the wind, either in tacking or to avert capsizing.

About—Changed from one tack to the other. You may *come about, go about,* or have the order *ready about* given.

Backstays—Stays which lead aft.

Bare poles—The condition of a sailing vessel when she has no sail set.

Beating to windward—Sailing close-hauled, first on one tack and then on the other, thereby working gradually up in the direction from which the wind is blowing.

Belay—To make fast.

Bend—To make fast. The sail is bent to a spar.

Bring to—The act of stopping a boat by bringing her head up into the wind.

Broach to—To slew around when running before the wind.

Cleat—A device with two arms on which a line may be belayed.

Close-hauled; by the wind or on the wind—Sailing a boat as close to the direction from which the wind blows as will gain the most distance to windward in a given time.

Douse—To lower quickly, as *dousing* a sail.

Down—Toward the lee side. It is used in connection with the tiller, which may be *put down* (up rudder), toward the lee side, or *up* (down rudder), toward the windward side. This wording was derived from the fact that a sailing vessel practically always lists away from the wind; therefore, the lee side is really down and the weather side up.

Downhaul—A tackle to exert a downward pull on a sail.

Draw—The sails are said to be *drawing* when they are filled with wind so as to give the boat headway.

Ease off—To slack away a line. To head off from the wind.

Free: sailing free; off the wind—Sailing with the sheets eased, on the desired course, without being close-hauled.

Full and by—With the sails as close to the wind as possible and yet filled with wind. This occurs when close-hauled.

Furl—To roll up snugly and secure, as a sail or awning.

Gate—A hinged, semicircular metal band attached to a thwart to help stay a mast.

Gybe—A sail is *gybed* when, in turning a boat's head away from the wind, the sail is allowed to swing from one side to the other; the wind being aft or nearly so, and the sail full, first on one side and then on the other.

Hauled flat—The condition of the sails when they are almost fore and aft, but still drawing.

Heave to—To put a vessel in the position of being stopped, but ready to proceed. Either power or sailing boats may do this.

In irons—Caught by the wind so that a turn cannot be made in either direction.

Jury mast—A temporary mast rigged in place of one lost or broken.

Lee side—The side away from the wind.

Lee shore—A shore onto which the wind is blowing. Dangerous.

Leeward—The direction toward which the wind is blowing; away from the wind.

Leeway—The lateral movement of a ship to leeward of her course, owing to the side thrust of the wind.

Lie to—To remain in practically the same position without anchoring. This may be done in a sailing vessel by *dousing sail, reducing sail,* or *heaving to.*

Loose sail—Unfurl sail and prepare for use.

Luff (verb)—To turn the boat's head into the wind as if to go about, causing the luff of the sail to shake. This should be done when a gust of wind heels the boat over and threatens to capsize her. When the tiller is put down and the boat heads up, the sails spill their wind, the heeling effect from them is lessened, and the danger of capsizing is temporarily averted. The sails should not be spilled completely, but just enough so that the luff begins to shake.

Pay off—To fall off from wind; said of the head of a sailing vessel. To *pay off,* or, preferably, to *pay out,* is also used to define the act of slacking line or sheet so that it may be free to run, but without letting go.

Port tack—Sailing with the wind coming over the port side.

Reach—A course that can be made good sailing off the wind. A straight run between bends in a river or canal.

Reef (verb)—To reduce the area of a sail when the wind is too strong to carry the whole sail. This is done to avert danger of capsizing or damage to sail or mast.

Reeve (verb)—To lead a rope through the proper fair-lead. Example: "Reeve the halyards through a sheave in the masthead, and lead down to a cleat on the mast."

Run—A course that can be made good sailing before the wind.

Running before the wind—Sailing free and with the wind abaft the beam.

Running rigging—Those ropes which reeve or lead through blocks or fair-leads, such as halyards, sheets, etc., by which the sails are controlled.

Sheet—A rope or tackle made fast to the clew of a sail or boom and used to control the angle the sail makes with the wind.

Shorten sail—To lessen or to *douse* sail; usually used as a command to take down sails.

Slack—To lessen tension on a rope by letting it run out.

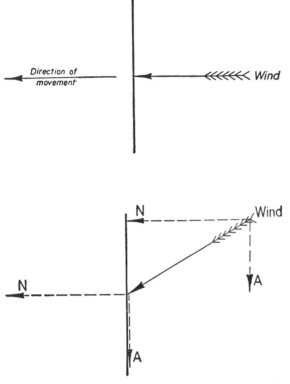

Figure 12-11. Principles of sailing (reaching).

Standing rigging—Those ropes which are stationary, and seldom require alterations, such as shrouds and stays.

Starboard tack—Sailing with the wind coming over the starboard side.

Sternboard—The motion of a vessel in a direction opposite to ahead. We say that a boat acquired *sternboard*, or more usually, *sternway*.

Strike—To shorten or douse; to *strike* sail.

Tack (verb)—To go about. Tiller down (helm alee), causing the boat's head to swing through the wind, and the sails to fill on the opposite side.

Tack (noun)—One leg of the zigzag course steered in beating to windward.

Trim—The difference in draft, forward and aft.

Wear (verb)—Tiller up (helm aweather) so that the boat's head falls off from the wind, sails gybe, and the boat comes by the wind on the other tack. Opposite of *tack*; in wearing, the boat's stern passes through the direction from which the wind comes, while in tacking, the bow passes through the wind.

Weather (verb)—In sailing, to pass to windward of another boat or object. It also means successfully to ride out a squall or storm.

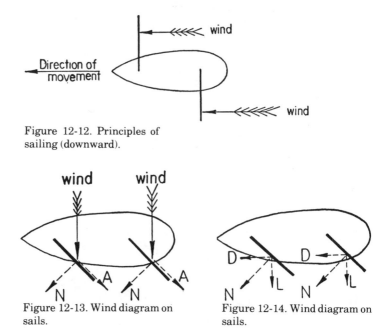

Figure 12-12. Principles of sailing (downward).

Figure 12-13. Wind diagram on sails.

Figure 12-14. Wind diagram on sails.

Weather side—The side toward the wind; opposite of lee side.

Wing and wing—With sails out on both sides. This is done in sailing right before the wind, and an oar or spar may even be used to extend the foot of a boomless sail if the breeze is not too strong.

Yaw—To veer suddenly and unintentionally off the course.

PRINCIPLES OF SAILING

Sails can be used to best advantage in the practical handling of a boat, if one has a general understanding of the theoretical principles of how sails apply the force of the wind in the direction of the keel line from aft, thereby driving the boat forward.

Consider the wind as blowing normal to the plate in Figure 12-10. The wind simply pushes on the plate, driving it in the direction of the wind.

Now consider the wind blowing on the plate at an angle as in Figure 12-11. Let the length of the arrow represent the scale of the force of the wind. Then the force of the wind may be resolved into two components, N normal to the plate and A along the face of the plate. Force component N tends to push the plate in the direction N, whereas A goes harmlessly off the edge of the plate.

Next mount two plates on a boat. When the wind is from aft, the boat will be driven ahead by the pressure of the wind on the plates as shown in Figure 12-12, as was the plate in the paragraph above.

If the boat is not to be driven in the direction of the wind but at an angle to it, the conditions are as shown in Figures 12-13 and 12-14. In Figure 12-13 the wind has been resolved into components normal to and along the faces of the plates.

Considering first the force component N and the fact that the plates are fixed rigid in the boat, it will be noted that this force component has itself two force components referred to the keel line of the boat, L and D (Figure 12-14). The force component L would give the boat leeway (move sideways), but is prevented from doing so by the resistance offered by the water pressure against the boat's side and keel. The component D moves the boat ahead, as the boat's construction has been designed to reduce the resistance offered by the water in this direction. The force component A blowing

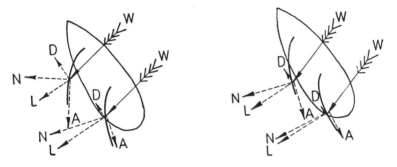

Figure 12-15. Wind diagram on sails.

along the face of the plate exerts no force to drive the boat. It does, however, play an important part in the efficiency of sails, as will be described later.

The A component (Figure 12-13) from the jib or foresail sweeps the eddy currents away from the mainsail and increases its efficiency. This is particularly true when the mainsail and jib overlap as they do when a large jib or genoa jib is used.

BENDING AND SHEETING SAILS

The belly or contour of the sails must be varied according to the force of the wind if the maximum drive is to be imparted to the boat. In light winds sails should have a very curved contour. As in the wings of propeller driven planes which have a maximum lift, the sail will have a maximum drive for the slow speed of the boat. When the breeze is stronger, sails should be flatter, simulating the almost flat wings of a jet plane. Variation of the contour of a rectangular sail is accomplished by giving the head and foot of the sail a slight fullness on hauling them taut when bending them to the gaff and boom. In the same manner is a jib-headed sail varied, except that the length of the leech must be adjusted by shifting the bending of the halyard in the head block. When the foot of such a sail is hauled taut on the boom, the leech must be lengthened, and vice versa. When the sail is being bent, great care must be taken not to spoil the shape of the sail by introducing hard spots, twists, or wrinkles, or by curling the leech.

The breaking in of a sail is important. It should first be bent with a moderate strain on outhauls and halyards and used in this manner until hard spots have stretched themselves out. The strain on boltropes should then be increased carefully to eliminate wrinkles, and thereafter the sail set in the same manner. It is important that the point of maximum curvature be kept close to the mast, or the boat will not sail well to windward. Should the boltrope at the luff be overstretched, not only will this point move aft, but the leech will tend to curl. Too much strain on boom or gaff outhaul creates a hard spot at the throat or tack.

It should be noted that when close-hauled, the *little drive* area parallels the keel of the boat and exerts no forward thrust. Thus, again, most of the forward thrust comes from the *much drive* area. Should the *little drive* area curl or be sheeted past the parallel of the keel, it will act as a drag.

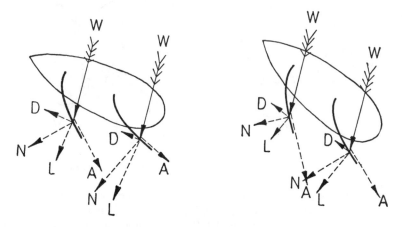

Figure 12-16. Wind diagram on sails.

Sails are sheeted to meet four general conditions: (*a*) On the wind; (*b*) Off the wind; (*c*) Running before the wind; (*d*) Give maximum drive to the mainsail.

(*a*) *On the wind*—It will be noted that, with a given force of the wind, the flatter the sails are sheeted the smaller is the D component and the greater the L component (Figure 12-15). In other words, as long as the boat remains on a course, the flatter the sails are sheeted the more the boat will tend to drift to leeward under the increased force of L, than to move ahead under the reduced force of D.

(2) When the sails have been set, it will be noted that the higher the boat is pointed into the wind the more are the driving force D and the leeway force L reduced. (See Figure 12-16.)

(3) Considering the above principles, the general rule for sailing on the wind is to keep the sails well full, sheets not too flat, but every one drawing and the boat alive. It is a common mistake to get the sheets so flat that the boat, while pointing high, actually makes a course to leeward of that she would make if kept away a little with sheets eased accordingly. Furthermore, as shown in (2) above, the efficiency of the sail is lost for a given sheet setting when the boat is too far off the wind as well as when held too close. The angle of heel is the indicator.

The action of the sails and the fill of the boat is the best indicator in determining the angle of the attack of the wind on the sail for the particular boat under the existing force of the wind and state of the sea. The best setting for the sheets comes from experiment, and improves with the experience of the helmsman. The use of a small pennant mounted on the masthead or one of the stays or shrouds is helpful in determining changes in wind direction. The relative angle that the pennant makes with the wake of the boat is somewhat of an indication of how the boat is pointing and can be used to advantage by beginners. Using fixed objects as ranges to check the course made good is a valuable aid in getting the most out of a set of sails. It must be constantly borne in mind that radical changes in the amount of the sheet are neither necessary nor desirable to improve conditions when pointing on a course. The sheet must be tended with the greatest delicacy for the best results. A boat must never be pointed so high that the luff of any sail flutters (the warning that eddy currents exist behind the sail and the area of greatest drive). When this occurs the drive from that part of the sail is being lost.

(b) *Off the wind*—when sailing off the wind, the boat is headed so that the wake lies along the course desired made good and the sails sheeted accordingly. The general rule is to ease off the sheets in order that the component D may be a maximum. This is accomplished practically by easing off the sheets until the luff of the mainsail quivers (not from the spill of the jib), and then to sheet in until the quivering stops.

(c) *Running before the wind*—When running before the wind the sail should be as nearly as possible at a 90-degree angle to the keel to prevent side thrust and loss of energy by moving the boat sideways through the water. However, very little will be lost in sheeting in the sails just sufficiently to clear the stays or shrouds. It is sometimes desirable to set the foresail or jib on the side opposite to the mainsail and thereby increase the drive area. A temporary boom is rigged by using a boat hook or oar. A boat sailing in this way is going *wing and wing*. The concern of one in charge of a boat running before the wind is not the set of the sails but the danger of gybing or perhaps capsizing. This is discussed later.

(d) *Give maximum drive to the mainsail*—(1) A sail is not a flat plate but has the curve of an airplane wing, and the area adjacent to the luff and along the forward part of the head and foot is the area of greatest drive. To get the most out of a boat, it is essential that the sail be bent so that the area of greatest drive is free from wrinkles which create eddy currents. Furthermore, when sheeting the mainsail, it is not the angle between the boom and the keel line of the boat that establishes the component D, drive of the sail, but it is rather the angle between that part of the sail having the greatest drive (just aft of the luff) and the keel line. The angle must never be such that this part of the sail quivers from eddy currents on the back surface.

(2) It has been stated herein that the spill of the foresail or jib tends, when properly set, to smooth out the eddy currents created by the mainmast on the back of the mainsail. When the foresail or jib is sheeted too flat,

the mainsail will be back sailed by this spill. It will show by a fluttering or dishing in of the mainsail luff. When this occurs, the jib or foresail must be eased at once by slacking off the sheets. As a general rule, because of the curve of the jib or foresail, the foot of these sails should make an angle of about 15 degrees more with the keel line of the boat than the angle of the foot of the mainsail. (See Figure 12-17.)

(3) In order to obtain a maximum drive from the foot of the sails, they should be raised as high above the gunwale as is practical and as the force of the wind will allow with the ballast available. They will then tend to be

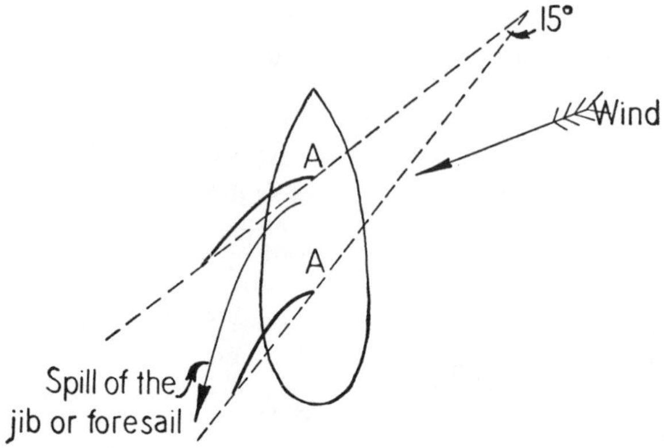

Figure 12-17. Spill of the jib or foresail.

clear of the eddy currents created by the hull of the boat. The ballast available (men) should be used in an effort to keep the boat on as near even keel as practicable. This will present a better angle of attack of the wind on the sail and reduce the blanketing effect of the hull on the foot of the sail. Also, the boat will offer less resistance with the keel against the leeward component, L. The exception is when in light airs a slight list to leeward is required to make the sails draw.

TRIM

By trim of the boat is meant the distribution of ballast, live or otherwise, after sails are set to best advantage. The boat should be trimmed athwartships so as to be kept as near on an even keel as is practicable. The desired fore-and-aft trim in a light or moderate breeze is obtained when the boat holds its course without the use of rudder. In a stiff breeze it is preferable, as a safety precaution, that the boat be trimmed fore and aft so that a slight amount of weather tiller is necessary to hold it on the course (the boat has a tendency to head up into the wind when the tiller is released).

Shifting ballast forward will give the boat a tendency to head up into the wind and will relieve a lee tiller. Shifting ballast aft will give the bow a tendency to drop off and will relieve a weather tiller. This is illustrated in Figure 12-18.

When running free, keep the ballast fairly well aft to hold the rudder deeper in the water and to give the boat a slight drag by the stern.

TACKING

In tacking the sails are sheeted in to bring the boat fairly close-hauled on the wind if not already so. At the moment when less head sea is encountered and the boat has good way on, the tiller is eased down and the mainsail sheeted in amidships gradually as the boat heads into the wind.

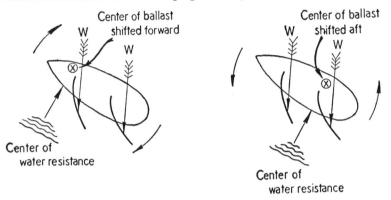

Figure 12-18. Center of water resistance.

The foresails are sheeted in, so as to be kept full, as long as they will draw. As the boat approaches heading directly into the wind, the critical moment of the maneuver occurs. At the instant the headsails cease to draw (luff flutters), their sheets should be cast off. The sails will flap. As the bow pays off on the new tack (crosses the wind), the headsails are shifted over and sheeted well in, and the mainsail sheets cast off. When the boat is well over on the new tack, the tiller is eased and sheets are adjusted to steady on the new course. When this maneuver is done properly the boat makes a good reach to windward and fills away on the new tack without for a moment losing headway. If, when almost headed into the wind, the boat seems about to lose headway, it is sometimes then desirable to hold the jib out on the old lee side with the sheets just cast off. The sail will act as a back sail to pay her head around. When this is done the main sheets must be cast off as soon as it ceases to draw. To hold the main sheets is liable to make a *back sail* of the mainsail, thereby putting the boat *in irons* or giving her sternboard. Weight should be shifted aft. If the boat gathers sternboard, shift over the rudder and do not sheet in the mainsail until the new tack has been made by backing around. The head sails should be eased over as the boat's stern backs up into the wind. When filling away on a new tack, it is advisable to run for a short time with slightly eased sheets in order to regain full headway quickly.

The use of an oar at any time with a boat under sail is lubberly and should only be resorted to in an emergency.

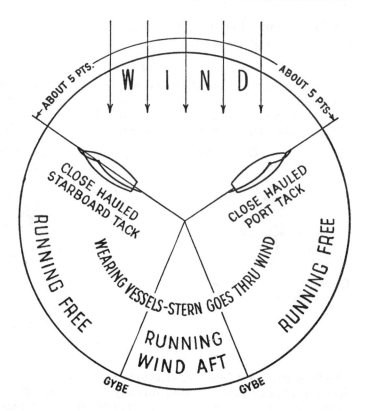

Figure 12-19. Sailing diagram close hauled and running free.

WEARING

How you wear a boat depends upon the force of the wind.

(1) *In a very light breeze* and when it is desired to come to the other tack by wearing, the tiller is put up slowly, and the mainsail sheets eased full off, roundly. As the bow pays off, the headsails are kept filled by gradually easing off the sheets. The boat goes off before the wind. Then as the boat comes to the other tack, the mainsail is sheeted in smartly, shifted over, and eased away steadily on the new lee quarter, the ballast shifted forward, and the headsail sheets cast off and allowed to flow. When well about, all sails and the ballast are trimmed to steady on the new course.

(2) *In a moderate or fresh breeze* the same procedure is followed except in the handling of the mainsail. The increased way on the boat will permit relying more upon the rudder than upon the sails to wear. Accordingly, when the tiller is put up, the mainsail is eased off only enough (about 60 degrees) to prevent the boat from heeling too deeply when well off the wind. Then, as the wind hauls aft, the mainsail is sheeted in gradually until amidships when the wind is astern. As the boat comes to the other

tack, the mainsail is eased away steadily on the new lee quarter. If the breeze is too strong to gybe safely—don't!

GENERAL PRECAUTIONARY NOTES

Reefing—When a boat begins to take water, it is time to reef; she should never, even in smooth water, be allowed to heel too much. A boat that is decked over may run her lee rail awash; but when an open boat is approaching this point it must be remembered that a fresher puff may bear the gunwale lower without warning, and that the moment it dips the boat will almost certainly fill and capsize. The details of reefing will depend upon the rig, but a few general rules may be laid down. The men should be stationed before beginning, and should all be required to remain seated. One lowers the halyards, as much as may be necessary, another hauls down on the leech and shifts the tack. The sheet is hauled in a little to let the men detailed for the reef points get hold of and gather in the foot. The sheet is then slacked and shifted, the reef points passed, the halyards manned, the sail hoisted, and the sheet trimmed. It is important to keep the boat under command while reefing, and for this she must have way enough to obey her rudder. If she can be luffed a little and still be kept going through the water sufficiently to obey the rudder, then it is unquestionably wise to luff, but not sufficiently to risk losing control.

If the boat has more than one sail, it is a safe plan to reef them one at a time when the sea is dangerously heavy.

Gybing—A boom sail is *gybed* when it swings from one side to the other, the wind being aft or nearly so, and the sail full, first on one side and then on the other. The gybe becomes dangerous when the sail is not kept under the control of a taut sheet or when the wind is of sufficient strength to list the boat and swing the stern violently when its force is shifted to the opposite side of the sail. Moreover, the violent sweep of the boom across the stern endangers everybody in its path. To avoid gybing because of an unexpected shift of wind or a deep yaw when running off the wind or running free, the sheets must be tended smartly and the tiller put hard down. By doing so, the swing of the boom may be controlled and checked.

If sitting to windward in a fresh breeze, the crew should move amidships when passing under the lee of a vessel or other object, where the wind may fail or even shift in an eddy.

The old rule of sailing was: "Never belay the main sheet." With modern quick-release cleats or a jam cleat you can safely make your sheet fast. But, you should always have it ready for running. If you have old fashioned cleats and make the sheet fast with several turns or figure eights, you are courting disaster and may have an unexpected swim.

The sails being properly sheeted and drawing full, a careful watch must be kept for squalls when sailing on the wind.

As the wind will vary more or less (in apparent if not real direction), it is necessary to be watchful and to bring the boat up or keep her away, from time to time, in order that she may be always at her best.

Advantage should be taken of the increased wind velocity of a squall in a light breeze. The boat should first be eased off slightly, and the sheets eased under the first impulse of the squall. When headway is obtained, sheet in the sails and luff up fully to gain way to windward.

In a stiff breeze the boat should be luffed for a moderate squall to prevent taking water. The luff should be only sufficient to shake, without spilling the sails, thus keeping headway enough to retain control, but with the sheets in hand. If the squall is a strong one, not only should the boat be luffed promptly but the sheets should be eased off at once. In a sudden emergency the sheets may be let go and control lost, but the longer the boat can be kept under control the better.

When running well off the wind or running free, squalls cannot be met by spilling the sails. More than a touch of the tiller would be required to do so. Accordingly, the only prudent thing is to slack the sheet while luffing.

The tendency of the wind to capsize the boat would be much reduced by running off. Ordinarily this is not a safe maneuver, for if the squall becomes too strong there is no recourse but to lower the sails, and the chances are they will bind against the shrouds. Moreover, there is always the danger of the wind shifting in the squall to such an extent as to gybe the mainsail with force.

If a heavy breaking sea is seen bearing down on a boat, she should be luffed up to meet it. The boat should be kept away again as soon as the sea has passed. The boat should not be luffed too high for if she loses way she becomes helpless at once.

It is dangerous to be caught by a heavy sea on the beam. Therefore, if the course to be made in rough water would bring the boat into the trough of the sea, the best plan is to run off for a time with the sea on the quarter, then bring her up with it on the bow, and so make good the course desired without actually steering it at any time.

Running before the wind in a fresh breeze in a rough sea is the most dangerous point of sailing. The danger of gybing is increased because the boat will certainly yaw considerably despite the very careful steering that will be demanded. As a precaution against gybing, the boom can be lashed to the rail or to a shroud by a *lazy guy*, which can be loosed quickly in an emergency.

A serious danger in running before a heavy sea is that of *broaching to.* The boat will yaw considerably, the rudder will be often out of water when it is most needed to meet her, and the sails will be becalmed in the trough of the sea. The situation here is much like that of a boat running in a surf. The yawing will be reduced by keeping the ballast aft and by steering with an oar. The jib should always be set, with the sheet hauled aft. It helps to meet and pay her off if she *flies to* against the rudder. A drag towed over the stern of the boat is also helpful. A long bight of heavy line used in this manner makes a rather effective drag.

A further danger is that the boom may dip in the water as the boat rolls and thus capsize the boat. The boom should be carried high enough to prevent this.

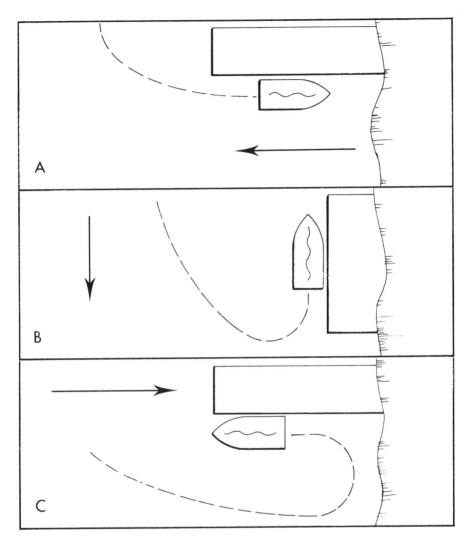

Figure 12-20. Approaching a dock under sail with wind from various directions. In sketch A the dock happens to be into the wind so that the boat has only to turn and luff into the wind. In sketch B the boat is originally on a broad reach and makes almost an 180° turn and luffs soon enough so that it has the way off just as it reaches the dock. Sketch C presents a more difficult situation. Going downwind, the boat has to turn and luff up into the wind soon enough to have all her way off when she reaches the dock. If she comes about too late, she will go aground on a lee shore. Not shown is a situation where the dock is on a lee shore and way must be killed as much as possible before going alongside. In this case the boat would have to make the approach running with the wind and then turn into the wind to luff. Sails would then be dropped and the boat permitted to drift down onto the dock. Dropping an anchor after way was lost and veering the anchor line will help cushion the landing on the dock.

Figure 12-21. Ocean sailing. Captain W.B. Hayler aboard the ketch *Velero* bound for Honolulu. Photo: John M. Keever.

Coming alongside under sail—Coming alongside a ship or a dock under sail requires skill, judgment, and experience. If there is any obstruction which the mast, stays, or shrouds can touch or become fouled on, it is wiser not to try to come alongside. In a small boat, unstep the mast and go alongside with oars or paddles. In a larger boat, lower the sails and turn on the engine.

No two situations are ever the same. The direction and force of the wind as well as the current will affect what happens. If you are under sail alone, you must lose your way to coast gently up to the dock without damage. If you kill your way too late, you will damage the boat. If you kill it to soon, you may not reach the dock, and you will have to try again. Figure 12-20 shows several examples which may face a small boat sailor when he is making a dock under sail. In sketch A the dock happens to be into the wind so the boat has only to turn and luff into the wind. In sketch B the boat is originally on a broad reach and makes almost an 180 degree turn and luffs soon enough so that it has the way off just as it reaches the dock. Sketch C presents a more difficult situation. Going down wind, the boat has to turn and luff up into the wind soon enough to have all her way off when she reaches the dock. If she comes about too late she will go aground on a lee shore. Not shown is a situation where the dock is on a lee shore and way must be killed as much as possible before going alongside. In this case the boat would have to make the approach running with the wind, and then turn into the wind to luff. Sails would then be dropped and the boat permitted to drift down onto the dock. Dropping an anchor after way was lost and veering the anchor line will help cushion the landing on the dock.

CHAPTER XIII

COMMUNICATIONS

THE UNITED STATES EDITION of the *International Code of Signals* (H.O. 102) is published by the U.S. Naval Oceanographic Office in one volume and is available from nautical book suppliers.

Methods of Communicating—Communications are sent by five methods:

1. Bridge-to-bridge radiotelephone.
2. Signal flags.
3. Flashing light signaling, using International Morse Code.
4. Sound signaling, using International Morse Code.
5. Signaling by semaphore.

BRIDGE-TO-BRIDGE RADIOTELEPHONE

Bridge-to-bridge radiotelephone communications have long been regarded as a valuable and necessary navigational safety tool. The use of voice radio, formerly voluntary, proved so successful that it has now become mandatory. It is required on navigable waters of the United States by law and on the high seas by the *International Rules of the Road* (1972). The requirements and procedures on the high seas and in the U.S. inland waters are compatible. More detailed information is contained in *U.S. Coast Guard Publication CG-439*. Individuals using bridge-to-bridge radiotelephone must possess a restricted radiotelephone operator's permit or a third class radiotelephone operator's license issued by the Federal Communications Commission.

The Bridge-to-Bridge Radiotelephone Act provides that practically all vessels must be capable of transmitting and receiving within the 156-162 Mega-Hertz (MHz) band. Included are:

a. Every power-driven vessel of 300 gross tons and upward while navigating;

b. Every vessel of 100 gross tons and upward carrying one or more passengers for hire while navigating;

c. Every towing vessel of 26 feet or over while navigating; and

d. Every dredge and floating plant engaged in or near a channel or fairway in operations likely to restrict or affect navigation of other vessels.

USE OF THE BRIDGE-TO-BRIDGE RADIOTELEPHONE

The watch on the radiotelephone is maintained on the 156-162 MHz band. The radiotelephone is for the exclusive use of the master, person in charge of the vessel, or a designated representative. It can be used only to transmit information necessary to the safe navigation of vessels such as a vessel's intentions. On a United States vessel no one can be assigned a radiotelephone watch unless he can speak the English language. Communications are to be kept as brief as possible and must be clear and concise. A voice radio log is maintained. Normal monitoring watch by international agreement is stood on channel 16 (156.8 MHz). U.S. ports have additional special requirements.

EMERGENCY SIGNALS

Three emergency signals are used on the radiotelephone:

MAYDAY—Used only when grave and imminent danger threatens a vessel and immediate help is required. It is a distress signal. MAYDAY could be used if a vessel were in collision, were sinking, or were on fire. A MAYDAY message is of the highest precedence.

PAN—This is an urgency signal and is next in precedence to MAYDAY. It is used to alert nearby ships or shore stations to a situation which may later require a MAYDAY but which does not yet warrant a distress signal. An example would be the loss of engine or rudder.

SECURITY—This is pronounced "Securité" and is a safety message. It indicates that the station is about to transmit a message concerning the safety of navigation or giving important meteorological warning. The precedence is just below PAN. In the United States the Coast Guard transmits notices to mariners and weather messages with this precedence. A merchant ship would probably not have occasion to transmit a SECURITY message but would be vitally interested in receiving any SECURITY transmission.

PHONETIC ALPHABET

The phonetic alphabet may be used when transmitting plain language or code and when it is necessary to spell words on radiotelephone. Its use for radiotelephone, as well as flaghoist and semaphore, is universal:

Letter	Word	Pronounced as	Letter	Word	Pronounced as
A	Alfa	AL FHA	N	November	NO VEM BER
B	Bravo	BRAH VOH	O	Oscar	OSS CAH
C	Charlie	CHAR LEE or	P	Papa	PAH PAH
		SHAR LEE	Q	Quebec	KEH BECK
D	Delta	DELL TAH	R	Romeo	ROW ME OH
E	Echo	ECK HO	S	Sierra	SEE AIR RAH
F	Foxtrot	FOKS TROT	T	Tango	TANG GO
G	Golf	GOLF	U	Uniform	YOU NEE FORM or
H	Hotel	HOH TELL			OO NEE FORM
I	India	IN DEE AH	V	Victor	VIK TAH
J	Juliett	JEW LEE ETT	W	Whiskey	WISS KEY
K	Kilo	KEY LOH	X	X-ray	ECKS RAY
L	Lima	LEE MAH	Y	Yankee	YANG KEY
M	Mike	MIKE	Z	Zulu	ZOO LOO

INTERNATIONAL FLAGS AND PENNANTS
WITH MORSE SYMBOLS

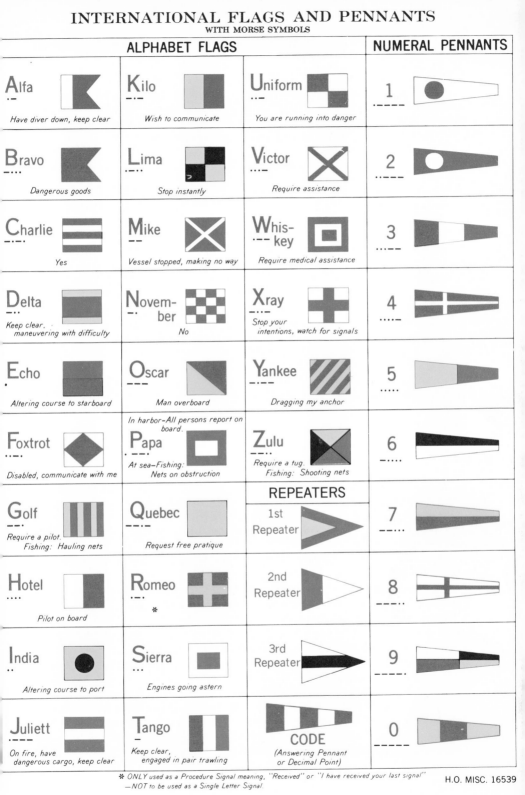

Figure 13-1. International flags and pennants. Courtesy: Defense Mapping Agency Hydrographic Center

PROCEDURE

A radiotelephone circuit can be compared with an old fashioned party line telephone. Only one person can speak at a time, and circuit discipline is essential. Since it is not possible to transmit and to receive at the same time, certain procedural words have become standardized, and you must know their meanings:

"Over"—Indicates that the transmission has ended and that a response is expected.

"Out"—Indicates that a transmission is completed and that no response is expected.

"Clear"—Has the same meaning as "Out."

"Roger"—Indicates that the immediately preceding message has been received, and is completely understood.

"Words Twice"—Is used to indicate that a series of words will be sent two times because of poor reception or other communications difficulty.

"Say again"—Means "repeat." Either expression is used.

"Break"—Is used to separate parts of a single transmission. It might be used as a pause between two parts of a long transmission.

TUNING

The tuning of the standard VHF marine radio is fairly simple. The volume should be set at a reasonable level with the squelch off. The squelch should be tuned until the point is reached where no more static is received. Tuning additional squelch will result in a loss of reception capability. Most sets have crystal controlled channel selection which only requires the selection of the proper numerical channel for the desired transmission.

VISUAL SIGNALS

Visual signaling can be conducted by the use of signal flags, semaphore, or flashing light. Before the days of voice radio this was the only means of communicating with a nearby ship. Experienced signalmen could pass messages quickly and reliably. Now that the radiotelephone is readily available to the mate on watch, visual signaling has largely fallen into disuse. The signal flags may remain neatly stowed during an entire voyage except when entering certain ports. However, ignorance of the techniques of visual signaling can become dangerous because a radio casualty or a radio silence imposed in time of war or emergency can suddenly make visual signals the primary—or only—way of communicating. Emergencies, by their nature, give little warning. Therefore, learning the fundamentals of visual signaling is very important.

INTERNATIONAL CODE FLAGS

By using the signal flags shown in Figure 13-1, messages may be spelled out letter by letter or by using the one, two, or three letter combinations contained in the *International Code of Signals* (H.O. 102).

Good visual discipline will result in a smart signalman who will be a source of pride to the ship concerned. Visual signals require practice since clarity and exactness in the transmission of messages are essential. A good signalman will choose the best background for transmitting his signals and avoid the use of a system when wind and weather make it unsatisfactory for use in both directions.

The signals used consist of one, two, or three letters. A ship's identity signal or call sign consists of four letters. Single letters have been allocated to either very common or very urgent situations. You should familiarize yourself with the single letter signals. Two and three letter signals require the use of H.O. 102.

SINGLE LETTER SIGNALS

(May be made by any method of signaling.)

A   I have a diver down: Keep well clear at slow speed.

B*   I am taking in, or discharging, or carrying dangerous goods.

C   Yes (affirmative or "The significance of the previous group should be read in the affirmative").

D*   Keep clear of me: I am maneuvering with difficulty.

E*   I am altering my course to starboard.

F   I am disabled: Communicate with me.

G   I require a pilot. When made by fishing vessels operating in close proximity on the fishing grounds, it means: "I am hauling nets."

H*   I have a pilot on board.

I*   I am altering my course to port.

J   I am on fire and have dangerous cargo on board: Keep well clear of me.

K[1]   I wish to communicate with you.

L   You should stop your vessel instantly.

M   My vessel is stopped and making no way through the water.

N   No (negative or "The significance of the previous group should be read in the negative"). This signal may be given only visually or by sound. For voice or radio transmission the signal should be "NO."

O   Man overboard.

P   In harbor—All persons should report on board as the vessel is about to proceed to sea.
        At sea—It may be used by fishing vessels to mean: "My nets have come fast upon an obstruction."

Q   My vessel is "healthy" and I request free pratique.

S*   My engines are going astern.

T*   Keep clear of me; I am engaged in pair trawling.

---

*Signals of letters marked by an asterisk (*) when made by sound may only be made in compliance with the requirements of the *International Regulations for Preventing Collisions at Sea* (1972), Rules 34 and 35.

[1]Signals "K" and "S" have special meanings as landing signals for small boats with crews or persons in distress. (*International Convention for the Safety of Life at Sea*, 1960, Chapt. V, Regulation 16.)

U	You are running into danger.
V	I require assistance.
W	I require medical assistance.
X	Stop carrying out your intentions and watch for my signals.
Y	I am dragging my anchor.
Z	I require a tug. When made by fishing vessels operating in close proximity on the fishing grounds, it means: "I am shooting nets."

TWO LETTER SIGNALS

Two letter signals have been allocated to operational situations and to instances pertaining to navigation, weather, and communications. In some cases a numeral pennant may follow the letters. The following examples illustrate the versatility of H.O. 102.

AE	I must abandon my vessel.
AL	I have a doctor on board.
AW	Aircraft should endeavor to alight where flag is waved or light is shown.
BB 2	You may alight on my deck: I am ready to receive you amidship.
CB 8	I require immediate assistance: Propeller shaft is broken.
CP	I am (or vessel indicated is) proceeding to your assistance.
DX	I am sinking.
EX	My position is doubtful.
FZ	You should continue search according to instructions and until further notice.
GS	I will attempt rescue with whip and breeches buoy.
HM	Survivors are in bad condition. Medical assistance is urgently required.
ID 1	Damage can be repaired at sea without assistance.
KI	There are no tugs available.
LP	There is not less than . . . (number) feet or meters of water over the bar.
LX 4	Where can I enter the canal?
MV	My vessel is releasing radioactive material and presents a hazard.
NF	You are running into danger.
OH	You should switch on your radar and keep radar watch.
PC	I have destroyed the drifting mine.
QI	I am going astern.
QX	I request permission to anchor.
SB	I am proceeding to the position of accident.
UI	Sea is too rough: Pilot boat cannot get off to you.
VB	Have you sufficient bunkers to reach port?
VY	One or more icebergs or growlers have been reported (with or without position and time).
ZA 6	I wish to communicate with you in Japanese.
ZI 8	I can receive but not transmit by radiotelephone 2182 kHz.

THREE LETTER SIGNALS

Medical advice should be sought and given in plain language whenever it is possible. If language difficulties are encountered, however, three letter signals are available and can be used. Medical signals are easily recognizable because they begin with the letter "M." As is the case with two letter signals, numeral pennants can be added. The following are a few examples:

MAK 39   I have a female aged 39 years.
MCF   The breathing is weak.
MER 58   Bleeding is present from bladder.
MTD 32   You should give aspirin tablets.

IDENTITY SIGNALS

All vessels are assigned four letter identity signals or call signs which are customarily flown when underway in harbor. Each maritime country is assigned a block of letters. All U.S. merchant ships have an identity signal beginning with the letter "K" or "W." These can be found in the Berne lists which are published by an international commission headquartered in Switzerland. These lists contain the identity signals of merchant ships of all nations. Identity signals of U.S. Navy ships begin with the letter "N."

FLAG SIGNALING PROCEDURE

As a general rule only one flag hoist should be shown at a time. Each hoist or group of hoists should be kept flying until it has been answered by the receiving station. When more groups than one are shown on the same halyard, they must be separated by a tackline. The transmitting station should always hoist the signal where it can be most easily seen by the receiving station, that is, in such a position that the flags will blow out clear and be free from smoke.

HOW TO CALL

The identity signal of the station(s) addressed is to be hoisted with the signal. If no identity signal is hoisted, it will be understood that the signal is addressed to all stations within visual signaling distance. If it is not possible to determine the identity signal of the station to which it is desired to signal, the group "VF" = "You would hoist your identity signal" or "CS" = "What is the name or identity signal of your vessel (or station)?" should be hoisted first; at the same time the station will hoist its own identity signal. The group "YQ" = "I wish to communicate" can also be used.

HOW TO ANSWER SIGNALS

All stations to which signals are addressed or which are indicated in signals are to hoist the answering pennant at the dip as soon as they see each hoist and close up immediately as they understand it; it is to be lowered to the dip as soon as the hoist is hauled down at the transmitting station, being hoisted close up again as soon as the next hoist is understood.

Figure 13-2. Flashing light signaling equipment. Photo: Midn. J.P. Jackson, California Maritime Academy.

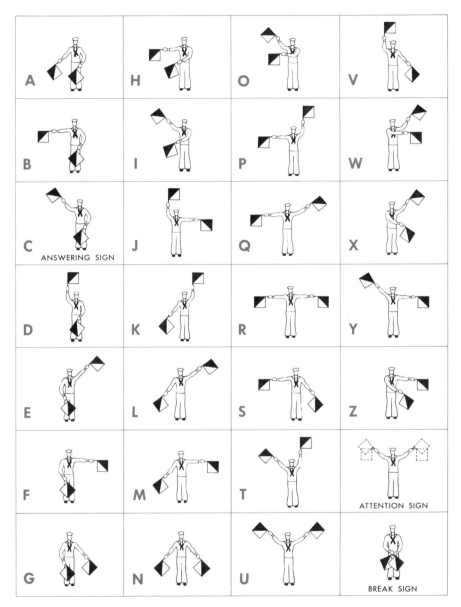

Figure 13-3. The semaphore alphabet.

HOW TO COMPLETE A SIGNAL

The transmitting station is to hoist the answering pennant singly after the last hoist of the signal to indicate that the signal is completed. The receiving station is to answer this in a similar manner to all other hoists.

HOW TO ACT WHEN SIGNALS ARE NOT UNDERSTOOD

If the receiving station cannot clearly distinguish the signal made to it, it is to keep the answering pennant at the dip. If the receiving station can distinguish the signal but cannot understand its meaning it can hoist the following signals: "ZQ" = "Your signal appears incorrectly coded. You should check and repeat the whole," or "ZL" = "Your signal has been received but not understood."

THE USE OF SUBSTITUTES

The use of substitutes is to enable the same signal flag, either alphabetical flag or numeral pennant, to be repeated one or more times in the same group, in case only one set of flags is carried on board. The first substitute always repeats the uppermost signal flag of that class of flags which immediately precedes the substitute. The second substitute always repeats the second signal flag and the third substitute repeats the third, counting from the top of that class of flags which immediately precedes them. No substitute can ever be used more than once in the same group. The answering pennant when used as a decimal point is to be disregarded in determining which substitute to use.

Example:

The signal "VV" would be made as follows:

V   first substitute

The number "1100" would be made by numeral pennants as follows:

1   first substitute
0   third substitute

The signal "L 2330" would be made as follows:

L
2
3   second substitute
0

In this case the second substitute follows a numeral pennant and therefore it can only repeat the second numeral in the group.

HOW TO SPELL

Names in the text of a signal are to be spelled out by means of the alphabetical flags. The signal "YZ" = "The words which follow are in plain language" can be used, if necessary.

FLASHING LIGHT SIGNALING

Flashing light signaling is accomplished by use of the Morse code which is shown in Figure 13-1 at the beginning of this chapter. Figure 13-2 shows typical flashing light signaling equipment used in the merchant service. A signal made by flashing light is divided into the following parts:

a. **The call**—It consists of the general call or the identity signal of the station to be called. It is answered by the answering signal.

b. **The identity**—The transmitting station makes "DE" followed by its identity signal or name. This will be repeated back by the receiving station which then signals its own identity signal or name. This will also be repeated back by the transmitting station.

c. **The text**—This consists of plain language or code groups. When code groups are to be used, they should be preceded by the signal "YU." Words of plain language may also be in the text, when the signal includes names, places, etc. Receipt of each word or group is acknowledged by "T."

d. **The ending**—It consists of the ending signal "AR" which is answered by "R."

If the entire text is in plain language the same procedure is to be followed. The call and identity may be omitted when two stations have established communications and already exchanged signals.

A list of procedure signals appears in H.O. 102. Although the use of these signals may be self-explanatory, the following notes might be found useful:

a. The General call sign (or call for unknown station) "AA AA AA" etc., is made to attract attention when wishing to signal to all stations within visual signaling distance or to a station whose name or identity signal is not known. The call is continued until the station addressed answers.

b. The Answering signal "TTTT" etc., is made to answer the call and it is to be continued until the transmitting station ceases to make the call. The transmission starts with the signal "DE" followed by the name or identity signal of the transmitting station.

c. The letter "T" is used to indicate the receipt of each word or group.

d. The Erase signal "EEEEEE" etc., is used to indicate that the last group or word was signaled incorrectly. It is to be answered with the erase signal. When answered, the transmitting station will repeat that last word or group which was correctly signaled and then proceed with the remainder of the transmission.

e. The Repeat signal "RPT" is to be used as follows:

   (i) by the transmitting station to indicate that it is going to repeat ("I repeat"). If such a repetition does not follow immediately after "RPT," the signal should be interpreted as a request to the receiving station to repeat the signal received ("Repeat what you have sent");

   (ii) by the receiving station to request for a repetition of the signal transmitted ("Repeat what you have sent");

   (iii) The Special Repetition signals are:

      AA = all after . . .
      AB = all before . . .
      BN = all between . . . and . . .
      WA = word or group after . . .
      WB = word or group before . . .

CHAPTER 4—SECTION 2

TABLE OF LIFESAVING SIGNALS

I Landing signals for the guidance of small boats with crews or persons in distress

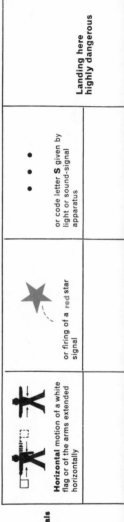

	MANUAL SIGNALS	LIGHT SIGNALS	OTHER SIGNALS	SIGNIFICATION
Day signals	**Vertical** motion of a white flag or of the arms	or firing of a green star signal	or code letter **K** given by light or sound-signal apparatus	This is the best place to land
Night signals	**Vertical** motion of a white light or flare	or firing of a green star signal	or code letter **K** given by light or sound-signal apparatus	

A range (indication of direction) may be given by placing a steady white light or flare at a lower level and in line with the observer

	MANUAL SIGNALS	LIGHT SIGNALS	OTHER SIGNALS	SIGNIFICATION
Day signals	**Horizontal** motion of a white flag or of the arms extended horizontally	or firing of a red star signal	or code letter **S** given by light or sound-signal apparatus	Landing here highly dangerous

Night signals		or firing of a red star signal	• •or code letter **S** given by light or sound-signal apparatus
Day signals	**1 Horizontal** motion of a white flag, followed by **2** the placing of the white flag in the ground and **3** by the carrying of another white flag in the direction to be indicated	**1** or firing of a red star signal vertically and **2** a **white** star signal in the direction towards the better landing place	**1** or signalling the code letter **S** (...) followed by the code letter **R** (. – .) if a better landing place for the craft in distress is located more to the *right* in the direction of approach **2** or signalling the code letter **S** (...) followed by the code letter **L** (. – . .) if a better landing place for the craft in distress is located more to the *left* in the direction of approach
Night signals	**1 Horizontal** motion of a white light or flare **2** followed by the placing of the white light or flare on the ground and **3** the carrying of another white light or flare in the direction to be indicated	**1** or firing of a red star signal vertically and a **2 white** star signal in the direction towards the better landing place	**1** or signalling the code letter **S** (...) followed by the code letter **R** (. – .) if a better landing place for the craft in distress is located more to the *right* in the direction of approach **2** or signalling the code letter **S** (...) followed by the code letter **L** (. – . .) if a better landing place for the craft in distress is located more to the *left* in the direction of approach

Landing here highly dangerous. A more favourable location for landing is in the direction indicated

SECTION 2.—TABLE OF LIFESAVING SIGNALS

TABLE OF LIFESAVING SIGNALS

II Signals to be employed in connection with the use of shore lifesaving apparatus

	MANUAL SIGNALS	LIGHT SIGNALS	OTHER SIGNALS	SIGNIFICATION
Day signals	Vertical motion of a white flag or of the arms	or firing of a green star signal		In general: affirmative Specifically: rocket line is held – tail block is made fast – hawser is made fast – man is in the breeches buoy – haul away
Night signals	Vertical motion of a white light or flare	or firing of a green star signal		
Day signals	Horizontal motion of a white flag or of the arms extended horizontally	or firing of a red star signal		In general: negative Specifically: slack away – avast hauling
Night signals	Horizontal motion of a white light or flare	or firing of a red star signal		

III Replies from lifesaving stations or maritime rescue units to distress signals made by a ship or person

Day signals		Orange smoke signal	or combined light and sound signal (thunder-light) consisting of 3 single signals which are fired at intervals of approximately one minute	You are seen – assistance will be given as soon as possible

(Repetition of such signal shall have the same meaning)

Night signals

White star rocket consisting of 3 single signals which are fired at intervals of approximately one minute

If necessary, the day signals may be given at night or the night signals by day

IV Signals used by aircraft engaged on search and rescue operations to direct ships towards an aircraft, ship or person in distress

PROCEDURES PERFORMED IN SEQUENCE BY AN AIRCRAFT **SIGNIFICATION**

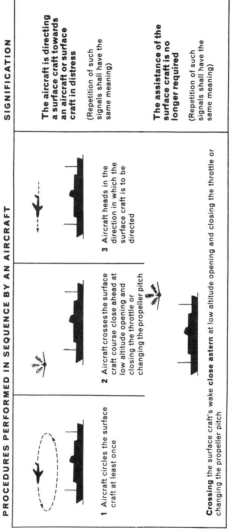

1 Aircraft circles the surface craft at least once

2 Aircraft crosses the surface craft course close ahead at low altitude opening and closing the throttle or changing the propeller pitch

3 Aircraft heads in the direction in which the surface craft is to be directed

The aircraft is directing a surface craft towards an aircraft or surface craft in distress

(Repetition of such signals shall have the same meaning)

Crossing the surface craft's wake **close astern** at low altitude opening and closing the throttle or changing the propeller pitch

The assistance of the surface craft is no longer required

(Repetition of such signals shall have the same meaning)

Figure 13-4. Continued.

DAYTIME SIGNALS

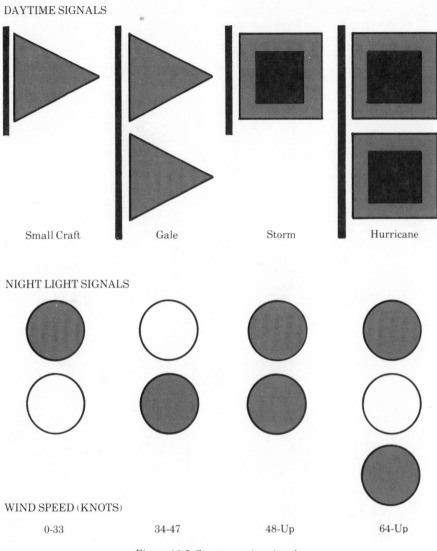

NIGHT LIGHT SIGNALS

| Small Craft | Gale | Storm | Hurricane |

WIND SPEED (KNOTS)

    0-33   34-47   48-Up   64-Up

Figure 13-5. Storm warning signals.

These are made by the receiving station as appropriate. In each case they are made immediately after the repeat signal: "RPT."

Examples:

"RPT AB KL" = Repeat all before group "KL."

"RPT BN 'boats' 'survivors' " = "Repeat all between words 'boats'; and 'survivors'."

If a signal is not understood, or, when decoded, it is not intelligible, the repeat signal is not used. The receiving station must then make the appropriate signal from the code, e.g. "Your signal has been received but not understood."

    f. A correctly received repetition is acknowledged by the signal "OK." The same signal may be used as an affirmative answer to a question ("It is correct").

    g. The Ending signal "AR" is used in all cases to indicate the end of a signal or the end of the transmission. The receiving station answers with the signal "R" = "Received" or "I have received your last signal."

    h. The transmitting station makes the signal "CS" when requesting the name or identity signal of the receiving station.

    i. The Waiting signal or Period signal "AS" is to be used as follows:

        (i) When made independently or after the end of a signal, it indicates that the other station must wait for further communications (waiting signal).

        (ii) When it is inserted between groups, it serves to separate them (period signal) to avoid confusion.

    j. The signal "C" should be used to indicate an affirmative statement or an affirmative reply to an interrogative signal; the signal "RQ" should be used to indicate a question. For a negative reply to an interrogative signal or for a negative statement, the signal "N" should be used in visual or sound signaling and the signal "NO" should be used for voice or radio transmission. When the signals "N" or "NO," and "RQ" are used to change an affirmative signal into a negative statement or into a question, respectively, they should be transmitted after the main signal.

Examples:

"CY N" (or "NO" as appropriate) = "Boat(s) is(are) not coming to you."

"CW RQ" = "Is boat/raft on board?" The signals "C," "N," or "NO," and "RQ" cannot be used in conjunction with single-letter signals.

SOUND SIGNALING

Although sound signaling is permitted by the *International Code of Signals*, it is archaic in the modern day. It is rarely, if ever used, and has not been experienced by the editors except with reference to the Rules of the Road.

Owing to the nature of the apparatus used (whistle, siren, foghorn, etc.) sound signaling is necessarily slow. Moreover, the misuse of sound signaling is of a nature to create serious confusion at sea. In fog it should be reduced to an absolute minimum. Signals other than the single letter signals should be used only in extreme emergency and never in frequented navigational waters.

The signals should be made slowly and clearly. They may be repeated, if necessary, but at sufficiently long intervals to insure that no confusion can arise and that one letter signals cannot be mistaken as two letter groups.

Masters are reminded that the one letter signals of the code, which are marked by an asterisk (*), when made by sound, may only be made in compliance with the requirements of the *International Regulations for Preventing Collisions at Sea* (1972).

SIGNALING BY SEMAPHORE

Semaphore was formerly the most used of all visual means of communication for short-range work. It is faster than flashing light. However, the advent of radio telephone has curtailed all visual signaling, and since semaphore can only be used at close range, it has largely dropped into disuse. The Coast Guard no longer requires that a candidate for a deck license be proficient in semaphore. Semaphore is still used by the Navy, its use is provided for in H.O. 102, and it still holds favor with old timers in the Merchant Marine. The semaphore alphabet is shown in Figure 13-3 which is reproduced from H.O. 102.

A station which desires to communicate with another station by semaphore may indicate the requirement by transmitting to that station the signal "K 1" by any method. If the stations are close to one another the attention sign may be made instead.

On receipt of the call the station addressed should hoist the answering pennant at the dip, make the answering sign, or, if unable to communicate by semaphore, reply with the signal "YS 1."

The sender will make the attention sign and wait until the anwering pennant is hoisted close up, or the answering sign is made by the station addressed, commencing transmission after a reasonable pause.

The signal should always be made in plain language and numbers occurring in a semaphore signal are always to be spelled out in words. At the end of each word the arms are to be dropped to the break position. When double letters occur, the arms are to be dropped to the break position after the first letter is made and then moved out to the second letter without pausing. The erase signal is a succession of E's.

The reception of each word is to be indicated by the receiving station making the letter "C." If this signal is not made the word is to be repeated.

All signals will end with the ending signal "AR."

DISTRESS SIGNALS

The Rules of the Road authorize certain visual, sound, and radio signals to indicate distress and need of assistance. These are listed in Chapter XIX. They are important and should be learned.

LIFESAVING SIGNALS

Over the years signals have evolved in the rescue of shipwrecked mariners. More recently standardized signals are used by aircraft engaged in search and rescue operations. These are contained in Figure 13-4, the "Table of Lifesaving Signals" which is reproduced from H.O. 102.

STORM WARNING SIGNALS

Whenever winds dangerous to navigation are forecast for an area, the flags and pennants shown in Figure 13-5 may be hoisted at the Weather Bureau and other shore stations. The signal indicates that the mariner can expect these weather conditions within the next twelve hours.

CHAPTER XIV

TANKERMAN'S GUIDE

TANKSHIPS AND TANK BARGES, TERMED "TANK VESSELS," are specially constructed or converted to carry liquid cargo in bulk. Tankships are equipped with means of self-propulsion; tank barges are not. Other types of ships, barges, and water craft designed to carry passengers or freight may also be permitted to carry certain classes of liquid bulk cargoes. If so, they are regulated in the same manner as tank vessels especially with regard to the conditions in which they are manned.

One or more men holding tankerman's certificates are required to be in the complement of every manned tank vessel provided that the holder of a license as master, mate, pilot, or engineer shall be considered as qualified to perform all of the duties of tankerman and shall not therefore be certified as tankerman.

Experience—Any applicant for a certificate as tankerman, not licensed as master, mate, pilot, or engineer, shall be eligible for examination after he has furnished satisfactory documentary evidence to the local inspectors that he is trained in, and capable to perform efficiently the necessary operations on tank vessels which relate to the handling of cargo.

Physical examination—Such applicant shall obtain from the United States Public Health Service, or a registered physician, a certificate that he is in good physical condition.

Written or **oral examination**—Before a certificate may be granted to such an applicant, he must prove to the satisfaction of the local inspectors, by an oral or written examination, that he is familiar with the general arrangement of cargo tanks, suction, and discharge pipe lines and valves, cargo pumps, and cargo hose, and has been properly trained in the actual operation of cargo pumps, all other operations connected with the loading and discharging of cargo, and the use of fire-extinguishing equipment.

Certificate—Each applicant successfully passing such examination shall receive a certificate as tankerman, stating the kinds or grades of liquid cargo the holder is qualified to handle. The back of such certificate and its stub shall each bear an imprint of the left thumb of the holder.

Suspension or **revocation**—Such certificates shall be subject to suspension or revocation on the same grounds and in the same manner and with like procedure as is provided for in the case of suspension or revocation of licenses of officers.

DANGERS OF ACCUMULATED GAS

Increased use on vessels in recent years of various kinds of oils as fuel and lubricants, and as stores, and the carriage of such oils in barrels, drums, and cases on cargo ships and tankers, as well as in bulk on tankers,

Figure 14-1. S.S. *Exxon North Slope* entering Valdez, Alaska. This ship, sistership of the *Exxon Benicia*, was built in 1979. She is 906 feet length overall, has a beam of 173 feet, and a draft of 55 feet. Her steam turbines develop 26,700 hp. Deadweight tonnage is 164,000. She has a crew of 24.

Photo: Courtesy Exxon Co. U.S.A.

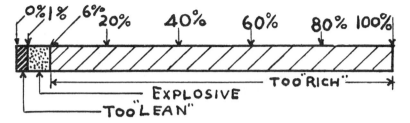

Figure 14-2. Explosive range of petroleum vapor.

renders it desirable if not imperative in the interests of safety that those persons directly responsible be familiar with established practice for the safe handling of such liquids.

With proper equipment, a reasonable diligence and adequate knowledge, cargoes of oil, in bulk or package, may be handled safely and with remarkable freedom from accident. The following pages contain the main requirements for such safe handling of oil cargoes. These principles must be well understood and practiced by everyone working such cargo.

Explosion of gas—While there is no doubt that a tanker is safer from the danger of explosion when gas free on the ballast voyage than when not gas free, the danger of an explosion can be minimized when the conditions necessary for an explosion are understood.

Many experiments have proved that the explosive range for petroleum vapors mixed with air starts at a point where 1 percent, by volume, of saturated petroleum vapors is mixed with 99 percent of air. The explosive range ends where the petroleum vapor is 6 percent and the air is 94 percent by volume. Fortunately this is a very narrow range in which it is possible to produce an explosion. This is apparent since in all possible mixtures of petroleum vapors and air from 1 to 100, only those are explosive which for petroleum vapors range from 1 to 6. Since the range from 1 to 6 is only a range of 5 percent in a possible 100 percent it is apparent that only one twentieth of the possible mixtures of petroleum vapors and air are explosive. This very narrow range necessary to produce explosive mixtures of petroleum vapors and air is evident in the delicate adjustment required for the carburetor of a gasoline motor and the ease with which an automobile engine becomes "flooded." The narrowness of this explosive range is illustrated in Figure 14-2.

We should also bear in mind the tremendous volume of explosive gases which are produced by one unit of petroleum product such as gasoline. One cubic foot of gasoline will produce 8,000 cubic feet of explosive vapors or gas. We should also bear in mind that volatile petroleum products which produce explosive mixtures with air at atmospheric temperatures give off these gases continuously and they fill the space above the liquid, and that in a tanker there is little difference between the density of gases at the surface of the liquid and at the top of the tank; that is, the diffusion of gases through the tank is nearly, but not quite, uniform at sea.

Figure 14-3. Main deck of *Exxon Benicia* from bridge. This view gives an idea of the immense size and complexity of the modern tanker. Main deck, cargo piping and vent stacks are clearly shown. Photo: Midn. R.L. Schopp, California Maritime Academy.

A tank of ordinary size, say, 25 × 30 × 30, would contain about 22,000 cubic feet of space. If empty, this amount of air could be made toxic (dangerous for men to enter) by only 1 gallon of gasoline; at the lower explosive limit by only 20 gallons of gasoline and well above the upper explosive limit by 120 gallons of gasoline. If the cargo was average Texas crude oil perhaps 240 gallons might be required to produce an atmosphere sufficiently "rich" to be well above the explosive limit.

Taking this investigation a little further, it will be seen that such a tank will have an interior surface of about 6,000 square feet (including all stiffening members). This would require only one fiftieth of a gallon of the Texas crude oil to wet each square foot of this surface and later by evaporation to render the air in the tank sufficiently above the upper explosive limit to make it too "rich" to explode.

The purpose of these calculations is to show, conclusively and based on well established facts, that the conditions prevailing within the cargo tanks after the discharge of volatile petroleum products are normally such that the atmosphere within tends to establish itself at a petroleum vapor concentration well above the upper explosive limit and that usually only a minute quantity of the volatile liquid is necessary to accomplish this result.

KINDS OF OILS

Liquids having the characteristic of being "greasy" are commonly called oils. In general, oils may be divided into the following 5 classes:

1. **Petroleum base**—This group includes those oils made by distillation (heating) of crude petroleum which produces such products as gasoline, kerosene, light fuel oils, heavy oils, lubricating oils, and asphalt.

2. **Coal base**—This group includes those oils made by distillation (heating) of coal and shale which produces such products as benzol, toluol, creosote, and coal tar.

3. **Vegetable oils**—This group includes such products as linseed, tung, cottonseed, olive, palm, and castor oils.

4. **Marine animal and fish oils**—This group includes cod, shark, fish, seal, whale, and porpoise oils.

5. **Animal oils**—This group includes such products as neat's-foot and lard oil.

While all of these oils are commonly transported in barrels and many of them are transported in bulk, those produced from crude petroleum are by far the most important because of the tremendous quantities which are transported.

CHARACTERISTICS OF OILS WHICH RELATE TO SAFETY

Oils of all kinds may be divided into two classes for purposes of safe handling:

Flammable—Those liquids which will give off flammable vapors at or below 80°F. Thus, if such an oil comes in contact with a flame when the oil temperature is at or below 80°F, it will "flash" (small flames will pass over its surface). At a temperature slightly above its "flash point" such an oil will burn steadily; this temperature is called its "fire point."

Combustible—Those liquids that will give off flammable vapors only above 80°F. Combustible oils are relatively safe to handle and include such petroleum products as kerosene, light and heavy fuels, lubricating oils, etc. Practically all of the animal, vegetable, and fish oils are combustible oils and therefore are relatively safe; however, it should be remembered that certain of these oils when mixed with other substances will sometimes ignite of themselves. Thus old rags smeared with linseed oil (or even paint) or sawdust or rags wet with fish oil and kept warm will often ignite from chemical action. Many fires on shipboard have been started in this way and the cause of such fires is referred to as spontaneous ignition, which means the capacity of some substances to ignite from chemical action without being brought in contact with flame.

It will be evident that this characteristic of certain vegetable and fish oils to ignite of themselves when smeared on wood, sawdust, rags, etc., and heated, should be clearly remembered when preparing a cargo hold for barrels of such oils or when wiping paint brushes or the hands on rags in the paint locker. Holds should be thoroughly swept up and oily rags should never be kept in a paint locker or other closed space.

For the purpose of regulating tank vessels the Coast Guard divides all oils into the five following grades:

FLAMMABLE LIQUIDS

Grade A—flammable liquids having a Reid vapor pressure of 14 pounds or more per square inch (psi) and a flash point of 80°F or lower. Some examples are casing head or natural gasoline, very light naphthas, and butane blends.

Grade B—flammable liquids having a Reid vapor pressure of more than 8 1/2 psi but less than 14 psi and a flash point of 80°F or lower. Most commercial gasolines are Grade B liquids.

Grade C—flammable liquids having a Reid vapor pressure of 8 1/2 psi, or less, and a flash point of 80°F, or lower, such as most crude oils, creosote, benzole, toluol, alcohol, aviation gasoline grade 115/145, JP-4 jet fuel.

In the three classes of flammable oils the expression "Reid vapor pressure" is used. This refers to a method of measuring the tendency of these oils to give off flammable vapors. If such oils are placed in tight containers to which pressure gauges are attached, it will be found that a moderate pressure exists in the container due to the pressure of the vapors which have escaped from the oil. The pressures given in the definitions of grades A, B, and C oils are "absolute."

Since the atmospheric pressure is about 14.7 pounds per square inch absolute, it will be seen that only grade A oils will give a vapor pressure greater than atmospheric. The Reid method of measuring vapor pressures consists of placing a small amount of the oil to be tested in a container which is then closed and heated to a temperature of 100°F at which temperature the pressure within the container is measured by a gauge. By this means the tendency of the oil to give off flammable vapors is measured.

COMBUSTIBLE LIQUIDS

Grade D—combustible liquids having a flash point above 80°F, but below 150°F such as kerosene, JP-5 jet fuel, light oils, distillates and a few heavy crude oils.

Grade E—combustible liquids having a flash point of 150°F or above, such as heavy fuel oils, bunker C, road oil, lubricating oil, asphalt, coal tar and fish, animal or vegetable oil.

Figure 14-4. Main cargo manifolds on *Exxon Benicia*. Tanker has capability of loading or discharging different products at the same time. Ship can be loaded in 15 hours and discharged in 20 hours. Photo: Midn. R.L. Schopp, California Maritime Academy.

OPERATIONS PRIOR TO TRANSFER OF OIL CARGO IN BULK

Upon joining a tank vessel, those whose duties require them to handle cargo should familiarize themselves as soon as possible with the arrangement of cargo pumps and the layout of suction and discharge piping and valves. Almost all tank vessels have individual peculiarities relating to the loading and discharging of cargo, and inquiry should be made as to the methods used for loading, "topping off," discharging, and draining.

Prior to starting the transfer of oil cargo in bulk the senior deck officer present should assure himself that the proper signals are displayed (a red flag by day and a red electric lantern by night if the vessel is at a dock). At the gangway or point of approach to the vessel a warning sign should be displayed reading as follows:

WARNING
NO OPEN LIGHTS
NO SMOKING
NO VISITORS

If cargo is being transferred, the sea valves should be tightly closed and lashed and main deck scuppers plugged to prevent oil from getting into the harbor. The signal system (telephone, walkie-talkies, bells or whistles) used on the dock and the deck should be tested.

No repair work should be permitted on the main deck or adjacent cargo spaces which might produce a spark. When loading flammable oils (grades A, B, and C) no fires or open flames should be permitted in any compartment which is on and open to that part of the deck on which the cargo hatches and hoses are located.

The cargo hoses or mechanical loading arms (chicks) should be properly connected and supported, and sufficient men should be available to handle properly the cargo transfer operations.

After the individuals in charge on the vessel and on the dock have done everything possible to prepare for cargo transfer, a "pre-transfer conference" is held to insure understanding between ship and shore. The following items are discussed:

1. Identity of products.
2. Sequence of transfer operations.
3. Transfer rates.
4. Names or titles and locations of each person in charge.
5. Particulars of transfering and receiving systems.
6. Critical stages of transfer operations.
7. Federal, state, and local regulations.
8. Emergency procedures.
9. Accidental discharge containment procedures.
10. Discharge reporting procedures.
11. Watch and shift arrangements.
12. Transfer shutdown procedures.

To insure that each person in charge understands fully the items discussed in the pre-transfer conference, a "Declaration of Inspection" must be signed at the beginning of each watch or shift of the person in charge. When an inspection by the senior deck officer on duty indicates that all is satisfactory on deck, and all paperwork and plans are secure, the cargo transfer may begin.

In accordance with pollution regulations all oil transfer systems must be connected to a fixed piping system both on the vessel and at the terminal. Although in the past grades D & E were "loaded overall" (through hoses leading directly into tanks), this is no longer permitted.

ACTUAL TRANSFER OF OIL CARGO IN BULK

The transfer of bulk oil cargo consists of either loading or discharging. During the loading operation the gases within the cargo tanks are expelled through the tank vents and the ullage (sounding) holes if open. It is usual after loading has started to proceed at a steady loading rate until all tanks are about 90 percent full and then to reduce the loading rate considerably and "top off," or complete the loading of each tank slowly in order to avoid an "oil spill" or overflow. An oil spill during loading presents one of the principal risks in handling oil cargoes and the topping-off operation should be watched with particular care.

The operation and setting of cargo valves during the loading of cargo is an important matter. The senior officer present should supervise the handling of all valves. The dock or terminal man should be given a "standby" order from 5 to 10 minutes before the loading is started, stopped,

Figure 14-5. Control panel of *Exxon Benicia*. Control of cargo loading and discharging is from the control room. Status of all tanks is continuously shown on the panel. Photo: Midn. R.L. Schopp, California Maritime Academy.

or reduced in rate. The quick closing of a ship valve may result in bursting the loading hose or mechanical loading arm.

When setting cargo valves in the "open" position it is a good practice first to open the valve all the way, and then to close it about one-fourth turn in order to be certain that the valve is not jammed in the open position. When closing cargo valves it is a good practice to close them tight and then open them one or two turns and then close them tight again. By this means any scale or foreign substance which may have become lodged under the valve gate or disk, preventing it from seating tightly, will be washed clear. As each tank is topped off and its valve is closed, it is a good practice to check the liquid level in it during the time the remaining tanks are being finished to make certain that the valves are not leaking. In the loading of tank vessels the opening and closing of some tank valves change the rate of flow of oil into those tanks where the setting of the valves is not changed.

Figure 14-6. Ullage meter on main deck. Reading is in feet and inches. Status of tank can be monitored from control room as well as locally at the meter. Handle at left makes it possible to insure that sounding tape is free. Photo: Midn. R.L. Schopp, California Maritime Academy.

The discharging of oil cargoes is relatively safe; however, the bursting of the cargo hose as a result of excessive pressure should be carefully guarded against by starting the cargo pumps slowly and observing the pressure gauges frequently.

In discharging oil cargoes (except where mixed grades are carried), it is usual to hold until the last one full tank of oil to be used for priming the cargo pumps when suction is lost in draining. During the draining operation the vessel is usually "trimmed by the stern" to assist the oil in running to the suctions.

During the transfer of oil cargo, the cargo hose and deck area should be frequently inspected to see that it is properly supported. Drip pans or buckets should be placed under the hose connections. When the transfer

Figure 14-7. One of three cargo pumps on *Exxon Benicia*. Pumps are located below the waterline just above the skin of the ship in the pumproom. They are remotely controlled from control room. Each has a capacity of 125,000 bbls/hr. Photo: Midn. R.L. Schopp, California Maritime Academy.

operation is completed, the cargo hose should be drained back into the vessel's tanks, or into the shore pipe lines or drainage system.

Cargo hoses—Only cargo hoses made for oil service and designed for a minimum working pressure of at least 150 psi should be used. The hoses for cargo and bunker transfer operations may be supplied by either the vessel or the terminal. In either case the same regulations cover their use. A hose which appears worn should not be used.

Particular care should be exercised to see that cargo hose is properly supported and protected against chafing. It should not be bent to too short a radius. Sufficient hose should be used to provide for the movement of the tank vessel, but constant care must be exercised to see that the "bight" of the hose is so supported that it cannot become pinched between the dock and the vessel's side.

Mechanical loading arms—Many terminals are replacing hoses with loading arms. These are steel pipes which are mechanically, electrically, or hydraulically controlled or are counterbalanced and are joined together with swivel joints. They are subject to the same testing as hoses.

Mechanical loading arms do require some extra precautions. Loading

Figure 14-8. Mechanical loading arms or "chickstands" at a modern terminal. Hoses are rarely used in modern commercial practice. Photo: Courtesy Exxon Co. U.S.A.

arms have limited movement fore and aft as well as limited reach. For this reason a constant watch must be made of mooring lines to keep the ship close alongside and in position.

Cargo pump relief valves—These valves should be tested at least once each year to make certain that they function properly at the pressure they are set for.

Cargo pump pressure gauges—These gauges should be tested at least once each year for accuracy.

Cargo discharge piping—Cargo discharging piping should be tested at least once each year at its maximum working pressure.

GENERAL SAFETY PRECAUTIONS

Matches—Safety matches only should be allowed on tank vessels.

Smoking—Smoking should not be allowed on the weather decks of any tank vessel when loading or discharging cargo, when gas-freeing tanks, or when lying at the docks of an oil terminal. The senior officer on each tank vessel should make his own rules for the guidance of the crew as to where and when smoking is permissible.

Figure 14-9. Close-up of one of the many tank tops which are shown in Figure 14-3. Access to all cargo tanks is made through tank tops for inspections. Photo: Midn. R.L. Schopp, California Maritime Academy.

Cargo tank hatches and ullage holes—Tank hatches and ullage (sounding) holes should not remain open without being fitted with flame screens, unless the tank is gas free.

Nonsparking tools—Tank vessels should be furnished with lead, copper, or other non-sparking hammers or tools for opening and closing cargo tank hatches.

Fresh air masks—On manned tank vessels, where the distance from the deck to the bottom of the cargo tank exceeds 15 feet, fresh air breathing apparatus (including belt and life line) is required to be carried.

Fresh air breathing apparatus and smoke helmets consist of a hand-operated air pump which supplies fresh air from an uncontaminated area through an air hose to a face mask. Use of this equipment is limited to the length of the hose the wearer can safely handle behind him.

Since there is a limitation due to hose length with the fresh air breathing apparatus, many tank vessels are equipped with self contained compressed air breathing apparatus such as the Scott Air Pack. This allows the wearer to enter any space with an air supply on his back. The only limitation is the size of the air canister and the length of time the air supply lasts.

Ventilation—Ventilation should not be confused with venting. Engine rooms, living quarters, and other spaces where members of crew normally may be employed have ventilation. Cargo tanks, bunker tanks, coffer-

Figure 14-10. Tanks are cleaned by the Butterworth system which involves spraying hot sea water against sides of tanks at high velocity. Crude oil wash system is also used. Machine can be operated either remotely from control room or manually from main deck. Photo: Midn. R.L. Schopp, California Maritime Academy.

dams, and water tanks are vented to protect them against excessive internal pressure or vacuum.

The importance of ventilation in working and living spaces where flammable vapors are likely to accumulate cannot be overemphasized. Even in pump rooms where precautions are taken to eliminate all sources of ignition, ventilation is of primary importance. In working spaces where grinding of tools, electrical sparks, and smoking are normally present, ventilation must often be depended on to prevent accumulation of flammable vapors.

Vapors are heavier than air and tend to settle to the lowest parts of any space. Therefore, it is desirable to see that ventilators are so set that vapors will be removed from these low places. Particular attention should be given to this fact in the ventilation of spaces containing gasoline engines.

Such spaces, as well as pump rooms and hold spaces containing independent cargo tanks, should have at least two ventilators, one extending to the lower part of the space and the other terminating in the upper part, to provide natural change of air. Where necessary, steam- or air-actuated ejectors or blowers may be installed to secure adequate ventilation.

Doors and ports which may be closed cannot be depended upon to ventilate enclosed spaces. Other openings provided for natural ventilation should never be shut off or closed. Where mechanical means for ventilation are provided for pump engine, or other engine rooms, it should be remembered to turn them on a sufficient length of time before starting engines to insure the removal of possible flammable vapors.

Electric bonding—At some terminals, especially those near cities or large refineries, stray electric currents from trolley tracks or grounded power lines sometimes follow the oil pipe lines down to the dock. Since the hull of the tank vessel offers an excellent ground for these stray currents and since the cargo hose contains metal reinforcing which provides an electrical conductor from flange to flange, it sometimes happens that an electric spark will pass between the hose and ship or shore flanges when the hose is being connected. If oil vapors are around in quantity, it is possible for such a spark to cause a fire.

In order to reduce the chance of fire from these stray currents, some terminals are fitted with electric bonding or grounding cables. These cables should be connected in the following manner: The shore end of the cable is already connected to or grounded on the dock pipe lines. A switch should be provided in the cable. The ship end of the cable should be bolted to a bright metallic part of the ship's hull or cargo lines within a few feet of the hose connection. The following should be the exact sequence of connecting and disconnecting the bonding cable:

When connecting cargo hose:

1. See that switch is *open*.
2. Connect bonding cable to ship.
3. *Close* switch.
4. Connect cargo hose.

When disconnecting cargo hose:

1. Disconnect and remove cargo hose from ship.
2. *Open* switch.
3. Remove bonding cable from ship.

In the use of an electric bonding cable the point to be remembered is that the ship should first be grounded before the cargo hose is connected and that this ground connection should be maintained until after the cargo hose is removed.

Handling of general cargo—No general cargo should be handled during the loading of flammable oils (grades A, B, and C) without the permission of the senior deck officer present.

EMERGENCIES

Under the tanker rules, the senior officer present on a tank vessel is allowed free exercise of his judgment in pursuing the most effective action in case of emergency. Where an emergency arises during the transfer of cargo, the safest procedure usually is to stop loading or discharging as soon as possible. In an emergency, such as an oil spill or broken cargo valves or pumps, a definite plan should be worked out in advance for correcting the trouble. It is generally best to develop such a plan by discussing the problem with the terminal representative and one or two others on the tank vessel. When the plan has finally been agreed to, every precaution should be taken to insure safety, and the work should proceed slowly and carefully.

If the nature of the emergency is such that the vessel, its crew, and surrounding property is hazarded (such, for example, as a serious oil spill) all hands should be called and the terminal executive should be notified. In the presence of known danger, every step should be carefully considered and action should, if possible, be slow and deliberate. Oil spilled on deck should be carefully bailed up with non-sparking bailers or buckets, and the deck should then be mopped up and washed down before loading is resumed.

If it becomes necessary to work on cargo pumps, the cargo pump room should be thoroughly ventilated and freed of gas. When a cargo pump is opened up for repairs it should first be washed out if possible by circulating water through it. After it has been opened up, the repair gang should leave the pump room until dangerous gases have been removed by ventilation. Under such conditions the use of tools or electric portables (extenders) which might produce a spark should be considered as a possible source of ignition.

Cargo tanks which are not known to be gas free should not be entered by anyone not provided with, and experienced in the use of, a fresh air (hose) mask or self-contained breathing apparatus. It should always be remembered that the usual "canister" mask is of no use in entering oil tanks. Only two types of mask can be used—the hose mask where fresh air is pumped to the user through a hose from the deck, and the oxygen breathing apparatus where a supply of oxygen for breathing is carried by the user. The wearer of either type of breathing apparatus should be provided with a safety belt and life line. The life line should be tended by two men from the deck above. Whenever possible, repairs in cargo tanks should not be made until the cargo tank has been gas freed. Under no circumstances should any repairs which require the use of open flames be attempted in cargo tanks until such cargo tanks are gas free.

Cargo transfer operations should be stopped during a severe electrical storm, if a fire takes place on the tank vessel or in the vicinity of the dock, or if a towboat should come alongside in the way of the cargo tanks while the tank vessel is loading flammable oils (grades A, B, and C).

CLEANING AND GAS-FREEING OF CARGO TANKS

When it is necessary to repair a tank vessel or, under certain conditions, when a different grade of oil is to be carried, it becomes necessary to clean and gas-free the cargo tanks, cofferdams, bunkers, pump rooms, etc. Tanks may be cleaned in various ways, but, regardless of the method used, only two principles are involved; first, the removal of as much of the oil as possible from the tanks, and, second, the ventilation of the tanks to drive out the remaining gases.

Today the main method of tank cleaning is through the use of portable cleaning machines. After the cargo tank has been thoroughly discharged and stripped dry, machines with rotating nozzles may be lowered into the

Figure 14-11. Safety is of prime importance on a modern tanker. This is one of many foam stations on the main deck. Photo: Midn. R.L. Schopp, California Maritime Academy.

tank through Butterworth openings on deck. The nozzles rotate slowly in both planes and direct two streams of very hot water at a high pressure on all parts of the interior tank surfaces. While this operation is in progress, the ship's cargo pumps should be used to continue stripping the tank dry to allow the bottom of the tank to be cleaned as well as the sides. After cleaned and opened, blowers may be fitted in the tank and good air allowed to circulate. Natural ventilation may also be used, but to do the job well, may require too much time. The time required to clean and gas-free a tank depends on its size and the extent to which it must be cleaned. If a ship is going into the shipyard it is sometimes necessary to go down into the tank after gas-freeing to remove any residue which may remain after tank-cleaning by machine.

The testing of air in a cargo tank to determine whether it is gas free as defined in the Rules for Tank Vessels, should be assigned only to persons trained and experienced in cleaning and gas-freeing a tank and in sampling and testing of the air in the tank to determine its toxic and explosive nature. Two methods of testing are in general use, namely:

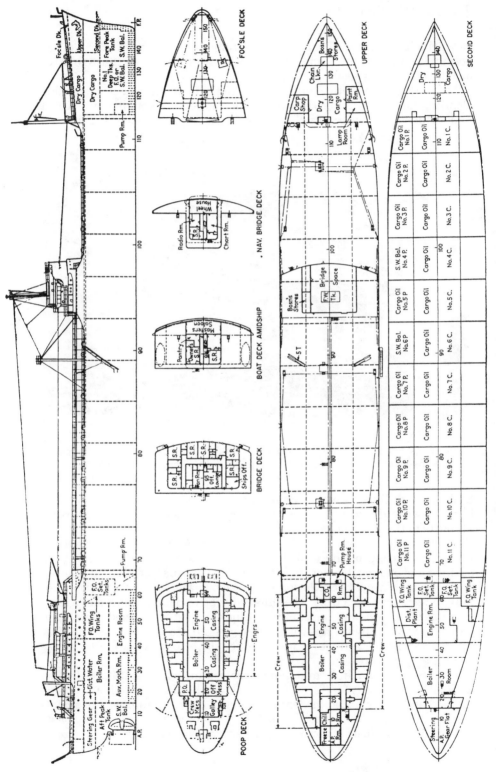

Figure 14-12. Profile, deck and tank arrangement plans of 38,000 DWT tanker.

1. Samples of the air of the tank are secured and taken to a laboratory where they are analyzed to determine the percentages of hydrocarbon vapors.

2. Samples of the air in a tank are drawn through a portable device known as a "gas indicator" which when properly calibrated will give a direct reading of the percentage of hydrocarbon vapor present in the air.

THE HANDLING OF OILS IN BARRELS, DRUMS, AND CASES

General—Before stowing oil in barrels, or cases, the holds should be thoroughly swept up and all paper, rags, sawdust, and water should be removed. Leaking barrels, drums and cases should be returned to the terminal for repair. Holds in which flammable oils (grades A, B, and C) in packages are stowed should be well ventilated during transit and especially before unloading. Ventilators to such holds should be screened. Before oil in barrels, drums, or cases is stowed in holds with other flammable or combustible cargo, the Interstate Commerce Commission regulations and Board of Underwriters rules should be consulted.

Stowage of combustible liquids in barrels—Lubricating oil, turpentine, kerosene, fish oil, and other combustible liquids in barrels should be stowed with the barrel on its side, bung up, and bilge free. Care should be taken that the chimes (ends of staves) are kept free from the sides of the vessel. No barrel should be stowed in a place where there is not sufficient room without bearing its weight on the bilge. All barrels should be stowed in straight tiers fore and aft. In no case should barrels be stowed with the sheer (round off) of the vessel's sides.

The middle of the barrel should be stowed over the four heads of the barrels in the under tier. This will bring the head of each barrel to the bung holes of the under barrels. In places where a barrel cannot be stowed in this manner, wood or suitable dunnage should be fitted in carefully in order to secure the barrels in the tier.

Barrels must not be stowed within 20 feet of a steam vessel's fidley or in any compartment where there is any likelihood of excessive heat.

Stowage of flammable liquids in steel drums—Steel drums containing gasoline, naphtha, or other flammable liquid should not be stowed more than seven high on end, and if the full quantity in height is not required, there should not be stowed on top of the drums any cargo the weight of which would exceed that of the drums and contents.

The drums should be well dunnaged between each tier and any broken wing stowage should be filled in with dunnage to equalize the pressure on the lower tiers and make a level. No drums containing flammable liquids should be used as fillers between the beams under the deck head.

Stowage of flammable and combustible liquids in cases—In stowing case oil, all cargo battens should be in place. Missing battens should be replaced with a 1-inch board.

Wings should be made up solid with planks or cordwood and boarded over top; also boarded fore and aft on sides to prevent cases being damaged by pressure of the cordwood.

All case cargo should be stowed in straight tiers fore and aft and under no circumstances should such cargo be stowed with the sheer of the vessel.

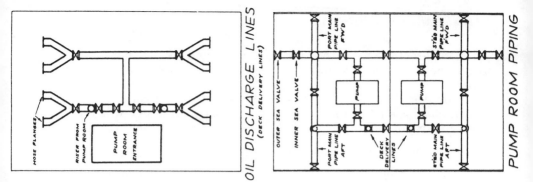

OIL DISCHARGE LINES
(DECK DELIVERY LINES)

PUMP ROOM PIPING

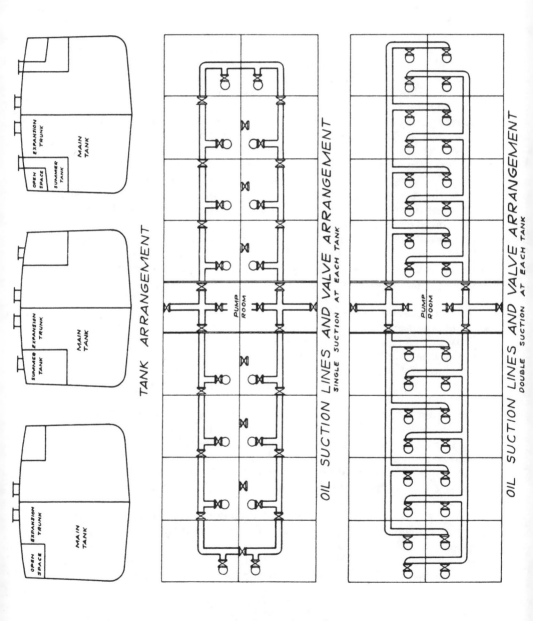

TANK ARRANGEMENT

OIL SUCTION LINES AND VALVE ARRANGEMENT
SINGLE SUCTION AT EACH TANK

OIL SUCTION LINES AND VALVE ARRANGEMENT
DOUBLE SUCTION AT EACH TANK

The first tier in all cases should be cross-boarded from wing to wing before the second tier is stowed. The after holds of steam vessels should be cross-boarded over the first tier and also cross-boarded over the tier that comes level with the top of the shaft tunnel. The tops of shaft tunnels should be made up solid to take the load of the cross-boarding, thus making a common level across the vessel. Split wood should be used in chocking cases on tiering height in both the lower hold and between decks.

Cases should be stowed on edge except in beam filling where one "flatter" of combustible oil is allowed. Flammable oil (gasoline, naphtha, benzene) should be stowed on edge and no "flatters" of this product should be allowed between the beams.

'Tween-deck spaces should be dunnaged 1 inch. 'Tween-deck hatch covers should be in place.

Lubricating oils and kerosene should be stowed under flammable oils (gasoline, naphtha, and benzene) or in blocks by themselves.

Flammable liquids (gasoline, naphtha, benzene) should not be stowed in a compartment or hold forward of the boiler room unless the bulkhead separating the hold from the boiler room is made of steel and watertight and with a separate bilge suction to such hold, and then only when approved general cargo such as machinery or oil in cases is stowed 20 feet forward of the bulkhead.

Flammable liquids in cases should not be stowed within 10 feet of the engine-room bulkhead, whether in the deep tank, 'tween decks, or hold.

Compartments in which flammable liquids in cases are stowed must be properly ventilated. Ventilators must be covered with flame screens.

Flammable liquids such as gasoline, naphtha, or benzene should not be stowed with ordinary general cargo.

EXTINGUISHING OIL FIRES

The crew of a tank ship or tank barge should be ready to fight fire at a moment's notice. Tank ships and tank barges are provided with special equipment for fighting oil fires which consist of:

1. A system of pipes and valves to convey steam, foam, carbon dioxide, or inert gas to the cargo compartments which may be operated from a protected control station, or,

2. A sufficient number of portable and semiportable foam or carbon dioxide extinguishers, located in various parts of the ship or barge.

All tank ships are provided with fire pumps, hydrants, hose, and nozzles. The use of water should, however, be restricted to fires in materials other than oils, except as mentioned in this section.

Foam—Foam extinguishes oil fires partly by the cooling from the water it contains, but more by cutting off the oil surface from the air, flames, and radiant heat, and retarding the formation of oil vapor necessary for the continuance of the fire. If the oil for a considerable depth below the surface has reached a temperature where vapor is given off freely, the vapor will penetrate the foam and burn above it.

◀ Figure 14-13. Tank, valve and piping arrangements.

Carbon dioxide—Carbon dioxide for fire extinguishing is stored at high pressure in steel cylinders in liquid form. When discharged, it immediately vaporizes to a carbon dioxide gas and snow at a temperature of about 110° below zero Fahrenheit. The cold snow materially aids in local cooling and smothers the fire. Spaces flooded with carbon dioxide gas should not be entered without proper oxygen-breathing apparatus. Carbon dioxide, being heavier than air, forms a layer of inert incombustible gas over the surface of the oil, thereby preventing the oxygen in the air from combining with the oil vapor.

Steam—Because steam has been found to be relatively ineffective in extinguishing fires, it will not be found on vessels constructed after 1962. However, to extinguish the fire an amount of steam must be supplied sufficient to reduce the oxygen content by the displacement of air.

Where large areas of oil are burning in the open air, foam should be used if available in preference to CO_2 for the reason that CO_2 vapor is likely to be blown from the surface of the oil by the slightest breeze which would probably allow the oil to reignite.

Directing streams of water into a tank of burning oil is ineffective for the reason that water does not remain on the surface of the oil long enough to extinguish the fire but sinks to the bottom of the tank immediately. If the use of water is continued, the tank will overflow and the burning oil, being on top, must then run out onto the deck through all available outlets. Water streams may be extremely useful, however, in cooling the decks and tops of other tanks which have not been ignited. A forceful stream quickly directed at small isolated puddles of burning oil may disperse and extinguish them.

The prompt and intelligent use of portable fire extinguishers will, in most cases, avert a serious oil fire. The two principal types of portable extinguishers suitable for oil fires are those containing foam or carbon dioxide. As usually supplied, these extinguishers contain 2 1/2 gallons of foam-producing liquid or 15 pounds of liquid carbon dioxide.

Foam should always be applied to the surface of the burning oil in as gentle a manner as possible in order that the foam may quickly float over the surface and form a continuous blanket. A point from which the foam blanket is to be laid on the surface of the oil should be selected and the foam stream directed in such manner as will continually advance the edge of the foam blanket over the surface of the oil. Since foam is a good conductor of electricity, if applied to live-electrical machinery, it will produce a severe shock to the operator. Therefore, foam should not be applied to such machinery except as a last resort. However, carbon dioxide extinguishers may be used safely on electrical fires.

Many large oil tankers are fitted with a fixed-foam system. This system consists of a series of large foam monitors on deck which can be aimed at the fire. The monitors are supplied by deck piping from a large tank containing foam. The foam, pumped to the monitors, provides a quick and efficient means of extinguishing a fire. These monitors may also be supplied with water to shoot out a large volume of water under pressure.

CHAPTER XV

SHIP CONSTRUCTION AND STABILITY

SHIP CONSTRUCTION as we find it today is the result of centuries of experience. It has changed over the years more through a process of evolution than of revolution. Many superfluous parts have been eliminated. Structural members have been reduced in size and strength. New materials have been developed, and testing has refined the size as well as the shape.

Many advancements in mathematical sciences have led to more sophisticated ship designing by the naval architect. No longer is trial and error the only means of determination. Precise calculations often with the use of computers have greatly aided the naval architect in the advancement of modern ship design.

SHIP STRUCTURE

The main structure of a ship is composed of a multitude of parts that are introduced either for strength, watertightness, safety, or, equally important, function. Many new requirements for vessels have led to radical departures from past design criteria. Formerly, the basic ship was designed for the carriage of cargo where no space could be wasted and weight was kept as low as possible. Craft for specialized industries such as offshore drilling and mining, research, and fishing have lead to new innovations in ship design.

Generally speaking, the cargo ship may be considered as a huge box girder, the sides of which are composed of shell plating and the deck. These parts are, in turn, strengthened by such members as the keel, frames, beams, keelsons, stringers, girders, and pillars. An understanding of the function of each of the above parts is essential.

The keel is primarily the backbone about which a ship is built. It consists of a rigid fabrication of plates or beams which run fore and aft along the centerline of the ship. At the forward end of the keel is connected the stem and at the after end are the sternframes which support both the rudder and the propeller.

The frames are the ribs of the ship. Their lower ends are attached at intervals along the keel, and their upper ends are attached through brackets to the beams which support the deck. Internal bracing is provided by keelsons and stringers which run fore and aft. The frames must determine the form of the ship and support and stiffen the shell plating.

The shell plating, although essentially necessary for watertightness, is one of the principal strength members of the ship. Running continuously from the stem to the stern frame and from the keel to the weather deck, it forms three of the sides of the box girder. The plating, aided by the frames, must be able to withstand the pressure of the water outside and the stresses which arise due to the buffeting of the waves or rubbing against a dock.

The main deck of the ship forms the fourth side of the box. For this reason it must be of strong construction. The deck plating is connected to beams

Figure 15-1. *Arco California* 188,500 DWT tanker under construction. Courtesy: National Steel & Shipbuilding Company.

which extend athwartships from one side of the ship to the other. In addition to supporting the deck plating, the deck beams tie into the tops of the frames and add support to the sides of the ship. The deck is strengthened by doubling plates in the regions where it is weakened by openings such as hatches and companionways, and also under all deck machinery, chocks and bitts. The deck is supported from the underside by girders and pillars. The bottom, sides, and main deck of the standard cargo ship would not be strong enough to stand the stress of an ocean voyage without some internal stiffening. This is provided by the lower decks and main traverse bulkheads.

In addition to furnishing support for the shell and decks, the main traverse bulkheads are made watertight, thus subdividing the vessel into watertight compartments, so that in the event of damage, the water can be confined. All doors through these bulkheads must be fitted with gaskets so that they can be made watertight, and must be kept clear at all times so that they can be closed instantly.

The first bulkhead aft of the stem is known as the collision bulkhead as its purpose is to limit the flooding that might occur after a collision. No

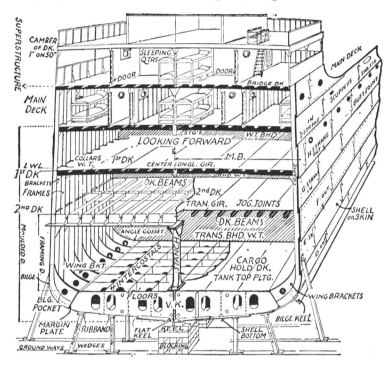

Figure 15-2. Midship section of a cargo vessel.

doors or other openings are permitted in this bulkhead below the main deck.

Further protection against damage is provided by the double bottom tanks. These are formed by a second complete layer of watertight plating located a few feet above the outer bottom and extending from bilge to bilge. Any grounding or similar damage which merely pierces the bottom plating will flood one or more of these tanks instead of allowing water to enter one of the main holds. Under ordinary service conditions these tanks are used to carry fresh water, fuel oil, or salt water ballast. The athwartship members that separate the bottom shell plating from the inner bottom plating or tanktops are called floors.

Modern tank vessels modify this basic design somewhat as they are devised to carry large volumes in tanks. In addition, they are often longer than a conventional cargo ship and are loaded deeper in the water. No 'tween decks are built into these vessels for added support to the side shell plating and so a system of much heavier frames, called web frames, is used. Fore and aft stringers are continuous or costal to provide maximum longitudinal strength. Since the ship is divided into tanks, the requirement for double bottoms has not yet been developed. Modern pollution laws are only beginning to deal with double bottoms as a requirement for new tank vessels. These ships have complex piping systems and thus require no hatch openings. A further discussion of this type vessel is found in Chapter XIV, Tankerman's Guide.

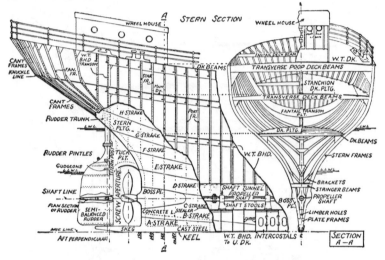

Figure 15-3. Side view and section of stern, looking aft.

The engine and boiler rooms have traditionally been amidships. However, this is no longer the case. Most new vessels have their machinery space aft to avoid interrupting the continuous cargo space, which is particularly important in container ships and tank vessels. In the machinery spaces special foundations are necessary for the support of the main engines and other main machinery components. 'Tween decks are often omitted in this area to allow sufficient overhead clearance for the machinery. To maintain the vessel's strength in the absence of these decks, several extra heavy web frames and traverse beams are fitted.

The propeller shaft extends through the after holds from the engine to the stern gland. As this must be accessible at all times for inspection and lubrication, it is enclosed in a narrow tunnel known as the shaft alley. The entrance to the shaft alley from the engine room is closed by a watertight door, and the sides are of watertight construction so that a fracture of the tail shaft or similar accident will cause only the tunnel to be flooded.

The necessity for good drainage requires special attention in the design and construction of a ship. Free water on the decks, in a hold, or in the bilges is detrimental to the stability of the vessel. Therefore, the drainage system must be as efficient as possible.

The decks are cambered to permit drainage to the scuppers which lead the water either overboard or to the bilges. Sufficient scuppers and suction must be provided so that the drainage will be effective in any condition of list or trim of the ship. Solid bulwarks, where fitted around a deck, are pierced by large freeing ports to allow any water that is shipped to escape quickly.

TONNAGE

Displacement tonnage is the actual weight of the entire vessel and everything aboard her, measured in long tons (2,240 pounds). The displacement tonnage is equal to the weight of the water displaced by the vessel. Displacement tonnage may be qualified as **Light**, indicating the weight of the vessel without cargo, fuel or stores; or **Heavy**, indicating the weight of the vessel fully loaded with cargo, fuel and stores.

Dead weight tonnage is the actual carrying capacity of a vessel and is equal to the difference between the Light displacement tonnage and the Heavy displacement tonnage.

Gross tonnage is the internal capacity of a vessel measured in units of 100 cubic feet.

Net registered tonnage is also the internal capacity of a vessel measured in units of 100 cubic feet but does not include the space occupied by boilers, engines, shaft alleys, chain lockers, officers' and crew's quarters and other spaces not available for carrying passengers or freight. Net registered tonnage is usually referred to as registered tonnage or net tonnage.

Under deck tonnage is the capacity of a vessel below the tonnage deck measured in units of 100 cubic feet. The tonnage deck is the upper deck on vessels that do not have more than two decks and the second deck from below on vessels of more than two decks.

Power tonnage is a measurement used to compare and classify vessels according to their importance. It is found by adding the gross tonnage to the indicated horsepower of the engines and is referred to in terms of *power-tons*.

DRAFT

The draft of a vessel is the distance that it is immersed in the water or the depth from the bottom of the keel to the water line.

Draft marks are painted on both sides of the stern and rudder posts in the following manner: The numerals are six inches high with six inches space between them and the bottom of each numeral rests on an even foot of draft. This method makes it possible to estimate by eye the inches of draft; thus if the water covered half of a number the draft would be equal to that number of feet plus three inches.

FREEBOARD AND LOAD LINES

The freeboard of a vessel is the height above the water level to the top of the freeboard deck measured amidships.

A load line is a line that limits the maximum mean draft so that there will be sufficient freeboard and reserve buoyancy to insure the safety of the vessel. The position of the load line on American ships is determined by the American Bureau of Shipping and indicated on the sides of the hull by Plimsoll marks (Figure 15-4).

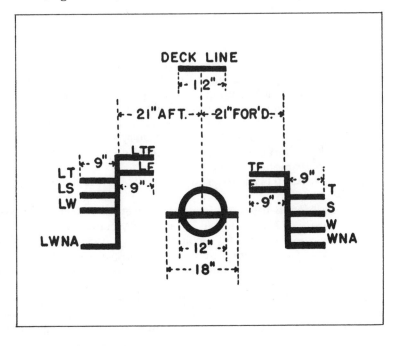

Figure 15-4. Standard load line.

Plimsoll marks consist of a disk with a horizontal line through its center, indicating the summer load line, and a series of other horizontal lines indicating the load lines for various waters and seasons. The abbreviations used to mark these lines are as follows:

F or **FW**—Fresh water.
   IS—Indian Ocean in summer.
WNA—North Atlantic in winter.
   S—Summer in waters other than Indian Ocean.
   W—Winter in waters other than North Atlantic.
   T—Tropical waters.
   TF—Tropical fresh waters.

PRINCIPAL DIMENSIONS

Length overall is the extreme length measured from the foremost part to the aftermost part of the hull.

Length between perpendiculars is the length measured between the forward and after perpendiculars. The forward perpendicular is a vertical line at the intersection of the fore side of the stem and the summer load line. The after perpendicular is a vertical line at the intersection of the summer load line and the afterside of the rudder post or stern post, or on the centerline of the rudderstock if there is no rudder post or stern post.

Breadth molded is the breadth of the hull at the widest part, measured between the outer surfaces of the frames.

Depth molded is the vertical distance from the molded base line to the top of the freeboard deck beam at the side, measured at the midlength of the vessel.

STABILITY OF SHIPS

In general, when the term "stability" is used by a ship's officer it refers to the ability of the ship to float upright and to its resistance to inclination by an external force. Stability is also used to refer to the tendency of the ship to return to its original position when inclined. Actually, there are two types of *stability*: transverse, which is in the athwartship plane, and longitudinal, which is in the fore and aft plane.

Another term often referred to when discussing stability is "trim." Trim, related to longitudinal stability, is the difference between the forward and after drafts. It is an important factor in loading modern ships because the depth of water in channels often requires that the ship enter the channel with the minimum possible draft. This means that the ship must be on an even keel and on zero trim. In tankers, trim and other factors in longitudinal stability such as stress and strain are far more important in loading the ship than transverse stability because loaded tankers are inherently stable.

The concept of stability and many of the formulae necessary for a full understanding of the subject are very complex. However, a few methods of handling stability on different types of ships are discussed in this chapter.

Several terms must be defined in order to discuss stability further:

Displacement —Displacement is the actual weight of a vessel, usually in tons. It is referred to as displacement because of "Archimedes principle." If a swimming pool were filled to the top, and a ship was then floated in the pool, water would overflow over the top of the pool. If it were possible to capture all the water that overflowed (was displaced by the ship), the weight of the water that was displaced would equal the weight of the ship. Furthermore, the *volume* of the water displaced would equal the underwater *volume* of the ship.

Center of gravity—The center of gravity of a block of uniform density is the geometric center. The center of gravity of a block or a shape of uneven density is the point through which all of the weight could be considered to act downward due to the force of gravity.

Center of buoyancy—The center of buoyancy is the point through which all upward force of buoyancy can be considered to act on a floating body. This is the geometric center of the underwater volume of all floating objects regardless of internal density. As the underwater volume changes (this happens when the ship rolls), the center of buoyancy changes.

The transverse metacenter—The transverse metacenter (the word "meta" is Greek for moving center) is the most complex of the points to be discussed in this text. It is calculated by the formula: **KM = KB + BM** where

　　KM is the metacenter
　　KB is the distance from keel to center of buoyancy
　　BM is the distance from center of buoyancy to metacenter

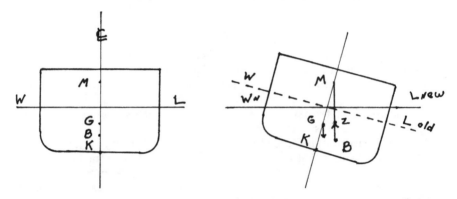

Figure 15-5. Shifting of the center of buoyancy. The center of buoyancy shifts to the right as the ship is inclined to starboard. This causes a righting moment between G acting *down* and B acting *up*. The distance from G to Z or perpendicular to the metacentric radius is called the righting arm. The righting arm × the displacement of the ship = the righting moment. The righting moment is the force in foot tons necessary to right the ship.

KB and BM may be calculated, but for most ships tables are available for extracting these numbers for a desired draft. The primary component of the metacenter is the beam of the vessel. The greater the beam, the higher the metacenter above the keel. The foregoing holds true, at least initially.

Many methods exist for calculating initial stability. The first one to be treated in this text is the use of the metacentric height. This is defined as the distance from the center of gravity (KG) to the metacenter (KM).

As a starting point, it is necessary to understand that the center of buoyancy rotates around the metacenter on a radius called the metacentric radius (KB). As the ship rolls, the center of buoyancy rotates around the metacenter at this distance. The *resulting* offset between the lines of force through the center of buoyancy and the center of gravity creates a righting arm. *The weight of the ship acting through this* righting arm is the basic force that acts upon the ship to set it upright (return it to an even keel).

Figure 15-5 gives the student a basic understanding of how and why the measurement of GM is effective in determining the initial righting force. The figure shows that as G moves up and the distance GM becomes smaller, GZ also becomes smaller. Thus there is less righting moment (force). As G moves down in the vessel (the weight being concentrated low in the hull), the distance GZ becomes larger. This creates a larger righting force.

The method of calculation used aboard ship is very simple. First, the center of gravity above the keel for each tank or compartment is calculated along with its total weight. A table is constructed as shown in Figure 15-6 on a standard ship's form which is generally provided by the steamship company.

Space	WT	Center of Gravity (KG)	Total Vertical Moments
#1	500	18	9000
#2	1200	21	25200
#3	1500	18	27000
#4	1250	17	21250
#5	1250	17	21250
light ship	2700	15	40500
crew & stores	250	22	5500
TOTAL	8650	(17.3)	149700

$$\text{KG for ship} = \frac{\text{TOTAL MOMENTS}}{\text{TOTAL WT}} = \frac{149700}{8650} = 17.3$$

This sample transverse stability form is a simplified version of the forms used on most ships. Most forms will include longitudinal stability information as well.

Figure 15-6. Sample transverse stability form, a simplified version of those used on most ships. Most of the forms include longitudinal stability information as well.

Figure 15-6 shows the basic method of determining the transverse stability by calculating the GM. A GM of 2 feet or more is normally necessary for a dry cargo ship because as fuel carried in the double bottom tanks is burned off, the center of gravity of the ship rises. This tends to decrease the stability and the GM. A final GM of 2 feet has been found to provide adequate stability and give good sea keeping qualities.

Free surface is an area which cannot be overlooked in any discussion of stability. Basically, when tanks are filled, but not to capacity ("pressed up"), the liquid in the tank is allowed to slosh from one side of the tank to the other. Generally the liquid goes to the low side of the tank as the ship rolls. This increases the intensity of the roll. The free surface effect is the same for a tank between 10 percent to 90 percent full. Calculations are made along the lines of the formula in Figure 15-7 to determine the effects of a loss in GM due to free surface.

1. GM by period of roll:

    $$GM = \left(\frac{.44 \times B}{t}\right)^2$$

t	= period of roll in seconds
B	= beam in feet

2. Inclining experiment:

    $$GM = \frac{WT \times distance}{displacement \times tangent\ of\ angle\ of\ heel}$$

    WT = weight shifted

3. Free surface:
    Effect

    $$GG' = \frac{rlb^3}{12V}$$

GG'	= reduction in GM
l	= length of tank
b	= breadth of tank
V	= Volumetric displacement of ship
r	$= \dfrac{specif.\ grav.\ of\ liquid}{specif.\ grav.\ sea\ water}$

    Constant salt water $= \dfrac{lb^3}{420}$

    Correction $= \dfrac{Free\ surface\ constant}{Displacement}$

4. Metacenter:

    KB = Block coefficient × Draft

    $$BM = \frac{I}{V}$$

I	$= L \times B^3 \times K$ (K = ship constant)
V	= Volumetric displacement of ship
	= 35 × displacement (in tons)

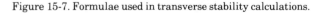

Figure 15-7. Formulae used in transverse stability calculations.

The block coefficient is a factor used to determine how close to a rectangular box the hull form actually is. For a ship the shape of the basic cargo vessel, a factor of about 0.53 is very common. However, larger container

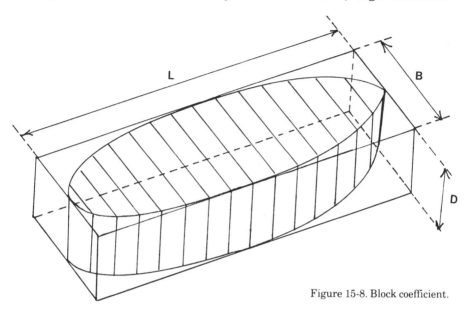

Figure 15-8. Block coefficient.

ships and very large tank ships have increased this figure somewhat. The block coefficient of a vessel of any particular draft is the ratio of the volume of the displacement to the volume of a rectangular box having the same length, breadth, and draft.

$$\text{Block Coefficient } (C_b) = \frac{\text{Volume of Displacement}}{\text{Volume of the block}}$$

or

$$(C_b) = \frac{\text{Volume of Displacement}}{\text{L x B x Draft}}$$

L x B x D   or
L x B x Draft x C_b = Volume of Displacement

In Figure 15-8 the shaded portion represents the volume of the vessel's displacement at a certain draft. The vessel is enclosed in a rectangle having the same dimensions of length, breadth, and draft.

TRIM

As ships have become longer, trim and a whole range of longitudinal factors have become increasingly important to the ship's officer. Ships with very deep drafts must be on an even keel in many areas to meet minimum draft requirements. Ships of excessive lengths must have the cargo carefully distributed in even amounts to avoid overstressing the hull.

Very simply, trim is the difference between the forward and after draft, and has nothing to do with the mean draft. A vessel with a forward draft of 7 feet and an after draft of 9 feet has the same 2 foot trim as a vessel with a 30 foot forward draft and a 32 foot after draft. Ships are normally loaded to be on an even keel or trimmed by the stern (after draft greater). If a vessel is trimmed by the head (forward draft greater) then the trim should be followed by the words "trim by the head."

The displacement of a vessel is the amount that the vessel actually weighs. It is also equal to the weight of the water the vessel displaces. If the draft and block coefficient of a vessel are known, the displacement may be found by the following formula. Conversely, the draft may be calculated if the intended displacement is known:

$$\text{Displacement} = \frac{\text{L x B x Draft x } C_b}{35 \text{ ft}^3/\text{ton (salt water)}}$$

$$\text{Displacement} = \frac{\text{L x B x Draft x } C_b}{36 \text{ ft}^3/\text{ton (fresh water)}}$$

$$\text{Draft (s.w.)} = \frac{\text{Displacement x 35 ft}^3/\text{ton}}{\text{L x B x } C_b}$$

Generally, once the intended draft or displacement is known, tables for longitudinal stability may be entered to find other necessary factors such as Tons per Inch Immersion (TPI) and Moment to Change Trim One Inch (MT1).

As was shown earlier, a moment is created when a weight is moved through a distance or added to a vessel away from the balance point. Thus if a 100 ton box is moved 120 feet aft on a ship, a moment to change the trim is created of:

$$100 \text{ tons x } 120 \text{ feet} = 12,000 \text{ foot tons.}$$

If the Moment to Change Trim One Inch (MT1) is 1000 foot tons, the change in trim can be calculated by:

$$\frac{\text{Trimming Moment}}{\text{MT1}} = \text{Change in trim (in inches)}$$

$$\frac{12,000 \text{ foot tons}}{1,000 \text{ foot tons}} = 12 \text{ inches (change in trim)}$$

The above change in trim, if the weight is moved aft and the vessel's tipping center is amidships, would mean that the forward draft would be 6 inches less and the after draft 6 inches more. This means a total difference between forward and aft of 12 inches.

When a weight is loaded aboard a ship, it first causes the ship to sink down in the water a small amount, depending on the size of the weight. If the weight is placed forward or aft of the tipping center, it also causes a trimming moment. The change is calculated as above and added or subtracted from the existing drafts. The vessel's sinkage is calculated by the use of the Tons Per Inch Immersion or TPI:

$$\text{Increase or decrease in mean Draft (inches)} = \frac{\text{Tons loaded or discharged}}{\text{TPI}}$$

Stress on the hull of a vessel is a very important part of the ship's officer's considerations in the loading of cargo. In the large and long ships of today, a poorly distributed load can cause the ship to break in half or crack. This is particularly true if the ship is in the heavy swells of the North Pacific or Atlantic.

Several means exist to determine stress. The stress factor and stress numeral are complex to calculate and tables are required for each vessel. On most new ships load calculators (or "loadacators") are installed to compute trim and stress. All the ship's officer must do is to enter the load that is to be placed in any hold at any particular time and he will receive an instantaneous readout of the stress on the vessel. In this way the stress can be monitored during the loading operation as well as when the load is complete.

GLOSSARY

Accommodation ladder—Stairs slung at the gangway.

Acorn—A solid piece of metal, shaped like an acorn, used to finish off the top of an upright in a railing constructed of pipe.

Aft, After—Toward the stern. Between the stern and the amidship section of a vessel.

Afterbody—The section aft of amidships.

After frames—Radiating cant frames fastened to transom plates.

Afterpeak—A compartment just forward of the sternpost. It is generally almost entirely below the load water line.

After perpendicular—The vertical line through the intersection of the load water line and the after side of the sternpost.

Afterrake—That part of the stern which overhangs the keel.

Air casing—A ring-shaped plate coaming surrounding the stack and fitted at the upper deck, just below the umbrella. It protects the deck structure from heat and helps ventilate the fireroom.

Air port—An opening in the side of a ship or a deckhouse, usually round in shape, and fitted with a hinged frame in which a thick glass light is secured. The purpose of the air port is to provide light and ventilation to the interior.

Airtight door—A door so constructed that, when closed, air cannot pass through. Fitted in air locks.

Aloft—Above the deck.

Altar—A step in a graving dock.

Amidship(s)—In the longitudinal, or fore-and-aft center of a ship. Halfway between stem and stern.

Anchor—An iron implement for holding a ship at rest in the water by means of a fluke or hook which grips the bottom.

Angle—Same as Angle bar.

Angle bar—A bar of angle-shaped section used as a stiffener; on riveted ships used to tie floors to the shell.

Angle collar—Angle bent to fit a pipe, column, tank or stack, riveted or welded to make a watertight joint.

Aperture—The space provided between propeller post and sternpost for the propeller.

Appendages—Relatively small portions of a vessel projecting beyond its main outline, as shown by cross sections and water sections. The word applies to the following parts of the stern and sternpost: the keel below its shell line; the rolling keel or fin; the rudder, rudder post, screw, and bilge keel.

Apron plate—A plate fitted in the continuation of the shell plating above the forecastle sheer strake at the stem. These plates are sometimes fitted one in each side of the stem, and serve as foundation for the bow mooring pipes.

Athwart—Same as Abeam.

Auxiliary foundations—Foundations for condensers, distillers, evaporators, pumps or any of the auxiliary machinery in the engine or boiler rooms.

Awash—Even with the surface of the water.

Balanced frames—The midship frames that are of equal shape and square flanged. There are thirty or more on a cargo vessel, equally divided between starboard and port sides.

Balanced rudder—A rudder with its axis halfway between the forward and after edge.

Ballast tanks—Tanks carried in various parts of a ship for water ballast, to keep the vessel on an even keel.

Base line—A horizontal fore-and-aft reference line for vertical measurements. This line is perpendicular to the vertical center line. A horizontal transverse reference line for vertical measurements. This line is perpendicular to both the vertical center line and fore-and-aft base line.

Batten—A narrow strip of wood for fairing in lines. Also a strip of wood to fasten objects together.

Beam knees—Angular fittings which connect beams and frames together.

Beam line—The line showing the top of the frame lines.

Beam plate angles—A beam made from a flat plate, with the flange bent at right angles by an angle-bending machine.

Beams—The athwartship members of the ship's frame which support the decks.

Bearding—The line of intersection of the plating and the stem or sternpost.

Bed plate—A structure fitted for support of the feet of the engine columns, as well as to provide support for crankshaft bearings. It also helps distribute engine weight and stresses to the ship's structure. The bed plate consists of a series of transverse girders, connecting fore-and-aft members of girders.

Bevel—The angle which one surface makes with another. Also to bevel a beam, flange, or plate for vee welding; to tilt a girder to make the sheer bevel.

Bevel square—A device that can be used to make a close bevel, less than 90°, or an open bevel, more than 90°.

Bilge—The rounded side of a ship where it curves up from the flat bottom plates to the vertical shell plating.

Bilge keel—Longitudinal angles welded and riveted back-to-back on the bilge of a vessel, to check the ship's tendency to roll.

Bilge plates—The curved shell plates that fit the bilge.

Bilgeway—Same as Bilge.

Bilge well—A bilge well is generally located in the lowest part of the compartment. It is used for drainage and is generally shaped like a box, and fitted to the underside of the inner bottom, with a strainer on top.

Birthmarks—Same as Plimsoll marks.

Bitts—Cast steel heads serving as posts to which cables are secured on a ship.

Bitumastic—A black, tarlike composition largely of bitumen or asphalt, and containing such other ingredients as rosin, Portland cement, slaked lime, petroleum, etc. It is used as a protective coating in ballast and trimming tanks, chain lockers, shaft alleys, etc.

Bleeders—A term applied to plugs screwed into the bottom of a ship to provide for drainage of the compartments when the vessel is in dry dock.

Block—The name given a pulley or sheave, or system of pulleys or sheaves mounted in a frame, and used to multiply power when moving objects by means of ropes run over the sheaves. Single, double or triple, when used with the word "block," indicates the number of sheaves it contains.

Block and tackle (Block and falls)—The complete unit of two or more blocks rove up with an adequate amount of rope.

Body plan—A pair of half transverse end elevations, with a common vertical center line. The right side gives the ship as seen from ahead, the left side from astern. Water lines, buttock and bow lines, diagonal lines, etc., are shown.

Boiler—Any vessel, container or receptacle that is capable of generating steam by the internal or external application of heat. There are two general classes of boilers, i.e., fire-tube and water-tube.

Boiler casing—A wall protecting the different deck spaces from the heat of the boiler room.

Boiler foundation—The structure upon which the boiler is secured. It generally consists of girders built up from plates and shapes. In a cylindrical boiler and the athwartship girders are often called saddles.

Boiler room—A compartment in the middle or after section of a vessel where the boilers are placed.

Bollards—Cast steel heads or short columns secured to a wharf or dock, and used for securing the lines from a ship. The bitts on a ship may also be called bollards.

Bolster plate—A piece of plate adjoining the hawse hole, to prevent the chafing of the hawser against the cheeks of a ship's bow. A plate for support like a pillow or cushion.

Booby hatch—The cover of a scuttleway or small hatchway, such as that which leads to the forecastle or forepeak of a vessel.

Boom—A term applied to a spar used in handling cargo, or as the lower piece of a fore-and-aft sail.

Boom table—An outrigger attached to the mast, or a structure built up around a mast from the deck, to support the heel bearings for booms. Boom tables are necessary to provide working clearances when a number of booms are installed on one mast.

Boot-topping—Special resistant paint or paints used to coat that portion of a vessel between light and load lines.

Boss—The part of the propeller to which blades are attached. Also the aperture in the stern frame where propeller shaft enters.

Boss frame—A frame bent around to fit the boss in way of the stern tube or shaft.

Boss plate—The plate fitted around the boss of a propeller post or around the curved frames in way of stern tubes.

Bottom plating—That part of the shell plating which is below the water line.

Bounding bar—A bar connecting the edges of a bulkhead to tank top, shell, decks, or another bulkhead.

Bow—The fore end of a ship.

Bow, bulbous—Bow with a large teardrop shape extending forward of the stem. This is a comparatively recent development which improves the seakeeping qualities of the ship as well as improving fuel efficiency because the ship disturbs the water less as it thrusts it aside.

Bow, clipper—A bow with an extreme forward rake, once familiar on sailing vessels.

Bow, flared—A bow with an extreme flare at the upper and forecastle deck.

Bow lines—Curves representing a vertical section of a ship's bow end.

Bow thruster—A large propeller mounted athwartships in a tunnel abaft the forefoot used to assist the ship in docking and undocking. Some ships may also have a thruster installed near the stern. This reduces or makes unnecessary the requirement for tugs. Thrusters are a comparatively recent innovation.

Bracket—A steel plate, commonly with a reinforcing flange, used to stiffen or tie beam angles to bulkheads, frames to longitudinals, etc.

Breadth—The side-to-side measurement of a vessel at any given place. The ends of the cross beams are considered the outward breadth measurements.

Break—Of poop or forecastle. The point at which the partial poop or forecastle decks are discontinued.

Breakwater—A term applied to plates fitted on a forward weather deck to form a V-shaped shield against water that is shipped over the bow.

Breast beam—The transverse beam nearest to midship on the poop and forecastle deck.

Breast hook—A horizontal plate secured across the forepeak of a vessel to tie the forepeak frames together and unite the bow.

Bridge—A partial deck extending from side to side of a vessel. Formerly placed forward or amidships, it is now frequently found aft on tank and container vessels. It is the control center of the ship which is used by the captain or pilot for conning. On older ships the term *bridge house* was used to define the bridge structure. It also contained the officers quarters and accommodations.

Brow—A small curved angle or flanged plate fitted on the outside of the shell of a ship over an air port to prevent water running down the ship's side from entering the open port. Also called a watershed.

Buckle plate—A plate that has warped from its original shape; also a plate that is wider at the center than at the ends.

Bulb plate—A narrow plate generally of mild steel, rolled with a bulb or swell along one of its edges. Used for hatch coamings, built-up beams, etc.

Bulkhead—A partition in a ship which divides the interior space into various compartments.

Bulkhead, collision—A watertight bulkhead approximately 25 feet aft of the bow, extending from the keel to the shelter deck. This bulkhead prevents the entire ship from being flooded in case of a collision.

Bulkhead sluice—An opening cut in a bulkhead just above the tank top connecting angle, and fitted with a valve which may be operated from the deck above.

Bulkhead stiffeners—A term applied to the beams or girders attached to a bulkhead for the purpose of supporting it under pressure and holding it in shape. Vertical stiffeners are most commonly used, but horizontal stiffeners or a combination of both may be used.

Bulkhead, swash—A partial bulkhead used for the same purpose as a swash plate.

Bulwark—The upper section of the frames and side plating, which extends above and around the upper deck. Often bulwarks.

Bulwark stay—A brace extending from the deck to a point near the top of the bulwark, to keep it rigid.

Bunker—Fuel oil space below decks.

Burr edge—The rough uneven edge of a punched or burnt hole or plate.

Butt joint—A joint made by fitting two pieces squarely together on their edges, which is then welded or butt strapped.

Buttock—Counter. The rounded-in overhanging part on each side of the stern in front of the rudder, merging underneath into the run.

Buttock lines—The curves shown by taking a vertical longitudinal section of the after part of a ship's hull, parallel to the keel.

Butt strap—A bar or plate used to fasten two or more objects together with their edges butted.

Camber—A slope upward toward the center of a surface, as on a deck amidships for shedding water. This deck camber is usually 1'' on 50''.

Cant—The inclination of an object from the perpendicular. As a verb, to turn anything so that it does not stand square to a given object.

Cant beam—Any of the beams supporting the deck plating or planking in the overhanging part of the stern of a vessel. They radiate in fan shape from the transom beam to cant frame.

Cant body—That portion of a vessel's body either forward or aft in which the planes of the frames are not at right angles to the center line of the ship.

Cant frames—The frames (generally bulb angles) at the end of a ship which are canted; that is, which rise obliquely from the keel.

Cargo port—An opening, in the side of a vessel of two or more decks, through which the cargo is received and discharged. Also called side port.

Carline—A short beam running fore and aft between or under transverse deck beams.

Carvel built—A type of plating made flush by vee-built welding or butt-strap riveting.

Casing—The extra case or bulkhead built around the ship's funnel to protect the decks from heat. See Air casing.

Caulk—To tighten a lap or other seam with a chisel tool, either by hand or mechanically.

Ceiling—The inside skin of a vessel between decks, or in a small vessel, from the deck beams to bilge.

Cellular double bottom—A term applied where the double bottom is divided into numerous rectangular compartments by the floors and longitudinals.

Center line—A horizontal fore-and-aft reference line for athwartship measurements, dividing the ship into two symmetrical halves. A vertical reference line in the center of the body plan, midship section or other sections.

Center line bulkhead—A fore-and-aft or longitudinal bulkhead erected on the center line or in the same plane as the keel. Also a reference line scrived on a transverse bulkhead to indicate the center of the ship.

Chain locker—The compartment for storing the anchor chains, located near the hawse pipes in the bow of the ship.

Chain locker manger—See Manger.

Chain locker pipe—The iron-bound opening or section of pipe leading from the chain locker to the deck, through which the chain cable passes.

Chains—Anchor chains.

Chamfer—A bevel surface formed by cutting away the angle of two faces of a piece of wood or metal.

Cheeks—The bilgeways, or curve of the bilges.

Chocks—Deck fittings for mooring line to pass through.

Cleat—A metal fitting having two projecting arms or horns to which a halyard or other rope is belayed. The deck, side plating, a stanchion, or other convenient structure serves as a support for securing the cleat.

Clip—A 4″-6″ angle bar welded temporarily to floors, plates, webs, etc. It is used as a hold-fast which, with the aid of a bolt, pulls objects up close in fitting.

Close butt—A joint fitted close by grinding, pulled tight by clips, and welded.

Club foot—The flattened, broadened afterend of the stem foot.

Coaming—Strictly speaking, coamings are the fore-and-aft framing in hatchways and scuttles, while the athwartship pieces are called head ledges; but the name coaming is commonly applied to all raised framework about deck openings. Coamings prevent water from running below and strengthen the deck about the hatches.

Cofferdam—A small space left open between two bulkheads as an air space, to protect another bulkhead from heat, fire hazard or collision.

Coffin plate—The plate used on an enclosed twin bossing, named for its shape. In reality it is an inverted boss plate.

Collar—A ring used around a pipe or mast, or a flat plate made to fit around a girder or beam passing through a bulkhead. They serve to make various spaces watertight.

Companionway—A set of steps or ladder leading up to a deck from below.

Composite vessel—A vessel with a steel frame and wooden hull and decks. Obsolete.

Conning tower—Protective structure built up of armor plates and having various shapes and sizes.

Counter—That part of a ship's stern which overhangs the sternpost.

Countersunk hole—A hole tapered or beveled around its edge to allow a rivet or bolt head to seat flush with or below the surface of the bolted object.

Cradle—A framing, built up on the ways, in which the ship rests while being launched.

Crater—A cup-shaped depression in a weld. The arc tends to push the molten metal away from the center of the point being welded, thus forming the crater.

Crutches—Same as Breast hook, but fitted at the afterend.

Cutwater—The forward edge of the stem or prow of a vessel at the water level.

Davits—A set of cranes or radial arms on the gunwale of a ship, from which are suspended the lifeboats.

Dead flat—The flat-surfaced midship section of a vessel on the sides above the bilge, or on the bottom below the bilge.

Deadlight—A shutter placed over a cabin window in stormy weather to protect the glass against the waves.

Dead rise—The upward slope of a ship's bottom from the keel to the bilge. This rise is to give drainage of oil or water toward the center of the ship.

Deck—A platform or horizontal floor which extends from side to side of a vessel.

Deck beam dimensions—The molding of a deck beam is its vertical dimension. Its siding is its horizontal dimension.

Deck, flush—A deck running from stem to stern without being broken by forecastle or poop.

Deck, forecastle—A deck over the main deck at the bow.

Deck, half—A short deck below the main deck.

Deckhouse—A small house on the after or midship section of a vessel.

Deck, main—The highest complete deck on a ship, in other words, the highest deck which runs the full length of the ship.

Deck, poop—The raised deck on the after part of a ship (obsolete).

Deck, shelter—The main deck.

Deep floor—A term applied to any of the floors in the forward or afterend of a vessel. Due to the converging sides of ships in the bow and stern, the floors become much deeper than in the main body.

Deep frame—A web frame or a frame whose athwartship dimension is over the general amount.

Deep tanks—These usually consist of ordinary hold compartments strengthened to carry water ballast. They are placed at either or both ends of the engine and boiler space. They usually run from the tank top up to, or above, the lower deck.

Development—The method of drawing on a flat surface the same lines which have already been drawn on a curved surface. The shapes and lines produced by development are the same as though the curved surface from which they are taken were a flexible sheet which could be spread out flat without change of area or distortion.

Diagonal line—A line cutting the body plan diagonally from the frames to the middle line in the loft layout.

Displacement—The weight in tons of the water displaced by a ship. This weight is the same as the total weight of the ship when afloat. A displacement ton equals 2,240 pounds.

Dog—A hold fast. Means of closing a watertight door.

Dog shores—The last supports to be knocked away at the launching of a ship.

Donkey engine—A small gas, steam or electric auxiliary engine, set on the deck, used for lifting, etc.

Double bottom—A tank whose bottom is formed by the bottom plates of a ship, used to hold water for ballast, for the storage of oil, etc.

Doubler plates—Extra plates (bars or stiffeners) added to strengthen sections where holes have been cut for hawse pipes, machinery, etc. Also placed where strain or wear is expected.

Draft markings—The water-line marks showing how deep the keel is in the water at stem or stern.

Drain well—The chamber into which seepage water is collected and pumped by drainage pumps into the sea through pump dales.

Dry dock—A dock into which a vessel is floated, the water then being removed to allow work to be done on the vessel's bottom.

Dutchman—A piece of steel fitted into an opening to cover up poor joints, or the crevices caused by poor workmanship.

Electrode—A pole or terminal in an electrical circuit. See Polarity.

Entrance—The forward underwater portion of a vessel at and near the bow.

Even keel—When a boat rides on an even keel its floating line coincides with the water line.

Expansion joint—A term applied to a joint which permits linear movement to take up the expansion and contraction due to changes in temperature.

Expansion trunks—Trunkways extending a short way into oil tanker compartments from the hatches. When the compartment is filled, the trunk is partly filled, and thus cuts down the free surface of the cargo, improving stability. Free space at the top is left for any expansion of the oil.

Eyebolt—A bolt having either a head looped to form a worked eye, or a solid head with a hole drilled through it forming a shackle eye. Use is similar to that of a pad eye.

Eyes—The forward end of the space below the upper decks of a ship which lies next abaft the stem, where the sides approach very near to each other. The hawse pipes are usually run down through the eyes of a ship.

Fabricate—To shape, assemble and secure in place the component parts in order to form a complete job.

Fair—To fair a line means to even out curves, sheer lines, deck lines, etc., in drawing and mold loft work.

Fair-lead—A term applied to fittings or devices used in preserving the direction of a rope, chain or wire, so that it may be delivered fairly or on a straight lead to the sheave or drum, etc.

Fairwater—Plating fitted, in the shape of a frustrum of a cone, around the ends of shaft tubes and struts to prevent an abrupt change in the stream lines. Also any casting or plate fitted to the hull for the purpose of preserving a smooth flow of water.

Fall—Commonly the entire length of rope used in a tackle, though strictly it means only the end to which the power is applied.

Fantail—The overhanging stern section of a vessel, from the sternpost aft.

Fathom—Six feet. A seagoing measure of length.

Fay—To unite closely two planks or plates, so as to bring the surfaces into intimate contact.

Fidley—A partially raised deck or framework over the engine and boiler room, usually around the smokestack (obsolete).

Fillet—The rounded edge of a rolled steel angle or bar.

Fin—A projecting keel.

Flange—The turned edge of a shape or girder, which acts to resist bending strain.

Flange, blank—A flange which is not drilled but which is otherwise complete.

Floating dry dock—A U-shaped dock with double skins which is filled by opening up the sillcocks, and allowed to settle so the middle section will be lower than the keel of the ship to be docked. The floating dry dock is then placed under the ship and the water pumped out, raising the ship so that repairs can be made on her hull.

Floor plan—A longitudinal section, showing the ship as divided at a water or deck line.

Floors—Vertical flat plates running transverse of the vessel, connecting the vertical keel with the margin plates or the frames to which the tank top and bottom shell is fastened.

Flux—A substance such as borax, used in welding to help in the melting of the metal. Flux also serves to stabilize the electric arc, steady the flow of the filler metal into the weld and protect the weld from oxidation.

Fore, forward—Toward the stem. Between the stem and amidships.

Forefoot—The forward end of a vessel's stem which is stepped on the keel.

Forepeak—The narrow extremity of a vessel's bow. Also the hold space within it.

Fork beam—A half beam to support a deck where hatchways occur.

Found—To fit and bed firmly.

Frame head—The section of a frame that rises above the deck line.

Frame lines—Lines of a vessel as laid out on the mold loft floor, showing the form and position of the frames. Also the line of intersection of shell with heel of frame.

Frames—The ribs of a ship.

Freeboard—The distance from the water line to the top of the weather deck on the side. Sometimes refers to the whole out-of-water section of a vessel's side.

Freeing ports—Holes in the bulwarks or rail, which allow deck wash to drain off into the sea. Some freeing ports have swing gates which allow water to drain off but which automatically close from sea-water pressure.

Gadget—A slang term applied to various fittings.

Gage—A standard of measure.

Galvanizing—The process of coating one metal with another, ordinarily applied to the coating of iron or steel with zinc. The chief purpose of galvanizing is to prevent corrosion.

Gangplank—A board with cleats, forming a bridge reaching from a gangway of a vessel to the wharf.

Gangway—The opening in the bulwarks of a vessel through which persons come on board or disembark. Also a gangplank.

Gear—Steering gear, running gear, etc. A comprehensive term used in speaking of all the implements, apparatus, machinery, etc., which are used in any given operation.

Girder—A heavy, main supporting beam.

Girth—The measurement around the body of a ship. The half-girth is taken from the center line of the keel to the upper-deck beam end.

Gooseneck—A return, or 180° bend, having one leg shorter than the other. An iron swivel making up the fastening between a boom and a mast. It consists of a pintle and an eyebolt, or clamp.

Gouge—A tool with a half-round cutting edge used to cut grooves.

Grating—An open iron latticework used for covering hatchways and platforms.

Graving dock—A dry dock. The vessel is floated in, and gates at the entrance closed. The water is pumped out, and the ship's bottom is graved or cleaned.

Grommet—A ring of fiber usually soaked in red lead or some other packing material, and used under the heads of bolts and nuts to preserve tightness.

Gudgeon—A metallic eye bolted to the sternpost, on which the rudder is hung.

Gunwale—The line where a shelter deck stringer meets the shell.

Gusset plate—A tie plate, used for fastening posts, frames, beams, etc., to other objects.

Gutterway—The sunken trough on the shelter deck outer edge which disposes of the water from the deck wash.

Guys—Wire or hemp rope or chains to support booms, davits, etc., laterally. Guys are employed in pairs. Where a span is fitted between two booms, for example, one pair only is required for the two.

Half-breadth plan—A plan or top view of half of a ship divided longitudinally. It shows the water lines, bow and buttock lines, and diagonal lines of construction.

Half model—A model of one side of a ship, on which the plate lines are drawn in.

Hard patch—A plate riveted over another plate to cover a hole or break.

Hatch bars—The bars by which the hatches are fastened down.

Hatches—Hatchway covers.

Hatchway—One of the large square openings in the deck of a ship through which freight is hoisted in or out, and access is had to the hold. There are four pieces in the frame of a hatchway. The fore-and-aft pieces are called coamings and those athwartships are called head ledges. The head ledges rest on the beams and the carlines extending between the beams. There may be forward, main and after hatchways, according to the size and character of the vessel.

Hawse—That part of a ship's bow in which are the hawse holes for the anchor chains.

Hawse hole—A hole in the bow through which a cable or chain passes. It is a cast steel tube, having rounded projecting lips both inside and out.

Hawse pipe—The tube lining a hawse hole in a ship's bow.

Hawse plug or block—A stopper used to prevent water from entering the hawse hole in heavy weather.

Hawser—A cable used in warping and mooring.

Height—Vertical distance between any two decks, or vertical distance measured from the base line to any water line.

Hog frame—A fore-and-aft frame, forming a truss for the main frames of a vessel, to prevent bending.

Hogged—A ship that is damaged or strained so that the bottom curves upward in the middle. Opposite of sagged.

Hold—An interior part of a ship, in which the cargo is stored. The various main compartments are distinguished as the forward, main, and after holds.

Hold beams—The beams that support the lower deck in a cargo vessel.

Hold-fast—A dog or brace to hold objects rigidly in place.

Holiday—Part of a ship's surface which has been accidentally missed in giving it a coat of paint or other protective preparation.

Hood—A covering for a companion hatch, scuttle or skylight.

Hulk—The dismantled hull of an old ship.

Hull—The body of a vessel, not including its masting, rigging, etc.

Inboard—Looking toward the center or toward midships from the outside of the ship.

Inboard profile—A plan representing a longitudinal section through the center of the vessel, showing heights of decks, location of transverse bulkheads, assignment of various spaces and all machinery, etc., located on the center or between the center and the shell on the port side.

Inner bottom—The tank top.

Intercostals—Plates which fit between floors to stiffen the double bottom of a ship. Intercostal comes from the Latin words *inter*, meaning between, and *costa*, meaning rib.

Isherwood system—A method of framing a vessel which employs closely spaced longitudinals, with extra heavy floors spaced further apart.

Jury—A term applied to temporary structures, such as masts, rudders, etc., used in an emergency.

Keel—A longitudinal beam or plate in the extreme bottom of a ship, from which the ribs or floors start. Different types of keel are described and illustrated in the main text.

Keel blocks—Blocks on which the keel of a vessel rests when being built, or when she is in a dry dock.

Keel bracket—A bracket, usually a triangular plate, connecting the vertical keel and flat keel plates, between the frames or floors of a ship.

Keel rider—A plate running along the top of the floors and connecting to the vertical keel.

Keelson—A large I-beam placed above the vertical keel on the rider plate for reinforcing the keel. The term may also apply to bottom fore-and-aft girders on the sides or at the bilge. See Side keelson.

Kerf—In joiner work, a slit or cut made by a saw. Kerfs are made where timber joints require adjusting. Also applied to the channel burned out by a cutting torch.

King posts—The main center pillar posts of the ship. May be used as synonym for samson post.

Knot—A nautical mile per hour.

Knuckle—An abrupt change in direction of plating, frames, keel, deck or other structure of a vessel. Most frequently used with reference to the line at the apex of the angle dividing the upper and lower part of the stern or counter.

Lap—A term applied to the distance that one piece is laid over the other in making a lap joint.

Lapstrake—Applies to boats built on the clinker system, in which the strakes overlap each other. The top strake always laps on the outside of the strake underneath.

Launch—To place a vessel in the water after completion, by means of sliding ways.

Laying out—Placing the necessary instructions on plates, shapes, etc., for planing, shearing, punching, bending, flanging, beveling, rolling, etc., from the templates made in the mold loft or taken from the ship.

Lazy guy—A light rope or tackle by which a boom is prevented from swinging around.

Lifting—Transferring marks and measurements from a drawing, model, etc., to a plate or other object, by templates or other means.

Lightening hole—A hole cut out of a plate to make it lighter and yet not reduce its strength. Also to make a passage through the plate.

Light load line—The water line when the ship rides empty.

Light port—An opening in a ship's side, provided with a glazed lid or cover.

Limber chains—Chains passing through the limber holes of a vessel, by which they may be cleared of dirt.

Limber holes—Holes in the bottoms of floors through which bilge water runs through tank sections to a seepage basin, where it is then pumped out. The row of holes constitutes the limber passage.

Liner—A piece of flat steel which may or may not taper to a point. Used to fill out a lap or to form a middle layer between two objects. Also for leveling foundations.

List—To lean to one side.

Load water line—The water line when the ship is loaded.

Locker—A storage compartment.

Magazine—Spaces or compartments devoted to the stowing of ammunition.

Main beam—The main longitudinal beam on a ship, running down the center line and supported as a rule by king posts. Sometimes there are two main beams, on each side of the center line.

Main body—The hull exclusive of all deck erections, spars, stacks, etc.—the naked hull.

Main breadth line—The greatest width of a ship amidships. If a ship's sides tumble home, the main breadth line will be considerably below the bulwarks.

Manger—The perforated, elevated bottom of the chain locker which prevents the chains from touching the main locker bottom, and allows seepage water to flow to the drains.

Manhole—A hole in a tank, boiler or compartment on a ship, designed to allow the entrance of a man for examination, cleaning and repairs.

Margin plate—A longitudinal plate which closes off the ends of floors along the midship section.

Marry—To join two ropes' ends so that the joint will run through a block; also to place two ropes alongside each other so that both may be hauled on at the same time.

Mast—A spar or hollow steel pipe tapering smaller at the top, placed on the center line of the ship. On cargo vessels they support cargo booms.

Mast hole—A hole in the deck to receive a mast. The diameter of the hole is larger than the mast for the purpose of receiving two rows of founded wedges to hold the mast in place.

Masts, pair—A pair of cargo masts stepped on either side of the center line, with their heads connected by spans.

Mast table—A structure built up around a mast as a support for the cargo boom pivots.

Middle body—That part of a ship adjacent to the midship section. When it has a uniform cross section throughout its length, with its water lines parallel to the center line, it is called the parallel middle line.

Midship—The middle of the vessel.

Midship beam—The longest beam transverse or longitudinal of the midship of a vessel.

Midship frame—The frame at midship, which is the largest on the vessel.

Mold—A pattern or template. Also a shape of metal or wood over or in which an object may be hammered or pressed to fit.

Molded breadth—The greatest breadth of a vessel, measured from the heel of frame on one side to heel of frame, on the other side.

Molded depth—The extreme height of a vessel amidships, from the top of the keel to the top of the upper deck beam.

Molding edge—The edge of a ship's frame which comes in contact with the skin, and is represented in the drawings.

Mooring line—Cable or hawse lines used to tie up a ship.

Mooring pipe—An opening through which hawse lines pass.

Non-watertight door—A term applied to a door that is not constructed to prevent water under pressure from passing through.

Oakum—A material made of tarred rope fibers obtained from scrap rope, used for caulking seams in a wooden deck.

Offsets—These are given in feet, inches, and eighths of an inch. They are taken from large body plans and give the horizontal distance from the center line to the molded frame line on each of the water lines, which are usually spaced 2'0'' to 4'0'' apart. Offsets also give the height of each buttock above the base line at each frame; the heights of decks from the base line; the location of sight edges of shell plates; location of longitudinals and stringers by half-breadths and heights, or heights above the base line intersecting the molded frame lines; and all dimensions such that the entire molded form of a ship and the location of all structural members are fixed.

Outboard—Away from the keel or center of a vessel on either side.

Outboard profile—A plan representing the longitudinal exterior of a vessel, showing the starboard side of the shell, all deck erections, masts, yards, rigging, rails, etc.

Overhang—Same as Counter.

Oxidation—The combination of a substance or element like wood, iron, gasoline, etc., with oxygen. The process is fundamentally the same whether wood is consumed with fire or iron is turned into rust (iron oxide). In welding, the oxygen of the air forms an oxide with the molten metal, thus injuring the quality and strength of the weld.

Pad eye—A fitting having an eye integral with a plate or base in order to distribute the strain over a greater area and to provide ample means of securing. The pad may have either a "worked" or a "shackle" eye, or more than one of either or both. The principal use of such a fitting is that it affords means for attaching rigging, stoppers, blocks, and other movable or portable objects.

Pale—One of the interior shores for steadying the beams of a ship while building.

Panting—The pulsation, in and out, of the bow and stern plating as the ship alternately rises and plunges deep into the water.

Panting beams—The transverse beams that tie the panting frames together.

Panting frames—The frames in the forepeak, usually extra heavy to withstand the panting action of the shell plating.

Partners—Similar pieces of steel plate, angles or wood timbers used to strengthen and support the mast where it passes through a deck, or placed between deck beams under machinery bed plates for added support.

Paying—Paying out, slackening away on a rope or chain. Also the operation of filling seams between planks after caulking, with melted pitch or marine glue, etc.

Peak—See Forepeak and Afterpeak.

Peak tank—Tanks in the forward and after ends of a vessel. The principal use of peak tanks is in trimming the ship. Their ballast is varied to meet required changes in trim. Should the afterhold be empty, the vessel would ride so high that the propeller would lie half out of water and lose much of its efficiency. Filling the afterpeak tank forces the propeller deeper into the water.

Peen—To round off or shape an object, smoothing out burrs and rough edges.

Pelican hook—A fastening used where security and great speed of removal are required.

Pendant—A length of rope, usually having a thimble or block spliced into the lower end for hooking on a tackle.

Perpendicular, after—A line perpendicular to the keel line, drawn tangent to the after contour of the stern.

Perpendicular, forward—A line perpendicular to the keel line, and intersecting the stem's forward side at the designed load water line.

Perpendicular, mid or midship—A line perpendicular to the keel line taken midway between the forward and after perpendiculars.

Pillars—Vertical columns supporting the decks. Also called stanchions.

Pintle—A metal pin secured to the rudder, which is hooked downward into the gudgeons on the sternpost, and affords an axis of oscillation as the rudder is moved from side to side for steering.

Plating—The steel plates which form the shell or skin of a vessel.

Plimsoll mark—The mark stencilled in and painted on a ship's side, designated by a circle and horizontal lines to mark the highest permissible load water lines under different conditions.

Polarity—The property possessed by electrified bodies by which they exert opposite forces in opposite directions. The current in an electrical circuit passes from the positive to the negative pole. In welding, more heat is generated on the positive pole than on the negative one, so that the welding rod is generally made the negative electrode.

Port—Same as Porthole.

Port flange—A protruding flange above a port to keep drip from entering.

Porthole—An opening in the ship's shell plating.

Port lid—A shutter for closing a porthole in stormy weather. It is hung by top hinges.

Port side—The left-hand side of the ship looking forward.

Propeller arch—The arched section of the hull above the propeller.

Prow—The part of the bow from the load water line to the top of the bow.

Punch, center—A small punch used to indent a piece of metal for centering a drill. Prick Punch: A small hand punch used to make a very small indentation or prick in a piece of metal.

Quarter—A side of a ship aft, between the main midship frames and stern. Also a side of a ship forward, between the main frames and the stem.

Rake—The forward pitch of the stem. The backward slope of the stern.

Rider plates—Bed plates set on top of the center keelson, if fitted, for the pillars to rest on.

Rolling chocks—Same as Bilge keel.

Rudder—A swinging flat frame hung to the sternpost of a ship, by which the ship is steered.

Rudder bands—The bands that extend on each side of a rudder to help brace and tie it into the pintles.

Rudder chains—The chains whereby the rudder is fastened to the stern quarters. They are shackled to the rudder by bolts just above the water line, and hang slack enough to permit free motion of the rudder. They are a precaution against losing a rudder at sea (obsolete).

Rudder flange—The flange which ties the main part of the rudder to the rudder stem. It may be horizontal or vertical.

Rudder frame—A frame within the inner shell, bolted through the latter into the main frame and shell, for the purpose of stiffening the rudder.

Rudder, pilot—a small rudder fastened to the after part of the regular rudder, which by a mechanical attachment pulls the main rudder to either side.

Rudder pintle—See Pintle.

Rudder post—The vertical post in the stern of a vessel on which the rudder hangs.

Rudder, streamlined—A rudder with a bullnosed round forward edge which tapers regularly to a thin after edge.

Rudder trunk or **case**—The well in the stern which holds the rudder stock.

Run—The narrowing of the beam of the ship from midships aft.

Sagged—Said of a ship which has been strained so that the bottom drops lower in the middle than it is at stem and stern. Opposite of hogged.

Samson post—Short heavy masts used as boom supports, and often used for ventilators as well.

Scantling—A term applied to the dimensions of the frames, girders, plating, etc., that go into a ship's structure. The various classification societies publish rules from which these dimensions may be obtained.

Scarfing—A method of cutting away two pieces so that they fit smoothly into each other to make one piece. They are fastened together by welding, bolting, riveting, etc.

Scupper—Any opening or tube leading from the waterway through the ship's side, to carry away water from the deck.

Scupper lip—A projection on the outside of the vessel to allow the water to drop free of the ship's side.

Scupper opening—A hole longer than an ordinary scupper with vertical bars, placed on the side of the ship at the deck line to allow deck wash to flow over the side of the vessel. Also called freeing port.

Scupper pipe—A pipe connected to the scupper on the decks, with an outlet through the side plating just above the water. The water thus diverted from the deck does not discolor the ship's side plating or damage the paint.

Scuttle—A small opening, usually circular in shape, and generally fitted in decks to provide access as a manhole or for stowing fuel, water and stores. A cover or lid is fitted so that the scuttle may be closed when not in use. Also applied to the operation of opening a sea valve or otherwise allowing the sea to enter a ship for the purpose of sinking her.

Seam—Joint.

Set bolt—A bolt used to force another bolt out of its hole.

Setup—To tighten the nut on a bolt or stud.

Shackle—A link with a bolt fastened through its eyes, used for fastening chains and eye loops together.

Shaft alley—A passageway along the shaft line between the after bulkhead of the engine room and the sternpost, affording a means of access to the propeller shaft.

Shaft coupling—A flange on the end of a shaft section connecting two sections by bolts.

Shaft pipe—A pipe which passes through a hole in the sternpost and through frames with a circular housing. In it are bearings supporting the after end of the propeller shaft and the propeller in twin- or multiple-screwed vessels having propeller shafts fitted off from the center line.

Shaft tunnel—See Shaft alley.

Shaping—Consists of cutting, bending and forming a structural member.

Shear legs—Usually two or more timbers or spars erected in the shape of an A-frame with lower ends spread out and upper ends fastened together, from which lifting tackle is suspended. Used for raising and moving heavy weights where a crane or derrick is not available.

Sheer—The upward curvature of the lines of a vessel toward the bow and stern.

Sheer plan—A vertical longitudinal midship section of a vessel, showing plan, elevation and end view, on which are projected various lines as follows: Water line; diagonal line; buttock and bow lines; main-breadth lines; top-breadth lines; topside sheer lines.

Shim—A piece of metal or wood placed under the bedplate or base of a machine or fitting for the purpose of truing it up. Also applied to pieces placed in slack spaces behind or under frames, plates or planks to preserve a fair surface.

Shoring or shoring timbers—Heavy timbers, usually 4x4s, which are used to shore up bulkheads damaged by collision or in battle. Also used to secure cargo.

Side keelson—A beam placed on the side of the hull about two-thirds the distance from the center line to the bilgeway. This is used as a stiffener longitudinally for the flat bottom of a vessel.

Skeg—The after part of the keel, upon which the sternpost rests.

Skin—The plating of a ship. The inside skin is sometimes called the ceiling, the outside skin the case. It consists of steel plates laid in alternate inside and outside strakes.

Sliding ways—One of the structures on each side of and parallel to the keel, supporting the cradle under the bilgeways on which the vessel rests in launching. The sliding ways form the inclined plane down which the vessel slides, made of planks laid on blocks of wood.

Sluice—An opening in the lower part of a bulkhead fitted with a sliding watertight gate or door having an operating rod extending to the upper deck or decks. These openings are useful in center-line bulkheads, as in case of damage to one side of the ship the water may be quickly admitted to the other side before the ship is dangerously listed.

Soft patch—A plate put on over a break or hole, and secured with tap bolts. It is made watertight with a gasket such as canvas saturated in red lead.

Spar—A pole used for a hoist or in scaffolding.

Spot-faced—Indicates that an annular facing has been made about a bolt hole to allow a nut or head to be recessed.

Square frame—A frame having no bevel on its flange. A midship frame.

Stanchion—An iron post or pillar for supporting the decks.

Starboard—The right side of a vessel looking forward.

Stealer or **steeler**—The foremost or aftermost plate in a strake, which is dropped short of the stem or sternpost of a vessel.

Steering engine room—Compartment above the rudder which contains the steering engine and related equipment.

Stem—The upright post or bar of the bow.

Stem foot—The forward end of the keel, into which stem is fitted.

Stern—The after part of the vessel.

Sternpost—The afterpost to which the rudder is hinged and placed on the skeg, with sufficient clearance for the propeller to revolve.

Stern tube—The bearing which supports the propeller shaft where it emerges from the ship. A cast iron or steel cylinder, fitted with brass bushings which are lined with lignum vitae or white metal bearing surfaces, upon which the propeller shaft, enclosed in a brass sleeve, rotates.

Stiffener—An angle bar or stringer fastened to a surface to strengthen it and make it rigid.

Stopwater—A wood plug driven through a scarf joint to stop water from leaking into the ship. The term is also applied to pieces of canvas soaked in oil, red lead, etc., placed between the faying surfaces of plates and shapes where water or oil is apt to work its way through.

Strake—A continuous line of plates on a vessel's side, reaching from stem to stern.

Strake, garboard—The range of plating nearest to the keel on both port and starboard sides.

Strake, landing—The second strake from the gunwale.

Strake, limber—The strake on the inner skin of a vessel which is nearest to the keel. Sheer strake: The top strake, just under the gunwale.

Stringer—A large beam or angle fitted in various parts of the vessel to give additional strength. Depending on their location, stringers are known as bilge stringers, side stringers, hold stringers, etc.

Stringer plate—A fore-and-aft member of deck plating which strengthens the connection between the beams and the frames, and keeps the beams square to the shell.

Superstructure—Any structure built above the uppermost complete deck, such as a pilothouse, bridge, etc.

Swash plates—Plates fixed in tanks to prevent excessive movement of the contained liquid.

Tackle—Any combination of ropes and blocks that multiplies power. A single whip, improperly called tackle, gives no increase in power, but a change in direction of the power applied.

Tail shaft—The aft section of the shaft, which receives the propeller.

Tank top—The plating laid on the bottom floors of a ship, which forms the topside of the tank sections or double bottom.

Template—A pattern made in the mold loft from wood strips or heavy paper.

Test head—The head of water corresponding to the pressure prescribed as a test for bulkheads, tanks, compartments, etc. Test heads are prescribed to insure satisfactory water- or oil-tightness, and also as tests of strength.

Toggle pin—A pin, usually having an eye worked on the head, and having a point so constructed, that a portion of it may turn on a pivot pin, forming a tee-shaped looking device to keep the pin in place.

Tongue—The tongue of a sternpost or propeller post is the raised middle section which is fastened to the vertical keel. As a rule the tongue is raised twice as high as the sides of the dished keel.

Tonnage openings—Openings in shelter-deck bulkheads for purposes of economy in tonnage rating.

Top breadth lines—The width of a vessel measured across the shelter deck.

Transom beam—A strong deck beam in the afterend of a vessel directly over the sternpost, and connected at each end to the transom frame. The cant beams supporting the deck plating in the overhang or the stern radiate from it.

Transom frame or **plate**—A horizontal frame, transverse bulkhead, etc. See also Abeam and Athwart.

Trunk bulkhead—The casing or partition that forms an enclosure running from deck to deck and surrounding the hatch openings.

Try square—A small and handy instrument for trying the square of surfaces while planing or fairing up with any tool. They come in various sizes and should be handled carefully to avoid knocking them out of true, and thus causing material to be spoiled by inaccurate work.

Tumble home—Said of the sides of a vessel when they lean in at the top. When vertical they are called wallsided; when they lean out, flaring.

Turnbuckles—Used to pull objects together. A link threaded on both ends of a short bar, one left-handed, the other right-handed.

'Tween decks—The space between any continuous decks.

Umbrella—A metal shield in the form of a frustum of a cone, fitted to the outer casing of the smokestack over the air casing to keep out the weather.

Unship—To remove anything from its usual place. To take apart.

Upper works—Superstructures, or deck erections located on or above the weather deck. Sometimes used with reference to a ship's entire above-water structure.

Uptake—A sheet metal conduit connecting the boiler furnace with the base of the smokestack. It conveys the smoke and hot gases from the boiler to the stack, and should be made double thickness with an air space between to prevent radiation. Swinging dampers for controlling the fires are fitted in the uptake.

Water lines—Lines drawn parallel with the surface of the water at varying heights on a ship's outline. In the sheer plan they are straight and horizontal; in the half-breadth plan they show the form of the ship at each successive height marked.

Watertight door—A door so constructed that, when closed, it will prevent water under pressure from passing through.

Waterway—A gutterlike recess on the shelter deck at the midship section of a ship, which delivers excess water to the scupper holes for discharge into the sea.

Ways—The timber sills upon which a ship is built.

Web—The plate or its equivalent in a beam or girder, which connects the upper and lower flat plates, or laterally extending members.

Weeping—The very slow issuance of water through the seams of a ship's structure or from a containing vessel in insufficient quantity to produce a stream.

Welding—The method of fastening steel objects together by fusing the metal with a gas flame or an electrical arc.

Welding bead—A seam made by closing a joint with molten metal applied with a welding stick.

Well deck—A sunken deck on a merchant vessel, fitted between the forecastle and a long poop or continuous bridge house or raised quarter deck.

Whaler—Any steel or wooden member used for temporarily bracing a bulkhead, deck section, etc.

Wing—The overhanging or outboard part (of a ship or deck). For example: The wing of the bridge or the wing tanks.

Wing tanks—Tanks located outboard and usually just under the weather deck. They are sometimes formed by fitting a longitudinal bulkhead between the two uppermost decks, and sometimes by working a diagonal, longitudinal flat between the ship's side and the weather deck.

Wire mesh bulkhead—A partition built up of wire mesh panel.

CHAPTER XVI

NAVIGATION

NAVIGATION IS DEFINED as "the process of directing the movement of a craft from one point to another." The purposes of this chapter are to give the merchant seaman an appreciation for what is involved in navigation, and a grounding in its fundamentals. The following pages are directed toward navigation requirements for the Coast Guard licensing examination for third mate, but will be of interest to anyone who intends to make his living at sea or to a yachtsman who wishes to prepare himself for ocean sailing or cruising in coastal waters. Although this chapter includes a description of instruments and accessories used in navigation, piloting, charts, and celestial navigation, a serious student should also become familiar with Bowditch's *American Practical Navigator* (1977), *Dutton's Navigation and Piloting* (1978), and other standard works.

Webster defines seamanship as "the art or skill of handling, working, and navigating a ship." Obviously seamanship and navigation are closely related and at times cannot be stowed neatly in separate lockers. But when a new seaman goes up to the bridge for his first watch he will find that the primary concern of the master and navigator (probably the second mate) is getting the ship to her next port safely and on time.

Navigation takes the following forms:

Dead reckoning—The determination of position by advancing a known position for courses and distances. A position so determined is called a dead reckoning position.

Piloting—Navigation involving frequent or continuous determination of a position relative to geographic points. This requires good judgement and almost constant attention on the part of the navigator.

Celestial navigation—Navigation using information obtained from celestial bodies.

Electronic navigation—Navigation by means of electronic equipment. This could be radio navigation which uses radio waves for determination of position or a line of position. It could be radar navigation which involves the use of radio waves, probably in the centimeter band, to determine the bearing and distance of a known object. It could be satellite navigation which uses the artificial earth satellites to determine the ship's position. The term could equally well refer to using the fathometer to assist in fixing the ship's position since a fathometer also uses electronics. Electronic navigation is a term so general it cannot be sharply defined. Rather, it can only be said that electronic navigation may be used to reinforce or to assist in piloting or in celestial navigation.

INSTRUMENTS AND ACCESSORIES USED IN NAVIGATION

Every occupation has its "tools of the trade" and navigation is no exception. These tools are many and vary from the extremely simple to the very complex, from the simple dividers which the navigator uses to measure a distance to the satellite navigator which can give a continuous read-out on a position in any part of the world.

Dividers and compasses—Dividers, or a "pair of dividers," are used for measuring distances. They consist of two hinged legs with pointed ends which can be separated to any required distance from each other. If one of the legs carries a pencil, the instrument is called a pair of compasses.

Parallel rules consist of two rulers connected together in such a manner that they remain parallel when one or the other is moved. They are used in chart work to determine courses and to lay off bearings.

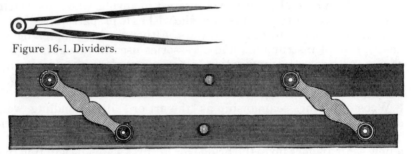

Figure 16-1. Dividers.

Figure 16-2. Parallel rulers.

Universal drafting machine—Most ships use a drafting machine or a parallel motion protractor instead of parallel rulers. It can be set for any bearing and makes plotting much easier.

COMPASSES

The two kinds of compasses found aboard ship are the magnetic compass and the gyrocompass (gyroscopic compass). The magnetic compass tends to align itself with the magnetic lines of force of the earth while the gyrocompass seeks the true (or geographic) meridian. Although the gyrocompass has largely superseded the magnetic compass, a vessel must have a reliable back-up system, and consequently all ships are required to carry a magnetic compass in addition to their gyrocompass. It is important to keep a record of the errors and performance of both types and compare their readings frequently when underway.

Magnetic compass—If a small magnet is pivoted at its center of gravity so that it is free to turn and dip, it will tend to line itself up with the earth's magnetic lines of force, or tend to point towards magnetic North.

In a mariner's compass, several magnets are mounted parallel to each other. A compass card made of light, nonmagnetic material is attached to the magnets. Both magnets and card are enclosed in a bowl which has a glass top. The bowl is weighted at the bottom and is suspended in gimbals

Figure 16-3. Universal drafting machine, reproduced from *American Practical Navigator.* Courtesy: Defense Mapping Agency Hydrographic Center.

so that it remains nearly horizontal when the vessel rolls and pitches. In most modern compasses the bowl is filled with a liquid that helps buoy up the compass card and reduce the friction on the pivot (a metal point in a jeweled bearing), and provides a means of damping the oscillations of the compass card. A mark called a lubber's line is placed on the inner surface of the bowl to indicate the bow of the ship when the bowl is correctly installed. The gimbals used for mounting the compass bowl are attached to a stand called a binnacle which is secured to the deck, usually on the center line.

The compass should be checked and overhauled at regular intervals. Discoloration of the liquid or the presence of a bubble should be investigated. If it is necessary to add liquid, it is probably a job for a professional. If it must be done aboard ship, the manufacturer's instructions should first be studied carefully.

On most modern compasses the card is graduated into equal parts of 360°, increasing clockwise. Some older cards may be graduated in "points" in addition to the degree graduations. There are 32 points to the compass, 11 1/4° apart. The four cardinal points are north, east, south, and west. The intercardinal points midway between these are northeast, southeast, southwest, and northwest.

	Points	Angular measure ° ′ ″		Points	Angular measure ° ′ ″
NORTH TO EAST			**SOUTH TO WEST**		
North	0	0 00 00	South	16	180 00 00
N¼E	¼	2 48 45	S¼W	16¼	182 48 45
N½E	½	5 37 30	S½W	16½	185 37 30
N¾E	¾	8 26 15	S¾W	16¾	188 26 15
N by E	1	11 15 00	S by W	17	191 15 00
N by E¼E	1¼	14 03 45	S by W¼W	17¼	194 03 45
N by E½E	1½	16 52 30	S by W½W	17½	196 52 30
N by E¾E	1¾	19 41 15	S by W¾W	17¾	199 41 15
NNE	2	22 30 00	SSW	18	202 30 00
NNE¼E	2¼	25 18 45	SSW¼W	18¼	205 18 45
NNE½E	2½	28 07 30	SSW½W	18½	208 07 30
NNE¾E	2¾	30 56 15	SSW¾W	18¾	210 56 15
NE by N	3	33 45 00	SW by S	19	213 45 00
NE¾N	3¼	36 33 45	SW¾S	19¼	216 33 45
NE½N	3½	39 22 30	SW½S	19½	219 22 30
NE¼N	3¾	42 11 15	SW¼S	19¾	222 11 15
NE	4	45 00 00	SW	20	225 00 00
NE¼E	4¼	47 48 45	SW¼W	20¼	227 48 45
NE½E	4½	50 37 30	SW½W	20½	230 37 30
NE¾E	4¾	53 26 15	SW¾W	20¾	233 26 15
NE by E	5	56 15 00	SW by W	21	236 15 00
NE by E¼E	5¼	59 03 45	SW by W¼W	21¼	239 03 45
NE by E½E	5½	61 52 30	SW by W½W	21½	241 52 30
NE by E¾E	5¾	64 41 15	SW by W¾W	21¾	244 41 15
ENE	6	67 30 00	WSW	22	247 30 00
ENE¼E	6¼	70 18 45	WSW¼W	22¼	250 18 45
ENE½E	6½	73 07 30	WSW½W	22½	253 07 30
ENE¾E	6¾	75 56 15	WSW¾W	22¾	255 56 15
E by N	7	78 45 00	W by S	23	258 45 00
E¾N	7¼	81 33 45	W¾S	23¼	261 33 45
E½N	7½	84 22 30	W½S	23½	264 22 30
E¼N	7¾	87 11 15	W¼S	23¾	267 11 15
EAST TO SOUTH			**WEST TO NORTH**		
East	8	90 00 00	West	24	270 00 00
E¼S	8¼	92 48 45	W¼N	24¼	272 48 45
E½S	8½	95 37 30	W½N	24½	275 37 30
E¾S	8¾	98 26 15	W¾N	24¾	278 26 15
E by S	9	101 15 00	W by N	25	281 15 00
ESE¾E	9¼	104 03 45	WNW¾W	25¼	284 03 45
ESE½E	9½	106 52 30	WNW½W	25½	286 52 30
ESE¼E	9¾	109 41 15	WNW¼W	25¾	289 41 15
ESE	10	112 30 00	WNW	26	292 30 00
SE by E¾E	10¼	115 18 45	NW by W¾W	26¼	295 18 45
SE by E½E	10½	118 07 30	NW by W½W	26½	298 07 30
SE by E¼E	10¾	120 56 15	NW by W¼W	26¾	300 56 15
SE by E	11	123 45 00	NW by W	27	303 45 00
SE¾E	11¼	126 33 45	NW¾W	27¼	306 33 45
SE½E	11½	129 22 30	NW½W	27½	309 22 30
SE¼E	11¾	132 11 15	NW¼W	27¾	312 11 15
SE	12	135 00 00	NW	28	315 00 00
SE¼S	12¼	137 48 45	NW¼N	28¼	317 48 45
SE½S	12½	140 37 30	NW½N	28½	320 37 30
SE¾S	12¾	143 26 15	NW¾N	28¾	323 26 15
SE by S	13	146 15 00	NW by N	29	326 15 00
SSE¾E	13¼	149 03 45	NNW¾W	29¼	329 03 45
SSE½E	13½	151 52 30	NNW½W	29½	331 52 30
SSE¼E	13¾	154 41 15	NNW¼W	29¾	334 41 15
SSE	14	157 30 00	NNW	30	337 30 00
S by E¾E	14¼	160 18 45	N by W¾W	30¼	340 18 45
S by E½E	14½	163 07 30	N by W½W	30½	343 07 30
S by E¼E	14¾	165 56 15	N by W¼W	30¾	345 56 15
S by E	15	168 45 00	N by W	31	348 45 00
S¾E	15¼	171 33 45	N¾W	31¼	351 33 45
S½E	15½	174 22 30	N½W	31½	354 22 30
S¼E	15¾	177 11 15	N¼W	31¾	357 11 15
South	16	180 00 00	North	32	360 00 00

Figure 16-4. Conversion of compass points to degrees, reproduced from *American Practical Navigator*. Courtesy: Defense Mapping Agency Hydrographic Center.

The use of points as a means of indicating direction has all but disappeared, but naming the various graduations of the compass by the use of the point system is called "boxing the compass" and is still included in the Lifeboatman's Manual (CG-175). Before condemning the system as completely obsolete, one should realize that it is much easier to see to steer a course of ENE on a dimly lit binnacle of a yawl on an ocean crossing than it is to see the graduation of 067°, and hold the boat on that heading. Table 2 of Bowditch reproduced as Figure 16-4 shows the conversion of compass points and quarter points to degrees, minutes, and seconds.

Figure 16-5. U.S. Navy 7 1/2 inch compass. Courtesy: Defense Mapping Agency Hydrographic Center.

The U.S. Navy 7 1/2-inch magnetic compass typical of those in use in the Merchant Marine and Navy has a liquid-filled bowl in which a 7 1/2'' aluminum card is pivoted. There may be either one or two pairs of magnets symmetrically placed. The card and magnet assembly has a central float or air chamber to reduce the weight on the pivot to between 0.14 and 0.21 ounce at 60°F when the correct compass fluid is used. Older compasses used a mixture of ethyl alcohol and distilled water, but newer ones used a refined petroleum product similar to varsol. A hollow cone with an open bottom extends into the underside of the float. The pointed top has a jeweled bearing, and the card assembly rests on an osmium-iridium tipped pivot at the center. This compass is shown in Figure 16-5.

The compass bowl is made of bronze, and has a tight glass top cover to prevent the liquid from leaking. A bellows-type expansion chamber allows for changes in volume of the liquid as the temperature changes. The top

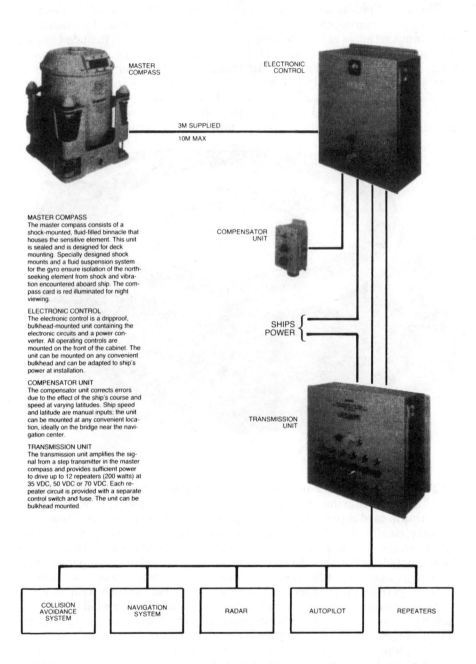

MASTER COMPASS

ELECTRONIC CONTROL

3M SUPPLIED

10M MAX

MASTER COMPASS
The master compass consists of a shock-mounted, fluid-filled binnacle that houses the sensitive element. This unit is sealed and is designed for deck mounting. Specially designed shock mounts and a fluid suspension system for the gyro ensure isolation of the north-seeking element from shock and vibration encountered aboard ship. The compass card is red illuminated for night viewing.

ELECTRONIC CONTROL
The electronic control is a dripproof, bulkhead-mounted unit containing the electronic circuits and a power converter. All operating controls are mounted on the front of the cabinet. The unit can be mounted on any convenient bulkhead and can be adapted to ship's power at installation.

COMPENSATOR UNIT
The compensator unit corrects errors due to the effect of the ship's course and speed at varying latitudes. Ship speed and latitude are manual inputs; the unit can be mounted at any convenient location, ideally on the bridge near the navigation center.

TRANSMISSION UNIT
The transmission unit amplifies the signal from a step transmitter in the master compass and provides sufficient power to drive up to 12 repeaters (200 watts) at 35 VDC, 50 VDC or 70 VDC. Each repeater circuit is provided with a separate control switch and fuse. The unit can be bulkhead mounted.

COMPENSATOR UNIT

SHIPS POWER

TRANSMISSION UNIT

COLLISION AVOIDANCE SYSTEM

NAVIGATION SYSTEM

RADAR

AUTOPILOT

REPEATERS

Figure 16-6. Sperry Mk 37 Mod D gyrocompass equipment. Courtesy Sperry Marine Inc.

ROUTINE OPERATION

Although the operation of the Master Compass is automatic, the following checks should be made during each watch.

Step 1. Check the 0-80 Latitude Control on Compensator Unit and reset as required.

Step 2. Check the N/S LATITUDE switch and reset as required.

Step 3. Check the SPEED KNOTS control on Compensator Unit and reset as required.

Step 4. Make periodic normal azimuth checks to verify the compass heading indication.

Figure 16-7. Routine operation of Mk 37 Mod D gyrocompass. Courtesy Sperry Marine Inc.

rim or bevel of the bowl is accurately machined so that an azimuth circle can be placed over it. The compass is mounted in gimbals for keeping it level when mounted in a binnacle. In addition to being a stand, the binnacle houses the correctors used to compensate the compass or to partially neutralize the local magnetic fields within the vessel.

The U.S. Navy 7 1/2-inch magnetic compass just described is called a liquid compass because the liquid in the bowl helps support the compass card. There is also a dry compass which has a compass card with the edge stiffened by aluminum held by 32 threads which radiate from a light aluminum base fitted with a sapphire bearing. The dry compass is rarely, if ever, seen aboard merchant ships.

The magnetic compass is basically simple and is not subject to mechanical failure. It does, however, have disadvantages. It points magnetic North instead of true North, and it does not have as much directional force as a gyrocompass does.

Gyrocompass—The gyrocompass is a mechanical compass that utilizes the forces of the earth's rotation and gravity in its operation and is entirely independent of, and unaffected by, the earth's magnetism or the magnetism in the iron and steel of the ship. When properly adjusted for latitude and the speed of the ship, the gyrocompass indicates the true North which eliminates the necessity of applying corrections for variation and deviation to the compass readings.

The gyrocompass consists essentially of a freely suspended rotor, driven at a high speed by an electric motor. The rotor when thus mounted so as to be free to turn about (1) its spinning axis, (2) its vertical axis, (3) its horizontal axis, becomes a free gyroscope and is subject to two natural phenomena, Gyroscopic Inertia and Precession.

Gyroscopic inertia is the phenomenon that causes a gyroscope to offer

considerable resistance to any force that tends to turn its spinning axle
into a new direction.

Precession is the phenomenon that causes a gyroscope, when a force is
applied to it, to move in a direction, at 90° from the applied force and in the
direction of rotation of the wheel.

Due to these phenomena, a gyroscope when placed with its axle parallel
with the axis of the earth, would retain its direction and serve as a compass

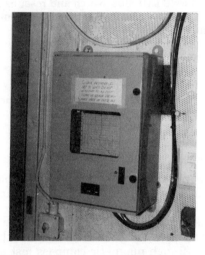

Figure 16-8. Course recorder. Photo: Midn. Steven Dirschel, California Maritime Academy.

if there was no friction at its support. Friction cannot be entirely eliminated, however, and for this reason, the gyro must be made to seek the
meridian.

This is accomplished by means of pendulous weights attached to the
rotor case. These weights are attached eccentrically, in such a manner that
the only position of rest that the gyro can find, is with its axle horizontal
and in line with the true meridian.

The directive force of a gyrocompass is much greater than that of a
magnetic compass. This strong directive force makes possible the operation of repeater compasses, course recorders and gyropilots.

Gyro repeaters—Repeating compasses are small compasses that repeat the indications of the master compass and are used for steering and
taking bearings. They are controlled electrically by the master compass
and may be placed in any part of the ship.

Course recorder—A course recorder is an instrument, operated electrically from the master compass, that makes a permanent record of the
exact courses steered. The exact courses steered are recorded in ink on a
moving strip of paper that is of sufficient length to last for a period of thirty
days.

Gyropilot—The gyropilot, or iron mike, is an instrument operated electrically from the master compass that steers the ship automatically, the gyropilot is discussed in Chapter IX.

Bearing circles and azimuth circles—Repeater compasses can be fitted with a bearing circle or an azimuth circle. These take a number of forms. If the device is simply a pair of sighting vanes attached to a ring which fits over the compass for taking bearings of objects on shore or other ships, it is called a bearing circle. If it also has a pivoted mirror to reflect the rays of the sun into a thin vertical slot half way between the sighting vanes, it would be known as an azimuth circle, and can be used for taking an azimuth or amplitude of the sun in addition to being used as a simple bearing circle. Figure 16-9 is an azimuth circle. You may occasionally see an azimuth prism which is simply a telescopic alidade (or bearing circle), but with provision for elevating the field of the telescope so that it can pick up a star or planet and let you read its azimuth.

Pelorus—The pelorus or "Dummy Compass," rarely if ever seen on a modern ship, is mentioned so that the reader will not confuse it with the name of Polaris, the North Star. Before ships were adequately fitted with repeater compasses, a pelorus was sometimes mounted on the bridge wing for taking bearings. It was really only a compass card which could be adjusted so that 000° was set on the ship's head, or so that it was set on the course being steered, depending upon the preference of the mate on watch. A bearing could be taken with the pelorus in the same way as with a bearing circle mounted on a repeater compass, but would have to be adjusted to correct for the amount the helmsman was off course when the bearing was taken, or to change a relative bearing to a true bearing if 000° was set on the ship's head or center line. It is shown in Figure 16-10.

Binnacles—Binnacles are the stands that support and protect the compass. They are made usually of wood and some nonmagnetic metal, usually brass, and are rigidly secured to the deck in such position that the lubber's line of the compass gives a true indication of the direction of the ship's head.

Binnacles consist of a stand, a compass chamber fitted to support the compass, and a protective hood containing lights for illuminating the compass at night.

Binnacles contain the appliances for carrying the various correctors used in the compensation of the deviation of the compass. These consist of (a) a system of permanent magnets for semi-circular deviation, placed in a tray immediately below the compass chamber, so arranged as to permit a variation in height and number of magnets employed; (b) a pair of arms projecting horizontally from the compass chamber and supporting soft masses of iron for quadrantal deviation; (c) a central tube in the vertical axis of the binnacle for a permanent magnet used to correct heeling error; (d) an attachment for securing a vertical soft iron rod or "Flinder's Bar" used in certain cases for the correction of vertical induced magnetism.

Hand lead—The hand lead is used for finding the depth of water not over 20 fathoms. It consists of a lead weight of 7 to 14 pounds and a line marked as shown in Figure 16-12.

Figure 16-9. Azimuth circle.

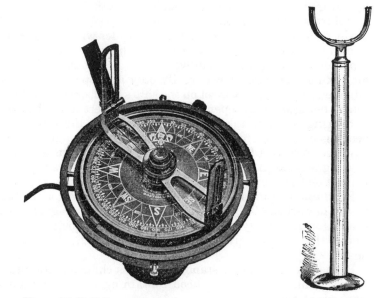

Figure 16-10. Pelorus and stand.

In taking soundings with the hand lead, the leadsman stands on a platform projecting from the side of the ship, called the chains. The line is held about two fathoms from the end, usually a toggle is provided for this, and the lead is swung to and fro in a fore-and-aft line, and when sufficient momentum is obtained the lead is thrown as far forward as possible. An expert leadsman will swing the lead in a complete circle over his head twice before releasing it. As the lead enters the water the slack in the line is taken in until the leadsman feels the lead on the bottom. When the line is stretched out in a straight line up and down, with the lead on the bottom, the sounding is read and called out to the bridge. With practice it is possible to feel the type of bottom and distinguish between a hard, soft, or sticky bottom. This information should also be reported to the bridge.

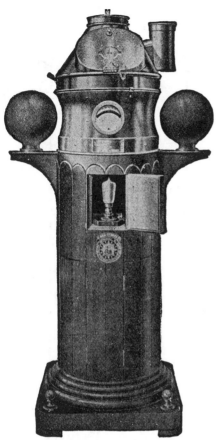

Figure 16-11. Binnacle.

In reporting the soundings to the bridge the following terminology should be used:

When the depth corresponds to any mark on the lead line it is reported as: "By the mark 7," "By the mark 10," etc.

When the depth corresponds to any fathom between the marks on the lead line it is reported as: "By the deep 6," "By the deep 8," etc.

When the depth is judged to be a fraction greater or less than that indicated by the marks it is reported as: "And a half 7," "And a quarter 5," "Half less 7," "Quarter less 10," etc.

Lead lines should be marked when wet and frequently checked for accuracy. When taking soundings at night and it is difficult to see the marks, accurate soundings may be taken by reading the line at the rail and subtracting the height of the rail above the water's edge.

The lead has its bottom hollowed out so that tallow can be inserted to get a sample of the bottom, called "arming the lead." In sailing-ship days "arming the lead" might give the ship her first indication of where the landfall was about to be made if her latitude was not known and if the chart

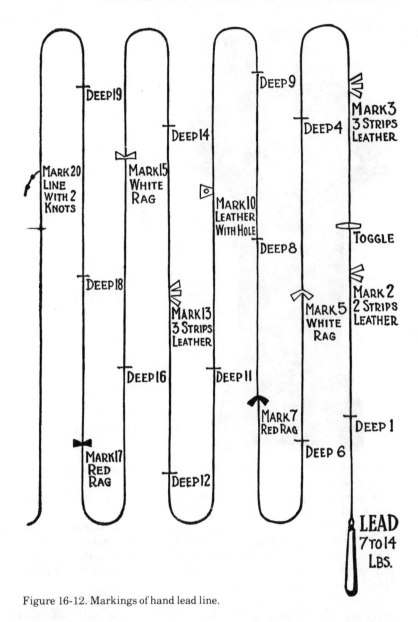

Figure 16-12. Markings of hand lead line.

showed that the character of the bottom changed rapidly from one location to another.

Although little used in the modern day, the lead line is important because it is not subject to mechanical or electronic failure and is always available as a last resort. All seamen should know the markings of the lead line and how to use it.

Older methods of taking soundings—Although no longer used, both the deep-sea lead and the sounding machine are worth mentioning so that the modern fathometer and Doppler log can be fully appreciated. The deep-sea (pronounced dipsey) lead was a lead up to 100 pounds weight which was armed and used with a deep-sea lead line. With this the ship could stop and take a sounding to 120 fathoms or more. The sounding

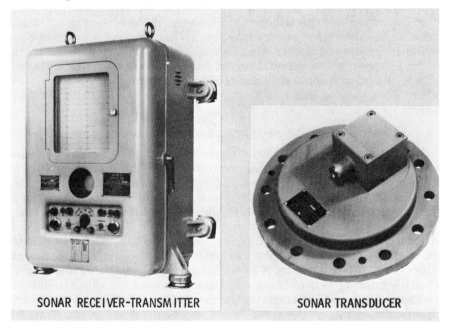

SONAR RECEIVER-TRANSMITTER   SONAR TRANSDUCER

Figure 16-13. Fathometer or echo sounder, reproduced from *American Practical Navigator*. Courtesy: Defense Mapping Agency Hydrographic Center.

machine was an advancement over the deep-sea lead because wire replaced the line and the ship did not have to stop. One sounding machine worked on a chemical principle and another recorded the depth which the lead reached based upon the pressure of the water when it hit bottom. Both required the wire to be retrieved before a reading could be made.

Fathometer—The modern fathometer or echo sounder is an enormous advance over earlier methods. Ships no longer have to stop, and depth readings are continuously recorded. A pulse of electrical energy is converted to sound energy and transmitted to the ocean floor by a transducer. When the pulse of electrical energy strikes the bottom, it bounces back to the transducer as an echo, is converted back to electrical energy, and the length of time it took to make the round trip is measured. This is possible because the speed of sound in the water is almost constant at 4,800 feet per second and the depth of water is thus a function of time. Depth information can be presented both on calibrated paper as shown in Figure 16-13 or by a cathode ray tube in which a beam of light will move about the dial of an indicator calibrated in feet or fathoms so that the position of the pencil of light will always be adjacent to the depth. The fathometer normally has three scales: One for depths up to 600 feet, another for depths up to 600 fathoms, and the third for depths up to 6,000 fathoms.

Although very reliable, the fathometer is subject to error. Probably the most obvious pitfall is reading the depth from the wrong scale, the fault of the operator, not the fathometer. However, if the bottom is soft mud, some of the sound-wave energy may reach a harder layer below, and give an indication of two bottoms. Also, if there is a distinct and rapid change in water temperature (a thermal layer), the sound wave may be deflected back to the transducer and a false reading will result. Schools of fish will return an echo, and so would a submarine if it were passing below your ship.

SPEED AND DISTANCE MEASURING DEVICES

Older systems—Before discussing modern methods of measuring speed and distance, two older systems are worth mentioning to give the new seaman a background. The oldest and very rudimentary method of measuring the speed of the ship through the water was the chip log, consisting of a "chip," a thin wood quadrant, weighted so that it would float upright, and a log line about 150 fathoms long made of hemp. The line was marked at about 15 fathoms from the chip with red bunting to allow for the chip to get clear of the wake, and then marked off with pieces of knotted line at intervals of 47 feet 3 inches. A 28 second sand glass was used and turned when the bunting went over the rail. The number of knots which went over the rail in 28 seconds was equal to the speed of the ship through the water. This is the origin of the term "knot" for nautical miles per hour. In sailing-ship days it was the custom to throw the log once a watch.

The patent log, or "Taffrail Log" shown in Figure 16-14, was an advance over the old chip log, and some are still in use. It is mechanical, comparatively inexpensive, very suitable for use on yachts or smaller craft, and records the distance actually run through the water. It consists of a rotator with blades arranged to form a spiral, a braided line from 30 to 100 fathoms in length for towing the rotator, and a mechanical recording device that registers the revolutions of the rotator and shows on a dial the distance run.

Although subject to error from various causes the taffrail log gives a good check on the vessel's speed through the water. The chief causes for error in the log are: the fouling of the rotator by seaweed or refuse from the ship, accidental bending of the blades of the rotator, a towing line that is too short, the action of a heavy head or following sea, and mechanical wear on parts of the register. The error in the reading of a patent log is usually constant and should be determined by careful observations and applied to all readings of the log.

Modern logs—Modern logs are of three general types and will usually record the distance traveled as well as the speed through the water. These are the pitot-static log, the electromagnetic log, and the impeller-type log. All are referred to, perhaps incorrectly, as "pitometer logs" although they work on different principles. All require the use of a rodmeter (sometimes called a pitometer sword) which extends through the bottom of the hull into the water. One type of rodmeter is fixed hull mounted and the other is retractable through a sea valve so that it will not be damaged by contact with the bottom or foreign objects.

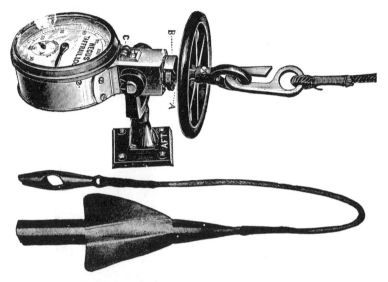

Figure 16-14. Patent log recording device and rotator.

The **pitot-static log** is the oldest of the modern logs. It requires a tube which extends 24 to 30 inches below the bottom of the hull where the water is undisturbed by hull motion. There are openings at the bottom of the tube. One faces forward and measures the dynamic water pressure as the ship moves forward. The pitot tube is surrounded by an outer tube which has openings along its athwartship sides. Whether the ship is stopped or in motion these athwartship openings are subject only to static pressure. The forward opening is subject to dynamic *and* static pressure if the ship is in motion, and static pressure only if the ship is stopped. The two pressures are led to separate bellows attached to opposite ends of a centrally pivoted lever. This lever controls the speed of a pump. When the ship is stopped, the pump stops, and the speed is registered as zero. When the ship is moving, the pump speed is proportional to the ship speed. Distance is obtained by means of a cam which is positioned by movement of the speed dial.

The **electromagnetic underwater log**, or "EM log," consists of a rodmeter, sea valve, indicator-transmitteer, and a remote control unit. A sensing device at the tip of the rodmeter develops a signal voltage proportional to the speed of the water through which the ship is passing. The principle on which the EM log works is that any conductor will produce a

Figure 16-15. Components of electromagnetic underwater log. Courtesy: Defense Mapping Agency Hydrographic Center.

voltage when it is moved across a magnetic field—or when a magnetic field is moved with respect to the conductor. The log will also give a read-out of distance. The components are shown in Figure 16-15.

The **impeller log** is a direct descendent of the old taffrail log. It can be hull-mounted in a rodmeter or towed astern. The impeller rotates as it moves through the water. Its number of revolutions is a measure of the distance the ship has traveled, and its speed of rotation is proportional to the ship's speed. The logs usually use a pulse frequency generator so that, except for the bearing surface, no physical contact is required between the impeller and the body of the instrument. These logs are relatively simple and accurate.

Unlike the first three speed measuring devices described, the **Doppler speed log** measures the speed over the bottom as opposed to speed through the water. It works on the principle of a frequency shift resulting from relative motion between a transmitter and receiver. The simplest explanation of the Doppler principle is that the sound of the whistle of an approaching train increases in pitch (becomes more shrill) because its frequency is increased by the speed of the train, but when the train has passed the

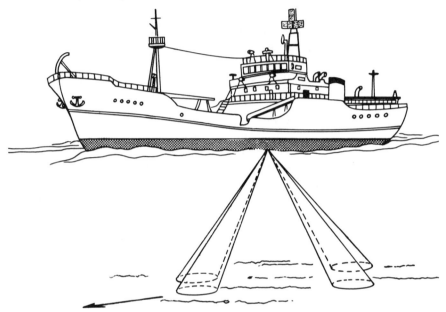

Figure 16-16. Operation of the Doppler speed log. Unlike the electromagnetic log or Pitot-Static log, the Doppler speed log measures speed over the bottom, not speed through water.

observer and is disappearing into the distance, the sound decreases in pitch (becomes lower) because the frequency is now decreased by the speed of the train. In addition to giving speed over the bottom, the Doppler log will also give a read-out in depth of water. There is also provision for giving the distance traveled. This log is a comparatively new development, and gives information necessary to the docking of very large vessels whose tonnage is 100,000 DWT or upwards. Their safe docking speed is about 0.2 feet per second because above that they may damage the dock. The Doppler log is sufficiently accurate to give the required information.

RADIO AND ELECTRONIC AIDS TO NAVIGATION

Radio direction finder—One of the older and more reliable radio aids to navigation is the radio direction finder (RDF). It is required equipment for merchant ships and is inspected annually by the Federal Communications Commision (F.C.C.). With the advent of radar, mariners may tend to neglect its use, but it remains a useful piece of equipment and is installed in the charthouse of merchant ships and frequently in yachts and smaller vessels. Radio direction finders have been in use since the early 1920s.

Although the shipboard RDF can take bearings on any radio signal, bearings are normally taken from marine radiobeacons which are built and operated solely for this purpose, and whose position is shown accurately on a chart.

The direction finder on older installations consists of a rotatable loop antenna mounted above the chartroom or pilothouse connected by a shaft to an indicating device which allows bearings to be taken directly from a compass card or gyro repeater. The RDF uses the directional properties of the loop antenna. If the antenna is parallel to the path of the radio waves, the signal is of maximum strength, and if it is perpendicular, the signal is of minimum strength if it is audible at all. The dial on the instrument is connected to the loop antenna so that the direction of the antenna and consequently the direction of the signal being received can be read directly. In practice the minimum reading, or "null," is used rather than the maximum bcause a more accurate or sharper reading is possible. Modern ships now use fixed loops rather than rotatable ones and read the angle by a goniometer. If bearings are obtained on two stations, the intersection of their lines of position gives a fix.

As indicated, the advent of radar, loran, and other more modern electronic aids to navigation has caused the RDF to be used less aboard ship. Its usefulness is more limited, and two shore stations are required to enable the navigator to fix his position. Only rarely is he close enough to two stations at the same time to do this. However, a wise navigator will use all the tools at his disposal, and RDF is one. One asset of the RDF is that it can take a bearing on any radio transmission, and consequently it has its greatest modern usefulness in homing in on a ship in distress at a far greater distance than radar range.

Old timers may remember that lightships used to send out submarine or sonar signals through the water at the same time that radio signals were transmitted from the bridge. By measuring the time difference between when the sound and radio signal were received, it was theoretically possible to determine how far you were from the lightship, and the RDF would give you the bearing. This equipment has long since been removed from the one remaining lightship in this country (Boston), and became obsolete with the advent of radar.

Radar (radio detecting and ranging), developed separately by the United States and Great Britain in the 1930s, was during World War II largely responsible for victory in the Battle of Britain, and in the Pacific campaigns against the Japanese. During World War II priorities prevented many merchant ships from having radar installed, but after 1945 it was made available to the merchant marine and is now required for all ships. Although different types of radar have been developed for many purposes, we will concern ourselves only with radar and its uses aboard ship. Commercial radar sets installed aboard merchant ships (Figure 16-18) are reliable, rugged, and require surprisingly little maintenance.

Radar depends upon the reflection of radio signals from a target, be it another ship, a point of land, or a buoy. Radars installed on merchant ships are in the 3 and 10 cm band and employ the same antenna for transmission of the outgoing signal as well as receiving the incoming signal. The time between the transmission of the outgoing signal and the return of the echo is extremely short and is measured in micro seconds. This is a function of distance and reads off on the range scale in yards or miles. Although the

Figure 16-17. Radio direction finder. Photo: Midn. R.L. Schopp, California Maritime Academy.

Figure 16-18. Radar installation on bridge. Photo: Midn. R.L. Schopp, California Maritime Academy.

transmission of outgoing signals is, in effect, continuous, the difference in time between any two signals is far enough apart so that an incoming signal from a target will be received before the next signal goes out. The direction of the target is read by noting the direction of the antenna at the time the signal is sent and received.

A radar set consists of five major parts, and you should know the general functions of each. The **transmitter** is an oscillator which produces electromagnetic waves in the super high frequency band (SHF). The **modulator** turns on and off the transmitter so the pulses of energy of about one micro second are sent out. The **antenna** is the rotating structure mounted on top of the pilot house, or perhaps forward of the mast. Its shape depends on the frequency of the set as does its rotation rate, but on a merchant ship the antenna is straight, and rotates between about 15 and 25 rpm. The

receiver is the circuitry which must amplify the weak incoming signal and prepare it for display. The **indicator** displays information so you can see and interpret it. It consists of a cathode ray tube which is called the scope. There are different types of scopes, but the one used for navigation is a PPI (Plan Position Indicator) scope. It is a mistake to think of radar as a television set, but a PPI scope presents the outline of a picture you would

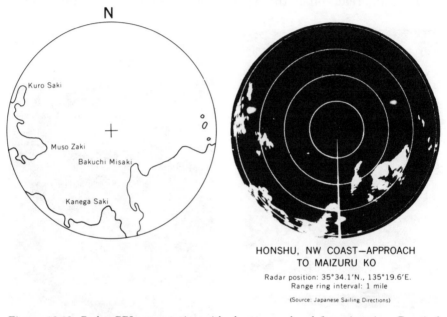

HONSHU, NW COAST—APPROACH
TO MAIZURU KO

Radar position: 35°34.1′N., 135°19.6′E.
Range ring interval: 1 mile

(Source: Japanese Sailing Directions)

Figure 16-19. Radar PPI presentation with chart, reproduced from American Practical Navigator. Courtesy: Defense Mapping Agency Hydrographic Center.

see if you were suspended several miles above your ship looking down on it. Figure 16-19 shows a typical PPI presentation.

Since radar is an invaluable aid to safety and navigation, all licensed deck officers are required to be examined in the use of it and must qualify for an endorsement as radar observer. Every five years when his license comes up for renewal, or when he raises the grade of his license, the deck officer must again qualify as a radar observer.

There are a number of basic considerations which the mariner must recognize about radar. Because of its extremely high frequency, range is limited to the horizon from the height of the radar antenna. By using Table 8 of Bowditch it is possible to determine the maximum possible radar range. If the target is a small ship or a fishing boat, the range is not as great as it would be for a large container ship or tanker. Targets close aboard are apt to be lost in the sea return, or clutter, which appears close to the center of the scope. While the set can be adjusted to cut down the sea return, the sensitivity of the set is to a degree affected, therefore, it is very possible to

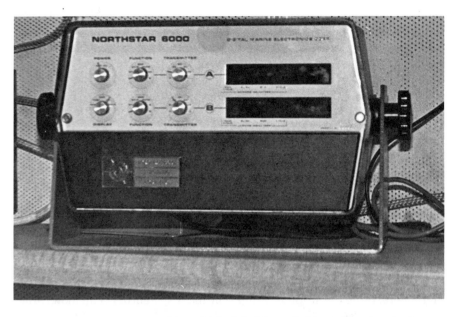

Figure 16-20. Loran receiver. Photo: Midn. R.L. Schopp, California Maritime Academy.

Figure 16-21. Omega navigation receiver. Photo: Midn. R.L. Schopp, California Maritime Academy.

lose a small craft (and sometimes a large vessel if the set is not properly adjusted) in the sea return. Weather affects radar reception. In typhoons, as an extreme example, the entire scope appears almost milky, and reception is very unreliable. Even in rain squalls which are clearly visible on the scope, it is possible for a ship to be hidden in the sea return. The effects of weather on the radar are, however, more pronounced on the 3 cm radar than the 10 cm radar. The editors recall one day of patchy rain squalls at sea when a passing island steamer was visible all afternoon, but frequently blocked out by sea return on the scope when it happened to be in a rain squall. Finally, while radar ranges are extremely accurate, radar bearings are less so. This is why, when piloting, it is always preferable to swing range arcs from prominent objects ashore than to obtain only the range and bearing of one object.

Loran is another World War II development which has been further refined and improved. The system uses medium frequency (MF) and measures the time-difference in the arrival of signals from two Loran stations. This establishes the ship's position as being somewhere along a hyperbola, and a reading of another set of stations would fix the position as being somewhere along another hyperbola. Where these two curved lines met would determine the ship's position. The older system of Loran, now called Loran A, was accurate to within 5-7 miles at distances of approximately 1,400 miles. This, however, depended upon several factors including the reception, the position of the ship with respect to the shore stations, and the time of day or night.

Loran A is now phasing out, the number of shore stations is being reduced, and the system is being replaced by Loran C. Loran C is a pulsed, hyperbolic system which operates on a single frequency of about 100kHz. This system became operational along the East Coast in 1957, and as coverage continues to increase, all U.S. coastal waters as well as much of the northern hemisphere will be under this system. Loran C gives considerably greater accuracy than Loran A.

Omega is another deep water system of electronic navigation. Developed by the U.S. Navy, it has similarities to Loran as well as distinct differences. It also depends upon shore stations but requires far fewer than Loran. The last Omega station is scheduled to go into operation in 1980, and then only eight stations will make up the system.

Unlike Loran which depends upon the difference in time of signals received from two stations, Omega depends upon phase-difference measurements of very low frequency (VLF) transmissions. There are no "master" and "slave" or "secondary" stations as there are with Loran. The operator can select any two stations whose signals will give him lines of position which cross at a right angle and thus give himself an accurate fix. The accuracy of Omega is between 1/2 and 1 mile in daytime, and 1 to 2 miles at night. An Omega receiver is shown in Figure 16-21.

The **Satellite navigation system** was also developed by the U.S. Navy, and has been available for use aboard merchant ships for about ten years. It is extremely accurate, fast, and can be used in any weather.

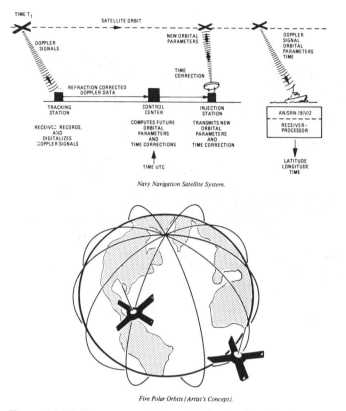

Navy Navigation Satellite System.

Five Polar Orbits (Artist's Concept).

Figure 16-22. Components of Navy Navigation Satellite System.
Courtesy: U.S. Navy.

It works on the Doppler principle discussed above under the Doppler speed log. The system consists of several parts, one of which is the shipboard receiver in the charthouse. The others are the satellites, the ground tracking stations, a computing center, an injection station, and the Naval Observatory time signals. These are shown in the sketch (Figure 16-22). Because of the Doppler principle as long as the position of the satellite is known, it is possible to obtain a very accurate position. The receiver gives a direct reading in latitude and longitude.

SEXTANT

The **sextant** is an instrument for measuring the altitude or height of a celestial body above the horizon. It may also be used for measuring the angle between two distant objects. It works because of the principle of optics known as double reflection: The angle between the first and last directions of a ray of light that has undergone two reflections in the same plane is twice the angle that the two reflecting surfaces make with each other.

Figure 16-23. Micrometer drum sextant, reproduced from *American Practical Navigator*. Parts are as follows: A. Frame, made of brass or aluminum; B. Limb, the teeth on outer edge each represent one degree of altitude; C. Altitude graduations along the limb called the arc; D. Index arm, a movable bar pivoted about the center of curvature of the limb; E. Tangent screw, mounted perpendicularly on the end of the index arm where it engages the teeth of the limb; F. The release, a spring-actuated clamp which keeps the tangent screw engaged with the teeth of the limb; G. Micrometer drum, graduated in minutes of altitude; H. Vernier, aids in reading fractions of a minute; I. Index mirror; J. Horizon glass, piece of optical glass silvered on its half nearest the frame; K. Shade glasses; L. Telescope; and M. Handle.
Courtesy: Defense Mapping Agency Hydrographic Center.

Instructions for reading the sextant—In order to facilitate the exact reading of a sextant, a *vernier*, a small scale similar in construction to the main scale of the sextant, is fitted and arranged to move alongside of and in contact with the main scale. The main scale of the sextant is divided into degrees. The vernier scale, or the scale on the micrometer drum, is divided into minutes, and the scale to the right of that indicates tenths of minutes. Therefore to read a sextant angle of 35°16.3', the 35° would be read from the arc of the sextant, the 16' would be read from the micrometer drum, and the .3' would be indicated by the line to the right of the drum. This last reading is made by estimate. Sextants vary in detail, but inspection will indicate any difference in particulars as to how they should be read.

Adjustments of the sextant—The theory of the sextant requires that for accurate indications, the following conditions be fulfilled:

(a) The two surfaces of each mirror and shade glass must be parallel planes.

(b) The graduated arc or limb must be a plane, and its graduations, as well as those of the vernier, must be exact.

(c) The axis must be at the center of the limb, and perpendicular to the plane thereof.

(d) The index and horizon glasses must be perpendicular, and the line of sight parallel to the plane of the limb.

Of these, only the last named ordinarily requires the attention of the navigator who is to make use of the sextant; the others, which may be called the permanent adjustments, should be made before the instrument leaves the hands of the maker, and with careful use will never be deranged.

Complete instructions for making the four adjustments that are required of the navigator are given below:

(a) The *first adjustment* consists of making the *Index Mirror* perpendicular to the plane of the instrument. To do this, place the index arm near the middle of the arc. Then, place the eye very nearly in the plane of the instrument and close to the index mirror, observe whether the direct image of the arc and its reflected image appear to form one continuous arc; if so, the index mirror is perpendicular to the plane of the sextant. If the reflected image does not form a continuous arc with the true image the index mirror should be adjusted by means of screws at the back of the mirror.

(b) The *second adjustment* consists of making the *Horizon Mirror* perpendicular to the plane of the instrument. To do this, hold the sextant vertically and bring the reflected horizon in line with the true horizon. Then incline the sextant until its plane makes a small angle with the horizon; if the true image and the reflected image form a continuous line, the horizon glass is perpendicular to the plane of the sextant. If they do not, the horizon mirror should be adjusted by means of screws attached to it.

(c) The *third adjustment* consists of making the *Horizon Mirror* parallel to the index glass when the vernier is set at zero. To do this, clamp the vernier on zero, hold the sextant vertically, and look at the horizon through the telescope ring; if the true and reflected images of the horizon form a continuous straight line, the horizon mirror is parallel to the index mirror. If the true image and the reflected image do not form a continuous straight line the horizon mirror should be adjusted by means of screws attached to it.

(d) The *fourth adjustment* consists of making the axis of the telescope parallel to the plane of the instrument. To do this, a telescope containing two parallel wires is used. Screw in the telescope so that the two wires are parallel to the plane of the instrument; then, after choosing two clearly defined objects, preferably stars that are more than 90 degrees apart, bring the reflected image of one object into exact coincidence with the direct image of the other at the inner wire. If the two objects remain together when, by a slight moving of the instrument, they appear on the outer wire, the telescope is parallel to the plane of the instrument. If the objects do not remain in coincidence, adjust the telescope ring by means of the screws holding it to the telescope bracket.

Index error—The sextant should be kept free of error, but if an error exists the amount of error must be determined and applied to all readings of the sextant. When the horizon mirror and the index mirror are parallel and the zero on the vernier does not correspond to the zero on the main scale, the difference is known as *index error*. Index error is most easily

Figure 16-24. A. Mechanical chronometer. Photo: Midn. R.L. Schopp, California Maritime Academy. B. Quartz crystal chronometer, reproduced from *American Practical Navigator*. Courtesy: Defense Mapping Agency Hydrographic Center.

determined by bringing the reflected image of the horizon in line with the true image of the horizon and then reading the sextant. If the zero on the vernier scale is to the right of the zero on the main scale, the error is *off* the arc and should be *added* to all readings of the sextant. If the zero on the vernier scale is to the left of the zero on the main scale, the error is *on* the arc and should be *subtracted* from all readings. To remember which way to apply the correction, it may help to keep the old saying in mind: If it's off (the arc), it's on (add the correction); and if it's on (the arc), it's off (subtract the correction).

Sextants should be handled carefully as any jarring may disturb the adjustment of the mirrors. They should be kept clean and all moisture or salt spray should be wiped off each time the sextant is used. Never use metal polish on the silver arc; a thin coating of light oil will protect the arc.

CHRONOMETER

Even the chronometer has not escaped the advancements of modern science. It is necessary to discuss both the traditional chronometer which is mechanical and wound like a clock, and the new quartz chronometer which is powered by a small flashlight battery.

Figure 16-25. Aneroid barometer, reproduced from *American Practical Navigator*. Courtesy: Defense Mapping Agency Hydrographic Center.

It is important for the navigator to know the time accurately or he will not be able to find his longitude. Before reliable chronometers were available, it was normal for a sailing ship to reach the latitude of its destination and then make her "eastings" or "westings"—sail along the proper parallel of latitude—until she reached her destination.

The invention of the chronometer early in the eighteenth century was important because it made it possible to determine longitude. The advent of radio time signals makes it always possible to know the chronometer error (CE) as compared to the Naval Observatory in Washington, D.C., or the Royal Observatory in Greenwich, England.

Traditional chronometer—A traditional chronometer is simply a fine, accurate clock which is compensated for changes in temperature and set in gimbals so that its working will not be disturbed by the motion of the ship. Chronometers should be carried as close to the center of motion of the ship as possible and be insulated against dampness and padded to reduce shocks. They should be wound daily, at the same time, preferably by the same person. They are checked daily by radio time signals, and a record is kept of the daily loss or gain and the accumulated error. The amount of gain or loss each day is known as the daily rate. Chronometers are set to GMT (Greenwich Mean Time).

Quartz chronometer—A very recent development is the quartz chronometer. The power source is a flashlight battery which will power it for about a year. The quartz crystal stabilizes the frequency of an electric oscillator. Quartz chronometers are far more accurate than mechanical chronometers; their average daily rate should not exceed 0.2 seconds and will probably be less. They do not require gimbals, can be mounted on a bulkhead, and are resistant to shock and vibration. They are less expensive than traditional chronometers, and in fact probably cost less to buy than the older types do to repair.

Stop watch, comparing watch, quartz wrist watch—The navigator must note the time of any sight he takes of the sun, planets, or stars. Since the chronometer must stay in the charthouse, he will use one of the above watches to note the time of the sight, and later compare it with the chronometer. For a yachtsman, backed up by a time tick, a quartz wrist watch makes an acceptable chronometer. Its rate may well be less than one or two seconds a day. But if it is being used as the boat's only chronometer it should be kept safely in the navigator's work area and out of harm's way. Time of celestial observations will be noted by a stop or comparing watch.

BAROMETER

The barometer is an instrument for measuring the pressure of the atmosphere and is used in determining weather conditions. There are two kinds of barometers, the mercurial and aneroid.

Mecurial barometer—The mercurial barometer consists of a glass tube sealed at the top and filled with mercury. The lower or open end is fitted into a cup so that the mercury is exposed to the air. The mercury falls in the glass tube until the atmospheric pressure on the mercury in the cup balances it against the vacuum at the top of the tube. The instrument reads in inches of mercury, the standard atmospheric pressure being 29.92 inches or 1013.2 millibars. Mercurial barometers are now rarely seen aboard ship and have become collector's items. They are fragile and if moved must be carried upright. They require a temperature correction found in Table 13 of Bowditch. They also require a correction for gravity which varies with the latitude, found in Table 12 of Bowditch.

Aneroid barometer—In practice the only type of barometer aboard ship is the aneroid. It consists of a small cylindrical metal box from which the air has been partially withdrawn, and which is mechanically connected to a pointer. The pointer indicates the atmospheric pressure on a graduated dial. The aneroid barometer is compensated so that it is not affected by changes in temperature, and consequently no temperature correction is necessary. Although frequently neglected aboard ship, all barometers require a correction for height above sea level, but unlike the mercurial barometers, this is the only correction used for aneroids.

THERMOMETER

The thermometer measures temperature. The usual form consists of a glass bulb filled with mercury, connected with a fine glass tube, and fitted

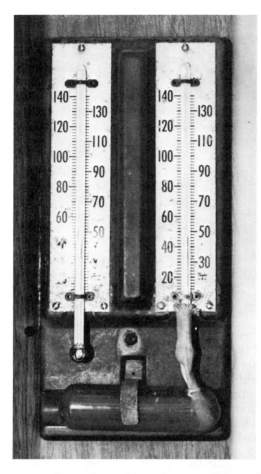

Figure 16-26. Psychrometer. The psychrometer is simply a wet and dry bulb thermometer set. It is kept on a slatted case on the open bridge to protect it from the weather.

to a scale graduated into degrees. Two scales are normally used. One is the Fahrenheit in which the freezing point of water is placed at 32° and the boiling point (under normal atmospheric pressure) at 212°. The other is the Celsius (formerly called Centigrade). In this the freezing point is taken as 0° and the boiling point as 100°. Table 15 of Bowditch can be used to convert from one to the other, or a formula can be used:

$F = 9/5C + 32°$ in which F = degrees Fahrenheit and C = degrees Celsius
$C = 5/9(F - 32°)$

Psychrometer—If two thermometers are mounted side by side in a wooden box or instrument shelter on a wing of the bridge and one of the thermometers has its bulb covered with a wet fabric and the other is exposed directly to the air, the resulting instrument is known as a psychrometer. Since the dry bulb thermometer shows the temperature of the

Figure 16-27. Anemometer.

free air and the wet bulb thermometer shows the temperature of evaporation, the relative humidity and the dew point of the atmosphere may be obtained from the different readings of the two thermometers. Table 16 of Bowditch gives the relative humidity, and Table 17 gives the dew point.

Anemometer—The anemometer is an instrument for measuring the velocity of the wind. It consists usually of three or more cups mounted on horizontal vanes which are attached to a vertical shaft. The revolutions of the shaft are recorded or indicated on a dial and show the wind's velocity. The readings of the anemometer are affected by the speed of the ship and must be corrected in order to determine the true velocity of the wind.

Calculators can save time and improve accuracy aboard ship in the charthouse. Calculators run from the simple ones that can multiply, divide, add and subtract to the more elaborate models that can be programmed. There are navigational calculators which can solve the celestial triangle or mercator or great circle sailing problems. We recommend a simple calculator that includes trigonometric functions. It makes interpolation faster, and does away with the use of logarithms and the slide rule.

The Coast Guard permits the use of calculators on licensing examinations, but does not permit the use of programmed calculators. This is as it should be. No mariner should be so dependent on a calculator that he is lost if he needs a new battery. We would hope *not* to read about the yachtsman who was lost at sea because his calculator needed new batteries or became inoperative because of salt water. Navigational tables such as H.O. 214, 229, 249 and the recently published *Star Sight Reduction Tables for 42 Stars* have not gone the way of Confederate money.

A **flashlight** is essential on the bridge. To protect dark-adapted vision it should be equipped with a red bulb or a red plastic or cellophane filter. A flashlight is necessary to help read a stop watch or any other instrument whose dial is not sufficiently bright. And in the event of an emergency on the bridge or anywhere else on the ship it might save your life.

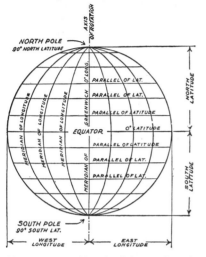

Figure 16-28. Sketch of the earth with meridians and parallels of latitude.

CHARTS

PRELIMINARY DEFINITIONS

The **earth** is a spherical body slightly flattened at the poles.

Axis of rotation is that diameter about which the earth rotates.

Earth's poles are the points at which the axis cuts the surface.

Great circle is any circle on the surface of the earth having its center at the center of the earth.

Equator is that great circle of the earth which lies midway between the poles. Every point on the equator is 90° from either pole.

Parallels of latitude are circles whose planes are parallel to the plane of the equator. They have their centers in the axis of rotation and the radii vary from zero at either pole to that of the equator. The equator is the only parallel of latitude which is a great circle.

Latitude of a plane on earth is its angular distance North or South of the equator, measured from 0° at equator to 90° at either pole.

Meridians of longitude are great circles on the surface of the earth which pass through both poles and which are used to establish location in East-West direction.

Prime Meridian is the meridian of longitude which passes through the observatory at Greenwich, England. It is the reference meridian for measuring longitude East or West from Greenwich.

Longitude of a place on earth is the arc of the equator intercepted between the Prime Meridian and the meridian of the place, measured from the Prime Meridian East or West through 180°.

Position of a place on earth is determined by its latitude and longitude; latitude being the distance North or South of the equator and longitude being the distance East or West of the Prime Meridian through Greenwich. Since latitude and longitude are measured in degrees, minutes and seconds, the position of Nantucket Shoals Lightship would be expressed as Latitude 40° 37' 05'' North and Longitude 69° 36' 33'' West. The position of the Melbourne Observatory would be expressed as Latitude 37° 49' 53'' South, Longitude 144° 58' 35'' East.

CHARTS: DEFINED

A chart is a representation on paper of a portion of the navigable waters of the world. Since the curved surface of the earth must be represented on a flat piece of paper, an exact reproduction is not possible. In order to overcome this difficulty a projection is used. There are three methods of projection: Mercator, polyconic, and gnomonic.

The **Mercator** is a projection of the earth's surface on a cylinder tangent to the earth at the Equator.

The **polyconic** is a projection of the earth's surface on a series of cones.

The **gnomonic** is a projection of the earth's surface on a plane tangent to the earth at some given point.

The Mercator projection is the one most generally used for navigational purposes. On a Mercator chart the meridians of longitude are parallel and cross the parallels of latitude at right angles. The length of each degree of latitude increases as the distance increases away from the equator.

Courses on Mercator charts are laid down in straight lines and intersect each meridian at the same angle. Distances are measured on the latitude scale directly opposite the position of the ship.

Charts are designed to give as much information to the navigator as possible. They show the outline of the water and adjacent land, the depth of the water, character of the bottom; location of all aids to navigation such as lighthouses, buoys, beacons, etc.; location of all dangers to navigation such as rocks, shoals, submerged wrecks, etc., and tidal and other currents.

Types of charts—Charts are various in character, according to the objects which they are designed to serve. The most important distinctions are the following:

1. Sailing charts. These are the smallest scale charts used for planning, fixing position at sea, and used on a long voyage. The scale is generally smaller than 1:600,000. The shoreline and topography are generalized and only offshore soundings and principal navigational aids visible at considerable distances are shown.

2. General charts are used for coastwise navigation outside outlying reefs and shoals. Scales range from about 1:150,000 to 1:600,000.

3. Coast charts are for inshore coastwise navigation where the course may lie inside outlying reefs and shoals, for entering and leaving bays and

harbors of considerable width, and for navigating large inland waterways. Scales range from about 1:50,000 to 1:150,000.

4. Harbor charts are for navigation and anchorage in harbors and small waterways. Scale is generally larger than 1:50,000.

5. Small-craft charts. Scale 1:40,000 and larger. These are special charts of inland waters including the Intracoastal Waterways, or special editions of conventional charts. They are printed on lighter weight paper and folded. They contain additional information of interest to small-craft operators.

In the classification system used by the Defense Mapping Agency Hydrographic Center the sailing charts are included in the general charts classification (smaller than 1:150,000), and coast charts which are especially useful for approaching confined waters are classified as approach charts.

DATES AND CORRECTIONS

The system of dates now used on charts published by the Defense Mapping Agency Hydrographic Center (DMAHC) and the National Ocean Survey (NOS) is as follows:

First edition—The original date of issue of a new chart. It is shown at the top center margin: 1st Ed., Sept. 1950.

New edition—A new edition is made when the corrections are too numerous or extensive to be reported in the *Notice to Mariners*. This makes previous printings obsolete. Date of the first edition is retained at the top margin. At the lower left-hand corner it is replaced by the number and date of the new edition. This date is the same as the one in the latest *Notice to Mariners* to which the chart has been corrected: 5th Ed., July 10, 1970.

Revised print—A revised print published by the National Ocean Survey may contain corrections which have been published in *Notice to Mariners* but does *not* supersede a current edition. The date of the revision is shown to the right of the edition date: 5th Ed., July 11, 1970; Revised 4/12/75.

Reprint—A chart may be reprinted when the stocks become low. It is a reprint of the chart with a limited number of corrections from the *Notice to Mariners*.

MAINTAINING CHARTS

The print date in the lower left-hand corner of the chart is the date of the latest *Notice to Mariners* used to update the chart. Corrections after that date are the responsibility of the user. Bowditch points out that an uncorrected chart is a menace, and this cannot be emphasized too strongly. The various issues of the *Notice to Mariners* after the print date contain all the information needed in maintaining charts. More urgent items are also broadcast by radio or contained in the *Daily Memorandum*. It is suggested that the *Notice to Mariners* corrections to charts aboard ship be noted on the 5 x 8 inch Chart/Publication Correction Record Card (DMAHC 8660/9). Periodically the DMAHC publishes a *Summary of Corrections*. When a new edition of a chart is published, the old one should be replaced.

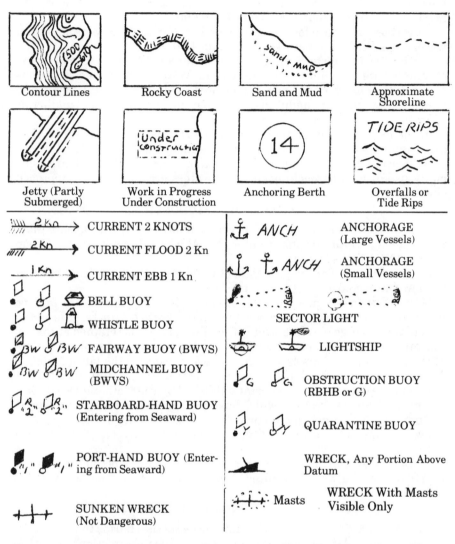

Figure 16-29. Chart symbols. These symbols are extracted from Chart No. 1, National Ocean Survey. Courtesy: Defense Mapping Agency Hydrographic Center.

SYMBOLS AND ABBREVIATIONS

Complete information on chart symbols and abbreviations is contained in Chart No. 1, prepared jointly by the National Oceanic and Atmospheric Administration (NOAA) and the Defense Mapping Agency Hydrographic Center (DMAHC). This information may be obtained separately and is also contained in both Bowditch and *Dutton's*.

Every symbol, figure and abbreviation on a chart has an important meaning which must be understood by the navigator. For instance: vertical lettering refers exclusively to topography, or features of the land, and slanted lettering refers to hydrography, or features of the areas covered by water at high tide. A few of some of the more important notations follow:

These abbreviations are used on charts to show the character of the bottom:

Cl.	Clay	Sh.	Shells	stf.	Stiff
Co.	Coral	rd.	Red	sft.	Soft
G.	Gravel	St.	Stones	bk.	Black
M.	Mud	Wd.	Weed	yl.	Yellow
rky.	Rocky	fne.	Fine	gy.	Gray
S.	Sand	crs.	Coarse		

Abbreviations, commonly used in presenting on the charts the essential characteristics of light, fog signals, and radio aids, are as follows:

F. fixed	G. green	R.Bn. radiobeacon
Fl. flashing	Sec. sector	Horn. fog horn
Occ. occulting	m. minute	Siren. fog siren
Alt. alternating	sec. seconds	R.D.F. Radio direction finder
Gp. group	Bell. fog bell	Whis. fog whistle
R. red	Dia. diaphone	
W. white	Gun. fog gun	

AIDS TO NAVIGATION

The term aid to navigation means any device not aboard a vessel which can assist the navigator in determining his position, safe course, or provide him with warning of dangers to navigation. This term includes lighthouses, beacons, lightships, sound signals, buoys, radiobeacons, and radio navigation systems.

The Coast Guard is charged with the maintenance of marine aids to navigation—including lighthouses, lightships, radiobeacons, Loran, buoys, and beacons—upon all navigable waters of the U.S. and its possessions.

Buoyage system of the United States—The following directions apply to all coasts and harbors of the United States and its possessions regarding the significance of buoys:

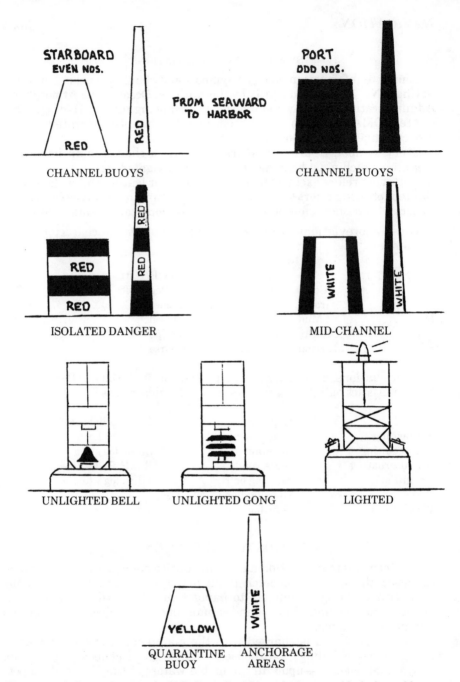

Figure 16-30. Buoys. In 1980 the U.S. Coast Guard is replacing some black channel buoys with green channel buoys to test the belief that green buoys can be detected at greater distances than black. If this test is successful, black buoys will probably be phased out in the future and replaced by green. Drawings: Midn. Eric Pett, California Maritime Academy.

1. In approaching the channel, etc., from seaward, red buoys, with even numbers, will be found on the starboard side of the channel, and must be kept on the starboard hand in passing (R.R.R. red on right on returning).

2. In approaching the channel from seaward, black buoys, with odd numbers, will be found on the port side of the channel and must be kept on the port hand in passing.

3. As a rule, starboard-hand buoys are nuns (conical) and port-hand buoys are cans (cylindrical), but spar buoys may replace either.

4. Red and black horizontally banded buoys mark obstructions, or a junction of one channel with another, and indicate that there is a channel on either side. If the topmost band is red, the principal channel will be followed by keeping the buoy on the right-hand side of the vessel, when entering from seaward. If the topmost band is black, the principal channel will be followed by keeping the buoy on the left-hand side of the vessel, when entering from seaward.

5. Buoys painted with white and black perpendicular stripes will be found in mid-channel, and must be passed close-to, to avoid danger.

6. Lighted buoys are used either on the right or left side of a channel at the entrance to the channel, to mark a turn in the channel or to mark a danger off the coast.

7. Red-lighted buoys are used to mark the right hand of a channel. ("Red, right, returning.") The light may be either white or red. Black-lighted buoys are used to mark the left side of a channel. The light may be either white or green.

8. Lighted buoys are almost always flashing or occulting.

9. Spar buoys may take the place of either nun or can buoys or be used as markers for other buoys.

10. Whistling buoys are usually placed off the entrances to channels or off the coast.

11. Bell buoys are sometimes placed at the entrance to small channels or more usually at turns in channels.

12. Yellow buoys mark quarantine stations or areas. White buoys mark anchorage areas.

13. If a light has the same durations of light and darkness it is known as Equal Interval (E. Int.) or Isophase. A light is occulting (Occ.) if it is totally eclipsed at regular intervals, the duration of light always being greater than the duration of dark. A light is flashing if it is flashing at regular intervals and at a rate not more than 30 flashes per minute.

Caution regarding buoys—Buoys are liable to be carried away, shifted, capsized, sunk, etc., lighted buoys may be extinguished, or whistling or bell buoys may not sound, as the result of storm, the accumulation of ice, running ice, or other natural causes, or collision, or other accidents. Buoys marking channels subject to frequent changes are moved as may be necessary and should be used only with local knowledge. Such buoys may not be charted. A prudent navigator will not rely solely on any single aid to navigation, particularly a floating aid.

SIGNIFICANCE OF BUOY LIGHT CHARACTERISTICS

Flashing characteristics are used on lighted buoys to distinguish their principal purposes, corresponding in part to the color distinctions that are made on unlighted buoys. The following table which is not in detail is helpful in showing how the system works.

Characteristics of Flashing	*Purpose Indicated*	*Color of Light*	*Color of Buoy*
1. Flashing, Quick Flashing, Occulting, Isophase, Fixed.	Channel sides and Coasts	White Green Red	Red or Black Black Red
2. Quick flashing. Not less than 60 flashes per minute.	Sudden constriction or sharp turns in channel. A distinctly cautionary significance indicated. Pass on one side only.	White Green Red	Red or black Black Red
3. Interrupted quick flashing (group). (I.Qk.Fl.) Shows a series of 6 quick flashes repeated at intervals of 10 sec.	Junctions in channels, wrecks, or other hazards that may be passed on either side.	White	Top band of buoy either red or black.
		Green	Top band of buoy black only.
		Red	Top band of buoy red only. (Buoy is red and black horizontally striped.)
4. Morse (A) lights. Groups consisting of a short flash and a long flash at intervals of 8 sec.	Fairways or mid-channels	White	Black and white vertical stripes.

Daymarks help make aids to navigation more visible and easily identifiable against daylight viewing backgrounds. In 1975 a revised system of daymarks was started. The changes included:

1. On port side daymarks, green is used instead of black or white. Green numbers and letters are used.

2. On starboard side daymarks, red numbers and letters are used instead of white numbers and letters.

3. On junction daymarks, green is used instead of black.

Lights—The distance at which a light may be seen as noted on a chart or in the *Light List* or *Coast Pilots* is the nominal range, or the maximum distance at which a light can be seen in clear weather as defined by the International Visibility Code (meteorological visibility of 10 nautical miles). Irrespective of the height of eye of the shipboard observer, the observer can never expect to see a light at greater than its nominal range unless the meteorological visibility is better than 10 miles. This does not happen often. In fact he will see it at less than half the nominal range if the conditions are less than ideal. The glare of a powerful light is often seen far beyond the limit of visibility of the actual rays of the light, but this must not be confounded with the true range of visiblity. Again, refraction may often cause a light to be seen farther than under ordinary circumstances. As the range of visibility increases with the elevation of the observer, it is often possible to obtain a bearing before the light is sighted from the bridge, by sighting the light from aloft, noting a star in range with it, and then obtaining a bearing of the star with compass or pelorus.

The actual power of a light should be considered when expecting to make it in thick weather. A weak light is easily obscured by haze, and no dependence can be placed on its being seen. The power of a light can be estimated by its candlepower as given in the light lists, and in some cases by noting how much its visibility in clear weather falls short of the range due to the height at which it is placed. Thus a light standing 200 feet above the sea and recorded as visible only 10 miles in clear weather is manifestly of little brilliancy, as its height would permit it to be seen over 20 miles if of sufficient power.

Fog Signals—Sound is conveyed in a very capricious way through the atmosphere. Apart from the wind, large areas of silence have been found in different directions and at different distances from the origin of the sound signal, even in clear weather. Therefore mariners should not be too confident of hearing a fog signal. Moreover, the apparatus for sounding the signal may require some time before it is in readiness to act. A fog often creeps imperceptibly toward the land and is not observed by those at a lighthouse until it is upon them, whereas a vessel may have been in it for many hours while approaching the land. In such a case no signal may be sounded. When sound travels against the wind it may be thrown upward; in such a case a man aloft might hear it when it is inaudible on deck. The conditions for hearing a signal will vary at the same station within short intervals of time. Mariners must not, therefore, judge their distance from a fog signal by the force of the sound and must not assume that a signal is not sounding because they do not hear it. Taken together, these facts should induce the utmost caution when nearing land or danger in fog. An echo-sounding instrument should be faithfully used.

In regions where the shores are high and rocky the echo of the whistle frequently warns of too close an approach to shore. In narrow passages it is often possible to keep in mid-channel by directing course so that the echoes from both shores are heard at approximately the same time.

An echo may sometimes be heard from the boarded side of a beacon (echo board) or from a flat surface of any structure. A megaphone is said to be helpful for detecting sound and for determining the direction of the source.

Soundings—In thick weather, when near or approaching the land or danger, soundings should be taken continually and at regular intervals, and with the character of the bottom systematically recorded. By marking the soundings on tracing paper, according to the scale of the chart, along a line representing the track of the ship, and then moving the paper over the chart parallel with the course until the observed soundings agree with those of the chart, the ship's position will in general be quite well determined.

Radiobeacons operate during fog or low visibility and also in clear weather at regular intervals.

In plotting long-range bearings on a chart of the Mercator projection a correction must be made, as the line of bearing is not a straight line excepting in the meridian.

For station identification simple characteristics consisting of combinations of dots and dashes are used. These combinations and the length of the dots, dashes and spaces are chosen for ease of identification when heard by the ship's navigating officer, who is not expected to be skilled in radiotelegraphy. They are not transmitted as code letters and are not referred to as such, but as: Two dashes (——); two dashes, dot (——.); four dashes (————); etc., depending on the combination used. Certain lowpower radiobeacons use a combination of high and low tone dashes to provide additional distinction in their characteristic.

Accuracy and use of bearings—Long experience with properly installed and correctly calibrated direction finders maintained in good condition indicates an average accuracy of 1° to 2°. Departures from this accuracy will sometimes be experienced when taking bearings from a position close to the shoreline and over land. Night effect, which is sometimes encountered, particularly near sunrise and sunset, and which is usually manifested in very wide or changing minimum, tends to limit the distance at which reliable bearings can be obtained. In observing marine radiobeacons night effect is not usually encountered at distances less than 30 to 50 miles. The existence of night effect can almost invariably be confirmed by rapidly taking repeated bearings, and when shown to be present, bearings should be used with extreme caution. Serious errors may result in bearings taken if other shipboard antennas are erected close to the direction finder after calibration, or if the direction finder, ship's rigging or other equipment affecting direction finder performance is not maintained in the condition existing at the time of last calibration. Regular and frequent use of the direction finder under all conditions is one of the best means of insuring ability to obtain accurate bearings and that the direction finder is at all times in proper condition. Clear weather operating periods provide ample opportunity for such use.

Radio weather broadcasts—Forecasts and general weather information are broadcast daily by the National Weather Service from a number of government and commercial radio stations for the benefit of marine, aviation, and commercial interests. Storm and hurricane warnings are broadcast whenever issued.

NOAA publication *Worldwide Marine Weather Broadcasts* furnishes a complete listing of weather broadcasts. Information on day and night visual storm warnings is found in sailing directions and coast pilots.

Radio time signals—The chronometer error and daily rate is normally obtained by radio time signals, otherwise known as "time ticks." Most maritime nations broadcast these several times daily, and little difficulty is experienced in obtaining a time tick anywhere in the world. At sea and in port chronometers should be checked daily, and the error and rate entered in the chronometer record book.

The U.S. Naval Observatory controls the transmissions of time signals from Naval Radio Stations. Beginning at five minutes before each even hour of GMT, dashes are transmitted every second, except the 29th and certain others near the end of each minute as shown. The seconds marked "60" indicate the start of the next minute. The final dash, marking the end of the hour, is considerably longer than any of the others. The beginnings of the dashes indicate the beginnings of the seconds, and the ends of the dashes have no meaning:

Minutes	Seconds										
	50	51	52	53	54	55	56	57	58	59	60
55	—		—	—	—	—					—
56	—	—		—	—	—					—
57	—	—	—		—	—					—
58	—	—	—	—		—					—
59	—										—

Further information is contained in DMAHC Pubs. 117A and 117B, Radio Navigation Aids.

GOVERNMENT PUBLICATIONS

The United States Government publishes much important information for mariners through its various agencies. It is essential that the navigator knows what is available, where it is published, and how he can use the information so that he can insure safe passage through all waters into which his ship may venture. Some of the more important publications follow:

Tide Tables are published by National Ocean Survey (NOS) in four volumes annually. Each volume contains data on high and low water as well as times of sunrise and sunset, moonrise, and moonset.

Tidal Current Tables, not to be confused with *Tide Tables*, are also published by NOS in two volumes. These are also published annually, and contain the times and strengths of flood and ebb currents as well as the time of slack water.

A *Table of Distances Between Ports* is published by NOS. One between U.S. and foreign ports is published by the Defense Mapping Agency Hydrographic Center (DMAHC).

The DMAHC publishes two much used sight reduction tables for celestial navigation. These are Pubs. 249 and 229. The latter is quite new. The DMAHC also publishes azimuth tables in Pubs. 260 and 261.

The *Nautical Almanac* which is vital in celestial navigation is prepared jointly by the U.S. Naval Observatory and the Royal Greenwich Observatory. It is published annually.

The *American Practical Navigator*, DMAHC Pub. 9, popularly called "Bowditch," was recommended at the outset of this chapter for any serious student of navigation. Although not a government publication, *Dutton's Navigation and Piloting*, should also be mentioned. *Dutton's* is published by the Naval Institute Press which is a private organization. Both books are thoroughly up-to-date and extremely well written and have been used as sources for this chapter.

Pilot Charts are published by DMAHC for the North Atlantic and North Pacific. *Atlases of Pilot Charts* are also issued for Central America and the South Atlantic, and for the South Pacific and Indian Oceans. These contain a wealth of information which is extremely useful in helping the mariner in planning a voyage. Included in graphic form is information on magnetic variation, currents, prevailing winds, weather, and iceberg limits. On the reverse side are articles of general information to the mariner.

Several agencies are involved in publishing nautical charts. NOS publishes charts of the coastal U.S. and its territories and possessions while charts of foreign waters and coasts are published by DMAHC. Charts of some inland rivers are prepared by the Army Corps of Engineers. Charts are organized into portfolios, and the chart numbering system based on regions and subregions provides a means of keeping track of charts issued by the various agencies and foreign countries.

The U.S. Coast Guard publishes *Light Lists* of the U.S. including island possessions, the Great Lakes, and the Mississippi. These are extremely complete, and come in five volumes. The detail contained in light lists is far greater than can be shown on charts. DMAHC publishes *Lists of Lights* in seven volumes which covers foreign coasts of the world.

The responsibility for *Coast Pilots* and *Sailing Directions* is split between NOAA and DMAHC as it is for the light lists. *Coast Pilots* (in nine editions) covers the United States and is published by the Coast Guard. *Sailing Directions* for foreign coasts and coastal waters is published by DMAHC.

From the scope of the publications discussed it is obvious that changes occur frequently and that corrections must be made. Some publications are reissued annually, and others have numbered "changes" issued.

Frequently the importance of updated information is so great that it cannot wait until the next regular change or new or revised edition. When this happens, the information is included in the weekly *Notice to Mariners* published by DMAHC with the cooperation of NOS and the Coast Guard. New charts, publications, and new revised editions are also announced. Small "paste in" corrections for charts are included in the weekly *Notices*. Information of general interest to navigation is also included. A separate *Notice to Mariners* for the Great Lakes is published.

A *Summary of Corrections* is published twice a year by DMAHC. These volumes contain the complete text of all changes to charts, *Coast Pilots*, and *Sailing Directions*.

Each Coast Guard District Commandant issues local *Notices to Mariners* for navigational material of local interest only.

When the safety of navigation requires, radio broadcast warnings are issued by the International Hydrographic Organization. For this purpose the world is divided into areas and sub-areas. The United States is responsible for the North Atlantic as far East as 40° and the Pacific as far West as 180°. These warnings are called "Hydrolants" and "Hydropacs." Information of continuing interest contained in *Broadcast Notices to Mariners* is reprinted in the local *Notices to Mariners*.

Finally, the DMAHC issued a *Daily Memorandum* for both the Atlantic and Pacific. These contain the text of pertinent NAVAREA WARNINGS and the Hydrolants or Hydropacs broadcast in the previous 24 hours.

Obviously the navigator has a full-time job keeping up with changes to his publications and charts. However, it is extremely important that he do so.

DEAD RECKONING AND PILOTING

DEFINITIONS

True North—The direction of the geographic North Pole from the ship. On a Mercator chart this is always straight up.

Magnetic North—The direction of the magnetic North Pole from the ship, or the direction in which the compass needle points when it is not affected by deviation.

Compass North—An imaginary point toward which the North end of the compass needle actually points. Its direction varies with both variation and deviation.

Variation—The angular difference at the ship between the direction of true North and magnetic North. It is an error of the compass caused by the fact that the magnetic needle points to the magnetic North Pole instead of the geographic North Pole.

Deviation—The angular difference at the ship between the direction of magnetic North and compass North. It is an error of the compass caused by the magnetic influence of the iron and steel within the ship itself. The ship acts as a magnet, and as the ship turns about the compass needle on the various headings the effect of this magnet on the needle varies, and the deviation therefore varies with the heading of the ship.

True course—The angle between true North and the intended track of the vessel over the bottom.

Magnetic course—The angle between magnetic North and the intended track of the vessel over the bottom.

Compass course—The angle between compass North and the intended track of the vessel over the bottom.

True heading—The angle between true North and the keel of the vessel. Due to current and leeway the true heading of the ship is sometimes

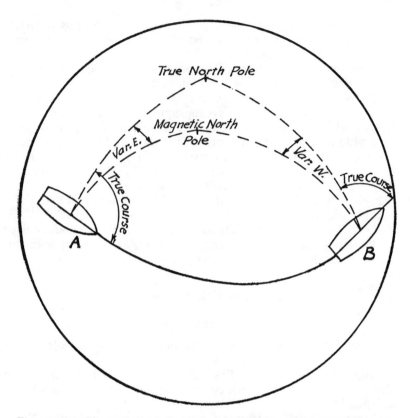

Figure 16-31. True and magnetic North Pole. A. The magnetic North lies to the right of true North, at B. the magnetic North is left of true North.

different from the true course. That is, to make good a certain course over the bottom it is necessary to head the ship on one side or the other to overcome current or wind.

Magnetic heading—The angle between magnetic North and the keel.

Compass heading—The angle between compass North and the keel. This is always the course given to the helmsman.

Course line—A line marked on the chart to show the intended track of the vessel.

Distance—The length of the line joining two points on the surface of the earth. Distance is always measured in nautical miles, one nautical mile being the length of the arc, on the surface of the earth, of one minute of latitude.

Difference of latitude—The difference of latitude of two places is the arc of a meridian intercepted between their parallels. If both places are in the same hemisphere, the difference of latitude is found by subtracting the smaller from the larger; if in opposite hemispheres, one in North and one in

South latitude, the difference in latitude is found by adding the two values together. Difference in latitude is measured in terms of arc, but the value can be converted into miles at will, one minute of latitude being equal to one nautical mile.

Difference of longitude—The difference of longitude of two places is the smaller arc of the equator intercepted between their meridians.

Departure—Departure is the length in nautical miles of an arc of a parallel of latitude. It is also expressed as the distance to the eastward or westward traveled by a ship in passing from one point to another.

Line of bearing—A line of sight, usually over a pelorus or compass, from the ship to an object. When properly plotted and laid down on the chart from the object in the direction of the ship, it becomes a line of position on which the ship was located at the instant the bearing was taken.

True bearing—The angle between true North and the line of bearing.

Magnetic bearing—The angle between magnetic North and the line of bearing.

Compass bearing—The angle between compass North and the line of bearing.

Relative bearing—The angle between the keel of the ship and the line of bearing.

Reciprocal true bearing—The reverse of the true bearing, found by adding 180° to the true bearing, dropping 360° if that figure is exceeded. It is actually the true bearing of the ship as observed from the object, and is used for plotting the bearing from a known object on the chart in the direction of the ship.

COMPASS ERROR

The magnetic compass needle is subject to two errors or influences which prevent it from pointing to the geographic North Pole, the direction of which has been defined as true North. These errors are known as *variation* and *deviation*.

Variation—The earth acts as a great spherical magnet and is surrounded by a magnetic field containing imaginary lines of force with which a freely suspended compass needle tends to align itself. These lines of force converge at two magnetic poles. The North end of the compass needle points to the magnetic North Pole which is located in northern Canada, some 1,150 miles from the geographic North Pole. This effect is called *variation*, and it is reckoned as an error of the compass. The *magnitude* of this error varies, depending on the position of the observer on the surface of the earth, but it has been carefully determined and is found noted inside the compass rose on every chart. The *direction* of the error also depends on location. If the position of the compass is such that the magnetic North Pole lies to the left of true North, the compass needle will point to the left, or West, of the true meridian, and the error is labeled *West*. If the magnetic North Pole lies to the right of true North, the variation is labeled *East*.

Figure 16-31 shows a ship in position *A*, where the magnetic North lies to the right of true North. The variation is therefore East and must be subtracted from the true course to get the magnetic course. As the ship sails to position *B*, the variation is constantly changing, and at *B* magnetic North lies to the left of true North. The variation is now West and must be added to the true course to obtain the magnetic course.

Deviation—If variation were the only error affecting the compass needle, the North end of the needle would always point to the magnetic North Pole. However, the metal in the ship itself also acts as a strong magnet, and the influence of the magnetic field of the ship will throw the compass needle either to the left or to the right of its alignment with magnetic North. The error resulting from this influence is called *deviation*. It varies in strength and direction, depending on the heading of the ship. It is partly eliminated by magnets placed around the compass, but it cannot be entirely removed, and the residual deviation is determined by placing the ship on a number of different headings, taking bearings on the sun or on known landmarks, and comparing these compass bearings with the actual known bearings. The difference between a known magnetic bearing and a compass bearing of the same object is the deviation for that heading of the ship. The deviation is recorded for each heading in a *deviation table*, which is kept at hand for consultation in the chart room at all times.

The direction in which the North point of the compass needle actually swings when influenced by both variation and deviation is called *compass North*. Thus we have three North poles or North directions in navigation: *true*, or *geographic North*, with reference to which all navigation is planned on the chart; *magnetic North*, which is the direction of the magnetic North Pole; and *compass North*, which is the direction in which the North point of the compass needle, or compass card, actually points. The angular difference at the ship between true North and magnetic North is variation. The difference between magnetic North and compass North is deviation.

If the variation and the deviation both tend to force the compass needle in the same direction, the total effect, called *total error*, is the sum of the two errors. If they act in opposite directions on the needle, the total error will be the difference between them, and in the direction of that of the larger value.

The direction of the effect of deviation is determined by the relationship between compass North and magnetic North, in the same manner in which we determined the direction of the variation. Thus, if compass North lies to the left of magnetic North, the deviation is called *West*, and is added to a magnetic course or bearing to get the corresponding compass course or bearing. If compass North lies to the right of magnetic North, the deviation is *East*, and it must be subtracted from a magnetic function to get a compass function.

These facts and rules must be thoroughly understood by the navigator. They can be summarized as follows:

When working from *true* to *magnetic* and from *magnetic* to *compass*, Add westerly errors, subtract easterly errors.

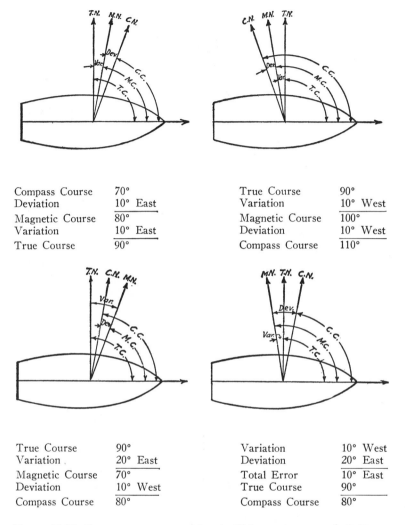

Compass Course	70°		True Course	90°
Deviation	10° East		Variation	10° West
Magnetic Course	80°		Magnetic Course	100°
Variation	10° East		Deviation	10° West
True Course	90°		Compass Course	110°

True Course	90°		Variation	10° West
Variation	20° East		Deviation	20° East
Magnetic Course	70°		Total Error	10° East
Deviation	10° West		True Course	90°
Compass Course	80°		Compass Course	80°

Figure 16-32. Compass course examples: A. With *true* to *magnetic*; B. From *magnetic* to *compass*.

When working from *compass* to *magnetic* and from *magnetic* to *true*, Subtract westerly errors and add easterly errors.

The algebraic sum of the variation and the deviation is called the *total error* or *compass error*. This can be applied to a true function to find the corresponding compass function, or vice versa, using the same rules just given, thus eliminating the magnetic function entirely.

These principles can be visualized by the examples given. Note in each case that the application of the total error will give the same result.

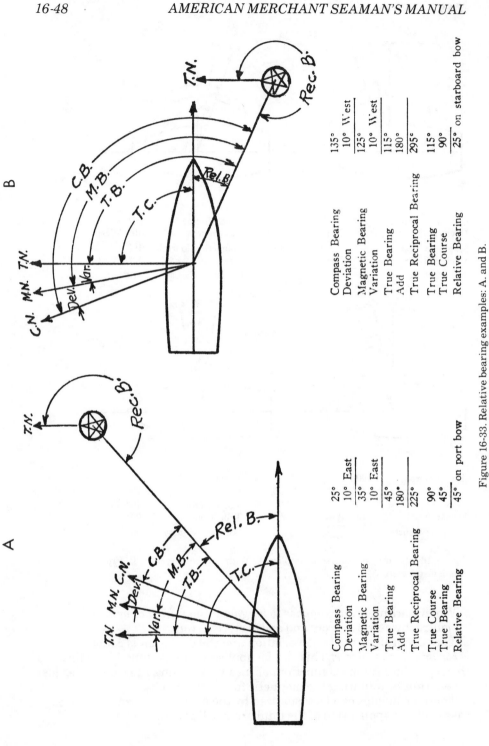

A		
Compass Bearing	25°	
Deviation	10°	East
Magnetic Bearing	35°	
Variation	10°	East
True Bearing	45°	
Add	180°	
True Reciprocal Bearing	225°	
True Course	90°	
True Bearing	45°	
Relative Bearing	45°	on port bow

B		
Compass Bearing	135°	
Deviation	10°	West
Magnetic Bearing	125°	
Variation	10°	West
True Bearing	115°	
Add	180°	
True Reciprocal Bearing	295°	
True Bearing	115°	
True Course	90°	
Relative Bearing	25°	on starboard bow

Figure 16-33. Relative bearing examples: A. and B.

In practice the navigator does not need to draw diagrams. He knows the rules, takes the variation from his chart and the deviation from the deviation table, and often makes the computation in his head. The examples shown in Figure 16-32A and 32B should be studied for practice.

If you understand these examples, but are afraid that you will forget when to add and when to subtract, it may help to remember the old saying: "*C*an *D*ead *M*en *V*ote *T*wice?"

Can	Dead	Men	Vote	Twice
(Compass)	(Deviation)	(Magnetic)	(Variation)	(True)

Then, by also remembering to add East and subtract West from going from compass to true, you can solve any conversion problem. Simply write down the formula and fill in what you know. This will show you that if you are going from true to compass you have to reverse the signs (subtract East instead of adding). Use the examples which follow to make sure you understand:

Compass Course or Bearing	Dev.	Magnetic Course or Bearing	Var.	True Course or Bearing	Total Error
75°	3° E	78°	10° E	88°	13° E
113°	3° W	110°	8° W	102°	11° W
192°	5° E	197°	5° W	192°	0
355°	5° E	000°	3° W	357°	2° E
230°	5° E	235°	10° W	225°	5° W
358°	4° E	002°	11° W	351°	7° W

BEARINGS

In practice when the navigator of a ship in pilot water fixes his position he will take bearings by using an azimuth or bearing circle mounted on a repeater from the gyrocompass. These are true bearings and he has only to plot them on the chart. His position or "fix" is where two or more bearings (or lines of position) intersect.

However, in the days before gyrocompasses were installed aboard ship, or before ships were so plentifully supplied with repeaters from the gyro, a pelorus or dumb compass was used. This is still the case with some yachts. Should there be a gyrocompass casualty, the navigator will have to use the repeater compass on the bridge wing as a pelorus, convert relative bearings to true bearings, and apply variation and deviation in order to convert to true bearings which he can plot. Consequently the Coast Guard requires that the candidate for a license demonstrate his ability to convert relative bearings to true bearings, and to convert magnetic to true bearings as necessary.

If the pelorus is adjusted so that the 000° point is opposite the lubber's line, or in line with the keel, the bearing taken will be the angle between the keel and the object. This is called a relative bearing since it is relative to the ship's head, and measured from 000° to 180° on either side of the ship. Figures 16-33A and 16-33B are examples of bearings taken on the port and starboard bow respectively. The ship is on a true course of 090°, or 090°(*t*). Studying these examples will show that a relative bearing on the port side,

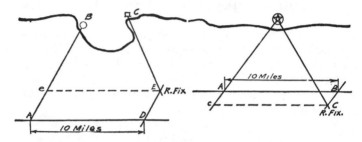

Figure 16-34. Running fix examples: A. and B.

subtracted from the true, magnetic or compass course, gives the true, magnetic or compass bearing of the landmark. On the starboard side the relative bearing is added to the course.

The reciprocal bearing is the reverse of the bearing, or the bearing of the ship, as measured by an observer at the landmark. It always differs from the bearing taken aboard ship by 180°. In Figure 16-33A the true bearing of the lighthouse is 045° and the reciprocal bearing is 225°. In Figure 16-33B the true bearing is 115° and its reciprocal is 295°.

The navigator lays down the reciprocal bearing as a line of position on the chart. Until he plots another line of position he only knows that he is *somewhere* along his first line of position. When he plots another line of position, he is assured that his ship is at the point where these two lines of position intersect. If he can plot three lines of position, or combine the two lines of position with a radar range, so much the better.

Running fixes—Often only one landmark is available for a fix at a certain time, but at a later hour another landmark becomes visible. It is then possible to obtain a so-called *running fix* by advancing the first line of position by the course and distance sailed, and crossing it with the new line of position. For instance, in Figure 16-34A, the navigator takes a bearing on landmark *B* and lays it down on the chart. He has no other good landmark for the time being, so he assumes that he is at position *A* where his course line is crossed by the line of position for *B*. He sails 10 miles farther on, when he gets another bearing on landmark *C*. He plots that also. He then marks out the distance sailed, 10 miles, along his course line from *A* to *D*, and through *D* draws a line parallel to the first line of position. This line intersects the second line of position from *C* to *E*, which is the running fix. Actually, when the bearing on *B* was taken, the ship was at *e*, farther inshore than the navigator intended to be.

Figure 16-34B shows a case where only one landmark is available, and two bearings are taken with a run between. The principle is the same as in Figure 16-34A. The first bearing is taken and laid down. It intersects the course line at *A*. The ship sails 10 miles farther on, and another bearing is

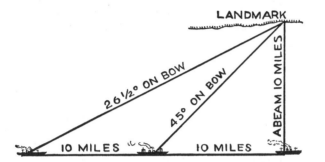

Figure 16-35. 26 1/2° - 45° bearing.

taken on the same landmark and is also plotted from the landmark in the direction of the ship. From *A* the distance sailed, or 10 miles, is laid off along the course line, reaching to point *B*, and through this point a line is drawn parallel to the first line of position. The intersection of this line with the second bearing gives the ship's position at the instant the second bearing was taken. In this case the ship had been set offshore from the intended course line, and actually the ship was at *c* when the first bearing was taken.

Since the advent of radar, running fixes are not as frequently used for piloting as they once were. Their usefulness is that they permit fixing the position of the ship by visual bearings if only one landmark is visible, or if one drops from view before the second is picked up. Now that radar can give an accurate range on prominent objects ashore, the necessity of taking running fixes when piloting rarely occurs. However, running fixes are still necessary in celestial navigation and the princple is the same. It must be thoroughly understood.

Distance off methods—The various distance off methods which are really only special cases of running fixes have also dropped into disuse now that radar is available to give ranges. However, they do provide a readily available means of verifying the distance offshore and should not be overlooked. Radars *have* been known to fail. Oldtime masters are inclined to require their mates to use a distance off method, at least as a back-up, and a yachtsman without radar or gyrocompass will find the method simple and convenient. An added reason for becoming familiar with distance off is that it is still a requirement on Coast Guard licensing examinations.

Bow and beam bearing—This is the most common of these short methods. The time is noted when a certain landmark bears 45° or 4 points off the bow. The time is again noted when that landmark is exactly abeam.

From the time interval, the distance traveled can be computed, and the distance traveled is the same as the distance off the landmark when it bears abeam.

7/10 Rule—If a bearing is taken and the time noted when a landmark bears 2 points, or 22 1/2°, on the bow and again when the same landmark bears 4 points, or 45°, on the bow, the distance off the landmark along the second line of bearing is equal to the distance traveled, and 7/10 of the distance traveled between the two bearings is the distance to the point where the ship will be abeam of the landmark. When abeam, the ship will also be 7/10 of that distance off the landmark.

26 1/2° and 45° Bearings—This combination of relative bearings is a favorite with many navigators. Take the time when the landmark bears 26 1/2° and again when it bears 45° on the bow, and figure the distance traveled between the two bearings. Then the ship will have to travel an equal distance before it will be abeam, and when abeam it will be this same distance off the landmark.

Table 7 of Bowditch—This table is a convenient means of figuring distance off. The table is entered with two angles: the angle on the bow of the first bearing and the angle on the bow of the second bearing. Two coefficients are found. The first is multiplied by the distance traveled between the two bearings to give the distance off the landmark along the second line of bearing, and the second coefficient, multiplied by the distance, gives the distance the ship will be off when abeam.

RADAR PILOTING AND RADAR FIXES

Radar now makes piloting far easier and safer than when it was necessary to depend upon visual bearings alone. A good navigator can bring a ship into a harbor in dense fog by radar alone and can follow his track line along a coast even though the features on shore are obscured or too indistinct for visual bearings.

Radar can be used in many ways when plotting a fix. How it is used will depend entirely on the circumstances, the contour of the coast, or the availability of known objects to range on. If a visual bearing can be obtained only on a single object ashore, a radar range can be secured either on that object, or upon an unseen feature of the coast. The fix is at the intersection of the visual line of position and the range arc drawn from the object or feature ranged on. Ranges can be obtained from two or more objects or features, and the results plotted either by themselves, or in addition to a visual line of position. A position obtained in this manner is highly accurate.

Finally, radar bearings can be used. However, radar bearings obtained from commercial radar sets are not nearly as accurate as radar ranges, and should only be used as a back-up, or a secondary source, if no means is available. If a radar bearing must be used, it should be used in conjunction with a bearing or range from another object or feature of the coastline. A navy surface search radar will give more accurate bearings than a commercial set, and a navy fire control radar is even better, but this does not help the merchant mariner who may occasionally have to fall back on radar bearings. He should, though, be aware of the limitations of his equipment.

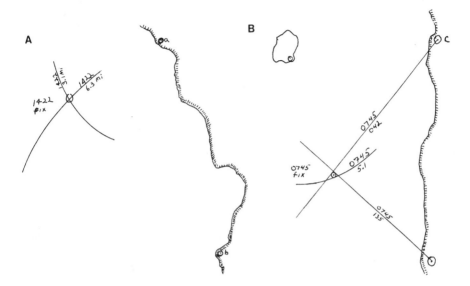

Figure 16-36. Radar piloting. In sketch A the navigator has obtained his position by taking radar ranges on objects "a" and "b" which are on the shoreline. The intersection of the arcs of these two ranges is labeled "1422 fix." Had either object been visible, he should have at least obtained one bearing. In sketch B the navigator has obtained his fix by taking visual bearings on objects "c" and "d" as well as obtaining a radar range on the nearest point of the island. This gives him a small triangle and reassures him that his visual bearings are plotted correctly. The result is labeled "0745 fix." Drawings: Midn. Eric Pett, California Maritime Academy.

THE SAILINGS

Bowditch defines "sailing" as "a method of solving the various problems involving course, distance, difference of latitude, difference of longitude, and departure."

This definition requires some discussion. Before starting on a voyage the navigator must determine the course or courses to be steered, and the distance between the latitude and longitude of his departure and the latitude and longitude of the port where he takes his arrival. He can do this in one of two ways, or by a combination of both. He may do all his planning on charts or plotting sheets. This is common in the Navy. Or he may mathematically compute the course and distance by knowing the position where he takes departure and where he expects to take arrival. If he uses this latter method, he is said to be working out "the sailings." In the merchant service emphasis is placed on the sailings. Obviously the merchant marine navigator will also do his chart work, but he is inclined to depend upon the mathematical solution of the sailings for the distance and his initial course.

In former days the solution of the sailings could be very cumbersome and time consuming, particularly with great circle sailings where accuracy required the use of logarithms. The advent of the hand-held calculator enables the navigator to multiply and divide large numbers directly without resort to logs. Furthermore, if a programmed or navigational calculator is used, there is an immediate read-out of course and distance after the initial inputs have been made. This is a real boon to the navigator because it makes it easier to check the distance as measued on the chart. Dividers have been known to slip, and a distance computed by working the sailings will be more accurate.

KINDS OF SAILINGS

There are seven kinds of sailings. Only parallel sailing and Mercator sailing are required on the third mate's licensing examination, but all will be defined and discussed to some degree. For more complete discussion of the sailings, the serious student is again referred to Bowditch.

Plane sailing—That part of the earth traversed is regarded as flat. Consequently this method should not be used for distances of more than a few hundred miles. A single course and distance, the difference of latitude, and departure are the only items involved. Plane sailing can be solved either by Table 3 of Bowditch or by trigonometry.

Parallel sailing—A ship sailing either directly East or West can use parallel sailing to advantage. In involves the interconversion of departure and difference of longitude. In the days of sail when vessels could not compute their longitude, they would reach the latitude of their destination and then make "eastings" or "westings."

Traverse sailing combines the plane sailing solutions when there are two or more course changes. When a sailing vessel was beating into the wind, traverse sailing was important but has lost its usefulness. It now warrants only a brief mention in Bowditch.

Mid-latitude (or **middle-latitude sailing**)—This involves the use of the mid-latitude of the point of departure and the point of arrival for converting departure to difference of longitude when the course is not due East or due West. It is somewhat simpler than Mercator sailing but not quite as accurate.

Mercator sailing—Mercator sailing provides a mathematical solution of the plot as made on a Mercator chart. It has similarities to plane sailing, but uses Table 5 of Bowditch for meridional difference and the difference of longitude instead of that of latitude and departure respectively.

Great Circle sailing—Great circle sailing treats the earth as a sphere and involves the solution of courses, distances, and points along a great circle between the point of departure and the point of arrival. It is required on the licensing examination for master, chief mate, and second mate.

Composite sailing is a modification of great circle sailing to limit the maximum latitude. Should a great circle take a vessel too far North or South, the track might be modified. It will not be discussed further.

DEFINITIONS AND SYMBOLS

The following definitions and symbols are needed in a discussion of the sailings. Several have been mentioned in the preliminary discussion.

1. Latitude (L). The latitude of the point of departure is L_1. Latitude of arrival is L_2.

2. Difference of latitude (l). The angular distance North or South between the parallels of latitude passing through two points on the surface of the earth, measured in degrees, minutes, and tenths of minutes or seconds. (One minute of latitude equals one nautical mile.)

3. Meridional parts (M). Meridional parts of point of departure (M_1), Meridional parts of point of arrival (M_2). See Table 5 of Bowditch.

4. Meridional difference (m). The difference between M_1 and M_2.

5. Longitude (λ). The longitude of the point of departure is designated λ_1. The longitude of the point of arrival is designated λ_2.

6. Difference of longitude (DLo). The angular difference East or West between the meridians of longitude passing through two points on the surface of the earth, measured on the plane of the equator in degrees, minutes, and tenths of minutes or seconds.

7. Departure (p). Distance East or West between two points on the surface of the earth, measured in nautical miles along a parallel of latitude.

8. Course or course angle (Cn or C). The angle between the track of the vessel and the true North meridian.

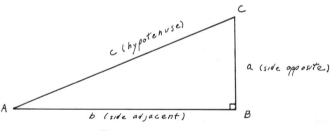

Figure 16-37. Right triangle.

TRIGONOMETRIC DEFINITIONS

In order to understand the sailings, you have to comprehend a few definitions in trigonometry. In the very excellent chapter on mathematics, Bowditch defines trigonometry as "that branch of mathematics dealing with the relations among the angles and sides of triangles."

A right triangle is shown in Figure 16-37.

From the trigonometric functions indicated in Figure 16-37 several other relations can be derived:

$$a = c \sin A \text{ (or c times sin A)}$$
$$b = c \cos A \text{ (or c times cos A)}$$
$$a = B \tan A \text{ (or b times tan A)}$$

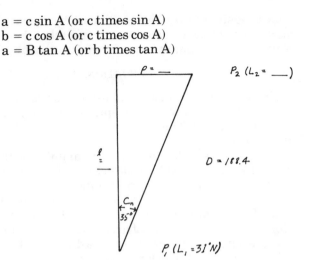

Figure 16-38. Plane sailing triangle.

Table 31 of Bowditch contains the natural trigonometric functions and Table 33, the logarithms of trigonometric functions. If accurate solutions to the problem c sin A were desired before the days of calculators and c = 2085.16 and A = 37°16.2′, it can be seen that a lot of long-hand arithmetic would be involved unless logarithms were used which simplified the job. Now with the hand-held calculator it is only necessary to write down the formula and substitute:

$$a = c \sin A$$
$$= 2085.16 \times \sin 37\text{-}16.2$$
$$= 1262.71$$

In the abbreviated discussion of the sailings which follows, no reference will be made to logarithms.

PLANE SAILING

The plane sailing triangle is shown in Figure 16-38. The lettering conforms to the definitions and symbols given earlier, but the right triangle can be solved in exactly the same way as the problem given in the brief trigonometric discussion in the previous paragraph.

Problem: A vessel departs latitude 31° N on course 035°t and steams 188.4 miles.

Required: (1) Difference of latitude (l). (2) Latitude of arrival (L_2). (3) Departure (p).

Solution: We know two parts of this right triangle, and we can solve for the others.

Two formulas look promising.

$$\text{Cos C} = \frac{1}{D} \qquad \text{and} \qquad \text{Sin C} = \frac{p}{D}$$

$$\text{Cos } 35° = \frac{1}{188.4} \qquad\qquad \text{Sin } 35° = \frac{p}{188.4}$$

$$1 = 188.4 \text{ Cos } 35° \qquad\qquad p = 188.4 \text{ Sin } 35°$$
$$= 154.3 \qquad\qquad\qquad = 108.06 \text{ or } 108.1$$

So. . . difference of latitude (l) = 154.3 = 2°34.3′

$$\text{latitude of arrival} = L_1 + 1$$
$$= 31° + 2°34.3′$$
$$= 33°34.3′$$
$$\text{departure (p)} = 108.6 \text{ miles}$$

PARALLEL SAILING

Parallel sailing is the simplest of the sailings. It can be solved either by trigonometric formulas or by Bowditch Table 3.

Two formulas can be used. They are really one formula, and differ in appearance only because the cosine is the reciprocal of the secant:

$$p = \text{DLo cos L} \qquad \text{DLo} = p \text{ sec L}$$

Problem: The DR latitude of a ship is 49°40.2′N. Course is 090°.
Required: Change in longitude (DLo) as ship steams for 136.4 miles.

$$\text{DLo} = p \text{ sec L}$$
$$= 136.4 \text{ sec } 49\text{-}40.2 = 210.8 = 3° + 30.8′ = 3\text{-}30.8$$

MID-LATITUDE SAILING

Plane sailing cannot be used on a voyage of any great distance, and parallel sailing can be used only when the course is due East or West. When a ship sails on a course in which latitude and longitude both change (this is most of the time), mid-latitude sailing is frequently used. Change in latitude is found as in plane sailing, and the average or middle latitude of the two places is used for converting departure into difference of longitude. Mid-latitude sailing problems can be solved either by computation or by the use of Table 3. The simpler computation method is shown in Figure 16-39 and can be used to solve the following:

Problem: A ship departs position A, L 49-57 N, λ 15-16 W bound for position B in L 47-18 N, λ 20-10 W.
Required: Find the course (C) and distance (D).

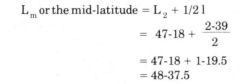

L_1	49-57 N		λ_1	15-16 W
L_2	47-18 N		λ_2	20-10 W
l	2-39 or 159'		DLo	4-54 or 4 x 60 + 54 = 294'

$$L_m \text{ or the mid-latitude} = L_2 + 1/2\,l$$

$$= 47\text{-}18 + \frac{2\text{-}39}{2}$$

$$= 47\text{-}18 + 1\text{-}19.5$$

$$= 48\text{-}37.5$$

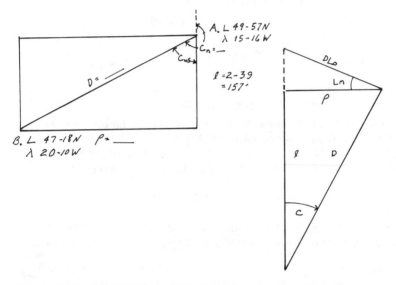

Figure 16-39. A. Mid-latitude sailing; B. Example of mid-latitude sailing. The relationships between the values used in mid-latitude sailing are shown in A. As is true for Mercator sailing, this is always drawn in the first quadrant.

The formula for plane sailing can be modified for mid-latitude sailing:

$$p = DLo \cos L_m$$

Substituting ... p = 294 cos 48-37.5 = 194.3
The Course angle must be measured in the Southwest quadrant since the vessel is heading in a southwesterly direction.

$$\text{Tan } C_{ws} = 1.220$$

$$C_{ws} = 50\text{-}39$$

$$Cn = 180 + 50\text{-}39 = 230\text{-}39.6$$

We must still find the Distance (D) . . .

$$\text{Sin } C_{ws} = \frac{194.3}{D}$$

$$D = \frac{194.3}{\sin 50\text{-}39.6}$$

$$= 251.2$$

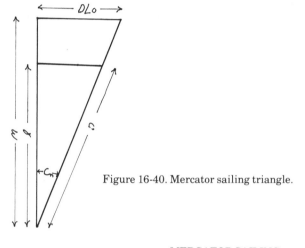

Figure 16-40. Mercator sailing triangle.

MERCATOR SAILING

Mercator sailing is a sailing in which the factors of latitude, longitude, course and distance are considered in relation to each other in the same manner as they are plotted on a Mercator chart. Mercator sailing can be used for great distances, and is more accurate than mid-latitude sailing. The relationships for Mercator sailing are shown in Figure 16-40. The formulas which can be used, based on the relationships of the sketch are as follows:

$$\tan C = \frac{DLo}{m} \qquad\qquad D = 1 \sec C = \frac{1}{\cos C}$$

$$DLo = m \tan C$$

$$p = \frac{1 \times DLo}{m}$$

The value "m" which we have not yet discussed is the number of meridional parts between L_1 and L_2. M_1 is the number of meridional parts equivalent to L_1, and M_2 is the number of meridional parts equivalent to L_2. See Table 5 of Bowditch. Note that the bottom part of Figure 16-40 is identical to Figure 16-38 which illustrates plane sailing.

Problem: Find the course and distance between position A, L 42-03 N/74-04 W and position B, L 36-59 N/25-10W.

L$_1$	42-03 N	M$_1$	2770.1	λ$_1$	70-04 W
L$_2$	36-59 N	M$_2$	2377.4	λ$_2$	25-10 W
l	5-04 S	m	392.7	DLo	44-54 E
	or 304'				or 2694'

Before going any farther it may be helpful to see how the actual track looks on a rough sketch (see Figure 16-41). Obviously the ship will take a course somewhat South of 090°, and a sketch will assist in not confusing the relationships:

$$\text{Tan C} = \frac{\text{DLo}}{\text{m}} = \frac{2694}{392.7} = 81\text{-}42.4$$

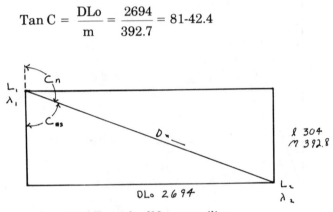

Figure 16-41. Example of Mercator sailing.

but remember that this is the course measured up to the East from 180°. Subtracting from 180° gives:

$$\begin{array}{r} 179\text{-}60.0 \\ -\ 81\text{-}42.4 \\ \hline 98\text{-}17.6 \end{array} \qquad \text{Cn of 98-17.6.}$$

This is also 8-17.6 South of 090°.

Looking back over the formulas given earlier, one in particular looks helpful:

$$D = l \sec C = \frac{l}{\cos C} = \frac{304}{.144241} = 2107.5 \text{ or } 2107 \text{ miles.}$$

Checking the solution on a programmed navigational calculator gives: C 98-19.7 and D 2098.8. In any case the difference between 2 minutes (not degrees!) in the course and 8 miles in a voyage of over 2,000 miles is not worth sneezing about. Aren't you glad that you don't have to solve the problem by using logarithms?

GREAT CIRCLE SAILING

Great circle sailing becomes important for a long voyage. The shortest distance between two points on the surface of the earth is a great circle, and is illustrated by stretching a string on a globe from one point to the other. On a regular Mercator chart this course will appear as a curved line because of the distortion of the Mercator chart. To sail this course exactly would mean that the ship would have to change its heading constantly by an insignificant amount. This is obviously impractical, and in actual practice a series of points along the track are selected, and straight lines (rhumb lines) are drawn between them. The ship will change course every day or two as the track goes from one rhumb line to the next.

The mathematical solution of a great circle track is shown in Bowditch. It is tedious and complicated. It can, however, be solved quickly by an eighth grade student with a programmed navigational pocket calculator even though he doesn't have the slightest idea what he is doing.

In practice the navigator will lay out his great circle track on a gnomonic chart on which all great circles appear as straight lines. He will pick out selected points, transfer them to a Mercator chart, and use these points to draw his rhumb lines. He can measure the lengths of the rhumb lines, add them up, and the total is the length of his voyage. However, his measurements still will not be as accurate as a mathematical solution to the great circle sailing problem. It is for this reason that the candidate for master, chief mate, or second mate must demonstrate his undersanding of great circle sailing. He can use a pocket calculator, but it cannot be already programmed.

CELESTIAL NAVIGATION

When you go topside on a clear night it looks as though the earth is surrounded by a huge concentric globe or sphere. Scattered around the sphere are the stars, and the center of the sphere is exactly at the center of the earth. A first year astronomy student will tell you that this is not true, but this concept makes some very useful definitions easy to understand and to remember.

The sphere you see is called the celestial sphere. If you extend the polar axis (a line passing through the earth's North and South Poles) until it reaches the edge of the celestial sphere, the celestial North and South Poles are located. If you extend the plane of the earth's equator indefinitely until it reaches the edge of the sphere (intersects it), you have located the celestial equator. The celestial sphere remains stationary, but inside it the earth spins about the polar axis from West to East, making it appear as though the stars are traveling from East to West. The celestial sphere is considered infinite in size because the nearest star is some 26 trillion miles away. This is so far that the motion of the earth in its orbit around the sun does not even materially affect the position of the center of the earth in relation to the center of the celestial sphere.

The positions of the stars in the celestial sphere are determined in the same manner in which your ship is located by latitude and longitude at sea. Celestial latitude is called *declination* and is measured North or South

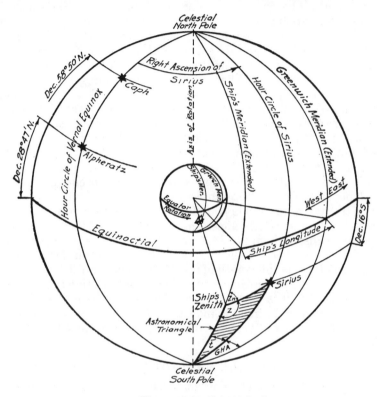

Figure 16-42. Celestial sphere.

from the celestial equator which is sometimes called the *equinoctial*. Celestial longitude is called *right ascension* and it is measured from a reference meridian in the sky called the *hour circle of the vernal equinox*. On the earth longitude is measured both East and West of the Greenwich meridian, but right ascension is measured only East, and is the angular distance the body is East of the vernal equinox. Right ascesion is customarily measured in units of time, 24 hours being equal to 360°.

A companion definition to right ascension, and one which is used far more in modern practice, is *sideral hour angle*. The difference between the two is the direction in which they are measured. *Sidereal hour angle* is the angular distance a body is *west* of the vernal equinox. It is measured on the arc of the celestial equator, or the angle at the celestial pole between the hour circle of the vernal equinox and the hour circle of the body. In the

Nautical Almanac you will notice that the position of stars is located by sideral hour angle (SHA) in degrees and declination.

The above two definitions are meaningless without a definition of *vernal equinox* which is the point of intersection in the path of the sun (the ecliptic) and the celestial equator which the sun occupies when it changes from south to north declination (or crosses the celestial equator) on or about March 21st each year.

These defiitions may become more clear by looking at Figure 16-42. The earth rotates about its axis once in 24 hours. During that period a star will appear to move completely around the earth in a circle of 360°. During 1 hour the star will move through an angle of 15°, and it will move through an angle of 1° in 4 minutes. Thus, angular measurement of celestial longitude can be expressed in time, and right ascension is measured in hours, minutes and tenths of minutes. Meridians of celestial longitude are called *hour circles*, and difference of celestial longitude is called *hour angle*. The *Nautical Almanac* prints a table for converting angles to time and vice versa.

In celestial navigation, to establish the relationship between a place on earth and a heavenly body, it is customary to project the meridian of the place on earth out to the celestial sphere and measure the hour angle between that meridian and the hour circle of the body. This establishes the relationship in the East-West direction. The North-South relationship is simply the difference between the latitude of the place on earth and the declination of the heavenly body.

The *zenith* of an observer is the point in the celestial sphere directly over his head. The opposite of the zenith is the point in the celestial sphere directly below the observer, called the *nadir*.

The *altitude* of a body is measured with the sextant, and is the angle between the body and the point in the horizon vertically below it.

The *zenith distance* of a celestial body is its angular distance from the zenith. Since the zenith is always 90° from the horizon, the zenith distance equals 90° minus the altitude.

The *polar distance* of a celestial body is its angular distance from the visible pole, measured along the hour circle which passes through the body. Since declination is also measured along this hour circle, but from the equinoctial toward the pole, it follows that the polar distance of a body equals 90° − declination, if the pole and the declination are of the same name (both North or both South), and equals 90° + declination if they are of opposite names.

The navigator is concerned mainly with two types of hour angle. The *Greenwich hour angle*, called GHA, is the angle at the pole between the Greenwich meridian projected out to the celestial sphere and the hour circle of the body observed. This angle is always measured westward and has a maximum value of 360°.

The *meridian angle*, called t, is the angle between the observer's local meridian, projected out to the celestial sphere, and the hour circle through the body, measured East or West, whichever gives the smaller angle. t has a maximum value of 180° and must always be labeled East or West according to the direction in which it is measured.

The *azimuth* of a celestial body, called Z, is the bearing of the body, reckoned from either true North or true South toward the East or the West.

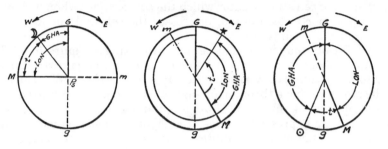

Figure 16-43. Time diagrams.

Z has a maximum value of 180°, but in modern navigation it is always converted to the bearing with respect to true North, called Z_n, according to the following rules:

1. If Z is North and East, $Z_n = Z$.
2. If Z is South and East, $Z_n = 180° - Z$.
3. If Z is South and West, $Z_n = 180° + Z$.
4. If Z is North and West, $Z_n = 360° - Z$.

HOUR ANGLES

Hour angles are shown on a diagram which assumes the observer to be out in space beyond the celestial South Pole and directly in line with the polar axis (see Figure 16-43). He sees the South Pole of both the earth and the celestial sphere as a single point in the center of the diagram, and he sees the equator and the equinoctial as concentric circles. All meridians and hour circles will appear as straight lines radiating from the South Pole. For convenience the Greenwich meridian is always shown as a solid line straight up from the pole and is labeled G. The part of the meridian which is on the other side of the earth from Greenwich, i.e. the 180th meridian, is shown as a dotted line and is labeled g. The solid line is called the *upper branch* of the Greenwich meridian, and the dotted line the *lower branch*.

With the Greenwich meridian so located, the local meridian of the observer can be drawn in according to the longitude of the observer. East longitude is marked off to the right of G in a clockwise direction while West longitude is marked off to the left of G in a counterclockwise direction. The local meridian is shown solid and labeled M for the upper branch, while the lower branch is shown dotted and labeled m.

The equatorial outline of the earth is omitted and the meridians are shown projected out to the celestial sphere. In this view, the celestial bodies will all appear to rotate around the diagram in a counterclockwise direction, or westward.

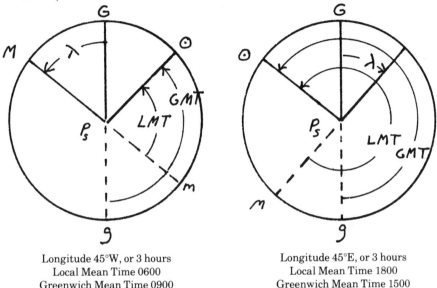

Longitude 45°W, or 3 hours
Local Mean Time 0600
Greenwich Mean Time 0900

Longitude 45°E, or 3 hours
Local Mean Time 1800
Greenwich Mean Time 1500

Figure 16-44. Time diagrams.

To use the diagram, draw in the Greenwich and the local meridian. The Greenwich hour angle, GHA, of the body is found from the *Nautical Almanac* and is marked out westward from G. The hour circle of the body is indicated and the angle *t* is labeled. Study of the diagram will show how to combine GHA and longitude to find *t*. *t* is labeled according to whether it is measured eastward or westward from M. In actual practice the longitude is obtained from the DR position and GHA from the *Nautical Almanac*.

TIME

Time, as told by the position of the sun in the sky, is called *apparent time*. This might be called sundial time. The seeming rotation of the sun around the earth, which is really caused by the rotation of the earth on its axis, is not quite uniform, and for navigational purposes an average or mean sun which travels at a uniform rate was invented. This is the time kept by the ship's chronometer. The difference between mean time and apparent time at any instant is called the *equation of time* and was formerly of great importance in navigation. Its greatest value is something over 16 minutes occuring in November. The value of the equation of time is given in the daily pages of the *Nautical Almanac*, and it may be used in determining the time of local apparent noon. However, in actual practice the equation of time is rarely, if ever, used and is of little direct use in modern celestial navigation.

The Greenwich meridian which passes through the Royal Observatory in Greenwich, England, has been adopted as the standard reference meridian. Greenwich mean time is the basis on which the *Nautical Almanac* is compiled. This was formerly called Greenwich civil time, and you may see this term in older texts and by older seadogs. Greenwich apparent time is the time at Greenwich determined by the position of the real sun with respect to that meridian. Local mean time is the time on any meridian determined by the position of the mean sun with respect to that meridian.

STANDARD OR ZONE TIME

Local mean time was formerly used by the various cities and towns which meant that each was keeping time based on its own local meridian. The introduction of zone time helped reduce the confusion caused by many different mean times. For convenience, the world has been divided up into 24 time zones within which people keep the same zone or standard time. Each zone extends over 15° of longitude, so that the time of adjoining zones will differ by one hour. The time of each zone is the local mean time of its central meridian. The central meridians around which the zones are planned are the Greenwich (0°), 15°, 30°, 45°, 60°, and so forth to 180° which is the International Date Line. If an area is on Daylight Saving, it simply means that if an area is normally on ZT + 5, it will be on ZT + 4. This extends the period of daylight, and makes the sun set later in the evening.

Time diagrams, exactly like those used to illustrate the hour angle, can be used to advantage. The rules can be stated as follows:

LMT = GMT − West longitude or LMT = GMT + East longitude
GMT = LMT + West longitude or GMT = LMT − East longitude
Examples are shown in Figure 16-44.

CHANGE OF DATE

It frequently happens that the local date of your position is different from the Greenwich date. Similarly, if you are in a different part of the world than another ship, you may have a different date than she does. When using the *Nautical Almanac*, it is extremely important to insure that you are going into the tables for the right day. Although there are short cuts, it is usually better to go through Greenwich Mean Time (GMT), insure that the zone description (ZD) is properly applied, and make sure that you are working on the proper day. A few examples may help:

	*San Francisco**	
GMT	21-00	21 Dec
ZD	+8	(R)
*ZT	13-00	21 Dec (same date)

	*Boston**	
GMT	00-00	5 July (midnight)
ZD	+5	(R)
*ZT	19-00	4 July (day before)

	*Istanbul**	
GMT	23-00	1 Oct
ZD	−2	(R)
*ZT	01-00	2 Oct (day later)

	*Taiwan**	
*ZT	04-00	1 Jan
ZD	−8	
GMT	20-00	31 Dec (day before)

This is not difficult, but a few rules will help cut down the mistakes:

Whether you are going from Greenwich (GMT) to zone time (ZT) or from zone to Greenwich (which is more usual), always write down the date.

If you are going from zone time to Greenwich, apply the zone description (ZD) exactly the way it appears. If you are going from GMT to ZT, reverse the sign (+ or −) of the time zone and place an (R) after the ZD as is done in the examples. When you get the answer, write down the date, whether it is the same or not.

Don't be afraid to taken an extra step if you have to. In the Istanbul example you actually add 2 hours to the 23-00 GMT of 1 October and get 25-00 on the 1st which is obviously 01-00 the next day, or 2 October. Similarly, in the Boston example, if you change the GMT of 00-00 on 5 July to a GMT of 24-00 on 4 July it is easier to subtract 5, and arrive at the ZT of 19-00 which is also obviously 4 July. In the Taiwan example it also might be easier to change the ZT of 04-00 on the 1st to 28-00 the 31st to make it easier to subtract 8 hours. GMT is then 20-00 31 December which is the day before.

It helps to remember that the sun travels from East to West. When it is 0800 in Boston people are still asleep in San Francisco because the sun hasn't gotten to the West Coast yet. It is only 0500 because there is a difference of three hours in the two time zones.

CHRONOMETER AND WATCH

When a navigator takes a sight he must know or be able to find the corresponding Greenwich time in order to look up the functions of the body observed in the *Nautical Almanac*. Since it is not convenient to look directly at the chronometer, he may use a stop watch which is started at the time of the sight and stopped at a convenient time after he has walked over to the chronometer box. Subtracting the reading of the stop watch from the reading of the chronometer will give him the chronometer time at the instant of the sight.

If a stop watch is not used, often an ordinary watch with a good second hand will be. Before taking his sights, the navigator notes simultaneously the reading of the chronometer and that of the watch. Subtracting the watch reading (W) from the chronometer reading (C) gives the difference known as C-W. This difference can then be added to the watch time of any sight taken shortly afterwards, and the result will be the chronometer time at the instant of the sight. To this must be applied the chronometer error (CE) to get the exact Greenwich mean time. If the chronometer is fast, the error is subtracted, and if it is slow, the error is added.

There is one other consideration. Since the chronometer reads only to 12 hours, and Greenwich time goes to 24 hours, it is necessary to know whether to add 12 hours to the chronometer time or not. It is easy to make a mistake, but with the help of a time diagram, and because you know what time zone (ZD or zone description) you are in, the problem is not really very hard. Since your day may be a day earlier or later than the Greenwich date, it is helpful if you write down the date everytime you write down a time.

Two examples may help:

Example No. 1. A ship is in Long. 150°E, and the navigator is getting ready to take a sight. The chronometer error (CE) is 2^{m}13^s fast. He wishes to find the value of C-W before he begins. His watch time (W) is 7-15-43 and the date is 4 July when the chronometer (C) reads 9-10-00. Since he is in 150°E, ZD is -10. He will want to find out two things: The value of C-W and also the approximate GMT so that he will know whether he is going to have to add 12 hours to CT and what day it is Greenwich time:

Chronometer (C)	09-10-00		ZT (approx)	7-15-43	July 4th
Watch time (W)	7-15-43	July 4th	ZD	−10	
C-W	1-54-17		GMT	21-15-43	July 3rd

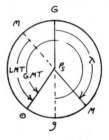

Figure 16-45. Time diagram (changing CT to GMT).

So we know the value of C-W and we also know that if we take our sight without too much delay the GMT will be about 2115, July 3. The time diagram (Figure 16-45) may make this clearer.

Now on to the actual time of taking the sight:

W	07-20-27	July 4th
C-W	1-54-17	
CT	09-14-44	(by addition)
CE	2-13	(F)
GMT	09-12-31	(if we don't have to add 12 hours)

but from applying the approximate ZT to the ZD earlier we know that the GMT is approximately 21-15 the day before so . . .

$$
\begin{array}{rl}
& 09\text{-}12\text{-}31 \\
+ & 12 \\
\hline
\text{GMT} \quad & 21\text{-}12\text{-}31 \quad \text{July 3rd (the day before).}
\end{array}
$$

Example No. 2. On August 15th the DR Long. of a ship is 124°E, and the zone time is about 0500. Chronometer error (CE) is 12^{m}15^s slow. What is the GMT and date when the chronometer reads 8-44-22?

ZT (approx)	05-00-00	August 15th
ZD	−8	(this is because Long. 124°E is in this time zone).
GMT (approx)	21-00-00	August 14th
C	08-44-22	
CE	12-15	(S)
GMT	08-56-37	(but from our example we know that we are 12 hours
	+ 12	in error, so . . .)
GMT	20-56-37	August 14th

A time diagram might help on this one also.

NAUTICAL ALMANAC

The *Nautical Almanac* is prepared jointly by the U.S. Naval Observatory and the Royal Greenwich Observatory in England. It is, however, printed separately by the Government Printing Office in this country and Her Majesty's Stationary Office in London. It lists the GHA (Greenwich hour angle) and declination for each hour of the day for the sun, moon, and certain planets. As a matter of convenience, even though the values of SHA (Sidereal hour angle) and declination for the stars vary only very slightly, they are listed on the daily pages. Tables listing the value of twilight, sunrise, sunset, moonrise, and moonset are also included.

An explanation of the tables is provided which gives examples of their use. This is followed by a table of Standard Times and Star Charts to assist in star identification. Polaris (North Star) tables provide a ready means of correcting the azimuth of Polaris to make it easy to compute a latitude by Polaris. Conversion of Arc to Time or Time to Arc can be read directly from a table which makes use of the fact that $1° = 4^m$. Since only hourly values of the GHAs for the bodies are listed on the daily pages, a table of increments and corrections makes it possible to interpolate these values to the nearest minute and second. Finally, altitude corrections are provided so that the altitude of the various bodies as read directly off the sextant can be corrected to give the observed altitude.

The format of the *Nautical Almanac* is straightforward and has altered little since the early 1950s when it underwent complete modernization and simplification. It is similar in format to the *Air Almanac*, used by aviators, but which has data for six months, one for January-June, and the second for July-December. Although the *Air Almanac* can be used by surface navigators and frequently is in the Navy, we recommend that aspiring merchant service navigators use the *Nautical Almanac* because it is more accurate and because it is used by the Coast Guard examiners in working up problems for licensing examinations.

ALTITUDE CORRECTIONS

The altitude of a body above the horizon (H_s) as read directly from the sextant cannot be immediately used for navigation because several corrections must be applied first. These corrections are found inside the front cover of the *Nautical Almanac*. After all corrections have been made, the result is known as the observed altitude (H_o). The difference between the observed altitude (H_o) and the computed altitude which is derived from tables when working out a sight is called "a." This value becomes very important, and consequently the navigator must take his sight with care and correct H_s properly unless his efforts are to be a waste of time.

Index error (IC)—This is sometimes called the Index Correction. It can be either plus or minus, and was discussed earlier in this chapter.

Dip of the horizon (HE)—Usually, simply called *Dip*, this is to correct for the error in the sextant altitude caused by the height of eye (HE). The greater the HE, the greater the H_s of any given body because the horizon is farther away, and the angle measured by the sextant will be larger than it would be closer to the surface of the water. The correction for HE is always negative.

Apparent altitude (H_a)—This is the result of applying IC and HE to the H_s. Strictly speaking, IC and HE should both be applied to H_s before applying the next correction, refraction (to be discussed in the following paragraph). In practice, and because it is easier, most navigators make up a form, total up all the corrections, plus (+) and minus(−), and apply the net result to H_s to obtain H_o. For practical purposes this works unless the H_s is very small as it is when the body is close to the horizon. In that case a small error might result. This minor point is brought up because for licensing examination purposes it is best to apply IC and HE to obtain H_a and then enter the table for refraction.

Refraction (R) is the final correction. It is caused by the bending of light as it passes from a medium of one density to another. The increasingly dense layers of the earth's atmosphere cause the rays to be bent more and more downward as they approach the surface. These corrections are the three left hand columns. Note that the first two columns are only for the sun, and the last is only for stars and planets. Be sure you use the correct column! Note further that there are two columns for the sun. One is for October to March, and the other April to September. This is because during some parts of the year the sun is farther away, and it makes a difference. Also note that there are different corrections for the lower limb (bottom part of the sun) and the upper limb (top part). Usually you shoot the lower limb, but if it is not visible and the top is, you can use the table for the upper limb.

One of the reasons that the refraction table for the sun differs from the star and planet table is that the sun is a large body which has a diameter which is measurable—unlike a star which is simply a point of light. Consequently there is a correction for this, the semi-diameter correction, which is included in the refraction table so you need not apply it separately. The slight additional correction for the few planets contained in the middle of the page is, in fact, semi-diameter.

Examples of correcting sextant altitudes of a few bodies are given below:

1. Sun's lower limb observed on February 20, 1979, H_s 36-45. HE 48 ft. IC - 2.5:

+	☉	−
IC		2.5
HE (48 ft.)		6.7
	−	9.2

H_s		36-45.0
corr.	(−)	9.2
H_a		36-35.8
R	(+)	15.0
H_o		36-50.8

2. A star was observed. H_s 73-27. HE 44 ft. IC + 1.5:

+	☆	−
IC 1.5		
HE (44 ft.)		6.4
	−	4.9

H_s		73-27.0
corr.	(−)	4.9
H_a		73-22.1
R	(−)	0.3
H_o		73-21.8

3. Venus was observed on November 9, 1979. H_s 25-52.4. HE 26 ft. IC - 0.8:

+	♀	−
IC		0.8
HE (26 ft.)		4.9
	−	5.7

H_s		25-52.4
corr.	(−)	5.7
H_a		25-46.7
R	(−)	2.0
		25-44.7
Addl	(+)	0.1
H_o		25-44.8

Note: The additional correction of + 0.1 for Venus is to be added March 4 - December 31. It is extremely minor, and shown only for the sake of completeness.

LATITUDE BY MERIDIAN ALTITUDE OF THE SUN (LAN)

Taking an "LAN" is the easiest way to obtain a sun line, and since the sun is on the meridian, the line obtained is a latitude line. It is only necessary to shoot the sun the instant it is at its highest altitude, after it has increased in altitude all morning, and before it starts its descent in the afternoon. The necessary computations are a bare minimum, and do not depend on the accuracy of your watch. It is ideal for a yachtsman and is done as follows:

1. Observe altitude of sun at noon and take highest value read on sextant. Correct H_s to obtain H_o.

2. Subtract H_o from 90° to get zenith distance. (The distance in degrees and minutes between the body and the point in the celestial sphere vertically overhead.)

3. By the use of the *Nautical Almanac*, find the declination of the sun at the time you took the observation. Follow the steps given in the example.

4. Find the latitude by combining the declination and the zenith distance according to the following rules:

a. If zenith distance and declination are the same name (North or South), add them. The result is your latitude.

b. If they are of different names, subtract the smaller from the larger, and the result is your latitude. Your latitude will take the name of the greater.

WATCH TIME OF LAN

The fact that there is a difference between local apparent time and zone time has been explained. Therefore, it should be no surprise to find that it is a very rare occurrence if LAN occurs exactly at 1200 ZT. It would only happen if the ship were on the meridian of the time zone at the moment the sun was directly overhead. Consequently LAN will occur some time before or after 1200 ZT depending on whether the ship is East or West of the meridian of the time zone. To save yourself half an hour waiting for LAN you can predict the time by a set of general rules or by a method easier to understand and shown as follows:

1200 DR Long.	82-03.9 W	DR Lat. 7-00.0 N
GMT 1700	82-03.9	
closest GHA	71-28.3	
difference	10-35.6	arc to time 42′22″

1700-00
+42-22
1742-22   First Estimate of LAN

1742-22 DR Long.	82-08.0	
closest GHA	71-28.3	
difference	10-39.7	arc to time 42′38″

1700-00
42-38
1742-38   Second Estimate of LAN

1742-38 (GMT)
1242-38 (LMT)

In this case the difference in time between the first estimate and the second estimate is not great. In practice you may not find it necessary to use a second estimate, but if you want to get the time down to a cat's whisker, this is the way it is done.

Figure 16-46. Taking a LAN (local apparent noon). Photo: Midn. J.P. Jackson, California Maritime Academy.

Now that we know when LAN is, let's go ahead and follow this navigator's work and see what he found when he worked out his sight:

H_s 67-08.4
c   −   6.9   ("c" here is the total of the IC and HE of eye)
H_a 67-01.5
c   +   15.8   ("c" is the altitude correction from cover page of *Nautical*
H_o 67-17.3   *Almanac*)
Dec   15-38.8 S
c   −   .6   (from *Nautical Almanac*)
Dec   15-38.2 S

$$
\begin{array}{r}
89\text{-}60.0 \\
-\ 67\text{-}17.3 \\
\hline
22\text{-}42.7 \quad \text{(zenith distance)} \\
-\ 15\text{-}38.2\text{S} \quad \text{(Dec at LAN)} \\
\hline
7\text{-}04.5\text{N} \quad \text{latitude at LAN}
\end{array}
$$

This is a good place to say a word about the importance of neatness and using a good format for your work. After you have taken your sights, working them out should be routine but the sight is useless unless you enter the tables correctly and write down the information accurately and legibly. Get a notebook to use as a navigation workbook, putting your work carefully in neat columns, making lines with a straight edge before adding

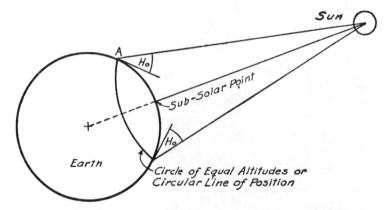

Figure 16-47. Circle of equal altitudes.

or subtracting, and using a quarter or other coin to draw a time diagram. Sloppy work causes mistakes and ultimately takes extra time. In correcting midshipmen's sights we find that a surprising number of budding navigators go wrong simply because they misread their own writing. The formats suggested on pages 16-79 and 16-80 are not the only ones, but they work.

LINE OF POSITION THEORY

The use of lines of position has long replaced laborious older methods of navigation. There are a number of methods of obtaining a line of position, and a few of the more common will be demonstrated. Once the line of position is obtained, the plotting begins. First it is necessary to explain what a line of position is. Figure 16-47 illustrates the basic principle. A line dropped from the center of the sun to the center of the earth pierces the surface of the earth at a point known as the sub-solar point. An observer at point A measures the altitude of the sun as H_o. A circle drawn with a sub-solar point as a center and the distance to A as a radius is called a *circle of equal altitudes*, because all observers located on this circle at that instant will read the identical altitude, H_o, for the sun.

It follows also that if, at that instant, an observer measures that altitude, he must be somewhere on this circle, and it can then be considered a line of position. Again, if at that instant he should measure an angle greater than H_o, he must of necessity be inside the circle, *toward* the sub-solar point. If he measures a smaller angle he must be outside the circle, *away* from the sub-solar point.

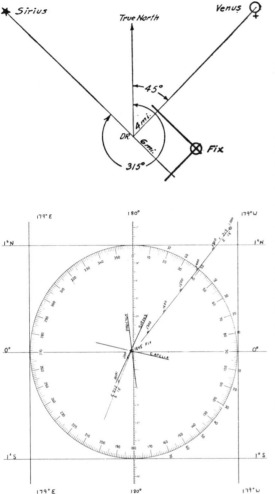

Figure 16-48. A. Solution of two LOP's; B. Three LOP's crossing at Equator and 180 degrees is another example of plotting lines of position. This one is very unusual. Procyon, Capella, and Sirius come together at a point which is within one mile of the intersection of the Equator and the 180 degree meridian. Sight was taken on 15 February, 1978 when T.S. *Golden Bear* was enroute Lahaina, Hawaii, to Noumea, New Caledonia. Courtesy: Midn. Phil Eichenberger, California Maritime Academy.

By means of tables the altitude and bearing of any navigational celestial body can be computed for any position on the surface of the earth, for any instant of time.

At any convenient time the navigator takes the altitude of the sun. Assuming that he is at his DR, or other convenient assumed position, he computes what the altitude and bearing of the sun, and consequently the bearing of the sub-solar point, would be if he were actually at that position. Comparison of the observed altitude, H_o, with the computed altitude, H_c, shows whether the actual line of position lies outside or inside the line of position passing through the DR or the assumed position. If the computed altitude is greater than the observed altitude, the observer is outside, or *away* from the sub-solar point. If less, the observer is inside, or *toward* the sub-solar point. The difference between the theoretical and the actual line of position is called the *intercept*. It can be shown that the intercept in nautical miles is equal to the difference between H_o and H_c in minutes.

Since the sub-solar point is usually at a very great distance away, it is not practical to mark it down. However, its true bearing called Z_n, is computed along with H_c, and the practice is to draw a line through the DR or assumed position in the direction of the body, mark out the intercept along this line either away from or toward the body, and at the point thus found draw a short heavy line at right angles to the line of bearing. This will be the line of position of the vessel for the instant when the sight was taken. Because the radius of a circular line of position is so great, it is safe to draw a line of position as a straight line for short distances, say not over 30 miles. Whether an intercept is marked toward or away can be remembered by the following connotation:

Computed	Greater	Away
Coast	Guard	Academy

If the navigator takes a single sight, he gets a single line of position, and he knows that for the instant of the sight he was somewhere on that line of position. In the absence of any better information he estimates he is at the intersection of the line of position and the bearing line along which the intercept was laid out. This point is called the *estimated position*.

A *running fix* can be obtained by advancing a morning sun line of position by the course and distance sailed (as explained under Bearings) to cross with an afternoon sun line of position. However, since this method of navigation can be used with all celestial bodies, an accurate fix can be obtained by taking simultaneous sights on two or more bodies in different quarters of the sky. The intersection of these several lines of position is the fix. They may not cross in a single point, but often form a small triangle. In that case the center of the triangle is taken as the fix.

Example: In Figure 16-48A simultaneous sights were taken on Venus and Sirius. For Venus, the azimuth, Z_n, was computed at 45° with an intercept of 4 miles toward. For Sirius the Z_n was 315° and the intercept 6 miles away. Plot fix from DR position.

MODERN SIGHT REDUCTION METHODS

Older methods, such as the time sight used for many years, have long been replaced by the more modern "short methods" in general use by the last two generations of seafarers. These tables are quite voluminous because the altitude and azimuth are computed for a given latitude, meridian angle, and declination. Interpolation is required to find the precise value required.

H.O. 214 is the first of the truly modern short methods of celestial navigation. Although now out of print, it is still aboard many ships and frequently used by older navigators. Reasonably rapid and not difficult, it can also be used to compute azimuths of the sun or other celestial bodies. The tables were conceived by Commander Richard Knight and Lieutenant Robert Jasperson, U.S.N. and were compiled by approximately 250 statis-

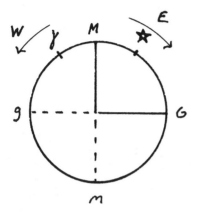

Figure 16-49. Example of time diagram for H.O. 214.

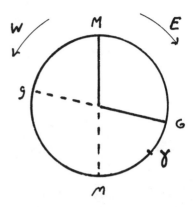

Figure 16-50. Example of time diagram for H.O. 249.

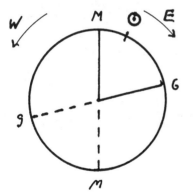

Figure 16-51. Time diagram for Pub. 229 - Sun.

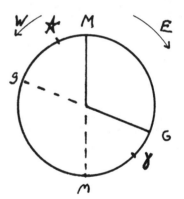

Figure 16-52. Time diagram for Pub. 229 - Star.

ticians furnished by the W.P.A. (Works Progress Administration, the agency which sponsored projects to provide work for the unemployed during the Depression of the 1930s). Since this was long before the invention of computers and calculators, all the work was done manually at an annual budget of $195,000. More than 9,000,000 calculations were involved, an enormous undertaking at a bargain price! DMAHC 249 (formerly H.O. Pub. No. 249) and DMAHC 229, in reality further modifications and developments of H.O. 214, are discussed briefly below.

DMAHC 249 entitled *Sight Reduction Tables for Air Navigation* came into general use in the late 1940s. Although intended primarily for air navigation, its accuracy is adequate for surface work. In three volumes only Volume I, which lists selected stars, will be discussed here. For the

Figure 16-53. S.S.*Argo Merchant* aground 28 miles southeast of Nantucket Island in December, 1976. This disaster was caused by a gross error in navigation. Ship was a total loss and an oil spill of 7.3 million gallons resulted. Courtesy: U.S. Coast Guard.

stars listed at any given time, DMAHC 249 is extremely fast and convenient to use. It is also very useful for the navigator as a star finder because those stars listed were selected because they were bright enough to see easily (first magnitude stars) and positioned so that they would give good intercepts.

An example will also be given from DMAHC 229. It has only come into general use in the last few years and is the replacement for H.O. 214. Somewhat more convenient and accurate than the older table, DMAHC 229 is not limited in scope as is 249. As the older mariners retire it will come into use more and more and will be the mainstay of celestial navigation for many years to come.

STAR H.O. 214		
Body	*Capella*	
CT	00-16-00	5 Feb 1979
SW	(−) 43	
GMT	00-15-17	
GHA γ	134-33.0	
SHA ☆	281-12.6	
corr.	3-49.9	
GHA ☆	419-35.5	
a Long.	90-35.5	W
t	31	E
a Lat.	12	N
dec.	45-58.7	N
Hₛ	47-06.5	
corr.	(−) 6.9	
Hₐ	46-59.6	
corr.	(−) 0.9	
Hₒ	46-58.7	
H_c	47-04.1	
"a"	5.4	away #
Hₜ	47-03.2	
corr.	(−) 0.9	
H_c	47-04.1	
d	67	
Z	N31.8E	
Zₙ	031.8	#

STAR H.O. PUB. No. 249		
Body	*Vega*	
CT	12-51-00	2 Feb 1979
CE	φ	
SW	(−) 27	
GMT	12-50-33	
GHA γ	312-05.1	
corr.	12-40.3	
GHA γ	324-45.4	
a Long.	103-45.4	W
LHA γ	221	
a Lat.	18	N
Zₙ	055	#
Hₛ	36-08.2	
corr.	(−) 6.9	
Hₐ	36-01.3	
Hₒ	36-00.0	
H_c	35-51.0	
"a"	9.0	towards #

Notes:

1. In both examples the intercepts which are used for plotting are marked with (#).
2. It can be seen that fewer computations are required for H.O. Pub. No. 249. For this reason it is very popular with navigators and is frequently used when the star which is observed is listed.

EXAMPLES OF MODERN SIGHT REDUCTION METHODS

In order to follow the examples given it is suggested that the *Nautical Almanac* and appropriate Sight Reduction Tables be broken out (see Figures 16-49, 16-50, 16-51 and 16-52).

Star Sight Reduction Tables for 42 Stars: Assumed Altitude Method of Celestial Navigation—A very recent addition to the modern methods of sight reduction is the *Star Sight Reduction Tables for 42 Stars:*

Assumed Altitude Method of Celestial Navigation by Rear Admiral Thomas D. Davies, U.S.N. (Ret) (Cornell Maritime Press, 1980).

Although it has similarities to H.O. Pub. No. 249, it covers 42 stars and does so in tables about the same size as H.O. Pub. No. 249. Its strength is that the method of entering the tables makes star identification unnecessary. It is fast and easy to use.

DMAHC 229						
Body	*Sun*			*Body*	*Arcturus*	
CT	17-01-00	6 Feb 1979		CT	14-09-00	30 Jan 1979
CE	0-00			CE	(−) 21	
SW	1-05					
GMT	16-59-55	6 Feb 1979		GMT	14-08-39	30 Jan
GHA o	56-28.3			GHA γ	339-12.6	
corr.	14-58.8			SHA ☆	146-19.5	
GHA	71-27.1			corr.	2-10.1	
a Long.	82-27.1	W		GHA ☆	487-42.2	
t	11	E		a Long.	116-42.2	W
				LHA	371	or 11
a Lat.	7	N		a Lat.	28	N
dec.	15-39.5	S		dec.	—	
corr.	(−) 0.8			corr.	—	
dec.	15-38.7	S		dec.	19-17.4	N
				H_t	76-29.7	
H_s	64-46.1			corr.	(+) 11.7	
corr.	(−) 6.9			H_c	76-41.4	
H_a	64-39.2			H_o	76-48.9	
corr.	(+) 15.8			"a"	7.5	towards #
H_o	64-55.0			Z	129.4	
H_c	64-52.1			corr.	(−) 0.9	
"a"	2.9	towards #		Az	N128.5	W
Z	N153.7E			Z_n	231.5	#
corr.	(+) 0.6					
Z_n	154.3	#		H_s	76-54.0	
				corr.	(−) 4.9	
H_t	65-26.8			H_a	76-49.1	
corr.	(−) 34.7			corr.	(−) 0.2	
H_c	64-52.1			H_o	76-48.9	

Note:

1. Pub. 229 has more similarities to H.O. 214 than it does to H.O. Pub. No. 249.

2. All navigation tables have explicit instructions for their use in the index or cover pages.

3. The explanation and examples contained in the *Nautical Alamanc* are particularly good.

CHAPTER XVII

MARITIME ENVIRONMENT

Yea, slimy things did crawl with legs
upon the slimy sea.
—*Samuel Taylor Coleridge*

A SHIP AT SEA is in the midst of a "maritime environment," a term defying precise description but including the phenomena of winds, weather, and the ocean itself. "Ocean, Winds, and Weather," the section on past Coast Guard licensing examinations, has been expanded in this chapter to include information about tides, tidal currents and ocean currents. The able seaman who wishes to prepare himself for his third mate's examination should turn to Bowditch's *American Practical Navigator* for a more comprehensive, broader coverage on this subject. The weather section of Knight's *Modern Seamanship* is also excellent.

WEATHER

GENERAL CIRCULATION

If we consider that on the surface of the earth we are surrounded by an ocean of air, we would have to say further that this ocean is divided into two main parts. The part nearest the earth is called the troposphere, and the upper part is the stratosphere. "Weather" is only in the troposphere which extends upwards about five miles at the poles and ten miles at the equator. This weather depends upon the season, latitude, and local topographic conditions. Air in the troposphere contains water vapor, dust, salt, and smoke particles. The dust particles are the nuclei of raindrops.

Varying temperatures, rotation of the earth, and variations of pressure cause movement of the air. If the movement is horizontal, it is known as wind; if it is vertical, it is known as current. The reflected rays of the sun are absorbed by the earth, and consequently the earth heats up. If the earth did not rotate, and if it had a uniform surface, the flow of air would be a simple circulation from the poles to the equator along the surface and from the equator to the poles aloft. Obviously the situation is a little more complex.

Figure 17-1 shows the pressure belts and general circulation of air in the world.

The **doldrums** is the belt of low pressure near the equator. Except for twice a day changes the pressure is almost uniform. With only a slight pressure gradient, the winds are light and variable. Days are hot and sultry. The sky is often overcast, and showers and thunderstorms are

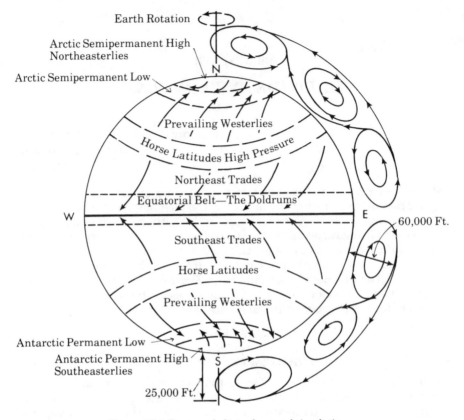

Figure 17-1. Pressure belts and general circulation.

frequent. Brief periods of strong winds occur, and this is what sailing ships needed to carry them through the doldrums.

The northeast and southeast trades blow from the belts of high pressure towards the doldrums. The rotation of the earth deflects the air toward the west. Consequently the trade winds in the northern hemisphere are from the northeast and in the southern hemisphere from the southeast. Trade winds are usually considered the most constant of winds.

North and south of each tradewind belt are high pressure areas known as the **horse latitudes**. These are areas of weak pressure gradients and as a consequence have light, variable winds. Compared with doldrums, periods of stagnation are fewer, and the area is less humid. Tradition tells us that horse latitudes got their name because at this point on a long voyage under sail, horses or other livestock in the cargo often died and had to be thrown over the side.

Poleward of the horse latitudes are the prevailing westerlies. They are partially blocked by large continents and are more pronounced over the Pacific than over the Atlantic. They are also somewhat stronger in winter than in summer. In the southern hemisphere the region between 40° and

50°-55° is known as the "roaring forties." Winds in this area are generally between 17-27 knots.

The low temperatures near the geographical poles tend to cause the surface pressure to be higher than in the surrounding regions. As a consequence the winds blow outward from the poles and are deflected westward by the earth's rotation. The result is the northeasterlies in the Arctic and the southeasterlies in the Antarctic.

Practically all the world's winds blow from areas of high pressure to areas of low pressure. Because of friction with the rotating earth they are deflected and will blow around these areas. In the northern hemisphere winds blow clockwise about and out of high pressure areas. If a region is one of low pressure, the wind will blow counterclockwise and toward the center. The direction of rotation of the wind about centers of high and low pressure is reversed in the southern hemisphere, but flow is still from high to low pressure.

Lines of equal pressure on weather maps are called **isobars**. When the isobars are close together, you can expect higher winds than when they are some distance apart.

A storm center is an area of low pressure. It can be located quite easily by using Buys Ballot's Law as stated in Bowditch:

> If an observer in the Northern Hemisphere faces the surface wind, the center of low pressure is toward his right, somewhat behind him; and the center of high pressure is toward his left and somewhat in front of him.
>
> If an observer in the Southern Hemisphere faces the surface wind, the center of low pressure is toward his left and somewhat behind him; and the center of high pressure is toward his right and somewhat in front of him.

Areas of low pressure are called **cyclones** while areas of high pressure are known as anti-cyclones.

WIND SYSTEMS AND LOCAL WINDS

The general circulation of the atmosphere is greatly modified by a number of conditions which have only been hinted at. The high pressure in the horse latitudes is not uniformly distributed and tends to remain in the same general areas. Semi-permanent lows occur in several places, among them the area west of Iceland and over the Aleutians in the winter. Land is another and important modifying influence because a landmass undergoes greater temperature changes than the surrounding sea.

The best example of a wind system produced by the alternate heating and cooling of a landmass is the monsoon of the China Sea and Indian Ocean. In summer the monsoon blows from the Indian Ocean into India with resulting wet and cloudy days. In winter the dry winter monsoon is a northerly wind carrying clear, dry air from the interior well out over the ocean. Monsoon characteristics are also present in the winds along the southeast coast of Asia and North America from 50° southward to 30°. Monsoons are not well developed in the southern hemisphere.

A **sea breeze** is a local mini-monsoon that reverses its direction daily. During the heat of the day it blows onshore, but with sunset it dwindles to a calm. Only where a warm soil and relatively cooler water lie adjacent to each other does a sea breeze develop. At night the process reverses itself and a land breeze develops. Neither land nor sea breezes extend any great distance from sea, but their presence is worth noting because a survivor in a lifeboat or life raft might wish to pull in his sea anchor during the daytime and let the wind blow him toward nearby land.

A warm dry wind with a downward component is called a **foehn**. On the west coast of the United States the best example is the Santa Ana in Southern California. It is normally of sufficient strength that it causes a small craft warning and is of concern to larger ships.

A cold dry wind blowing down an incline is called a **fall wind**. This occurs when cold air spills over the windward side of a mountain and blows out to sea from the nearby coast. These winds can be violent. The example best known to American seamen is the Tehuantepecer which occurs in the Eastern Pacific in the Gulf of Tehuantepec.

CYCLONES

There are two kinds of cyclones of concern to the mariner. The extratropical cyclone is the common storm of the temperate zones while the tropical cyclone is the storm we know as a hurricane or typhoon. The mariner must have a basic understanding of both types of cyclones.

EXTRATROPICAL CYCLONES

In the temperate zones of the prevailing westerlies, the mariner will frequently encounter cyclones (lows) and anti-cyclones (highs). The extratropical cyclone is not as violent as the tropical cyclone. However, it is important because it is more frequently encountered by the seaman. Formation can occur over both land and sea. The lows tend to intensify as they move poleward, and the highs weaken as they move toward the equator.

Symptoms of the approach of an extratropical cyclone are:

1. Falling barometer.

2. Increasing wind usually from a direction between east and south in the northern hemisphere and between east and north in the southern hemisphere.

3. Increasing cirrus clouds which thicken into altostratus (sometimes altocumulus), accompanied by rain (or snow in season).

Extratropical cyclones are frequently accompanied by both warm and cold fronts. Steady, light to moderate precipitation often accompanies the warm front while heavy, showery precipitation is more usual with a cold front. Between the warm and cold fronts lies an area called the warm sector which has generally fair weather.

When the extratropical cyclone passes, the barometer becomes steady and then will rise. This will be accompanied by a wind shift (either through south or north) to a direction between west and north in the northern hemisphere and east and south in the southern hemisphere. Finally the rain or snow ends and skies clear slowly.

TROPICAL CYCLONE

Seamen dread the tropical cyclone and with good reason. A tropical cyclone has its origin in the tropics or subtropics. It is similar to the extratropical cyclone which has its origin in higher latitudes, but it is apt to be more violent. This is a general term which includes tropical distrubance, tropical depression, tropical storm, and hurricane or typhoon as

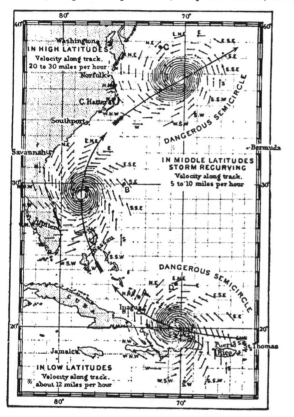

Figure 17-2. Characteristic track and wind system of tropical cyclone of northern hemisphere. Note the position of the dangerous semicircle on the right of the track of the storm. Not only does the velocity of the storm center add itself to the strength of the wind, but also the wind direction tends to push the ship into the storm track. Hurricane tracks can be unpredictable. The 1938 New England hurricane began on a track like the one shown but then curved left unexpectedly causing severe damage and loss of life in southern New England.

listed in order of increasing severity. Hurricanes and typhoons are identical. The only difference is in the title. In the North Atlantic and Eastern Pacific they are known as hurricanes. In the Western Pacific they take the name of typhoon. In the Philippines they are called *baguios*, and in Australia the term is willy-willy. However, they are all tropical cyclones and obey the same laws.

Tropical cyclones originate 5° to 15° from the equator over the North Atlantic Ocean and over the Pacific, both north and south of the equator. They travel north and westward from the equator over the Atlantic and Pacific in the northern hemisphere, but south and westward if they originate south of the equator. All tropical cyclones lying north of the equator slowly change their paths from one toward the northwest to one toward the northeast as illustrated in Figure 17-2; those lying south of the equator recurve as shown in Figure 17-3.

The approach of a tropical cyclone is foretold by a rapidly falling barometer and a long swell coming from the direction of the storm. The presence of

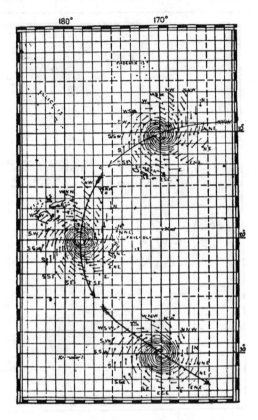

Figure 17-3. Characteristic track and wind system of tropical cyclone of the southern hemisphere. Note that in the southern hemisphere the storm curves to the left, but that in the northern hemisphere (see Figure 17-2), the curvature is to the right.

cirrus clouds which lower and thicken gradually into cirrostratus, altostratus, and stratus is further evidence of the storm's approach. Thick, dark cumulonimbus clouds accompany the center of the storm.

Rough seas of high swells and gigantic waves, strong and sometimes disastrous winds, and very grim and ugly weather accompany the tropical storm over an area varying from 200-300 miles to 1,000 miles in diameter. The intensity of the storm increases until it reaches latitudes 30° to 35° from the equator, after which it slowly subsides. At the very center, the "eye of the storm," near calm prevails, but the sea remains extremely confused. That half of the storm lying to the right of its path in the northern hemisphere, and to the left of its path in the southern hemisphere, is the *dangerous semicircle* because it is here that the velocity of the storm in its path and its counterclockwise winds (clockwise south of the equator) are added to each other to produce the highest velocities.

No matter how large or seaworthy it may be, no ship is immune from storm damage at the hands of a typhoon or hurricane. A ship should avoid the center of the storm. If it is in the dangerous semicircle, it should maneuver to get out. The center and probable path should be plotted.

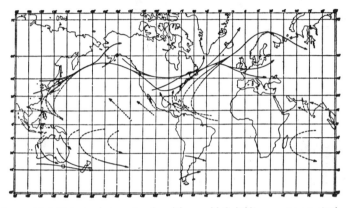

Figure 17-4. Principal storm tracks of the world. Solid lines, extratropical cyclones. Dashed lines, tropical cyclones..

Regular radio and facsimile weather broadcasts should be monitored and taken into account. If weather reports are lacking, the prudent seaman should be alert to note the symptoms of an approaching storm. A rapidly falling barometer is a prime indication.

Changes in wind direction are important to notice. In the northern hemisphere a veering wind (one which changes in direction to the right or clockwise) is an indication that you are in the dangerous semicircle. If the wind backs (moves in a counterclockwise direction) it is an indication that you are in the safe or navigable semicircle. In the southern hemisphere, the reverse is true.

RULES FOR MANEUVERING TO AVOID A TROPICAL STORM

NORTHERN HEMISPHERE

Right or **dangerous semicircle**—Bring the wind on the starboard bow and make as much way as possible. If obliged to heave to, do so head to the sea.

Left or **navigable semicircle**—Bring the wind on the starboard quarter, note the course and hold it. If obliged to heave to, place the stern to sea.

On the storm track in front of center—Bring the wind two points on the starboard quarter, note the course and hold it. Run for the left semicircle. When in the left semicircle, bring the wind on the starboard quarter.

Beaufort number or force	Wind speed — knots	Wind speed — mph	Wind speed — meters per second	Wind speed — km per hour	World Meteorological Organization (1964)	Effects observed far from land	Effects observed near coast	Effects observed on land	Sea State — Term and height of waves, in meters	Sea State — Code
0	under 1	under 1	0.0–0.2	under 1	Calm	Sea like mirror.	Calm.	Calm; smoke rises vertically.	Calm, glassy, 0	0
1	1–3	1–3	0.3–1.5	1–5	Light air	Ripples with appearance of scales; no foam crests.	Fishing smack just has steerage way.	Smoke drift indicates wind direction; vanes do not move.	Calm, rippled, 0–0.1	1
2	4–6	4–7	1.6–3.3	6–11	Light breeze	Small wavelets; crests of glassy appearance, not breaking.	Wind fills the sails of smacks which then travel at about 1–2 miles per hour.	Wind felt on face; leaves rustle; vanes begin to move.	Smooth, wavelets, 0.1–0.5	2
3	7–10	8–12	3.4–5.4	12–19	Gentle breeze	Large wavelets; crests begin to break; scattered whitecaps.	Smacks begin to careen and travel about 3–4 miles per hour.	Leaves, small twigs in constant motion; light flags extended.	Slight, 0.5–1.25	3
4	11–16	13–18	5.5–7.9	20–28	Moderate breeze	Small waves, becoming longer; numerous whitecaps.	Good working breeze, smacks carry all canvas with good list.	Dust, leaves, and loose paper raised up; small branches move.	Moderate, 1.25–2.5	4
5	17–21	19–24	8.0–10.7	29–38	Fresh breeze	Moderate waves, taking longer form; many whitecaps; some spray.	Smacks shorten sail.	Small trees in leaf begin to sway.	Rough, 2.5–4	5
6	22–27	25–31	10.8–13.8	39–49	Strong breeze	Larger waves forming; whitecaps everywhere; more spray.	Smacks have doubled reef in mainsail; care required when fishing.	Larger branches of trees in motion; whistling heard in wires.	Very rough, 4–6	6
7	28–33	32–38	13.9–17.1	50–61	Near gale	Sea heaps up; white foam from breaking waves begins to be blown in streaks.	Smacks remain in harbor and those at sea lie-to.	Whole trees in motion; resistance felt in walking against wind.		
8	34–40	39–46	17.2–20.7	62–74	Gale	Moderately high waves of greater length; edges of crests begin to break into spindrift; foam is blown in well-marked streaks.	All smacks make for harbor, if near.	Twigs and small branches broken off trees; progress generally impeded.	High, 6–9	7
9	41–47	47–54	20.8–24.4	75–88	Strong gale	High waves, sea begins to roll; dense streaks of foam; spray may reduce visibility.		Slight structural damage occurs; slate blown from roofs.		
10	48–55	55–63	24.5–28.4	89–102	Storm	Very high waves with overhanging crests; sea takes white appearance as foam is blown in very dense streaks; rolling is heavy and visibility reduced.		Seldom experienced on land; trees broken or uprooted; considerable structural damage occurs.		
11	56–63	64–72	28.5–32.6	103–117	Violent storm	Exceptionally high waves; sea covered with white foam patches; visibility still more reduced.		Very rarely experienced on land; usually accompanied by widespread damage.	Very high, 9–14	8
12	64 and over	73 and over	32.7 and over	118 and over	Hurricane	Air filled with foam; sea completely white with driving spray; visibility greatly reduced.			Phenomenal, over 14	9

Note: Since January 1, 1955, weather map symbols have been based upon wind speed in knots, at five-knot intervals, rather than upon Beaufort number.

Figure 17-5. Beaufort wind scale with corresponding sea state codes, reproduced from *American Practical Navigator*. Courtesy: Defense Mapping Agency Hydrographic Center.

SOUTHERN HEMISPHERE

Left or **dangerous semicircle**—Bring the wind on the port bow and make as much way as possible. If obliged to heave to, do so head to sea.

Right or **navigable semicircle**—Bring the wind on the port quarter, note the course and hold it. If obliged to heave to, do so stern to sea.

On the storm track, in front of center—Avoid the center by the best practicable route, having regard for the tendency of cyclones to recurve to the southward and eastward.

STATE OF WEATHER

A ship at sea makes hourly entries in the log giving the meteorological data such as wind force and direction, barometric pressure, reading of wet and dry bulb thermometers, cloud forms, visibility, and sea conditions. These entries are standardized, and the Beaufort scale for wind as well as sea state is used. Figure 17-5 which is reproduced from Bowditch is extremely comprehensive and complete. Even though a ship has an anemometer, a glance at the appearance of the sea should confirm the recorded force of the wind.

Symbols are also used to record the weather. The common code is as follows:

b—Blue sky, cloudless.
bc—Blue sky with detached clouds.
c—Sky mainly cloudy.
d—Drizzling, or light rain.
e—Wet air, without rain.
f—Fog, or foggy weather.
g—Gloomy, or dark, stormy-looking.
h—Hail.
l—Lightning.
m—Misty weather.
o—Overcast.
p—Passing showers of rain.

q—Squally weather.
r—Rainy weather, or continuous rain.
s—Snow, snowy weather, or snow falling.
t—Thunder.
u—Ugly appearance, or threatening weather.
v—Variable weather.
w—Wet, or heavy dew.
z—Hazy weather.

Visibility is obviously important, and the mate on watch will record the visibility by using the following scale:

0. Prominent objects not visible at 50 yards.
1. Prominent objects not visible at 200 yards.
2. Prominent objects not visible at 500 yards.
3. Prominent objects not visible at 1/2 mile.
4. Prominent objects not visible at 1 mile.
5. Prominent objects not visible at 2 miles.
6. Prominent objects not visible at 4 miles.
7. Prominent objects not visible at 7 miles.
8. Prominent objects not visible at 20 miles.
9. Prominent objects visible above 20 miles.

The amount of cloud cover is also important, and it is recorded in the following code which lists the coverage in eights:

Code figure	eights
0	0
1	1 or less
2	2
3	3
4	4
5	5
6	6
7	7 or more but not 8
8	8 (overcast)
9	obscured, or cloud amount cannot be determined

CLOUDS

Clouds are defined as visible collections of numerous tiny droplets of water or ice crystals formed by condensation of water vapor in the air with their bases above the surface of the earth.

Although there is almost an infinite variety of clouds, they can be grouped into three general types: high, middle, and low. High clouds have bases which begin from 16,500 feet to 45,000 feet. Common types of high clouds are: **cirrus** (Ci), **cirrocumulus** (Cc), and **cirrostratus** (Cs).

Middle clouds have bases which begin from 6,500 feet to 23,000 feet. Common types are **altocumulus** (Ac), **altostratus** (As), and **nimbostratus** (Ns).

Low clouds have bases which may begin between the earth's surface and 6,500 feet. Common types are **cumulus** (Cu), **cumulonimbus** (Cb), **stratocumulus** (Sc), and **stratus**(St).

The appearance of a cloud depends upon how it was formed, and is an indication of what is happening—or what has happened—in the atmosphere. Being able to recognize cloud types is a valuable asset for any seaman and extremely useful in predicting future weather.

Cloud charts are frequently posted on or near the bridge to assist the mate in identifying cloud types. They are far more comprehensive than the examples given here.

FOG

Fog is a cloud whose base is low enough to restrict visibility. It is formed by the condensation or crystallization of water vapor in the air.

Radiation fog is formed over low-lying land on clear, calm nights. As the land loses heat, it cools the air immediately above it. This causes a temperature inversion: The temperature above the land increasing with altitude. If the air is cooled to or below its dew point, fog forms. After sunrise the fog frequently lifts. At sea there is little change in water temperature between day and night, and radiation fog is seldom encountered any distance from land.

Figure 17-6. Cirrus (Ci). Detached high clouds of delicate and fibrous appearance, without shading, generally white in color, often of a silky appearance. Composed entirely of ice crystals. Courtesy: National Oceanic and Atmospheric Administration.

Figure 17-7. Cirrus spissatus (Ci sp). Dense Cirrus in patches or entangled sheaves which usually do not increase and sometimes seem to be the remains of the upper parts of Cumulonimbus. Courtesy: National Oceanic and Atmospheric Administration.

Figure 17-8. Cirrocumulus (Cc). Composed of small white flakes or scales, or of very small globular masses, usually without shadows and arranged in groups, lines, or ripples. Known as a "mackerel sky."

Figure 17-9. Altocumulus (Ac). A layer of large, ball-like masses that tend to merge together. The balls or patches may vary in thickness and color from dazzling white to dark gray, but they are more or less regularly arranged. Courtesy: National Oceanic and Atmospheric Administration.

Figure 17-10. Cumulus (Cu). Brunswick, Georgia. Dense clouds with vertical development (clouds formed by rising air which cools as it reaches greater heights). A horizontal base and dome-shaped upper surface with protuberances extending above the dome. Appear in small patches and never cover the entire sky. Courtesy: National Oceanic and Atmospheric Administration.

Figure 17-11. Stratocumulus (Sc). Soft, gray, roll-shaped masses. They may be shaped in long, parallel rolls like altocumulus, moving with the wind. Motion is in the direction of short dimension like ocean waves. Vary greatly in altitude. Usually followed by clear skies during the night. Courtesy: National Oceanic and Atmospheric Administration.

Figure 17-12. Cumulonimbus (Cb). Massive cloud with vertical development. Upper part consists of ice crystals and often spreads out into the shape of an anvil. Frequently produces showers of rain, snow, or hail which are often accompanied by thunder. Popularly called "thunderhead" or "thundercloud." Courtesy: National Oceanic and Atmospheric Administration, photograph by Ralph Kresge.

Figure 17-13. Waterspout. A small, whirling storm over the water. In appearance it is a funnel-shaped cloud. When fully developed it reaches from the surface to the base of a cumulus-type cloud. Found most frequently in the tropics. Over land it would be called a tornado. Waterspouts have been known to destroy small vessels and damage larger ones.

Advection fog occurs when warm, moist air blows over a colder surface and is cooled below its dew point. This is commonly encountered at sea and can be very persistent. Advection fog is common over cold ocean currents.

If very cold air moves over warmer water, wisps of visible water vapor rise from the surface, and the water appears to "steam." This is commonly called **sea smoke** or **arctic smoke**.

Haze consists of fine dust or smoke particles in the air. It reduces visibility and can cast a bluish or yellowish veil over the landscape.

Mist and drizzle mean the same thing in the United States. This is somewhere between haze and fog in its make-up.

Smog is a mixture of smoke and fog.

WEATHER REPORTS

At sea most ships transmit weather observations to the National Weather Service every six hours at 0000, 0600, 1200, and 1800 GMT. These are sent in a coded form provided by the weather service. As a result sufficient data is accumulated so that commercial and government radio stations can broadcast weather forecasts and storm warnings.

National Weather Service forecasts are transmitted both in plain language, in a weather code, and also by facsimile transmitters. If a ship has a facsimile receiver, it can receive a completed weather map or forecast almost instantaneously. Figures 17-14 and 17-15 are examples of facsimile transmissions.

Figure 17-14 shows the surface forecast sent by the San Francisco station of the National Weather Service at 0000 GMT on 25 January 1980. The low pressure area centered at about latitude 45°N and longitude 165°W has gale force winds. At its eastern edge is a stationary front. Well to the east at about 33°N is a stationary high pressure area whose center has a barometric pressure of 1,024 millibars. North of that is another, smaller low pressure area at whose eastern edge is a cold front. Ships in the high pressure area can probably expect good weather for a while, but those further north cannot expect much improvement in weather conditions.

Figure 17-17 is a wind and sea state analysis sent out by the San Francisco station of the National Weather Service based on information received from both surface as well as satellite observations. The broad arrows indicate the period as well as the height and direction of the swells. For example, the 9/10 at the bottom of the map means that the period, or length of time it takes between the time one crest passes through a given point until the next one passes is 9 seconds. Wave height is 10 feet. Single arrows indicate wind velocity and direction. Arrows at the bottom of the map indicate that wind is from WNW to W varying between 20, 15, and 10 knots respectively. What appear to be cloud forms indicate scattered (SCT) and isolated (ISOLD) showers.

TIDES, TIDAL CURRENTS, AND OCEAN CURRENTS
TIDES

Tides are the periodic rising and falling of the height of the sea caused by the gravitational attraction of the moon and the sun. Although the major

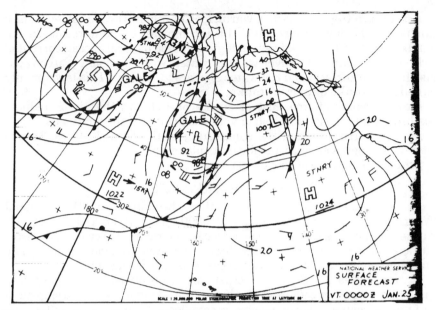

Figure 17-14. Surface forecast. 0000Z January 25, 1980, weather map from the facsimile receiver. Courtesy: National Weather Service.

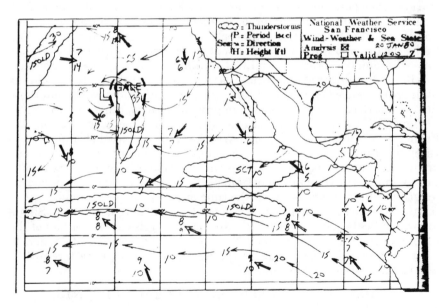

Figure 17-15. Surface forecast. 1200Z January 20, 1980, weather analysis from the facsimile receiver. Courtesy: National Weather Service.

factor which causes tides is the moon, the sun's effect is approximately two-fifths that of the moon.

The relative positions of the sun and the moon will effect the difference in height between any two successive high or low tides (range of tide). If the sun and moon are pulling together as happens when the moon is either new or full, high tides are going to be higher, and low tides will be lower than average. This is what is called a **spring tide**, and obviously not a tide that occurs in the spring of the year as is the common misconception.

If the sun and moon act at right angles, the difference between the high and low tides will not be as great. This occurs when the moon is in its first or third quarter, or is said to be in quadrature. The name given for the tides which occur at this time of the month is **neap tide**.

Since the attraction of two objects toward each other increases as the distance between them decreases, we would expect that the range of tide would vary as the distance between the moon and the earth decreases and increases. In fact, this is what happens. When the moon is in its orbit at the point closest to the earth, it is said to be at **perigee**. When this happens, the high tides are higher, and the low tides are lower. When the moon is in its orbit at the maximum distance from the earth, it is said to be in **apogee**. At this time the range of tide will be least. It should be emphasized that whether the moon is in apogee or perigee is not related to whether it is new, full, or in its first or third quarter. A spring tide will occur when the moon is new or full, but if it occurs when the moon is in perigee, the range of tide will be greater than at any other time. This would be called a **perigean spring tide**.

All charts must have a sounding datum so that you know what reference plane was used when the area was sounded. This information is printed on the chart. A number of reference planes are in use. The most common are mean low water (MLW) which is used on the U.S. Atlantic Coast, mean lower low water (MLLW) which is used on the Pacific Coast, and mean low water springs (MLWS) which is used in Great Britain, Germany, and Denmark. Mean low water is the average height of all low waters at a place. Mean lower low water is the average of the lowest of the two waters of each tidal day, and mean low water springs is the average of the low waters that occur on spring tides.

The heights of land features on U.S. charts is the height above mean high water. In the event the question came up as to whether the mast would pass under a bridge shown on the chart, this would become of extreme interest.

TIDAL CURRENTS

Tidal current is the periodic horizontal flow of water accompanying the rise and fall of the tide. Where the direction of flow is restricted by the channel, the current is reversing. Slack water is said to occur when there is no horizontal movement of the water. The current is said to be ebbing when the direction of the current is away from the land, and flooding when its direction is towards the land. Technically, even though the expression "ebb tide" is used frequently, it is incorrect because the current ebbs, not the tide.

Tidal currents have periods and cycles much like those of the tides. They are subject to similar variations, but flood and ebb currents will probably not occur at the same times as the rise and fall of the tide. In many places there is a relationship, but this is complex. The strength of the current varies with the variations in the range of the tide.

TIDE TABLES AND TIDAL CURRENT TABLES

Tide Tables and *Tidal Current Tables* are published annually by the National Ocean Survey (NOS) as stated in Chapter XVI. In order to find the height of tide or the strength of current at any time at any given place these tables must be consulted. Directions for the use of these tables are contained in the tables themselves. Although the directions are not difficult to follow, they must be followed exactly or erroneous information will result. To insure accuracy, the user must practice their use. The prudent mariner who consults the tide and current tables prior to entering port will first work out his data the day before, and do so again just before entering. If the results agree, he can be sure he has made no mistakes.

OCEAN CURRENTS

Wind is the principle cause of an ocean current, but the direction, depth, strength, and permanency of the current depends upon a variety of factors. Among these is the presence of land and shoal water, the meeting of conflicting currents and tides, and the difference in density of the sea water in diverse regions. The difference in atmospheric pressure on the water in dissimilar areas is also a contributing factor.

Wind blowing across the ocean causes the surface layer of water to move, the motion being transmitted to each succeeding layer of water. It is generally considered that a steady wind for about 12 hours is needed to cause an ocean current.

Wind-driven currents do not flow in the direction of the wind because they are deflected by the Coriolis force which is caused by the rotation of the earth. This deflection is to the right in the northern hemisphere, and to the left in the southern hemisphere. It varies from about 15° in shallow water to 45° in deep water.

If ocean currents are caused by winds, it should not be surprising that they are greatly influenced by the general circulation which was shown earlier in Figure 17-1. Pilot charts published by the Defense Mapping Agency Hydrographic/Topographic Center show the ocean currents along with other phenomena and should be studied in order to gain an insight into the factors which will influence a voyage.

A complete discussion of the various currents is beyond the scope of this text. Therefore, we will limit ourselves to mentioning only two as representative of currents the seaman may encounter throughout the world.

In the Atlantic, the Gulf Stream originates in the Straits of Florida and moves north to latitude 30°. From there it travels ENE to latitude 32°, then a little north of NE to Cape Hatteras. Its maximum current occurs 11-20 miles outside the 100 fathom curve. Its velocity varies from 3-5 knots off Fowey Rocks to 1.5 off Hatteras. A large volume of water flows north in the Gulf Stream. It is deep blue-indigo in color which is in contrast to the dull green of the surrounding water.

In the Pacific, the Japan Stream, or Black Current, has many similarities to the Gulf Stream. It carries large quantities of warm tropical water to higher latitudes, and then curves toward the east as a major part of the clockwise circulation of the northern hemisphere. As it moves east, it widens and slows. The major portion continues on between the Aleutians and the Hawaiian Islands where it becomes known as the North Pacific Current.

CHAPTER XVIII

SHIP SANITATION AND
MEDICAL PROCEDURES*

QUARANTINE IS MAINTAINED by the Federal Government to prevent the entry of persons, animals or insects carrying disease. Quarantine regulations vary in different countries. In the United States, typhus, cholera, yellow fever, leprosy, plague, anthrax and smallpox are quarantinable diseases.

Every vessel bound from a foreign port must have a consular bill of health showing prevalence of any quarantinable diseases at port of clearance. If any, special care is taken that no diseased person enters, or, if the disease is one carried by animals or insects, the ship is quarantined and fumigated.

Disinfection—Any object carrying germs able to produce disease is *infected*, and the process by which germs are destroyed is *disinfection*.

Disinfestation—Any object carrying in it or on it insects such as lice, fleas, or bedbugs, also rats and mice, is *infested*. The process of destroying these is *disinfestation*. Usually only a small part of the vessel must be disinfested to prevent spread of disease.

Fumigation—Disinfection or disinfestation by a gaseous agent is called *fumigation*. Most of the gases used are for disinfestation, and have little value as a disinfectant. Carbon monoxide, cyanide, sulphur gas and formaldehyde are generally used in fumigation. Carbon monoxide and cyanide are very dangerous, and should be used only by experienced men. Of these agents, only sulphur gas or sulphur dioxide is a reliable disinfectant. It is produced by burning sulphur in the presence of plenty of moisture. For every 5 pounds of sulphur burned 1 pint of water should be vaporized. All ventilators and ports should be closed and paper pasted over keyholes and cracks. The sulphur should be placed in broad pans to insure complete burning. Pans should be thick enough not to melt and start a fire.

HYGIENE AND SANITATION ON SHIPBOARD

The object of hygiene is to keep people in good health and to prevent accidents and diseases. Sanitation involves the place where people work and live. Personal hygiene concerns those things the individual must do for himself to preserve his health. Public health includes the teaching of sanitation, public hygiene, and the whole science of hygiene so that the individual will acquire health habits.

*Frank A. M. Bryant, M.D., and Louis C. Jacobi, H.M.C., USN (Ret) of the Medical Department T.S. *Golden Bear*, California Maritime Academy have contributed the Emergency Medical Procedures section of this chapter.

Ship sanitation is one of the oldest branches of public health. The ship is no more than a floating house, and sanitary rules are the same. This means mechanical cleanliness, adequate provision for disposal of waste products of the ship and her company, and adequate apparatus and opportunity for frequent baths. Water for drinking and cooking must be from a supply known to be pure.

Sanitation also means sound, wholesome food, unspoiled, and sufficiently cooked to kill parasites and disease germs which may be in it.

It also means ventilation of forecastles, cabins, galleys, and firerooms, and complete protection of passengers and crew against vermin.

One of the great health menaces on shipboard is the cockroach, which can be routed by cleanliness and frequent fumigations. Cockroaches hang around the "heads," and unless these are kept absolutely clean they may eat the discharges of sick men or apparently well men who are carriers of disease germs, and thus spread disease.

Ants, while not proven disease carriers, are a nuisance aboard ship. Several good ant poisons are available, whose basis is arsenic and honey. The poison is put in a small baking powder can, with the top bent in at one place, and the lid replaced.

There are three kinds of lice: head louse, body louse, and pubic louse (crabs). The infested person, his clothes and his surroundings should be deloused, for lice may carry disease from one person to another. Head lice are destroyed by washing hair with a mixture of equal parts of kerosene and vinegar, taking care that it does not run down over the face or neck. A preparation called *Kwell* is effective for all three types of lice.

Bedbugs spread disease and mean dirty sleeping quarters. To get rid of them, pour boiling water or kerosene in cracks, especially around bunks. Bedding should be boiled or sterilized, and living quarters fumigated.

In port, flies may be a nuisance or danger. The ship should be rid of them.

Mosquitoes seldom breed on a modern ship; the danger is from shore mosquitoes. They spread malaria, yellow fever, and dengue. Make every effort to keep the ship free of them; when they are present, it is wise to sleep in a screened compartment or under a bed net.

Fleas are a menace on ship because they usually come from rats dying of bubonic plague. Fleas carry the germs to men. If rats are on the ship, they should be killed by fumigation. Rats should be kept off the vessel by breasting off in port, putting rat guards on all mooring lines, and raising the gangplank at night. Before sailing, the entire ship should be kept carefully checked for sanitary condition, especially the quarters, galleys, mess halls, and heads, the presence of vermin being noted and corrected.

DRINKING-WATER DISTRIBUTING SYSTEM AND ITS CARE

The drinking-water system, seacocks, pumps, storage tanks, and piping should be independent of all other water systems aboard. Also, measures should be taken to kill any possible disease germs.

Water tanks should be cleaned and flushed at the start of the season and at least every two weeks that the vessel is in service. After mechanical cleansing they should be filled and 1 pound hypochlorite of lime added for each 5,000 gallons water. After standing 24 hours, the water is discharged and the tank filled with water known to be pure. The piping system should be cleansed in the same way.

Chlorination—Hypochlorite of lime or bleaching powder effectively sterilizes drinking water. It deteriorates quickly when exposed to air, so it should be purchased in airtight cans. To be effective, the powder should be dry. Ordinarily 1/4 teaspoonful to 50 gallons of water will make water safe without affecting taste.

If this is not available, drinking water may be disinfected by adding 1 tablespoonful of tincture of iodine to 1 barrel of water (55 or 60 gallons), stirring, and letting stand for half an hour before using.

Distillation—Distilled water is the purest form of water obtainable. It tastes flat unless well mixed with air.

ANATOMY OF THE BODY

Bones of skeleton—The human body is built over a framework of bones bound together by tough fibrous bands called ligaments, which act like hinges. The bones are very dense on the outside, but a fine lattice work on the inside makes them light but very strong. The skeleton (Figure 18-1) consists of 206 bones.

The *skull*, placed on top of the spinal column, contains the brain, which sends out nerves to all parts of the body. The skull consists of the cranium and the face. The cranial bones are flat, firmly mortised into one another, and are rarely dislocated.

The face proper begins with the eyebrows and ends with the lower jaw. The orbits are cavities containing the eyes. The bulge above each eye marks the frontal sinuses, which are connected with the nose.

The *nasal* bones are thin plates of bone, easily broken by a direct blow.

The *clavicle* (collar-bone) is a long bone fastened on one end to the top of the *sternum* (breast-bone) and on the other to the *scapula* (shoulder blade) and the *humerus* (arm-bone).

The *humerus* is a long bone from shoulder to elbow. The *ulna* extends from the prominent part of the elbow to the wrist. The *radius* is located on the thumb side of the lower arm.

The *femur*, the longest bone in the body, extends from hip to knee. Fracture of this bone is very common.

The *tibia* extends from knee to ankle. The *fibula* (calf-bone) extends from a point just below the knee. This bone is more frequently fractured than the tibia.

The **muscles** compose about one half the body weight and are of three kinds: (1) those, like the arm muscles, controlled by the will; (2) the muscles of the intestines, not controlled by the will; and (3) the heart muscle, which is not controlled by the will and possesses a cellular structure different from the other types.

The point where a muscle arises is called the *origin*. The point where a muscle exerts force is called the *insertion*. The muscles often end in a small, strong, inelastic band called a *tendon*.

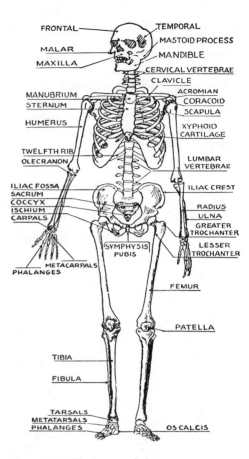

Figure 18-1. The human skeleton.

Blood vessels—The circulatory system consists of the heart, the arteries, which carry the blood from it, and the veins, which bring the blood to it. Blood from the veins is pumped by the right half of the heart to the lungs, where it is purified and returned to the left half as arterial or purified blood.

The arteries divide and subdivide until invisible to the naked eye, and reach every part of the body. When the heart contracts, it forces blood into the arteries, causing them to expand. This alternate expansion and contraction produces the pulse, readily felt if the finger is placed over a point where the artery is near the surface. Usually, the pulse is taken at the wrist.

Taking the pulse shows the rate at which the heart is beating. In the sitting adult this is about 70 per minute. It is faster when one is standing, working, in a fever, taking a warm bath or a hot drink. The pulse may be described as slow or fast, strong or weak, regular or irregular.

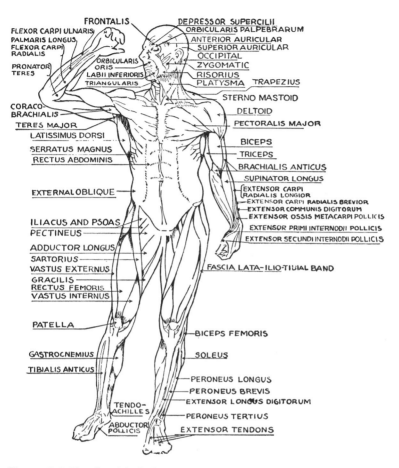

Figure 18-2. Muscles of the body.

The veins have thinner walls than the arteries and are provided with valves. They carry the venous (impure) blood to the heart. They usually accompany the arteries, but have no pulse.

There are two lungs, one on either side of the heart, where impure blood from the veins carries carbon dioxide to exchange it for oxygen to carry back to the tissues. The lungs are enclosed in a sac of smooth membrane, the *pleura*, which protects these delicate organs and helps their movement inside the chest. The pleura is sometimes inflamed, producing *pleurisy*, in which there is fever and pain in the side on breathing.

Abdominal cavity—The weakest part of the abdomen (belly) is the *groin*, where *hernia* (rupture) most often occurs. The abdomen is lined by a closed sac of membrane, the *peritoneum*. This may become inflamed, causing *peritonitis*.

In this general region are the stomach and intesines, liver, spleen, pancreas, the kidneys and their ureters (tubes) leading to the urinary bladder.

The *stomach* is in the upper part of the abdomen, associated with the liver, spleen, and pancreas. The tube carrying food and drink to the stomach is the *esophagus* (gullet). The stomach empties into the first part of the small intestine, the *duodenum.*

The *small intestine* is about 23 feet long. In its first part the food is mixed with the secretions of the liver (bile) and the pancreas. The interior is generally roughened to aid in the digestion and absorption of food products which have been prepared by the action of the digestive juices.

The *large intestine*, about 5 feet long, begins in the right flank, runs upward, crosses abdomen in its upper part, descends along the left flank, and empties into the rectum, which ends at the anus. Where it begins it is pouch-shaped, and has the *appendix*, which may become inflamed, causing *appendicitis.*

The *kidneys* lie in the back part of the abdomen just under the lowest ribs, and empty into the urinary bladder, just behind the pubic bone.

FIRST AID

First aid, in any situation, consists of the emergency treatment of the sick and/or injured until competent medical or surgical help can be obtained. At sea, however, YOU may well be the only medical help available.

There are some general rules to keep in mind in almost any situation.

1. Keep the patient lying down until the extent of his injuries can be determined.

2. Check for breathing, bleeding, and signs of shock.

3. Remove only enough clothing to get a clear idea of the extent of the injury.

4. Reassure the casualty. Tell him that you have everything under control and that he is going to be fine.

5. Avoid allowing the casualty to see his injury. Even a minor injury may appear severe to the injured person.

6. Never attempt to give an unconscious person anything by mouth, not even water.

7. Do not move the casualty until first aid measures are complete.

8. Always move a casualty feet first, except when going up a ladder.

Before discussing the care of different types of injuries, a few words about YOU. When an injury occurs, whether one or many, excitement and confusion arise. In these situations you will have to force yourself to KEEP CALM. Never permit yourself to become overly excited and confused. Act quickly with efficiency and confidence. Doing this will reassure the casualty that everything that can be done is being done.

If there are many casualties, enlist the help of those individuals not seriously injured. This will keep them occupied and from feeling sorry for themselves.

CARDIOPULMONARY RESUSCITATION

Cardiopulmonary resuscitation (CPR) is the root treatment for any illness or injury. If you spend time working on the injury itself, whether bleeding, fracture, wounds, etc., and the casualty is not breathing and his heart is not pumping blood through his veins, you may be patching up a dead person. In short, the FIRST thing to be checked on any casualty is breathing and pulse. This is because if the brain, which is the computer that tells the rest of the body what and how to do it, is without oxygen for a period of 4 - 6 minutes, its cells start to die. These cells can never be regenerated. After about 10 minutes, it is possible that a significant number of brain cells have died so that even if "lucky" enough to get heart and breathing started, the casualty may already be a "vegetable." There-fore, if breathing and/or pulse are absent—CPR *must* be started IMMEDIATELY.

A. **Airway**—The tongue is the most frequent cause of an airway obstruc-tion (Figure 18-3). When a person is unconscious, the lower jaw relaxes and falls back. The tongue being attached to the lower jaw also falls back and blocks the passage of air to the lungs. With certain exceptions the best way to correct this obstruction is to hyperextend the head which will thrust the jaw forward lifting the tongue from the back of the throat, allowing a free flow of air to and from the lungs. This may be all that is needed for the casualty to start breathing on his own. If breathing is in doubt, place your ear over the casualty's mouth so you may feel and/or hear any breathing. If not, blow four (4) full deep breaths into the casualty's mouth (hold nose closed) not allowing the lungs to deflate completely then check the carotid pulse.

B. **Breathing**—If the casualty still is not breathing, start mouth-to-mouth artificial ventilation at the rate of one (1) breath every five (5) seconds or twelve (12) times per minute until spontaneous breathing starts.

C. **Circulation**—To see if the heart is beating—check the carotid pulse. (See Figure 18-4.) The carotid arteries are on either side of the "Adam's apple." Place two (2) fingers on the Adam's apple and slide them to the cleft on either side and press lightly to feel the pulse. If you do not feel a pulse—start artifical circulation by placing the heel of your hand on the lower half of the sternum (breast-bone), NOT the xyphoid, which is the very tip of the sternum. Compress the chest 1 1/2 to 2 inches.

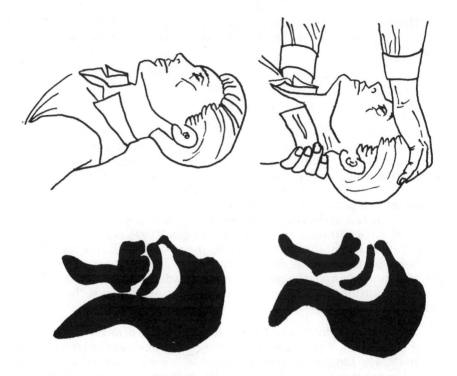

Figure 18-3. The airway. The two sketches on the left show patient when assistance first arrives on scene. Lower jaw is relaxed, and passage of air to the lungs is blocked. Sketches on right show how airway is opened by hyperextending the head. This is the first step in the administration of CPR (Cardiopulmonary resuscitation). CPR has taken the place of all older forms of reviving the unconscious or apparently drowned.

If you are alone you must compress the chest at the rate of 80 times per minute. This is done by compressing the chest 15 times then giving 2 full ventilations (breaths) into the casualty until he becomes conscious, or the heart starts beating on its own and spontaneous breathing returns.

If available have someone help you. The chest should be compressed at the rate of 60 times per minute or once each second by one person. The other person should impose one (1) breath on the upstroke of each fifth (5th) compression. This will give the casualty five (5) compressions (heart beats) and one (1) breath. The heart is beating 60 times a minute and the lungs are being filled 12 times every minute.

NEAR-DROWNING

Drowning or near-drowning is caused by asphyxiation due to submersion. All near-drowning victims suffer from acute asphyxia. There is a

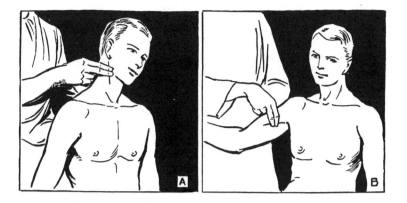

Figure 18-4. A. Point of compression for carotid artery; B. for brachial artery.

lowering of arterial oxygen (hypoxemia) and an increase in the metabolic acidosis which persists in those who have aspirated fluid.

Treatment—It is useless to attempt to drain water from the lungs of either a fresh water or a sea water near-drowning victim. But placing the patient in the Trendelenburg position (head and shoulders lower than the abdomen and pelvis) may promote drainage.

Often victims of submersion swallow water which fills the stomach and prevents movement of the diaphragm. Roll the victim face down and lift him just anterior to the pelvis. Any water will drain out of his stomach by gravity. Roll the victim over and begin the routine CPR.

A) Establish an airway.

B) Check carotid pulse.

C) Closed chest cardiac massage, alternating with positive pressure mouth to mouth ventilation.

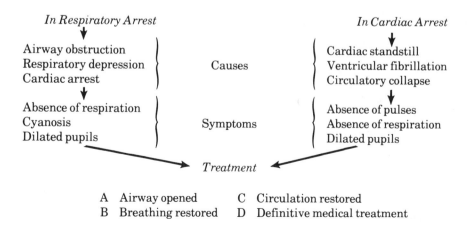

MANAGEMENT OF WOUNDS AND INJURIES

By definition, a wound is a break in the continuity of body tissues involving an opening in the skin; and an injury is the disruption in the continuity of body tissues not necessarily involving the skin. With this in mind, you can see that all wounds may be classified as injuries, but not all injuries may be classified as a wound.

Wound prophylaxis—In a sentence—KEEP IT CLEAN! This can be accomplished by doing the following:

1. Make sure hands are clean—scrub them thoroughly with soap and hot water.

2. Place a piece of sterile bandage over the wound while cleaning the surrounding area.

3. If the wound is in a hairy area, shave the hair off 2 to 3 inches around the wound. (Never shave off any part of the eyebrow, as it may not grow back.)

4. If possible flush the wound thoroughly with sterile saline solution. This will wash out any loose debris.

5. Apply a dry sterile dressing, using only sufficient pressure to stop bleeding.

6. If the casualty has not had a tetanus booster within the past 6 months, give 0.5 cc. of tetanus toxoid, injected into the arm to prevent "lock-jaw."

7. Start antibiotic therapy as indicated.

CONTROL OF HEMORRHAGE

Hemorrhage, or bleeding, is the escape of blood from arteries, veins, and capillaries because of a break in their walls. Control of active bleeding is urgent.

Symptoms—While external bleeding is very demonstrative, internal bleeding can be just as serious. The following symptoms will usually be present in both types of hemorrhage, but perhaps disregarded in external bleeding:

1. Pale skin or pale mucous membranes.

2. Subnormal temperature.

3. Increased pulse rate. Possibly feeble and easily compressed or lost.

4. Blood pressure lowered.

5. Dilated pupils and slow in reacting to light.

6. Ringing in ears.

7. Faintness or fainting (may be first symptom).

8. Thirst due to dehydration.

9. Air hunger (yawning).

10. Impaired vision.

Treatment

Internal Hemorrhage—can only be controlled by surgery. Until a patient reaches a hospital, he must be kept alive with the aid of blood volume expanders (I.V.'s) that can be used until whole blood is available at the hospital. Blood loss can produce "Hemorrhagic Shock."

External Hemorrhage

1. Local pressure by use of pressure dressings.

2. Pressure on the pressure points can control bleeding in that region.

3. A tourniquet is a constricting bond that can be placed around an extremity and tightened until the escaping blood flow stops. Should be used ONLY AS A LAST RESORT!

MANAGEMENT OF SHOCK

Shock is a state of circulatory deficiency associated with depression of the vital processes of the body.

Symptoms

1. Eyes—glassy, lack luster, dilated pupils, suggest fear and/or apprehension.

2. Breathing—shallow and irregular.

3. Lips maybe pale or cyanotic (bluish grey).

4. Skin—pale, cool, and moist or waxy.

Treatment

1. Keep patient lying down in supine position.

2. Raise feet 10 to 12 inches higher than head.

3. Keep patient warm.

   (a) remove wet clothing

   (b) cover with a blanket

4. Ascertain cause and contact a physician.

MANAGEMENT OF BURNS

Burns are classified in several ways; by the extent of body surface burned; by the depth of the burn; and by the causative agent. Of these, extent of body surface burned plays the greatest role in survival. This is calculated by what is called the "Rule of Nines" (Figure 18-5).

Using this as a basis, an adult having 15 percent of body surface burned or a small child having 10 percent of body surface burned, can go into shock. If more than 20 percent of body surface is burned, it can endanger life. If 30 percent or more of body surface is burned, it is usually fatal.

Keeping the above in mind and adding another factor or classification of depth or degree, will intensify the mortality rate of burn injuries.

First-degree burns involve only the outer layer of skin or epidermis. Mild sunburn is a good example.

Second-degree burns extend through the epidermis and involve the inner layers of skin or dermis, but not enough to prevent rapid regeneration of the skin. It is characterized by blisters and moderately severe pain.

Third-degree burns destroy both the epidermis and dermis along with underlying tissues. Severe pain may be absent because nerve endings have been destroyed. The color may range from white and lifeless, as in scalds, to black and charred, as in thermal or gas explosions. Skin grafts are generally required before complete healing can take place.

The first aid treatment for all burns involves three (3) main considerations: (1) Relieve pain; (2) prevent or treat shock; and (3) prevent infection. These can be accomplished by doing the following:

Ice-water treatment—If the burn involves 20 percent or less of body surface burned, immerse the part in ice-water. Where immersion is impractical, repeated applications of ice-cold moist towels to the burned area is advisable. Continue this ice-water treatment until no pain is felt. This could take anywhere from 30 minutes to 5 hours.

Treatment for pain of a first-degree burn should require no more than 1 or 2 aspirins for relief of discomfort. For moderately severe pain as with second-degree burns, codeine 1/2 grain (32 mgm.) orally or by injection.

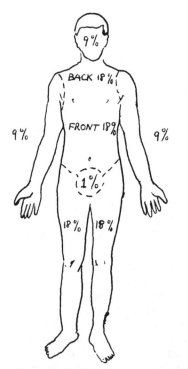

Figure 18-5. "Rule of Nines" for analysis of burn treatment. Head = 9%, each arm = 9%, front of body = 18%, back of body = 18%, genital area = 1%, each leg = 18%. Drawing: Midn. Eric Pett, California Maritime Academy.

For pain from extensive burns (third-degree), 8 - 20 mgm. of morphine injected subcutaneously. Morphine should not be injected intermuscularly because of the probability of reduced peripheral circulation and possible morphine poisoning.

In burns as with other things that happen to, and within, the body, the body's own mechanisms take over and try to help right the wrong. In the case of burns, the body rushes fluid in the form of plasma to the site of the burn to help cool it. This causes a loss of fluid in other important parts of the body including the blood stream. With a decrease in blood volume, shock is imminent. Therefore, these fluids must be replaced. If the casualty is conscious, he may be given liquids (coffee, tea, water, etc.) with salt added (about 1/4 teaspoon to 8 ounces). If unconscious, an I.V. of sterile normal saline should be started (8 - 10 drops per minute).

Prevention of infection is a never ending process. While infection seems to be frequent and early in development, there are measures to help slow it down. Make-shift wrappings such as sheets and towels may be used to cover the burn to keep out dust and dirt from the air. *Never* put ointments, creams, or other medicines directly on or into a burn. Casualties with burns of over 20 percent of the body surface should receive a prophylaxis to combat infection. Procaine Penicillin in the amount of 600,000 units intramuscularly every 12 - 24 hours OR 0.5 grams of Streptomycin, intramuscularly, daily is recommended.

ENVIRONMENTAL EMERGENCIES

Injuries due to heat and cold are often found among seafaring people due to the extremes in climate they encounter. Injuries due to heat are more prevalent, especially among engineers. This is not only because of climate, but because of the sometimes excessive heat generated in the engine room by the machinery that powers the vessel.

The three (3) injuries occuring from heat are, in order of their severity, heat exhaustion, heat cramps, and heat stroke. **Heat exhaustion** is a physiologic disturbance following exposure to heat, characterized by peripheral vasomotor collapse. This is usually not fatal. The casualty will appear "shockish" in that the skin will be pale, cool, and clammy. He will be perspiring profusely. Nausea, vomiting, headache, and restlessness are also common. The casualty should be laid down in a cool environment (air conditioned or well ventilated space), and cool (not iced) drinks with 1/4 teaspoon of salt added to 8 ounces, orally as tolerated, should be administered.

Heat cramps are painful contractions of various skeletal muscles brought about by the depletion of sodium chloride (salt) from the body fluids via excessive sweating. This occurs very suddenly and most frequently in the flexor muscles (Figure 18-2) of the arms and legs. The skin will be pale and moist due to the excessive sweating. In touching the muscle, a knot or spasm will be able to be felt, along with localized heat over the spasm. The casualty should be given aspirin for pain, but most importantly, cool liquids containing salt (1/2 teaspoon in 16 ounces of water). An ace wrap applied to the limb will help control pain.

Heat stroke, the most dangerous of heat disorders, is an extreme elevation of body temperature, due to a failure of the sweating mechanism. It occurs whenever heat regulation is dependent upon sweating for long periods of time. The casualty's skin will appear flushed, hot, and dry. Body temperature will be elevated to 105°F possibly 106°F. Convulsions, vomiting, and profound shock develop and are followed by circulatory collapse and death. In treating the casualty, you must reduce the body temperature immediately. Immerse the casualty in an "ice-water" bath if practical, or cover with "ice-water" and alcohol-moistened towels until the temperature is reduced to at least 102°F. Continue checking the temperature every ten (10) minutes until normal. Since this casualty will normally be unconscious, an I.V. of sterile normal saline should be started immediately. Full recovery is very slow, often taking several weeks.

Of the injuries due to cold, **immersion foot** is the most frequently encountered. This is a condition occuring in persons who have spent long periods of time in water-logged boots or shoes. It does not necessarily have to be cold. This type of injury can occur in 70°F weather. Prevention and treatment for this is the same; keep the feet warm and dry by changing socks and shoes frequently, at least daily.

Chilblains is a painful swelling of sores on the feet and/or hands caused by exposure to cold. Children get this most frequently when playing in the snow making snowballs, etc. Never take cold injuries lightly because of possible tissue loss and nerve damage. Restrict the patient from usual activities until the extent of the injury can be determined. Mild stimulants such as coffee and tea may be given. NEVER give alcohol or tobacco to a cold injury. DO NOT administer snow or ice-water, grease, dry heat, or massage the injured part. DO NOT break any blisters. For chilblains get the person into a dry warm atmosphere. Benadryl 50 mgm. as needed for hives should be administered.

INJURIES OF MUSCLES, JOINTS, AND BONES

These can be classified into five (5) main classes: contusions, strains, sprains, dislocations, and fractures. Fractures will be explained separately and definitively.

Contusions which result from the crushing or tearing of muscle tissue or tendons are the most common. A patient with a contusion will have localized swelling and tenderness at the site of the injury. Normally, discoloration of the area is due to the rupture of blood vessels. This discoloration will range from red (immediately) through blue or black and finally change to yellow or green progressively over several days. These changes are due to the breakdown of blood pigments which are gradually being reabsorbed. Treatment of contusions is generally unnecessary. In large contusions ice or cold applications will help prevent and reduce swelling at the onset. Ace wraps on the limbs will help control swelling, however, pulse must be checked frequently to insure sufficient circulation.

Strains result when a muscle or tendon is stretched to the point of partial or possible complete rupture. With this condition, patients will have pain in the affected part with stiffness and lameness together with localized swelling over the area. If a complete rupture occurs, there would be a possible loss of power of the affected muscle. On examination of a complete rupture, a distinct gap may be felt at the site of the rupture, and there may be swelling above where the muscle has retracted. To treat minor strains a supportive adhesive strapping or bandaging combined with rest is indicated. In severe strains, particularly with complete ruptures, the part should be immobilized so that the affected muscle is in a relaxed position.

A **sprain** is an injury in or about a joint due to wrenching or twisting of its ligaments and adjacent soft parts. This is often caused by a momentary dislocation and an automatic reduction of a joint. There will be pain and swelling about the joint. To treat this type of injury, the part should be elevated and cold applied in the form of moist packs or ice bags for about one (1) hour to allay hemmorrhage. Immobilization is the key to the healing of a sprain as it is with a fracture.

When the bones which form a joint slip away from each other, beyond their normal relationships it is called a **dislocation**. Pain and muscle spasm are almost always present. A dimple effect will be seen caused by the misalignment of the joint. Treat a dislocation as if it were a fracture, by immobilizing the joint and the part.

MANAGEMENT OF FRACTURES

All injuries produced by force should be examined with fracture in mind. A fracture is a broken bone and should not be regarded as an isolated phenomenon.

There are five (5) classifications/types of fractures:

1. **Simple (closed) fracture**—The bone is broken and normally in good alignment, but the skin is not broken.

2. **Compound (open) fracture**—There is an open wound so that the broken bone *may* be see through the opening in the skin. The bone may or may not protrude through the opening.

3. **Greenstick fracture**—The bone shaft is bent and cracked, but is not completely broken through.

4. **Comminuted fracture**—The bone is crushed, splintered, or broken into a number of fragments.

5. **Impacted fracture**—One fragment of bone is forcibly driven into another and remains more or less fixed in that position.

The treatment of any fracture is IMMOBILIZATION. The pre-formed splints are outstanding for immobilizing a fracture, but just because there aren't any available or handy, do not lose time looking for one. There are many items that can be used as a splint. A pillow, magazine, or board will all immobilize a fracture when properly applied.

DISEASES AND THEIR THERAPY

GENERAL

It is simply not possible to give all the details of every medical condition or of every disease that you may encounter aboard a merchant ship or fishing vessel. It is necessary to limit yourself to general principles so that you can be of assistance. The book, *Ship's Medicine Chest and Medical Aid at Sea*, H.E.W. Publication (HSA) 78-2024, available from U.S. Government Printing Office and nautical book suppliers, contains detailed information beyond the scope of this chapter and is the leading text in this field.

The diseases and conditions selected for discussion in this chapter are:

Acute Alcoholism	Dysentery	Rash
Acute Appendicitis	Epilepsy (Convulsions)	Scabies
Angina Pectoris	Erysipelas	Sunburn
Asthma	Eye	Tetanus
Bladder (Cystitis)	Fainting	Toothache
Bronchitis	Headaches	Typhoid Fever (Enteric
Bubonic Plague	Hemorrhoids (Piles)	Fever)
Chicken Pox	Hysteria	Typhus Fever
Cholera	Indigestion (Heartburn)	Ulcers (Gastric or
Common Colds	Influenza (La Grippe)	Duodenal)
Coronary Thrombosis	Malaria	Undulant Fever
Delirium Tremens	Measles	(Brucellosis)
Diabetes Mellitus	Mental Disorders	Venereal Disease
Diabetic Coma	Mumps	Whooping Cough
Diarrhea	Pneumonia	(Pertussis)
Diphtheria	Radiation Exposure	Yellow Fever

The following explanation of common abbreviations and definitions will help in clarifying the suggested treatment:

Abbreviation or term	*Meaning*
subcutaneously	injected just below the skin
I.M.	intramuscular
I.V.	intravenous
mg. or mgm.	milligram
gm.	gram
gr.	grain

Abbreviation or term	*Meaning*
U	unit
x d.	daily
cc.	cubic centimeters
gtts.	drops
p.r.n.	as needed or necessary
1:1000	one part per thousand
oz.	ounce
q.	every
b.i.d.	twice a day
t.i.d.	three times a day
q.i.d.	four times a day
q.v.	vital signs
tab	tablet

The essential rules to follow are:

1. Isolate and put the patient to bed. If anyone has a temperature without an obvious cause, isolate until a diagnosis is made.

2. Make a thorough examination with the patient stripped. Include temperature, pulse rate, respiratory rate, and blood pressure. Look for a rash in an effort to establish diagnosis.

3. Liquid or light diet.

4. If temperature is 103°F (39.4°C), give a tepid sponging.

5. Designate someone to look after the patient and to arrange the control of eating and drinking utensils and their sterilization after use. Provide for use of bed pan and the urinal.

6. Radio consultation: (a) patient is seriously ill and (b) any doubt as to diagnosis.

7. Treat symptoms as they arise.

8. Keep patient in bed during convalescence.

9. When approaching port, contact the Port Authority by radio to make necessary arrangements including ambulance and isolation of patient and contacts as appropriate.

10. Log patient's name and identification number and the sequence of events or course of illness, including any medications given (how much and how often).

ACUTE ALCOHOLISM

Intoxication is a temporary disturbance accompanied by muscular incoordination, inability to walk steadily or to talk in a coherent manner. The patient has difficulty in focusing his eyes which are usually bloodshot.

He has a rapid pulse. He may vomit. This is a sign of alcohol poisoning. Usually he is in a happy or excited mood, but is liable to cry and to be easily depressed. His mood is unpredictable.

Impairment of consciousness is gradual. However, coma may occur with unexpected rapidity. Death may occur suddenly after several hours of coma.

Deaths from alcoholism are recorded every year either as a result of excessive drinking of liquor or from accidents which seem to befall those with impaired judgment or poor muscular coordination secondary to ingestion of alcohol. Before beginning treatment, be sure that other possible causes of the patient's stuporous or comatose condition are ruled out. Alcohol breath does not always mean a person is "drunk."

Patients should not be put to bed to sleep it off alone. Too often they may rouse to vomit, be unable to get out of bed, and then be choked by their own vomitus, i.e., asphyxiated.

Take vital signs every half hour until they stabilize (that is, until they do not vary from one reading to the next).

Place in a prone position. Attempt to get patient to drink some hot, black coffee.

If unruly, restless or agitated give paraldehyde one half ounce if able to drink. If not, give paraldehyde 4 cc. I.M.; Vistaril 50 mg. I.M. may be substituted and repeated every 4 - 6 hours as indicated.

ACUTE APPENDICITIS

An inflammatory process which is brought about by a stopping up of the lumen of the appendix with fecal material.

Symptoms—Generalized abdominal pain (that later localizes in the right lower quadrant of the body); nausea and vomiting (not usually diarrhea) are predominant. There is a slight elevation of temperature to about 101°. Further elevations in temperature are often indicative of gangrene, rupture, or spreading peritonitis.

Treatment—As soon as appendicitis is suspected, contact a physician and arrange to get the patient transferred to a hospital for surgery. Surgery is the *only cure*. In the meantime give NOTHING by mouth. Not even water. An ice bag may alleviate some of the abdominal pain. If the patient cannot be transferred for 3 to 4 hours, and pain is intense, give 15 mgm. of morphine. I.V. fluids of 5% dextrose in normal saline and 5% dextrose in water (2000 cc.) should be x.d. 600,000 U of procaine penicillin should be given I.M. q. 3 - 4 hours, and 0.5 gm. of streptomycin q. 6 hours to help slow the spread of infection.

ANGINA PECTORIS

Occurs in persons of middle age or older. It is due to a slackened or insufficient supply of fresh oxygenated blood to the heart muscle, causing a spasm of the blood vessels supplying the muscle. (See also Indigestion.)

Symptoms—The attack comes on suddenly, usually when the patient has over-exerted, eaten too much, or has had a sudden emotional strain. The pain radiates over the anterior chest wall, down the left arm, up into the neck and sometimes over the upper abdomen. There is sweating, and the patient has a cold, clammy skin. The attack usually passes off in two or three minutes, but sometimes sudden death may occur.

Treatment—This is a grave medical emergency and requires expert care. Do not move the patient during the attack. Allow him to remain in whatever position he finds most comfortable. The chest will feel as though crushed in a vice. Use an amyl nitrite capsule crushed in a handkerchief and hold it over the nose and mouth. Place a tablet of nitro-glycerine gr. 1/150 under the tongue. Morphine gr. 1/4 or Dermol 50 mg. should be injected subcutaneously for relief of pain. Hospitalize or remove to patient's cabin as soon as possible. Monitor the vital signs—blood pressure, pulse, respirations until the patient is stabilized. Log the sequence of events, the vital signs, and the medications given.

ASTHMA

Patient has periodic attacks of difficulty in breathing accompanied by a feeling of tightness in the chest.

Causes

1. Exposure to irritants patient is sensitive to such as dust, cold air, fumes, drugs.

2. Mental stress.

3. Some chest diseases—e.g., emphysema.

4. Certain heart conditions.

Treatment

1. Patient who knows he has sensitivities will usually have remedies with him.

2. Patient with no remedies—one (1) ephedrine or one (1) aminophyllin tablet 3 x d. for as long as wheezing continues.

3. Severe attacks—give ephedrine (or adrenalin) 1:1000, gtts. 3, subcutaneously. If not relieved in 20 minutes, repeat injection of gtts. 3.

BLADDER (CYSTITIS)

This may arise from exposure to cold, infection by a germ (*Escherichia coli*), as a complication of stricture of the bladder, or an enlarged prostate gland, as a result of gonorrhea.

Symptoms—Pain in bladder region, pain on urination, and urgency and frequency to empty the bladder.

Treatment—If secondary to gonorrhea, treat this disease. Force fluids to 2 - 3 quarts every day. Ganatol 500 mg. tablets, 2 tablets, q.i.d.

Prevention—May be caused by exposure to cold, as a result of intercourse with a new partner, or as one result of gonorrhea.

Symptoms—There is pain in the region of the bladder, with frequent and constant desire to pass urine which is passed in small quantities with pain and straining. There may be temperature rise to 100°F (37.8°C). If there is a rise to 102°-104°F (38.9°-40.0°C) with shivering and pain in the back, just under the rib area, it indicates inflammation in the kidneys (pyelitis). (This is often called "a cold in the kidneys.")

Treatment—Fluids up to 2 - 3 quarts in 24 hours. Fruit juices, with cream of tartar—one heaping teaspoonful to 2 quarts. Bowels shold be kept open. Sulfamethoxazole (Ganatol) 1 gm. q.i.d. for 6 days.

BRONCHITIS

Inflammation of the wind-pipes or the bronchi.

Symptoms—Onset of a head cold, hard dry cough, mild fever 100° - 102°F (37.8°-38.9°C) occasionally some productive sputum.

Treatment—Put patient to bed in a warm room. Diet as desired. Aspirin gr. 10 q. 6 hours for aches and discomfort. Elixir Benadryl drams 1, q. 3 - 4 hours, p.r.n. or elixir terpin hydrate with codeine, same dosage.

BUBONIC PLAGUE

Incubation—2 - 6 days.

Segregation—6 days.

Prevention—Bubonic plague is caused by the bite of a flea from a diseased rat. Ships must be kept free of rats by fumigation. All ships engaged in foreign trade must be fumigated at least every 6 months. This is done by a quarantine officer, usually with cyanide sulphur gas or carbon monoxide.

Symptoms—Chief symptom is formation of buboes, or swelling of lymph glands in the groin, armpits, and neck. The onset is abrupt, associated with chills, with the temperature rising to 103°-106°F. The pulse gradually weakens, and the patient may become delirious or unconscious.

Treatment—Isolation of the patient and disinfection of his bed and personal articles. Tetracycline or chloramphenicol 500 mg. I.V. q. 3 hours for 48 hours (may be given I.M.), then give 4 gm. per day orally for the next 2 days; then 3 gm. per day, orally for an additional 4 to 5 days. For pain, morphine gr. 1/4 or Demerol 50 mg. q. 4 hours p.r.n. Aspirin gr. 10 q.i.d. will combat fever and relieve pain.

Isolation—3 weeks.

Port Quarantine—None.

CHICKEN POX

Chicken pox is caused by a virus and is spread by direct contact with a patient. It is very contagious. Only prevention is isolation of patient and quarantine of those exposed. There is no vaccination against chicken pox. One attack gives life-long immunity.

Symptoms—Early signs are fever, headache, backache, loss of appetite, and weakness. The first *real* sign is a rash, appearing as a faint red spot, usually on the trunk. A small blister appears in the center. It contains clear fluid, the size of a pinhead. It breaks easily and forms a crust (scab). Thereafter blisters (or pocks) come out in crops of 10 or more, scattered over the body, usually more on the abdomen, chest, back, and face, than on the arms and legs. As each new crop of pocks comes out, temperature rises for a few hours. New crops may erupt for 5 - 7 days. Then temperature remains normal.

After the rash is about a week old, pocks are in various stages and sizes, temperature remains normal, and no new crops appear. Patient may then safely be released from isolation. In another week scabs fall off, leaving a superficial red mark which usually disappears leaving no scar.

Treatment—Chicken pox is rarely serious unless pocks become infected from itching attached to pocks in the early stage. Scratching must be avoided to prevent infection. Calamine or Caladryl lotion is very effective for this. Neomycin and/or Bacitracin ointment will also help clear up the pocks. Patient should be kept in bed until (a) temperature remains normal for two days—or—(b) no new crops of pocks have appeared for 48 hours. Isolation may be ended even though some crusted lesions remain. Nightly tub or shower baths in tepid water will hasten removal of crusts. Boric acid ointment may also be used.

Isolation—No new pocks for 48 hours.

Port Quarantine—None.

CHOLERA

Incubation—2 - 3 days.

Segregation—5 days.

Prevention—Cholera vaccine is of benefit in endemic areas; booster injections are required every 6 months. Cholera is spread by the ingestion of water and foods contaminated by the excrement of patients. Boil all drinking water and cook all vegetables where the disease is suspected.

Symptoms—Abdominal pains may suddenly begin with looseness of bowels, headache, and perhaps vomiting. The watery stools may lose as much as 1 liter of fluid each time patient goes to stool. The severe dehydration and electrolyte depletion leads to intense thirst, and decrease in the amount of urine. Muscle cramps then ensue with weakness, loss of skin turgor and sunken eyes. Because of loss of electrolytes, there may be circulatory collapse.

Uncomplicated cholera is typically a self-limited disease, recovery being apparent by the third to the sixth day. Temperature may be several degrees below normal. On the other hand, the patient may become delirious, with pulse feeble and rapid. Death occurs with coma.

Treatment—Patient should rest in bed and be given a fluid diet. It is essential to combat dehydration and circulatory collapse and restore the electrolyte balance by giving parenteral fluids, I.V. The following may be used: 5 percent dextrose in normal sodium chloride; Ringer's Solution, with or without dextrose; 1/6 molar lactate. But give from 1 to 6 liters each day, depending upon the patient's condition and the amount of urinary output. The continued appraisal of the patient during this time is critical: temperature, pulse rate, blood pressure. Solid food is withheld until vomiting is controlled and food is desired. With continued diarrhea, compazene suppositories will be of little value to suppress vomiting. Tetracycline 250 mg. orally, q. 6 hours is effective. If vomiting, give equivalent dose I.M.

Isolation—4 - 6 weeks.

Port Quarantine—5 days.

COMMON COLD

More prevalent than any other disease, a cold is an inflammation of the upper respiratory system caused by lowered resistance, insufficient rest, exposure to cold and wet, and contact with someone who has a cold or is coming down with one.

Incubation—12 - 24 hours.

Segregation—3 days.

Treatment—Avoid persons who have a cold or upper respiratory infection. Force fluids up to 2 - 3 liters each 24 hours. Rest in bed. Aspirin or Tylenol, gr. 10, q. 4-6 hours. Ascorbic acid (Vitamin C) therapy is questionable.

Isolation—To prevent spread to others.

Port Quarantine—None.

CORONARY THROMBOSIS

This is due to clot in one of the arteries supplying the heart muscle. Arterio sclerosis usually plays a part in causing this. (See also Indigestion and Angina Pectoris.)

Symptoms—The symptoms are very similar to those of angine pectoris. The pain is not so likely to be associated with activity and may even come on when the patient is resting.

1. There is a squeezing, compressing, constricting, vicelike pain which radiates down the anterior chest wall, to the upper abdomen and down the left arm.

2. The patient may vomit early in the attack.

3. There is a drop in blood pressure, the pulse is weak and rapid.

4. The skin is cold and clammy and has an ashen look.

5. If the pain lasts more than 10 minutes, it should be assumed to be an attack of coronary thrombosis.

Treatment—This is a grave emergency and requires expert medical care.

1. Put the patient in his bunk by stretcher as soon as possible.

2. Give morphine 15 mg. subcutaneously, or Demerol 50 mg., subcutaneously or I.V.; repeat in 1/2 hour if pain is still severe, or patient is distressed and restless.

3. No stimulating drinks.

4. Nitroglycerine tablet, gr. 1/150, may be put under patients tongue, in an attempt to relieve spasm of angina pectoris.

5. Arrange for professional medical help as quickly as possible.

DELIRIUM TREMENS

Delirium tremens, "D.T.s," commonly attacks only the chronic drinker and usually follows a prolonged or heavy drinking orgy. It may also follow sudden withdrawal of liquor from an habitual drinker.

Symptoms—Muscular trembling, talkative, very noisy actions. As the attack develops, patient becomes wildly excited, waves his arms in meaningless gestures, talks incoherently possibly about "green-eyed monsters" or "snakes" that are after him. Patient will not eat or sleep and must be guarded to prevent injury to himself or to others. He must be considered *temporarily insane*.

Treatment—Paraldehyde 10 cc. orally, q. 4 hours. The same amount may be given I.M. Chloral hydrate 1 gm. orally, q. 6 hours may also be used. Either regime should be maintained for several days, keeping the patient adequately sedated. When the attack is over, Librium (chlordiazepoxide) 50 mg. q.i.d. should be given. Keep the patient warm; encourage him to take food. If patient becomes assaultive, it may be necessary to use four point restraints for his own protection and the protection of others. On no account give the patient any more alcohol, even beer.

DIABETES MELLITUS

A constitutional disorder in which the normal ability of the body to utilize the sugar which circulates in the blood is diminished or lost. In consequence, the sugar accumulates in the blood and is passed out in the urine.

Symptoms—Onset may be abrupt in children or young adults. In older people it is usually insidious, with evidence of diabetes discovered on routine urine and blood examinations. Symptoms include polyuria, thirst, itching, hunger, weakness and weight loss. Large amounts of urine are passed day and night.

Boils and carbuncles are common due to poor vitality of the tissues.

Treatment—In many cases a strict diet is all that is required. No alcoholic beverages are allowable. Persons who have diabetes are familiar with the details of their treatment and diet.

When diabetes is suspected, test the urine for sugar: (a) first specimen in the morning and (b) two or three hours after a large meal.

This is carried out by dipping a urine testing stick for sugar into the urine. If sugar is present, the stick will turn blue. It can then be assumed the patient is suffering from diabetes. Place patient on a strict diet avoiding starchy or sugary foods until diagnosis and treatment can be done under medical supervision.

DIABETIC COMA

With a patient in whom the disease is under control with diet or insulin or both, the disease may suddenly get out of control and give rise to extreme weakness, collapse, and unconsciousness. This may happen if the patient does not take his regularly prescribed insulin and keep to his diet, if he overindulges in alcohol, or if he suffers from boils or some feverish illness.

Treatment—Test the urine as above, and if found to contain sugar the following treatment should be started at once or the patient will become unconscious:

1. If the patient has his own supply of insulin, this may be given under medical advice, obtained by radio as quickly as possible.

2. Give the patient large quantities of water to drink containing a level teaspoonful of soda bicarbonate to the pint.

3. If the patient has an infection or a fever, give the patient a course of penicillin, if he is sensitive to this, a course of tetracycline.

Overdosage with Insulin—If too much insulin is taken by a patient, a condition approaching collapse will occur with hunger, sweating, trembling and breathlessness. In this case the urine will be found to contain no sugar. Patient will respond to fruit juices, cola drinks. This should be followed with a balanced meal.

DIARRHEA

Looseness of the bowels is not a disease in itself, but a symptom that intestines are inflamed or irritated.

Common Causes

1. Partaking of unsuitable food, or drink, e.g. unripe or overripe fruit.

2. Partaking of unwholesome food or drink contaminated by harmful bacteria and their toxins.

3. Partaking of iced drinks where ice cubes may come from contaminated water supply.

4. Typhoid Fever.

5. Dysentery.

6. Cholera.

Treatment—Lomotil tablets—4 tab at onset, then 2 tab after each movement until stool becomes pasty. Paregoric and bismuth sub-nitrate equal parts, oz. 1 may be given instead. Kaopectate, oz. 1, may be tried but is not reliable nor effective enough.

DIPHTHERIA

Incubation—2 - 4 days.

Segregation—7 days.

Prevention—An acute contagious bacterial disease characterized by the formation of a fibrinous pseudomembrane on the mucosa, usually of the respiratory tract. It is transmitted by direct contact with someone ill with the disease. Patient must be isolated. Most people have been immunized by Diphtheria-Pertussis-Tetanus (DPT) vaccine at an early age.

Symptoms—Onset is gradual. Slight sore throat, slight rise in temperature, slight feeling of tired muscles and loss of appetite. Examination of the throat will show, at first, white spots in tonsillar areas or back of the throat. These grow forward. Glands of neck below ears enlarge as well as the submandibular area. If antitoxin is withheld for more than 4 days, death rate climbs rapidly. Death results from heart failure and inability to breathe, to exchange oxygen and carbon dioxide, because of the pseudo-membranous layer blanketing the air passages.

Treatment—Isolate the patient in bed and administer diphtheria antitoxin, if it is available. The patient must lie quietly and be fed lying on his back or side. He must not sit up. Keep nose and throat clean by irrigations with warm salt water (1 teaspoonful to 8 oz. of water). Aqueous procaine penicillin, 2,000,000 U per day, I.M. for 7 - 10 days. Tube feeding may be necessary.

Antitoxin must be skin tested before using. If no reaction, give diphtheria antitoxin I.M. in graduated doses, beginning with 0.05 cc. of the 1:20 dilution. If in 15 minutes no reaction has occurred, double the dose every 15 minutes thereafter until a dose of 1.0 cc. of undiluted antitoxin has been given. It is advisable to have epinephrine 1:1000 at hand, or adrenalin 1:1000, for immediate injection of 0.3 cc. subcutaneously, I.M. or even I.V. (slowly) in untoward symptoms appear.

Recovery from diphtheria is slow—up to 8 weeks. Strict bed rest. Diet as tolerated, beginning with fluids.

A tracheotomy may have to be performed if breathing is greatly embarrassed.

Isolation—2 weeks.

Port Quarantine—None.

DYSENTERY

Incubation—1 - 7 days.

Segregation—None.

Prevention—An infection of the bowel, perhaps by an amoeba, taken into the system through water and food, contaminated by infected excreta. Flies may also carry the contamination. The parasite causes severe inflammation of the mucous membrane lining the intestines.

Crews should be warned when going ashore in tropical or semi-tropical countries not to eat salads, uncooked vegetables, ice cream, or unpeeled fruit and not to drink any water or use ice in any drinks. Only bottled soft drinks or club soda are acceptable.

Symptoms—Slight attacks of diarrhea, gripping pain in the abdomen, chills and fever. Diarrhea may be severe and very frequent in the early stages and soon progress to blood and mucus. Temperature is not high.

Treatment—Rest, force fluids as much as possible. Lomotil (Lonox) tab 4 at onset, repeat 2 tab after each movement until stools become pasty. Also the following may be used: Sulfadiazine 500 mg. tab, 6 tab t.i.d.; paregoric oz. 1; or paregoric and bismuth subnitrate or each oz. 1.

Isolation—None.

Port Quarantine—None.

EPILEPSY (CONVULSIONS)

This is a violent, involuntary series of contractions of great muscle masses of the body, occurring singly or in a series, often accompanied by sudden loss of consciousness. It is due to an acute disturbance in brain function.

Petit Mal—Brief, fleeting attacks (1-30 seconds) not involving loss of consciousness, with or without loss of muscular tone.

Grand Mal—This type of seizure is characterized by a cry, a loss of consciousness, falling, contraction of muscles, urinary and fecal incontinence, frothing at the mouth, and biting the tongue.

Treatment—During an attack, prevent patient from biting tongue, place a bit of wood, or a wad of cloth in the corner of the jaw. Turn the head so that the mucus flows from the mouth; do not restrain.

After the attack, give the patient phenobarbital 15 or 30 mg. t.i.d. Dilantin 100 mg. I.M. may be given during or after the attack. Record how long the seizure lasts, the confusion of the patient, any excesses of alcohol, drugs, or tobacco. Arrange to have patient consult a doctor as soon as the ship reaches port.

ERYSIPELAS

Incubation—1 - 7 days.

Segregation—None.

Symptoms—An acute streptococal inflammation of the skin caused by the germ invading through a scratch or an abrasion. Sudden onset with headache, rigor, rapidly rising temperature to 103°-104°F (39.4°-40.0°C) and a general feeling of malaise. The skin affected becomes hot, red, swollen and the edges spread rapidly.

Treatment—Isolate the patient and keep in bed during the acute stage (until temperature is normal and the skin lesion abates). Penicillin 2,400,000 U I.M. daily until temperature is normal. Erythromycin 500 mg. at onset, then 250 mg. q.i.d. until temperature is normal. Cold packs may be used locally on the skin.

Isolation—Until temperature and skin are normal.

Port Quarantine—None.

EYE—DISEASES AND INJURIES

Conjunctivitis—An inflammation of the conjunctiva due to irritation, eyestrain, exposure to cold, dust, wind, and smoke; or from a foreign body or from infection with a germ.

The eye may have been infected with the germ of gonorrhea; therefore question the patient about a penile or vaginal discharge.

Symptoms—The eye feels as if it has grit in it. There is pain and a sensation of heat. The eye looks bloodshot and watery. The lids may be swollen and tend to stick together.

Treatment—First irrigate the eye with tepid water. Ophthalmic Pontocaine affords relief. This should be followed with ophthalmic Bacitracin ointment or ophthalmic Neomycin ointment. The patient may feel more comfortable if the affected eye is bandaged. Always apply the same treatment to the unaffected eye.

Foreign Body—The eye should be irrigated as above. Pull up the upper lid and have the patient look to left and right, then up and down. If a particle is seen, an attempt to remove it may be made, using a Q-Tip gently. The same examination should be made with the lower lid pulled down.

Ophthalmic Pontocaine ointment should be applied to afford relief. This should be followed as outlined above. Again, the patient may feel more comfortable with the eye bandaged. If the foreign particle cannot be removed easily, apply Pontocaine ointment several times a day, and keep the eye bandaged.

Stye—This is a tiny boil on the eyelid. Ophthalmic Gantrisin ointment should be applied several times a day until the inflammation clears up.

Perforating Injuries—These may be caused by blows from sharp instruments, flying particles of metal or by explosions. With this type of injury a most careful inspection should be made. Anesthetic agents, such as Pontocine ointment, ophthalmic type, should be used and repeated as often as necessary to reduce pain. Patient should have absolute bed rest on his back. The eye should be bandaged, and it is best for both eyes to be covered or bandaged. Morphine 15 mg. or Demerol 50 mg. may be used for pain. The patient should be seen by an eye specialist as soon as possible.

FAINTING

This is a very common medical emergency. Usually there is sudden, complete loss of consciousness with loss of normal muscular power. There are many types of fainting (see Petit Mal, above) but the mechanism is fundamentally the same; there is a deficiency of blood circulating through the brain. It can be brought on by a sudden unpleasant sight, a sudden emotional upset, receiving bad news, to name a few.

Treatment—Loosen any tight or constrictive clothing, place the patient in prone position, break an ampule of amyl nitrite (smelling salts) in a handkerchief and let the patient whiff it. Or use aromatic spirits of ammonia.

HEADACHE

Merely a symptom headache is not of itself an illness. An attempt must be made to find the cause. The following should be considered:

1. Psychological—The headaches are often of long standing. Patient claims it is continuous "like a band around the head."

2. Onset of feverish illness.

3. Sinusitis.

4. High blood pressure—The throbbing is made worse by exertion.

5. Diseases of the brain: (a) Cerebrospinal meningitis—In most cases, patient has a high fever, projectile vomiting, can't bear light and has a stiff neck. (b) Brain hemorrhage, apoplexy or stroke—Onset is sudden but without fever. Patient may well be paralyzed. (c) Migraine—Usually af-

fects only one side of the head, vomiting, avoids light. Treatment—Cafergot or Fiorinal, tab 1, repeat in 4 - 6 hours. (d) Head injury, heat stroke or concussion—q.v.

HEMORRHOIDS (PILES)

These consist of dilated blood vessels at the lower end of the rectum. Bleeding is the main symptom. Occasionally there is mild itching of the skin around this area.

Treatment—Bowel movements should be kept soft with mineral oil, 1/2 oz. b.i.d. morning and at bedtime. Apply Nupercaine ointment locally and after each bowel movement. Suppositories, such as Anusol or Rectal Medicone, should be inserted in the rectum morning and evening. Witch Hazel compresses, applied locally, will also afford some relief.

HYSTERIA

An illness in which the patient produces symptoms of illnesses somehow to his advantage although he does not consciously or maliciously produce these symptoms. The pattern is characterized by dramatic and attention-seeking behavior, excitability, emotional instability, overreacting, self centeredness, and provocativeness.

Hysterical symptoms are among the most difficult to diagnose and should be treated as ordinary genuine complaints. In hysterical attacks, rest and quiet are essential. Meprobamate 200 mg. t.i.d. or q.i.d. is useful. Valium 5 mg. t.i.d. or q.i.d. is used as an alternate.

INDIGESTION (HEARTBURN)

A symptom complex including nausea, heartburn, upper abdominal pain, flatulence, burping, a sense of fullness and a feeling of abdominal distention, occurring during or after the ingestion of food. (See also Angina Pectoris and Coronary Thrombosis.)

Causes and Symptoms
1. Organic disease in the gastro-intestinal tract.
2. Eating too much or too rapidly.
3. Inadequate mastication (perhaps due to poor dentition).
4. Eating during emotional upsets or during severe mental strain.
5. Swallowing large amounts of air.
6. Excessive smoking.
7. Constipation.
8. Ingestion of poorly cooked foods.
9. Nausea and vomiting.

Treatment—Mild cases recover in 24 hours or less and require no treatment beyond one or two doses of an effervescent alkaline powder (Alka-Seltzer). An effervescent saline cathartic, such as Sal Hepatica, is effective. Baking soda is also suggested. In severe cases, withhold all food for 24 hours, giving only small sips of water, plus one of the two medications mentioned above.

INFLUENZA (LA GRIPPE)

Incubation—1 - 3 days.

Segregation—None.

Prevention—An upper respiratory infection involving nose, throat and the upper portions of the lungs, perhaps due to a virus. It often occurs in epidemics. Influenza vaccine may modify or prevent an attack.

Symptoms—Sudden onset, with or without a chill, rise in temperature, sore throat, generalized aches and pains in bones and muscles, and headache. Occassionally there is nausea and vomiting. Symptoms persist for 2 - 5 days, then gradually subside, leaving patient very weak and fatigued.

Treatment—Mainly absolute bed rest until temperature is normal. Isolate the patient. Give Epsom salts—2 level teaspoons in 8 oz. of warm water. Aspirin gr. 10 q. 4 hours relieves aches and helps reduce the temperature. Diet—light and as patient desires.

Isolation—Until temperature is normal.

Port Quarantine—None.

MALARIA

Malaria is a common disease in tropical and semi-tropical countries, caused by the bite of the *Anopheles* mosquito which has fed on an infected person.

Incubation—10 days.

Segregation—None.

Prevention—While in places where malaria exists, take 5 - 10 gr. of quinine daily as a preventive. As an alternative, amodiaquin dihydrochloride dihydrate (Aralen) 400 mg. once a week, taken on the same day. Start before entering malaria country and should be continued until 2 weeks after leaving the area.

Symptoms—Chill, followed by fever, then sweating. Sometimes preceded by headache and vomiting. During chill, temperature may rise to 105°-106°F. Rigor begins gradually and increases until the whole body shakes. Skin is cold and bluish. This stage may last from 10 - 60 minutes. Gradually the hot stage is reached; skin becomes dry and very hot. Face becomes flushed, pulse strong and then usually a severe headache. This stage last from one-half - 2 hours. After the discomfort wears off, patient appears to be well until the next attack, which will be within 24, 48 or 72 hours, depending on the type of malaria.

Treatment—Quinine is a specific remedy for malaria. Safe dosage in acute cases is 30 gr. x d. for 2 weeks, 20 gr. x d. for a month, then reduce to 10 gr. x d. for 2 or 3 months.

Discontinue quinine if these symptoms appear: deafness, ringing in the ears, skin rash, eye trouble, severe pounding in the head.

Rest is essential. Diet as tolerated. Stimulating drinks may be given. Chloroquine diphosphate or sulfate 300 mg. twice a week is found effective.

MEASLES

Incubation—10 - 15 days, usually 12.

Segregation—14 days.

Prevention—A virus transmitted by contact with a patient exposed or ill with the disease. Those who have never had measles are almost certain to contract the disease if they come in direct contact with a measles patient.

One attack usually confers life time immunity. Therefore only those who have had measles may safely take care of a patient. However, measles vaccine is available, so that immunity can be had without an actual attack of the disease.

The danger of measles is that it is often accompanied by bronchitis or bronchal pneumonia, and this must be treated vigorously.

Symptoms—The first symptoms are like a head cold, with sneezing, running of the nose and eyes, headache, cough, and slight fever, 99.5°-100°F (37.5°-37.8°C). Two days after the onset of symptoms, minute, white pin-head-size spots appear on the inside of the lips and cheeks (koplick spots). At this stage the disease is highly contagious. On the third or fourth day, the temperature increases to 102°-104°F (38.9°-40.0°C), and a pink, smooth papular rash appears, beginning behind the ears and on the forehead. The eruption spreads rapidly to the cheeks, neck, chest, abdomen, and extremities and finally to the palms of the hands and soles of the feet. In four or five days, the rash or eruption begins to fade, beginning with the regions where it first appeared. Occasionally some peeling accompanies the disappearance of the rash. The temperature becomes normal, and the symptoms disappear, barring complications.

Treatment—Isolate the patient, and put him to bed. Force fluids, such as water, fruit juices, tea, coffee, and milk. Soft diet is recommended. Keep patient in bed for 3 days after fever has subsided. Aspirin gr. 10 q. 4 hours for headache and discomfort. Otherwise treatment is symptomatic. Itching may be relieved by calamine lotion.

Isolation—7 days after disappearance of rash.

Port Quarantine—None.

MENTAL DISORDERS

While psychotherapy is beyond your scope, it may be necessary to cope with someone with mental abnormalities, ranging from childish immaturity to suicidal tendencies.

Symptoms of Mental Disorder

1. Abnormal or altered behavior observed by others, e.g., a cheerful, likeable person may become irritable and morose; an outgoing person may keep to himself.

2. Complaints of physical or mental disabilities, e.g., dyspepsia, headache, palpitations, "stomach ache," insomnia.

The patient developing an **immature personality** often seems to be incapable of adjusting to new situations and accepting new responsibilities. Such changes in a person's character may be relatively mild, but are sometimes excessive, perhaps giving rise to one or other of the following kinds of insanity:

Mania—The patient is excited, with extraordinary ideas. He may be noisy, wild, indecent, quarrelsome, and often violent.

Depression—Depression is the opposite of mania. The essential symptom is extreme and unreasonable depression which at first may be mild but becomes so severe constant observation is necessary. Precautions to prevent the patient seizing an opportunity to commit suicide need to be taken. The patient may have delusions and think himself unworthy. He may think he has committed some crime and thereby be very anxious and agitated.

Delusions—The patient may have fixed delusions about something without being obviously excited or depressed. He often has a sense of persecution; he thinks he is being watched; that he has an animal inside him; or that he is receiving secret, coded messages, usually with special instructions for him. The patient's conversation and behavior, apart from the delusions, may be reasonable, but he is capable of planning and carrying out vengeance on his supposed persecutors.

Dementia—This is simply loss of mental power, such as poor memory, weak judgment, and loss of self-control. Dementia may occur in old age or in chronic alcoholic cases. The patient may show childish behavior.

Treatment—Whatever the symptoms, NEVER make the mistake of thinking you can predict a reaction or anticipate a move. In dealing with a mentally disturbed patient, do not be dictatorial. Patience, tact, firmness, common sense, and sympathy are required.

If the patient is acutely psychotic (out of touch with reality) or if he is uncommunicative, has delusions, hallucinations, and perhaps suicidal tendencies, he must be closely supervised so that he cannot harm himself. The cabin where he is to be placed should have all furniture removed except the mattress which should be placed on the floor or deck. Remove his belt, tie, and shoe laces.

Restraints only aggravate the condition and should not be used unless necessary. If, however, the patient is violent and combative, restraints may be necessary for his own protection and the protection of others. These may be either folded sheets or towels and should be placed at the ankles, above the knees, under the armpits and about the wrists. Avoid restraints over the chest or abdomen.

Never leave a patient alone with any means of destroying himself or inflicting a wound on others. If the patient is violent, he should be given a sedative. Paraldehyde 4 cc. I.M.; Thorazene 100 mg. I.M.; Vistaril 100 mg. q. 4-6 hours as needed. Contact a physician for advice on drugs to administer prior to and during the evacuation period. With mentally-ill patients, be sure to log the sequence of events, the medications given, and the vital signs as monitored.

MUMPS

Incubation—12-26 days, usually 18.
Segregation—22 days.

Prevention—Mumps is caused by a virus and is spread by direct contact with a patient. One attack of mumps usually immunizes for life. Mumps vaccine is available for protection but not for treatment.

Symptoms—Accompanied by a slight fever, onset is usually sudden with pain and/or stiffness on moving the lower jaw. The patient notices swelling on the side of his face where the salivary glands have now become swollen and tender. One or both sides may be affected. While swelling and fever exist, patient is considered contagious.

In adult males one or both testicles are frequently involved with considerable pain and swelling. This will happen, if it does, about 10 days after mumps begin. In adult females one or both ovaries are frequently involved with considerable pain in the lower abdomen. The pancreas (in the upper abdomen) may be involved or inflamed, about a week after the onset, causing severe abdominal pain, above the umbilicus.

Treatment—Isolate the patient with complete bed rest with a fluid or soft diet. If the testicles are involved, support by a jock strap or a small pillow. Use only warm applications to the testicles. If the ovaries are involved, apply ice bags to the lower abdomen. Ice bags are comforting to the cheek swellings also. Isolation ends when the fever and swelling have subsided for 48 hours. Aspirin gr. 10, q. 4 hours for relief of pain and discomfort.

Isolation—3 weeks.

Port Quarantine—None.

PNEUMONIA

Incubation—24-48 hours.

Segregation—7 days.

Prevention—In most cases pneumonia is preceded by an upper respiratory infection or what seems to be a head cold. If treated within the first one to three days, 90 to 95 percent are cured. Patient may carry germs in nose and throat or the patient may have had direct contact. Pneumonia often is a complication of measles.

Symptoms—Usually begins abruptly with severe chills, followed by rapidly rising temperature. The face is flushed and has an anxious look. Patient complains of headache and generalized aching and malaise. Breathing is hurried. Temperature 103°-105°F (39.4°-40.6°C); pulse rate 110 - 130. Cough is dry at first, persistent and patient develops a sticky sputum.

Treatment—Keep the patient in bed. Force fluids, may have a semi-soft diet. Patient should have constant nursing. He may breathe easier if he is propped up in bed. Give crystalline penicillin G 300,000 U I.M. q. 12 hours for 4 days, or tetracycline 250 mg. q. 6 hours for 4 days. Distressing cough may be relieved by elixir Benadryl teaspoonful q. 3-4 hours or elixir terpin hydrate with codeine as a substitute. Aspirin gr. 10 q. 4 hours will ease aches, help combat fever and aid general discomfort. Keep patient in bed until temperature is normal for 2 or 3 days. Convalescence is slow.

Isolation—3 days after temperature is normal.

Port Quarantine—None.

RADIATION EXPOSURE

1. Visible contamination should be removed at once by washing or wiping with towels which should then be thrown overboard.

2. Wash the patient thoroughly and all over with a gentle stream of water while the patient lathers himself over and over. Dilution is the greatest factor at this point.

3. Wash eyes with a gentle stream of plain water.

4. Isolate the patient. He may still be radioactive enough to contaminate shipmates.

5. Radio for medical advice as soon as possible.

RASH

A change in the normal condition of the skin. (See also Chicken Pox and Measles.) Possible causes and treatment as follows:

Chapping and/or **Chilblains**—Due to exposure of the skin to cold winds, salt water, or washing in cold water without adequate drying. Cracks appear on the backs of the hands, feet, toes, lips, and ears.

Treatment—Protect hands, feet, ears, and face as much as possible. Dry hands thoroughly. Neomycin and Bacitracin ointment should be applied and rubbed in, as with hand lotion.

Eczema, Contact Dermatitis, Urticaria—Occur in healthy people without any known cause or may be due to contact with irritants found in occupational environment. They may be caused by certain oils in perfumes, poison ivy, or poison oak and from some dyes in fabrics. Also they may be caused by failure to rinse out detergents. At first there is a reddened area that is hot and itches. The skin then develops minute blisters or vesicles. These burst, help spread the rash, and cause a "weeping rash."

Treatment—Avoid washing the area especially when in the "weeping" stage. Give an anti-allergy remedy such as Pyribenzamine 50 mg. b.i.d., Benadryl 50 mg. b.i.d., or chlor-tri-miton 4 mg. b.i.d. Apply calamine or Caladryl lotion for itching as needed. Kenalog creme or ointment may be applied locally.

Herpes simplex (Shingles)—A painful affliction caused by a virus. It appears as vesicles on the skin along the course of some nerve and can be very painful.

Treatment—Calamine lotion applied locally on the rash. Painting the rash with tincture of benzoin to avoid irritation from air and/or clothing is helpful. For pain, aspirin, gr. 10 q. 4 hours; but add codeine gr. 1/2 q. 4 hours if pain is intense.

Impetigo—A very infectious skin eruption caused by staphylococcus or streptococcus. Consists of one or several red spots which develop into blisters. These blisters break and exude fluid which forms a yellow crust.

Treatment—Avoid contact with other personnel. Tincture of Merthiolate or tincture of iodine applied locally b.i.d. is very effective. Neomycin and Bacitracin are also effective. Keep area covered to avoid exposure to others.

Prickly Heat—Commonly affects persons in tropical climates with a high humidity. There is a macular red rash in the armpits, elbow areas, back of the knees, in the groins or where clothing rubs tightly or is compressed.

Rash will disappear spontaneously if the patient moves to cooler climates. Air conditioned atmosphere will have the same effect.

Avoid any exercise that leads to sweating. Wear loose, porous clothing. Frequent tepid or cool showers are helpful. Dry gently and apply calamine lotion or medicated baby powder.

Ringworm—A skin disease due to a fungus. There is a circle or circles of a reddened area that itches. Minute pimples or vesicles appear. These extend outward, leaving the center apparently healed.

Treatment—Whitfield's Ointment or 5 percent ammoniated mercury ointment applied q.i.d. These, combined with applications of tincture of Merthiolate and/or tincture of iodine are very effective. Exposure to sunlight (ultra violet rays) daily is effective.

SCABIES

A transmissable parasitic skin infection, scabies are characterized by superficial burrows, intense pruritus, and occasionally secondary inflammation. This entity is seldom seen in hygienic environment. Transmitted by intimate contact.

Symptoms—Intense itching, especially at night. The lesions occur on the genitalia. Other common areas are inner surface of the elbows, the axillary folds, umbilicus, folds of the buttocks. In women, under the folds of the breasts. The inflammatory lesions are secondary to the scratching which the patient feels compelled to do.

Treatment—Patient is instructed to take a long (up to 30 minutes) hot shower, using a good soapy lather. He should thoroughly clean the areas affected. Following this, after drying gently, he should apply Eurax, or a lotion containing benzocaine, and benzyl-benzoate from the chin down, covering the entire body. Then don clean clothing. Be sure that there is fresh bed linen. Patient should be isolated for 24 hours as a precaution. No baths during this period. After 24 hours, re-apply Eurax, or the lotion mentioned above, and change all clothing and linen once again. Forty-eight hours after last application the patient should take another hot, cleansing shower. This should assure complete eradication. After this time, calamine lotion may be used as a soothing lotion.

SUNBURN

Do not expose the skin more than a few minutes a day when in a warm or hot climate. When on the beach or in the water, take appropriate intervals in the shade during the first few days when acquiring a sun tan. *Slow and easy.*

Sun tan lotions are useful, but do not prevent or protect from a really bad burn from over exposure in the sun, whether on the beach, in the water, or on the deck of the ship. For a blistering burn, apply Nupercaine ointment.

TETANUS

Incubation—2 - 6 days.

Segregation—Not necessary.

Prevention—Tetanus or lockjaw is a very serious disease and prevention is the best treatment. It is caused by a wound or scratch on the body, thereby introducing a clostridium tetani, usually found in soil and/or manure. Frequently occurs in ships carrying livestock. The disease is characterized by painful muscular contractions which start in the jaw and neck muscles.

Treatment—Clean the wound well, and apply an antiseptic. Give a booster injection of tetanus anti-toxin (1.0 cc.). For painful muscular contractions give morphine 15 mg. by injection q. 6 hours. Seek immediate advice by radio.

Isolation—Until recovery.

Port Quarantine—None.

TOOTHACHE

Caused by decay of a tooth, by a tooth abscess, or by gingivitis (inflammation of the gums).

Prevention—Teeth should be checked regularly by patient's dentist.

Treatment—This is only a temporary expedient. Apply oil of cloves on a Q-Tip or a piece of cotton. The mouth should be rinsed out with a warm salt solution (teaspoonful of salt to 8 oz. of water) after each meal and at bedtime. Aspirin gr. 10 q. 4-6 hours may be given for pain. If the pain worsens and there is throbbing and swelling of the face or jaw, give penicillin 250 mg. q.i.d. for 4 days.

TYPHOID FEVER (ENTERIC FEVER)

Incubation—7 - 14 days.

Segregation—14 days.

Prevention—Typhoid fever is caused by drinking water or eating food containing the typhoid bacilli. It is a constant source of danger to seamen and travelers. Avoid all food and drink served by dirty-looking people. Stall restaurants, food stands in bazaars, and similar establishments are suspect. Water from questionable sources should be boiled. All food should be cooked. Avoid iced drinks because the water from which the ice is made may be contaminated. All travelers should have typhoid and para-typhoid immunization injections.

Symptoms—At first the patient feels off-color and apathetic. He may have a headache, poor appetite, and vague discomfort. Soon the patient develops a high, continuous fever lasting from 3 to 5 weeks. Stools are offensive, sometimes bloody and greenish in color, and usually not formed, "diarrhealike." The patient develops a rash which appears at first as faint rose-colored spots on the abdomen. He becomes emaciated and dehydrated and may be too weak to turn himself over in bed.

Treatment—Strict confinement to bed from the start. Careful nursing is essential. Force fluids and a soft diet if desired. If dehydrated, give 1 liter of 5 percent dextrose in normal saline solution or Ringer's lactate I.V. Continue this until patient is able to take adequate amount of fluids by mouth. Chloramphenicol 4 capsules, q. 8 hours, for 4 days, or until temperature is normal; then 2 capsules q. 8 hours for 14 days. After temperature reaches normal, keep patient on soft food for 7-10 days. Urine and stools of patient should be passed into a disinfectant.

Isolation—Variable. Until declared free from infection by bacteriological exam.

Port Quarantine—None.

TYPHUS FEVER

Incubation—6 - 15 days, usually 12 days.

Segreation—14 days.

Prevention—Typhus fever is carried by lice and is spread very easily in overcrowded conditions. If it breaks out on shipboard, all clothing and baggage should be fumigated. Patient's clothing should be sterilized by heat and liberally sprinkled with an insecticide powder.

Symptoms—Usually begins suddenly with chills followed by fever, vomiting, and headache. Temperature may reach 104°-105°F (40.0°-40.6°C). The patient becomes prostrated and may be confused and delirious. About the fifth day a rash, as dusky red spots, giving the skin a blotchy appearance, appears on the front of the body, spreading to the back and the limbs. The disease lasts 2 - 3 weeks. The temperature then falls, and recovery is rapid.

Treatment—Isolate the patient. Sprinkle his clothing, particularly his under-clothing, with an insecticide powder. Force fluids and give frequent small feedings of soft diet. Chloramphenicol, 2 capsules q. 4 hours until temperature becomes normal and then one day more. Tetracycline 500 mg. q. 4 hours may be used also. If the patient is seen to have lice in his hair or on his body, cut the hair, burn it, and then use an insecticide on his body. Convalescence is slow and protracted.

Isolation—3 days after the temperature is normal.

Port Quarantine—14 days.

ULCERS (GASTRIC OR DUODENAL)

Some people suffer from chronic indigestion. If the pain in the upper part of the abdomen has a regular relation to the time of meals, and/or is eased by small amounts of food, only to return later, an ulcer should be suspected.

Treatment—Bed rest is preferable. Diet consists of small drinks of milk, every 2 hours and gradully increases to porridge, cereals, toast, weak tea, eggs (poached) and cheese. Fried foods and fatty foods, strong tea, coffee, spiced food are prohibited. Alcohol and smoking will only aggravate the condition. An anti-acid, such as a combination of aluminum hydroxide and magnesium trisilicate (Maalox or Gelusil, for example) may be alternated with the milk. Phenobarbital gr. 1/2 q.i.d. is useful in allaying tenseness.

Complications

1. The ulcer may penetrate a blood vessel in the wall of the stomach, causing an internal hemorrhage. The patient will then vomit blood.

2. The ulcer may penetrate through the wall of the stomach causing perforation and peritonitis.

In either of these events start an intravenous solution on the patient (any will do), and radio for advice.

UNDULANT FEVER (BRUCELLOSIS)

Incubation—2 - 3 weeks.

Segregation—Unnecessary.

Prevention—Undulant fever is a widespread disease attacking both humans and animals. In humans it is seldom conveyed from one person to another but is generally contracted by drinking raw milk or other products from dairy cattle infected with the organism. Goats or goat milk are not excluded.

Symptoms—There are feverish periods of from 10 - 12 days with a temperature up to 104°F (40.0°C) followed by periods of 6 - 8 days without fever. It may be confused with tuberculosis, typhoid fever, and malaria. Patient will not appear to be acutely ill. There is some irritability, weakness, headache and malaise. Diagnosis can be made by following the temperature course.

Treatment—Patient should be isolated. His feeding utensils should be sterilized. Treat the symptoms as they arise. Diet—as the patient chooses. Aspirin gr. 10 q. 4 - 6 hours as indicated for headache and malaise.

Prevention—This disease can readily be prevented by boiling all milk taken on board the vessel while abroad.

Isolation—During the illness.

Port Quarantine—None.

VENEREAL DISEASE

Of the many venereal diseases we will discuss the most common: Gonorrhea, Syphilis, Chancroid, Trichomonas Vaginalis, and Herpes Venerealis.

Venereal diseases can be prevented. Of course, the surest way is to abstain from sexual activity. If you should participate, the best method to help prevent venereal disease is to:

1. *Immediately* get up and wash *thoroughly* with soap and hot water.

2. Urinate.

Other aids which also may help include the use of condoms and/or vaginal creams. These are not foolproof, and soap and hot water should be used also.

All venereal diseases can be treated and, with very few exceptions, can be cured completely. The worst thing anyone can do is to ignore the signs and symptoms of venereal disease. In doing so, extremely serious medical problems can come about—sterility, arthritis, heart trouble, brain damage, to name a few.

Gonorrhea (Clap, Strain, Dose, Morning Drop, Drip, G.C.)—The symptoms in the male are usually burning during urination and a discharge containing pus. The burning is most prevalent with the first urination in the morning but may occur with each urination. The puslike discharge will be more noticeable prior to the first morning urination. In the female, there may or may not be a mild burning on urination. There is usually a foul uterine discharge. Later, an infection of the uterus and tubes may cause severe abdominal pain. These symptoms, in both male and female, usually appear about 10 days after sexual contact.

The recommended treatment of gonorrhea is penicillin, 4,800,000 U (divided into two (2) shots) given in the buttocks. This single treatment should be all that is needed to completely cure gonorrhea. The patient should abstain from all sexual contact for a period of 14 days. If an allergy to penicillin is present, 500 mgm. of tetracycline, q.i.d. for 14 days is recommended. The patient should abstain from sexual contact for a period of 21 days.

Syphilis—Syphilis is a progressive venereal disease, that evolves by stages. In order to obtain a positive diagnosis of syphilis, a blood test must be completed.

First or Early Stage (Bad Blood, Siff, Haircut, Old Joe, Lues)—The symptoms of the first stage usually are a painless ulcer or chancre on or about the sex organs. These can appear anywhere on the body where contact has been made with an infected person. The chancre will usually disappear with or without treatment. Frequently, the chancre stage is not noticeable. The chancre normally appears 10 - 90 days after sexual contact.

Second or Middle Stage (Bad Blood, Pox, Siff, Old Joe, Lues)—The symptoms of the second stage can vary from a fever, sore throat, patches of baldness, to a rash over the entire body. The important difference between this rash and any other is that the syphilitic rash is present on the palms of the hands and the soles of the feet. Syphilitic rash usually appears 3 - 6 weeks after the chancre of the first stage disappears.

Third or Late Stage (General Paralysis of the Insane, Vascular Lues, Neuro Lues)—The symptoms of the third stage are varied and numerous. This is why syphilis has been called "the Great Pretender." In this stage the heart, brain, spinal cord, and/or muscles can be involved. They can all be involved or can be singly involved. Any of the following may occur:

Heart Trouble (heart attack).

Paralysis from muscle or spinal cord involvement.

Brain disease ranging from a "personality disorder" to "insanity."

These symptoms usually appear from 1 - 20 years after the first stage.

Treatment—The treatment and cure of syphilis depends on when it is discovered. The earlier it is diagnosed and treated, the better the chances for a complete cure. In the first and second stages, the chances for a complete cure are excellent. As the third stage progresses, the chances of a complete cure lessen, but treatment can arrest the progress of the disease.

A total of 7,200,000 U of Bicillin penicillin should be given. This should consist of three (3) separate shots of 2,400,000 U every five (5) days. If an allergy to penicillin exists, either tetracycline or erthromycin, 500 mgm. q.i.d. for twenty (20) days. Abstaining from sexual activity is a must.

Chancroid (Soft Chancre)—The symptoms are painful, ulcerating sores on the sex organs called chancres. Unlike the chancre of syphilis, this chancres will be painful and will weep a puslike discharge. These are later accompanied by tender, swollen glands in the groin. The most common sites of the chancres in the male are on the edge of the foreskin, the groove just behind the head of the penis, and the base of the shaft of the penis. In the female, the chancres normally appear on the external lips of the vagina. Unlike the chancre of syphilis, the chancres in chancroid are generally multiple.

In treating chancroid, the ulcer should be thoroughly cleaned with soap and water daily. The ulcer should also be soaked for 20 - 30 minutes q.i.d. with a saline solution (2 teaspoonsful of salt to a quart of water).

If the patient is not allergic to sulfa drugs, give Sulfisoxazole 1000 mgm. (1 gm.), q.i.d. until the lesions are completely healed. *Remember*: when taking any sulfa drug, it is very important to drink copious amounts of water.

If allergic to sulfa drugs, administer 500 mgm. of tetracycline q.i.d. until the lesions are completely healed.

Trichomonas Vaginalis—By the name of this disease, one may think that it is a disease of only the female. It is NOT. Both the male and female can contact and carry this disease. This is a protozoan (unicellular organism) infection of the vagina and/or cervix of the female and in the bladder and urethra of the male. In the female there can be a "frothy" and foul smelling discharge. There may also be an itching sensation in the vagina. The male is normally free from symptoms, except he may have a slight burning or tingling sensation when urinating.

The most important thing to remember in treating this disease is that both the male *and* female MUST be treated at the same time. This is true even though no symptoms are present in the male. If you should treat the female and not the male, you will cure her, only to have her reinfected when she has sexual relations with her male partner again.

The above statement does not mean that the female is the culprit. It is simply that the male is usually symptom-free, and the diagnosis is nearly always made from a specimen from the female. Consequently, if the male is not treated, he will reinfect the female.

The drug of choice is Flagl, 250 mgm. q.i.d. for 10 days. During this period sexual acitivities should be eliminated.

Herpes Venerealis—An irritating rash, usually circumscribed (localized), containing minute punctate red areas, similar in appearance to Poison Ivy or to Poison Oak, found on the penis in men and in and around the vagina (the labia, or "lips of the vagina") in women. The affected area itches and so demands attention. Because of the location, fear of having been infected with Gonorrhea or Syphilis is aroused. Other areas, non-venereal, often appear. For example, the affected area, when seen on the lips of the mouth, also is irritating. Here, it is called a "Cold Sore." When these red areas appear along the rib cage, or on the forehead, with the usual punctate red areas, it is called "Shingles." When fear of a breast tumor is indicated by tenderness near the breast, this same syndrome is known as "Tietze's Disease" (after a Dr. Tietze). The virus that causes this discomfort is actually the Herpes Simplex Type I, but more usually, Type II.

Incubation—2 - 8 days.

Symptoms—Itching sensation in the area affected, which, when examined, will show the rash (as above). This may be accompanied by a low grade fever (99.4°-100.6°). In both men and women, there is usually a burning on urination. The course of the affliction lasts about 10 days.

Treatment—Wash the afflicted area, gently, with warm water and soap. Dry. Apply a hydrocortisone cream, 0.5 to 1.0%, or Triamcinolone Acetonide Cream 0.025% locally, 3 or 4 times x.d. Reassure the patient. Urge him to be checked for both Gonorrhea and Syphilis, when he returns to home port.

Prevention—In Herpes Venerealis, abstain from intercourse. Males afflicted with the rash should be cautioned to use a condom. For females, there is nothing that can protect them from acquiring it or transmitting it, if they are afflicted.

Port Quarantine—None.

Virus vaccines are being developed. However, these are not practical for use in treatment aboard ship.

WHOOPING COUGH (PERTUSSIS)

Incubation—7 - 21 days.

Segregation—21 days.

Prevention—Whooping cough or pertussis is caused by a coccobacillus. It is a droplet infection acquired by contact when a patient coughs or sneezes. One attack gives life-time immunity. Vaccines are available for prevention but not for treatment.

Symptoms—Starts as a head cold or bronchitis. The "whoop" is caused by sharp inhalation after a paroxysm of coughing. There is bronchial tree spasm.

Treatment—Isolate the patient. He should be cared for by those who are immune. Complete rest and a nutritious diet are important. Medicated steam inhalations are helpful, using tincture of benzoin, a pinch of menthol crystals, or eucalyptus.

For the cough—Elixir Benadryl or elixir terpin hydrate, a teaspoonful q. 3 - 5 hours as needed. Medicated lozenges are helpful.

Isolation—4 weeks.

Port Quarantine—None.

YELLOW FEVER

Incubation—3 - 6 days.

Segregation—6 days.

Prevention—Serious and often fatal disease caused by the bite of the mosquito *Stegomyia* which has fed on an infected person. It is apt to occur in tropical and subtropical countries. All countries in yellow fever infected territory require persons to be inoculated against the disease. A single inoculation lasts 10 years. Mosquito repellant on the skin is useful but not prevention-proof.

Symptoms—Sudden onset. The patient suffers from shivering and heat flushes alternately. Fever up to 105°F (40.6°C). Headache and backache are severe. There is tenderness and nausea in the pit of the stomach (upper abdomen). After a day or two vomiting occurs, tinged with bile and blood—"black-vomit."

Stomach pains increase, and the patient becomes constipated. About the fourth day the skin and eyes become yellow (jaundiced). There may be some delirium. After the fifth or sixth day the symptoms may abate, and the temperature may fall. This is the critical period.

Treatment—Isolate the patient. Give an enema every 12 hours of 2 pints of water containing 2 teaspoonsful of salt. Sponge baths while the temperature lasts. During the first 3 or 4 days, give only fluids, up to 2 quarts (2.114 liters) a day.

Convalescence is slow and solid food should be given with great caution. Intravenous solutions of 1 liter of 5 percent dextrose in normal saline (or Ringer's solution or 1/6 molar lactate) should be given continuously until patient can retain fluids.

There is no specific remedy for Yellow Fever. Compazene 5 mg. to 10 mg. orally, or I.M., or rectally q. 4 - 6 hours to alleviate nausea and vomiting.

Isolation—6 days.

Port Quarantine—6 days.

MEDICAL RELIEF FOR SEAMEN

The following excerpts from TITLE 42, U.S. CODE *Chapter 1 Public Health Service, U.S. Department of Health, Education, and Welfare: Part 32— Medical Care for Seamen and Certain Other Persons* states the requirements which must be met by American seamen in order to be provided medical services by the United States Public Health Service (USPHS).

§32.6   Persons eligible. (a) Under this part the following persons are entitled to care and treatment by the Service as hereinafter prescribed:

1. Seamen employed on vessels of the United States registered, enrolled, or licensed under the maritime laws thereof, other than canal boats engaged in the coasting trade, hereinafter designated as American seamen;

2. Seamen employed on United States or foreign flag vessels as employees of the United States;

3. Seamen, not enlisted or commissioned in the military or naval establishments, who are employed on State school ships or on vessels of the United States Government of more than five tons burden;

4. Seamen on vessels of the Mississippi River Commission;

5. Officers and crew members of vessels of the Fish and Wildlife Service;

6. Enrollees in the United States Maritime Service on active duty and members of the Merchant Marine Cadet Corps;

7. Cadets at State maritime academies or on State training ships;

8. Seamen-trainees while participating in maritime training programs to develop or enhance their employability in the maritime industry;

9. Seamen on foreign flag vessels other than those seamen employed on foreign flag vessels specified in subparagraph (2) of this paragraph;

10. Non-beneficiaries for temporary treatment and care in case of emergency;

11. Persons who own vessels registered, enrolled, or licensed under the maritime laws of the United States, who are engaged in commercial fishing operations, and who acompany such vessels on such fishing operations, and a substantial part of whose services in connection with such fishing operations are comparable to services performed by seamen employed on such vessel or on vessels engaged in similar operations.

AMERICAN SEAMEN

§32.11 Scope of benefits. (a) American seamen shall, on presenting evidence of eligibility, be entitled to medical, surgical, and dental treatment or hospitalization at medical care facilities operated by the Service or, in accordance with these regulations, at Service contract medical facilities at the expense of the Service.

(b) Where medical facilities of the Service are not available, medical care and services may be obtained from contract medical providers designated by the Service. Expenses for medical care and services obtained from non-Service providers or in non-Service facilities not arranged for by the Service in behalf of seamen is not an obligation of the Service and will not be paid.

§32.12 Provision of services. (a) When a seaman requires medical, surgical and dental treatment or hospitalization which the Service is unable to provide in the local Service operated facility, or in the case of an emergency, arrangements for such medical, surgical, and dental treatment or hospitalization at the expense of the Service shall be made by an authorizing official.

(b) If eligibility cannot be established at the time of application by the seaman or by the person who applies in his behalf, the applicant shall be notified that the authorization for treatment is conditional and the payment of reasonable expenses by the Service for such treatment shall be subject to proof of eligibility.

(c) The authorizing official shall keep himself informed regarding the progress of the case in order that treatment or hospitalization shall not be unnecessarily prolonged.

§32.13 Application for treatment. (a) In nonemergency cases, a sick or disabled seaman, in order to obtain the benefits of the Service, must apply in person, or by proxy if too sick to do so, to an authorizing official as specified in §32.12, and must furnish satisfactory evidence of his eligibility for such benefits.

(b) In emergency cases, a sick or disabled seaman shall, upon admission for such condition or as soon thereafter as is practicable under the circumstances, either personally or by proxy, notify the nearest authorizing official of the fact of such admission and treatment and shall furnish appropriate identification and satisfactory evidence of eligibility for such benefits.

§32.14 Evidence of eligibility. (a) As evidence of his eligibility a seaman must present a properly executed Master's Certificate, or a continuous discharge book, or a certificate of discharge, showing that he has been employed on a registered, enrolled, or licensed vessel of the United States. The certificate of the owner or accredited commercial agent of a vessel as to the facts of the employment of any seaman on said vessel may be accepted in lieu of the Master's Certificate where the latter is not procurable. When an applicant cannot furnish any of the foregoing documents, his certification as to the facts of his most recent (including his last) employment as a seaman, stating names of vessels and dates of service, may be accepted as evidence in support of his eligibility. Documentary evidence of eligibility, excepting continuous discharge books and certificates of discharge, shall be filed at the medical care facility of the Service where application is made. Where continuous discharge books and certificates of discharge are submitted as evidence of eligibility, the pertinent information shall be abstracted therefrom, certified by the officer accepting the application, and filed at the station.

(b) Except as otherwise provided in §§32.11 to 32.23, inclusive, documentary evidence of eligibility must show that the applicant has been employed for 60 days of continuous service on a registered, enrolled, or licensed vessel of the United States, a part of which time must have been during the 180 days immediately preceding application for relief. There may be included as a part of such 60 days of continuous service as a seaman time spent in training as:

1. an active duty enrollee in the United States Maritime Service;
2. a member of the Merchant Marine Cadet Corps;
3. a cadet at a State maritime academy; or
4. a cadet on a State training ship. The phrase "60 days of continuous service" shall not be held to exclude seamen whose papers show brief intermissions between short services that aggregate the required 60 days: Provided, that any such intermission does not exceed 60 days. The time during which a seaman has been treated as a patient of the Service shall not be considered as absence from the vessel in determining eligibility. When the seamen's service on his last vessel is less than 60 days, his oath or affirmation as to previous service may be accepted.

§32.15 *Sickness or injury while employed.* A seaman taken sick or injured on board or ashore when actually employed on a vessel shall be entitled to care and treatment without regard to length of service.

§32.16 *Seamen from wrecked vessels.* Seamen taken from wrecked vessels of the United States and returned to the United States, if sick or disabled at the time of their arrival in the United States, shall be entitled to care and treatment without regard to length of service.

§32.17 *Lapse of more than 180 days since last service.* (a) Where more than 180 days have elapsed since an applicant's last service as a seaman, he will no longer be eligible for benefits from the Service: *Provided,* That if he can show that he has not definitely changed his occupation, such period of time shall not exclude him from receiving care and treatment (1) if due in whole or in part to closure of navigation or economic conditions resulting in decreased shipping with consequent lack of opportunity to ship, or (2) if he provides satisfactory evidence that he has been under continuous medical supervision and treatment at other than Service expense for a condition which occurred or arose during any period of treatment at a Service facility or at Service expense.

(b) Where a seaman receives care and treatment by the Service or at Service expense during a period of eligibility for a condition or illness which requires, in the opinion of the attending physician, continuing and recurring care and treatment on a regular and frequent basis, such periods of continuing and recurring care and treatment whether obtained privately by the seaman or at Service facilities or Service expense shall not be included in the computation of the 180 day period above.

§32.18 *Procedure in case of doubtful eligibility.* When a reasonable doubt exists as to the eligibility of an applicant for service, the matter shall be referred immediately to the appropriate authorizing official or Hospital Director for decision. If, in the opinion of such person the applicant's condition is such that immediate care and treatment is necessary, temporary care and treatment shall be given pending the decision as to eligibility.

§32.19 *False document evidencing service.* The issue or presentation of a false document as evidence of service with intent to produce the treatment of a person as a seaman shall be immediately reported to the Headquarters of the Service.

§32.20 *Treatment during voyage.* The Service shall not be liable for expenses incurred during the voyage for the care of sick and disabled seamen.

§32.21 *Care while in custody.* Seamen shall not be provided treatment at the expense of the Service while in police custody.

§*32.22 Reconsideration of eligibility denial.* A decision of the authorizing official or Hospital Director denying eligibility shall be communicated to the seaman in writing, shall set forth the reasons therefor, and shall state that such decision may be reconsidered by the Secretary upon written request setting forth the facts in support of such request.

§*32.23 Certificate of discharge from treatment.* A certificate of discharge from treatment may, at the discretion of the officer in charge, be given to a hospital patient, but such certificate, when presented at another medical care facility shall not be taken as establishing the seaman's eligibility for further care and treatment, but may be considered in connection with other documentary evidence of eligibility submitted by the seaman.

SEAMEN: STATE SCHOOL SHIPS AND VESSELS OF THE UNITED STATES GOVERNMENT

§*32.46 Conditions and extent of treatment.* Seamen, not enlisted or commissioned in the military naval establishments, who are employed on State school ships, on vessels of the United States Government of more than five tons burden, or on vessels of the Mississippi River commission or of the Fish and Wildlife Service, shall be entitled to care and treatment by the Service under the same conditions, where applicable, and to the same extent as is provided for American seamen.

OWNER-OPERATORS OF COMMERCIAL FISHING VESSELS

§*32.57 Conditions and extent of treatment.* Persons who own vessels registered, enrolled, or licensed under the maritime laws of the United States, who are engaged in commercial fishing operations, and who accompany such vessels on such fishing operations, and a substantial part of whose services in connection with such fishing operations are comparable to services performed by seamen employed on such vessel or on vessels engaged in similar operations shall be entitled to care and treatment by the Service under the same conditions, where applicable, and to the same extent as is provided for American seamen.

MARITIME SERVICE ENROLLEES AND MERCHANT MARINE CADETS

§*32.61 Use of Service facilities.* (a) Enrollees in the United States Maritime Service on active duty and member of the Merchant Cadet Corps shall, upon written request of the responsible officer of the station or training ship to which such enrollees or cadets are attached, identifying the applicant, be entitled to medical, surgical, and dental treatment or hospitalization at medical care facilities of the Service or at Service expense. Whenever an enrollee or cadet applies for care without the above-mentioned written request and in the opinion of the responsible Service officer the applicant's condition is such that immediate care and treatment is necessary, temporary care and treatment shall be given pending verification of the applicant's status as an enrollee or cadet.

(b) If eligibility cannot be established at the time of application by the enrollee or cadet or by the person who applies in his behalf, the applicant shall be notified that the authorization for treatment is conditional and that the payment of reasonable expenses by the Service for such treatment shall be subject to proof of eligibility.

(c) The authorizing officer shall keep himself informed regarding the progress of the case in order that treatment or hospitalization shall not be unnecessarily prolonged.

§*32.62 Injury while in custody.* Enrollees on active duty or cadets shall not be provided treatment at the expense of the Service while in police custody.

§*32.63 Absence without leave.* Enrollees on active duty or cadets shall not be entitled, when absent without leave, to receive medical care except at a medical care facility of the Service or under contract to the Service.

CADETS AT STATE MARITIME ACADEMIES OR ON STATE TRAINING SHIPS

§32.76   *Conditions and extent of treatment.* Cadets at State maritime academies or on State training ships shall be entitled to care and treatment by the Service under the same conditions and to the same extent as is provided for American seamen. Provided, however, that the written request of the superintendent or other responsible officer of an academy, including the Master of a training ship, shall be accepted in lieu of the documentary evidence of eligibility required of American seamen.

SEAMEN ON FOREIGN FLAG VESSELS

§32.106   *Conditions and extent of treatment; rates; burial.* (a) Seamen on foreign flag vessels may, when suitable accommodations are available and on application of the Master, owner, or agent of the vessel, be provided treatment at medical care facilities of the Service at rates prescribed by the Secretary.

(b) Upon application, the Service may assist in arranging for private hospitalization of such seamen or private services in connection with their treatment at the expense of the Master, owner, or agent of the vessel.

(c) If any such seaman dies while receiving treatment by the Service, the expenses of burial shall be paid directly to the vendors by the Master, owner, or agent.

U.S. PUBLIC HEALTH SERVICE HOSPITALS AND OUTPATIENT CLINICS

The U.S. Public Health Service operates eight hospitals and 30 outpatient clinics which provide emergency and followup general medical care for eligible merchant seamen:

HOSPITALS

Baltimore, Maryland 21211	3100 Wyman Park Drive
Boston, Mass. 02135	77 Warren Street
Nassau Bay, Texas 77058	2050 Space Park Drive
New Orleans, La. 70118	210 State Street
Norfolk, Virginia 23508	6500 Hampton Blvd.
San Francisco, Calif. 94118	15th Ave. and Lake St.
Seattle, Washington 98144	1131 14th Ave. So.
Staten Island, N.Y. 10304	Bay St. and Vanderbilt Ave.

OUTPATIENT CLINICS

Atlanta, Georgia 30333	1600 Clifton Road, N.E.
Balboa Heights, Canal Zone	--
Buffalo, New York 14203	50 High Street, Rm. 609
Charleston, S.C. 29403	214 Fed. Bldg., 334 Meeting St.
Charlotte Amalie	U.S. Federal Office Bldg.
Virgin Islands 00801	Veterans Blvd.
Chicago, Illinois 60605	1439 S. Michigan Avenue
Cincinnati, Ohio 45202	P.O. and Courthouse Bldg.
	5th and Walnut Sts.
Cleveland, Ohio 44113	New P.O. Bldg., West 3rd St.
	and Prospect Ave.

Detroit, Michigan 48215	14700 Riverside Drive
Galveston, Texas 77550	4400 Avenue N
Honolulu, Hawai 96807	591 Ala Moana Boulevard
Houston, Texas 77002	204 U.S. Customs Building
	701 San Jacinto St.
Jacksonville, Fla. 32201	P.O. Bldg., Suite 118
	311 W. Monroe St.
Juneau, Alaska 99801	Bartlett Mem. Hosp.
	419-6th Street
Memphis, Tennessee 38104	969 Madison Ave.
Miami, Florida 33130	51 S.W. 1st Ave., Rm. 712
Mobile, Alabama 36602	125 Federal Bldg.
New York, N.Y. 10014	245 West Houston St.
Philadelphia, Pa 19106	U.S. Custom House, Rm. 700
	2nd and Chestnut Streets
Pittsburgh, Pa. 15219	U.S. Post Office and Courthouse
	7th Ave. and Grant St.
Port Arthur, Texas 77640	Fed. Office Building, Rm. 209
	5th St. and Austin Ave.
Portland, Maine 04103	331 Veranda St.
Portland, Oregon 97205	220 Courthouse
	Broadway and Main St.
St. Louis, Missouri 63103	1520 Market St.
San Diego, Calif. 92101	2105 Fifth Ave.
San Juan, Puerto Rico 00904	8 1/2 Fernandez Juncos Ave.
San Pedro, Calif. 90731	825 S. Beacon St.
Savannah, Georgia 31401	1602 Drayton Street
Tampa, Florida 33601	601 Florida Ave.
Washington, D.C. 20201	Switzer Bldg.
	4th and C Sts., S.W.

NOTE

Except in wartime when radio silence is imposed on ships at sea the Master can and should radio the U.S. Public Health Service for medical advice when it is needed.

A merchant seaman can obtain information on the location of the nearest U.S. Public Health Service hospital or clinic by dialing one of the following toll free telephone numbers:

AC 800 - 231-SHIP from anywhere except Texas.

AC 800 - 392-SHIP from Texas.

CHAPTER XIX

RULES OF THE ROAD

> A collision at sea can ruin your entire day.
> —*Anon.*

MANY LANDSMEN AND SMALL BOAT OWNERS think that a vessel underway on the high seas or in a harbor can respond to every whim of its owner or master and still be operated safely and legally. A seaman realizes this is not true and understands that just as his car must observe traffic regulations on city streets and freeways, so must his ship obey certain laws and regulations when underway. However, there is far more complexity to the laws and regulations a vessel must observe than there is to the relatively simple traffic laws enacted by cities and states. Furthermore, the headlines of newspapers remind us with disturbing frequency that the consequences of ignoring the Rules of the Road afloat are far more serious than disregarding a traffic regulation ashore. The loss of life and property will be far greater as the collision of the *Andrea Doria* and the *Stockholm* indicated.

Some complexity of the Rules of the Road is due to the fact that there are essentially two different "rules" to be observed depending upon the location of your vessel. If you are on the high seas, you are subject to the International Rules, known as the *International Regulations for Preventing Collisions at Sea, 1972* (72 COLREGS), in force since 1977. If you are in New York Harbor or San Francisco Bay, on the Mississippi River or the Great Lakes, you are subject to the new Unified Inland Rules.

There are still many older masters who remember the Rules of the Road examination they took for their original third mate's license. There were only two questions. The first: "Write the International Rules;" the second: "Write the Inland Rules." The applicant who could not do this verbatim did not get his license. Although this is no longer required, an individual who does not thoroughly understand the International, Inland, and pertinent Pilot Rules will not receive his license. This is as it should be. Human life is irreplaceable.

HISTORY OF THE RULES OF THE ROAD

The International Rules go back more than 100 years when France and England adopted a set of rules to govern the conduct of vessels on the high seas. In 1864 the United States adopted a similar set. This led to a conference of maritime nations in Washington, D.C., which modified the earlier rules and became effective for United States vessels in 1897. With very little change these rules remained in effect until the 1948 International Conference on Safety of Life at Sea met in London.

Although it was apparent changes were required because of increased size and speed of vessels, comparatively few modifications were made and these rules became effective in 1954. Another conference was held in London in 1960, and in 1965 this version of the rules became effective. Again, there was little basic change although radar was mentioned for the fiirst time.

The most recent International Conference held in London in 1972 made major revisions. A new format was adopted resulting in a completely reorganized set of rules in a form which was far easier to learn and understand. Although the substance of the rules was not greatly changed, some of the archaic provisions were dropped, and the presentation became far more logical. These rules, referred to simply as the 1972 Rules, went into effect on July 15, 1977. They have been acclaimed by mariners as a real contribution to safety on the high seas.

Rule 1(b) of the International Rules authorizes special rules for inland waters connected with the high seas and navigable by seagoing vessels with the proviso that these rules conform as closely as possible to the International Rules. The United States, alone among the leading seafaring nations, has enacted a complete set of rules the mariner must learn in addition to the International Rules. In late 1981 a new body of U.S. Inland Rules became effective. These replaced the older and sometimes archaic Inland Rules which had been in force since the turn of the century. Although the new Rules are modeled on the International Rules and are frequently identical, there are distinct differences in the use of whistle signals and in navigation lights of which the mariner must be aware. As a consequence there is no shortcut or easy way to master the Rules of the Road. It requires application and effort.

LEARNING THE RULES OF THE ROAD

Occasionally texts appear which present an "abbreviated" or "simplified" version of the Rules of the Road. Although these texts may have their place, it is our view that an aspiring mariner or cadet who limits himself to studying such a text is doing himself a disservice in preparing for a licensing examination. The primary authority for a study of Rules of the Road in this country is the U.S. Coast Guard *Navigation Rules* (COLREGS), due to be published in 1990 as Commandant Instruction M16672.2B. Formerly distributed free of charge, it is now sold to the public through the Government Printing Office. It is complete with illustrations and comments. To supplement a study of the Rules, *Farwell's Rules of the Nautical Road,* 6th Edition, published in 1982 by the United States Naval Institute is invaluable. In addition to containing the Rules themselves, *Farwell's* furnishes background information and court interpretations which assist the aspiring mariner, as well as the experienced master, with a wealth of information enabling him to observe the Rules more intelligently. Also very helpful is *Nautical Rules of the Road* by Farnsworth and Young, published in 1990 by Cornell Maritime Press. It is compact, prints the International and Inland Rules side by side, and provides an excellent commentary. It is for these reasons we have not tried to duplicate the Rules which are better presented elsewhere. What follows are extracts of the steering and sailing rules, whistle signals for vessels within sight of one another, fog signals, and distress signals. Where it is deemed essential, the Inland Rule follows the corresponding International Rule. In these extracts the emphasis is placed on International Rules. The treatment of lights is limited to Rules 23 and 24 and to a few plates portraying various situations both on the high seas and inland. After reading and digesting these extracts, the serious student, it is stressed, must turn to Commandant Instruction M16672.2B, *Farwell's,* or Farnsworth and Young.

Rule 2—International

RESPONSIBILITY

(a) Nothing in these Rules shall exonerate any vessel, or the owner, master or crew thereof, from the consequences of any neglect to comply with these Rules or of the neglect of any precaution which may be required by the ordinary practice of seamen, or by the special circumstances of the case.

(b) In construing and complying with these Rules due regard shall be had to all dangers of navigation and collision and to any special circumstances, including the limitations of the vessels involved, which may make a departure from these Rules necessary to avoid immediate danger.

STEERING AND SAILING RULES

CONDUCT OF VESSELS IN ANY CONDITION OF VISIBILITY

Rule 4—International

APPLICATION

Rules of this Section apply in any condition of visibility.

Rule 5—International

LOOK-OUT

Every vessel shall at all times maintain a proper look-out by sight and hearing as well as by all available means appropriate in the prevailing circumstances and conditions so as to make a full appraisal of the situation and of the risk of collision.

Rule 7—International

RISK OF COLLISION

(a) Every vessel shall use all available means appropriate to the prevailing circumstances and conditions to determine if risk of collision exists. If there is any doubt such risk shall be deemed to exist.

(b) Proper use shall be made of radar equipment if fitted and operational, including long-range scanning to obtain early warning of risk of collision and radar plotting or equivalent systematic observation of detected objects.

(c) Assumptions shall not be made on the basis of scanty information, especially scanty radar information.

(d) In determining if risk of collision exists the following considerations shall be among those taken into account:

(i) such risk shall be deemed to exist if the compass bearing of an approaching vessel does not appreciably change;

(ii) such risk may sometimes exist even when an appreciable bearing change is evident, particularly when approaching a very large vessel or a tow or when approaching a vessel at close range.

Rule 8—International

ACTION TO AVOID COLLISION

(a) Any action taken to avoid collision shall, if the circumstances of the case admit, be positive, made in ample time and with due regard to the observance of good seamanship.

(b) Any alteration of course and/or speed to avoid collision shall, if the circumstances of the case admit, be large enough to be readily apparent to another vessel observing visually or by radar; a succession of small alterations of course and/or speed should be avoided.

(c) If there is sufficient sea room, alteration of course alone may be the most effective action to avoid a close-quarters situation provided that it is made in good time, is substantial and does not result in another close-quarters situation.

(d) Action taken to avoid collision with another vessel shall be such as to result in passing at a safe distance. The effectiveness of the action shall be carefully checked until the other vessel is finally past and clear.

(e) If necessary to avoid collision or allow more time to assess the situation, a vessel shall slacken her speed or take all way off by stopping or reversing her means of propulsion.

Rule 9—International

NARROW CHANNELS

(a) A vessel proceeding along the course of a narrow channel or fairway shall keep as near to the outer limit of the channel or fairway which lies on her starboard side as is safe and practicable.

(b) A vessel of less than 20 meters in length or a sailing vessel shall not impede the passage of a vessel which can safely navigate only within a narrow channel or fairway.

(c) A vessel engaged in fishing shall not impede the passage of any other vessel navigating within a narrow channel or fairway.

(d) A vessel shall not cross a narrow channel or fairway if such crossing impedes the passage of a vessel which can safely navigate only within such channel or fairway. The latter vessel may use the sound signal prescribed in Rule 34(d) if in doubt as to the intention of the crossing vessel.

(e)(i) In a narrow channel or fairway when overtaking can take place only if the vessel to be overtaken has to take action to permit safe passing, the vessel intending to overtake shall indicate her intention by sounding the appropriate signal prescribed in Rule 34(c)(i). The vessel to be overtaken shall, if in agreement, sound the appropriate signal prescribed in Rule 34(c)(ii) and take steps to permit safe passing. If in doubt she may sound the signals prescribed in Rule 34(d).

Editorial Comment: Rule 34(c)(i) prescribes two prolonged blasts followed by one short blast to mean, "I intend to overtake you on your starboard side" and two prolonged blasts followed by two short blasts to mean, "I intend to overtake you on your port side." Rule 34(d) prescribes the danger signal—5 or more short blasts.

(ii) This Rule does not relieve the overtaking vessel of her obligation under Rule 13.

(f) A vessel nearing a bend or an area of a narrow channel or fairway where other vessels may be obscured by an intervening obstruction shall navigate with particular alertness and caution and shall sound the appropriate signal prescribed in Rule 34(e).

(g) Any vessel shall, if the circumstances of the case admit, avoid anchoring in a narrow channel.

Editorial Comment: **Rule 34(e) prescribes one prolonged blast. Under Inland Rules on the Great Lakes or in Western Rivers a vessel proceeding downbound with a following current has the right-of-way over an upbound vessel.**

Rule 10—International

TRAFFIC SEPARATION SCHEMES

(a) This Rule applies to traffic separation schemes adopted by the Organization.

(b) A vessel using a traffic separation scheme shall:

(i) proceed in the appropriate traffic lane in the general direction of traffic flow for that lane;

(ii) so far as practicable keep clear of a traffic separation line or separation zone;

(iii) normally join or leave a traffic lane at the termination of the lane, but when joining or leaving from the side shall do so at as small an angle to the general direction of traffic flow as practicable.

(c) A vessel shall so far as practicable avoid crossing traffic lanes, but if obliged to do so shall cross as nearly as practicable at right angles to the general direction of traffic flow.

(d) Inshore traffic zones shall not normally be used by through traffic which can safely use the appropriate traffic lane within the adjacent traffic separation scheme.

(e) A vessel, other than a crossing vessel, shall not normally enter a separation zone or cross a separation line except:

(i) in cases of emergency to avoid immediate danger;

(ii) to engage in fishing within a separation zone.

(f) A vessel navigating in areas near the terminations of traffic separation schemes shall do so with particular caution.

(g) A vessel shall so far as practicable avoid anchoring in a traffic separation scheme or in areas near its terminations.

(h) A vessel not using traffic separations scheme shall avoid it by as wide a margin as is practicable.

(i) A vessel engaged in fishing shall not impede the passage of any vessel following a traffic lane.

(j) A vessel of less than 20 meters in length or a sailing vessel shall not impede the safe passage of a power-driven vessel following a traffic lane.

CONDUCT OF VESSELS IN SIGHT OF ONE ANOTHER

Rule 11—International

APPLICATION

Rules in this Section apply to vessels in sight of one another.

Rule 12—International

SAILING VESSELS

(a) When two sailing vessels are approaching one another, so as to involve risk of collision, one of them shall keep out of the way of the other as follows:

(i) when each has the wind on a different side, the vessel which has the wind on the port side shall keep out of the way of the other;

(ii) when both have the wind on the same side, the vessel which is to windward shall keep out of the way of the vessel which is to leeward;

(iii) if a vessel with the wind on the port side sees a vessel to windward and cannot determine with certainty whether the other vessel has the wind on the port or on the starboard side, she shall keep out of the way of the other.

(b) For the purposes of this Rule the windward side shall be deemed to be the side opposite to that on which the mainsail is carried or, in the case of a square-rigged vessel, the side opposite to that on which the largest fore-and-aft sail is carried.

Rule 13—International

OVERTAKING

(a) Notwithstanding anything contained in the Rules of this Section any vessel overtaking any other shall keep out of the way of the vessel being overtaken.

(b) A vessel shall be deemed to be overtaking when coming up with another vessel from a direction more than 22.5 degrees abaft her beam, that is, in such a position with reference to the vessel she is overtaking, that at night she would be able to see only the sternlight of that vessel but neither of her sidelights.

(c) When a vessel is in any doubt as to whether she is overtaking another, she shall assume that this is the case and act accordingly.

(d) Any subsequent alteration of the bearing between the two vessels shall not make the overtaking vessel a crossing vessel within the meaning of these rules or relieve her of the duty of keeping clear of the overtaken vessel until she is finally past and clear.

Rule 14—International

HEAD-ON SITUATION

(a) When two power-driven vessels are meeting on reciprocal or nearly reciprocal courses so as to involve risk of collision each shall alter her course to starboard so that each shall pass on the port side of the other.

(b) Such a situation shall be deemed to exist when a vessel sees the other ahead or nearly ahead and by night she could see the masthead lights of the other in a line or nearly in a line and/or both sidelights and by day she observes the corresponding aspect of the other vessel.

(c) When a vessel is in any doubt as to whether such a situation exists she shall assume that it does exist and act accordingly.

Rule 15—International

CROSSING SITUATION

When two power-driven vessels are crossing so as to involve risk of collision, the vessel which has the other on her own starboard side shall keep out of the way and shall, if the circumstances of the case admit, avoid crossing ahead of the other vessel.

Rule 15—Inland

CROSSING SITUATION

(a) When two power-driven vessels are crossing so as to involve risk of collision, the vessel which has the other on her starboard side shall keep out of the way and shall, if the circumstances of the case admit, avoid crossing ahead of the other vessel.

(b) Notwithstanding paragraph (a), on the Great Lakes, Western Rivers, or water specified by the Secretary, a vessel crossing a river shall keep out of the way of a power-driven vessel ascending or descending the river.

Rule 16—International

ACTION BY GIVE-WAY VESSEL

Every vessel which is directed to keep out of the way of another vessel shall, so far as possible, take early and substantial action to keep well clear.

Rule 17—International

ACTION BY STAND-ON VESSEL

(a) (i) Where one of two vessels is to keep out of the way the other shall keep her course and speed.

(ii) the latter vessel may however take action to avoid collision by her maneuver alone, as soon as it becomes apparent to her that the vessel required to keep out of the way is not taking appropriate action in compliance with these Rules.

(b) When, from any cause, the vessel required to keep her course and speed finds herself so close that collision cannot be avoided by the action of the give-way vessel alone, she shall take such action as will best aid to avoid collision.

(c) A power-driven vessel which takes action in a crossing situation in accordance with sub-paragraph (a) (ii) of this Rule to avoid collision with another power-driven vessel shall, if the circumstances of the case admit, not alter course to port for a vessel on her own port side.

(d) This Rule does not relieve the give-way vessel of her obligation to keep out of the way.

Rule 19—International

CONDUCT OF VESSELS IN RESTRICTED VISIBILITY

(a) This Rule applies to vessels not in sight of one another when navigating in or near an area of restricted visibility.

(b) Every vessel shall proceed at a safe speed adapted to the prevailing circumstances and conditions of restricted visibility. A power-driven vessel shall have her engines ready for immediate maneuver.

(c) Every vessel shall have due regard to the prevailing circumstances and conditions of restricted visibility when complying with the Rules of Section I of this Part.

(d) A vessel which detects by radar alone the presence of another vessel shall determine if a close-quarters situation is developing and/or risk of collision exists. If so, she shall take avoiding action in ample time, provided that when such action consists of an alteration of course, so far as possible the following shall be avoided:

(i) an alteration of course to port for a vessel forward of the beam, other than for a vessel being overtaken;

(ii) an alteration of course towards a vessel abeam or abaft the beam.

(e) Except where it has been determined that a risk of collision does not exist, every vessel which hears apparently forward of her beam the fog signal of another vessel, or which cannot avoid a close-quarters situation with another vessel forward of her beam, shall reduce her speed to the minimum at which she can be kept on her course. She shall if necessary take all her way off and in any event navigate with extreme caution until danger of collision is over.

LIGHTS AND SHAPES

Rule 21—International

DEFINITIONS

(a) "Masthead light" means a white light placed over the fore and aft centerline of the vessel showing an unbroken light over an arc of the horizon of 225° and so fixed as to show the light from right ahead to 22.5° abaft the beam on either side of the vessel.

(b) "Sidelights" means a green light on the starboard side and a red light on the port side each showing an unbroken light over an arc of the horizon of 112.5° and so fixed as to show the light from right ahead to 22.5° abaft the beam on its respective side. In a vessel of less than 20 meters in length the sidelights may be combined in one lantern carried on the fore and aft centerline of the vessel.

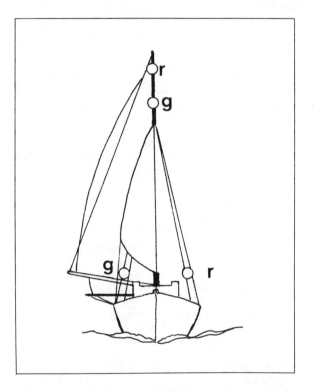

Figure 19-1. Sailing vessel underway in international or inland waters. This vessel is carrying optional all-round red and green lights on her mast. She also carries a sternlight. Drawing: Midn. Eric Pett, California Maritime Academy. Adapted from *Farwell's Rules of the Nautical Road* by permission of Naval Institute Press.

(c) "Sternlight" means a white light placed as nearly as practicable at the stern showing an unbroken light over an arc of the horizon of 135° and so fixed as to show the light 67.5° from right aft on each side of the vessel.

(d) "Towing light" means a yellow light having the same characteristics as the "sternlight" defined in paragraph (c) of this Rule.

(e) "All round light" means a light showing an unbroken light over an arc of the horizon of 360 degrees.

(f) "Flashing light" means a light flashing at regular intervals at a frequency of 120 flashes or more per minute.

LIGHTS FOR VESSELS UNDERWAY

Rules 22-29, INTERNATIONAL, set forth in detail the requirements for lights and shapes to be shown by vessels underway. These are important and are a matter of law. Only Rules 23 and 24 are reproduced below since they are deemed to be of most interest to the seaman. Although many of the differences between INTERNATIONAL and INLAND lights have been resolved, the student is cautioned that some differences continue to exist. The student is referred to *CG-169* , to *Farwell's*, or to Farnsworth and Young, *Nautical Rules of the Road* for a complete explanation.

Rule 23—International

POWER-DRIVEN VESSELS UNDERWAY

(a) A power-driven vessel underway shall exhibit:

(i) a masthead light forward;

(ii) a second masthead light abaft of and higher than the forward one; except that a vessel of less than 50 meters in length shall not be obliged to exhibit such light but may do so;

(iii) sidelights;

(iv) a sternlight.

(b) An air-cushion vessel when operating in the nondisplacement mode shall, in addition to the lights prescribed in paragraph (a) of this Rule, exhibit an all-round flashing yellow light.

(c) A power-driven vessel of less than 7 meters in length and whose maximum speed does not exceed 7 knots may, in lieu of the lights prescribed in paragraph (a) of this Rule, exhibit an all-round white light. Such vessel shall, if practicable, also exhibit sidelights.

Rule 24—International

TOWING AND PUSHING

(a) A power-driven vessel when towing shall exhibit:

(i) instead of the light prescribed in Rule 23(a)(i), two masthead lights forward in a vertical line. When the length of the tow, measuring from the stern of the towing vessel to the after end of the tow exceeds 200 meters, three such lights in a vertical line;

(ii) sidelights;

(iii) a sternlight;

(iv) a towing light in a vertical line above the sternlight;

(v) when the length of the tow exceeds 200 meters, a diamond shape where it can best be seen.

(b) When a pushing vessel and a vessel being pushed ahead are rigidly connected in a composite unit they shall be regarded as a power-driven vessel and exhibit the lights prescribed in Rule 23.

(c) A power-driven vessel when pushing ahead or towing alongside, except in the case of a composite unit, shall exhibit:

(i) instead of the light prescribed in Rule 23(a)(i), two masthead lights forward in a vertical line;

(ii) sidelights;

(iii) a sternlight.

(d) A power-driven vessel to which paragraphs (a) and (c) of this Rule apply shall also comply with Rule 23(a)(ii).

(e) A vessel or object being towed shall exhibit:

(i) sidelights;

(ii) a sternlight;

(iii) when the length of the tow exceeds 200 meters, a diamond shape where it can best be seen.

(f) Provided that any number of vessels being towed alongside or pushed in a group shall be lighted as one vessel,

(i) a vessel being pushed ahead, not being part of a composite unit, shall exhibit at the forward end, sidelights;

(ii) a vessel being towed alongside shall exhibit a sternlight and at the forward end, sidelights.

(g) Where from any sufficient cause it is impracticable for a vessel or object being towed to exhibit the lights prescribed in paragraph (e) of this Rule, all possible measures shall be taken to light the vessel or object towed or at least to indicate the presence of the unlighted vessel or object.

Rule 30—International

ANCHORED VESSELS

(a) A vessel at anchor shall exhibit where it can best be seen:

(i) in the fore part, an all-round white light or one ball;

(ii) at or near the stern and at a lower level than the light prescribed in sub-paragraph (i), an all-round white light.

(b) A vessel of less than 50 meters in length may exhibit an all-round white light where it can best be seen instead of the lights prescribed in paragraph (a) of this Rule.

(c) A vessel at anchor may, and a vessel of 100 meters and more in length shall, also use the available working or equivalent lights to illuminate her decks.

(d) A vessel aground shall exhibit the lights prescribed in paragraph (a) or (b) of this Rule and in addition, where they can best be seen:

(i) two all-round red lights in a vertical line;

(ii) three balls in a vertical line.

(e) A vessel of less than 7 meters in length, when at anchor or aground, not in or near a narrow channel, fairway or anchorage, or where other vessels normally navigate, shall not be required to exhibit the lights or shapes prescribed in paragraphs (a), (b) or (d) of this Rule.

SOUND AND LIGHT SIGNALS

Rule 32—International

DEFINITIONS

(a) The word "whistle" means any sound signalling appliance capable of producing the prescribed blasts and which complies with the specifications in Annex III to these Regulations.

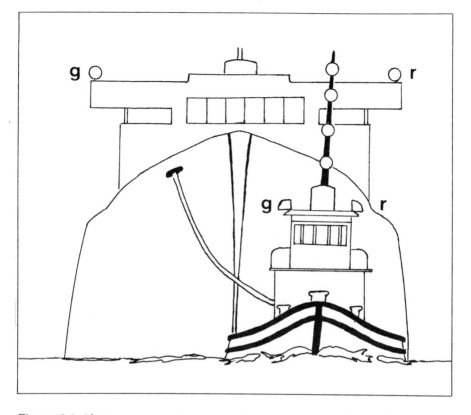

Figure 19-2. *Above,* tug towing a large vessel. The bow on view would be similar for inland and international waters, but there are differences in the manner in which the white lights to indicate towing are displayed. This is only one reason why a detailed study of the Rules of the Road is necessary for a licensed officer. In any event, in neither inland nor international waters, does a vessel being towed show masthead or range lights. Drawing: Midn. Eric Pett, California Maritime Academy. Adapted from *Farwell's Rules of the Nautical Road* by permission of Naval Institute Press.

(b) The term "short blast" means a blast of about one second's duration.

(c) The term "prolonged blast" means a blast of from four to six seconds' duration.

Editorial comment: Rules 34 INTERNATIONAL and INLAND follow. The student must understand there is a vast difference in the meaning of whistle signals between International and Inland Rules. In International Rules whistle signals are sometimes called "rudder signals" because whenever two ships are within sight of one another and one changes course, the vessel changing course must sound her whistle. In Inland Rules the meaning depends upon the situation. Generally, the first ship to sound her whistle "proposes" and the other ship "answers," or "agrees."

Rule 34—International

MANEUVERING AND WARNING SIGNALS

(a) When vessels are in sight of one another, a power-driven vessel underway, when maneuvering as authorized or required by these Rules, shall indicate that maneuver by the following signals on her whistle:

—one short blast to mean "I am altering my course to starboard;"

—two short blasts to mean "I am altering my course to port;"

—three short blasts to mean "I am operating astern propulsion."

(b) Any vessel may supplement the whistle signals prescribed in paragraph (a) of this Rule by light signals, repeated as appropriate, whilst the maneuver is being carried out:

(i) these light signals shall have the following significance:

—one flash to mean "I am altering my course to starboard;"

—two flashes to mean "I am altering my course to port;"

—three flashes to mean "I am operating astern propulsion;"

(ii) the duration of each flash shall be about one second, the interval between flashes shall be about one second, and the interval between successive signals shall be not less than ten seconds;

(iii) the light used for this signal shall, if fitted, be an all-round white light, visible at a minimum range of 5 miles, and shall comply with the provisions of Annex I.

(c) When in sight of one another in a narrow channel or fairway:

(i) a vessel intending to overtake another shall in compliance with Rule 9(e)(i) indicate her intention by the following signals on her whistle:

—two prolonged blasts followed by one short blast to mean "I intend to overtake you on your starboard side;"

—two prolonged blasts followed by two short blasts to mean "I intend to overtake you on your port side."

(ii) the vessel about to be overtaken when acting in accordance with Rule 9(e)(i) shall indicate her agreement by the following signal on her whistle:

—one prolonged, one short, one prolonged and one short blast, in that order.

(d) When vessels in sight of one another are approaching each other and from any cause either vessel fails to understand the intentions or actions of the other, or is in doubt whether sufficient action is being taken by the other to avoid collision, the vessel in doubt shall immediately indicate such doubt by giving at least five short and rapid blasts on the whistle. Such signal may be supplemented by a light signal of at least five short and rapid flashes.

(e) A vessel nearing a bend or an area of a channel or fairway where other vessels may be obscured by an intervening obstruction shall sound one prolonged blast. Such signal shall be answered with a prolonged blast by any approaching vessel that may be within hearing around the bend or behind the intervening obstruction.

Figure 19-3. *Above right,* power driven vessel underway in inland or international waters. Vessel has a slight starboard bow aspect. Range light in international rules is 225 degrees or 20 points. Drawing: Midn. Eric Pett, California Maritime Academy. Adapted from *Farwell's Rules of the Nautical Road* by permission of Naval Institute Press.

Figure 19-4. *Below right,* vessel not under command, international waters only. This vessel is underway and making way through the water. Note that she does not show masthead or range lights. If vessel were stopped and not making way she would not have her sidelights on. Drawing: Midn. Eric Pett, California Maritime Academy. Adapted from *Farwell's Rules of the Nautical Road* by permission of Naval Institute Press.

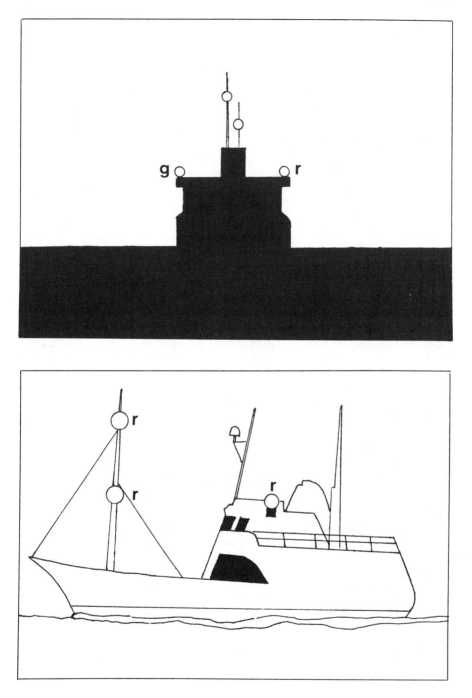

(f) If whistles are fitted on a vessel at a distance apart of more than 100 meters, one whistle only shall be used for giving maneuvering and warning signals.

Rule 34—Inland

MANEUVERING AND WARNING SIGNALS

(a) When power-driven vessels are in sight of one another and meeting or crossing at a distance within half a mile of each other, each vessel underway, when maneuvering as authorized or required by these Rules:

(i) shall indicate that maneuver by the following signals on her whistle: one short blast to mean "I intend to leave you on my port side"; two short blasts to mean "I intend to leave you on my starboard side"; and three short blasts to mean "I am operating astern propulsion".

(ii) upon hearing the one or two blast signal of the other shall, if in agreement, sound the same whistle signal and take the steps necessary to effect a safe passing. If, however, from any cause, the vessel doubts the safety of the proposed maneuver, she shall sound the danger signal specified in paragraph (d) of this Rule and each vessel shall take appropriate precautionary action until a safe passing agreement is made.

(b) A vessel may supplement the whistle signals prescribed in paragraph (a) of this Rule by light signals:

(i) These signals shall have the following significance: one flash to mean "I intend to leave you on my port side"; two flashes to mean "I intend to leave you on my starboard side"; three flashes to mean "I am operating astern propulsion";

(ii) The duration of each flash shall be about 1 second; and

(iii) The light used for this signal shall, if fitted, be one all-round white or yellow light, visible at a minimum range of 2 miles, synchronized with the whistle, and shall comply with the provisions of Annex I to these Rules.

(c) When in sight of one another:

(i) a power-driven vessel intending to overtake another power-driven vessel shall indicate her intention by the following signals on her whistle: one short blast to mean "I intend to overtake you on your starboard side"; two short blasts to mean "I intend to overtake you on your port side"; and

(ii) the power-driven vessel about to be overtaken shall, if in agreement, sound a similar sound signal. If in doubt she shall sound the danger signal prescribed in paragraph (d).

(d) When vessels in sight of one another are approaching each other and from any cause either vessel fails to understand the intentions or actions of the other, or is in doubt whether sufficient action is being taken by the other to avoid collision, the vessel in doubt shall immediately indicate such doubt by giving at least five short and rapid blasts on the whistle. This signal may be supplemented by a light signal of at least five short and rapid flashes.

(e) A vessel nearing a bend or an area of a channel or fairway where other vessels may be obscured by an intervening obstruction shall sound one prolonged blast. This signal shall be answered with a prolonged blast by any approaching vessel that may be within hearing around the bend or behind the intervening obstruction.

(f) If whistles are fitted on a vessel at a distance apart of more than 100 meters, one whistle only shall be used for giving maneuvering and warning signals.

(g) When a power-driven vessel is leaving a dock or berth, she shall sound one prolonged blast.

(h) A vessel that reaches agreement with another vessel in a meeting, crossing, or overtaking situation by using the radiotelephone as prescribed by the Bridge-to-Bridge Radiotelephone Act (85 Stat. 165; 33 U.S.C. 1207), is not obliged to sound the whistle signals prescribed by this Rule, but may do so. If agreement is not reached, then whistle signals shall be exchanged in a timely manner and shall prevail.

Rule 35—International

SOUND SIGNALS IN RESTRICTED VISIBILITY

In or near an area of restricted visibility, whether by day or night, the signals prescribed in this Rule shall be used as follows:

(a) A power-driven vessel making way through the water shall sound at intervals of not more than 2 minutes one prolonged blast.

(b) A power-driven vessel underway but stopped and making no way through the water shall sound at intervals of not more than 2 minutes two prolonged blasts in succession with an interval of about 2 seconds between them.

(c) A vessel not under command, a vessel restricted in her ability to maneuver, a vessel constrained by her draft, a sailing vessel, a vessel engaged in fishing and a vessel engaged in towing or pushing another vessel shall, instead of the signals prescribed in paragraphs (a) or (b) of this Rule, sound at intervals of not more than 2 minutes three blasts in succession, namely one prolonged followed by two short blasts.

(d) A vessel towed or if more than one vessel is towed the last vessel of the tow, if manned, shall at intervals of not more than 2 minutes sound four blasts in succession, namely one prolonged followed by three short blasts. When practicable, this signal shall be made immediately after the signal made by the towing vessel.

(e) When a pushing vessel and a vessel being pushed ahead are rigidly connected in a composite unit they shall be regarded as a power-driven vessel and shall give the signals prescribed in paragraphs (a) or (b) of this Rule.

(f) A vessel at anchor shall at intervals of not more than one minute ring the bell rapidly for about 5 seconds. In a vessel of 100 meters or more in length the bell shall be sounded in the forepart of the vessel and immediately after the ringing of the bell the gong shall be sounded rapidly for about 5 seconds in the after part of the vessel. A vessel at anchor may in addition sound three blasts in succession, namely one short, one prolonged and one short blast, to give warning of her position and of the possibility of collision to an approaching vessel.

(g) A vessel aground shall give the bell signal and if required the gong signal prescribed in paragraph (f) of this Rule and shall, in addition, give three separate and distinct strokes on the bell immediately before and after the rapid ringing of the bell. A vessel aground may in addition sound an appropriate whistle signal.

(h) A vessel of less than 12 meters in length shall not be obliged to give the above-mentioned signals but, if she does not, shall make some other efficient sound signal at intervals of not more than 2 minutes.

(i) A pilot vessel when engaged on pilotage duty may in addition to the signals prescribed in paragraphs (a), (b) or (f) of this Rule sound an identity signal consisting of four short blasts.

Editorial Comment:

1. In inland waters the danger signal may be used even though vessels cannot see each other. In international waters the danger signal can be used *only* if vessels *can* see each other.

2. The term, "a vessel constrained by her draft" does not appear in Inland Rules.

3. A fishing vessel or a vessel restricted in her ability to maneuver sounds the same signal at anchor as she does underway.

Annex IV—International

DISTRESS SIGNALS

1. The following signals, used or exhibited either together or separately, indicate distress and need of assistance:

(a) a gun or other explosive signal fired at intervals of about a minute;

(b) a continuous sounding with any fog-signaling apparatus;

(c) rockets or shells, throwing red stars fired one at a time at short intervals;

(d) a signal made by radiotelegraphy or by any other signalling method consisting of the group ...---... (SOS) in the Morse Code;

(e) a signal sent by radiotelephony consisting of the spoken word "Mayday;"

(f) the International Code Signal of distress indicated by N.C.;

(g) a signal consisting of a square flag having above or below it a ball or anything resembling a ball;

(h) flames on the vessel (as from a burning tar barrel, oil barrel, etc.)

(i) a rocket parachute flare or a hand flare showing a red light;

(j) a smoke signal giving off orange-coloured smoke;

(k) slowly and repeatedly raising and lowering arms outstretched to each side;

(l) the radiotelegraph alarm signal;

(m) the radiotelephone alarm signal;

(n) signals transmitted by emergency position-indicating radio beacons.

2. The use or exhibition of any of the foregoing signals except for the purpose of indicating distress and need of assistance and the use of other signals which may be confused with any of the above signals is prohibited.

3. Attention is drawn to the relevant sections of the International Code of Signals, the Merchant Ship Search and Rescue Manual and the following signals:

(a) a piece of orange-coloured canvas with either a black square and circle or other appropriate symbol (for identification from the air);

(b) a dye marker.

The damaged bow of the USNS *Asterion* after collision with the *Kokoku Maru* in fog off Point Reyes in June 1963. (Courtesy John Meadows).

CHAPTER XX

SAFETY

SAFETY IS THE BUSINESS OF ALL HANDS. The consequences of neglect of safety measures can be tragic. It is difficult to talk about safety without repeating trite phrases everyone has heard many times, but the fact that more than 50 percent of all accidents aboard ship are caused by slips, trips, and falls indicates that safety practices are not always observed. Surprisingly, the vast majority of trips and falls occur in good weather simply because an individual aboard ship was not using the handrail, was going up or down a ladder two rungs at a time, or was carrying so heavy a load he could not spare one hand for the rail. The old saying taught the apprentice before he went aloft on a sailing vessel still holds true: "One hand for yourself, the other for the ship."

No matter how good the new safety equipment, how well written the safety instructions, or how well the mate or bos'n checks you out on the equipment, if you do not carry out the instructions and use common sense you are an accident about to happen. Capable, safety-conscious personnel are the best devices aboard ship. On the other hand, if seamen are careless, foolhardy, or ill trained, their vessel will be an accident trap.

Probably the most important precautions are the easiest. You should know your ship. Know where all the exits and entries are to every space. If there are two means of escape from a compartment and you know only one, your chances of getting out alive if that exit is blocked by fire or flooding are very poor. It doesn't take a war to cause fire or damage to a ship. Peacetime disasters can be no less tragic. The fate of the *Titanic* or the recent collision in New York Harbor between the *Sea Witch* and the *Esso Brussels* are classic examples.

There is one thing that every seaman can do for the safety of the ship and crew immediately after he has signed the articles. That is to locate the station bill and ascertain his station and duties in case of fire or an order to man the boats. It is not enough for the seaman to know the location of his station and an enumeration of his duties. He must know what equipment is available and precisely how to use it. He must also know his ship so that he can get to his station from any part of the ship on a moment's notice.

Preparation for an emergency may mean the difference between life and death; forethought and precaution which will prevent the emergency from arising are even more important. Following is a check-list for officers and personnel assigned to the duty of checking safety, fire-fighting, and life-saving equipment:

GENERAL SAFETY CHECK-UP

Hatches—Are tarpaulins in good condition, neatly spread and tucked at corners, and secured with battens and wedges to maintain hatches watertight?

Watertight doors and weather doors—Are they kept securely closed and "dogged" or securely hooked in the open position except when actually in use? A heavy door can crush an unsuspecting foot or hand when the ship rolls in a heavy seaway.

Figure 20-1. Annual test of fire hose aboard T.S. *Golden Bear*. Photo: Midn. R.L. Schopp, California Maritime Academy.

Air ports—Are gaskets and dogs in good condition so that ports can be closed down tight if weather conditions so demand? Are the deadlight covers of proper fit and kept at hand ready for use?

Deck cargo—Are all the lashings taut and in good condition? Are the chocks and shores in place and secure?

FIRE-FIGHTING EQUIPMENT

General—Is equipment provided as required by regulations?

Fire hose—Is the hose in good condition? Is it properly racked? Are the valve handles, valves, and spindles in good order? Are the clamps or pins in the racks free? If in cabinets, can the door latch be readily opened? Are gaskets kept at hand or proper fit and in good order? Are the nozzles and spanners in place and ready to use? Is hose readily accessible?

Portable fire extinguishers—Are the hoses in good condition? Are extinguishers properly filled, tagged and dated, and located in a place where they can be easily seen and readily removed for use? Are extinguishers of the proper type for hazard involved?

Fire-extinguishing system—Are the control valves legibly marked, in good order, and accessible for prompt use? Do not operate valves. Are strainers clean? Are fire pumps in good operable condition?

Fire axes—Are they in a position where they are readily accessible and handy for use? Are handles smooth and free of rough edges? Do the handles fit snugly to the heads, and are the cutting edges smooth and sharp?

Figure 20-2. Equipment for one lifeboat laid out for annual Coast Guard inspection aboard T.S. *Golden Bear.* Photo: Midn. R.L. Schopp, California Maritime Academy.

Air and gas masks—Are they in good condition, ready for immediate use, and located where they will be easily obtainable when needed in an emergency?

Oxygen-breathing apparatus—Is the chamber filled with Cardoxide? Is there sufficient oxygen in the bottle? Has the apparatus been tested for leaks in the connections? Is the crew familiar with proper operation of all fire-fighting equipment?

LIFEBOATS

Equipment—Was equipment thoroughly examined in port? Are you checking it frequently at sea?

Are the oars, boathooks, radio masts, etc., in good condition and properly lashed in boats?

Are the row locks properly secured and ready for shipping into the sockets?

Does the rudder fit properly into the gudgeons, and is it properly attached to the boat with a lanyard to prevent loss?

Water and provisions—Are the hermetically sealed cans containing fresh water in good condition?

Are the provision containers in good condition and watertight?

Security and readiness—Are the boat painters properly attached and led out and not chafing on any portion of the hull or superstructure?

Are frapping lines provided for lifeboat falls?

Are the crank handles for the davits in place and of proper fit?

Are the lifeboat fall reels clear for running?

Has the motorboat engine been operated frequently?

Has the hand-propelling gear been operated and lubricated frequently (if the boat is so fitted)?

Are there any stores or other gear stowed on the boat deck in way of lifeboats? If so, is it properly secured so that it will not fall into the boats if vessel should be suddenly and rapidly listed?

Are the embarkation nets properly secured and stowed in such a manner that they shall be ready for dropping promptly into position?

Are the embarkation ladders properly placed and readily available for use where required?

Has the length of the life lines for the davit heads been regulated to the draft of the vessel so that there will not be too much surplus to entangle and capsize the boat if the vessel is rolling or a heavy sea is running?

LIFE RAFTS

Is the operating cord securely attached to the rail or other part of the ship's structure?

Are the instructions mounted near each lifeboat station? Are they legible?

Does the pod or case appear to be in good condition? Does it have any cracks?

LIFE FLOATS

Stowage—Are the life floats stowed so that they will float free, and can also be launched directly overboard?

Ring buoys—Are all the ring buoys properly distributed and stowed ready for immediate use?

Water lights—Are all the water lights properly attached and will they ignite? (Test in daytime.)

LIFE PRESERVERS

Are they at hand, in good condition, and ready for each individual's immediate use?

Are an additional number of life preservers provided for personnel on watch in the engine room, pilothouse, and the bow lookout?

LIGHTS

Portable emergency lights—Are all portable emergency lights in their respective position and in good condition, and will they light? (Test in daytime.)

Are all stationary emergency lights in their proper positions and in good order? Will they light?

Flashlights—Are all emergency flashlights in good order and will they light?

Life-preserver lights—Has each seaman taken care of his life-preserver light and seen that it will burn, and renewed the battery when necessary?

MISCELLANEOUS

Portable radio transmitter—Is this fitted with a lanyard for lowering and kept handy for placing in the lifeboats?

Whistles—Are all police whistles kept in good order? Has every man tested out his own?

Jackknives—Has every man oiled and cleaned the blade of his jackknife, and does he carry it on his person or keep it close at hand?

Reflector tape markings—Is all this tape effectively and properly maintained?

Emergency escapes—Are they all free and clear of obstruction? Are emergency ladders kept in place and properly secured? Are emergency escapes properly marked and readily visible?

HARMFUL GASES

One of the common hazards on shipboard is represented by accumulations of harmful gases in tanks, holds, and voids. Spaces containing such gases will also sometimes contain less than the normal percentage of oxygen. A man entering such a space unprotected is consequently in danger of asphyxiation or suffocation both from lack of air and from the poisonous effects of the harmful gases which he breathes.

Breathing cycle—An average man at rest will breathe about every 5 seconds, drawing in about one quart of air at a breath. The air is spread out in the lungs, enters small cells through the walls, where the impure blood gives off carbon dioxide and takes up oxygen from the inhaled air. The breath leaving the lungs then carries away the carbon dioxide. The re-oxygenated blood goes from lungs to heart, from which it is pumped through the body again. The oxygen carried in the blood is used in reaction with the body tissues. The result of this reaction, which is actually a form of combustion, is to use up the oxygen and produce carbon dioxide. The blood then carries the carbon dioxide back through the heart to the lungs, thus completing the cycle.

To cut off or replace this vital supply of oxygen with other gases is to bring about starvation of the body tissues, beginning with the brain. As a result unconsciousness comes early in the process of asphyxiation.

The lower processes of the body, or those which go on automatically, such as respiration, circulation of the blood, etc., can and do go on even when the person is unconscious, but usually in asphyxiation, soon after unconsciousness develops, respiration also ceases, so that most asphyxiated persons are not only unconscious but also are not breathing. In this stage of asphyxiation, provided that the heart has not yet been sufficiently affected to prevent its functioning, the patient can be benefited by cardiopulmonary resusitation (CPR) as described in Chapter XVIII.

By making a person breathe artificially we get oxygen back into the lungs where it can be absorbed by the blood and taken to the various vital centers of the body. Those parts that were affected last usually recover first, which is the reason, during artificial respiration, that the patient may begin to breathe even before he wakes up or becomes conscious. As respiration improves and more oxygen is brought to the vital centers of the body, the higher centers are finally reoxygenated and the person becomes conscious once more.

EFFECT OF GASES

Breathing carbon dioxide—Since carbon dioxide is the gas which the impure blood gets rid of in the lungs, to breathe air which is heavily charged with this gas and correspondingly low in oxygen is bound to starve the blood and produce eventual suffocation. Fires, with their heavy consumption of oxygen and production of carbon dioxide, are the common cause of such a dangerous atmosphere. A concentration of more than 2 or 3% of carbon dioxide will force a man to breathe rapidly and with more or less discomfort.

Breathing carbon monoxide—The most dangerous of all common gases is carbon monoxide. A few seconds of breathing air containing 2% of this gas will bring unconsciousness, and death will follow in 3 or 4 minutes. A few hours' exposure to carbon monoxide in a concentration of 0.02% can produce headache, and a feeling of dullness. A concentration of 0.2% may bring about death in 2 to 4 hours.

The reason for this rapid action is that the blood absorbs carbon monoxide 300 times more quickly than it absorbs oxygen. The oxygen is simply choked out and cannot get into the blood stream, which is soon saturated to a dangerous point with carbon monoxide.

Carbon monoxide gives no sign of its presence. It cannot be seen or smelled.

Breathing other gases—Many other harmful gases, chlorine, ammonia, hydrogen sulphide, sulphur dioxide, etc., are produced by various conditions. A cargo fire may create an atmosphere which is not only dangerous because of smoke produced and oxygen used up, but also because of the harmful gases generated by the combustion of the materials making up the cargo. Burning wood gives off a high percentage of carbon monoxide. Burning rubber produces both sulphur dioxide and carbon monoxide.

Breathing smoke—In case of fire, smoke presents another hazard in addition to the lack of oxygen and the presence of harmful gases. Smoke is very irritating to the air passages. The choking and coughing which results from breathing smoke-filled air sometimes prevents nearly all the inhaled air from reaching the lungs. Since this air is generally poor to begin with, quick suffocation can result if there is no escape to the open air.

But even in a smoke-filled compartment it is possible to survive by finding the lowest spot, staying there, breathing slowly, and using as little energy as possible until rescued. After severe damage to a ship one of the editors served aboard during World War II, half a dozen men in a two-level machinery space retreated before the smoke to the bilges where they remained until the next day when they were rescued. The dozen men who remained on the upper level suffocated.

Breathing through a damp rag should not be overlooked even if it means urinating to dampen the rag.

Danger in empty tanks—Ships' tanks which have remained sealed for long periods should be considered unsafe to enter even though they contain no oil or other cargo residues. Such tanks should be ventilated by a portable blower and then entered only with extreme caution. A self-contained breathing apparatus or fresh air hose mask, properly tended with people standing by, is a wise precaution. Steel surfaces consume oxygen by rusting, and substances other than iron or steel may remove oxygen from the atmosphere in an enclosed space. Whether or not carbon monoxide is present, a gas hazard still exists.

Petroleum gases—The gases and vapors arising from petroleum products in fuel bunkers and other tanks are both toxic and explosive. Safety codes and Coast Guard regulations quite properly require that such spaces be tested before being entered.

RESPIRATORY SAFETY EQUIPMENT

Assistance in breathing or protection for breathing is furnished by two general classes of equipment. These are gas masks and breathing apparatus. The difference between them is extremely important: Gas masks protect against some kinds of poison gas but do not furnish oxygen. Breathing apparatus provides air or oxygen independent of the atmosphere surrounding the wearer. In short—if there is a lack of oxygen in a compartment, a gas mask will not do any good, but breathing apparatus will keep you alive. Some gases such as ammonia (NH_3) or hydrocyanic gas (HCN) which are used for fumigating require protective clothing in addition to breathing apparatus because these gases are absorbed through the skin. A gas mask, however, does furnish some limited protection against smoke. All shipboard personnel should be thoroughly familiar with the use of the type of gas masks and breathing equipment aboard. The best equipment in the world is of no value if you do not know how to use it.

GAS MASKS

A gas mask consists of a facepiece with glass eyepieces which is held in place by head bands and is connected by corrugated tubing to a canister held against the chest and supported by a harness about the neck and body. (See Figure 20-3.)

In use, the head bands are so adjusted that the facepiece is held very tightly against the face so as to prevent the entrance of gases under the mask. The facepiece should be tested for tightness by holding the palm of the hand over the bottom of the canister and inhaling strongly. The facepiece should collapse against the face and remain there as long as the breath is held and the hand remains in place.

Figure 20-3. Gas mask.

Air or gases enter the canister through a check valve in its bottom, pass through the purifying chemicals contained in it, and then leave the top of the canister, being inhaled through the corrugated tube. The inhaled dry air enters the facepiece through tubes and is discharged over the eyeglasses to prevent fogging.

Canisters should be kept absolutely dry, as moisture causes deterioration of the contents.

The date on which the seal of a canister is broken and the canister attached to the mask should be recorded on the label of the canister. No canister should be continued in service for more than one year from such date, regardless of the amount of use it has had.

Timer—The service time of the canister in protecting the wearer against carbon monoxide fumes is about 2 hours, either continuous or intermittent. A timer fitted to the canister registers the number of respirations on a dial. One complete revolution of the pointer marks roughly two hours of use, after which the canister should be replaced, and the used canister marked to prevent re-use by mistake. Never forget to reset the dial pointer of the timer to zero when a new canister is connected to the mask.

The facepiece and tube can be sterilized by immersing for a few minutes in any of the following solutions: 3% solution of carbolic acid; 2% solution of Lysol; 70% solution of denatured alcohol.

Gas masks simply purify the air breathed through them, and should not be used in an atmosphere containing less than 16% of oxygen. An open light—a candle or lantern—will not burn in an atmosphere containing a smaller amount of oxygen. Consequently, when any doubt exists as to the oxygen content of the atmosphere, it should be tested by the use of a flame safety lamp, which because of its construction will not ignite flammable gases. Compartments in which a flame safety lamp is extinguished should not be entered when using a gas mask.

BREATHING APPARATUS

There are two types of breathing apparatus. One is the self-contained breathing apparatus, sometimes called an oxygen breathing apparatus (OBA), and the other is the fresh air hose mask.

Self-contained apparatus consists of a mouthpiece or facepiece with tubes, inhalation and exhalation valves, and other necessary fittings. One type contains a breathing bag and canister to purify the air and provide it to the wearer in accordance with his needs. This equipment is shown in Figure 20-4. A timer is provided so that the wearer can set it before entering a compartment and be assured of not overstaying his time.

The second type contains oxygen under high pressure in a cylinder. A reducing valve brings the pressure down so that the oxygen is usable and goes into a breathing bag. Another variation of this type has no breathing bag, and the air or oxygen goes directly through a reducing valve to the head piece.

The fresh air hose mask is simply a face mask which is supplied with fresh air through a rubber hose operated by a pump. An obvious precaution with the fresh air breather is to make sure that the pump is placed where the air taken in is pure. The hose cannot be more than 150 feet long.

In using any type of respiratory equipment, the wearer should have a safety line or lifeline attached to him when he enters a space. The lifeline should be tended by someone who is alert for signals and who can pull his shipmate back to safety. The standard signals which should be written on a plate attached to the lifeline are:

One Pull—Okay
Two Pulls—Advance
Three Pulls—Coming Out
Four Pulls—Help

FLAME SAFETY LAMP

A flame safety lamp is used to discover if the atmosphere in a compartment has sufficient oxygen to sustain life. The lamp will not burn if there is a lack of oxygen. It should not be lighted in a location which is not known to be safe. The operation of the flame safety lamp should be understood by all shipboard personnel.

Normal air contains 21% oxygen. Candles or flame safety lamps cease to burn when the oxygen content is lowered to 16%. (Unconsciousness occurs in humans when the oxygen content drops to 10%). Therefore, the user is warned of oxygen deficiency in time to withdraw to a place of safety.

Flame safety lamps should be used to test the oxygen content before men are allowed to enter places where oxygen deficiency is liable to occur, such as holds in which a fire has been smoldering, or where solid CO_2 has been used as a refrigerant, or in deep tanks which have been filled with oil or molasses and which have not been thoroughly aired out; or in fuel or water tanks which may have been sealed for some time, etc.

As a special safety precaution men wearing gas masks in any part of the vessel where a deficiency of oxygen might be encountered should carry a flame safety lamp.

Fuel specifications—Successful operation of the flame safety lamp depends in large part on use of proper fuel. Gasoline that contains tetraethyl lead is not satisfactory nor is the so-called third structure white gasoline even though this latter is lead free. In order to light the cold lamp with the re-lighting device, a fuel having a flash point sufficiently low to insure the presence of a flammable fuel-vapor mixture at the open end of the wick is required. The U.S. Bureau of Mines recommends the following fuel for permissible safety lamps (Koeler & Wolf):

"Trade Name of Fuel: Atlantic 70 Naphtha; Freedom safety lamp fuel; Gulf safety lamp fuel; Waverly safety lamp fuel.

"Lamps for which these fuels are suitable are often referred to as 'naphtha-burning lamps' or just 'naphtha lamps.' 'Naphtha' is an indefinite term, in that there is no general agreement as to what constitutes a naphtha. However, to some refiners it means a straight-run distillate, one that has no part produced by cracking. In this respect all of the above fuels may be classed as naphthas."

Container for reserve fuel—Even though the lamp is not used there will be a gradual loss of fuel through evaporation from the wick. It is, therefore, advisable to have available a reserve supply of fuel. One satisfactory method of keeping a small reserve handy is to use a one pint copper-plated engineer's filler with screw cap on the filler spout. This filler should be kept filled with fuel and stored near the lamp.

Precautions in using—The following precautions should be observed in using a flame safety lamp:

Be sure that the lamp is locked.

Examine the lamp carefully to see that it is in good condition before using it. Do not carry the key which opens the lamp with you.

Do not attempt to open the lamp in hold or tank. Always take into fresh air.

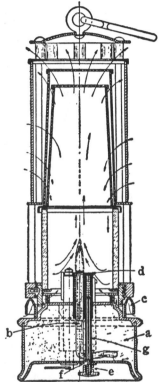

Figure 20-4. Cannister-type oxygen breathing appa-   Figure 20-5. Flame safety lamp.
ratus. Photo: Midn. R.L. Schopp, California Maritime
                          Academy.

Be sure that lamp gauze is clean. Do not use one with rust, dirt, or oil on gauze.

Do not let lamp smoke. Soot may fill up the gauze.

Lamps that have not been used for some time may have rusty gauzes and hardened wick or gummy fuel. Do not use such a lamp.

Action of fuel in lamp—Figure 20-5 shows a sectional view of a typical flame safety lamp. The parts shown are:

a) Cotton in base of lamp which absorbs the fuel.

b) Wick.

c) Bottom inlet ring through which most of the air that supports combustion enters.

d) Cover cap to tube in which wick adjuster is contained.

e) Control handle for wick adjuster.

f) Rod connecting control handle with wick adjusting mechanism.

g) Tube containing wick adjusting mechanism.

The arrows show the path of air into and out of the lamp.

Assembling errors—When properly assembled, a flame safety lamp may be introduced into an explosive mixture of gases and air. However, it should not be so used unless absolutely necessary. It should not be used in cofferdams fouled by fuel oil or in atmospheres that may contain hydrogen or acetylene gas. If possible, the space should be first tested with a com-

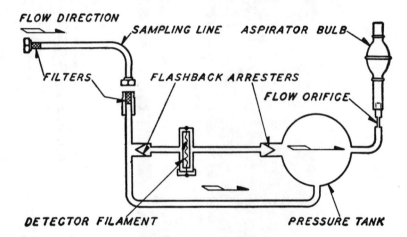

Figure 20-6. Combustible gas indicator, diagrammatic layout.

bustible gas indicator. A flame safety lamp is safe only when in perfect condition and used with care and discretion. The following errors may be made in assembling lamps:

1. Leaving out one or both gaskets or using a broken glass.

2. Placing gaskets in underfeed lamps so the inlet passage under the glass is obstructed.

3. Leaving out one of the gauzes in double-gauze lamps.

4. Placing on top of glass an expansion ring designed to be placed under the glass.

5. Placing expansion ring upside down, thus destroying its usefulness.

6. Failure to screw the fuel vessel far enough in to make a tight fit between the glass globe and the gaskets.

7. Leaving off the deflection rings that prevent air from flowing directly into the lamp.

8. Leaving off the shield or bonnet when the lamp is to be used in a strong air current.

9. Placing a defective gauze in a lamp.

Care of wicks—The wick should be renewed when it is believed that it has become stiff and when there is a characteristic gummy deposit around the wick and wick tube. The cotton in the fuel reservoir should be renewed about once a year. In packing the lamp the base should be filled with cotton uniformly distributed and a wick trailed out through the cotton in intimate contact with the fuel supply. No more fuel should be placed in the base than can be absorbed in the cotton. After filling the fuel reservoir it should be inverted and any free liquid allowed to drain out. Be certain that filler cap is screwed on tightly.

Flame safety lamps are gas testing devices and dependable only when properly assembled, properly fueled, and properly used. They indicate deficiency in oxygen as well as explosive atmospheres. Keep them in good condition and test them frequently.

COMBUSTIBLE GAS INDICATORS

Combustible gas indicators measure the degree of explosive gases present in any space, tank, compartment, etc. By means of a sampling line, a length of small tubing, an air sample is drawn out of the space and through the measuring instrument. A meter indicates the concentration of the explosive gas in the air under test. It is graduated to read in percentage of the low explosive limit concentration.

The gas sample may be drawn into the instrument by means of a small piston-type hand pump, an aspirator bulb, or motor-driven pump in the case of the non-portable gas alarm. The sample flows over a hot platinum wire which forms a part of a balanced electrical circuit. Current for the circuit is supplied by two small dry cell batteries. This detector unit is balanced against the filament of a small electric light bulb burning in an inert gas. The combustible gas in the air sample burns easily in the presence of the platinum detector filament, which heats up during the combustion according to the amount of gas burned. This increases the wire's resistance and causes the electrical circuit to become unbalanced. The unbalancing of the circuit in turn causes a movement of the pointer of the electrical meter which is directly proportional to the concentration of combustible gas in the sample.

Combustible gas alarm—The combustible gas alarm operates in the same manner as the portable instrument. When the combustible gas concentration exceeds that for which the instrument is set to operate, the alarm circuit closes and the alarm signal (bell, light, horn or siren) operates until the gas concentration is lowered.

Two small pilot lights indicate normal operation. When the alarm circuit closes, these lights go out and a red warning light inside the instrument case flashes on.

Like the portable indicator, the alarm may be specially calibrated for any particular gas and adjusted to give alarm at any desired degree of concentration. It may also be hooked up to operate ventilating fans or blowers.

FIRES AND FIRE-FIGHTING SYSTEMS

How fires burn—Fire occurs whenever a given material is heated in the presence of oxygen to a temperature corresponding to the kindling point of the material. Thus there are three factors, *all* of which must be present, if fire is to exist: the *material*, plus a supply of *oxygen*, plus sufficiently high *temperature*. These three make fire burn. Education in fire fighting starts with this simple fact, because fires may be extinguished by removing one of these essential elements.

Figure 20-7. Fireman's exposure suit, part of the equipment contained in the damage control locker, taken in the shaft alley of T.S. *Golden Bear*. Photo: Midn. R.L. Schopp, California Maritime Academy.

Rules for fighting fire—From the above statement, three simple rules for fighting fire evolve:

1. *Remove the material*—If you want to extinguish the fire in a gas burner, you simply turn off the gas. This removes the material, and there is nothing to burn. Here is how this simple rule was applied to a serious fire by a quick-thinking fire chief:

A ruptured connection on the outside of a tank car of gasoline spilled onto the track under the car and ignited. When the fire department arrived, the blaze was seemingly beyond control. As fast as the fire was extinguished, the gasoline running down from the car caught fire again. Recalling his high school physics, the fire chief had an inspiration. He directed a hose stream into the open hatch on top of the tank car. Water, he recalled, is heavier than gasoline. After the firemen had poured water into the tank car for a few minutes, the water sank to the bottom of the tank and came through the opening below instead of gasoline. As soon as this happened, it was an easy matter to control the blaze. The chief, in other words, had removed the material.

2. *Remove the temperature*—The chief value of water as an extinguishing agent is that it cools the material below its kindling point. Consequently, tanks containing flammable liquid, if near a fire which cannot be brought under control immediately, may be saved by turning the hose on them and keeping them cool.

3. *Remove the oxygen*—Place a lighted candle on the table and lower a milk bottle over it. As soon as the flame uses up the oxygen inside the bottle, the fire goes out. In fire fighting, the removal of oxygen is ordinarily a blanketing operation. This is what you do when a person's clothes catch fire, and you roll him in a rug. Foam kills fire by blanketing it with a gummy substance which keeps the air away. A water spray has a blanketing effect. Vaporizing liquid extinguishers produce a heavy vapor which cuts off a fire's air supply. The carbon dioxide extinguisher hits the blaze with a barrage of carbon dioxide which drives away the oxygen, killing the fire.

Classification of fires—It is important to know what type of fire you are fighting and what rules to follow in fighting it:

Class A—Fires in ordinary combustible materials such as mattresses, dunnage, piles of wood and shavings, and canvas. They are best extinguished by the quenching and cooling effects of quantities of water or fog.

Class B—Fires in flammable liquids such as grease, gasoline, fuel oil, lubricating oil, diesel, and tar. The blanketing or smothering effect of the extinguishing agent is of prime importance.

Class C—Fires in electrical equipment where the use of a non-conductive extinguishing agent is of first importance.

Class D—This class of fire was recently deemed of sufficient importance that fires in combustible metals such as magnesium, sodium, titanium, and lithium are now called Class D fires. These metals contain their own oxygen and burn independent of the atmosphere. Materials of this nature have been used in fire bombs.

Spontaneous combustion—One of the causes of fire aboard ship is spontaneous combustion. The term spontaneous combustion means simply combustion or fire which starts without aid from outside sources, such as a spark, open flame, overheated wall, etc.

Such occurrences seem unnatural until we remember that combustion is not limited to the production of open flames but is happening all the time all around us. Copper turned green is in a state of combustion. So is rusting iron, rotting wood, and oil which is open to the air. As mentioned in regard to the breathing process, the body tissues are in a constant state of combustion.

And in every case heat is given off, whether or not it can be measured. For combustion is a chemical process in which oxygen combines with another chemical substance or compound. The combining process releases energy which takes the form of heat.

Combinations of hydrogen and carbon, called hydro-carbons, oxidize readily and are familiar agents of spontaneous combustion. The familiar story of the oily waste which was tossed in a box and later caught fire is an example of oxidation of the hydro-carbons in oil.

Several things make this possible. First, the waste presented a large surface to the air which was covered with oil, making the amount of oxidation comparatively large. As the chemical process started the heat given off was very slight, but enough to make the oxidation proceed a little faster. More heat was given off, speeding up the process more and more until the waste became hot enough to break out into flames. The oxidation or combustion process became violent and visible.

Spontaneous combustion requires favorable conditions, a closed space and still air to prevent the generated heat from being carried away from the oxidizing material. The hydro-carbon must be exposed in a vapor or a thin film.

Explosions—Explosions in vessels or pipe lines sometimes are the end result of spontaneous combustion. For example, a heated vessel containing a hydro-carbon vapor, air, and perhaps a coating of finely divided carbon on its surface may be as dangerous as a bomb. Under such conditions the hydro-carbon oxidizes quickly, building up a large amount of heat. When the vapor ignites it burns fairly slowly at first. The contents of the vessel expand under the heat. The pressure resulting from this expansion also produces heat until all at once the whole body of unburned vapor takes fire, building up a tremendous pressure, and blows out the vessel.

FIRE EXTINGUISHERS

Portable fire extinguishers on modern ships are either CO_2 or dry chemical. Older ships may still have soda-acid type extinguishers, but these are no longer being installed. Formerly carbon tetrachloride extinguishers were also used, but because the gas formed when the stream of chemical strikes the flame is dangerous to human life, they are now forbidden.

CO_2 extinguishers are located in spaces where "Class B" and "Class C" fires are a danger. There are two general types. One is operated by a small wheel at the top and the other by a squeeze grip. When the CO_2 is discharged, the liquid CO_2 is forced out of the discharge hose and enters the horn-shaped nozzle where rapid expansion takes place. It now becomes a gas, and the temperature decreases dramatically. Extinguishers should be weighed annually and recharged if the weight loss exceeds 10 percent of the weight of the charge.

Dry chemical extinguishers look much like CO_2 extinguishers and are used in a similar manner. However, the powdery chemical must reach the base of the fire. The chemical should be directed across, but not into the fuel surface, to avoid splashing the fuel and enlarging the fire area. Extinguishers should be recharged if the pressure is low or if dry chemical is needed.

Figure 20-8. CO $_2$ fire extinguisher. Photo: Midn. R.L. Schopp, California Maritime Academy.

Figure 20-9. Dry chemical fire extinguisher. Photo: Midn. R.L. Schopp, California Maritime Academy.

Machinery spaces may have semiportable CO_2 systems installed. The semiportable system is simply a large bottle connected to a long hose. The hose is taken to the fire and the bottle remains in its permanent location. The CO_2 should be applied to the base of the flames from as close a distance as possible with a slow sweeping motion in a vertical up and down direction.

FIXED CO2 SYSTEM

A battery of CO_2 cylinders, manifolded and equipped for simultaneous release, provides protection for the engine and fire rooms. All ship's officers should be familiar with the location of the pull boxes for the engine room system and any other system with which the ship is provided. CO_2 is not poisonous, but it will suffocate anyone in a space which is flooded by CO_2. All personnel must be warned to vacate the space before CO_2 is released.

If the fire is in the engine room or boiler room, the fixed CO_2 system should be the last resort. The fire in the boiler should be extinguished, auxiliaries stopped, and the ventilation system should be secured.

Figure 20-10. Fixed CO ₂ system installed aboard T.S. *Golden Bear.* This system provides protection for fireroom and engine room. Photo: Midn. R.L. Schopp, California Maritime Academy.

CARGO PROTECTION SYSTEMS

Cargo and passenger ships may be fitted with a system for the protection of cargo spaces. Several types are in use. They consist of a combination of a detecting system and a CO_2 extinguishing system. The system has a smoke detector and a fire gong which rings automatically at the first trace of smoke in a cargo hold so that the fire can be put out immediately.

Pipe lines are run from all individual cargo spaces and terminate in the chamber of the detector which is installed on the bridge. Duplicate exhaust fans draw a continuous sample of air through each line into the detector. Any trace of smoke in an air sample is illuminated giving a visual warning of fire and locating the actual space on fire. The air samples are discharged into the wheelhouse, if desired, thus enabling smell detection also.

The detector also rings one or more fire gongs to attract the attention of the watch to the detector when fire breaks out.

In the detector, the air samples from the cargo spaces are passed between a photovoltaic cell and a source of light for "smoke inspection." If there is any smoke in an air sample, the amount of light reaching the cell is reduced, thus causing the cell to operate the alarm gong and indicate the number of the space in trouble. The detector is equipped with a voltage regulator that compensates for voltage variations in the ship's lines, preventing false alarms due to variations in the intensity of the light source. A light intensity control makes it possible to compensate for aging of the light source and for any dirt that might collect and reduce the amount of light reaching the cell.

Figure 20-11. Quick-acting watertight door. Photo: Midn. R.L. Schopp, California Maritime Academy.

Figure 20-12. Fire screen door. Photo: Midn. R.L. Schopp, California Maritime Academy.

WATERTIGHT DOORS AND HATCHES

A ship's ability to withstand damage and contain flooding and fire depends to a large degree on its watertight doors and other closures. Not only do the doors have to be in good operating condition, but the crew must be trained to close them during fire and emergency drills so that in time of emergency they will be closed automatically.

There are several types of watertight doors. Some are closed by individual dogs and some have a hand wheel or lever which controls all the dogs as shown in Figure 20-11. In this case it is simply necessary to spin the lever or wheel to close the door. Some ships have watertight doors which can be operated remotely from the bridge.

Watertightness of the door is insured by rubber gaskets which are forced against the knife edges when the dogs are secured. Chalk testing the fit by

Figure 20-13. Watertight door operated remotely between shaft alley and engine room of T.S. *Golden Bear.* Door is controlled manually by a handwheel from two levels above shaft alley. It is checked annually in the Coast Guard inspection. Photo: Midn. R.L. Schopp, California Maritime Academy.

placing chalk on the knife edge, dogging the door, and then checking to see that chalk comes off uniformly on the gasket will insure that the closure is in fact watertight. Gaskets should not be painted, and any paint which slops over on the gasket when the door is being painted should be removed with the wooden handle of a wire brush.

Another type of door installed on passenger ships is the firescreen door (Figure 20-12). It is not watertight but is designed to check the spread of fire. Normally firescreen doors are open, but a magnetic switch permits them to close when power is lost for any reason, or when the master switch is operated on the bridge.

On most merchant ships the shaft alley is a long compartment of large cubic capacity opening into the engine room. If the shaft alley is flooded, it would severely impair the safety of the ship. The size of the shaft alley can be seen in Figure 20-7. In order to insure that the shaft alley can be closed in an emergency, Coast Guard regulations require that a heavy watertight door be installed which can be operated remotely from the engine room. Figure 20-13 shows the installation on the *Golden Bear.* This is operated by hand or by "Norwegian Steam," as it is sometimes called. Other installations may be hydraulic.

EMERGENCY SQUAD

The emergency squad, mentioned briefly in Chapter X, will be discussed in more detail here. In the Navy the emergency squad would be called the

"Damage Control Party" or "Fire and Rescue" squad. These names indicate the types of emergencies which may arise and the kind of training and skills required of a good emergency squad.

The master of the ship designates a signal for calling the emergency squad which will assemble at the scene within a few minutes with the designated equipment. If a ship is fitted with loudspeakers, the nature and location of the emergency will be announced. The chief mate will take charge, estimate the situation, and keep the master informed by messenger, telephone, or walkie-talkie radio. Keeping the bridge informed is of prime importance because the master cannot help unless he knows what is going on. He may wish to stop the ship to help prevent the spread of fire, send extra assistance to the emergency squad, shut off the ventilation, or radio for help. He has to be informed so he can make his own evaluation of the extent of danger.

If the emergency is a fire, the first men on the scene lead out hoses and start fighting the fire. It may be that the fire is small enough to be put out by CO_2 extinguishers. If that is the case the hoses will simply be led out and charged in the event they are needed.

The members of the emergency squad take such immediate steps as the occasion requires to fight the fire, close adjacent firescreen doors and airports, arrange for the stopping of the ventilation system in that part of the ship, and warn the passengers in adjacent accommodations.

If the general fire alarm has sounded, the squad directs all members of the crew assigned to adjacent hoses to lead in all hoses possible to bear, without delay, in order to apply as large a volume of water as possible on the fire. Hoses may be coupled together, some may be passed from deck to deck, and streams from as many hoses as reach played on the fire.

The emergency squad provides fire axes, crowbars, fire extinguishers, spare lengths of fire hose, nozzle and spanners, flashlights, gas masks and oxygen-breathing apparatus, and a safety flame lamp.

All members of the squad should be thoroughly trained in the use of gas masks for rescue purposes, and instructed in the limitations of possible use of the all-service gas masks, and use of the safety flame lamp. The oxygen-breathing apparatus should be reserved for service when it is necessary to furnish oxygen to the would-be rescuer, in cases of oxygen depletion within a compartment. Instructions for the use of this equipment should be carefully observed. Men entering smoke-filled compartments should wear a safety belt fitted with a line, to enable them to be dragged to safety.

The emergency squad responds to all man-overboard calls and prepares to swing out the emergency boat on the designated or lee side, assists the emergency boat crew into life preservers, tends the falls and frapping lines, and, if necessary, men from the squad fill in vacant thwarts to expedite launching of the boat. If necessary to use storm oil, a man from the squad is detailed for the purpose, and at least one man keeps watch on the person overboard until relieved by regular lookouts. At night time the searchlights are manned. The squad can hang an ordinary rope net cargo sling over the side, aft of the emergency boat, for picking up the boat crew

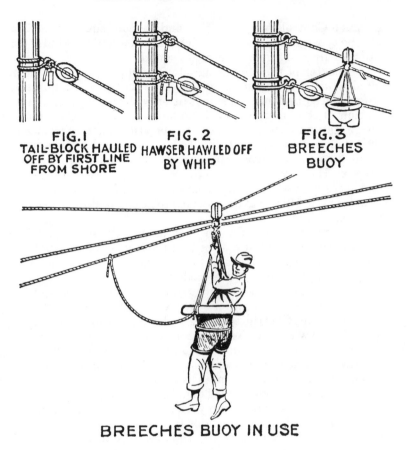

FIG. 1
TAIL-BLOCK HAULED
OFF BY FIRST LINE
FROM SHORE

FIG. 2
HAWSER HAWLED OFF
BY WHIP

FIG. 3
BREECHES
BUOY

BREECHES BUOY IN USE

Figure 20-14. Breeches buoy in use.

in case the boat is overturned when launching. As soon as one boat is cleared away and lowered, the remainder of the squad prepares the other boat for lowering, and then provides heaving lines to pass the sea painter to the boats and arranges for hoisting the boat or boats upon their return. A pilot's ladder is also hung over the side to take the crew aboard.

In case of collision, the squad reports to the scene and immediately starts closing hand-operated watertight doors adjacent to the damage, closes air ports and ventilation ducts passing through the boundary watertight bulkheads, and makes every effort to localize the damage and to enhance the watertight integrity of the ship adjacent to the damage. The chief officer instructs his messenger to report the extent of the damage to the master or mate on watch, with such recommendations as are necessary. All overboard discharges in the vicinity are closed and preparations are made to effect temporary repairs, if feasible. Soundings are taken of adjacent compartments to determine if leakage has occurred.

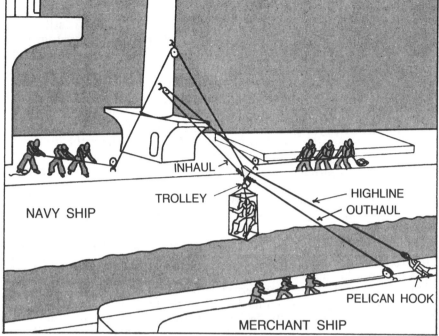

Figure 20-15. Manila highline rig. Drawing: Scott Duncan.

The emergency squad is thoroughly familiar with shifting steering control from the bridge to the steering engine room as discussed in Chapter IX. All deck and engineering officers as well as able seamen should understand how this is done. The importance of good communications between the bridge and steering engine room is vital.

The emergency squad has proven itself invaluable aboard ship. In many cases emergencies have been met successfully without having to call the entire crew to emergency stations. However, when the word is passed for the emergency squad, the prudent seaman will get ready for the general alarm bell. It may not be far behind.

BREECHES BUOY AND HIGHLINE

All U.S. flag ships are required to have "Lifesaving Signals and Breeches Buoy Instructions" posted on the bridge. This is a standard Coast Guard form which must be mounted behind glass or clear plastic. The illustration in the instructions is identical to Figure 20-14.

The illustration in Figure 20-14 is one that has not been changed for almost a century. It was the original used by the old U.S. Life Saving Service on Cape Cod. In that era the Life Saving Service patrolled the beaches where wrecks were apt to occur. At considerable risk to themselves they took survivors off wrecked and stranded ships. The functions of the Life Saving Service have long since been taken over by the Coast Guard. The possibility that a breeches buoy might be used is still considered great enough to warrant the instructions being posted on the bridge. You should become familiar with them as well as the "Lifesaving Signals" contained in Chapter XIII.

The use of the breeches buoy for rescue of stranded mariners is admittedly rare in the modern day, but you should know how it works and how to rig it, because its use for an emergency transfer of a sick or injured man to a Coast Guard or Navy ship at sea is a distinct possibility. There are at least two recent instances in the San Francisco Bay area where the breeches buoy or highline (to use the modern term) was used for rescue or salvage operations. The brother of one of the editors owes his life to a highline transfer which was conducted in the gathering darkness of an approaching storm. On his way over to the other ship he was still receiving blood plasma. The transfer was accomplished without interrupting the administration of blood plasma which was in the process at the time.

If the weather is too bad for helicopters or if boating is not possible for the same reason, you may find a Navy or Coast Guard vessel making an approach on your ship for a highline transfer. Figure 20-15 shows the highline rigged. Highline transfers of both personnel and stores are extensively used by the civilian manned Military Sealift Command ships.

The similarity between this drawing and the older one are apparent. The merchant ship will be asked to steady up on a course and speed so that she rides as easily as possible. Generally the course selected will bring the wind and sea one or two points on the starboard bow. The Navy or Coast Guard will make the approach and provide all the transfer gear. Instructions will be given by signal or more probably by loud hailer. A heaving line or shot line is passed to the merchant ship. This is followed by a larger line and snatch block. A 3 inch or 5 inch manila or synthetic highline follows. The highline will be tended by the Navy ship so that the only manpower required on the merchant ship will be to tend the outhaul or inhaul line. The method is quick and safe, but all hands should stay alert and pay attention. Spectators must stay clear, and all hands should wear life jackets and hard hats.

CHAPTER XXI

CONSULAR AFFAIRS

THE UNITED STATES MAINTAINS A CONSULATE in most major foreign seaports. The consulate is usually headed by a career foreign service officer called the consul-general. He is a member of the United States diplomatic team assigned to each foreign country which is headed by the ambassador. Among other duties, the consul-general is charged with looking out for United States shipping interest, including the protection, relief, and repatriation of America's seamen aboard.

The responsibilities and duties of the United States consul with respect to shipping and seamen are described in Volume 7 of the *Foreign Affairs Manual* published by the State Department. The following parts of this chapter are extracted and condensed from this publication. Only information deemed of vital interest to the merchant seaman is presented.

STATUS AS AN AMERICAN SEAMAN

A United States citizen or national acquires status as an American seaman by shipping on a vessel of the United States. After three or more years of reasonably continuous service on American merchant vessels he may retain his status even though not engaged as a seaman for a period of up to one year.

A foreign citizen can acquire status as an American seaman only by shipping on a United States vessel in a United States port. He may then reship on any United States vessel in either a United States or foreign port without losing his status. However, if he becomes a deserter or abandons his calling as a seaman he forfeits this status.

The status of an American seaman carries certain privileges of protection and relief under the laws of the United States and depends on whether or not the seaman has actually served on United States vessels, not simply on his possession of United States Merchant Marine documents. In the event of doubt as to a seaman's status, the State Department should verify his alleged service before the consul furnishes relief at the expense of the United States taxpayer.

A United States citizen employed on a foreign flag vessel is subject to the jurisdiction of the country whose flag the vessel flies and can have no claim at foreign ports to the special protection which the United States affords seamen employed on United States flag ships.

DOCUMENTS

A United States Merchant Mariner's Document has no expiration date and need not be renewed. However, if a seaman who is shown as a United States citizen loses his American citizenship, his document must be surrendered to the consulate for return to the Coast Guard. Should a document be lost in a foreign country and returned to the consulate, it will be sent to the Commandant, United States Coast Guard, not to the seaman.

In previous years a seaman who had become separated from or who was joining his ship needed only his Merchant Mariner's Document for travel to a foreign country where that ship was expected to be. Sometimes this is still possible, but more often than not foreign countries now require passports. A merchant seaman is well advised to have a valid passport. It will help insure that he is not delayed if he has to leave his ship for an emergency at home when he is in a foreign port.

CONSULAR SERVICES PROVIDED FOR SHIP AND CREW

A consulate may accept mail addressed to seamen on United States vessels. It will be held for pickup or forwarded as appropriate. The consulate will post pilot charts and *Notices to Mariners*. He will assist seamen who wish to vote by absentee ballot, and send their ballots to the United States by diplomatic pouch.

SHIPPING OF SEAMEN

In foreign ports the consul has responsibilities in signing seamen on and off articles. If a master engages a seaman in a foreign port where there is a United States consul, he must report the fact immediately to the consul. If no consul is present, the report should be made to the nearest United States consul. When a seaman is discharged in a foreign port, the master must make the required entries in the continuous discharge book and on the shipping articles. The entries must be attested to by the consular officer in ports where available.

If a master considers that he needs one or more seamen to continue the voyage, and no documented seamen are available, he may ship a person who is a United States citizen with no document provided the concurrence of the consul and the approval of the commandant of the Coast Guard is given. When a seaman is shipped before a consular officer at a foreign port, the consul must see that the seaman understands the contract. The seaman is not bound by a clause in the contract not read and explained to him.

The master of a vessel cannot discharge a seaman in a foreign port without the intervention of the consul whether or not the discharge is with the seaman's consent, whether or not the seaman has been guilty of misconduct, or if the seaman is not a citizen of the United States. The consul must be satisfied that the seaman has completed his shipping agreement or is entitled to his discharge according to the general principles or usages of maritime law. A seaman must be physically present to be discharged. Grounds for discharge include mutual consent of master and seaman, illness or injury, transfer to another vessel, or disrating.

The regulations for the payment of seamen discharged in the presence of the consul are complex, but in general the consular officer shall collect the wages from the master and in turn pay the seaman who must sign a receipt.

DESERTION AND FAILURE TO REJOIN SHIP

Desertion means the quitting of the vessel and her service without leave, against the obligation of the party, and with an intent not to return again to duty on the vessel. Neglect or refusal to rejoin the ship after authorized absence is desertion.

It is not considered desertion if a seaman has overstayed his time of leave because of excess of indulgence and has not refused or has neglected to comply with an order to return. Neither is it desertion if a seaman leaves his ship because of cruel or oppressive treatment, or for want of sufficient provisions in port when they could be procured by the master, or when the voyage is altered in the articles without his consent. A casual overstay of leave is not desertion, and neither is going ashore without permission, but with the intent to return.

Deserters forfeit all of the clothes or effects they leave on board as well as the pay which they may have earned up to the time of desertion. If the desertion occurs in a foreign port, the master must report the fact to the consul within 48 hours if possible. An alleged desertion shall be carefully investigated by the consul.

Although the imprisonment of merchant seamen charged with desertion in the United States is forbidden, deserters are subject to the laws of the country where they may be. Foreign authorities not infrequently detain deserters as persons who have not been lawfully admitted to the country under its immigration laws. When this occurs, consular officers procure as liberal treatment as possible for the seamen who are detained.

PROTESTS, DISPUTES, AND OFFENSES

American seamen are entitled to make complaints to consular officers concerning provisions, condition of water, the unseaworthiness of the vessel, or continuance of the voyage contrary to agreement. Although consular officers are authorized to protect seamen's rights under the statutes, they are not permitted to inject themselves into disputes between parties who have signed collective bargaining agreements.

When a dispute arises between the master and crew of a United States flag vessel or between seamen, a consular officer shall investigate the circumstances. He may act as arbiter, but has no authority to try or punish offending parties.

Less serious offenses committed aboard a merchant vessel in a foreign port are usually left by local governments to be adjusted by officers of the vessel and the diplomatic or consular representatives of the nation of registry. More serious ones will be handled by the local government. The foreign government has jurisdiction over offenses commited by seamen while ashore in its ports.

RELIEF AND REPATRIATION OF SEAMEN

United States shipowners or operators are responsible for relief and repatriation of all seamen separated from their vessels at foreign ports for any reason except desertion or shipwreck. However, the consular officer must furnish relief and repatriation to any destitute American seaman or to any shipwrecked, ill, or injured American seaman. He is also responsible for certified deserters.

A seaman applying to a consul for relief will be examined closely to insure that he is in fact entitled to relief. A seaman is not destitute when he has any arrears of wages or extra wages or is earning his own living. The exception to this is when he is shipwrecked, ill, or injured, or if his vessel has been abandoned by its owners and no funds are available for wages or maintenance.

An American seaman in jail in a foreign country or under indictment and out on bond is not entitled to relief. When a seaman leaves the United States as a passenger on a vessel bound for a foreign country and becomes destitute, he is entitled to no relief or aid from government funds as an American seaman. If a seaman has been furnished transportation from a foreign port to the United States and deserts at some intermediate port, he is not entitled to further relief from the United States government.

Any person who conceals himself on board a vessel and is discovered when the vessel is at sea is a stowaway. Unless the stowaway has been signed on the articles (which is extremely unlikely), a consular officer shall not extend relief to him as a destitute seaman in case he is put ashore. Seamen on undocumented vessels, unless they have individual status as American seamen, are not eligible for relief.

When seamen from United States flag vessels arrive at a foreign port after shipwreck, the consul shall make immediate arrangements for their relief. This is true whether or not an individual has status as an American seaman or has funds in his possession. In addition, American seamen, if they cannot be reshipped, should be provided with passage to the United States or an intermediate port where employment may be had or passage obtained.

When a seaman becomes ill or is injured in the service of a United States vessel and is formally discharged before a consul, relief may be furnished by the consul regardless of the cause of his illness or injury and whether or not he has funds of his own. Should the disability not be the result of misconduct, maritime usage has placed the responsibility of furnishing relief upon the operator of the ship.

It is important that a seaman who becomes ill or injured be discharged before a consular officer because otherwise the consular officer is not required by law to furnish relief unless the seaman is found destitute. A seaman who fails to rejoin his vessel but without intent to desert is termed a "straggler." Responsibility for his maintenance and repatriation remains with the shipowner.

The primary purpose of repatriation at government expense is to make seamen available once again to the American Merchant Marine. Consequently, a destitute seaman who is not a survivor of a shipwreck is only entitled to repatriation to a convenient port in the United States, while a shipwreck survivor will be transported to his port of shipment if he so desires.

Do not expect the consul to put you up at the best hotel if you are a shipwreck survivor. The following is a direct quote from the *Foreign Affairs Manual*:

> The lodging should be in a healthful locality, removed, if possible, from scenes of temptation and vice. The subsistence should be simple but sufficient...The clothing should be as inexpensive as is consistent with strength and durability.

A seaman must, if he is able to travel, accept the first offer of repatriation. Refusal deprives him of his right to further assistance.

DECEASED SEAMEN AND THEIR EFFECTS

The owner of a United States flag vessel is normally responsible for the payment of burial expenses of a seaman and may not deduct these expenses from his wages. Burial expenses are paid by the government only where the circumstances would have warranted expenditure of government funds for maintenance and repatriation had death not occurred. No government funds are available for the shipment of remains, but if the family desires the return of the body, the same procedure will be followed as in returning the bodies of other United States citizens.

When knowledge of the death of any American seaman or United States citizen serving on a foreign vessel reaches a consular officer, information shall be telegraphed to the State Department for transmittal to the next of kin.

If an American seaman dies aboard ship, the master should take charge of all monies, clothes, and effects left on board by the seaman. Should the ship touch at a foreign port before returning to the United States, the master is obliged to report the case to the consular officer there. If death occurs on foreign shore, the consular officer shall claim and take charge of any money or effects not on board the victim's vessel.

CONSULAR POWERS OF THE COMMANDING OFFICER OF A NAVAL VESSEL

The following quotation from *Title 10*, UNITED STATES CODE, ANNOTATED, Section 5948 concerns the consular powers vested in the commanding officer of a naval vessel or the senior officer of more than one vessel:

> In any foreign port where there is no resident consul of the United States, or on the high seas, the senior officer present afloat has the powers of a consul in relation to mariners of the United States.

CHAPTER XXII

LAWS PERTAINING TO MERCHANT SEAMEN

THIS CHAPTER COVERS THE NAVIGATION LAWS which affect the shipment, protection, disciplinary conduct, and discharge of seamen in the American Merchant Marine. Complete information on these and other laws pertaining to shipping is given in the U.S. CODE ANNOTATED which is simply a notated edition of the U.S. CODE. The latter in turn is the codified product of the REVISED STATUTES—the basic written laws of our country.

Reference to the various statutory laws usually takes the form of, for example, R.S. 4449 (*Title 46*, U.S.C., 240). This means that the REVISED STATUTE 4449 has been set in the U.S. CODE under *Title 46*, Section 240. Pertinent sections of the code are kept available at any steamship company, union headquarters, Coast Guard Officer in Charge, Marine Inspection (OCMI), or large public library. In addition the Commandant of the Coast Guard is required by statute to furnish copies of those laws dealing with vessel inspection and safety. As a result a library of Coast Guard publications has grown up which contains sections of the U.S. CODE appropriate to the subject matter of the pamphlet. The material which follows in this chapter is contained in *Laws Governing Marine Inspection, CG-227*. Examples of other Coast Guard publications are *Rules and Regulations for Cargo and Miscellaneous Vessels* (Sub-Chapter 1), *CG-257* and *Navigation Rules (International—Inland), CG-169*.

A seaman's first contact with the Articles of Agreement, or Shipping Articles, is experienced upon his "signing on" for a foreign voyage at a United States port.

Formerly these articles were signed before the shipping commissioner to insure that the nation could control the engagement, discharge, and protection of, as well as keep a record of, her merchant seamen. In 1979 this practice was terminated, and the Coast Guard and United States Customs were relieved of any responsibilities for the shipment and discharge of seamen.

The laws governing shipment and discharge of seamen were enacted in the nineteenth century as a result of serious abuses to mariners on ocean vessels. At that time there were few, if any, organized unions, no government agency to oversee safety, no National Labor Relations Board, and few public or private agencies to promote the welfare of the United States merchant seaman. Shipowners and masters who historically abused the rights of seamen now assume a much higher sense of responsibility, and as a result, the role of the "shipping commissioner" has become outmoded. Provision for his activities was officially dropped from the Department of Transportation's appropriations bill. The new Coast Guard procedures for the shipment and discharge of seamen have not been published in their final form, but "signing on" will probably take place with the master and the representatives of the owner as well as the maritime unions involved in attendance.

The rules concerning shipping articles with respect to the responsibilities formerly assigned the shipping commissioner are in a process of revision. Consequently, in the extracts of the code which follow, where the term "shipping commissioner" or "Coast Guard official to whom the duties of shipping commissioner have been delegated" appears, it must be understood that this function will be carried out in some other manner. Without doubt the rights of seamen will be preserved, and any change in shipment and discharge will be more apparent than real.

Shipping articles—The master of every vessel bound from a port in the United States to any foreign port other than vessels engaged in trade between the United States and the British North American possessions, or the West Indian Islands, or Mexico, or of any vessel of the burden of seventy-five tons or upward, bound from a port on the Atlantic to a port on the Pacific, or vice versa, shall, before he proceeds on such voyage, make an agreement, in writing or in print, with every seaman whom he carries to sea as one of the crew, in the manner hereinafter mentioned; and every such agreement shall be, as near as may be, in the form given . . ., and shall be dated at the time of the first signature thereof, and shall be signed by the master before any seaman signs the same, and shall contain the following particulars:

1. The nature and, as far as practicable, the duration of the intended voyage or engagement, and the port or the country at which the voyage is to terminate.

2. The number and description of the crew, specifying their respective employments.

3. The time at which each seaman is to be on board to begin work.

4. The capacity in which each seaman is to serve.

5. The amount of wages which each seaman is to receive.

6. A scale of the provisions which are to be furnished to each seaman.

7. Any regulations as to conduct on board, and as to fines, short allowance of provisions, or other lawful punishments for misconduct, which may be sanctioned by Congress and not contrary to or not otherwise provided for by law, which the parties agree to adopt.

8. Any stipulations in reference to advance and allotments of wages, or other matters not contrary to law. (*Title 46*, U.S.C., 564.)

Rules for shipping articles—The following rules shall be observed with respect to agreements:

1. Every agreement, except such as are otherwise specially provided for, shall be signed by each seaman in the presence of a Coast Guard official to whom the duties of shipping commissioner have been delegated.

2. When the crew is first engaged the agreement shall be signed in duplicate, and one part shall be retained by such Coast Guard official, and the other part shall contain a special place or form for the description and signatures of persons engaged subsequently to the first departure of the ship, and shall be delivered to the master.

3. Every agreement entered into before such Coast Guard official shall be acknowledged and certified under the hand and official seal of same. The certificate of acknowledgment shall be endorsed on or annexed to the agreement; and shall be in the following form:

"State of . . . . County of . . . . :

"On this . . . . . . day of . . . ., personally appeared before me, a Coast Guard official in and for the said county, A.B., C.D., and E.F., severally known to me to be the same persons who executed the foregoing instrument, who each for himself acknowledged to me that he had read or had heard read the same; that he was by me made acquainted with the conditions thereof, and understood the same; and that, while sober and not in a state of intoxication, he signed it freely and voluntarily, for the uses and purposes therein mentioned." (*Title 46,* U.S.C., 565.)

Shipping seamen to replace those lost by desertion or casualty—In case of desertion or casualty resulting in the loss of one or more of the seamen, the master must ship, if obtainable, a number equal to the number of those whose services he has been deprived of by desertion or casualty, who must be of the same or higher grade or rating with those whose places they fill, and report the same to the United States consul at the first port at which he shall arrive, without incurring the penalty prescribed by sections 567 and 568 of this title. This section shall not apply to fishing or whaling vessels or yachts. (*Title 46,* U.S.C., 569.)

Shipping seamen in foreign ports—Every master of a merchant vessel who engages any seaman at a place out of the United States, in which there is a consular officer shall, before carrying such seaman to sea, procure the sanction of such officer, and shall engage seamen in his presence; and the rules governing the engagement of seamen before a Coast Guard official to whom the duties of shipping commissioner have been delegated in the United States, shall apply to such engagements made before a consular officer; and upon every such engagement the consular officer shall endorse upon the agreement his sanction thereof, and an attestation to the effect that the same has been signed in his presence, and otherwise duly made. (*Title 46,* U.S.C., 570.)

Period of engagement—A master of a vessel in the foreign trade may engage a seaman at any port in the United States, in the manner provided by law, to serve on a voyage to any port, or for the round trip from and to the port of departure, or for a definite time, whatever the destination. The master of a vessel making regular and stated trips between the United States and a foreign country may engage a seaman for one or more round trips, or for a definite time, or on the return of said vessel to the United States may reship such seaman for another voyage in the same vessel, in the manner provided by law. (*Title 46,* U.S.C., 572.)

Voyage or term of seaman shipped in foreign port; reshipment; bond—Every master of a vessel in the foreign trade may engage any seaman at any port out of the United States, in the manner provided by law, to serve for one or more round trips from and to the port of departure, or for a definite time, whatever the destination; and the master of a vessel clearing from a port of the United States with one or more seamen engaged in a foreign port as herein provided shall not be required to reship in a port of the United States the seamen so engaged, or to give bond, to produce said seamen before a boarding officer on return of said vessel to the United States. (*Title 46,* U.S.C., 573.)

Copy of agreement to be posted—A legible copy of the Shipping Articles, omitting signatures, shall be placed or posted up in such part of the vessel as to be accessible to the crew, at the commencement of the voyage or engagement. (*Title 46,* U.S.C., 577.)

List of crew for collector of customs—Before clearance is granted to any vessel bound on a foreign voyage or engaged in the whale fishery, the master of such vessel shall deliver to the collector of customs a list containing the names, places of birth and residence, and description of the persons who compose his ship's company; to which list the oath of the captain shall be annexed, that the list contains the names of his crew, together with the places of their birth and residence as far as he can ascertain them; and the collector shall deliver him a certified copy thereof. (*Title 46,* U.S.C., 674.)

Requirements, qualifications, and regulations as to crews—Qualifications—(a) No vessel of one hundred tons gross and upward, except those navigating rivers exclusively and the smaller inland lakes and except as provided in section 569 of this title, shall be permitted to depart from any port of the United States unless she has on board a crew not less than 75 per centum of which, in each department thereof, are able to understand any order given by the officers of such vessel, nor unless 65 per centum of her deck crew, exclusive of licensed officers and apprentices, are of a rating not less than able seamen. Every person shall be rated an able seaman, and qualified for service as such on the seas, who is nineteen years of age or upward, and has had at least three years' service on deck at sea or on the Great Lakes, on a vessel or vessels to which this section applies, including decked fishing vessels, and vessels in United States Government service; and every person shall be rated an able seaman, and qualified to serve as such on the Great Lakes and on the smaller lakes, bays, or sounds who is nineteen years of age or upward and has had at least eighteen months' service on deck at sea or on the Great Lakes or on the smaller lakes, bays, or sounds, on a vessel or vessels to which this section applies, including decked fishing vessels and vessels in the United States Government service; and graduates of school ships approved by and conducted under rules prescribed by the Commandant of the Coast Guard may be rated able seamen upon graduation in good standing from said school ships: *Provided,* That no boy shall be shipped on any vessel to which this section applies unless he meets the physical qualifications contained in regulations to be prescribed by the Commandant of the Coast Guard and that no boy shall be placed on the lookout or at the wheel except for the purpose of learning, and that in narrow and crowded waters or in low visibility none below the rating of able seaman shall be permitted at the wheel; *Provided further,* That no deck boy shall be held qualified to fill the place of ordinary seaman until he has had at least six months' service as deck boy: *Provided further,* That upon examination, under rules prescribed by the Coast guard as to eyesight, hearing, and physical condition, such persons or graduates are found to be competent: *Provided further,* That upon examination, under rules prescribed by the Coast Guard as to eyesight, hearing, physical condition, and knowledge of the duties of seamanship, a person found competent may be rated as able seaman after having served on deck twelve months at sea or on the Great Lakes, but seamen examined and rated able seamen under this proviso shall not in any case compose more than one-fourth of the number of able seamen required by this section to be shipped or employed upon any vessel.

Certificate of service as able seaman—(b) Application may be made to the Coast Guard for a certificate of service as able seaman, and upon proof being made to the Coast Guard by affidavit and examination, under rules approved by the Commandant of the Coast Guard, showing the nationality and age of the applicant, the vessel or vessels on which he has had service, that he is skilled in the work usually performed by able seamen, and that he is entitled to such certificate under the provisions of this section, the Coast Guard shall issue to said applicant a certificate of service as able seaman, which shall be retained by him and be accepted as prima-facie evidence of his rating as an able seaman.

Record of certificates of service—(c) Each Coast Guard official shall keep a complete record of all certificates of service issued by him and to whom issued and shall keep on file the affidavits and records of examinations upon which said certificates are issued.

Muster of the crew on motion or information; rules and regulations; examination of applicant for certificate of service as able seaman; surrender of certificates; new certificates—(d) The collector of customs may, upon his own motion, and shall, upon the sworn information of any reputable citizen of the United States setting forth that this section is not being complied with, cause a muster of the crew of any vessel to be made to determine the fact, at which muster said reputable citizen must be present; and no clearance shall be given to any vessel failing to comply with the provisions of this section: *Provided,* That the collector of customs shall not be required to cause such muster of the crew to be made unless said sworn information has been filed with him for at least six hours before the vessel departs, or is scheduled to depart: *Provided further,* That any person that shall knowingly make a false affidavit for such purpose shall be deemed guilty of perjury and upon conviction thereof shall be punished by a fine not exceeding $500 or by imprisonment not exceeding one year, or by both such fine and imprisonment, within the discretion of the court. Any violation of any provision of this section by the owner, master, or officer in charge of the vessel shall subject the owner of such vessel to a penalty of not less than $100 and not more than $500: *Provided further,* That the Commandant of the Coast Guard shall make such rules and regulations as may be necessary to carry out the provisions of this section, and nothing herein shall be held or construed to prevent the Commandant of the Coast Guard from making rules and regulations authorized by law as to vessels excluded from the operation of this section: *And provided further*, That no certificate of service as able seaman shall be issued by the Coast Guard until after examination of the applicant therefor, under rules and regulations prescribed by the Commandant of the Coast Guard, as to his efficiency, and upon proof, as a result of such examination, that he has been trained in and is acquainted with the duties entitling him to such rating. No seaman shall be considered an "able seaman" within the meaning of the laws of the United States relating to the manning of vessels unless he is in possession of such certificate issued by the board of local inspectors of the Coast Guard. All certificates as "able seaman" and "lifeboatman" issued by the several boards of local inspectors or other Federal officers prior to June 25, 1936, shall, within six months thereafter, be surrendered to such boards of local inspectors for cancellation, and there shall be issued in lieu thereof to all able seamen and lifeboatmen found qualified by such examination new certificates as required by law: *Provided,* That if due to inability on the part of the Department of Commerce to carry out the provisions of this subsection with regard to all seamen, the Secretary of Commerce may, in his discretion, extend the time for a period not to exceed three months. Such new certificates shall be stamped with the seal of the board of local inspectors or the Coast Guard, placed partially over the signature of the applicant for such certificate; and there shall be attached thereto a photograph of the applicant. Any other safeguards which, in the judgment of the Commandant of the Coast Guard, may be necessary and advisable to establish the authenticity of the certificate, are authorized.

Members of engine department—(e) No vessel to which this section applies may be navigated unless all of the complement in her engine department above the rating of coal passer or wiper and below the rating of licensed officer shall be holders of a certificate of service as a qualified member of the engine department. The Coast Guard shall, upon application and examination as to competence and physical condition, as prescribed by the Commandant of the Coast Guard, issue such a certificate of service. An applicant for such rating shall produce to the Coast Guard definite proof of at least six months' service at sea in a rating at least equal to that of coal passer or wiper in the engine department of vessels required by this section to have such certificated men or proof that he is a graduate of a school ship approved by and conducted under rules prescribed by the Commandant of the Coast Guard.

Rules as to certificates of service or efficiency—(f) As to the certificates of service or efficiency, the Commandant of the Coast Guard shall promulgate rules covering the form, contents, and manner of issuance, which shall include a provision that copies of these and all documents pertaining thereto be filed in the local offices and in the central office in Washington.

Certificates of service for other ratings—(g) The Coast Guard shall, without examination (except food handlers who must be free from communicable disease), issue to all members of the crews of merchant vessels of the United States (except licensed officers), certificates of service for ratings other than as able seaman or a qualified member of the engine department, which certificates shall authorize them to serve in the capacities specified in such certificates: *Provided,* That such certificates shall not issue before oath has been taken before a Coast Guard official that the applicant therefor will faithfully and honestly perform all the duties required of him by law, and carry out the lawful orders of his superior officers on shipboard and, in the case of a radio operator, shall produce to the Coast Guard his unexpired license issued by the Federal Communications Commission to act in that capacity: *And provided further,* That when a certificate has been revoked or suspended under the provisions of subsection (h) of this section, a new certificate shall not be issued until the Coast Guard shall determine that the issue of such new certificate is compatible with the requirements of good discipline and safety at sea.

Suspension or revocation of certificates of service or efficiency—(h) All certificates of service or efficiency issued by the Bureau of Marine Inspection and Navigation or the Coast

Guard shall be subject to suspension or revocation on the same grounds and in the same manner and with like procedure as is provided in the case of suspension or revocation of licenses of officers under the provisions of section 239 of this title.

Penalty for serving without certificate of service—(i) It shall be unlawful to employ any person, or for any person to serve aboard any merchant vessel of the United States, below the rating of licensed officer, who has not a certificate of service issued by a board of local inspectors or the Coast Guard, and anyone violating this section shall be liable to a penalty of $100 for each offense.

Effect of section on other laws—(j) This section is not to amend or repeal any of the provisions of chapter 3 of *Title 47.*

Freedom of seamen unimpaired—(k) Nothing in this section shall be construed to impose, sanction, or permit any condition of involuntary servitude nor to prevent any seaman from leaving the service of any vessel when in a safe harbor to the same extent and with like effect as under the provisions of existing law.

Effective date of section—(l) This section shall take effect six months after June 25, 1936; *Provided,* That if it is found impracticable on the part of the Department of Commerce to furnish the certificates herein provided, the Secretary of Commerce may, in his discretion, extend the effective date for a period not exceeding three months. (*Title 46,* U.S.C., 672.)

Exception to section 672, certain sail vessels—The provisions of section 672 of this title, relating to the manning of certain vessels, shall not apply to any sail vessel of less than five hundred tons registered tonnage, while not carrying passengers for hire, and while not operating outside the line dividing inland waters from the high seas, as defined in section 151 of *Title 33.* (*Title 46,* U.S.C., 672-1.)

Exceptions to section 672; certain persons as able seamen—Notwithstanding any provision of section 672 of this title, every person may be rated as an able seaman for the purpose of serving on vessels of not more than five hundred gross tons, on bays and sounds, when such vessels are not carrying passengers, who is nineteen years of age and upward and who has had at least twelve months of service on deck at sea or on the Great Lakes or on the bays and sounds connected directly with the seas. (*Title 46,* U.S.C., 672-2.)

Nationality of crews—Officers and pilots—(a) From and after June 25, 1936, all licensed officers and pilots of vessels of the United States shall be citizens of the United States, native-born, or completely naturalized.

Seamen—(b) From and after six months after June 25, 1936, upon each departure of any such vessel from a port of the United States, 75 per centum of the crew, excluding licensed officers, shall be citizens of the United States, native-born, or completely naturalized, unless the Commandant of the Coast Guard shall, upon investigation, ascertain that qualified citizen seamen are not available, when, under such conditions, he may reduce the above percentages.

Vacancies on foreign voyage—(c) If any vessel while on a foreign voyage is for any reason deprived of the services of any member of the crew, such position or vacancy caused by the promotion of another to such position may be supplied by a person other than defined in subsection (a) and (b) of this section until the first call of such vessel at a port in the United States where such replacements can be obtained.

Penalty for violating section—(d) The owner, agent, or officer of any such vessel, who shall employ any person in violation of the provisions of this section, shall be subject to a penalty of $500 for each offense. (*Title 46,* U.S.C., 672a.)

Exceptions to section 672; unrigged vessels, tugs, and towboats—The provisions of section 672 of this title, requiring the manning of certain merchant vessels by persons holding certificates of service or efficiency issued by the Bureau of Marine Inspection and Navigation or the Coast Guard shall not apply as to unrigged vessels, except seagoing barges, and, insofar as said provisions apply to tugs and towboats, the said provisions are modified as follows:

Able seamen; rating—(a) Able seamen shall not be required in the deck crew of tugs and towboats on the bays and sounds connected directly with the seas, and every person may be rated an able seaman for the purpose of serving on tugs and towboats on the seas who is nineteen years of age and upwards and who has had at least eighteen months of service on deck at sea or on the Great Lakes or on the bays and sounds connected directly with the seas; and

Service and rating equal to coal passer or wiper—(b) Service and rating at least equal to that of coal passer or wiper in the engine department of tugs and towboats operating on the seas or Great Lakes or on the bays and sounds connected directly with the seas shall be considered as meeting the requirement of subsection (e) of section 672 of this title which requires that an applicant for rating under that subsection shall produce to the Coast Guard definite proof of at least six months' service at sea in a rating at least equal to that of coal passer or wiper in the engine department of vessels required by said section to have such certificated men.

Nothing in this section shall restrict or modify any of the other provisions of section 672 of this title which must be complied with before the certificates therein authorized can be granted. (*Title 46*, U.S.C., 672b.)

Exceptions to section 672; seagoing barges—Notwithstanding any provisions of section 672 of this title, every person may be rated as an able seaman for the purpose of serving on seagoing barges who is nineteen years of age and upward, and who has had at least twelve months of service on deck at sea or on the Great Lakes or on the bays and sounds connected directly with the seas. (*Title 46*, U.S.C., 672b-1.)

Requirements as to watches; duties of seamen; hours of work; penalty; right of seamen to discharge; effective date—In all merchant vessels of the United States of more than one hundred tons gross, excepting those navigating rivers, harbors, lakes (other than Great Lakes), bays, sounds, bayous, and canals, exclusively, the licensed officers and sailors, coal passers, firemen, oilers, and water tenders shall, while at sea, be divided into at least three watches, which shall be kept on duty successively for the performance of ordinary work incident to the sailing and management of the vessel: *Provided,* That in the case of radiotelegraph operators this requirement shall be applicable only when three or more radio officers are employed. No licensed officer or seaman in the deck or engine department of any tug documented under the laws of the United States (except boats or vessels used exclusively for fishing purposes) navigating the Great Lakes, harbors of the Great Lakes, and connecting and tributary waters between Gary, Indiana; Duluth, Minnesota; Niagara Falls, New York; and Ogdensburg, New York, shall be required or permitted to work more than eight hours in one day except in case of extraordinary emergency affecting the safety of the vessel and/or life or property. The seamen shall not be shipped to work alternately in the fireroom and on deck, nor shall those shipped for deck duty be required to work in the fireroom, or vice versa; nor shall any licensed officer or seaman in the deck or engine department be required to work more than eight hours in one day; but these provisions shall not limit either the authority of the master or other officer or the obedience of the seamen when in the judgment of the master or other officer the whole or any part of the crew are needed for maneuvering, shifting berth, mooring, or unmooring, the vessel or the performance of work necessary for the safety of the vessel, her passengers, crew, and cargo, or for the saving of life aboard other vessels in jeopardy, or when in port or at sea, from requiring the whole or any part of the crew to participate in the performance of fire, lifeboat, or other drills. While such vessel is in a safe harbor no seaman shall be required to do any unnecessary work on Sundays or the following-named days: New Year's Day, the Fourth of July, Labor Day, Thanksgiving Day, and Christmas Day, but this shall not prevent the dispatch of a vessel on regular schedule or when ready to proceed on her voyage. And at all times while such vessel is in a safe harbor, eight hours, inclusive of the anchor watch, shall constitute a day's work. Whenever the master of any vessel shall fail to comply with this section and the regulation issued thereunder, the owner shall be liable to a penalty not to exceed $500, and the seamen shall be entitled to discharge from such vessel and to receive the wages earned. But this section shall not apply to vessels engaged in salvage operations: *Provided,* That in all tugs and barges subject to this section when engaged on a voyage of less than six hundred miles, the licensed officers and members of crews other than coal passers, firemen, oilers, and water tenders may, while at sea, be divided into not less than two watches, but nothing in this proviso shall be construed as repealing any part of section 222 of this title. This section shall take effect six months after June 25, 1936. (*Title 46*, U.S.C., 673.)

Offenses and punishments—Whenever any seaman who has been lawfully engaged or any apprentice to the sea service commits any of the following offenses, he shall be punished as follows:

1. For desertion, by forfeiture of all or any part of the clothes or effects he leaves on board and of all or any part of the wages or emoluments which he has then earned.

2. For neglecting or refusing without reasonable cause to join his vessel or to proceed to sea in his vessel, or for absence without leave at any time within 24 hours of the vessel's sailing from any port, either at the commencement or during the progress of the voyage, or for absence at any time without leave and without sufficient reason from his vessel and from his duty, not amounting to desertion, by forfeiture from his wages of not more than two days' pay or sufficient to defray any expenses which shall have been properly incurred in hiring a substitute.

3. For quitting the vessel without leave, after her arrival at the port of her delivery and before she has been placed in security, by forfeiture from his wages of not more than one month's pay.

4. For willful disobedience to any lawful command at sea, by being, at the option of the master, placed in irons until such disobedience shall cease, and upon arrival in port by forfeiture from his wages of not more than 4 days' pay, or, at the discretion of the court, by imprisonment for not more than one month.

5. For continued willful disobedience to lawful command or continued willful neglect of duty at sea, by being, at the option of the master, placed in irons, on bread and water, with full rations every fifth day, until such disobedience shall cease, and upon arrival in port by forfeiture, for every 24 hours' continuance of such disobedience or neglect, of a sum of not more than 12 days' pay, or by imprisonment for not more than three months, at the discretion of the court.

6. For assaulting any master, mate, pilot, engineer, or staff officer, by imprisonment for not more than two years.

7. For willfully damaging the vessel, or embezzling or willfully damaging any of the stores or cargo, by forfeiture out of his wages of a sum equal in amount to the loss thereby sustained and also, at the discretion of the court, by imprisonment for not more than 12 months.

8. For any act of smuggling for which he is convicted and whereby loss or damage is occasioned to the master or owner, he shall be liable to pay such master or owner such a sum as is sufficient to reimburse the master for such a loss or damage, and the whole or any part of his wages may be retained in satisfaction or on account of such liability, and he shall be liable to imprisonment for a period of not more than 12 months. (*Title 46*, U.S.C., 701.)

Entry of offense in logbook—Upon the commission of any of the offenses enumerated in section 701 an entry thereof shall be made in the official log book on the day on which the offense was committed, and shall be signed by the master and by the mate or one of the crew; and the offender, if still in the vessel, shall, before her arrival at any port, or, if she is at the time in port, before her departure therefrom, be furnished with a copy of such entry and have the same read over distinctly and audibly to him, and may thereupon make such a reply thereto as he thinks fit; and a statement that a copy of the entry has been so furnished, or the same has been so read over, together with his reply, if any, made by the offender, shall likewise be entered and signed in the same manner. In any subsequent legal proceedings the entries hereinbefore required shall, if practicable, be produced or proved, and in default of such production or proof the court hearing the case may, at its discretion, refuse to receive evidence of the offense. (*Title 46,* U.S.C., 702.)

It is the duty of consular officers to discountenance insubordination by every means in their power, and, where the local authorities can be usefully employed for that purpose, to lend their aid and use their exertions to that end in the most effectual manner. In all cases where seamen or officers are accused, the consular officer shall inquire into the facts and proceed as provided in section 685 of this title; and the officer discharging such seaman shall enter upon the crew list and shipping articles and official log the cause of such discharge and the particulars in which the cruel or unusual treatment consisted and subscribe his name thereto officially. He shall read the entry made in the official log to the master, and his reply thereto, if any, shall likewise be entered and subscribed in the same manner. (*Title 46,* U.S.C., 703).

Disposal of forfeitures—All clothes, effects, and wages which, under the provisions of Title 53 of the REVISED STATUTES, are forfeited for desertion, shall be applied in the first instance, in payment of the expenses occasioned by such desertion, to the master or owner of the vessel from which the desertion has taken place, and the balance, if any, shall be paid by the master or owner to any Coast Guard official to whom the duties of shipping commissioner have been delegated resident at the port at which the voyage of such vessel terminates; and such Coast Guard official shall account for and pay over such balance to the judge of the district court within one month after such Coast Guard official receives the same, to be disposed of by him in the same manner as is prescribed for the disposal of the money, effects, and wages of deceased seamen. Whenever any master or owner neglects or refuses to pay over to such Coast Guard official in the same manner that seamen's wages are recovered. In all other cases of forfeiture of wages, the forfeiture shall be for the benefit of the master or owner by whom the wages are payable. (*Title 46,* U.S.C., 706.)

CRIMES

Other serious offenses are designated as crimes and are punishable when committed upon the high seas or on any other waters within the admiralty and maritime jurisdiction of the United States. Punishments are provided in the Criminal Code of the United States:

Manslaughter, murder
Mayhem
Asault
Attempted murder or manslaughter
Death caused by negligence of employer
Rape
Carnal knowledge of minor
Ill-treatment of crew
Abandonment of seaman
Inciting mutiny on shipboard
Revolt and mutiny
Yielding or running away with vessel or cargo
Robbery
Larceny
Receiving stolen property
Obtaining money by false pretenses
Forgery
Perjury

Conspiracy against United States
Barratry
Arson
Wrecking
Laying violent hands on commander
Plundering vessel
Breaking and entering vessel
Destroying vessel at sea by owner
Destroying vessel at sea by person other than owner
Piracy, crimes deemed
Piratical crew, robbery on shore by
Piracy under color of foreign commision
Piracy by aliens
Pirates, confederating with, and confining master
Shipping packages of liquor in interstate commerce not plainly marked
Reproducing United States official insignia

PROTECTION AND RELIEF

Coast Guard official as arbiter—Every Coast Guard official to whom the duties of shipping commissioner have been delegated shall hear and decide any question whatsoever between a master, consignee, agent, or owner and any of his crew, which both parties agree in writing to submit to him; and every award so made by him shall be binding on both parties, and shall, in any legal proceedings which may be taken in the matter, before any court of justice, be deemed to be conclusive as to the rights of parties. And any document under the hand and official seal of such Coast Guard official purporting to be such submission or award, shall be prima facie evidence thereof. (*Title 46,* U.S.C., 651.)

Complaint that vessel is unseaworthy—If the first and second officers under the master or a majority of the crew of any vessel bound on any voyage shall, before the vessel shall have left the harbor, discover that the vessel is too leaky or is otherwise unfit in her crew, body, tackle, apparel, furniture, provisions, or stores to proceed on the intended voyage, and shall require such unfitness to be inquired into, the master shall upon the request of the first and second officers under the master or such majority of the crew, forthwith apply to the judge of the district court of that judicial district, if he shall there reside, or if not, to some justice of the peace of the city, town, or place for the appointment of surveyors, as provided in section 654 of this title, taking with him two or more of the crew who shall have made such request; and any master refusing or neglecting to comply with these provisions shall be liable to a penalty of $500. This section shall not apply to fishing or whaling vessels or yachts. (*Title 46*, U.S.C., 653.)

Proceedings on examination of vessel—The judge, or justice, in a domestic port, shall, upon such application of the master or commander, issue his precept, directed to three persons in the neighborhood, the most experienced and skillful in maritime affairs that can be procured; and whenever such complaint is about the provisions, one of such surveyors shall be a physician or a surgeon of the Public Health Service. If such service is established at the place where the complaint is made, it shall be the duty of such surveyors to repair on board such vessel and to examine the same in respect to the defects and insufficiencies complained of, and make reports to the judge, or justice, as the case may be, in writing, under their hands or the hands of two of them whether in any or in what respect the vessel is unfit to proceed on the intended voyage, and what addition of men, provisions, or stores, or what repairs or alterations in the body, tackle, or apparel will be necessary; and upon such report the judge or justice shall adjudge and shall endorse on his report his judgment whether the vessel is fit to proceed on the intended voyage, and, if not, whether such repairs can be made or deficiencies supplied where the vessel then lies, or whether it is necessary for her to proceed to the nearest or most convenient place where such repairs can be made or deficiencies supplied; and the master and the crew shall, in all things, conform to the judgment. The master or commander shall, in the first instance, pay all the costs of such review, report, or judgment to be taxed and allowed on a fair copy thereof, certified by the judge or justice. But if the complaint of the crew shall appear upon the report and judgment to have been without foundation, the master or commander, or the owner or consignee of such vessel shall deduct the amount thereof and of reasonable damages for detention, to be ascertained by the judge or justice, out of the wages of the complaining seamen. This section shall not apply to fishing or whaling vessels or yachts. (*Title 46*, U.S.C., 654.)

Refusal to proceed when vessel found seaworthy—If, after judgment that such vessel is fit to proceed on her intended voyage, or after procuring such men, provisions, stores, repairs, or alterations as may be directed, the seamen, or either of them, shall refuse to proceed on the voyage, he shall forfeit any wages that may be due him. This section shall not apply to fishing or whaling vessels or yachts. (*Title 46*, U.S.C., 655.)

Appointment of inspectors by consul in foreign port—Upon a complaint in writing, signed by the first and second officers or a majority of the crew of any vessel, while in a foreign port, that such vessel is in an unsuitable condition to go to sea because she is leaky or insufficiently supplied with sails, rigging, anchors, or any other equipment, or that the crew is insufficient to man her, or that her provisions, stores, and supplies are not or have not been during the voyage sufficient or wholesome, thereupon, in any of these or like cases the consul shall cause to be appointed three persons of like qualifications with those described in section 654 (*46*, U.S.C.), who shall proceed to examine into the cause of complaint and who shall proceed and be governed in all their proceedings as provided by said section. (*Title 46*, U.S.C., 656.)

Report of inspectors—The inspectors appointed by any consul, in pursuance of the preceding section, shall have full power to examine the vessel and whatever is aboard of her, so far as is pertinent to their inquiry, and also to hear and receive any other proofs which the ends of justice may require; and if, upon a view of the whole proceedings, the consul is satisfied therewith, he may approve the whole or any part of the report, and shall certify such approval; or if he dissents he shall certify his reasons for dissenting. (*Title 46*, U.S.C., 657.)

Discharge of crew on account of unseaworthiness—The inspectors in their report shall also state whether in their opinion the vessel was sent to sea unsuitably provided in any important or essential particular, by neglect or design, or through mistake or accident; and in case it was by neglect or design, and the consular officer approves of such finding, he shall discharge such of the crew as request it, and shall require the payment by the master of one month's wages for each seaman over and above the wages then due, or sufficient money for the return of such of the crew as desire to be discharged to the nearest and most convenient port of the United States, or by furnishing the seamen who so desire to be discharged with employment on a ship agreed to by them. But if in the opinion of the inspectors the defects or deficiencies found to exist have been the result of mistake or accident, and could not, in the exercise of ordinary care, have been known and provided against before the sailing of the vessel, and the master shall in a reasonable time remove or remedy the causes of complaint, then the crew shall remain and discharge their duty.

If any person knowingly sends or attempts to send or is a party to the sending or attempting to send an American ship to sea, in the foreign or coastwise trade, in such an unseaworthy state that the life of any person is likely to be thereby endangered, he shall, in respect of each offense, be guilty of a misdemeanor, and shall be punished by a fine not to exceed $1000 or by imprisonment not to exceed five years, or both, at the discretion of the court, unless he proves that either he used all reasonable means to ensure her being sent to sea in a seaworthy state, or that her going to sea in an unseaworthy state was, under the circumstances, reasonable and justifiable, and for the purposes of giving that proof he may give evidence in the same manner as any other witness. (*Title 46*, U.S.C., 658.)

Payment of inspection charges—The master shall pay all such reasonable charges for inspection under such complaint as shall be officially certified to him under the hand of the consul; but in case the inspectors report that the complaint is without any good and sufficient cause, the master may retain from the wages of the complainants, in proportion to the pay of each, the amount of such charges, with such reasonable damages for detention on that account as the consul directing the inquiry may officially certify. (*Title 46*, U.S.C., 659.)

Inspection of crew quarters—Time and extent—Local marine inspection officers shall inspect the crew quarters of every American vessel, at least once in each month, or at such time as such vessel shall enter an American port, and shall satisfy themselves that such quarters are of the size required by law or regulations issued thereunder, are properly ventilated and in a clean and sanitary condition, and are equipped with the proper plumbing and mechanical applicances required by law or regulations issued thereunder, and that such plumbing and mechanical appliances are in good working order and condition. (*Title 46*, U.S.C., 660a.)

Paragraph (*b*) of this section provides that, upon proof that such improper condition as shall have been willingly or negligently permitted in violation of these requirements by the licensed officer in charge of such vessel, a penalty will be assessed of not more than $500.

Medicines—Every vessel belonging to a citizen of the United States, bound from a port in the United States to any foreign port, or being of the burden of 75 tons or upward, and bound from a port on the Atlantic to a port on the Pacific, or vice versa, shall be provided with a chest of medicines; and every sailing vessel bound on a voyage across the Atlantic or Pacific Ocean, or around Cape Horn, or the Cape of Good Hope, or engaged in the whaling or other fisheries, or in sealing, shall also be provided with, and cause to be kept, a sufficient quantity of lime or lemon juice, and also sugar and vinegar, or other antiscorbutics, to be served out to every seaman as follows: The master of every such vessel shall serve the lime or lemon juice, and sugar and vinegar, to the crew, within 10 days after salt provisions mainly have been served out to the crew and so long afterward as such consumption of salt provisions continues; the lime or lemon juice and sugar daily at the rate of half an ounce each per day; and the vinegar weekly at the rate of half a pint per week for each member of the crew. (*Title 46*, U.S.C., 666.)

Clothing and heat—Every vessel bound on any foreign voyage exceeding in length 14 days shall be provided with at least one suit of woolen clothing for each seaman, and every vessel in the foreign or domestic trade shall provide a safe and warm room for the use of seamen in cold weather. Failure to meet such provision shall subject the owner or master to a penalty of not less than $100. This section shall not apply to fishing or whaling vessels or yachts. (*Title 46*, U.S.C., 669.)

Slop chest—Every vessel mentioned in Section 666 of this title shall also be provided with a slop chest, which shall contain a complement of clothing for the intended voyage for each seaman employed, including boots or shoes, hats or caps, underclothing and outer clothing, oil clothing, and everything necessary for the wear of a seaman; also a full supply of tobacco and blankets. Any of the contents of the slop chest shall be sold, from time to time, to any or every seaman applying therefor, for his own use, at a profit not exceeding 10 per centum of the reasonable wholesale value of the same at the port at which the voyage commenced. And if any such vessel is not provided, before sailing, as herein required, the owner shall be liable to a penalty of not more than $500. The provisions of this section shall not apply to vessels plying between the United States and the Dominion of Canada, Newfoundland, the Bermuda Islands, the Bahama Islands, the West Indies, Mexico, and Central America. (*Title 46*, U.S.C., 670.)

EFFECTS OF DECEASED SEAMEN

Duty of master where seaman dies during voyage—Whenever any seaman or apprentice belonging to or sent home on any merchant vessel, whether a foreign-going or domestic vessel, employed on a voyage which is to terminate in the United States, dies during such voyage, the master shall take charge of all moneys, clothes, and effects which he leaves on board, and shall, if he thinks fit, cause all or any of such clothes and effects to be sold by auction at the mast or other public auction, and shall thereupon sign an entry in the official log book, and cause it to be attested by the mate and one of the crew, containing the following particulars:

1. A statement of the amount of money so left by the deceased.

2. In the case of a sale, a description of each article sold, and the sum received for each.

3. A statement of the sum due to deceased as wages, and the total amount of deductions, if any, to be made therefrom. (*Title 46*, U.S.C., 621.)

Proceedings in regard to effects—In cases embraced by section 621 of this title, the following rules shall be observed:

1. If the vessel proceeds at once to any port in the United States, the master shall, within forty-eight hours after his arrival, deliver any such effects remaining unsold, and pay any money which he has taken charge of or received from such sale, and the balance of wages due to the deceased, to the Coast Guard official to whom the duties of shipping commissioner have been delegated at the port of destination in the United States.

2. If the vessel touches and remains at some foreign port before coming to any port in the United States, the master shall report the case to the United States consular officer there, and shall give to such officer any information he requires as to the destination of the vessel and probable length of the voyage; and such officer may, if he considers it expedient so to do, require the effects, money, and wages to be delivered and paid to him, and shall, upon such delivery and payment, give to the master a receipt; and the master shall within forty-eight hours after his arrival at his port of destination in the United States produce the same to the Coast Guard official to whom the duties of shipping commissioner have been delegated there. Such consular officer shall, in any such case, endorse and certify upon the agreement with the crew the particulars with respect to such delivery and payment.

3. If the consular officer does not require such payment and delivery to be made to him, the master shall take charge of the effects, money, and wages, and shall, within forty-eight hours after his arrival at his port of destination in the United States, deliver and pay the same to the Coast Guard official to whom the duties of shipping commissioner have been delegated there.

4. The master shall, in all cases in which any seaman or apprentice dies during the voyage or engagement, give to such office or Coast Guard official an account, in such form as they may respectively require, of the effects, money, and wages so to be delivered and paid; and no deductions claimed in such account shall be allowed unless verified by an entry in the official log book, if there be any; and by such other vouchers, if any, as may be reasonably required by the officer or Coast Guard official to whom the account is rendered.

5. Upon due compliance with such of the provisions of this section as relate to acts to be done at the port of destination in the United States, the Coast Guard official to whom the duties of shipping commissioner have been delegated shall grant to the master a certificate to that effect. No officer of customs shall clear any foreign-going vessel without the production of such certificate. (*Title 46*, U.S.C., 622.)

Effects of seaman dying within the United States—Whenever any seaman or apprentice dies in the United States, and is, at the time of his death, entitled to claim from the master or owner of any vessel in which he has served, any unpaid wages or effects, such master or owner shall pay and deliver, or account for the same, to the Coast Guard official to whom the duties of shipping commissioner have been delegated at the port where the seaman or apprentice was discharged, or was to have been discharged or where he died. (*Title 46*, U.S.C., 625.)

Unclaimed wages or effects—A district court may, in its discretion, at any time direct the sale of the whole or any part of the effects of a deceased seaman which it has received, and shall hold the proceeds of such sale as the wages of deceased seamen are held. When no claim to the wages or effects, or proceeds of the sale of the effects of a deceased seaman received by a district court, is substantiated within six years after the receipt thereof by the court, it shall be in the absolute discretion of the court, if any subsequent claim is made, either to allow or refuse the same. Such courts shall, from time to time, pay any moneys arising from the unclaimed wages and effects of deceased seamen, which in their opinion it is not necessary to retain for the purpose of satisfying claims, into the Treasury of the United States, and such money shall form a fund for, and be appropriated to, the relief of sick, disabled, and destitute seamen belonging to the United States Merchant Marine service. (*Title 46*, U.S.C., 628.)

SEAMEN'S WAGES

Commencement of wages—A seaman's right to wages and provisions shall be taken to commence either at the time at which he commences work, or at the time specified in the agreement for his commencement of work or presence on board, whichever first happens. (*Title 46*, U.S.C., 591.)

Wages not dependent on freight earned—No right to wages shall be dependent on the earning of freight by the vessel; but every seaman who would be entitled to demand and receive any wages if the vessel on which he has served had earned freight, shall, subject to all other rules of law and conditions applicable to the case, be entitled to claim and recover the same of the master or owner in personam, notwithstanding that freight has been earned. But in all cases of wreck or loss of vessel, proof that any seaman or apprentice has not exerted himself to the utmost to save the vessel, cargo, and stores shall bar his claim. (*Title 46*, U.S.C., 592.)

Wages terminate upon loss of vessel; transportation to place of shipment—In cases where the service of any seaman terminates before the period contemplated in the agreement, by reason of the loss or wreck of the vessel, such seaman shall be entitled to wages for the time of service prior to such termination, but not for any further period. Such seaman shall be considered as a destitute seaman and shall be treated and transported to port of shipment as provided in Sections 678 and 679 of this title. This section shall apply to fishing and whaling vessels but not to yachts. (*Title 46*, U.S.C., 593.)

Right to wages in case of improper discharge—Any seaman who has signed an agreement and is afterward discharged before the commencement of the voyage or before one month's wages are earned, without fault on his part justifying such discharge, and without his consent, shall be entitled to receive from the master or owner, in addition to any wages he may have earned, a sum equal in amount to one month's wages as compensation and may, on adducing evidence satisfactory to the court hearing the case of having been improperly discharged, recover such compensation as if it were wages duly earned. (*Title 46*, U.S.C., 594.)

Right to wages affected by conduct—No seaman shall be entitled to wages for any period during which he unlawfully refuses or neglects to work when required, after the time fixed by the agreement for him to begin work, nor, unless the court hearing the case otherwise directs, for any period during which he is lawfully imprisoned for any offense committed by him. (*Title 46*, U.S.C., 595.)

Time wages shall be paid—The master or owner of any vessel making coastwise voyages shall pay to every seaman his wages within two days after the termination of the agreement under which he was shipped, or at the time such seaman is discharged, whichever first happens; and in case of vessels making foreign voyages, or from a port on the Atlantic to a port on the Pacific, or vice versa, within 24 hours after the cargo has been discharged, or within 4 days after the seaman has been discharged, whichever first happens; and in all cases the seaman shall be entitled to be paid at the time of his discharge on account of wages a sum equal to one-third part of the balance due him. Every master or owner who refuses or neglects to make payment in the manner hereinbefore mentioned without sufficient cause shall pay to the seaman a sum equal to two days' pay for each and every day during which payment is delayed beyond the respective periods, which sum shall be recoverable as wages in any claim made before the court; but this section shall not apply to masters or owners or any vessel the seamen of which are entitled to share in the profits of the cruise or voyage. This section shall not apply to fishing or whaling vessels or yachts. (*Title 46*, U.S.C., 596.)

Payment at ports—Every seaman on a vessel of the United States shall be entitled to receive on demand from the master of the vessel to which he belongs one-half part of the balance of his wages earned and remaining unpaid at the time when such demand is made at every port where such vessel, after the voyage has been commenced, shall load or deliver cargo before the voyage is ended, and all stipulations in the contract to the contrary shall be void: Provided, such a demand shall not be made before the expiration of, nor oftener than once in five days nor more than once in the same harbor in the same entry. Any failure on the part of the master to comply with this demand shall release the seaman from his contract and he shall be entitled to full payment of wages earned. And when the voyage is ended every such seaman shall be entitled to the remainder of the wages which shall be then due him, as provided in section 596: Provided further, that notwithstanding any release signed by any seaman under section 644 (rules for settlement of wages), any court having jurisdiction may, upon good cause shown, set aside such release and take such action as justice shall require; and provided further, that this section shall apply to seamen of foreign vessels while in harbors of the United States, and the courts of the United States shall be open to such seamen for its enforcement. This section shall not apply to fishing vessels or yachts. (*Title 46*, U.S.C., 597.)

Advances and allotments—(a) It shall be unlawful in any case to pay any seaman wages in advance of the time when he has actually earned the same, or pay such advance wages, or to make any order, or note, or other evidence of indebtedness therefor to any other person, or to pay any person, for the shipment of seamen when payment is deducted or to be deducted from a seaman's wages. Any person violating any of the foregoing provisions of this section shall be deemed guilty of a misdemeanor, and upon conviction shall be punished by a fine of not less than $25 nor more than $100, and may also be imprisoned for a period of not exceeding six months, at the discretion of the court. The payment of such advance wages or allotment, whether made within or without the United States or territory subject to the jurisdiction thereof, shall in no case except as herein provided absolve the vessel or the master or the owner thereof from the full payment of wages after the same have been actually earned, and shall be no defense to a libel suit or action for the recovery of such wages. If any person shall demand or receive, either directly or indirectly, from any seaman or other person seeking employment as seaman, or from any person on his behalf, any remuneration whatever for providing him with employment, he shall for every such offense be deemed guilty of a misdemeanor and shall be imprisoned not more than six months or fined not more than $500.

(b) It shall be lawful for any seaman to stipulate in his shipping agreement for an allotment of any portion of the wages he may earn (1) to his grandparents, parents, wife, sister, or children; (2) to an agency duly designated by the Secretary of the Treasury for the handling of applications for United States Savings Bonds, for the purpose of purchasing such bonds for the seaman; or (3) for deposits to be made in an account for savings, or investment opened by him and maintained in his name either at a savings bank or a United States postal savings depository subject to the governing regulations thereof, or a savings institution in which such accounts are insured by the Federal Deposit Insurance Corporation or the Federal Savings and Loan Insurance Corporation.

(c) No allotment shall be valid unless in writing and signed by and approved by the Coast Guard official to whom the duties of shipping commissioner have been delegated. It shall be the duty of the said Coast Guard official to examine such allotments and the parties to them and enforce compliance with the law. All stipulations for the allotment of any part of the wages of a seaman during his absence which are made at the commencement of the voyage shall be inserted in the agreement and shall state the amounts and the times of the payments to be made and the persons to whom the payments are to be made, or by directing the payments to be made to a savings bank or a United States postal savings depository in an account maintained in his name.

(d) No allotment except as provided for in this section shall be legal. Any person who shall falsely claim to be such relation, as above described, or to be a savings bank or a United States postal savings depository and as such an allottee of the seaman under this section, shall for every such offense be punished by a fine not exceeding $500 or imprisonment not exceeding six months, at the discretion of the court.

(e) This section shall apply as well to foreign vessels while in waters of the United States, as to vessels of the United States, and any master, owner, consignee, or agent of any foreign vessel who has violated its provisions shall be liable to the same penalty that the master, owner, or agent of a vessel of the United States would be for similar violation. The master, owner, consignee, or agent of any vessel of the United States, or of any foreign vessel seeking clearance from a port of the United States, shall present his shipping articles at the port of clearance, and no clearance shall be granted any such vessel unless the provisions of this section have been complied with.

(f) The Commandant of the Coast Guard shall make regulations to carry out this section. This section shall not apply to fishing or whaling vessels or yachts.

(g) The provisions of this section shall not apply to, or render unlawful, deductions made by an employer from the wages of a seaman, pursuant to the written consent of the seaman, if (1) such deductions are paid into a trust fund established for the sole and exclusive benefit of seamen employed by such employer, and their families and dependents (or of such seamen, families, and their dependents jointly with seamen employed by other employers and their families and dependents); and (2) such payments are held in trust for the benefit of providing, either from principal or income or both, for the benefit of such seamen, their families, and dependents, medical and/or hospital care, pensions on retirement or death of the seamen, life insurance, unemployment benefits, compensation for illness or injuries resulting from occupational activity, sickness, accident, and disability compensation, or any one or more of the foregoing benefits, or for the purpose of purchasing insurance to provide any one or more of such benefits. (*Title 46,* U.S.C., 599.)

Limit of sum recoverable during voyage—No sum exceeding $1 shall be recoverable from any seaman, by any one person, for any debt contracted during the time such seaman shall actually belong to any vessel, until the voyage for which such seaman engaged shall be ended. (*Title 46,* U.S.C., 602.)

DISCHARGE

Mode—All seamen discharged in the United States from merchant vessels engaged in voyages from a port in the United States to any foreign port, or being of the burden of seventy-five tons or upward, from a port on the Atlantic to a port on the Pacific, or vice versa, shall be discharged and receive their wages in the presence of a duly authorized Coast Guard official to whom the duties of shipping commissioner under *Title 53* of the REVISED STATUES have been delegated, except in cases where some competent court otherwise directs; and any master or owner of any such vessel who discharges any such seaman belonging hereto, or pays his wages within the United States in any other manner, shall be liable to a penalty of not more than $50. (*Title 46,* U.S.C., 641.)

Rules for settlement—The following rules shall be observed with respect to the settlement of wages:

1. Upon the completion before a Coast Guard official to whom the duties of shipping commissioner have been delegated, of any discharge and settlement, the master or owner and each seaman, respectively, in the presence of such Coast Guard official, shall sign a mutual release of all claims in respect of the past voyage or engagement, and the shipping commissioner shall also sign and attest it, and shall retain it in a book to be kept for that purpose, provided both the master and seaman assent to such settlement, or the settlement has been adjusted by such Coast Guard official.

2. Such release, so signed and attested, shall operate as a mutual discharge and settlement of all demands for wages between the parties thereto, on account of wages, in respect of the past voyage or engagement.

3. A copy of such release, certified under the hand and seal of such Coast Guard official to be a true copy, shall be given by him to any party thereto requiring same, and such copy shall be receivable in evidence upon any future question touching such claims, and shall have all the effect of the original of which it purports to be a copy.

4. In cases in which discharge and settlement before a Coast Guard official to whom the duties of shipping commissioner have been delegated are required, no payment, receipt, settlement, or discharge otherwise made shall operate as evidence of the release or satisfaction of any claim.

5. Upon payment being made by a master before a Coast Guard official to whom the duties of shipping commissioner have been delegated, such official shall, if required, sign and give to such master a statement of the whole amount so paid; and such statement shall, between the master and his employer, be received as evidence that he has made the payments therein mentioned. (*Title 46,* U.S.C., 644.)

UNITED STATES MERCHANT MARINER'S DOCUMENT

According to the U.S.CODE, no one may sail aboard a United States flag merchant vessel without certain identification documents. Until shortly after World War II such documents were called a "certificate of identification" or a "certificate of service." These terms are still mentioned in the U.S.CODE and a few documents with these titles may still be in use. But the vast majority were exchanged in 1945 for the United States Merchant Mariner's Document.

All personnel who have been documented since 1945 have been issued United States Merchant Mariner's Documents, the certificate of service or identification mentioned in the code. Figure 22-1 shows an actual document.

The document, popularly called a "Z" card, shows an individual's qualifications together with certain descriptive information. The Z card carries an identifying number which in recent years is simply the individual's Social Security account number. Only unlicensed ratings are shown on the Z card. An individual who starts sailing as an ordinary seaman will be issued a new document when he qualifies as lifeboatman or is upgraded to able seaman. On the other hand, if an individual has a license as a master or chief engineer, that fact will not be apparent from an examination of his Z card. His qualification as a licensed officer is separate and distinct from his unlicensed qualification stated on his Z card.

The Merchant Mariner's Document is laminated in plastic; altering or tampering with it is a federal offense. The Z card is something like a passport for a seaman. You must present it when you go ashore in a foreign

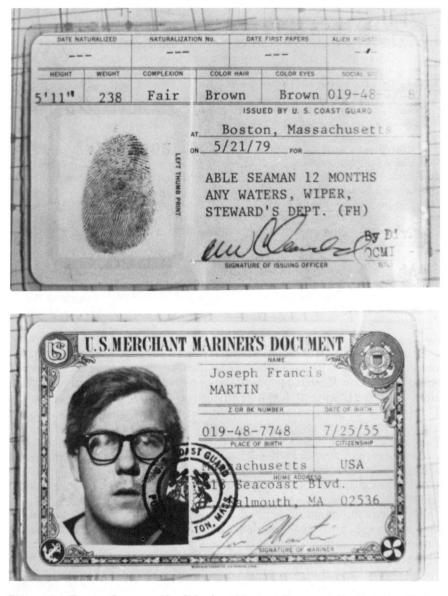

Figure 22-1. Front and reverse side of Merchant Mariner's Document. Martin is identified as an Able Seaman with 12 months' experience. He may also sign on as Wiper in the Engine Department or as a food-handler in the Steward's Department. Photo: Midn. R.L. Schopp, California Maritime Academy.

port. However, it no longer serves all identification needs. Most foreign countries now require that you have a regular passport for certain contingencies, for example, entering the country to join your ship or departing from the country after signing off to go home. One of the wisest moves you can make at the outset of your maritime career, therefore, is to get a passport.

CERTIFICATE OF DISCHARGE AND CONTINOUS DISCHARGE BOOK

From reading the Code it is apparent that a seaman who is discharged from a ship must be provided with evidence that he was employed aboard the vessel and the date and place where he was discharged. Whether the evidence of discharge takes the form of a certificate or a continuous discharge book depends upon the wishes of the individual. With a continuous discharge book the record of employment is readily apparent at a glance. But this has often caused resentment. Many seamen simply do not want a record of their professional life laid bare before each employer on whose ship they happen to sail. Furthermore, the continuous discharge book had a reputation of being open to abuse in that masters might enter comments on the seaman's character or proficiency even though this would be a violation of *Title 46,* U.S.C., 643. As a consequence many seamen prefer to receive an individual certificate of discharge when they sign off each ship. By filing his discharge certificates in chronological order, the seaman has the benefit of a continuous discharge book for his own use while being protected from what he may consider to be an invasion of privacy.

CHAPTER XXIII

GENERAL INFORMATION

THIS CHAPTER CONTAINS MISCELLANEOUS INFORMATION of interest to seamen. Since the subject matter presented varies so widely, an index for the chapter is provided with the material listed in the order in which it appears. Where appropriate, acknowledgements appear after each item:

INDEX

Merchant Marine Act of 1970	U.S. Maritime Administration
U.S. Merchant Marine Academy	U.S. Maritime Administration
State Maritime Academies	
Harry Lundeberg School of Seamanship	Harry Lundeberg School of Seamanship
National Maritime Union Upgrading and Retraining School	National Maritime Union
U.S. Naval Academy	U.S. Naval Academy
U.S. Coast Guard	U.S. Coast Guard
U.S. Coast Guard Academy	U.S. Coast Guard
National Ocean Survey	N.O.A.A.
National Weather Service	N.O.A.A.
Military Sealift Command	Military Sealift Command
Requirements for Qualified Members of the Engine Department	*Manual for Lifeboatmen, Able Seamen, and Qualified Members of the Engine Department, CG-175*

The Day at Sea
Organization Diagram of A Merchant
Ship

The World Almanac & Book of Facts, 1979 edition. Newspaper Enterprise Association, New York, NY, 1978.

WEIGHTS AND MEASURES

The United States is the only industrial country in the world not yet on the metric system. However, slowly and with mixed feelings the United States is moving in this direction. In 1971 the Secretary of Commerce recommended a gradual changeover during a ten year period, and in 1975 the Metric Conversion Act stated that national policy was to coordinate the increased use of the Metric System. A Metric Board was established to assist in voluntary conversion. The recent appearance in some states of highway signs in both miles or miles per hour as well as in kilometers and kilometers per hour will help ease the transition and help the public "think metric."

Sometimes the word "English" is used to differentiate between the metric system and the system which *has been* commonly used in Great Britain and the United States. Normally the British and United States measures are identical. Sometimes they differ as in the case of the British gallon of 277.274 cubic inches and the United States gallon which is 231 cubic inches. When this occurs, the notation "U.S." or "British" will appear.

TABLES OF EQUIVALENT MEASURES

Length

12 inches	= 1 foot
3 feet	= 1 yard
5280 feet or 1760 yards	= 1 statute mile
6076.1 feet	= 1 nautical mile

Volume

```
1728 cu. inches  = 1 cu. foot
27 cu. feet      = 1 cu. yard
1 cord of wood   = 128 cu. feet or (4 × 4 × 8 feet)
1 shipping ton   = 40 cu. feet merchandise
1 shipping ton   = 42 cu. feet lumber
```

Surface

```
144 sq. inches = 1 sq. foot
9 sq. feet     = 1 sq. yard
```

Weight

```
16 ounces     = 1 pound
2000 pounds = 1 short ton
2240 pounds = 1 long ton
```

Liquid Measure

```
4 gills        = 1 pint
2 pints        = 1 quart
4 quarts       = 1 gallon       U.S. 231 cu. inches
31.5 gallons = 1 barrel       British 277.274 cu. inches
```

Board Measure

Number of feet = length in feet × width in feet × thickness in inches

Circular or Angular Measure

```
60 seconds  = 1 minute
60 minutes  = 1 degree
90 degrees  = 1 quadrant or right angle
4 quadrants = 1 circumference
```

METRIC AND U.S. CONVERSION TABLES

Measures of Length

Metric to U.S.

```
1 millimeter    = 0.03937 inch
1 centimeter    = 0.3937 inch
1 meter         = 39.37 inches
1 meter         = 3.2808 feet
1 kilometer     = 0.6214 mile
```

U.S. to Metric

```
1 inch = 25.4 millimeters
1 inch = 2.54 centimeters
1 inch = 0.0254 meter
1 foot  = 0.3048 meter
1 mile = 1.609 kilometers
```

Measures of Surface

Metric to U.S.

1 sq. millimeter = 0.0155 sq. inch
1 sq. centimeter = 0.155 sq. inch
1 sq. meter   = 10.764 sq. feet
1 sq. meter   = 1.196 sq. yards
1 sq. kilometer = 0.3861 sq. mile

U.S. to Metric

1 sq. inch = 645.2 sq. millimeters
1 sq. inch = 6.452 sq. centimeters
1 sq. foot = 0.0929 sq. meter
1 sq. yard = 0.8361 sq. meter
1 sq. mile = 2.59 sq. kilometers

Measures of Volume and Capacity

Metric to U.S.

1 cu. centimeter = 0.061 cu. inch
1 cu. meter   = 35.314 cu. feet
1 cu. meter   = 1.308 cu. yards
1 liter   = 1 cu. decimeter = 61.023 cu. inches

U.S. to Metric

1 cu. inch = 16.39 cu. centimeters
1 cu. foot = 0.0283 cu. meter
1 cu. yard = 0.7645 cu. meter
1 cu. foot = 28.32 liters

Liquid Measure

Metric to U.S.

1 liter   = 1.0567 quarts
1 liter   = 0.2642 gallon
1 cu. meter = 264.17 gallons

U.S. to Metric

1 quart = 0.9463 liter
1 gallon = 3.7854 liters
1 gallon = 0.0038 cu. meter

Dry Measure

Metric to U.S.   U.S. to Metric

1 liter = 0.908 quart   1 quart = 1.1013 liters

Weights

Metric to U.S.

1 milligram = 0.0154 grain
1 gram   = 15.432 grains
1 kilogram = 2.2046 pounds (avoir.)
1 metric ton = 1.1023 short tons (2000 lbs.)
1 metric ton = 0.9842 long ton (2240 lbs.)

U.S. to Metric

1 pound (avoir.) = 0.4536 kilogram
1 short ton   = 0.9072 metric ton
1 long ton   = 1.0161 metric tons

The gram is the weight of 1 cu. cm. of pure distilled water at a temperature of 39.2°F; the kilogram is the weight of 1 liter of water; the ton is the weight of 1 cu. m. of water.

Compound Units

Metric to U.S.

1 kilogram per meter	= 0.6720 pound per foot
1 kilogram per sq. centimeter	= 14.223 pounds per sq. inch
1 kilogram per sq. meter	= 0.2048 pound per sq. foot
1 kilogram per cu. meter	= 0.0624 pound per cu. foot
1 kilogram-meter	= 7.233 foot-pounds
1 kilowatt	1.341 horsepower
1 kilogram-meter per sq. centimeter	= 46.58 ft.-lbs. per sq. inch

COMMON CONVERSION FACTORS

Multiply	By	To Obtain
Barrels (fuel oil)	42.	gallons (fuel oil)
British gallon	1.2	U.S. gallons
B.t.u.	778.	foot-pounds
Centimeters	0.3937	inches
Centimeters of mercury	0.1934	pounds per sq. inch
Cubic feet	1728.	cu. inches
Cubic feet	7.48	gallons, U.S.
Cubic feet (fresh water)	62.5	pounds of fresh water
Cubic feet (sea water)	64.	pounds of sea water
Cwts., U.S.	45.36	kilograms
Fathoms	6.	feet
Feet	30.48	centimeters
Feet	0.3048	meters
Feet of water	0.434	pounds per sq. inch
Force de cheval	0.98633	horsepower
Gallons, U.S.	231.	cu. inches
Gallons of water, U.S.	8.33	pounds of water
Gallons per min.	0.1337	cu. feet per min.
Grams	15.432	grains
Grams	0.035274	ounces
Horsepower	33000.	foot-pounds per minute
Horsepower	550.	foot-pounds per second
Horsepower	0.746	kilowatts
Horsepower (boiler)	33472.	B.t.u. per hour
Horsepower-hours	2245.	B.t.u.
Inches	2.54	centimeters
Inches of mercury	0.491	pounds per sq. inch
Inches of mercury	2.540	centimeters

Multiply	By	To Obtain
Kilograms	35.274	ounces
Kilograms	2.2046	pounds
Kilometers	3281.	feet
Kilometers	1093.633	yards
Kilometers per hour	0.621	miles per hour
Kilowatts	1.34	horsepower
Kilowatt-hours	1.34	horsepower-hours
Knots per hour	1.152	miles per hour
Liters	35.2	fluid ounces (imp.)
Liters	0.2642	gallons, U.S.
Liters	1.760	pints
Meters	3.281	feet
Meters	1.0936	yards
Miles	1.609	kilometers
Miles (land)	5280.	feet
Miles (nautical)	6076.1	feet
Miles per hour (land)	88.	feet per minute
Miles per hour (land)	0.8684	knots per hour
Ounces (avoir.)	28.35	grams
Ounces (troy)	31.1035	grams
Pints	0.56793	liters
Pounds	453.6	grams
Pounds	0.4536	kilograms
Pounds per sq. inch	2.307	feet of water
Pounds per sq. inch	2.036	inches of mercury
Pounds per sq. inch	144.	pounds per sq. foot
Quarts (dry), U.S.	67.20	cu. inches
Quarts (liquid), U.S.	57.75	cu. inches
Square miles	640.	acres
Square miles	259.02	hectares
Tons (long)	2240.	pounds
Tons (short)	2000.	pounds
Tons (long) fresh water	35.84	cu. feet of fresh water
Tons (long) sea water	35.	cu. feet of sea water
Yards	0.9144	meters

U.S. to Metric

1 pound per foot	= 1.4882 kilograms per meter
1 pound per sq. inch	= 0.0703 kilogram per sq. centimeter
1 pound per sq. foot	= 4.8825 kilograms per sq. meter
1 pound per cu. foot	= 16.0192 kilograms per cu. meter
1 foot-pound	= 0.1383 kilogram-meter
1 h.p.	= 1.014 cheval vapeur (metric h.p.)
1 h.p.	= 0.746 kilowatt

FAHRENHEIT AND CELSIUS TEMPERATURE SCALES

F.	C.	F.	C.	F.	C.	F.	C.	F.	C.
−40	−40.	70	21.1	185	85.	950	510.	2100	1149.
−35	−37.2	75	23.9	190	87.8	1000	537.8	2150	1176.5
−30	−34.4	80	26.7	195	90.6	1050	565.5	2200	1204.
−25	−31.7	85	29.4	200	93.3	1100	593.	2250	1232.
−20	−28.9	90	32.2	205	96.1	1150	621.	2300	1260.
−15	−26.1	95	35.	210	98.9	1200	648.5	2350	1287.5
−10	−23.3	100	37.8	212	100.	1250	676.5	2400	1315.5
− 5	−20.6	105	40.6	215	101.7	1300	704.	2450	1343.
0	−17.8	110	43.3	225	107.2	1350	732.	2500	1371.
+ 5	−15.	115	46.1	250	121.2	1400	760.	2550	1399.
10	−12.2	120	48.9	300	148.9	1450	788.	2600	1426.5
15	− 9.4	125	51.7	350	176.7	1500	816.	2650	1455.
20	− 6.7	130	54.4	400	204.4	1550	844.	2700	1483.
25	− 3.9	135	57.2	450	232.2	1600	872.	2750	1510.
30	− 1.1	140	60.	500	260.	1650	899.	2800	1537.5
32	0	145	62.8	550	287.8	1700	926.	2850	1565.
35	+ 1.7	150	65.6	600	315.6	1750	954.	2900	1593.
40	4.4	155	68.3	650	343.3	1800	982.	2950	1621.
45	7.2	160	71.1	700	371.1	1850	1010.	3000	1648.5
50	10.	165	73.9	750	398.9	1900	1038.	3050	1676.
55	12.8	170	76.7	800	426.7	1950	1065.5	3100	1705.
60	15.6	175	79.4	850	454.4	2000	1093.	3150	1732.
65	18.3.	180	82.2	900	482.2	2050	1121.	3200	1760.

Temperature Scale Conversions

$$F = (C \times 1.8) + 32°$$
$$C = (F - 32°) \times .55$$

WATER

1 cu. foot of sea water	= 64.00 pounds
1 cu. inch of sea water	= 0.037037 pounds
1 cu. foot of water	= 6.23 imperial gallons
1 cu. foot of water	= 28.375 liters
1 cu. foot of water	= 62.35 pounds
1 cu. inch of water	= 0.03616 pounds
1 cylindrical foot of water	= 48.96 pounds
1 cylindrical inch of water	= 0.0284 pound
Capacity of a 12″ cube	= 6.232 gallons
1 cu. foot of ice	= 57 pounds

Vol. of 1 ton of 2240 pounds of fresh water = 35.84 cu. feet, or 1 cu. meter (approx.),
(specific gravity, 1.000; density 1000 oz.   or 269 U.S. gallons, or 1000 liters
per cu. foot, or 62 1/2 pound per cu. foot)   (approx.)

Vol. of 1 ton of 2240 pounds of sea water   = 35 cu. feet
(specific gravity, 1.025; density 1025 oz.
per cu. foot., or 64 pounds per cu. foot)

AREAS AND CIRCUMFERENCES OF CIRCLES FROM 1/32 TO 10

Dia.	Area	Circum.	Dia.	Area	Circum.	Dia.	Area	Circum.
1/32	0.00077	0.098175	2	3.1416	6.28319	5	19.635	15.7080
3/64	0.00173	0.147262	1/16	3.3410	6.47953	1/16	20.129	15.9043
1/16	0.00307	0.196350	1/8	3.5466	6.67588	1/8	20.629	16.1007
3/32	0.00690	0.294524	3/16	3.7583	6.87223	3/16	21.135	16.2970
1/8	0.01227	0.392699	1/4	3.9761	7.06858	1/4	21.648	16.4934
5/32	0.01917	0.490874	5/16	4.2000	7.26493	5/16	22.166	16.6897
3/16	0.02761	0.589049	3/8	4.4301	7.46128	3/8	22.691	16.8861
7/32	0.03758	0.687223	7/16	4.6664	7.65763	7/16	23.221	17.0824
1/4	0.04909	0.785398	1/2	4.9087	7.85398	1/2	23.758	17.2788
9/32	0.06213	0.883573	9/16	5.1572	8.05033	9/16	24.301	17.4751
5/16	0.07670	0.981748	5/8	5.4119	8.24668	5/8	24.850	17.6715
11/32	0.09281	1.07992	11/16	5.6727	8.44303	11/16	25.406	17.8678
3/8	0.11045	1.17810	3/4	5.9396	8.63938	3/4	25.967	18.0642
13/32	0.12962	1.27627	13/16	6.2126	8.83573	13/16	26.535	18.2605
7/16	0.15033	1.37445	7/8	6.4918	9.03208	7/8	27.109	18.4569
15/32	0.17257	1.47262	15/16	6.7771	9.22843	15/16	27.688	18.6532
1/2	0.19635	1.57080	3	7.0686	9.42478	6	28.274	18.8496
17/32	0.22166	1.66897	1/16	7.3662	9.62113	1/16	29.465	19.2423
9/16	0.24850	1.76715	1/8	7.6699	9.81748	1/8	30.680	19.6350
19/32	0.27688	1.86532	3/16	7.9798	10.0138	3/16	31.919	20.0277
5/8	0.30680	1.96350	1/4	8.2958	10.2102	1/4	33.183	20.4204
21/32	0.33824	2.06167	5/16	8.6179	10.4065	5/16	34.472	20.8131
11/16	0.37122	2.15984	3/8	8.9462	10.6029	3/8	35.785	21.2058
23/32	0.40574	2.25802	7/16	9.2806	10.7992	7/16	37.122	21.5984
3/4	0.44179	2.35619	1/2	9.6211	10.9956	7	38.485	21.9911
25/32	0.47937	2.45437	9/16	9.9678	11.1919	1/16	39.871	22.3838
13/16	0.51849	2.55254	5/8	10.321	11.3883	1/8	41.282	22.7765
27/32	0.55914	2.65072	11/16	10.680	11.5846	3/16	42.718	23.1692
7/8	0.60132	2.74889	3/4	11.045	11.7810	1/4	44.179	23.5619
29/32	0.64504	2.84707	13/16	11.416	11.9773	5/16	45.664	23.9546
15/16	0.69029	2.94524	7/8	11.793	12.1737	3/8	47.173	24.3473
31/32	0.73708	3.04342	15/16	12.177	12.3700	7/16	48.707	24.7400
1	0.78540	3.14159	4	12.566	12.5664	8	50.265	25.1327
1/16	0.88664	3.33794	1/16	12.962	12.7627	1/16	51.849	25.5224
1/8	0.99402	3.53429	1/8	13.364	12.9591	1/8	53.456	25.9181
3/16	1.1075	3.73064	3/16	13.772	13.1554	3/16	55.088	26.3108
1/4	1.2272	3.92699	1/4	14.186	13.3518	1/4	56.745	26.7035
5/16	1.3530	4.12334	5/16	14.607	13.5481	5/16	58.426	27.0962
3/8	1.4849	4.31969	3/8	15.033	13.7445	3/8	60.132	27.4889
7/16	1.6230	4.51604	7/16	15.466	13.9408	7/16	61.862	27.8816
1/2	1.7671	4.71239	1/2	15.904	14.1372	9	63.617	28.2743
9/16	1.9175	4.90874	9/16	16.349	14.3335	1/16	65.397	28.6670
5/8	2.0739	5.10509	5/8	16.800	14.5299	1/8	67.201	29.0597
11/16	2.2365	5.30144	11/16	17.257	14.7262	3/16	69.029	29.4524
3/4	2.4053	5.49779	3/4	17.721	14.9226	1/4	70.882	29.8451
13/16	2.5802	5.69414	13/16	18.190	15.1189	3/8	72.760	30.2378
7/8	2.7612	5.89049	7/8	18.665	15.3153	3/4	74.662	30.6305
15/16	2.9483	6.08684	15/16	19.147	15.5116	7/8	76.589	31.0232

NAUTICAL MEASURES

6 feet	= 1 fathom
120 fathoms	= 1 cable
6076.1 feet	= 1 sea or nautical mile

A sea or nautical mile is a unit of distance equal to 1,852 meters (6,076.11549 feet). This is approximately equal to the length of one minute of latitude.

A knot is a speed of one nautical mile per hour. The term is often incorrectly used as meaning a nautical mile.

NAUTICAL MILES TO KILOMETERS

Nautical Miles	Kilometers	Nautical Miles	Kilometers
1	1.8532	20	37.064
2	3.7064	30	55.596
3	5.5596	40	74.128
4	7.4128	50	92.660
5	9.2660	60	111.190
6	11.1190	70	129.720
7	12.9720	80	148.250
8	14.8250	90	167.880
9	16.7880	100	185.320
10	18.5320	110	203.850

KILOMETERS TO NAUTICAL MILES

Kilometers	Nautical Miles	Kilometers	Nautical Miles
1	.5396	20	10.792
2	1.0792	30	16.188
3	1.6188	40	21.584
4	2.1584	50	26.980
5	2.6980	60	32.375
6	3.2375	70	37.771
7	3.7771	80	43.167
8	4.3167	90	48.563
9	4.8563	100	53.959
10	5.3959	110	59.355

SPECIFIC GRAVITY OF DIFFERENT SUBSTANCES
(Compared with Water as 1.00)

Liquids, etc.		Timber		Metals	
Alcohol	.80	Apple	.79	Bar Iron	7.79
Beer	1.02	Ash	.84	Brass	8.40
Cider	1.02	Beech	.85	Cast Iron	7.21
Granite	2.72	Cedar	.61	Copper	8.69
Gravel, Sand	2.65	Cherry	.72	Gold	19.26
Olive Oil	.92	Cork	.24	Lead	11.35
Petroleum	.78-.94	Ebony	1.33	Mercury	13.57
Porter	1.04	Fir	.55	Platinum	19.50
Sea Water	1.03	Mahogany	1.00	Silver	10.51
Turpentine	.99	Maple	.75	Steel	7.83
Wine	1.00	Oak	1.17	Tin	7.29
		Pear	.66	Zinc	7.19
		Poplar	.38		
		Walnut	.70		

SPECIFIC GRAVITY AND API (AMERICAN PETROLEUM INDUSTRY) GRAVITY AT 60°F OF LIQUIDS

Liquid	Specific Gravity	API Gravity 60°F
Acid, Acetic	1.03	5.9
Acid, Hydrochloric	1.19	-
Acid, Nitric	1.50	-
Acid, Sulphuric	1.84	-
Oil, Light Lubricating	.900	25.7
Oil, Medium Lubricating	.908	24.3
Oil, Heavy Lubricating	.912	23.6
Oil, Linseed	.95 - .97	17.4 - 14.3
Oil, Whale	.94	19.0
Water, Fresh	1.00	10.0
Water, Sea	1.026	6.4
Gasoline	.75 - .78	57.2 - 49.9
Paraffin	.87	31.1

SAFE WORKING LOADS (new gear)

C = circumference in inches d = diameter in inches

Manila rope: $SWL = \dfrac{B}{S.F.}$

Wire: $SWL = C^2 \times .4 = tons$
(B = Breaking Strain; S.F. = Safety Factor)

Note: See Chapters I and II.

Chain: $8d^2 = tons$
Hook: $2/3d^2 = tons$ (d = diameter at lower quarter)

Shackle: $3d^2 = tons$
Ring-bolt: $2d^2 = tons$

AVERAGE RISE AND FALL OF TIDE

Places	Feet	Inch	Places	Feet	Inch	Places	Feet	Inch
Balboa, Panama	12	7	Mobile, Ala.	1	7	San Diego, Cal.	4	2
Baltimore, Md.	1	2	New London, Conn.	2	6	Sandy Hook, N. J.	4	7
Boston, Mass.	9	5	New Orleans, La.	None	None	San Francisco, Cal.	3	11
Charleston, S. C.	5	2	Newport, R. I.	3	6	Savannah, Ga.	7	5
Colon, Panama	0	11	New York, N. Y.	4	5	Seattle, Wash.	7	7
Eastport, Me.	18	2	Old Pt. Comfort, Va.	2	6	Tampa, Fla.	1	10
Galveston, Tex.	1	0	Philadelphia, Pa.	5	2	Washington, D. C.	2	11
Key West, Fla.	1	4	Portland, Me.	8	11			

Okhotsk Sea, in Northeastern Asia, has a tide only once a day. On one occasion the rise was 37 feet. The average is 28 feet.

There are a few places on the Gulf Coast, Alaska, the Philippines and the coast of China where the tide also rises but once in 24 hours, but the degree of the daily rise is not striking. Sometimes the Okhotsk Sea breaks its rule. The Soviet scientists state that on a few days in the month there are actually two tides.

In Passamaquoddy Bay, which is the outlet of the St. Croix River and lies between Maine and the Canadian Province of New Brunswick, the maximum rise of the tide at St. Andrews is 25 feet, and that only 3 days a month. The average head of water is about 15 feet, for power purposes.

In the upper part of the Bay of Fundy, which lies between New Brunswick and Nova Scotia, the tide-rise varies from 30 to 50 feet.

USEFUL INFORMATION

Rope. Weight of Manila (in pounds) $= .2 \times C^2 \times$ fathoms
       $= 2/11 \times$ weight of same size wire
       Weight of wire (in pounds) $=$ fathoms $\times C^2$

Chain. Weight of chain cable (in pounds) $= 60 \times d^2$
        Links per fathom, chain cable $= 18 \div d$
        (d = diameter of iron in link)

Carrying capacity of lifeboat. 1/10 (length $\times$ breadth $\times$ depth $\times$ .6) = number of persons.

Sea water pressure. Pounds per sq. inch = 4/9 depth (in feet)

Area of wetted surface (approx.) Length $\times$ (breadth + depth) = sq. feet

Anti-corrosive paint covers about 270 sq. feet per gallon

Anti-fouling paint covers about 240 sq. feet per gallon

DISTANCE OF THE HORIZON
(Extracted from Table 8, *American Practical Navigator*)

Height of eye (feet)	Nautical miles	Statute miles	Height of eye (feet)	Nautical miles	Statute miles
5	2.6	2.9	85	10.5	12.1
10	3.6	4.2	90	10.9	12.5
15	4.4	5.1	95	11.2	12.8
20	5.1	5.9	100	11.4	13.2
25	5.7	6.6	110	12.0	13.8
30	6.3	7.2	120	12.5	14.4
35	6.8	7.8	130	13.0	15.0
40	7.2	8.3	140	13.5	15.6
45	7.7	8.8	150	14.0	16.1
50	8.1	9.3	200	16.2	18.6
55	8.5	9.8	250	18.1	20.8
60	8.9	10.2	300	19.8	22.8
65	9.2	10.6	350	21.4	24.6
70	9.6	11.0	400	22.9	26.3
75	9.9	11.4	450	24.3	27.9
80	10.2	11.8	500	25.6	29.4

Note:

1. Roughly speaking, the distance of visibility in nautical miles is equal to eight-sevenths of the square root of the height of eye above sea level.

2. This table was computed by means of the formulas: nautical miles: $D = 1.144 \sqrt{h}$; statute miles: $D = 1.317 \sqrt{h}$.

SHORTEST NAVIGABLE DISTANCES BETWEEN PORTS

Source: Distances Between Ports, 1965. Defense Mapping Agency Hydrographic Center

Distances shown are in nautical miles (1,852 meters or about 6,076.115 feet). To get statute miles, multiply by 1.15.

TO FROM	New York	Montreal	Colon[1]
Algiers, Algeria	3,617	3,600	4,745
Amsterdam, Netherlands	3,438	3,162	4,825
Baltimore, Md.	417	1,769	1,901
Barcelona, Spain	3,714	3,697	4,842
Boston, Mass.	386	1,308	2,157
Buenos Aires, Argentina	5,817	6,455	5,472
Cape Town, S. Africa[2]	6,786	7,118	6,494
Cherbourg, France	3,154	2,878	4,541
Cobh, Ireland	2,901	2,603	4,308
Copenhagen, Denmark	3,846	3,570	5,233
Dakar, Senegal	3,335	3,566	3,694
Galveston, Tex.	1,882	3,165	1,492
Gibraltar[3]	3,204	3,187	4,332
Glasgow, Scotland	3,086	2,691	4,508
Halifax, N.S.	600	895	2,295
Hamburg, W. Germany	3,674	3,398	5,061
Hamilton, Bermuda	697	1,572	1,659
Havana, Cuba	1,186	2,473	998
Helsinki, Finland	4,309	4,033	5,696
Istanbul, Turkey	5,001	4,984	6,129
Kingston, Jamaica	1,474	2,690	551
Lagos, Nigeria	4,883	5,130	5,049
Lisbon, Portugal	2,972	2,943	4,152
Marseille, France	3,891	3,874	5,019
Montreal, Quebec	1,460		3,126
Naples, Italy	4,181	4,164	5,309
Nassau, Bahamas	962	2,274	1,166
New Orleans, La.	1,708	2,991	1,389
New York, N.Y.		1,460	1,974
Norfolk, Va.	294	1,700	1,779
Oslo, Norway	3,827	3,165	5,053
Piraeus, Greece	4,688	4,671	5,816
Port Said, Egypt	5,123	5,106	6,251
Rio de Janeiro, Brazil	4,770	5,354	4,367
St. John's, Nfld.	1,093	1,043	2,695
San Juan, Puerto Rico	1,399	2,445	993
Southampton, England	3,189	2,913	4,576

TO FROM	San. Fran.	Vancouver	Panama[1]
Acapulco, Mexico	1,833	2,613	1,426
Anchorage, Alas.	1,872	1,444	5,093
Bombay, India	9,794	9,578	12,962
Calcutta, India	8,991	8,728	12,154
Colon, Panama[1]	3,298	4,076	44
Jakarta, Indonesia	7,641	7,360	10,637
Haiphong, Vietnam	6,496	6,231	9,673
Hong Kong	6,044	5,777	9,195
Honolulu, Hawaii	2,091	2,423	4,685
Los Angeles, Cal.	371	1,161	2,913
Manila, Philippines	6,221	5,976	9,347
Melbourne, Australia	6,970	7,343	7,928
Pusan, S. Korea	4,914	4,623	8,074
Saigon, Vietnam	6,878	6,664	10,017
San Francisco, Cal.		812	3,245
Seattle, Wash.	807	126	4,020
Shanghai, China	5,396	5,110	8,566
Singapore	7,353	7,078	10,505
Suva, Fiji	4,749	5,183	6,325
Valparaiso, Chile	5,140	5,915	2,616
Vancouver, B.C.	812		4,032
Vladivostok, USSR	4,563	4,378	7,741
Yokohama, Japan	4,536	4,262	7,682

TO FROM	Port Said	Cape Town[2]	Singa- pore
Bombay, India	3,049	4,616	2,441
Calcutta, India	4,695	5,638	1,649
Dar es Salaam, Tanzania	3,238	2,365	4,042
Jakarta, Indonesia	5,293	5,276	525
Hong Kong	6,462	7,006	1,454
Kuwait	3,360	5,176	3,833
Manila, Philippines	6,348	6,777	1,330
Melbourne, Australia	7,842	5,963	3,844
Saigon, Vietnam	5,667	6,263	649
Singapore	5,018	5,614	
Yokohama, Japan	7,907	8,503	2,889

(1) Colon on the Atlantic is 44 nautical miles from Panama (port) on the Pacific. (2) Cape Town is 35 nautical miles northwest of the Cape of Good Hope. (3) Gibraltar (port) is 24 nautical miles east of the Strait of Gibraltar.

NOTABLE OCEAN PASSAGES BY SHIPS

Time	From	To	Naut. mi.	Date		Ship
			Sailing Vessels			
16d	Liverpool	New York	3,150	Nov.	1846	Yorkshire
76d 6h	San Francisco	Boston	...		1853	Northern Light
12d 6h	Boston Light	Light Rock	...		1854	James Baines
89d	New York	San Francisco	15,091		1854	Flying Cloud
89d 20h	New York	San Francisco	13,700		1860	Andrew Jackson
63d 18h 15m	Liverpool	Melbourne	...		1868-69	Thermopylae
13d 1h 25m	New York	Liverpool	3,150		...	Red Jacket
36d	50 S. Lat	Golden Gate	...		...	Starr King
12d 12h	Equator	San Francisco	...		...	Golden Fleece
12d 4h 1m	Sandy Hook	England	3,013		1905	Atlantic
			Atlantic Crossing by Power Vessels			
29d 4h	Savannah	Liverpool	...	May 22,	1819	Savannah (Amer.) (a)
15d	Bristol	New York	...	Apr.	1838	Great Western (Br.)
14d 8h	Liverpool	New York	3,150	July	1840	Britannia (Br.) (b)
9d 13h	Liverpool	New York	3,054	Aug.	1852	Baltic (Amer.)
5d 15h 20m	Southampton	New York	3,189		1898	Kaiser Wilhelm Der Grosse (Ger.)
5d 7h 38m	Sandy Hook	Plymouth	3,082	Sept.	1900	Deutschland (Ger.)
4d 11h 42m	Queenstown	New York	2,780		1909	Lusitania (Br.)
5d 6h 21m	New York	Cherbourg	3,227	Oct.	1924	Leviathan (Amer.)
4d 17h 42m	Cherbourg	Ambrose Lt.	3,164	July	1929	Bremen (Ger.)*
4d 14h 30m	New York	Plymouth	3,082	July	1929	Bremen (Ger.)
4d 16h 48m	Cherbourg	New York	3,149	July	1933	Europa (Ger.)
4d 13h 58m	Gibraltar	Ambrose Lt.	3,181	Aug.	1933	Rex (Ital.)
4d 14h 27m	Cherbourg	Ambrose Lt.	3,092	Nov.	1934	Bremen (Ger.)
3d 23h 02m	Bishop's Rock	Ambrose Lt.	2,906	July-Aug.	1937	Normandie (Fr.)
3d 22h 07m	New York	Southampton	2,936	Aug.	1937	Normandie (Fr.)
3d 20h 42m	Ambrose Lt.	Bishop's Rock	3,120	Aug. 10-14,	1938	Queen Mary (Br.)
3d 21h 48m	Bishop's Rock	Ambrose Lt.	3,120	Aug. 3-8,	1948	Queen Mary (Br.)
3d 10h 40m	Ambrose Lt.	Bishop's Rock	2,942	July 3-7,	1952	United States (U.S.)* (e)
3d 11h 24m	Bishop's Rock	Ambrose Lt.	2,912	Aug. 20,	1973	Sea-Land Exchange (U.S.) (k)
			Other Ocean Passages			
3d 00h 36m	San Pedro	Honolulu	2,226	June	1928	U.S.S. Lexington
86d	Halifax	Vancouver	7,295	July-Sept.	1944	St. Roch (Can.) (c)
3d 2h 30m	San Francisco	Oahu, Hawaii	2,091	July 16-19,	1945	U.S.S. Indianapolis (d)
4d 8h 51m	Gibraltar	Newport News	3,360	Nov. 26,	1945	U.S.S. Lake Champlain
7d 18h 36m	Japan	San Francisco	5,000	July-Aug. 4,	1950	U.S.S. Boxer
7d 13h	Yokosuka	Alameda	5,000	June 1-9,	1951	U.S.S. Philippine Sea
8d 11h	Nantucket	Portland, Eng.	3,161	Feb. 25-Mar. 4,	1958	U.S.S. Skate (f)
7d 5h	Lizard Head	Nantucket, Mass.	...	Mar. 23-29,	1958	U.S.S. Skate (f)
15d	Pearl Harbor	Iceland (via N. Pole)	...	July 23-Aug. 7,	1958	U.S.S. Nautilus (g)
34d	New London	Rehoboth, Del.	41,500	Feb. 16-May 10,	1960	U.S.S. Triton (h)
6d	Baffin Bay	NW Passage, Pac.	850	Aug. 15-20,	1960	U.S.S. Seadragon (i)
12d 16h 22m	New York	Cape Town	6,786	Oct. 30-Nov. 11,	1962	African Comet*
5d 6h	Kobe	Race Rock, B.C.	4,126	Aug. 24,	1973	Sea-Land Trade (U.S.)

*Maiden voyage. (a) The Savannah, a fully rigged sailing vessel with steam auxiliary (over 300 tons, 98.5 ft. long, beam 25.8 ft., depth 12.9 ft.) was launched in the East River in 1818. It was the first ship to use steam in crossing any ocean. It was supplied with engines and detachable iron paddle wheels. On its famous voyage it used steam 105 hours. (b) First Cunard liner. (c) First ship to complete NW Passage in one season. (d) Carried Hiroshima atomic bomb in World War II. (e) Set world speed record; average speed eastbound on maiden voyage 35.59 knots (about 41 m.p.h.). (f) First atomic submarine to cross Atlantic both ways submerged. (g) World's first atomic submarine also first to make undersea voyage under polar ice cap, 1,830 mi. from Point Barrow, Alaska, to Atlantic Ocean, Aug. 1-4, 1958, reaching North Pole Aug. 3. Second undersea transit of the North Pole made by submarine USS Skate Aug. 11, 1958, during trip from New London, Conn., and return. (h) World's largest submarine. Nuclear-powered Triton was submerged during nearly all its voyage around the globe. It duplicated the route of Ferdinand Magellan's circuit (1519-1522) 30,708 mi., starting from St. Paul Rocks off the NE coast of Brazil, Feb. 24-Apr. 25, 1960, then sailed to Cadiz, Spain, before returning home. (i) First underwater transit of Northwest Passage. (k) Fastest freighter crossing of Atlantic.

UNITED STATES OCEANGOING MERCHANT MARINE
DECEMBER 1, 1989
(TONNAGE IN THOUSANDS)

	TOTAL			PRIVATELY OWNED			GOVERNMENT OWNED a/		
	NUMBER SHIPS	GROSS TONS	DEADWEIGHT TONS	NUMBER SHIPS	GROSS TONS	DEADWEIGHT TONS	NUMBER SHIPS	GROSS TONS	DEADWEIGHT TONS
Active Fleet									
Passenger	7	96	55	2	41	14	5	55	41
General Cargo	38	614	574	37	607	563	1	7	11
Intermodal	126	3624	3742	125	3621	3739	1	3	3
Bulk Carriers	22	561	972	22	561	972	-	-	-
Tankers	192	6874	12556	191	6863	12539	1	11	17
Total	385	11769	17899	377	11693	17827	8	76	72
Inactive Fleet									
Passenger	13	191	107	2	53	23	11	138	84
General Cargo	169	1557	2012	7	86	88	162	1471	1924
Intermodal	41	884	948	4	81	82	37	803	866
Bulk Carriers	4	179	298	4	179	298	-	-	-
Tankers	47	1727	3178	16	1057	2173	31	670	1005
Total	274	4538	6543	33	1456	2664	241	3082	3879
Total Fleet									
Passenger	20	287	162	4	94	37	16	193	125
General Cargo	207	2171	2586	44	693	651	163	1478	1935
Intermodal	167	4508	4690	129	3702	3821	38	806	869
Bulk Carriers	26	740	1270	26	740	1270	-	-	-
Tankers	239	8601	15734	207	7920	14712	32	681	1022
Total U.S. Flag	659	16307	24442	410	13149	20491	249	3158	3951

a/ Includes 241 NDRF vessels, of which 90 belong to the RRF.

Courtesy U.S. Maritime Administration

EMPLOYMENT OF U.S. FLAG MERCHANT FLEET VESSELS OF 1,000 GROSS TONS AND OVER AS OF 1 JANUARY 1989[1]

Status and Area of Employment	Total No.	DWT Tons
Grand Total	659	24,442
Active Vessels	385	17,899
Privately Owned	377	17,827
U.S. Foreign Trade	134	4,881
Foreign-to-Foreign	26	2,247
Domestic Trade	163	9,267
Coastal	89	3,590
Noncontiguous	74	5,677
M.S.C. Charter	54	1,432
Government Owned	8	72
B.B. Charter & Other Custody	8	72
Inactive Vessels	274	6,543
Privately Owned	33	2,664
Temporarily Inactive	2	246
Laid-up	24	2,269
Laid-up (MARAD Custody)	7	149
Government Owned (MARAD Custody)	241	3,879
National Defense Reserve Fleet	238	3,657
Ready Reserve Force (RRF)	89	1,542
Other Reserve	136	1,928
Special Programs[2]	7	141
Non-Retention[3]	6	46
In Processing for RRF	–	–
Other Government Owned	3	222

[1] – Excludes vessels operating exclusively on the Great Lakes, inland waterways, and those owned by the United States Army and Navy and special types such as cable ships, tugs, etc.

[2] – Vessels unavailable for activation due to special status

[3] – Vessels not actively maintained

MAJOR MERCHANT FLEETS OF THE WORLD—JANUARY 1, 1989

Country	No. of Ships[1]	Rank by No. of Ships	Deadweight Tons	Rank by Deadweight Tonnage
Liberia	1,405	3	89,200,000	1
Panama	3,304	1	72,977,000	2
Japan	1,118	6	39,699,000	3
Greece	974	7	37,130,000	4
Cyprus	1,140	5	31,832,000	5
U.S.S.R.	2,434	2	25,481,000	6
British Independent Territories	545	9	24,180,000	7
United States (Private)	424	13	21,601,000	8
Norway (NIS)	366	15	19,335,000	9
China	1,235	4	18,437,000	10
Nassau Bahamas	430	12	16,547,000	11
Philippines	562	8	14,770,000	12
Singapore	417	14	11,752,000	13
Korea (South)	434	11	11,382,000	14
Italy	500	10	10,765,000	15
All Others[2]	8,180		156,831,000	
Total	23,468		601,919,000	

[1]Oceangoing merchant ships of 1,000 gross tons and over.

[2]Includes 251 United States Government-Owned ships of 3,975,000 dwt.

Courtesy of U.S. Maritime Administration

PANAMA CANAL

The Canal Zone has been, in effect, a United States government reservation. It is a strip of land extending 5 miles on each side of the axis of the Canal, under jurisdiction of the United States by treaty with the Republic of Panama in 1903.

Two new treaties governing the future operation and defense of the Panama Canal were signed by the United States and Panama in a ceremony at OAS headquarters in Washington on September 7, 1977. They were approved by Panama in a plebiscite on October 23d of that year and the United States Senate gave its advice and consent to their ratification in March and April, 1978. The 2 countries exchanged the instruments of ratification on June 16, 1978. The exchange becomes effective March 31, 1979. Six months later, October 1, 1979, the Canal Zone will cease to exist; Panama will have full sovereignty over the area, except for limited United States police and legal authority during a 30-month transition period.

The canal connects the Caribbean with the Bay of Panama on the Pacific. Because of the geographic loop made by the Isthmus of Panama, the Caribbean end of the canal, which could be called the eastern end, is actually further west than the Pacific end.

The zone has an area of 647 sq. mi. of which 372 are land. Population (1978 est.) was 39,000. About 9,100 United States army, air force, and navy personnel are normally stationed in the zone. Government headquarters in Balboa Heights.

The Canal Zone government and the Panama Canal Co. are the 2 operating agencies, both headed by an individual who acts as governor of the Canal Zone and president of the company. The governor is appointed by the president of the United States. As governor he reports directly to the secretary of the army; as president of the company he reports to its board of directors, appointed by the secretary of the army. The Canal Zone government maintains civil government. The company operates the canal, the Panama Railroad, terminals, employee services, and utilities.

A French company under Ferdinand de Lesseps failed to complete a canal, 1880-89, and a second French company failed in 1899. The United States bought their rights for $40 million, paid private owners $4 million, and offered Colombia compensation for a canal zone, but Colombia failed to ratify the treaty, October 1903. Panama declared itself independent of Columbia November 3, 1903, and was recognized by President Theodore Roosevelt November 6. American naval forces discouraged action by Colombia. On November 18 Panama granted the canal strip to the United States by treaty, ratified February 26, 1904, compensation $10 million, with annual payments of $250,000 after 9 years, and a guarantee of Panama's independence.

Under terms of the 1903 treaty, Panama granted the United States perpetual sovereignty over the Canal Zone.

The canal was opened to traffic August 15, 1914. In 1922, Colombia accepted $25 million from the United States plus special land transportation privileges, and agreed to recognize Panama. The United States increased its annual payment to Panama to $430,000 and withdrew its guarantee of independence.

A further treaty regulating relations between the United States and Panama was signed January 25, 1955, increasing the annuity paid Panama to $1.9 million (actually increasing it to $2.3 million because of devaluation of the United States dollar). In addition, the United States gave Panama $28 million worth of real estate and buildings. United States citizen and non-citizen employees were guaranteed equality of pay and opportunity. In addition, the United States agreed to build a high level bridge over the Pacific entrance to the canal. The bridge was opened October 12, 1962, as a link in the Inter-American Highway.

Negotiations for a new treaty began after Panamanian riots protesting the 1903 and 1955 treaties caused the death of 20 Panamanians and 4 United States soldiers, January 9, 1964. Preliminary agreement was reached in 1967, but in 1970, after a change of government, Panama rejected the proposal.

Under the new Panama Canal Treaty, the United States will retain primary responsibility for defense and administration of the canal until the year 2000, but with Panama assuming an increasing role in both until the final turnover date, December 31, 1999. The Panama Canal Co. will be replaced with a new United States agency with a board of 9, composed of 5 Americans and 4 Panamanians. Until 1990 the chief administrator will be American and his deputy Panamanian; in 1990 the positions will be reversed.

On October 1, 1979, the United States will turn over some 65% of the zone to Panamanian jurisdiction. Times for withdrawal of United States troops and disposal of bases will be up to the United States. The United States will pay Panama $50 to $70 million a year from canal revenues.

STANDARD TIME, DAYLIGHT SAVING TIME, AND OTHERS

STANDARD TIME

Standard time is reckoned from Greenwich, England, recognized as the Prime Meridian of Longitude. The world is divided into 24 zones, each 15° of arc, or one hour in time apart. The Greenwich meridian (0°) extends through the center of the initial zone, and the zones to the east are numbered from 1 to 12 with the prefix "minus" indicating the number of hours to be subtracted to obtain Greenwich Time.

Westward zones are similarly numbered, but prefixed "plus" showing the number of hours that must be added to get Greenwich Time. While these zones apply generally to sea areas, it should be noted that the Standard Time maintained in many countries does not coincide with zone time. A graphical representation of the zones is shown on the Standard Time Zone Chart of the World published by the Defense Mapping Agency Hydrographic Center, Washington, DC 20390.

The United States and possessions are divided into eight Standard Time zones, as set forth by the Uniform Time Act of 1966, which also provides for the use of Daylight Saving Time therein. Each zone is approximately 15° of

STANDARD TIME DIFFERENCE—UNITED STATES CITIES

At 12 o'clock noon U.S. Eastern Standard Time, the clocks in the cities of the United States are:

City	Time	City	Time
Atlanta, Ga.	12.00 NOON	Memphis, Tenn.	11.00 A.M.
Baltimore, Md.	12.00 NOON	Milwaukee, Wis.	11.00 A.M.
Birmingham, Ala. ...	11.00 A.M.	Minneapolis, Minn. ..	11.00 A.M.
Boston, Mass.	12.00 NOON	Newark, New Jersey .	12.00 NOON
Buffalo, N.Y.	12.00 NOON	New Haven, Conn. ...	12.00 NOON
Charleston, S.C.	12.00 NOON	New York, N.Y.	12.00 NOON
Chicago, Ill.	11.00 A.M.	New Orleans, La.	11.00 A.M.
Cincinnati, Ohio	12.00 NOON	Norfolk, Va.	12.00 NOON
Cleveland, Ohio	12.00 NOON	Omaha, Neb.	11.00 A.M.
Columbus, Ohio	12.00 NOON	Philadelphia, Pa.	12.00 NOON
Dallas, Tex.	11.00 A.M.	Pittsburgh, Pa.	12.00 NOON
Denver, Col.	10.00 A.M.	Portland, Oregon	9.00 A.M.
Des Moines, Iowa	11.00 A.M.	Providence, R.I.	12.00 NOON
Detroit, Mich.	12.00 NOON	Richmond, Va.	12.00 NOON
El Paso, Tex.	11.00 A.M.	St. Paul, Minn.	11.00 A.M.
Galveston, Tex.	11.00 A.M.	Rochester, N.Y.	12.00 NOON
Hartford, Conn.	12.00 NOON	Salt Lake City, Utah .	10.00 A.M.
Houston, Texas	11.00 A.M.	San Francisco, Cal. ..	9.00 A.M.
Indianapolis, Ind.	11.00 A.M.	Savannah, Ga.	12.00 NOON
Kansas City, Mo.	11.00 A.M.	Seattle, Wash.	9.00 A.M.
Los Angeles, Cal.	9.00 A.M.	St. Louis, Mo.	11.00 A.M.
Louisville, Ky.	11.00 A.M.	Washington, D.C.	12.00 NOON

longitude in width. All places in each zone use, instead of their own local time, the time counted from the transit of the "mean sun" across the Standard Time meridian which passes near the middle of that zone.

These time zones are designated as Atlantic, Eastern, Central, Mountain, Pacific, Yukon, Alaska-Hawaii, and Bering, and the time in these zones is basically reckoned from the 60th, 75th, 90th, 105th, 120th, 135th, 150th, 165th meridians west of Greenwich. The line wanders to conform to local geographical regions. The time in the various zones is earlier than Greenwich Time by 4, 5, 6, 7, 8, 9, 10, and 11 hours respectively.

24-HOUR TIME

24-hour time is widely used in scientific work throughout the world. In the United States it is used also in operations of the Armed Forces. In Europe it is used in preference to the 12-hour a.m. and p.m. system. With the 24-hour system the day begins at midnight and hours are numbered 0 through 23.

INTERNATIONAL DATE LINE

The Date Line is a zig-zag line that approximately coincides with the 180th meridian and it is where each calendar day begins. The date must be advanced one day when crossing in a westerly direction and set back one day when crossing in an easterly direction.

The line is deflected between north latitude 48° and 75°, so that all Asia lies to the west of it.

DAYLIGHT SAVING TIME

Daylight Saving Time is achieved by advancing the clock one hour. Under the Uniform Time Act, which became effective in 1967, all states, the District of Columbia, and United States possessions were to observe Daylight Saving Time beginning at 2 a.m. on the last Sunday in April and ending at 2 a.m. on the last Sunday in October. Any state could, by law, exempt itself; a 1972 amendment to the act authorized states split by time zones to take that into consideration in exempting themselves. Arizona, Hawaii, Puerto Rico, the Virgin Islands, American Samoa, and part of Indiana are now exempt. Some local zone boundaries in Kansas, Texas, Florida, and Michigan have been modified in the last several years by the Dept. of Transportation, which oversees the act. To conserve energy Congress put most of the nation on year-round Daylight Saving Time for two years effective January 6, 1974 through October 26, 1975; but a further bill, signed in October, 1974, restored Standard Time from the last Sunday in that month to the last Sunday in February, 1975.

A BRIEF HISTORY OF THE UNITED STATES MERCHANT MARINE

Merchant ships have played an important part in the history of the United States from the beginning. The American colonists who became skillful sailors, shipbuilders, and shrewd traders, sailed all over the world. The schooner and clipper ship were American developments. American ships were sold to other countries, earning needed foreign exchange. By the end of the eighteenth century American ships carried most of the country's trade.

Shipping was both dangerous and difficult. Charts were poor and navigation aids almost lacking. Living conditons were primitive. Quarters were cramped, and food was monotonous and frequently bad. Every war meant vessel losses because after the American Revolution the United States no longer had the protection of the British Navy and had no real Navy until after 1800.

After the War of 1812 with Great Britain, when the United States objected to the seizing of American Seaman for British service, American shipping enjoyed 40 prosperous years accompanied by many improvements in shipbuilding and navigation.

Ships helped knit America together. They brought goods and people from the East Coast to the West Coast and made possible the rapid development of California following the discovery of gold in 1849. Ships sailed when cargo was offered, and often the captain and crew undertook to sell the cargo on shares. Cargo was later carried at fixed rates for merchants and regular sailings were established. A "packet" service was established

STANDARD TIME DIFFERENCES—WORLD CITIES

The time indicated in the table is fixed by law and is called the legal time, or, more generally, Standard Time. Use of Daylight Saving Time varies widely. *Indicates morning of the following day. At 12.00, Eastern Standard Time, the standard time (in 24-hour time) in foreign cities is as follows:

City	Time	City	Time
Alexandria	19 00	Lisbon	18 00
Amsterdam	18 00	Liverpool	17 00
Athens	19 00	London	17 00
Auckland	5 00 *	Madrid	18 00
Baghdad	20 00	Manila	1 00 *
Bangkok	0 00	Melbourne	3 00 *
Belfast	17 00	Montevideo	14 00
Berlin	18 00	Moscow	20 00
Bogota	12 00	Nagasaki	2 00 *
Bombay	22 30	Oslo	18 00
Bremen	18 00	Paris	18 00
Brussels	18 00	Peking	1 00 *
Bucharest	19 00	Prague	18 00
Budapest	18 00	Rangoon	23 30
Buenos Aires	14 00	Rio De Janeiro	14 00
Calcutta	22 30	Rome	18 00
Cape Town	19 00	Saigon	1 00 *
Caracas	13 00	Santiago (Chile)	13 00
Copenhagen	18 00	Seoul	2 00 *
Dacca	23 00	Shanghai	1 00 *
Delhi	22 30	Singapore	12 30 *
Djakarta	0 00	Stockholm	18 00
Dublin	17 00	Sydney (Australia)	3 00 *
Gdansk	18 00	Tashkent	23 00
Geneva	18 00	Teheran	20 30
Havana	12 00	Tel Aviv	19 00
Helsinki	19 00	Tokyo	2 00 *
Hong Kong	1 00 *	Valparaiso	13 00
Istanbul	19 00	Vladivostok	3 00 *
Jerusalem	19 00	Vienna	18 00
Johannesburg	19 00	Warsaw	18 00
Karachi	22 00	Wellington (N.Z.)	5 00 *
Le Havre	18 00	Yokohama	2 00 *
Leningrad	20 00	Zurich	18 00
Lima	12 00		

by the Black Ball Line in 1816 and made regular passages from New York to Liverpool in 18 to 20 days.

The famous clipper ships appeared in the 1840's and often sailed at speeds of 18 to 19 knots. These ships were used principally on the long voyages to the West Coast, India, and China.

Although American developments such as Robert Fulton's *Clermont* and the *SS Savannah* helped usher in the era of steam-powered ships, America lost her lead among maritime nations. She lacked abundant coal close to the sea as well as skilled iron workers. In addition, the Civil War seriously damaged shipping. Many vessels were lost or sold abroad. After the war high prices and taxation hampered efforts to revive shipping. England took the lead in building iron and steel-hulled vessels powered by steam using screw propellors instead of paddlewheels.

The United States government attempted to help merchant shipping by granting contracts for carrying mail or by permitting the import of ship-building materials without tariffs. But even with this help the beginning of the twentieth century found only one American trans-Atlantic line in operation and American ships carrying less than 10 percent of American trade.

It took World War I to arouse the nation to correct the shortcomings of its Merchant Marine. Finally, the Shipping Act of 1916 was passed, and the first major attempt to develop a national maritime policy established a United States Shipping Board, the forerunner of the present Maritime Administration. Various kinds of discrimination were prohibited, and unfair practices by common carriers in coastwise trade and foreign commerce were curtailed. The Board's authority was expanded when the United States entered the war. Between 1918 and 1922 about 2,300 vessels were constructed, but few were delivered in time to see wartime service. After the war these ships were found to be poorly suited to peacetime use.

The Merchant Marine Act of 1920 was passed to help dispose of these surplus vessels and, for the first time, established as a national maritime policy the creation and maintenance of a merchant marine, "ultimately to be owned and operated by private citizens of the United States." It provided for a construction loan fund, and a tax exemption on earnings deposited in special funds for the purpose of building new vessels. It required that United States mails be transported in American vessels whenever possible. An important section of this act, still in force, commonly referred to as the Jones Act, reserves all domestic waterborne commerce for United States built, registered, and citizen-owned vessels.

The Merchant Marine Act of 1928 was designed to hasten the transfer of the government fleet to private firms since the 1920 act had not been entirely successful. It reaffirmed the policy of the 1920 act, increased the construction loan fund, and imposed a United States citizenship requirement on the crew of any vessel receiving mail contracts.

In 1936, legislation which became the cornerstone of United States maritime policy was passed. The Merchant Marine Act of 1936 declared it to be national policy to foster the development and maintenance of a merchant marine sufficient to carry domestic waterborne commerce and a substantial portion of the foreign commerce of the country. It also provided that the American Merchant Marine be capable of serving as a naval and military auxiliary in time of war, and that it should be owned and operated to the extent possible by United States citizens. The fleet was to be composed of the best equipped, safest, and most suitable types of vessels built in the United States and to be manned by American civilian personnel.

In order to do this the act provided for construction and operating subsidies to be paid to American shipping lines engaged in foreign trade. These subsidies were designed to equalize the difference between the cost of building and operating the ships under the American flag and the lower costs of foreign flags. Construction subsidies replaced the old system of awarding mail contracts which had been difficult to regulate and had done nothing to insure any modernization of the merchant fleet. The subsidies provided for government assistance in building new ships but required that the owners set aside funds to build a new ship at the end of the useful life of the old one. A United States Maritime Commission was established which made a survey of the industry and laid out a long-range program of shipbuilding designed to construct 500 ships within ten years.

Before the program was well started, World War II broke out in Europe. Once again ships were in great demand and the number to be built was doubled and redoubled.

By concentrating on a simple, standard type of vessel, the Liberty ship, American yards were able to use mass production methods. Within a year and a half after entering the war, shipyards were building vessels faster than the enemy was sinking them. From 1942 through 1945, 5,592 merchant ships were built, of which 2,701 were Liberty ships and 414 were the faster Victory ships, 651 were tankers, 417 were C-type standard cargo ships, and the remaining 1,409 were military or other types.

The government also took over the direction of ship operations, and established the War Shipping Administration (WSA) for this purpose. The head of the WSA was also the head of the Maritime Commission and this insured close cooperation between the two departments. Ships were taken over from private operators, foreign ships were purchased, and enemy ships seized. Thousands of seamen were recruited and trained. The WSA carried four-fifths of the supplies for the entire war effort and brought back essential raw materials needed to maintain the civilian economy. The Army and Navy used many merchant ships as hospital ships, naval oilers, repair ships, and even small aircraft carriers.

At the end of World War II, half of the seven million troops overseas were brough back home within three months aboard merchant ships. Cargo ships were now needed to carry food, clothing, and machinery to start the rebuilding of foreign countries shattered in the war.

The effort was made to restore the United States flag merchant fleet to private control as quickly as possible. The WSA was dissolved in 1945 and its remaining functions absorbed by the Maritime Commission. By 1947 all surviving vessels which had been taken over from private operators were returned to their owners. War-built ships were offered for sale and the best, the C-types, were purchased by American flag operators. Many

Liberty ships were sold to foreign flag operators to help rebuild their fleets and strengthen their economies. By 1951, 843 ships had been sold to American and 1,113 to foreign flag operators for a total of almost two billion dollars. Surplus vessels were laid up in reserve fleets where they were preserved for emergency use.

In 1950 war broke out in Korea, and the United States sent troops and supplies to help the South Koreans. Added to the need for military shipments was a sudden and urgent demand for ships to carry coal and grain to countries in Europe and Asia which were suffering from a severe winter. All available privately-owned ships were chartered, and hundreds of government-owned vessels were withdrawn from the reserve fleets. By 1952 over 500 government-owned ships were in operation. As the requirements diminished, the Maritime Administration withdrew its vessels from service and returned them to the reserve fleets.

In 1965 the Defense Department requested the reactivation of about 20 reserve fleet ships to carry cargoes to Viet Nam. Additional ships were requested, and by the end of 1966, about 172 Maritime Administration ships, most of them from the reserve fleets, were assigned to private companies appointed to act as agents for the government. In addition there were about 300 privately-owned ships under charter to the military for the Southeast Asian supply program. By the end of 1970 the requirements for military shipments were being handled by the Navy's Military Sealift Command and privately-owned ships. All government-owned vessels had been withdrawn from operation.

THE MARITIME ADMINISTRATION

The Maritime Commission was abolished in a 1950 reorganization, and its place taken by a Federal Maritime Board and the Maritime Administration which were placed under the Department of Commerce. The Maritime Board was assigned the regulatory and subsidy determination of the old Commission and the Maritime Administration (MarAd) was given the function of administering the various Merchant Marine programs. This arrangement was found undesirable, and in 1961 the Maritime Board was abolished and a separate and independent Federal Maritime Commission was established to handle regulatory matters, to hear complaints against shipping lines or conferences, to approve or disapprove freight rate agreements and to carry out other functions. The responsibilities of the Maritime Administration were enlarged to administer the shipbuilding and ship operating subsidies and other promotional programs.

MarAd is the agency charged with fostering the development and encouraging the maintenance of the United States Merchant Marine. MarAd pays ship operating- and construction-differential subsidies to make up the difference between United States costs of building and operating ships and the estimated costs of foreign competitors.

In return for the government aid received, United States operators must provide regular, adequate service in United States foreign trade. The Administration also determines, after investigating their qualifications, which companies shall receive operating subsidy.

At the present time there are seven liner companies with subsidy contracts, which operate about one-third of the active fleet. Operating subsidy payments of $303 million were made in fiscal year 1978.

The subsidized operator must agree to replace his obsolete ships with new ships found to be suitable for trade routes to be served and for emergency use as naval and military auxiliaries. The Administration pays a percentage of the domestic cost of such ships, so that the operator pays no more than the estimated cost of building a similar ship in a representative foreign shipyard. The Administration may pay for any national defense features found to be in excess of commercial requirements. Construction subsidy may be paid for any ship to be used in United States foreign trade, whether or not the owner receives operating subsidy. The government also may guarantee ship construction loans or mortgages obtained from private sources.

The Maritime Administration maintains a National Defense Reserve Fleet of ships available for emergency use. Ships no longer of use to the government are sold for scrap.

Transfers of United States ships to foreign flag must be approved by the Maritime Administration, which may grant permission if the transfer is in accordance with policies established from time to time. Such policies limit the types of ships which may be transferred and generally require that the ships not be needed by the United States or that they will be made available to the United States in an emergency.

The Maritime Administration operates the United States Merchant Marine Academy at Kings Point, Long Island, New York, where young men and women are trained to become Merchant Marine officers. The curriculum covers a four-year course leading to a Bachelor of Science degree and a third mate's or third engineer's license. The Administration also supervises the government grants and student aid given to the six State Merchant Marine schools.

The Maritime Administration also promotes and coordinates the development of port facilities and intermodal transportation systems, and is responsible for coordinating emergency operation programs of the ports.

The agency cooperates in international programs and meetings in such matters as prevention of pollution of the seas by oil, the liability for damage from nuclear powered ships, simplification of shipping documents, standard container sizes, and improved safety and navigation regulations.

THE MERCHANT MARINE ACT OF 1970

Although the 1936 Act was a landmark in maritime history and was largely responsible for preparing the Merchant Marine for its tremendous growth in World War II, it had become outmoded by the late 1960's. The United States fleet had declined, and foreign nations had built large fleets of modern vessels that gradually monopolized trade. By 1969, obsolete United States bulk ships were carrying less than 5 percent of United States foreign trade. To reverse this trend, and in order to restructure and redirect our national maritime policy, the Merchant Marine Act of 1970 was passed.

The 1970 Act provided incentives to encourage the application of advanced technology to increase the productivity and competitiveness of the American Merchant Marine. It streamlined the administration of the subsidy programs, expanded the ship guarantee program, accelerated research and development programs, and extended the full range of government subsidies.

The 1970 Act stimulated many improvements in the maritime industry. An encouraging number of shipbuilding orders, both subsidized and unsubsidized, have been placed with American shipyards. The vessels being constructed under the Act include the best-equipped, safest, and most productive types. The vessels being delivered are improving the performance and efficiency of the United States flag merchant fleet. Research projects are developing new technologies, systems, and equipment to further improve the maritime industry.

The financial programs and incentives of the 1970 Act are also helping the orderly growth of the fleet. In addition, a new spirit of cooperation between maritime labor and management has contributed to the development of a stronger and more stable American maritime industry.

Merchant ships are indispensable to the economy of a powerful trading nation such as the United States with its world-wide markets. Experience in two World Wars, the Korean conflict, and in Southeast Asia has demonstrated that the United States must depend upon its own merchant fleet and shipbuilding and repair industries for ocean transportation. The maintenance of a strong and efficient Merchant Marine continues to be essential to our country's trade and defense.

UNITED STATES MERCHANT MARINE ACADEMY, KINGS POINT, NEW YORK

The United States Merchant Marine Cadet Corps was established on March 15, 1938, following passage of the Merchant Marine Act of 1936. Training was first given aboard merchant ships and later at temporary shore establishments pending the acquisition of permanent facilities. The Walter P. Chrysler estate at Kings Point, New York was selected as the permanent site for the Academy in March 1942, and construction was begun the following May. Fifteen months later the task was virtually completed and the United States Merchant Marine Academy was dedicated on September 30, 1943.

World War II required the Academy to forego normal operation and devote all of its resources toward meeting the emergency personnel needs of the Merchant Marine. The enrollment was increased to 2,700 and the planned course of instruction was reduced in length from four years to twenty-four months. Notwithstanding the war, shipboard training continued to be an integral part of the Academy curriculum, and midshipmen served at sea in combat zones the world over. Two hundred and twelve midshipmen and graduates gave their lives in service to their country and many others survived torpedoings and bombings. Seven midshipmen and one graduate were awarded the Merchant Marine Distinguished Service

Medal, the nation's highest decoration for conspicuous gallantry and devotion to duty, and by the end of the war, the Academy had graduated 6,634 officers.

In the closing days of World War II, plans were formulated to establish a four-year college-level program to meet the peacetime needs of the Merchant Marine. At the end of the War, in August 1945, the four-year course was immediately instituted with the September class of midshipmen.

Figure 23-1. U.S. Merchant Marine Academy, Kings Point, New York. Photo: U.S. Merchant Marine Academy.

The Academy has since grown in stature and has become one of the world's foremost institutions in the field of maritime education. Authorization for awarding graduates the degree of Bachelor of Science was granted by the 81st Congress in a law approved August 18, 1949, and the Academy was fully accredited as a degree-granting institution by the Middle States Association of Colleges and Schools on November 26, 1949. Made a permanent institution by an Act of Congress on February 20, 1956, its operation was placed under the authority of the Department of Commerce. Today, Kings Point graduates are serving with distinction in all sectors of the maritime industry—as ships' officers, steamship company executives, admiralty lawyers, marine underwriters, naval architects, oceanographers, and career officers in the United States Navy and Coast Guard. With the 1974-75 academic year the Academy opened its doors to young women who will find broad opportunities for satisfying careers in the maritime industry.

Without regard to race, color, sex, or national and ethnic origin, candidates for admission must be citizens of the United States, at least 17 years of age and not have passed their 22nd birthday on July 1 of the year of admission. A candidate must obtain a nomination from Members of Congress from the candidate's home state, must be physically fit with special emphasis on vision, and must have acceptable academic qualifications.

Tuition, room and board, medical and dental care are provided. While assigned aboard ship for the shipboard training portion of the curriculum, midshipmen are provided with a salary of $351 per month, paid by the steamship companies. For further information write: Office of External Affairs, United States Merchant Marine Academy, Kings Point, N.Y. 11024.

Figure 23-2. View of the campus, Maritime College of the State University of New York, Fort Schuyler, Bronx, N.Y. T.S. *Empire State* is shown at left.

STATE MARITIME ACADEMIES

State maritime academies are specialized college-level schools which receive most of their funding from their parent states and the balance from the federal government. They exist for the purpose of training and educating future masters and chief engineers of the American Merchant Marine. In addition, the student acquires the knowledge and background which will fit him for positions ashore of increasing responsibility in the maritime industry.

There are six academies which point a student towards a license and a maritime career. The oldest is in New York, located at Fort Schuyler across Long Island Sound from J.F. Kennedy Airport. Now officially the Maritime College of the State University of New York, it was established in 1875 through the efforts of Admiral Stephen B. Luce who also founded the Naval War College and wrote Luce's *Seamanship*. The next academy founded, in 1891, is in Massachusetts, located on Buzzard's Bay. Also on the East Coast is the Maine Maritime Academy at Castine which dates from 1941. On the Gulf Coast at Galveston is the Texas Maritime College, a part of Texas A&M, founded in 1962. Finally, on San Francisco Bay in

Vallejo is the California Maritime Academy founded in 1929. The newest addition to this group is the Great Lakes Maritime Academy which is a division of the Northwestern Michigan College in Traverse City, Michigan. It is a three year school, and graduates are qualified to sit for their Great Lakes First Class Pilot's license or their Third Assistant Engineer's license.

The curricula of the state maritime academies differ from one school to the next, but all strive to produce a highly qualified mate or assistant engineer who will be useful the day he reports to his first ship. It is no longer enough to be able to "splice, reef and steer." All the academies have broadened their offerings and lengthened their course to four years (except Great Lakes Maritime Academy) in recognition of this fact.

Unlike the Naval Academy, and in keeping with Coast Guard licensing requirements, midshipmen are split into prospective deck officers and prospective engineering officers. There is very little cross-training. A few midshipmen may complete the program with both deck and engineering licenses, but this is highly unusual. As a consequence, the training can be in depth within the midshipman's chosen specialty. An engineering midshipman must receive sufficient time in a diesel laboratory to learn how to operate a diesel, diagnose its ills, and repair it, possibly by machining a new part. Later the same day he may attend a class in thermodynamics or electricity. Deck midshipmen receive similar training. A Merchant Marine deck officer is his own bosn's mate and quartermaster. It follows that he must be far more familiar with the practice and theory of navigation and deck seamanship than his Naval Academy counterpart.

A Merchant Marine license as third mate or third assistant engineer is issued by the United States Coast Guard as a part of its function of Merchant Marine safety. To qualify for a license a candidate must be a graduate of one of the maritime academies or have served for three years at sea in an unlicensed capacity. An officer who comes up by the latter route is said to "have come up through the hawsepipe." The path of advancement in the Merchant Marine is third mate, second mate, first mate and finally master. Time at sea is required in each grade before a candidate is permitted to "sit" for his next higher license. The technical training at the state academies is rigorous, and a graduate would have the capability of passing his examinations for master or chief engineer on completion of his course of study. This the Coast Guard does not permit, but occasionally an academy graduate presents himself at the examining room and has sufficient time at sea in a responsible billet to sit immediately for his license as second mate or second assistant engineer.

The Naval Reserve program offered at the state academies is not a primary source of reserve officers, and the graduate is not ordered to active duty unless he so requests. Some academies have a full NROTC program, others have a smaller Naval Science Department which offers courses to provide the midshipman with sufficient familiarity with the Navy should he ever operate with Navy ships or be called to active duty in time of war. Most graduates receive inactive Naval Reserve commissions, but very few go on active duty. The number appears to depend upon the economic climate as well as the programs which the Navy may offer.

Self-discipline and a keen sense of responsibility are traits which maritime academy midshipmen and cadets must develop before they can graduate and receive licenses certifying competency in their chosen fields.

After cutting his teeth at sea and raising his license many possibilities open up to the qualified licensed officer. One of the more attractive is that of a pilot. To receive pilotage for a particular area an officer must have acquired specialized knowledge and experience in that area in addition to his master's or mate's license. Probably the most elite group of pilots in the world is composed of the Panama Canal pilots. State maritime academies may be a little short on frills and on pre-World War II military spit and polish, but they can give unmatched training and education to those interested. The opportunities at sea are as limitless as the ocean.

For detailed information concerning the course and entrance requirements of the state maritime academies, address:

The President
Maine Maritime Academy
Castine, ME 04421

The President
Massachusetts Maritime Academy
Buzzard's Bay, MA 02532

The President
Maritime College of the State
  University of New York
Fort Schuyler
Bronx, NY 10465

The President
Texas Maritime College
P.O. Box 1675
Galveston, TX 77553

The President
California Maritime Academy
P.O. Box 1392
Vallejo, CA 94590

The President
Great Lakes Maritime Academy
Northwestern Michigan College
1701 East Front Street
Traverse City, MI 49684

THE HARRY LUNDEBERG SCHOOL OF SEAMANSHIP, PINEY POINT, MARYLAND

The Harry Lundeberg School of Seamanship, named in honor of the first president of the Seafarers' International Union (SIU), was founded on its present site in 1967. In the years since it has grown to become the largest educational facility for seafarers and boatmen in the United States.

The purpose of the school is to train, guide, and encourage young people to make careers for themselves on America's network of inland and coastal waters and on the high seas as well as to upgrade seamen and boatmen to higher ratings.

In order to achieve these goals, the school emphasizes both academic and vocational education. The basic vocational education program at the Lundeberg School is a 12-week course which provides a continuing source of manpower for SIU-contracted vessels. The students learn the fundamental skills to work aboard their first vessels and perform their duties competently. The training courses emphasize discipline, personal hygiene, and basic professional skills. Students also learn the safety practices and cargo-handling skills which the United States Coast Guard requires of tankermen.

Upon successful completion of the basic training course, graduates receive their seamen's documents from the United States Coast Guard and their certification of completion of tankerman and lifeboatman training.

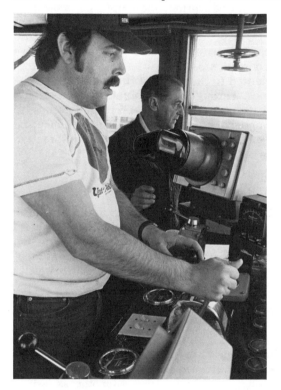

Figure 23-3. Instruction to prepare students for tugboat or towboat command at the Harry Lundeberg Seamanship School. Young people are prepared for careers in inland and coastal waters as well as on the high seas. Courtesy: Harry Lundeberg Seamanship School, Inc.

When the graduate acquires the necessary work time aboard a vessel, he is eligible for these endorsements without further testing. Every graduate is placed in his first job aboard an SIU-contracted ship, boat or barge.

The advanced and specialized programs assist experienced seafarers and boatmen with sufficient work experience to advance their professional skills and increase their earning potential. These training programs are designed to increase the student's professional ability, protect their job security, and provide highly qualified manpower to the water transportation industries.

Through the upgrading programs, a seafarer can earn any or all of the unlicensed ratings for the department—deck, engine or steward—in which he works. Boatmen may earn any licensed or unlicensed rating for the inland and offshore shipping industries.

Complementing the vocational education curricula are a variety of programs for academic advancement. The school offers a remedial reading program, an independent study program and a high school equivalency program. Independent study college programs allow students to continue their college course ambitions.

In both academic and vocational education, the emphasis is on individualized instruction tailored to meet the needs of the student. Personal study guides based on diagnostic tests and a low student-to-teacher ratio are examples of this approach to learning and are factors which have contributed to the success rate of students.

The Lundeberg School is oriented to the needs of the students and the needs of the maritime industries. Through its combination of vocational and academic education and its policy of flexibility and responsiveness to technological advances, the Lundeberg School is successfully educating and securing employment for seafarers and boatmen aboard the ships and boats of America's privately-owned, civilian-manned fleets.

NATIONAL MARITIME UNION UPGRADING AND RETRAINING SCHOOL

The National Maritime Union (NMU) Upgrading and Retraining School, located at 346 West 17th Street, New York, NY 10011, offers instruction to members to enable them to upgrade the endorsements on their Merchant Mariner's documents. The school is also available to seamen who may hold a rating endorsement or a position aboard ship for which they have no formal training.

COURSES OFFERED AND THEIR REQUIREMENTS

Course	Requirement for Admission
Able Seaman	One year of sea time as an Ordinary Seaman.
Electrician	Fireman, Watertender, and Oiler endorsement, *plus* at least one year of sea time in these or other skilled engine room ratings.
Deck Engine Mechanic	Fireman, Watertender, and Oiler endorsement, *plus* at least one year of sea time in these or other skilled engine room ratings.
Diesel, Machinist/ Pumpman	Same as for Deck Engine Mechanic.
Liquefied Natural Gas	Demac endorsement, *plus* at least one year of sea time as a Demac and/or Pumpman. *OR* Able Seaman's endorsement, *plus* at least 18 months of sea time as an Able Seaman.
Basic Food Preparation	At least 18 months of sea time in the Steward Department.
Chief Steward/Cook	At least 18 months of sea time in the Steward Department, including one year as Chief Cook.
Shipboard Medical Care Program	9-week course offered to Chief Stewards.

HOW TO APPLY FOR ADMISSION TO THE SCHOOL

Periodically the school notifies all NMU branches of the courses currently being offered, the date they begin, and the requirements for each. This information also appears in "The Pilot," the official monthly publication of the NMU. Written application for admission to a course must be made by the seaman on a special form provided. These application forms are available from the school or from any NMU branch. Application for a course should be made at least two months before it is scheduled to begin. The completed application should be submitted to the agent at the NMU branch where application is made.

UNITED STATES NAVAL ACADEMY, ANNAPOLIS, MARYLAND

The United States Naval Academy is the Navy's undergraduate professional college. The 4,400 men and women at Annapolis are called midshipmen. Graduates of the four-year course receive B.S. degrees and embark on careers as officers in the Navy or Marine Corps. The majority of the 18 majors offered are engineering or science-oriented. Military, moral, professional, and physical development are stressed throughout the curriculum.

All midshipmen participate in an extensive sports program which includes 28 varsity sports and 26 intramural sports. Over 80 different extracurricular activities are offered. Religious services are available on campus and in the city of Annapolis. Professional summer training is conducted at the Naval Academy and at other United States military bases, as well as aboard naval units at sea. Aviation, submarine, amphibious, and surface warfare-training, and visits to foreign countries are included.

Race, creed, sex, religion, or national origin are not factors in eligibility. Basically, a candidate must be a United States citizen; of good moral character; at least 17 and not past the 22nd birthday on July 1, year of entry; and unmarried and have no children. A candidate *must obtain a nomination*, qualify academically (acceptable SAT or ACT, class-standing, transcript, etc.), qualify medically (eyes are the principal problem area), qualify physically, and be selected by the Academy for an appointment.

Nominations are available from Members of Congress from the candidate's home state. Write United States senators and representatives directly; it is not necessary to know them. Other nominations are available to various categories of servicemen (active and reserve) and to children of career members of the armed services, active, retired, or deceased. Nominations are also provided for children of deceased/disabled veterans, Medal of Honor winners, and POW's/MIA's, and to residents of Puerto Rico, the Canal Zone, American Samoa, Guam, and the Virgin Islands.

Tuition, room and board, medical and dental care, and a monthly salary of $375 for uniforms, books and personal needs are provided. A five-year active duty service obligation is incurred at graduation. For further information about the Naval Academy and its entrance requirements, write the

Director of Candidate Guidance, United States Naval Academy, Annapolis, Maryland 21402.

UNITED STATES COAST GUARD

The origin of the Coast Guard dates from August 4, 1790, when it was created by Act of Congress and was then known as the Revenue Marine and later as the Revenue-Cutter Service. Under the Act of January 28, 1915, the Revenue-Cutter Service and Life-Saving Service were merged into one single organization—the United States Coast Guard—which constitutes, by law, a part of the military forces of the United States, operating under the Department of Transportation in time of peace, and as a part of the Navy, subject to the orders of the Secretary of the Navy, in time of war, or when the President shall so direct.

The duties of the Coast Guard include the enforcing of Federal law upon the navigable waters of the United States and its insular possessions and upon the high seas which may be within the jurisdiction of the United States. It renders assistance to vessels in distress and assists in protecting life and property on the seas and the navigable waters of the United States and its insular possessions and along the coasts thereof. The Coast Guard is responsible for pollution control and prevention in the coastal waters, shorelines, and navigable waterways of the United States. It takes part in the international ice patrol in the North Atlantic, enforces the agreements of international conventions regarding fishing on the high seas, and extends relief to flood victims along the Ohio and Mississippi Rivers and their tributaries.

The United States Shipping Commissioners and the Marine Safety Office, which deal with the certification of vessels and the licensing and certification of merchant seaman, are also under the United States Coast Guard.

COAST GUARD ACADEMY, NEW LONDON, CONNECTICUT

The Coast Guard Academy accommodating about 200 cadets, offers a four-year course of study embracing engineering, military science, cultural and other professional subjects. A well-rounded program of athletics is carried out, and each year a practice cruise, usually touching at foreign ports, is made.

Upon graduation, a cadet is commissioned by the President as an ensign in the Coast Guard, receiving the same pay and allowances as an ensign in the Navy. Cadets are paid a monthly salary set by Congress.

Entrance is by competitive examination, held about the second week in June of each year at designated cities. Applicants should be graduates from a high school. A sound body is a requisite, with age limits from 17 to 22 years.

Further information may be obtained from the Commandant, United States Coast Guard, Washington, D.C., 20590, or from the Superintendent, United States Coast Guard Academy, New London, Connecticut, 06320.

NATIONAL OCEAN SURVEY

The National Ocean Survey (NOS), a part of the National Oceanic and Atmospheric Administration (NOAA), is an engineering and scientific organization which acquires, processes, analyzes, and disseminates solid earth and ocean data. The main services of the Survey are the publication of nautical and aeronautical charts which are basic tools in maintaining the nation's air and sea transportation systems.

The NOS National Geodetic Survey (NGS) is concerned with establishing and maintaining national geodetic networks, the precise positional reference for all local, regional, and national surveys and maps. The vertical and horizontal control points established by NGS serve as a basis for surveying, mapping, large engineering projects, coastal base lines, urban planning, and land management.

Staffed by scientists, engineers, and technical personnel, NOS has additional capabilities in photogrammetry, chart reproduction processes, seismology, geomagnetism, gravity, marine engineering, naval architecture, astronomy, marine research, and modern seamanship.

The surveys and studies are produced at NOS headquarters in Rockville, Maryland. Issued in various forms, NOS publications include nautical and aeronautical charts, annual tables of predicted tides and currents, charts showing magnetic declination, and *Coast Pilots*. *Coast Pilots*, a series of nine volumes, supplement the nautical charts and supply descriptions of the coasts, sailing directions, port, harbor and anchorage information, and emphasize any conditions which might be hazardous to water-borne traffic, including recreational boaters.

Besides the main office of the NOS in Rockville, there are marine centers in Norfolk, Virginia, and Seattle, Washington, where the NOAA fleet of 25 vessels is maintained to conduct ocean research and hydrographic surveys in coastal waters and the deep sea.

Catalogs of nautical and aeronautical charts and related publications may be obtained from National Ocean Survey, Distribution Division (C44), Riverdale, MD 20840.

NATIONAL WEATHER SERVICE

The National Weather Service (NWS) is an agency under the National Oceanographic and Atmospheric Administration (NOAA). It has over 400 facilities which are found in the 50 states, and about 5,000 employees who are concerned with meteorological, hydrological, and oceanographic observations. It is supported by an extensive international communications system.

The mission of the National Weather Service is to provide forecasts and weather warnings to the general public and special users. The offices most involved in the production of forecasts are the Weather Service Forecast Offices (WSFOs) and the River Forecast Centers (RFCs).

Forecasts issued by the WSFOs include state, zone (areas the size of several counties that can expect the same weather), local, agricultural, environmental quality (air stagnation, forest fire weather), and other specialized products. A sizable effort at WSFOs concerns meteorological support for the aviation industry. The National Meteorological Center (NMC) located near Washington, D.C., provides WSFOs with material used in developing forecasts.

Warnings from both WSFOs and WSOs are issued for severe weather such as hurricanes, tornadoes, thunderstorms, flash flooding, and extreme winter weather. The National Severe Storms Forecast Center (NSSFC) in Kansas City and the National Hurricane Center (NHC) in Miami provide the main support for the warning program.

NWS activities also include oceanographic, overseas, and space operation support services. Another important aspect of NWS operations is the acquisition of meteorological data collected from on the land, on the sea, and in the upper atmosphere by people from many countries. Additionally, satellite information is sent to many receiving stations on the ground. The NOAA Weather Wire Service (NWWS) provides direct teletypewriter service to many radio and TV stations which link the NWS to the public.

THE MILITARY SEALIFT COMMAND

The United States Navy's Military Sealift Command (MSC), activated October 1, 1949, as the Military Sea Transportation Service, was renamed August 1, 1970. The command's missions are to provide contingency sealift for military forces worldwide, to develop plans and to provide assets for emergency expansion, to provide sealift support of United States military forces in peacetime, to operate Naval Fleet Auxiliary force ships, and to operate ships supporting scientific and other non-transportation missions.

MSC controls a force of more than 100 ships, with approximately two thirds of that force consisting of government-owned or long-term chartered ships that are involved in dry cargo and tanker operations, in direct support of the Navy fleet—including underway replenishment—and in special operations such as support of space flight, cable laying, or ocean research. In addition, the command books military cargo on regularly scheduled commercial ships, and systems it contracts for include intermodal delivery from supply point to the customer in the field.

Pay and work rules for the 4,000 MSC seagoing personnel are based on the pay and work rules prevalent in the maritime industry. At the same time the MSC civil service employees receive normal civil service benefits.

Information on employment opportunities, can be obtained by writing the MSC Atlantic Employment Office, Military Ocean Terminal Building 42, Bayonne, N.J. 07002, or the MSC Pacific Employment Office, Oakland, Calif. 94625.

REQUIREMENTS FOR QUALIFIED MEMBERS OF THE ENGINE DEPARTMENT

Certification required:
    (a) Every person employed in a rating as qualified member of the engine department on any United States vessel requiring certification shall produce a certificate for the shipping commissioner, United States Collector

or Deputy Collector of Customs, or master before signing articles of agreement.

(b) No certificate as qualified member of the engine department is required of any person employed on any unrigged vessel, except seagoing barges.

General requirements:

(a) A qualified member of the engine department is any person below the rating of licensed officer and above the rating of coal passer or wiper, who holds a certificate of service issued by the Coast Guard or predecessor authority.

(b) The rating of "assistant electrician" is considered a rating not above that of coal passer or wiper, but equal thereto.

(c) An applicant, to be eligible for certification shall be able to speak and understand the English language as would be required in the rating of qualified member of the engine department and in an emergency aboard ship.

Physical requirements:

(a) An applicant for a certificate of service as a qualified member of the engine department shall present a certificate of a medical officer of the United States Public Health Service, or other reputable physician attesting that his eyesight, hearing, and physical condition are such that he can perform the duties required.

(b) The medical examination for qualified member of the engine department is the same as for an original license as engineer. All applicants shall be required to pass a physical examination given by a medical officer of the United States Public Health Service and present a certificate executed by this Public Health Service Officer to the Officer in Charge, Marine Inspection. This certificate shall attest to the applicant's acuity of vision, color sense, and general physical condition. In exceptional cases where an applicant would be put to great inconvenience or expense to appear before a medical officer of the United States Public Health Service, the physical examination and certification may be made by another reputable physician.

(1) Epilepsy, insanity, senility, acute veneral disease or neurosyphilis, badly impaired hearing, or other defect that would render the applicant incompetent to perform ordinary duties at sea are causes for certification as incompetent.

(2) Applicants shall be examined only as to their ability to distinguish the colors red, blue, green, and yellow. No applicant shall be disqualified for failure to distinguish colors if any of his required experience is served prior to May 1, 1947.

(3) Applicants must have uncorrected vision of at least 20/100 in both eyes correctable to at least 20/30 in one eye and 20/50 in the other.

(4) Persons serving or intending to serve in the Merchant Marine Service are recommended to take the earliest opportunity of ascertaining, through examination by an ophthalmic surgeon, whether their vision, and color vision where required, is such as to qualify them for service in that profession.

(c) Where an applicant is not possessed of the vision, hearing, or general physical condition necessary, the Officer in Charge, Marine Inspection, after consultation with the Public Health Service physician or other examining physician, may make recommendation to the Commandant for an exception to these requirements, if in his opinion, extenuating circumstances warrant special consideration. Any requests for a decision by the Commandant must be accompanied by all pertinent correspondence, records, and reports. In this connection recommendations from agencies of the Federal Government operating government vessels, as well as owners and operators of private vessels, made in behalf of their employees, will be given full consideration in arriving at a decision.

(d) An applicant holding a certificate of service for a particular rating as qualified member of the engine department and desiring certification for another rating covered by this same form of certificate may qualify therefor without a physical examination unless the Officer in Charge, Marine Inspection, finds that the applicant obviously suffers from some physical or mental infirmity to a degree that would render him incompetent to perform the required duties. In this event the applicant shall be required to undergo an examination to determine his competency.

Service or training requirements:

(a) An applicant for a certificate of service as qualified member of the engine department other than as deck engine mechanic or engineman shall furnish the Coast Guard proof that he possesses one of the following requirements of training or service:

(1) Six months' service at sea in a rating at least equal to that of coal passer or wiper in the engine department of vessels required to have such certificated men, or in the engine department of tugs or towboats operating on the high seas or Great Lakes, or in the bays or sounds directly connected with the seas; or

(2) Graduation from a schoolship approved by and conducted under rules prescribed by the Commandant; or,

(3) Satisfactory completion of a course of training approved by the Commandant and served aboard a training vessel; or,

(4) Graduation from the United States Naval Academy or the United States Coast Guard Academy.

(b) The requirements for deck engine mechanic and for engineman are as follows:

(1) Deck engine mechanic.

(a) An applicant for a certificate as "deck engine mechanic" shall be a person holding a Merchant Mariner's Document endorsed as "junior engineer." The applicant shall be eligible for such certification upon furnishing one of the following:

(1) Presentation of a temporary letter that was issued to the holder to serve as "deck engine mechanic" by an Officer in Charge, Marine Inspection, dated prior to December 1, 1966; or,

(2) Satisfactory documentary evidence of sea service of 6 months in the rating of "junior engineer" on steam vessels of 4,000 horsepower or over; or,

(3) Documentary evidence from an operator of an automated vessel that he has completed satisfactorily at least 4 weeks indoctrination and training in the engine department of an automated steam vessel of 4,000 horsepower or over; or

(4) Satisfactory completion of a course of training for "deck engine mechanic" acceptable to the Commandant.

(b) The Officer in Charge, Marine Inspection, who is satisfied that an applicant for the rating of "deck engine mechanic" meets the requirements specified in this section, will endorse this rating on the current Merchant Mariner's Document held by the applicant.

(c) Any holder of a Merchant Mariner's Document endorsed for "any unlicensed rating in the engine department" or "QMED-any rating" is qualified as a "deck engine mechanic" and that endorsement will not be entered on his document.

(2) Engineman.

(a) An applicant for a certificate as "engineman" shall be a person holding a Merchant Mariner's Document endorsed as "fireman/watertender" and "oiler," or "junior engineer." The applicant shall be eligible for such certification upon furnishing one of the following:

(1) Presentation of a temporary letter that was issued to the holder to serve as "engineman" by an Officer in Charge, Marine Inspection, dated prior to December 1, 1966; or,

(2) Satisfactory documentary evidence of sea service of 6 months in any one or combination of "junior engineer," "fireman/watertender" or "oiler" on steam vessels of 4,000 horsepower or over; or,

(3) Documentary evidence from an operator of a "partially automated" steam vessel that he has completed satisfactorily at least 2 weeks indoctrination and training in the engine department of a "partially automated" steam vessel of 4,000 horsepower or over; or

(4) Satisfactory completion of a course of training for "engineman" acceptable to the Commandant.

(b) The Officer in Charge, Marine Inspection, who is satisfied that an applicant for the rating of "engineman" meets the requirements specified in this section, will endorse this rating on the current Merchant Mariner's Document held by the applicant.

(c) Any holder of a Merchant Mariner's Document endorsed for "any unlicensed rating in the engine department," "QMED-any rating" or "deck engine mechanic" is qualified as an "engineman" and that endorsement will not be entered on his document.

General provisions respecting Merchant Mariner's Documents endorsed as qualified member of the engine department:

(a) The holder of a Merchant Mariner's Document endorsed with one or more qualified member of the engine department ratings may serve in any unqualified rating in the engine department without obtaining an additional endorsement. This does not mean that an endorsement of one qualified member authorizes the holder to serve in all qualified member ratings. Each qualified member of the engine department rating for which a holder of a Merchant Mariner's Document is qualified must be endorsed separately. When however, the applicant qualifies for all ratings covered by a certificate as a qualified member the certification may read "QMED-any rating." The ratings are as follows:

(1) Refrigerating engineer.

(2) Oiler.

(3) Watertender.

(4) Fireman.

(5) Deck engineer.

(6) Junior engineer.

(7) Electrician.

(8) Boilermaker.

(9) Machinist.

(10) Pumpman.

(11) Deck engine mechanic.

(12) Engineman.

Examination requirements:

(a) Applicants for certification as qualified members of the engine department in the ratings of oiler, watertender, fireman, deck engineer, refrigerator engineer, junior engineer, electrician, and machinist shall be examined orally or in writing and only in the English language on the subjects listed in paragraph (d) of this section. The applicant's general knowledge of the subjects must be sufficient to satisfy the examiner that he is qualified to perform the duties of the rating for which he makes application.

(b) Applicants for certification as qualified member of the engine department in the ratings of boilermaker and pumpman shall, by written or oral examination, demonstrate sufficient knowledge of the subjects peculiar to those ratings to satisfy the Officer in Charge, Marine Inspection, that they are qualified to perform the duties of the rating.

(c) Applicants for certification as qualified members of the engine department in the rating of deck engine mechanic or engineman, who have proved eligiblity for such endorsement will not be required to take a written or oral examination for such ratings.

THE DAY AT SEA

The day at sea is divided into six watches of four hours each. The midwatch or middle watch is from midnight to 4:00 A. M.; the morning watch is from 4:00 A. M. until 8:00 A. M.; the forenoon watch is from 8:00 A. M. until 12 noon; the afternoon watch is from noon until 4:00 P. M.; the evening watch is from 4:00 P. M. until 8:00 P. M.; and the first watch is from 8:00 P. M. until midnight.

In earlier days the evening watch was divided into a first and a second "dog watch" of two hours each. This is still the custom in the Navy where it is found to be a convenient means of providing reliefs for the evening meal. In the Merchant Marine, however, where fewer personnel are on watch, meal reliefs are provided on an individual basis.

Although the ship's bell is rarely ever struck aboard a merchant ship to note the passage of time today, passenger ships, training ships, and naval vessels still observe the custom. Bells are struck every half hour on each watch beginning thirty minutes after the hour when the watch has begun. An additional bell notes the passage of each half hour until the end of the watch when eight bells are struck and the sequence begins over. Thus, on the afternoon watch, the bells are sounded as follows:

12 noon	1200	eight bells
12:30 P. M.	1230	one bell
1:00 P. M.	1300	two bells
1:30 P. M.	1330	three bells
2:00 P. M.	1400	four bells
2:30 P. M.	1430	five bells
3:00 P. M.	1500	six bells
3:30 P. M.	1530	seven bells
4:00 P. M.	1600	eight bells

ORGANIZATION DIAGRAM OF A MERCHANT SHIP

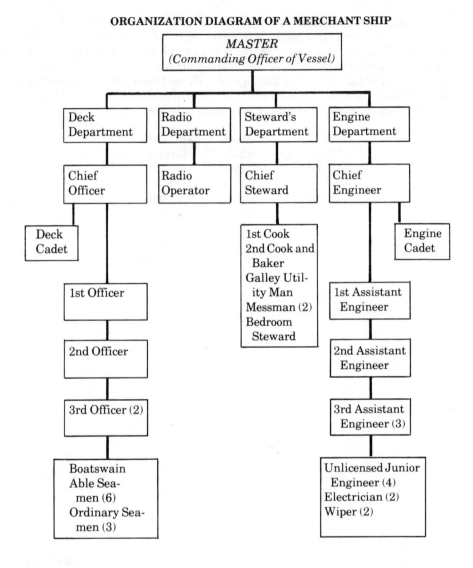

The manning of a merchant vessel depends upon many factors and will vary according to the type, size, minimum Coast Guard requirements, and employment of the ship as well as the union agreements in force. In this respect the differences in agreements between the Atlantic and Pacific coasts result in some variations in job descriptions. If the vessel were a tanker, she would probably not have an electrician but would have at least one pumpman. This diagram is representative of a medium sized, automated ship in the Pacific.

INDEX

ABOUT THE EDITORS

William B. Hayler began his naval service during World War II when he was aboard the aircraft carrier *Franklin*, the vessel renowned for sailing home under its own power after receiving the most severe damage of any ship which still remained afloat. Subsequently, Captain Hayler commanded the LST 859, the LSMR 403, the high speed transport *Balduck*, the destroyer *Buck* and the C-3 repair ship *Cadmus*. He was awarded the British Distinguished Service Cross during the Korean War. Educated at Phillips Academy in Andover, Massachusetts, he graduated from the U.S. Naval Academy in 1944 and received an M.A. from George Washington University in 1964. In 1969 he obtained his Master Mariner's license and since 1970 has been on the faculty of the California Maritime Academy where he teaches seamanship, navigation, ship handling, and rules of the road. Bill Hayler is a frequent contributor to journals of maritime interest. His articles have appeared in the *Naval Institute Proceedings*, *Sealift*, and *Shipmate*.

A 1970 graduate of the California Maritime Academy, John M. Keever lost little time in raising his license from third mate to Master. He has been on the faculty at the Academy since 1972 with frequent official absences to acquire seatime. In 1980 he received his Master's in Public Administration from Golden Gate University. He is a Lieutenant Commander in the Merchant Marine Reserve of the U.S. Navy. Currently, he is Chief Mate and Head of the Deck Department of the T.S. *Golden Bear*. An enthusiastic sailor, Keever sailed his own 35-foot ketch to Honolulu in 1973 accompanied by Captain Hayler and two midshipmen.

Paul M. Seiler retired from the U.S. Coast Guard as a Chief Warrant Boatswain. He began his service career in the Army but soon found the sea more to his liking. During World War II he worked as a longshoreman and then saw service aboard Coast Guard attack transport *Hunter Liggett* in the Pacific and on the U.S.S. *Etamin*, a Liberty Ship. After the war he spent eight years at the Coast Guard Academy as Chief Boatswain of the *Eagle*, the 295-foot barque which makes the annual training cruises for Coast Guard midshipmen. His last active duty in the Coast Guard was as skipper of the buoy tender *Columbine* based in San Francisco. Joining the faculty of the California Maritime Academy in 1967, he is Boatswain of the T.S. *Golden Bear* as well as an instructor in seamanship.